BUILDING A MAIL ORDER BUSINESS
A Complete Manual for Success

Second Edition

Other books by William A. Cohen

The Executive's Guide to Finding a Superior Job
The Principles of Technical Management
How to Sell to the Government
Successful Marketing for Small Business (with Marshall Reddick)
The Entrepreneur and Small Business Problem Solver
Direct Response Marketing
Top Executive Performance (with Nurit Cohen)

BUILDING A MAIL ORDER BUSINESS

A Complete Manual for Success

Second Edition

WILLIAM A. COHEN

JOHN WILEY & SONS

New York   Chichester   Brisbane   Toronto   Singapore

Library of Congress Cataloging in Publication Data:

Cohen, William A., 1937–
    Building a mail order business.

    Includes index.
    1. Mail-order business—Handbooks, manuals, etc.
I. Title.

HF5466.C56   658.8'72   81-16071
ISBN 0-471-81062-2   AACR2

Printed in the United States of America

10 9 8 7 6 5 4 3

*To my wife, Nurit,
who has participated
in every venture
and every adventure*

Preface

When Steve Kippur, then my editor at John Wiley, asked me to prepare this second edition of *Building a Mail Order Business*, I wasn't too surprised. Why not? We're talking about a form of business and marketing that is growing so fast that stories appear almost every week in newspapers such as the *New York Times* and *Los Angeles Times*. Business media such as *Fortune*, the *Wall Street Journal*, *Business Week*, *Advertising Age* and many others are all discussing what was once the "Cinderella of business": that system of marketing called direct marketing, which includes mail order. Even our own professional magazines—*Direct Marketing*, *Zip*, and *Direct Marketing News*—are expanding their readerships of folks involved in this business every day.

But what did surprise me was the time interval since the last edition . . . only two years! But Steve was absolutely right. In the last two years there have been massive changes in the industry. In this short time period, mail order sales have increased by billions of dollars. Technology has improved the tools available to the entrepreneur or practitioner that wants to make his or her fortune in mail order. Many new ideas are available from the firing line. As an educator in the field, the experience which I have gained in teaching hundreds of students about mail order since I wrote the first edition, as well as having the satisfaction of hearing about, and in some cases being able to witness, their successes, has provided material for new approaches both to improve your chances for success and decrease wasted time, money, and effort in getting there. Because of this, almost every chapter has been revised and much material added. As a result, comprehensive as the first edition of *Building a Mail Order Business* was, this edition has been expanded by more than 100 pages. The appendixes have also been enlarged, and important information about the Federal Trade Commission's 30-day mail order rule and the Direct Marketing Association's *Guidelines for Ethical Business Practices* are included. Also included are many new advertisements, success stories, and explanations, and even a complete sample marketing plan for a business service promoted through the mail!

Shortly after I completed the first edition, I wrote a short article which was published by newspapers and other professional journals around the country entitled, "Can Anyone Make a Million Dollars in Mail Order?" The conclusion of this article was, basically, that there were no guarantees of success, but there were few limitations, and many people from all walks of life, backgrounds, and geographical locations had become wealthy through mail order. The number of those whom I have heard about who made their fortunes in mail order since I wrote that article would fill many more articles. My wish for you is that I will be able to add your name to that list.

WILLIAM A. COHEN

Pasadena, California
December 17, 1984

Foreword

Mail order is one of the truly exciting frontiers of the free enterprise system.

It is still possible to start a business on a shoestring from your basement or on your kitchen table. And it's still possible to build that business into a profitable company giving you independence and freedom—the goals that embody the American Dream.

I know firsthand that it can be done. I started in the basement of my home and built a sizable company, and I know others who have done the same. Mail order companies are generally started not by big corporations but primarily by entrepreneurs who have an idea or a dream and pursue it with vigor and determination.

But to pursue that dream, you've got to have knowledge—a road map showing where to go and how to get there. You need the basics and an overall perception of the factors involved in conducting a mail order business.

Bill Cohen's book gives you these basics in a straightforward and understandable way. He continually raises questions—the same questions you'd naturally raise as you read his book. And then he answers them very clearly.

Dr. Cohen has also done his homework well. He has studied all the current and past books on mail order, clipped many advertisements, and gleaned from this material the truly important details to make his book an outstanding primer for our industry.

Building a Mail Order Business gives you the "nuts and bolts" necessary to carry you through almost every aspect of mail order marketing from the very rudimentary basics to the same techniques used by the pros.

When I started JS&A in the basement of my home, I had a little head start. I had my own advertising business, and I was able to write my own advertisements. Despite the head start, I made many mistakes—many totally avoidable had I known much of the information in this book.

Even with this book the road to success will not be easy, but given the determination, a concept, and persistence, you can indeed succeed in the mail order business. Bill Cohen has just made it a little easier.

JOE SUGARMAN

Northbrook, Illinois
January 1982

Preface to the First Edition

Not long ago I was in your shoes. I had picked up a book on mail order because I'd heard there was a lot of money to be made in that business and I wondered whether I could make it. The writer was kind of skimpy on details, but he seemed certain enough that it was easy to succeed, so I jumped in and immediately lost several hundred dollars. Discouraged, but far from down and out, I went to the library and took out every single book I could find on mail order or direct mail operations. Some were packed with technical information, but they were very difficult for me, as a beginner, to understand. Others were intended more for the giant company already engaged in other operations, companies on the *Fortune* 500 list, and senior managers; they talked about concepts that were a complete mystery to me, with my limited knowledge of mail order operations. Meanwhile, I tried again and lost more money. In fact, I fell victim to several mail order scams through which I sent off small sums of money against promises that such and such an individual would help me get established in one sort of mail order deal or another. The bottom line was that I lost money, even though I tried to learn as much as I could from the books that were available.

Eventually, and with considerable difficulty, I learned how to make money in the mail order business. I learned how the business should be started and what tricks could be used to start it in the most profitable manner and in the easiest way possible. I learned what the big companies were doing that was really necessary and how to actually beat the big companies in mail order by using my advantages, and how to develop mail order techniques and apply them to other business operations, such as job finding. Direct mail techniques that I perfected not only worked in marketing oneself for a new job, but they worked so well that my book *The Executive's Guide to Finding a Superior Job* went through five printings in two years. I heard from people all over the country who had used these techniques successfully. In addition, I began to apply mail order techniques to obtaining research for the university with which I became associated. One mailing gave us a response in excess of 30%, and in one short period I sold more in funded research through direct mail techniques than we were able to obtain over the previous three years through other methods. And, of course, I myself began selling products successfully by mail.

There are other books on mail order and many that I can recommend because of the specialized nature of the various subjects and topics they discuss. However, this book is intended to be both basic and comprehensive. Therefore, I recommend most heartily that you read this book first. It is organized in a special way, to take you right from the start through every single concept you need to be successful in mail order. Further, not only is every concept thoroughly explained with examples, but you will find each chapter easy to follow since it is made up of many short subtopics. The subtopics are building blocks you can use to absorb the material at your own pace and then refer back to it later as you need it. To assist you in referring back, there is a comprehensive subject index, which lists the mail order topics covered in the text. Finally, there are appendixes that contain some extremely important information you will need in your mail order business, including a list of mail order associations, sources of mailing lists, and other material that will greatly assist you in achieving your goals in mail order as rapidly as possible.

If you already have a mail order business in operation, you may want to skip some of the basic chapters or some chapters with which you are already familiar and go right on to advanced techniques in other areas. If you don't already have a mail order business, I would recommend that you proceed from the first chapter to the last in the order in which they appear. Chapter 1, "How You Can Make Your Fortune in the Multimillion-Dollar Mail Order Industry," tells a great deal about the business and just how much money there really is in it, along with just a few of its opportunities. In Chapter 2, I tell you how to get your mail order business started at once. If you've always wanted to start your own mail order business but never seemed to get around to it, read this chapter for all the details. In Chapter 3, I talk about avoiding legal problems in mail order and maintaining your professional ethics. Some of the most successful mail order people are also those with the highest professional ethics, but even an honest person must know how to avoid legal problems in his or her profession. In Chapter 4, I tell you exactly how to find profitable products to sell by mail if you don't have a product already. You will learn of more sources of new products and services than you ever dreamed possible. And you will also learn how to increase your chances of picking a product that will prove successful. Chapter 5 discusses the critical importance of the mail order offer—what's special about it and how to develop it. I must tell you right now that even if you have a great product, you can make a lot of money or lose money, depending upon how this product is offered to your potential customers. Mathematics is a key to mail order operations, and in Chapter 6 I tell you essential cost and profit calculations for your business, and I do so in a way that you can understand easily. This is the downfall of many books for beginners and others on mail order: Because mathematics can be painful, they either avoid the subject altogether or make it so complicated that no one can understand it. Here is complete coverage in a way that everyone can understand.

The next chapter, Chapter 7, tells you how to develop a marketing plan that works, and this is important because many people don't bother with marketing plans and thus spend much of their time fighting those daily fires that could have been avoided. A marketing plan will help you avoid much firefighting and will provide you with a road map to show you exactly where to go to reach mail order success. Chapter 8 is important for beginners, especially because it tells you how to make money with classified ads, probably the most inexpensive advertising you can start with. But eventually you'll want to get into other types of advertising and this is explained in Chapter 9, "How to Develop and Use Display Ads Profitably." Chapter 10 shows you where the big money is in direct mail; Chapter 11 shows you how to reach this money with lists; and Chapter 12, which is absolutely essential for mail order, tells you how to use other methods of mail order marketing, including radio, television, and the telephone. You will need these if you really want to hit it big.

Following the types of advertising, in Chapter 13 we talk about how to write copy that creates sales. Copy is crucial; it can cause you to lose sales as well as create them. In Chapter 14 we talk about art and graphics and how to get all types of illustration done for you as inexpensively as possible. In Chapter 15, I do the same for printing, and tell you the different printing methods that are better for various types of operations and what type of work you need to have done. Chapter 16 is one of the most important in the book, for it is on mail order testing, and testing is the heart of mail order. Proper testing will not allow you to build a profitable business, but if you do it correctly, it can almost guarantee mail order success. Chapter 17 is also important and is left out of too many books on mail order operations. It concerns fulfillment—how you fulfill your commitment to your customer after your customer has placed the order. Major mail order businesses have foundered or gone on to success solely because of the ways in which they dealt with this aspect of the business. Chapter 18 is concerned with mail order catalogs—how to use them to your best advantage. Chapter 19 is a potpourri of special selling techniques for mail order—techniques many firms are using to multiply their profits, including sales to other mail order firms and special tools little known outside the industry. In Chapter 20, I discuss mail order management and record keeping. Many firms with successful products or services, firms making profit in mail order, ultimately fail because of an inability to keep correct and accurate records and to manage their business properly. No need for this to happen if you read Chapter 20. Finally in Chapter 21 you will see where mail order is going and get some ideas as to how to apply high technology to mail order today.

Let's start right in with Chapter 1. I'm eager for you to start and succeed in your own mail order business, and I'm eager to hear about your success. But success begins with the first step, which you are about to take.

WILLIAM A. COHEN

Pasadena, California
January 1982

Acknowledgments

I would like to thank some of the many mail order entrepreneurs, businesspeople, scholars, students, and experts who have assisted me in preparing this book: Ed Burnett, Melvin Powers, Mark Varnes, Steve Popkin, Freeman Gosden, Jr., Henry R. "Pete" Hoke, Jr., Leonard Carlson, E. Joseph Cossman, Joe Sugarman, Paul Muchnick, and the late Joe Karbo, who spoke before the first graduate academic course in mail order at his home.

Cohen's Maxims*

Risk.   Never be afraid to take risks. If you work for someone, that is part of what you are getting paid for. If you work for yourself, it is the only way you can become successful.

Responsibility.   If you are assigned a task, you are responsible for its successful completion. There are no acceptable excuses for failing to fulfill this responsibility and the responsibility cannot be shifted to others.

Self-Confidence.   Self-confidence comes from successfully completing increasingly difficult tasks and assignments. Give your maximum to every project, no matter how insignificant or formidable.

Leadership.   A leader accepts responsibility for others. This means that the welfare of those that you lead must always come before your own well being. Therefore, while your primary duty is the accomplishment of your organization's mission the welfare of your subordinates comes second, and your own welfare last.

Success.   Success does not come from working hard. Success comes from playing hard. Therefore, if you want success, you must position yourself so that the duties that you perform, no matter how difficult or challenging, are considered play to you and not work. If you do this, not only will you gain success, but you will have fun doing it.

Compensation.   Compensation, whether in the form of profit, salary, or job satisfaction, is the by-product of your contribution to society and is in direct proportion to this contribution. It is an error to make compensation the focus of your life's work. You will not reach your full potential and will have cheated society of the full benefit of your talent and ability.

Individual Ability. Every individual has the potential to do great things. To reach this potential it is necessary to discover your special abilities and qualifications. This means that you should always attempt new tasks and accept responsibility for untried assignments whenever they are offered.

Duty. Whatever your occupation, you have a duty to the society of which you are a member. If you are a soldier, your duty is to protect that society. If you are in business or industry, your duty is to create and manage the jobs, wealth, and products of that society. Therefore, failure will not only be harmful to you, but also to society, just as success will not only be beneficial to you, but also to society.

Planning. Successful actions are not results of accidents or luck, but rather of an analysis of the situation and the preparation and proper execution of plans. Because of a changing environment and other variables, plans will not always succeed as originally conceived. But planning will maximize your successes and minimize your failures.

Contents

How You Can Make Your Fortune in the Multibillion-Dollar Mail Order Industry

WHO'S DOING WHAT IN MAIL ORDER TODAY?

As I sit here today, writing these words, I look at my own daily mail and I'm amazed at the wide variety of products and services being sold in the incredible mail order industry.

First, here's an offer for $6 worth of cheeses free, by mail, to entice me to join a cheese lovers' monthly club. Here is an industrial offer. Someone has sent me literature on a fantastic new cutter that cuts and fabricates all thermal plastics. Next I have an offer that includes a free sample of a keychain that can be imprinted with my company's name. The offer states that if I pay the standard price for several hundred, I will receive an equal number free. And here is a catalog of limited plate editions. These plates are ceramic and go for as much as $75 or more per copy. Next I see an intriguing envelope, which when opened proves to be a booklet describing a system for winning at blackjack. Another somewhat bulky envelope advertises a complete set of nuts, bolts, and sheet metal screws. Included in the envelope and creating a huge bulge are a sample screw, bolt, and nut for my examination. This particular mailing I am familiar with: I have seen it before and I know it to be one of the most successful mailings of the previous year. The next offer is for a booklet on how to win regularly at the racetrack. Now here's an interesting one— this individual researches patents and, noting that I have a patent for an invention, he has sent me a postcard stating that my patent has been cited during the issuing of a new patent. The card goes on to state that I will undoubtedly want to know whether my patent dominates later patents or any state of the art advances shown by the later patents. This company will send me a list of patent numbers at a cost of $15 each. Next I have a large envelope from American Airlines, which advertises all sorts of products, ranging from a Yashika SLR camera outfit to a computer to a vacuum cleaner. Here's a brochure describing a special science magazine for children. And right under it is a mailing from the American Management Association asking me to join the President's Association. Another thick brown envelope contains multicolor photographs of jackets, trousers, suits, shoes, and all sorts of wearing apparel. And a final package contains an offer to join a tape or record club, the immediate attraction being an offer of six tapes or records for only 1¢ plus postage and handling. Truly, the variety of goods and services sold through the mail today is incredible.

This amazing group of products offered in my daily mail is indicative of the great size of the mail order market. According to a *New York Times* article it is currently in excess of $140 billion a year. I want to say again, that's *billions* of dollars. Why, if you had only 1% of that market, you would have a billion dollars in sales. This huge volume has attracted major companies as well as individual entrepreneurs. In fact, today, over half the *Fortune* 500 companies in the United States have mail order divisions and sell products and services by mail. These include such firms as American Airlines, whose mailing I received today, Time-Life Books, Hewlett-Packard, Montgomery Ward, American Express, Gulf Oil, and thousands of other major companies.

But if you think that the mail order business is only for the giants, against whom you cannot compete, you are wrong. There are thousands of entrepreneurs who either started small and grew big and who are right now making a fortune by mail, or who are well on their way to becoming rich and are knocking down incomes of $20,000, $30,000, or $50,000 a year or more. We'll talk about some of them—Joe Sugarman, Joe Karbo, Ben Suarez, and others—later. Further, in the coming chapters in this book I will tell you how you can meet, and beat, the competition of the giants as a small work-out-of-your-home mail order businessman or businesswoman.

MAIL ORDER . . . WHAT ARE WE TALKING ABOUT?

Before we get down to business, however, we need to get a couple of terms straight. Because the mail order, or direct response marketing industry is growing at such a rapid pace, new terms are continually being coined and the meanings of older terms are being changed. Therefore, even before proceeding we need to take a few minutes to develop a common language. The Direct Marketing Association (DMA), which is the largest and oldest trade association having to do with mail order, likes the term *direct marketing* to describe the activities of its members. Only last year it changed its name to the present one; its old name was the Direct Mail/Marketing Association.

According to the *Fact Book on Direct Response Marketing* published by the DMA direct marketing is "the total of activities by which products and services are offered to market segments in one or more media for informational purposes or to solicit a direct response from a present or prospective customer or contributor by mail, telephone or other access."

Martin Baier, Henry R. Hoke, Jr., and Robert Stone, three well-known experts in the field, developed some concepts and definitions worthy of note that were published in the April 1982 issue of *Direct Marketing* magazine. They defined *mail order* as "a Method of Selling, which relies on direct response advertising alone, to effect a measurable response and/or transaction by mail, telephone or other interactive medium," and *direct response advertising* as "that which effects a measurable response and/or transaction at any location."

In this book, the terms *mail order* and *direct response marketing* will be used interchangeably. Important here is that while the term is *mail order*, common usage and technology have combined to make the term applicable not only to mail, but also to telephone, radio, television, and so on, and not only to order, but also to fulfillment of the product ordered.

One final word about a term that is sometimes used to mean *mail order* but does not. The term *direct mail* describes a medium of *direct-response advertising*, the same as newspaper, magazine, radio, or television.

WHY THE MAIL ORDER BUSINESS IS GROWING AND WILL CONTINUE TO GROW

Even though the mail order business is currently in excess of $140 billion a year in gross sales, it is still growing at an enormous percentage growth rate, currently estimated at as much as 12 to 16% every single year. In fact, it grew even during the recent recession. This phenomenal growth is due to several factors. First is the growth in education in the United States. Mail order requires that your customer be able to read and understand the message you are trying to communicate to him or her. Unless the customer understands your message, he or she cannot buy. As the educational level of the United States has risen, mail order sales have also increased.

Along with the rise in education levels, there has been an increase in incomes. This means that individuals have more disposable income items that are essentially luxuries, not basic requirements of life. Most of those items I saw advertised in my own mail this morning—even food items, such as those special cheeses for cheese lovers—were marginal luxuries that require a higher-income buyer. As the income levels have increased in the United States, and in the world, so has your potential market for the purchase of mail order items.

Personal selling costs is another factor that has favored the growth of mail order. Personal selling costs have skyrocketed. The costs of many consumer items that could previously have been sold door to door and in- dustrial products that could be sold through personal sales calls have gone up greatly, because of higher gasoline prices and higher incomes of salespeople, among other reasons. Each face-to-face call made by a sales- person costs much more today than it did 10 years ago, even in noninfla- tion dollars. As a result, mail order has become extremely attractive, compared to personal selling, as a means of selling all sorts of products, both consumer and industrial. At the same time, various forms of mail order techniques have been used to assist personal selling, so that each expensive call can be made more easily and with a higher success rate.

Social changes have acted to influence mail order buying. Today, women hold down better than 40% of the jobs in the United States, a tre- mendous change from just a few years ago. And because women are working today, they no longer have the opportunities they once had for daily shopping. This change has extended by many times the products that people are willing to buy through the mail.

Technological and communications advances have also served to in- crease mail order growth. Such innovations and inventions as the com- puter and the WATS line telephone service have made tremendous changes in the mail order industry. Through the use of the computer, for example, costs of selling can be greatly reduced. And as the computer has developed further, even small companies can use it profitably to lower their costs and thus increase their profits. In a similar fashion, WATS lines have made it much easier for mail order customers to order. Order- ing by mail is not a completely trouble-free task. A potential customer seeing your advertisement or receiving your direct mail piece must not only make the decision to buy, but must then sit down, write a letter, find a stamp, find an envelope, put together the entire package with the check, and mail it. Then he or she must wait a certain amount of time before receiving what was ordered. Through the use of a WATS line, a buyer can make a toll-free call. With a credit card (which, as we will see, has also increased mail order sales), he or she not only places the order much more easily but also shortens the period of waiting before receiving the order. Other technological advances that both lower costs for the mail order operator and make it easier for the potential mail order buyer to place the order are continually being made.

Consumer credit has also had a remarkable effect on mail order. Consumer credit, as exemplified by credit cards, not only makes it possible to order more easily by mail, but also provides a means for time payment on higher-priced items. Stop and think about this for a moment. Whereas once the mail order businessperson had to carry credit and perhaps act as a collection agency for the sale of a higher-priced item to a mail order customer, now the consumer has a credit system readily and immediately available to him or her.

Finally, the energy crisis has helped the growth in mail order sales. Since energy, in the form of gas for the car, must be expended by a consumer almost every time he or she shops, it is much easier and less expensive simply to order many items through the mail.

WHY THE MAIL ORDER BUSINESS
IS A PERFECT PLACE TO MAKE YOUR FORTUNE

The mail order business is a perfect place to make your fortune as an entrepreneur. This is true not only if you have not yet entered business, but even if you have an ongoing, established business that has little to do with mail order. Here's why:

1. *Low Barrier to Enter.* If you want to enter the mail order business or employ mail order techniques to assist a business you already have in operation, there is little to prevent your entry. As a matter of fact, the U.S. Post Office, which benefits from mail order sales, will assist you in every way possible. Unless you deal with certain restricted types of goods, there are no licenses to obtain other than a local business license, which we'll discuss fully in chapter 2. There are no tests you must take to qualify you. There are no educational requirements you must have completed to become a mail order practitioner. As a result, most people can enter the mail order business more easily and with less difficulty than any other business.

2. *Low Capital Requirement.* Although you cannot get into mail order without at least some money, this initial amount is really quite low, compared to other businesses you might choose to enter. For example, it will require several hundred thousand dollars or more for you to enter the restaurant business with a single restaurant, and yet, you won't even know whether you have been successful for a year or longer. A machine shop will typically require a large capital investment, for various types of tools and machinery. A retail store requires not only an outlay for the store itself but also for inventory and sales personnel. However, a mail order business can be started with little capital equipment, no special offices or facilities, and no employees except yourself to begin with. In fact, as we will point out in a later chapter, you can start part-time and maintain a very low investment and overhead until the cash flow is right and you are successful enough for the business to become full-time. Or, if you wish, you may keep it a part-time business for as long as you desire and bring in thousands of extra dollars a year as a welcome addition to compensation coming from whatever else it is you are doing. Tyler Hicks, famous for his books on entrepreneurship, makes a fortune through his mail order business while holding down an executive position in the publishing industry.

3. *Success or Failure, You'll Find Out Fast.* With most other businesses, unless you have misplanned for your capital requirements and go bankrupt very early on, you may not know for years if your business is really a viable moneymaker with great profit potential or if you will be forever "barely making it." A man in New York didn't realize for three years that the specialty restaurant he had started was wrong for the area in which he was located. An engineer worked for seven years on a robot lawnmower and finally succeeded in getting it into production, only to discover that a market did not exist for that item at that time. With a mail order business, regardless of the product or service sold, you can find out very quickly whether you have a winner or a loser. I will show you exactly how to do this in a later chapter. Further, even if you have a number of losers, you can control your expenses so that once you hit a big winner, you will more than make up for your losses many times over. No other business will permit you to experiment in this fashion while you test and modify your products and concepts until eventually you achieve success.

For the established business, mail order also offers a number of distinct advantages.

First, you can target your specific market. For example, let us say you have developed a calculating device that is useful for everyone, but is especially useful for engineers. Through mail order techniques, you can either advertise in places such as engineering magazines, where those engineers are most likely to read your advertisement, or you can obtain specialized mailing lists and send direct mail pieces to reach your market directly. This is one of the reasons that Hewlett-Packard was so much more successful with its electronic calculators than its competition.

You can get to your market fast. If you have a retail business selling a certain item—let's say, a special wrist radio—and if you advertise, your customers must come to you to purchase your item through your retail outlet. And without special advertising or promotion, you can sell the wrist radio only as word is passed from one person to another that you have it for sale. But in mail order, if you are successful with a certain item during a test, you can expand your promotion rapidly and nationally to get to the entire market. For example, the Hewlett-Packard people tested the sales potential of their electronic computers through the mail in a relatively small mailing to engineers, and when they found it successful, they expanded immediately and rapidly, getting to their entire market fast through a mailing to as many engineers as they could find. You can do the same thing.

You can time your promotion through the mail to coincide with other promotional activities. Let's say you are selling a special item at a trade show. A direct mailing campaign promoting this item before the show can coincide with your trade show promotion and both can work together to increase your sales dramatically.

You can test at a relatively low cost. Again, what does it cost to test other types of business or other types of product through other media? Sometimes, quite a lot. If you sell plants through a retail store, it will be a long time before you know whether the location and product are correct for the market you are trying to reach. Further, this "test" will cost not only the price of the inventory, but the price and rent of the store and other equipment. If you sell plants through mail order, through drop-ship arrangements, you may have no inventory cost whatsoever. The cost of your test will be limited to your mailing. If the mailing is successful, you have a winner and can expand immediately. If it's a loser, you can drop it at once and your only cost is the cost of your test.

You can exploit winners fast, which goes along with getting to your market quickly. Let's say that your plant shop or your restaurant, as described above, is successful. How long will it take, then, to acquire another location or build another shop and open it up, even if you know that you have a winner with this type of operation? Not overnight, that's certain. But through the mail, you can exploit your winners the very next day after learning of your success.

For all of the above reasons, the mail order business is a perfect place for you to make your fortune. One word of caution: You are not guaranteed success in mail order by these facts, nor is success in mail order easy in the sense that you do no work or need not apply yourself to achieve it. However, I feel that in no other business is it as easy to be successful, nor do you have better control over your future, the amount of success, and how quickly you can obtain it. Paul Muchnick, writing in a U.S. government Small Business Administration booklet on mail order, says this: "The success stories are countless of people who have not only made a good living selling products and services by mail, but have amassed fortunes—starting on a kitchen table, in a garage, or spare room."

WHY YOUR CUSTOMER WILL BUY BY MAIL

One basic principle in mail order selling is always to go to your market first, and then look for a product or service to offer to the market, not the other way around. So, in going to our market first, let's look and see why people buy by mail. Joseph H. Rhoads, writing in an earlier U.S. government Small Business Administration booklet entitled *Selling by Mail with Limited Capital,* puts mail order buyers into the following four categories.

1. *Those Interested in Novelties.*   These are buyers who want things that are different from their neighbors. According to Rhoads, these people actually look over magazines for items of this sort that are different and that appeal to them. When they find products that are novel and relatively inexpensive, and that are not owned—or are thought not to be owned—by their neighbors, they purchase them.

2. *Those Pursuing a Hobby or Some Particular Interest.*   These are people with special interests, such as gardening, stamp or coin collecting, financial investments, making money, and many other different hobbies or activities.

3. *Those Who Buy by Mail as a Matter of Convenience.*   These are buyers or potential buyers who find it easier to buy by mail, especially if they live in a location somewhat removed from adequate shopping facilities. Very frequently, these people will send away for merchandise to benefit from a larger and wider selection of items than they can find at their local stores.

4. *Those Who Buy by Mail Purely for What They Consider to Be a Price Advantage.* These are individuals who are buyers because they look over mail order catalogs or see other advertisements and direct mail pieces, compare them with retail store selections, and order through the mail because they are certain that the cost in dealing by mail is a bargain, compared to the prices in their local stores.

Len Carlson, the founder of Sunset House and many other successful mail order ventures, developed a list of 29 reasons why people buy, a list of 13 reasons why people prefer to order by mail or by telephone. Here are Len's lists:

There are 29 psychological reasons why people buy
1. to be more comfortable
2. to make work easier
3. to safeguard self and family
4. to protect family's future
5. to be well liked and loved
6. to add to life's pleasures
7. to be in fashion
8. to fulfill fantasies
9. to own attractive things
10. to collect valuable possessions
11. to protect possessions
12. to satisfy ego
13. to accumulate money
14. to preserve money already accumulated
15. to save time
16. to protect reputation
17. to appease appetite
18. to enjoy exotic tastes
19. to live in a clean atmosphere
20. to be strong and healthy
21. to get rid of aches and pains
22. to find new and uncommon things
23. to be more beautiful
24. to attract opposite sex
25. to satisfy sexual desires

26. to bring back "good old days"
27. to be "lucky"
28. to live longer
29. to save money

Why people prefer to order by mail/telephone

1. It's convenient.
2. It offers unusual items they can't find elsewhere.
3. Variety is bigger, with more complete selections.
4. Price is lower.
5. It saves time.
6. Product description is more complete.
7. It avoids contact with inept salespersons.
8. It saves gas, parking, security problems.
9. Liberal guarantee provides comfort.
10. "Surprise" element is fun.
11. It avoids embarrassment.
12. Additional credit is sometimes available.
13. Activity counteracts mailbox loneliness.

Researcher–writer Melodie Cingolani, writing in an issue of Bank of America's *Small Business Reporter* entitled *Mail Order Enterprises,* says that mail order buying retains appeal because many customers find it easy and pleasant, and because it has the advantage of convenience, selection, anonymity, economy, and fun.

Some years ago, *Better Homes and Gardens* did a special study on mail order buyers from their publication. One of the questions they asked was, "Why do you purchase items by mail?" Respondents were invited to check one of five different reasons, and 63.3% indicated that they purchased items by mail because they couldn't find them elsewhere. Next highest was the 49.3% who said they purchased items by mail because of convenience. Price was third, with 25.2%. And finally, "Simply enjoy buying by mail" pulled in 12.1%. Only 4% checked "Other," and .5% did not respond to this question.

Similar results were reported by Jim Kobs, who is president of the direct marketing agency of Kobs & Brady and the author of the book *Profitable Direct Marketing.* Kobs analyzed the same question in an earlier *Better Homes and Gardens* survey. He compared the responses with those of a second, more recent study done by a leading direct marketing catalog house, which limited its study to its own customer lists. The results were similar, but not idential, to those of the *Better Homes and Gardens* study: 49% said they shopped for convenience; 37% indicated they could not find the items elsewhere; 16% said they shopped for variety, 14% for price, 12% for service, 11% because of a desire for gifts or items for personal use, and 10% for quality. Ten percent in this survey indicated a variety of "other" reasons, including free gifts and utility items. If you have counted and are wondering why this total exceeds 100%, it is because the survey permitted multiple answers.

In the survey mentioned earlier, *Better Homes and Gardens* also looked into the energy problem and its affect on mail order buying through two questions: "How has the energy problem changed your style of shopping?" and "Have you or do you think that you will be shopping more by mail now?" In partial answer to the first question, 15.5% of the respondents indicated that they would be making use of mail order more. And to the second question, 30.5% answered yes, they thought that they would be shopping more by mail now. So to the traditional answers as to why people purchase by mail, we must now add energy, and this will no doubt also be a partial explanation for the significant increase every year in mail order buying.

What do these studies suggest about products in mail order selling? Well, the fact that so many people buy by mail because they feel they cannot find these items elsewhere should be ample evidence that you should seek a product that is not easily found elsewhere by mail. Conversely, it is much more difficult to sell a staple item, such as bread, by mail unless there is something unique about it. Perhaps if it is homemade, if you can keep it fresh, and if it can be obtained nowhere else, it can be sold by mail. Or perhaps a bread that is self-warming as you open the package could be sold by mail. But the ordinary bread that can be found at your store, at almost every store, cannot be sold profitably by mail. The same is true for similar types of item.

Price is also clearly very important to the mail order buyer. However, it is a little known fact that mail order selling is actually a very expensive way to sell. Therefore, one of your challenges as a mail order dealer is to find a way in which you can supply the item less expensively to your customer, or at least your customer perceives the item to be less expensive than what he or she can buy in a store.

All the reasons that mail order buyers do purchase by mail should be carefully considered by anyone who wants to enter the mail order business. They should be used as a guide to selecting a product and service, and further, to how entering this market so as to maximize your chances for success. We'll explain exactly how to do this in some detail in the chapters to come.

SMALL BUSINESSPERSONS WHO BECAME
MILLIONAIRES THROUGH MAIL ORDER

As was pointed out earlier, mail order is not necessarily as easy way to success, nor does the mere fact that you enter mail order guarantee your success. It certainly does not guarantee that you will become a millionaire. Nevertheless, it is a fact that a number of small businesspeople who have entered the mail order business have gone on to become millionaires from very humble beginnings. I would like to talk about a few of these individuals here, just to show you how it can be done and to show you that such success is possible for you, too. While certainly no one can say that you will be as successful as these individuals, certainly no one can say that you can't do better than they have, either.

Joe Cossman

Joe Cossman is the author of *How I Made One Million Dollars in Mail Order.* Joe actually made more than $25 million selling mail order ant farms, toy soldiers, garden sprinklers, fly poison, potato spud guns, and even toy shrunken heads. He has spent the last few years giving seminars around the country and helping others get started in their own businesses. Joe started after World War II, working after-hours from his $35-a-week job with a beat-up typewriter on his kitchen table. He tells an incredible story of his first success. After one year of writing letters all over the world, attempting to find customers for exports from the United States, he saw a large ad for soap. Writing his contacts abroad, he received a letter of credit for $180,000, which would be good when he delivered the soap at the ship and presented the bills of lading at the bank. At first he couldn't get leave from his job, and he had to go so far as to threaten to quit. Taking his life's savings of $300, he went to New York City and approached the soap company, only to discover that the soap company was nonexistent, and that the soap that was advertised did not exist. He went to the library and, using the *Thomas Register of Manufacturers,* called soap companies all over the country until he found one that made the soap that had been advertised. He then made arrangements to purchase the soap and persuaded a trucking company to drive from New York to Alabama to pick it up without payment up front. In the meantime, he had run up a telephone bill of $810. When he returned to New york with the soap, time was running out. The letter of credit was good for 30 days and if the bills of lading were not presented at the bank, the letter of credit would be worthless and he would be unable to collect the $180,000. In addition to his other debts, he also owed a great deal of money to the soap company for the 30,000 cases of soap. But even as the soap was being loaded onto the ship, Joe realized that, with less than an hour remaining until the letter of credit would expire, time had run out. Making a last desperate attempt to succeed, he barged into the office of the president of the steamship line and was able to convince the president to give him bills of lading and assume responsibility for the soap, even though it had not been loaded onto the ship. In fact, the president had his own limousine take Joe to the bank before it closed to present the bills of lading. Cossman made almost $30,000 on this first mail order project, and $30,000 was worth a great deal more after World War II than it is today. This venture launched him on his multimillion-dollar mail order success trip, which is still going on.

Joe Cossman's story also illustrates some important principles if you are going to be successful in mail order. First, mail order is not necessarily a quick success. Although Joe made $30,000 with his first victory, it required a year's worldwide correspondence before the soap venture came together. Second, you need perseverance. The fact that Joe Cossman worked for a year says much for his perseverance by itself. The incredible difficulties that Cossman met and conquered to win the $30,000 says even more. Look at the steps Cossman had to follow to make this "easy money." First, he had to write numerous letters abroad attempting to locate a customer for products in general, and, finally, for the soap product itself. Second, he had to get a leave of absence from the company where he worked to make the trip to New York. Third, he had to meet the disappointment of finding the company that had advertised the soap to be nonexistent. Fourth, he had to spend the time and take the trouble and expense to locate a soap company that actually manufactured soap that could be exported. Fifth, he had to get the trucking firm to drive down and get the soap on credit. Sixth, he got back to New York and then realized only a desperate meeting with the president of the steamship line could save the deal, and then he made that last desperation attempt. Is it any wonder that Joe Cossman won and eventually became a multimillionaire? Joe Cossman says this: "I know of no business in the world that requires such a small investment to start, and yet holds promise of such tremendous financial gains as mail order."

Benjamin Suarez

Benjamin Suarez (also spelled Swarez) is the author of *Seven Steps to Freedom* and the genius behind numerous successful mail order campaigns, such as "How to Get What the U.S. Government Owes You," "The Secret of Having Good Luck," "Why People in Vermont Are

Healthier, Less Overweight, Stay Younger Longer, Live Longer Than People of Any Other State in the Union," "The Machine That Peels Off Pounds While You Sit Back and Enjoy It," "Fountain of Youth Discovered by Little Known Civilization," "Famed Physicist Proves That Sitting in a Pyramid Causes Unexplainable Good Things to Happen," "The International Astrological Association," "Ohio Man Discovers the Secret of How to Escape the American Rat Race," and many others.

Benjamin Suarez started as a computer programmer and systems analyst with a major company. Assigned to a project for working with nuclear reactors and power generation equipment, he ran into trouble with his bosses over his work innovations and he decided in 1970 that he would begin a part-time business and eventually become fully independent. His first project was a food delivery system, started in April 1970, that failed. In July of 1970, he started a computerized poker system, which also failed. In October of 1970, he started two different projects—special financial tables published in book form, and a calculator. He attempted to market these in several ways, including mail order. After he invested in huge amounts of inventory and attempted to sell these products in the wrong way to the wrong list, these projects also failed. Finally, in October of 1971, he started an astrology club, which he attempted to sell by direct mail. He got a 3% response. Although he only broke even, he still felt that he could make money. This he did by implementing an idea that he pioneered. Every flier he sent out was personalized by having the potential customer's name handwritten after the words "Memo to," and there was a real signature after the word "From." This innovation doubled Suarez's response to 6% and the American Astrological Association was born in December 1971. Comfortable with his cash flow, Suarez resigned his job with the major corporation and went into the mail order business full-time. Still, even with this success, he went through a lawsuit with partners, a suit to get his company name back, and many other tribulations, until 1974, when he really made it big—and paid himself a bonus of $80,000 in one month, in September of 1974. Since that time Benjamin Suarez has gone on to earn hundreds of thousands of dollars a year and become a great mail order success.

Again, Ben Suarez's experiences underline the need for persistence and the fact that you must go to the market first and find out what your market wants, rather than try to sell something you want to sell.

Jerry Buchanan

Jerry Buchanan of Vancouver, Washington, started with his *Writer's Utopia Formula Report* and his *Towers Club Newsletter* on self publishing in 1973 and hit on instant success, making another rags-to-riches story through mail order. For 18 years he had been a traveling salesman, almost always working for educational institutions and having only moderate success in selling. Prior to 1973, he and his wife had been live-in, full-charge resident managers of a large garden court apartment complex for four years. His wife's and his combined earnings were around $700 a month, for working seven days a week. One day his direct superior said, "Jerry, you know what your trouble is? You read too damned much," at which point, Jerry Buchanan quit his job and decided to go into self-publishing and sell through mail order full time. He had had some experience over a seven-year period earning from $1500 to $2500 a year by selling a one-page report he had written, entitled "How to Eliminate Moles and Gophers from Your Garden." Spending little money and learning the tricks of the trade through classified advertising, he had slowly acquired expertise during this period, so that when he sold the first *Writer's Utopia Formula Report,* which was only 10 pages long, he was able to document his experiences, tell how to do the same, and get a whopping $10 for his advice. At the same time, he received numerous testimonials attesting to just how good this information was. Today, there are many reports and books on the market having to do with self-publishing, but back in 1973 few had written down their inside secrets and attempted to sell them through the mail. Jerry Buchanan was one of the first and certainly the most successful. To help his report buyers keep up-to-date on what he was learning about the direct mail business himself, and to provide other information that would be useful to individuals selling reports through the mail, he started publishing a monthly newsletter soon after the first *Writer's Utopia Formula Report.* This also brought in huge profits. Today, Jerry Buchanan is a highly successful and wealthy mail order publisher.

Jerry Buchanan's success demonstrates, once again, some important mail order principles, which I will explain in this book. If you follow these principles, you will greatly enhance your chances of reaching success as quickly as possible. First, there is the length of Jerry Buchanan's report. Today, this report has grown to many times the original length, but is is important to realize that initially the *Writer's Utopia Formula Report* was only 10 pages long. If you are in the business or want to get into the business of selling information, what you are selling is the information, not paper or ink by weight. The length of the report you are selling is irrelevant. What is important is the information it contains. Jerry Buchanan's success also demonstrated the importance of the back-end business of mail order. Back-end profits are those made to the same customer after the first sale. In fact, the first sale to a customer may result only in your breaking even or even sustaining a loss. But the big profits are made with what happens after you get your customer to make his or her initial purchase. In Jerry Buchanan's case, the back-end business was the *Towers Club Newsletter,* which was (and is) sold to the buyers of the original report. After all, someone purchasing the report on how to publish oneself and sell by mail is certainly interested in getting updated information on the same subject. As I was working on this chapter, I received a letter from Jerry. He has started another newsletter, called *Information Age Letter,* and it is doing well, too. The concept of back-end profits is extremely important in mail order, and, regardless of the product or service you offer, you should keep it in mind as we discuss this concept further in the chapters to come.

Richard Thalheimer

Richard Thalheimer is the founder and president of the Sharper Image, a prestigious San Francisco mail order catalog house. Graduating from college and yearning for the excitement of the far west, he arrived in San Francisco in the early 1970s. Unfortunately, although San Francisco was everything he had hoped it would be, try as he might he couldn't find a job. Desperate, Richard finally found work selling office supplies door to door. Somewhere he heard about the exciting possibilities of selling through the mail. He started a small company, the Ribbon House, to sell office supplies in this manner. Not only was his business successful, but in the hopes of learning a high-paying profession, he put himself through law school at night with his profits. In 1977, the well-known Japanese firm, Seiko, introduced the wristwatch chronograph, selling for several hundred dollars. Richard found another watch, made in Asia at a much lower cost. Using his mail order know-how, he placed a small ad and made $600 profit in one month. Now, Richard Thalheimer is a jogger, and he immediately thought he saw a potential market in joggers, especially since his small ad had been so successful.

With some trepidation because of the higher risk, he placed a full-page ad in *Runner's World.* This ad resulted in 3000 orders, each of which represented $30 in profits . . . an incredible $90,000 in profits from a single ad! Not bad for a mail order entrepreneur who was not yet 30 years old!

Unfortunately, there was just one small problem: Because of the demand, his source had run out of product, Thalheimer had lots of orders and nothing to fulfill them with. He immediately sat down and wrote the best letter he could to his customers, giving them a chance to cancel the deal, but stressing the advantages of waiting for the product. In this way, he stalled for six months. Finally, his father found an alternative source, and, three months later, the 3000 watches arrived in Thalheimer's office.

But when he opened the shipping container, he found that these watches were of lower quality. In almost every case, the watch face had separated from the rest of the watch.

As quickly as he could, he called around town and found a source of glue that was the correct type for reattaching the watch faces, and he laboriously reattached every one of the 3000 orders. This project launched the Sharper Image, and the very fist year, in addition to locating a source for high-quality chronograph watches, his new company hit $3 million in sales. Less than two years later, in 1979, he published his first catalog. Last year his company had reached $100 million in sales . . . and he never did get the opportunity to practice law.

Thalheimer's story also illustrates the virtue of persistence and the willingness to take risks after a thorough analysis of the situation. Like other successful mail order entrepreneurs, Richard Thalheimer knows that his success comes from the value he provides to his customers, and as he told a recent gathering of mail order pros, "the success of the Sharper Image is due to our outstanding customer relations."

Len Carlson

Len Carlson founded Sunset House and was its president for 20 years. But he didn't start as president of a multimillion-dollar mail order company. Len worked in advertising and promotion at Topps Bubble Gum in New York City. One of the products he developed as a premium was a small rubber stamp that was made up with a child's name. This premium was advertised in comic books to help promote the bubble gum. Before the campaign was well under way, Len left the bubble gum business to live and work in California. After a year after he had left Topps, he became curious about how the rubber stamp item had worked out. Much to his amazement, he discovered that the promotion had failed and that the company still had 75,000 rubber stamps in its warehouse.

But somehow, the idea of the personalized rubber stamp as a unique mail order item just wouldn't leave his mind. He approached a local manufacturer and was told, "Young man, we are the largest manufacturer of rubber stamps in the world, and my father was in the business before me—believe me, you can't sell rubber stamps through the mail. We know . . . we've tried." But Carlson couldn't be deterred. He worked out a deal with the manufacturer to supply rubber stamps that he would sell by mail. However, Len didn't call his device a rubber stamp; he promoted it as a personal name stamp and advertised it in *House and Garden* and *Sunset Magazine* for $1.00 When he checked his mailbox, he found it stuffed with envelopes containing dollar bills. Knowing he had to sell something to his customers after this first sale to really have a business, he studied every competitor's catalog he could get his hands on, and the very first year he was mailing his catalog to 50,000 names.

Carlson built Sunset House into one of America's largest specialty mail order companies. Since selling Sunset House in 1969, he has headed up several mail order operations, including Lenca, Inc., of Beverly Hills, a product development firm that has developed over 100 unusual items sold in the United States, Europe, and Asia; Perma Plaque Corporation, which offers a unique lamination process to preserve documents; New Silken/Sheer, which sells pantyhose by mail; and Better Life, Inc., a Japanese mail order joint venture that sells American health and beauty aids through mail order in Japan. Over the past 30 years he has pioneered and merchandised almost 10,000 new and unique mail order products.

Charles Atlas

Charles Atlas was a poor immigrant boy from Calabria, Italy, whose real name was Angelo Siciliano. Beaten and humiliated by bullies, he resolved to strengthen himself such that no one would ever pick on him again. He began a series of experiments with body building, none of which were entirely satisfactory to him. One day while visiting the Prospect Park Zoo in Brooklyn he saw a lion stretching in its cage. He was amazed at the muscles on the lion, which seemed to tense and bulge as the lion exercised. Atlas realized that the lion must be exercising, and that in some natural way, the lion had developed a strong, muscular body.

From this visit to the zoo, Charles Atlas developed a whole series of exercises which he called Dynamic-Tension. In short order he doubled his weight and become an artist's model and a famous strongman. Then one day he learned that physical culturist Bernarr MacFadden was sponsoring a contest for the "World's Most Beautiful Man." Atlas won. The following year, MacFadden sponsored a new contest for "America's Most Perfectly Developed Man." Atlas won that one, too. Now, feeling that he had something to sell and a message to impart, Atlas put together his own physical culture course and began selling his course through mail order. At first the business did well, but then sales fell off and the business was in trouble. Atlas consulted with his advertising agency and was assigned a new account executive who had just graduated from New York University, Charles Roman. Roman thought he knew what was wrong with the ads. The business was failing, and the advertising agency didn't seem to care much about the account. But Roman did, and Atlas was convinced that Roman knew what he was talking about. Atlas offered Roman half the business as a working partner. In short order these two men were selling thousands of Charles Atlas courses every year, and when Charles Atlas died in 1972 they were selling more than 20,000 courses every year. Both the poor immigrant who had sand kicked in his face and his partner were millionaires several times over, and Charles Atlas was perhaps the most well-known strongman in the world. They had trained literally hundreds of thousands of students to be strong . . . all by mail.

Joe Karbo

Joe Karbo's *The Lazy Man's Way to Riches* is one of the biggest success stories in mail order of the 1970s. Like many mail order operators who are successful today, Joe Karbo never finished college; his college education was interrupted by World War II and service in the armed forces. On returning, Joe went into an advertising agency, and by the early 1960s he and his wife ran one of the first all-night, 24-hour television stations in the United States. Joe would come on at midnight and, with talk shows, movies, and so forth, go through the night, until the daytime regulars began their cycle. Through the sale of advertising time, Joe was slowly but surely acquiring a fortune, earning $5000 a week. Suddenly, the station from which Joe rented the time was acquired by a large corporation, and Joe was cut out of the business. He went from a net income of $5000 a week to being $50,000 in debt. His attorney advised bankruptcy, but instead Joe called together his creditors, telling them that there was presently no money to pay them off, but that he fully intended to do so. If they did not believe him, they could take him to court. Since he had no money, this would not have helped them. Even if they sent him to jail, there was still no money to be had. However, Karbo promised his creditors that he would pay them every penny he owed them, and he did have a business idea he felt could make him successful and allow him to pay his creditors everything. Karbo asked only that the payments be made on a regular schedule and that his creditors not jeopardize the business each time he accumulated a little cash. Joe was able to persuade his creditors, and in a short period he had written and published a booklet called *The Power of Money Management,* for which he wrote an ad headlined "Get Out of Debt in 90 Minutes without Borrowing." He soon sold over 250,000 copies. Joe had many other mail order products, so that by 1972 or 1973, when he embarked on his "Lazy Man's Way to Riches" campaign, he had an income of several hundred thousand a year, a Rolls Royce, several homes, and other adornments of the very rich. For some time he'd had the concept of a success booklet based on his own success story, a combination of what Joe calls "Dyna Psych" and mail order marketing methods. One night he got up, unable to sleep, and within two hours wrote the ad that was to take him from an income of several hundred thousand dollars a year to multimillions. He then published his famous ad for his book, *The Lazy Man's Way to Riches,* and received $50,000 in orders and sales before he sat down to write the book itself. *The Lazy Man's Way to Riches* has been translated into many languages and sold in many countries around the world. To date, it has sold over a million copies and is still going strong. Further, this isn't Joe's only product. He has sold a book on handicapping, has a newsletter, has sold a skin care product, and a device for seeing through doors, among many other successful products.

Joe's successful advertisement for *The Lazy Man's Way to Riches* was the first of many similar ads by advertisers who have sought to imitate him. His ads contained a number of innovations that have since been adopted in the industry as standard practice. Among these are the use of large space advertisements in the classified sections of newspapers, the request for postdated checks, which are not to be cashed by the seller for a month while the merchandise is examined, and the use of an accountant's statement verifying what is said in the ad to add to credibility. We'll be talking about these concepts and others later on.

Joe's success again points out the importance of the market-before-the-product concept, and, like others before him, Joe Karbo advertised and tested to make sure that his market existed before he acquired the product in large inventory.

Len and Rick Hornick and Bay County Woodcrafts

From the pages of the June 1981 issue of *Direct Marketing* magazine comes the story of the Hornick brothers, Len and Rick, who started a part-time business in high school. The part-time business grew out of a hobby of making duck hunting decoys by hand. After a couple of years, both realized that what they really enjoyed making was not duck decoys, but far more detailed and artistic decorative ducks—real art objects. They moved from their basement to their garage and stayed there five years, doing everything themselves including carving the birds, sanding them, and painting them. In those early days, they didn't have a single employee. The first years were tough, and they had difficulty finding their market for these unusual "birds." At first they wholesaled to department stores and gift shops. Finally, in 1970, they began to sell direct. They ran small twelfth of a page ads in mail order sections of magazines selling the sanded ducks unpainted. These successful ads got them hooked on selling through mail order. Slowly, reinvesting the money they made, they built their business. Today, the two brothers employ over 100 expert artisans to make their ducks. They produce a beautiful 32 page catalog that is mailed out four times a year. The September mailing alone is mailed to three quarters of a million potential customers. Their company, Bay County Woodcrafts, makes about 1000 ducks every day. While the price for an individual duck may be $85 or more, they sell many kits in the $20 to $30 range. From their high school hobby, the two brothers have built a multimillion dollar business. They did something that they liked to do and that they were expert in doing—and they persisted until the business was successful.

Melvin Powers

Today Melvin Powers, author of *How to Get Rich in Mail Order*, is president of the Wilshire Book Company and the dean of mail book publishing. But 25 years ago he was a disappointed author who wrote a book on hypnotism that no publisher would publish. He placed a small ad in *Popular Science* for $119. After nine days, only 12 orders had come in and Melvin wrote off the $119 and another $250 he had spent for printing the book. The twelfth day after the ad had appeared, Melvin's wife called him at work. He had no less than 201 letters requesting his book. At $5 each, this was more money than Melvin made at his job in a month. Melvin started his operation in a garage, grew out of it, and moved into a small office rented from an advertising agency on Sunset Strip. Today, Melvin has a building of 15,000 square feet and with additional storage space and carries 400 different book titles. He sells more than 100,000 books every month. He has sold millions of books by mail, including such well-known big sellers as *Psycho-Cybernetics, Magic of Thinking Big,* and *Think and Grow Rich.*

Melvin Powers was fortunate in making money from the start, but not all of his projects have been successful. Here's what he says about success in the mail order business: "Don't expect success with every mail order campaign. It just doesn't happen, not even to the experts. If you have given your best effort to a mail order idea and it doesn't work, put your energy into the next project."

Brainerd Mellinger

Brainerd Mellinger came from a mail order family. But his father once said that Brainerd would never learn to write copy, so perhaps partly to prove his father wrong, he too started out on a shoestring—less than $100 and a rented garage. Brainerd's ideas ran to import-export. During World War II, he had seen products he knew to be in demand in the United States firsthand. A little luck, timing, and genius gave him a big boost toward success. Recalling products he had seen in Europe, he hit on one of the greatest of import mail order success products. Further, he discovered he could have this product drop-shipped directly to a customer from Germany for less than a dollar. The product? A miniature version of the famous Black Forest cuckoo clock. The product was so successful that Brainerd tied up almost the entire production of these cuckoo clocks in Germany. Success at importing other products and selling them through the mail soon led Brainerd to the concept of training others through a mail order course for import and mail order selling, while he continued to do all three activities profitably himself. Furthermore, his concept had a new twist: He would locate dealers worldwide who would wholesale thousands of different products to his students. Brainerd's business grew tremendously and expanded into seminars, newsletters, and worldwide trips for his mail order students. While he no longer writes advertising himself, his success is due in no small part to the fact that he indeed learned how to write copy.

Gerardo Joffe

Gerardo Joffe is an engineer who came to the United States from Germany via Bolivia; unlike the other mail order millionaires we have talked about, he is very well educated indeed. Joffe has a BS in mining engineering from the Missouri School of Mines and an MBA from Harvard. Gerardo got into the mail order business by accident. He had invented a gadget, and someone told him that he could sell it by mail order. He couldn't, but meanwhile he found some other products that he could sell. These he put into a catalog, and five years after forming this company, Haverhills, he sold it to Time, Inc., for just over $1 million. He then started another mail order company, Henniker's, which he sold for more than a million dollars also. In his book *How You Can Make At Least $1 Million (but Probably Much More) in the Mail Order Business,* Gerardo says, "Sometimes, in looking back at those very early days, I wonder how I survived in business. But I did ... I made a decent living and good profit."

Joe Sugarman

Joe Sugarman is the author of *Success Forces.* His book is well titled, for Joe's success is unique and motivating
    Joe Sugarman is another college dropout who started a little mail order business in the basement of his home. In a copy of *Business Week,* he read that a manufacturer was reducing the size and cost of electronic

calculators so that they would fit in your pocket and cost $240. At the time, Joe was in the advertising business. He suggested that a client sell the $240 calculators, but the idea was rejected. Joe then went out and raised $12,000 from friends to sell the calculators through direct mail— that is, letters direct to prospective customers. He was looking for a 2% return and needed only 2% to break even. No one was more dismayed than Joe when he failed to break even and lost most of his investors' money. However, he did some quick analysis and realized that two of the 10 lists he had mailed to were actually far above the breakeven point. It was the other eight lists that were unprofitable. Joe reduced the price to $180 and remailed. His tactic was very successful. He has since changed his advertising from direct mail to large space ads in the *Wall Street Journal, Popular Science, Scientific American,* and other publications. His company, JS&A, is the trendsetter in electronic gadgetry, and it is said that the giant firms of Sears, Montgomery Ward, Radio Shack, and others stock their goods according to what Joe sells.

I said that Joe Sugarman's success was big as well as fast, and this is true—Joe's annual sales are currently $50 million every year, and he reached this level in only seven years.

SUMMARY

In this chapter, we've talked about the incredible size of this multimillion-dollar mail order industry and how you can make your fortune in it, just as others have before you. The individuals I have discussed are all real-life people, but they are not the only ones who have gone on to become millionaires through mail order, nor are they necessarily even the largest. One can, of course, cite the examples of Sears, Montgomery Ward, Sunset House, the Franklin Mint, Fingerhut Corporation, and hundreds of other large corporations, all of which started as small entrepreneurial companies headed by one individual who knew how to make the mail order concept of marketing work.

No one can promise you success or guarantee it in the mail order business, but if you read this book carefully and apply its principles, your chances of reaching success in mail order, making a significant contribution to your present income, or, if you will, becoming fabulously wealthy are greatly increased. Now, let's not waste any more time. Turn to chapter 2 and see how to get your mail order business started.

2

How to Get Your Mail Order Business Started

You may feel that starting your own business is something very difficult and mysterious and requires an attorney and an accountant watching over your shoulder every step of the way. Actually, many, if not most, small mail order businesses will require a minimum of help from either of these specialists at the start. In fact, you can even incorporate your mail order business legally, without an attorney. In this chapter, we're going to discuss, step by step, exactly how to start your own mail order business. I'm going to cover the legal forms of businesses—the proprietorship, the partnership, and the corporation—and give you the advantages and disadvantages of each. I will explain exactly how to get a business license, how to obtain fictitious name registration if it is necessary, how to go about handling state sales tax, how to borrow money and sources of capital, and how to maintain a low overhead. By the end of the chapter, you will know exactly what you must do to start your own business and how to go about it with a minimum of fuss, problems, and expense.

WHICH FORM OF BUSINESS ORGANIZATION?

Let's look at the three legal forms of businesses first: the sole proprietorship, the partnership, and the corporation.

Sole Proprietorship

Of the three legal forms of ownership, the sole proprietorship is the simplest and easiest to start, and it is also the form which the majority of new businesses take.

Let's look at the advantages of the sole proprietorship. First, it's the easiest and quickest to initiate. Assuming your mail order business doesn't require a special license because of the product you sell (drugs and certain other types of product are controlled and regulated by the federal government), all you must do is visit your city or county clerk and obtain a business license. It takes just a few minutes and often costs less than $25, if anything. You can start to do business immediately. If you plan on doing business under your own name, there is no additional cost involved in setting up the business. You save on legal fees with a proprietorship because no special contracts must be drawn up or developed, as is the case with a corporation or a properly established partnership.

Another advantage is that you run the entire business as you wish. There is no board of directors or any other boss (except your customers) to direct you, supervise the decisions you make, or criticize your errors. Win, lose, or draw, you are the whole show, and what you say goes. You personally receive all the benefits and pay the costs of running and managing your new business.

It is also fairly easy to close down your operation and terminate your sole proprietorship. You liquidate your assets, pay your debts, and turn out the light, and that finishes the entire operation. Or, of course, you can sell your business. The point is, winding down the business is as easy to do as getting into it: It normally requires little, if any, legal assistance.

In terms of taxes, the government treats you and your sole proprietorship as one, and this can be very beneficial because you may or may not make money over the first few months of your mail order operation. If you end up losing money over the first year, you may deduct these losses on your tax return against any other income you may have earned during the year. This is especially valuable if you are running your new business part-time while holding a full-time position with another company.

However, a sole proprietorship is not advantageous in all situations. There are some disadvantages that you should consider before deciding definitely on this form of business organization. One major disadvantage is that you have unlimited personal liability in your business. Since you and your business are legally one and the same, all the liabilities that may occur to your enterprise are your own. For example, if for some reason you are sued as a result of some actions of your business, and you lose this lawsuit, you are personally responsible for payment. If the money available in your business does not cover that which you are required to pay, your personal assets—those items that you personally own outside of the business—can be taken to pay this debt. In the same way, if your business fails and it fails owing money to various creditors, those monies still owed to these creditors can be collected from your personal assets.

Certain circumstances may reduce the importance of these drawbacks in your situation. If you must borrow money for your business, the bank will usually require that you personally guarantee your loan. In this way and for this purpose, the bank has succeeded in "piercing the corporate shield." Even if you are incorporated, the bank may be able to reach your personal assets through this guarantee. And if the type of product you are selling is not likely to lead to a lawsuit, the protective function of a corporation may not be important. For example, if you are handling products such as greeting cards, it is not very likely that anyone will sue you for product failure. If, on the other hand, you are selling a product such as protective body armor, a product I have handled, it would probably behoove you not to use a sole proprietorship organization since, by the very nature of your product, product failure can lead to a lawsuit.

As a sole proprietorship, you are essentially limited to your own skills and capabilities. This means that you must wear many hats and do many jobs by yourself; you are limited to those resources you can provide. What happens should you become ill and unable to work? Under such circumstances, your business will generally suffer. Finally, as a major disadvantage, should you wish to borrow capital for your business, you will find it more difficult to attract investors as a sole proprietor than if you were either a partnership or a corporation, because the individual, individuals, or institution that lends you money must rely on you and you alone to make good this debt. A partnership, where there are at least two of you, doubles the chances of the investors' receiving their money back. The bottom line is that an investor, recognizing the risk, will be less likely to lend money to an individual.

The Partnership

I am against partnerships for a variety of reasons. In fact, almost every attorney I have talked to about forming a partnership has advised against it. Yet, strange though it may seem, most attorneys, when they band together to form a law firm, are organized as—you guessed it—a partnership. Clearly, the partnership is somewhat controversial. Let's look at the advantages and disadvantages and we'll see why.

With a partnership, it is also fairly easy to start your business. Legally, a business license from your county clerk or city clerk is required, just as in the sole proprietorship. This business license generally costs no more than the license for a sole proprietorship. The difficulty comes in an examination of who does what in the partnership—but we'll get to that after we finish looking at the advantages.

Another advantage of the partnership is that the person with whom you are teamed is an excellent source of additional capital.

Although this one can also be a disadvantage, a third advantage is that you can count on one or more of your partners to help you share in the decision making, the responsibilities, and the work. This advantage fits with the old saying that two heads are better than one. Having additional partners also makes it easy to take an annual vacation.

In the sole proprietorship, you had only your own resources to rely on. However, partners, having different experiences, skills, and strengths, add their own talent to the business, and if the partners' backgrounds are complementary, the chance of success is increased. For example, if your own background is in creating copy, one partner is an accountant, and another partner is skilled in marketing, the sum total is a definite asset to your business.

As with the sole proprietorship, there is a minimum of paperwork associated with the partnership, as opposed to the corporation. You must file Form 1065, *U.S. Partnership Return of Income,* each year for the IRS. But basically, the monies that you receive from the partnership are treated as ordinary income, as are the monies that you receive from the sole proprietorship. And you can deduct losses in the partnership from another source of income when you complete your income tax form.

Along with these considerable advantages, there are some decided disadvantages of the partnership. First, since you are not running your own show, there can be serious problems in decision making. Who has the final say? Who makes decisions about what? So serious is this aspect of a partnership that it has been described as having all the disadvantages of a marriage with none of the advantages. Indeed, if you decide on a partnership, tasks and divisions of responsibility and decision making should be decided very early on. One individual should be designated as the chief executive officer, so that continuous bickering and arguing about daily decisions do not cause you to become disorganized and unsuccessful. In fact, I would say that if you do decide to choose a partnership form of organization, this should be your first step—decide who will be doing what.

Another disadvantage, and a serious one, of a partnership is that you are liable for the actions and commitments of your partners. For example, if, while you are on vacation, your partner takes it into his head to use all the funds you have accumulated to purchase a new car, you are responsible for the debt incurred, even though you did not participate in this decision. The same applies, of course, to decisions concerning an addressing machine, word processor, mailings, hirings, firings, and so forth.

Just as with the sole proprietorship, you run the risk of incurring personal liability, and my comments regarding a potential lawsuit or obligation to creditors if your business should fail hold true for the partnership.

There is one additional aspect of the partnership organization that should be discussed here, and that is that there may be both general and limited partners. Limited partners do not participate in the day-to-day operation of the business and are not held personally liable for business debts, except to the extent of their investments. If the business loses money, the limited partner can lose only to the amount of his or her investment. But, of course, profits are also limited by the amount of his or her investment. A general partner is a full, participating partner and is personally liable beyond his or her investment. The general partner participates in the day-to-day operation of the business and usually receives compensation for his or her services. The general partner may own a greater share of the business at less investment in money because of his or her active participation and greater assumption of risks.

If you want to start and own a mail order business, you probably want to be a general partner, but to attract capital, you may offer limited partnerships.

All of these facts mean that this form of business organization is more complex. Therefore, some kind of written agreement or contract regarding the operation of the partnership should be drawn up with the assistance of an attorney.

The Corporation

The third major legal form of business ownership is the corporation. To set up a corporation, three or more individuals must usually apply for a charter in the state in which they intend to conduct their business and in which the principal office is located. However, there are exceptions to this rule.

Corporate law is very complicated. As a consequence, incorporation is usually accomplished by an attorney. The attorney's fee, which may be $1000 or more, may be one reason that new mail order entrepreneurs do not incorporate. But there are ways of incorporating by yourself. One good book on this subject is *How to Form Your Own Corporation without a Lawyer for under $50,* by Ted Nicholas, published by the Enterprise Publishing Company, 1000 Oakfield Lane, Wilmington, Delaware 19810. Since state laws differ regarding incorporation, many books describing how to incorporate in individual states have been written. These books may even contain tear-out forms for you to use. For example, in California, there is *How to Form Your Own California Corporation,* by Anthony Mancuso, among others.

Incorporation provides advantages for many companies in the mail order business. First, you generally avoid the problem of personal liability. With a corporation, your liability is limited to the amount of your investment. Your creditors cannot take your personal holdings or assets if the corporation fails or is sued for more funds than are available in corporation coffers. This fact alone is probably the major reason for many incorporations of small businesses. Remember, however, that, depending upon your product and whether it is necessary to borrow capital for your corporation against a personal guaranteed signature, this "advantage" may not be important to you.

Another major advantage of incorporating is related to income taxes. A corporation pays taxes on a maximum 48% of its net profits, compared to 90% for personal income tax. The money you would normally pay in taxes can be used to make your company grow, and at some time in the future, you can sell your much larger business and pay capital gains, rather than income taxes. Since capital gains taxes are lower, the net result is that if the business is really big when you sell it, like Geraldo Joffe's "Haverhills," you can really make a fortune.

A third major advantage of incorporating is that lenders—including banks, venture capitalists, and others—are generally much more willing to give you loans if you are a corporation that has been operating successfully than if you are an individual sole proprietorship, or even a partnership. In fact, as a corporation, you can sell stock to the public and raise money for further expansion or to "cash in" without selling the whole business.

There are also advantages in the area of fringe benefits and perks, such as pension plans, stock plans, insurance, company cars, and so forth, although many of these can also be made available to the proprietorship or the partnership.

Now let's look at the disadvantages. One major disadvantage of the corporation is the immense amount of paperwork and other complications that are part and parcel of running a corporation. Maintenance of this paperwork takes time, effort, and money that you might otherwise spend in building your business.

As was explained earlier, if you lose money in your proprietorship or your partnership, these losses can be taken as deductions from other earned income on your income tax. However, if the corporation loses money, these losses cannot be taken against other earned income, until such time as you sell your stock or the business fails.

Corporations are very closely regulated by the state in which you have registered. This regulation not only requires the paperwork mentioned earlier but may also restrict your business activities. Furthermore, the corporation is required to have a board of directors and hold stockholders' meetings. Obviously, you can stack this board of directors so that you still run your company, but your control of your company and your ability to run your own show are certainly more complicated and difficult than with a sole proprietorship. If the profits from your business are not sufficiently high, the low tax rate that was an advantage becomes a disadvantage in the form of double taxation: Corporate profits are taxed once through the corporation itself as a taxable legal entity and then a second time, through your salary or when profits are distributed to you or a stockholder.

You should make the decision as to which legal form of business organization to adopt for your company after carefully considering your product and your own situation, and perhaps consulting with your attorney and accountant. In most situations you will find that the easiest route is that of the sole proprietorship because it is so easy to set up. In fact, unless you are reading this on a weekend, you can probably set up a sole proprietorship, complete with business license, this very day. Such is not necessarily true with a partnership, and most definitely not true of the corporation.

IT'S EASY TO GET A BUSINESS LICENSE

What is a business license? It is simply a permit granted by a local governmental body, generally for a small fee, that allows you to carry on some business, subject to local regulations. In some areas, the governing body, whether city or county, does not even require a business license. However, it may require special permits for businesses of a certain type. So your first step is to determine whether a business license is required for your area and your particular type of mail order business. To find out, simply contact the chamber of commerce, city hall, city licensing department, or whatever body is applicable for the area in which you live. If you live in an unincorporated area of a county, contact the county licensing department. They can also tell you whether a state license is required. In this case, you will be contacting the state licensing board or some similar department.

If a business license is required, you will have to visit the appropriate agency and fill out an application. In general, it is relatively simple to complete: The typical information required is your name, type of business—in this case, you would put mail order—a fictitious name if you have one, the business address, the mailing address, your telephone number, your personal residence address, when the business is starting, the type of organization of your business, the number of employees, and partners' names, if any.

Sometimes your new business will require zoning, fire, and police department notification, and clearance before your new business license will be issued. However, for a mail order business, it is usually necessary to state only that you will not maintain large amounts of inventory or have large package deliveries made to the residence if you are conducting the mail order business from your own home.

HOW TO GET FICTITIOUS NAME REGISTRATION

You may or may not need fictitious name registration when starting your new mail order business, depending on the law in your area of operations. Usually, you must file a fictitious name registration statement if the business name you select is within the definition of "fictitious business name" used in your area. Generally, a fictitious business name is any name other than your own or those of partners with whom you may be associated. Therefore, if I use the name William A. Cohen and describe my operation as "mail order and direct mail," I would generally not need fictitious name registration. However, if I use the name William A. Cohen and Associates, or the William A. Cohen Company, fictitious name registration would be required. Of course, any name other than your own— such as "the ABC Company" or "the Magic Peanut Company"—would definitely require fictitious name registration.

Obtaining fictitious name registration is also relatively easy and the fact that you must register it should not be considered an impediment to selecting a name that people will notice and associate with your business. To find out the law in your state, contact the appropriate agency listed in your telephone book under city, county, or state government and they will tell you what the requirements are. Usually they involve nothing more than completing a simple form, which asks for your fictitious business name and the business address, your own name and home address, and a description of the business you are in. This information must be published within 30 days after filing the statement, usually in a newspaper, and it usually must be published once a week for four consecutive weeks. Thirty days after the publication has been accomplished, an affidavit of publication is filed with the county clerk. This procedure is a lot easier than it sounds. Usually it can be done by simply going to the newspaper yourself and telling the newspaper that you want to publish fictitious name registration. The forms are frequently available right there on the spot, and the newspaper itself will take care of all of the work for you by helping you to prepare the statement and filing it with the county clerk for you after publication. The cost will vary, but it is usually minimal:

The filing fee will probably be about $10, and the newspaper publication cost can range from $15 to $100. To minimize these publication costs, you should pick the newspaper with the smallest circulation possible within the area in which you are doing business, and of course, in accordance with any other legal requirements of the particular jurisdiction in which you are doing business.

Another tip is to file for registration for more than one fictitious name, which is usually permitted, sometimes without additional cost. You can easily get more than one fictitious name at once if you write small and squeeze all the names you can or want to use on the fictitious business name statement form. Since this statement form is published exactly as you write it, the additional names you have managed to write on the form will also be given to you. These names can be used for a variety of different purposes. For example, for some types of promotions it may be advantageous to use some name other than your regular fictitious name. A very large and successful mail order company does exactly this when testing new products.

The advantage of doing this is that, if the promotion fails, the failure will not be associated with the main name under which the company is doing business. Mail order consultants will sometimes use such fictitious names to test new products for their clients. In any case, you never know when you may wish to use another fictitious name for some special purpose, such as an in-house advertising agency, as described later in this book, and my general advice is to get all the fictitious names you can all at once.

Some small businesspeople I know in mail order, although operating under fictitious names, have never filed for a fictitious name statement. Probably they will not be apprehended, even though they may operate for years. I don't recommend this practice, but the truth is that penalties for failing to register are generally small, and most violators do not get caught. One very large mail order operator I know does considerable testing under various and assorted fictitious names, and, to quote him, he "forgets to file" fictitious name registrations for these one-time tests of new products. Although this has been his practice for the last 25 years, he has yet to be taken to task by the law. However, there is one major disadvantage of not registering: Some other mail order operator may beat you to the name you want!

Regardless of what name or names you decide to select for your business and then register as fictitious, the best possible name is one that best describes your product or services. An unusual or fancy name that does not describe your product or service will confuse your customer and may cause you to lose potential customers, or at the very least, may cause you to miss business that your name alone might otherwise attract. My friend, Melvin Powers, president of The Wilshire Book Company, clearly must have something to do with books—publishing, retailing, or wholesaling them. In fact, he does all three, and some business does come to him because his company name alone tells potential customers the kind of product and service he is involved with.

WHAT A SELLER'S PERMIT IS AND HOW TO OBTAIN ONE

A seller's permit, which can be obtained from your state board of equalization or similar organization, gives you the right to buy certain personal property that you intend to resell without having to pay sales tax or so-called use tax to your vendor for purchasing this property. Instead, you give the seller a resale certificate that indicates your seller's permit number. When you sell the property, you collect the tax from the consumer and pay the tax collected to your state board of equalization. If you intend to sell any tangible personal property to which this tax can apply, you must obtain this seller's permit; otherwise, you will have to pay the tax to your vendor every time you buy property for your business—office supplies, inventory, or whatever. This applies whether you are a wholesaler or a retailer through our mail order business. The only exception is if you are in a service business, in which case you may be exempt from this requirement since services are usually not taxed.

To obtain a seller's permit, contact the sales and use tax department of your state, as listed in Figure 2-1. If a fee is required for a seller's permit, the appropriate office will inform you. Sometimes the board of equalization may require some security from you for the payment of future tax. If so, the amount is determined at the time you make your application for the permit. This security deposit assures the state that if you fail to pay any sales tax due, the state can deduct the amount you owe from the security you have posted.

Since the required security can run as high as several thousand dollars, it is to your advantage not to post it for your seller's permit if at all possible. How much security is required, or whether any is required at all, depends on the information you provide the board on your application form. In some cases, if the security deposit is very high, an installment payment arrangement can be made. Small business consultant Wayde T. Gilliam, Jr., has made an extensive study of the security deposit and ways of minimizing it while receiving a seller's permit. In his

ALABAMA
Department of Revenue
Sales and Use Taxes
Montgomery, Alabama 36130

ALASKA
Department of Revenue
Pouch S
Juneau, Alaska 99801

ARIZONA
Sales Tax Division
Phoenix, Arizona 85007

ARKANSAS
Sales and Use Tax Division
Department of Finance and Adminis-
tration
Little Rock, Arkansas 72201

CALIFORNIA
Department of Business Taxes
State Board of Equalization
P.O. Box 1799
Sacramento, California 95808

COLORADO
Department of Revenue
State Capitol Annex
Denver, Colorado 80203

CONNECTICUT
Sales, Use and Excise Tax Division
Hartford, Connecticut 06115

DELAWARE
State Division of Revenue
Wilmington, Delaware 19801

DISTRICT OF COLUMBIA
Department of Finance and Revenue
300 Indiana Avenue, N.W.
Washington, D.C. 20001

FLORIDA
Sales Tax Bureau
Department of Revenue
Tallahassee, Florida 32304

GEORGIA
Sales and Use Tax Unit
Department of Revenue
Atlanta, Georgia 30334

HAWAII
Department of Taxation
State Tax Office Building
425 Queen Street
Honolulu, Hawaii 96813

IDAHO
Sales Tax Division
State Tax Commission
Boise, Idaho 83707

ILLINOIS
Department of Revenue
Springfield, Illinois 62706

INDIANA
Sales Tax Division
Department of Revenue
100 N. Senate Avenue
Indianapolis, Indiana 46204

IOWA
Division of Retail Sales and Use Tax
Department of Revenue
Lucas State Office Building
Des Moines, Iowa 50319

KANSAS
Sales and Compensating Tax Division
State Revenue Building
Department of Revenue
Topeka, Kansas 66612

KENTUCKY
Sales Tax Division
Department of Revenue
Frankfort, Kentucky 40601

LOUISIANA
Collector of Revenue
Baton Rouge, Louisiana 70821

MAINE
Sales Tax Division
Bureau of Taxation
Augusta, Maine 04330

MARYLAND
Retail Sales Tax Division
Treasury Department
301 W. Preston Street
Baltimore, Maryland 21201

MASSACHUSETTS
Sales and Use Taxes
Department of Corporations & Taxation
Boston, Massachusetts 02133

MICHIGAN
Sales and Use Taxes
Department of Treasury
Revenue Division
Treasury Building
Lansing, Michigan 48922

Figure 2-1. Locations of state sales and use tax departments.

MINNESOTA
Sales and Use Tax Division
Department of Taxation
Centennial Office Building
St. Paul, Minnesota 55101

MISSISSIPPI
Sales and Use Tax Division
State Tax Commission
Jackson, Mississippi 39205

MISSOURI
Sales and Use Tax Bureau
P.O. Box 840
Jefferson City, Missouri 65102

NEBRASKA
Sales and Use Tax Unit
Department of Revenue
Box 4818, State Capitol
Lincoln, Nebraska 68509

NEVADA
Nevada Tax Commission
Carson City, Nevada 89701

NEW JERSEY
Division of Taxation
Department of the Treasury
Trenton, New Jersey 08625

NEW MEXICO
Revenue, Bureau of Revenue
Santa Fe, New Mexico 87501

NEW YORK
Sales Tax Bureau, State Tax
Commission
Department of Taxation and Finance
Tax and Finance Building 9,
State Campus
Albany, New York 12226

NORTH CAROLINA
Sales and Use Tax Division
Main Office—Revenue Building
Raleigh, North Carolina 27611

NORTH DAKOTA
Enforcement Director (Sales Tax)
State Capitol Building
Bismarck, North Dakota 58501

OHIO
Sales and Excise Division
Department of Taxation
68 East Gay Street
Columbus, Ohio 43151

OKLAHOMA
Sales and Use Taxes
Oklahoma Tax Commission
2101 Lincoln Blvd.
Oklahoma City, Oklahoma 73105

PENNSYLVANIA
Bureau of Taxes for Education
Department of Revenue
Harrisburg, Pennsylvania 17128

RHODE ISLAND
Department of Administration
49 Westminster Street
Providence, Rhode Island 02903

SOUTH CAROLINA
Sales and Use Tax Division
South Carolina Tax Commission
Columbia, South Carolina 29201

SOUTH DAKOTA
Sales and Use Tax Division
Department of Revenue
Pierre, South Dakota 57501

TENNESSEE
Sales and Use Tax Division
Department of Revenue
War Memorial Building
Nashville, Tennessee 37219

TEXAS
Comptroller of Public Accounts
Austin, Texas 78711

UTAH
Auditing Division (Sales Tax)
State Tax Commission
201 State Office Building
Salt Lake City, Utah 84114

VERMONT
Department of Taxes
State of Vermont
P.O. Box 547
Montpelier, Vermont 05602

VIRGINIA
Sales and Use Tax Division
Department of Taxation
P.O. Box 6L
Richmond, Virginia 23215

WASHINGTON
Department of Revenue
Olympia, Washington 98501

Figure 2-1. (Continued)

WEST VIRGINIA
Sales and Use Taxes
State Tax Department
Charleston, West Virginia 25305

Business and Occupation Tax
State Tax Department
Charleston, West Virginia 25305

WISCONSIN
Income, Sales, and Excise Tax Division
Department of Revenue
P.O. Box 39
Madison, Wisconsin 53702

WYOMING
Sales and Use Tax Division
State Tax Commission
Cheyenne, Wyoming 82002

Figure 2-1. (Continued)

book *How to Increase Your Standard of Living with a Small Business,* he lists seven facts on your application form that can affect the security deposit required:

1. If you own a home
2. If you have a substantial equity in your home
3. If your estimated monthly expense are low
4. If your estimated monthly sales are low
5. If you are presently employed and this is a part-time business
6. If you have no employees
7. If you have only one place of business

If you think the board of equalization in your state is setting too high a security deposit requirement, you should discuss it with the official and try to negotiate a more reasonable deposit. In my own first mail order business, the board wanted me to deposit $2000. We negotiated until eventually the requirement was no security deposit at all! So talking personally with the members of the board of equalization when you obtain your seller's permit is worthwhile.

HOW TO SELECT A BANK AND OPEN A BANK ACCOUNT

From the very start, it is to your advantage to select a bank that will help you and your mail order business to be successful. The best service for your needs is usually available at an independent bank with no branches, or a small chain of banks. Here's why. In a small bank, your account may be very important, whereas in a large bank, you may not even be noticed. Also, a small bank will assist you in becoming acquainted with as many of the employees in the bank as possible. In the course of your business, people who know you can be extremely helpful in assisting your operation and in acquiring business loans for expansion or just for operating capital.

A large bank is useful if your mail order business is involved in international trade. For example, if the item you are going to sell is being imported from abroad or you are selling abroad through export, having a large bank can help you because most very large banks have international departments. They can assist you through the various mazes of payments, letters of credit, insurance, and so forth. One large international bank that we know actually assisted an entrepreneur by having a member of its Hong Kong branch give free seminars in international trade to an international business group the entrepreneur was leading on a guided tour through the Orient. Obviously, such services would not be available with a small independent bank.

Regardless of what bank you decide to do business with, you should not move your account from bank to bank, if at all possible. Your bank reference can be very important for you in obtaining credit from suppliers, and in some cases, can be very useful in acting as a reference to your customers as well, as we will discuss later in building credibility in your ads.

Your bank will not allow you to register a bank account in your fictitious name until you have already obtained fictitious name registration. To open the account, a small deposit of $100 or less is usually all that is required.

When you have your own bank, feel free to discuss various financial problems with your banker. This person can be of much help in running your mail order business, in finding an attorney or accountant, and in supplying various other services that will help you to succeed.

When you have your bank account, it's good to start building credit right away, rather than waiting until you actually need it. Most small mail order businesses will sometimes need capital to grow, or to take advantage of opportunities that present themselves suddenly in the marketplace. One way of establishing credit is to take a small loan you don't need—for, say, $1000 or less—and then to pay back the amount borrowed with regular payments. In this way, you will have built a track record of paying off a bank loan, which can help later on when you need greater sums of money from your bank. Naturally, you should make certain that your payments are made exactly on time and when required.

Having your own business bank account is evidence of the fact that you are really in business for yourself, whether it is a part-time or full-time business.

BORROWING MONEY AND SOURCES OF CAPITAL
FOR YOUR MAIL ORDER BUSINESS

The best source of capital for your new business is you—that is, money that you currently control. It is the easiest to make use of, and the quickest. Further, you need not surrender equity in your business or worry about paying it back.

The second best source for new capital is close friends or relatives. Why are close friends and relatives a good source of money? Because, except for your own money, it is usually the fastest, easiest, and cheapest way to raise cash that you need, and it also involves less paperwork and fewer legal problems. Larry O., a friend of mine, started his new mail order business in Canada, selling a cosmetic product he had developed himself and patented. His sales suddenly boomed from a few dollars a month to $50,000 with one large wholesale order. He needed money immediately for raw materials, machinery to manufacture in large quantities, rental of work space, and so forth. Larry raised $20,000 in less than two weeks, almost entirely from friends at his former place of employment, from which he had resigned upon receiving the $50,000 order. Larry's cosmetic business grew rapidly, and within two years he was able to cash in and sell out at a huge profit. One cautionary note here, however: If you do borrow money from friends or relatives, be certain not to cut them in on your business. You are borrowing money, not making them partners. Close friends or relatives are very difficult to control in managing your business.

If you have money in a savings account, you can borrow against it. Usually the cost of this type of loan is low and the reason, of course, is that the savings institution in which you have the money can keep it as collateral until you repay what is borrowed. One additional advantage for this type of borrowing is that the money you have in the savings account continues to draw interest while you have the loan, even while it is held as collateral. So if your money is normally earning 7½% interest and if the loan is costing you 11½%, the real cost of the loan is only 4%.

A life insurance loan may also be possible. If your life insurance policy has cash value, you can generally obtain a loan of up to 95% of the value that has accumulated. An unusual aspect of a life insurance loan is that you don't actually have to repay the loan. You pay only the interest each year along with your premium. Of course, if you don't replace the money you borrowed, that amount is deducted from the face value of the policy paid to a beneficiary.

Getting a loan from a regular bank to start a new business is usually pretty difficult. However, if your credit is good, you can sometimes get a signature or personal loan for several thousand dollars almost immediately. Sometimes you can get more if you have dealt with a bank for some time and it feels that you are a good risk. Usually these are short-term loans, which must be paid off within a three-year period. Such loans can be paid off in installments, or the lump sum can be paid at a specified time.

Along the same lines, credit unions, which are really nonprofit banks, are an excellent source of loans for relatively small sums. Of course, you must already belong to the credit union to get a loan. Membership frequently depends upon place of employment or similar factors. The main advantage of dealing with a credit union over dealing with a bank is that the interest rates are usually several points lower than those of banks.

A finance company or loan company is also a source of money and can lend you from several thousand dollars up to much more, depending upon the individual state laws and how much collateral in real estate or other property you're able to put up and it is willing to accept. However, the most frequent loans from finance and loan companies are small—for a maximum of a couple of thousand dollars—and are granted providing you already have a job and a good credit rating. The advantage of dealing with a finance company is that the loan usually comes fairly fast—in a day if you already have a credit rating, or several days if you haven't dealt with this particular loan or finance company before. However, the interest rates from finance and loan companies are fairly high, much higher than those of a bank or credit union.

Credit cards are a frequently overlooked source of credit. Depending upon the credit limit with every credit card you have—MasterCard, Visa, and so on—you can usually get at least $500 worth of credit. Here again, annual interest charges vary and have risen greatly in the last few months, but they are a ready source of credit in paying for many of your raw materials, products, and so forth, whether you order face to face or by mail.

Your suppliers are a frequently overlooked source of loans. For example, if you order stationery and printing supplies and you do not have to pay until delivery, this is, in effect, a loan for that period. Further, if your supplier will grant you 30, 60, or 90 additional days to pay for the material you have purchased, this is a loan as well. Occasionally, suppliers give a discount for early payment, usually something like 2% for payment within 10 days, but this discount should be weighed against your need for immediate funds, and you should never be afraid of asking for credit, if you need this money for some valid business purpose.

For really large sums of money you should know about venture capital companies, the Small Business Administration, and small business investment corporations (SBICs) and business development corporations (BDCs). Small Business Administration loans are usually extremely limited, and even though you may be able to obtain a loan for several hundred thousand dollars, complete business plans will be required and a lead time of from nine months to a year or more is required. Similarly, a business plan is required with venture capital companies, SBICs, and BDCs. All of these types of firms with the potential for lending you money can be found either by contacting the Small Business Administration, or by checking in the *Wall Street Journal* or your local big-city paper in the business opportunities column of the classified section. SBICs, BDCs, and venture capital companies will want equity capital and controlling interest in your business. Further, the likelihood of their investing in your mail order company before your company has a track record is rather remote. Therefore, these sources should not be considered until you have already had a certain amount of success and you have demonstrated a clear potential for future growth. Finally, you must be willing to surrender a controlling interest in your company in exchange for the capital you need.

One final method of obtaining money to start your new business should be noted. This is the finder. The finder is a financial broker who locates sources of investment capital for you in exchange for receiving a percentage of that capital. For example, if you wanted to start a mail order business and required $20,000, you might engage a finder to help you find this money in exchange for 5%, or $1000, when you receive the loan. Thus, if you are using a finder, you must be certain to allow additional money in the loan to pay the finder himself. Of course, the finder's fee is in addition to the interest rate you must pay to the individual who is lending you the money or investing in your company. Finders themselves can be located through your accountant, attorney, or bank, or sometimes through various business publications such as the *Wall Street Journal* and weekend editions of major newspapers in the *Financial* or *Loans Available* columns of the classified sections.

THE IMPORTANT PRINCIPLE OF MAINTAINING A LOW OVERHEAD IN YOUR NEW MAIL ORDER BUSINESS

It is absolutely critical to your success that you maintain a low overhead in your new mail order business. Overhead eats into all funds that you have available as your profits. In 1973, a very successful manager in a large aerospace company quit to start his own mail order business, even though it would have been very easy to start the business part-time while he still had a large salary coming in from his regular work. To compound his mistake, he insisted upon renting a large office in a prestigious neighborhood and buying top-quality furniture and office equipment, even before he started. Because of the tremendous overhead with which this man saddled himself, his business was doomed to failure before he even started, and in fact, he sold not one single item before he was bankrupt.

Do not make this mistake. To maintain a low overhead from the beginning, you should do the following.

1. Do not give up your regular source of income, but start your mail order business part-time until it is off the ground and you are earning sufficient income to support yourself and your family.
2. Do not be afraid of working out of your home. Many mail order millionaires have started their businesses on the kitchen table or have used portions of their garage or a spare bedroom.

One of the great mail order success stories of the last 10 years is that of Benjamin Suarez. He says that fixed overhead breeds silently and rapidly to destroy your business because: (1) the enterpreneur or business owner wants to feed his or her ego by having fancy business accommodations and a lot of subordinates; (2) subordinates also want to feed their egos and make their jobs easier with fancy accommodations, extra help, and work-saving equipment; (3) government and institutions will encourage increases in fixed overhead and play upon the entrepreneur's ego because such increases feed the government more taxes and provide good business for the institutions; and 4) businesses that sell to businesses are constantly bombarding the entrepreneur or business owner with sales pitches for larger and fancier accommodations and equipment.

Richard H. Buskirk and Percy J. Vaughn, Jr., professors of business management, say in their book *Managing New Enterprises:* "The management of overhead is one key to success in small business. In fact, it is the very reason that small business can frequently compete against bigger enterprises." So if you want to have a successful mail order business, keep your overhead low.

SHOULD YOU USE A BOX NUMBER OR A STREET ADDRESS FOR YOUR MAILING ADDRESS?

Many new mail order enterpreneurs worry about whether they should use a box number instead of their street address. When I started out, I had the same concern. I was afraid that if I used my home address, I would be bothered by would-be customers, or even dissatisfied customers. On the other hand, some literature on mail order told me that I could not be successful if I used a box number because potential customers would think that I was a fly-by-night operator. Finally I decided to try a box anyway. No sooner had I rented the box than I tried to place my initial advertisement and discovered that California requires a street address to be listed in your advertisement, whether you use a post office box for mailing or not! Since my initial advertisement was in the *Los Angeles Times Magazine,* I didn't have much choice. But this situation turned out to be a great mini-test because my out-of-state advertisements used the box address only. Here's what happened.

1. Some folks who had seen my ad came to my house to see the merchandise close up—and bought!
2. In my out-of-state ads, I didn't suffer one iota because of the postal box address.

After this experience, I used the following guidelines; if I advertised within the state, I used my home address; if I advertised out-of-state, I also used my home address, except in a classified ad, where each word means more dollars. With a classified ad, I could save several words, which translated into several dollars, by using a box number.

If you still have concerns about using your home address, consider Joe Karbo's experience. Joe thought long and hard about whether to expose his family to any wrongdoing by putting his home address in his "Lazy Man's Way to Riches" ads. But in seven years of carrying a street address, he's had no difficulties.

WHETHER YOU NEED TO CARRY MASTERCARD OR VISA, AND HOW TO DO IT

Another question that has probably crossed your mind is whether to use credit cards, such as MasterCard or Visa, in your business. My suggestion is to do it. Here's why.

1. When you first start your business, your name is unknown. To use the old cliché, people don't know you or your business from Adam. But MasterCard or Visa? Everyone knows them, and the association with them is very good for your credibility.
2. If you sell high-cost, or so-called "big-ticket," items, you are going to have to provide some kind of time payment plan. Otherwise,

you just aren't going to be able to get together enough customers. The sad fact is that if you provide this time payment plan yourself, even with a series of dunning and threatening letters, you will never collect from all your customers. What percentage will you be able to collect from? With luck, maybe 60 or 70%. To avoid this unpleasantness and get the money owed you from each and every customer, use the major credit cards.

3. It is a fact, that, for most products in most situations, your returns will be better if you offer a credit card option. Part of the reason is the credibility factor noted above. But beyond that, it's just a little easier to order, with fewer immediate demands on your customer's financial treasure.

4. For some operations, a credit card is essential. A major example here would be those late-night television advertisements for tapes, records, kitchenware, or whatever. When used in conjunction with a toll-free telephone number, which I discuss shortly, those advertisements can really pull.

Despite all these favorable reasons for using the major credit cards, there are some drawbacks. The first is that it's not free. It's going to cost you something. At this particular time, the percentage it will cost you for each order is changing. However, it is always negotiable, and if your monthly sales are smaller, you can expect to pay a higher percentage than if they are huge.

The second drawback is that, contrary to what you might think, neither Visa nor MasterCard is wildly enthusiastic about dealing with new mail order operators because they have been burned in the past. People with little training and no preparation have gotten into the business, and the result has been a lot of dissatisfied customers, to whom the credit card people would rather not be responsible, even in an indirect way. As a result, you are going to have to be ready to present a pretty good story, business plan, personal background, and so on to convince these people that you know what you are doing so that they let you join their system. Naturally, it helps if you were already in business and selling your product even before you decided to enter the mail order business. Also, be ready for some high-level negotiating. After being turned down by both cards at the local level, I took my story to the corporate offices and succeeded with an argument that went something like this: "I'm sure your competitor is going to approve my application, so I'll be advertising with his card only. Now, my sales are forecast to be low the first year, but don't try to convince me to add your card when my sales reach $1,000,000." Usually the facts, some possibilities, and a good argument presented forcefully, but tactfully, will win the day. If you can't get either credit card for your business, don't despair. Numerous multimillion-dollar mail order businesses have been built without the use of credit cards, and many still don't use them.

If your application is approved, the use of these cards is simple. In your advertisement, you simply ask for the buyer's card number and expiration date in addition to his or her name and address. When you get this information, you can check whether the person's credit is good by use of a toll-free number. You then fill out a credit card form given to you by MasterCard or Visa. You can save these forms and send them in once a month, and you will be credited with the amount less the percentage owed, or you can take them to the bank and get your cash immediately.

SHOULD YOU USE A TOLL-FREE NUMBER?

Toll-free numbers are another way of increasing response. Why does response increase? Because they make it easier for your customer to order. Again, some operations, by their very nature, make the use of toll-free numbers a must: think about late-night television shows again. However, the toll-free number is free to your *customer,* not to you. So before signing up, you should think about it a little. True, a toll-free number will probably help your credibility, but not as much as a credit card, and probably not enough to make it worthwhile for this reason alone. In general, toll-free numbers are useful when:

You have a lot of business

You are selling a relatively high-ticket item

It is customary to provide a toll-free number for the product, industry, or method you are using to sell (records on TV again)

Many people have tried toll-free numbers for their mail order businesses and found that, for their situations, it wasn't worthwhile. Joe Karbo is one outstanding example.

If you want a toll-free number, there are two ways of getting it. One is to rent the toll-free line from the telephone company yourself. This is the most expensive way, but it is worthwhile if your phone is going to be ringing all the time: It gives you the greatest control over the calls to ensure that your incoming orders are handled as you want them handled. If you decide to go this way, the telephone company will give you several options to choose from. You can use a measured rate service, which provides for 10 hours of use per month plus overtime. Cost varies, depending on area, from $205 plus $15.45 for each additional hour to $337 plus $19.32

for each additional hour. Another way to go is to rent the line for a full business day. In that case, you'll pay $950 to $1750 per month plus $2.60 to $8.75 per additional hour.

The alternative is to participate in a toll-free service offered by a firm that has rented a line from the telephone company. In this case, you pay less, since you are sharing the line with other users. A typical ad response service may cost you $100 to $200 per month for 24-hour service. If you are interested in this option, here are two companies that offer a toll-free service:

> The National Communications Center, 3939 Cambridge Road, Suite 104, Shingle Springs, California   95682

> Communication Response Service, Inc., 140 Washington Street, Reno, Nevada   89503

SUMMARY

In this very important chapter, we discussed how to get your mail order business off the ground. First, we talked about the three basic legal forms of business: the sole proprietorship, the partnership, and the corporation. We concluded that you must pick the form that best fits your needs, your situation, and the products you intend to sell by mail. Next, we discussed how to get a business license so that you meet the basic legal requirements for your new business. Then we discussed fictitious name registration, when it is required and how to apply for it, and what a name means to your mail order business. Looking at the seller's permit, we learned how to apply for it and where to write in your particular state to obtain information about getting one. We also talked about what factors minimize the deposit required by your state board of equalization. Our next subject was banking, and we talked about getting your bank account and how to select a bank that will be most suitable to your operation. Then we discussed sources of money and capital for starting your mail order business. We talked about maintaining a low overhead so that you will maximize your opportunities for immediate success. This is most important. Finally I gave you the alternatives in three relevant issues: box versus street addresses, credit cards versus none, and use or nonuse of toll-free numbers and your options if you use them.

Following the instructions outlined in this chapter, you will get your business off and running on the right foot for profitability. Do not shortchange yourself by failing to apply these basics in your business. Following the principles discussed in this chapter can make you a mail order millionaire.

3

Avoiding Legal Problems in Mail Order and Maintaining Your Professional Ethics

You can make a fortune in mail order, and you can do so honestly and without deceiving your customers. Believe me, it is not worth the legal headache or legal penalties should you, intentionally or unintentionally, break the law. But above and beyond the law, deception goes against all standards and ideals of those engaged in marketing by mail. The potential exists to make a fortune in mail order not because you can rip off the customer, but because you can satisfy his or her needs. Therefore, do not be tempted to rush through this chapter without reading it carefully, for not only are the penalties for breaking the law severe, but, as Joe Karbo says, "It is you who must view yourself in the mirror on rising and before going to bed and be satisfied with what you see."

The Direct Marketing Association publishes a list of no less than 40 operating guidelines for ethical business practice for all direct response marketers, whether they are selling products or services or raising funds for nonprofit organizations. Perhaps the basic guideline is this one: "Direct response marketers should make their offers clear and honest. They should not misrepresent a product, service, publication, or program and should not use misleading, partially true, or exaggerated statements. All descriptions and promises should be in accordance with actual conditions, situations and circumstances existing at the time the promotion is made. Direct response marketers should operate in accordance with the

Better Business Bureau's basic principles contained in the Better Business Bureau's Code of Advertising and be cognizant of and adhere to the Postal Laws and Regulations and all other laws governing advertising in transactions of business by mail, telephone, and the print and broadcast media." Certainly this is a mouthful, but the essence is contained in the first sentence: Your offer should always be clear and honest. The complete list of *The Direct Marketing Association's Guidelines for Ethical Business Practices* is contained in Appendix B.

The main agencies that must be dealt with regarding the laws of mail order and direct mail marketing are the U.S. Postal Service and the Federal Trade Commission. Either of these two government agencies can do you considerable harm if you go astray, and it is possible to stray from the regulations without ill intent. An advertisement that you place may be illegal if there is the smallest chance that your customer may be deceived by a statement or classification that is misleading. For example, at one time I wished to sell information regarding job finding through the mail. I wanted to try something new. The idea was to place a short classified ad under the classification for various types of help wanted in the Sunday edition of the newspaper. My plan was a small test ad in the *Los Angeles Times,* and, if successful, I would expand into many different papers across the country. The first thing I discovered in attempting this was that it is illegal to advertise information on job finding in a column headed *Help Wanted.* The only legal way around this was to advertise "See Our Announcement under *Announcements"* and make the promotion for the information that I wished to sell in the *Announcements* column.

Whether your ad is legal or illegal may not be determined directly from the ad itself. For example, if you advertise a course for writers in which you state, "You can make $50,000 a year," the ad's legitimacy would really depend upon whether writers of this category make $50,000 a year and whether graduates of your correspondence course make this much.

BEWARE OF DECEPTIVE PRICING

The Federal Trade Commission (FTC) has issued several guides and advisory opinions pertaining to how you may advertise pricing. These concern price comparisons with former prices, price comparisons with retail items, advertising prices that have been established or suggested by manufacturers or other nonretail distributors, bargain offers based on the purchase of other merchandise, and various other price comparisons.

Price Comparisons with Former Prices

If you offer an item at a bargain price, compared with its former price, the former price must actually have been offered to the public on a regular basis for a reasonably substantial period. If you establish a price that is obviously inflated and artificial for the specific purpose of offering the item later at a large reduction or as a "bargain," this former price is considered false by the FTC and is illegal. On the other hand, a former price is not necessarily fictitious merely because you made no sales at that price. For example, if you established a valid price for an item, advertised it at $12.95, but sold only a few, you could legally advertise a price reduction to, say, $9.95. The basic point here is that it is illegal to advertise a bargain price or reduction price if you never really intended to make any sales at the first price.

Retail Price Comparisons

If you advertise that you are selling at a price below that charged in your geographic area for a certain product, you must be reasonably certain that your price does not appreciably exceed the price at which substantial sales for the article are being made in that area. According to an advisory opinion by the FTC, there are two fundamental requirements for determining the validity of savings claims based upon the sale of the same or comparable merchandise. First you should be certain that the retail merchandise advertised is of essentially similar quality in all material respects to the product you are advertising. The second requirement is that you must be reasonably certain that the price advertised does not exceed the price at which such merchandise is being offered by representative retail outlets in the area.

Advertising Prices That Have Been Established or Suggested by Manufacturers or Other Nonretail Distributors

Many a product has a suggested price set by the manufacturer that is totally disregarded when sold by a retailer. In fact, everyone in your area may sell the product at a much lower price. So when you are advertising by mail, if you suggest that your price is much lower than the manufacturer's or distributor's suggested retail price, you must be careful to offer a reduction from the price at which the product is generally sold in the area to which you are selling. If a number of retail establishments are selling this product at the list or suggested retail price, you are all right. However, according to the FTC, if they are selling at a lower price, you cannot suggest in your advertising that your price is a bargain by comparing it to the manufacturer's list or suggested price.

Bargain Offers Based on the Purchase of Other Merchandise

As we will point out in a later chapter, there are many ways to make an offer, some of which will be much more interesting to your potential customer than others. Some offers are more profitable to make even though they are essentially the same as the less interesting offers. For example, two for $1 or one for $1 and one free are the same offer presented differently. This is fine unless you advertise in such a manner that you increase the regular price of the one article you are requiring to be bought to obtain the second, or decrease the quantity and quality of that product or otherwise put such conditions on the offer that it is no longer the same. If you do any of these things, you may be deceiving the customer, and may therefore be liable for FTC action. Let's say that you are selling tape cassettes for $5 and you advertise, "Our regular tape cassette, 2 for $5." If you actually send your customers a cheaper tape cassette of lower quality than your standard cassette and don't tell them, this is deception.

Miscellaneous Price Comparisons

Other common deceptions in advertising prices upon which the FTC definitely frowns are advertising a retail price as a wholesale price when, in fact, it isn't or a factory price when you are not selling the items at the price actually sold by the manufacturer, or offering seconds or irregular merchandise at a reduced price without telling your customer that the merchandise is not in perfect condition. Do any of these things in pricing and you have violated the basic principle of mail order marketing, and you will be in lots of trouble with the FTC.

DELIVERY OF MAIL ORDER MERCHANDISE

One of the most important regulations affecting people engaged in mail order selling was passed by the FTC on February 2, 1976. It is called the Thirty Day Delay Delivery Rule, and it says, basically, that if there is a reasonable basis on which to believe that the product you are selling will not be shipped within 30 days of receiving a properly completed order, your advertisement must include a clear and conspicuous notice of the time in which you expect to make shipment. If you make no statement, this rule requires that your shipment be made within 30 days.

Now, what happens if you cannot make the shipment within an unstated 30-day period or the period you've stated specifically in your advertisement? In that case, you must send a notice of revised shipment date to the buyer by first class mail before expiration of the original 30-day period. This statement must include a postage-paid reply form that notifies the buyer of the new shipping date and offers the option of agreeing to the delay or canceling the order and obtaining a refund. Your notice must also inform your buyer that, unless you receive a response rejecting the delay, the buyer will have consented to the delayed shipment. Finally, some states, such as New York, have delivery rules stricter than that of the FTC! So you should check state laws about this if there is any doubt.

There are other important aspects of this 30-day rule. Recently Joe Sugarman was fined heavily by the FTC because of violation of the 30-day rule when the computer that handled Joe's orders went out during a winter storm. Sugarman has fought this tooth and nail, with blistering ads exposing the FTC's ability to destroy legitimate mail order businesses. In an article entitled "FTC: Change Your Mail Order Rule or Face Court Challenge" in the June 1980 issue of *Direct Marketing*, Sugarman explains the reasons for his opposition and his proposals for a fair rule that mail order people can live with. The point here is not that Sugarman is right or wrong in his attack on or defense against the FTC's contentions regarding the 30-day rule under extenuating circumstances, but that you must be aware of the rule and obey it to the best of your ability as it exists now. Figure 3-1 shows a typical letter used by Joe's company, JS&A, for a late shipment.

The FTC rule is so important that you will find *A Business Guide to the Federal Trade Commission's Mail Order Rule* by the FTC printed in its entirety in Appendix A.

ENDORSEMENTS AND TESTIMONIALS IN ADVERTISING

The FTC has proposed several guidelines for use of endorsements and testimonials in advertising. This is most important because endorsements and testimonials lend a tremendous amount of credibility to whatever your proposition is. Some of these guidelines, quoted directly, are as follows:

1. Every endorsement must reflect the honest view of the endorser and may not use statements in endorsements that could not be supported if presented in the advertiser's words rather than the endorser's.

One JS&A Plaza, Northbrook, Illinois 60062

(312) 564-7000 Telex 72-4498

August 25, 1980

We're late in sending you Mr. Sugarman's Success Forces book that you recently ordered.

Although we expect to ship the book to you within the next thirty days, we want you to know that you can always cancel your order if you wish.

If you prefer to cancel your order, simply call our toll-free number, (800) 323-6400, or return the Release of Order Form below to us in the self-addressed, postage-free envelope enclosed.

Again, our sincere apologies for being late, but be assured that we are concerned about your order and are doing everything we can to expedite its shipment.

Sincerely,

JS&A Group, Inc.

Mary Stank

P.S. If you placed the order using your credit card, the credit card will not be charged until such time that the book is shipped.

RELEASE OF ORDER

Please cancel my order for the Success Forces book and return my money.

Name _____
     (signature)
Address _____

City _____ State ____ Zip _____

Date _____

Figure 3-1. JS&A explaining delayed delivery.

2. The advertiser may not distort the endorser's opinion or experience with the product by rewording the endorsement or by presenting it out of context. Further the advertiser may continue to use the endorsement only as long as he or she has good reason to believe that the endorser continues to subscribe to the views presented.

3. Where the advertisement represents that the endorser uses a product, he or she must actually be a bona fide user of the product. Further, such endorsement may be used only as long as the advertiser has good reason to believe the endorser continues to be a bona fide user of the product.

4. Endorsements that reflect the experience of an individual consumer will be interpreted as representing the typical performance of the product under similar circumstances. If the represented performance is atypical, the advertisement must disclose what typically would be in the depicted circumstances.

5. Advertisements that represent endorsements of "actual consumers" must use actual consumers or disclose that the persons appearing in the advertisement are professional actors appearing for compensation.

6. Endorsements concerning the effectiveness of drug products shall not be made by laypersons.

7. When there is a connection between the endorser and the seller that might materially affect the weight or credibility of the endorsement, such connection must be fully disclosed.

These rules are frequently enforced by the FTC. Gordon Cooper, the former astronaut, was named in an FTC settlement involving ads for an automotive valve. The FTC said that Cooper represented himself as an automotive engineering expert when he endorsed the valve, when, in fact, he didn't have such experience, and that he failed to disclose the fact that he had a financial interest in the product's sales. Pat Boone was similarly charged by the FTC when he endorsed a product called Acne-Statin, and he had to pay $5000 toward a $200,000 refund pool.

When celebrities like Cooper and Boone can get in trouble with the FTC—and these are men of known integrity and service to their country and the community—you know that folks like you and me must be careful.

Figure 3-2 shows an endorsement that former radio and television personality Art Linkletter makes for the National Home Life Assurance Company. Note that Linkletter signs his endorsement letter as "Member of the Board of Directors with a financial interest in the Company." In this way, both he and the company avoid running afoul of the FTC.

Figure 3-2. Art Linkletter's endorsement for National Home Life Assurance Company.

Shortly after publication of the first edition of *Building a Mail Order Business* I received a call from a reader who had read this chapter and was concerned with what he had read. "You mean all those testimonials must be real?" he asked. "I thought people just made them up . . . and that's what I've been doing in advertising my product for the last six months." I assured him that testimonials must be "real," and I recommended that he cease his advertising at once. The government takes a very dim view of such fraudulent advertising. And the truth is, if your product or service has value it is not difficult to obtain actual and honest testimonials boosting your product, which you can legally use in your advertising. I will explain fully how to obtain these testimonials in chapter 10.

DRY-TESTING

Dry-testing is extremely important in mail order because it allows the marketer to start promoting a product by mail before the product has been manufactured or stocked as inventory. Obviously, this is a tremendous advantage, since you, as a mail order seller, need not invest money in the product until you are certain that the demand exists and that the size of the response of the solicitation is sufficient to be profitable. Dry-testing is still legal in mail order. However, the FTC has issued an opinion—so far, it is an *advisory* opinion—in which it allows dry-testing under strict guidelines to ensure that the potential customer is in no way misled about the terms of the offer. This opinion involved a promotion of a continuity book series by mail order and is the only opinion on the subject issued by the FTC known to the author at the time of this writing.

Specifically, the FTC stated that it did not object to the use of dry-testing the continuity book series marketed by mail order as long as the following conditions were observed:

1. No representation expressed or implied could be made in promotional material that would mislead the public into believing that the books were or would definitely be published, or that by expressing an interest in receiving a book, a prospective purchaser would necessarily receive them.

2. Clear and conspicuous disclosures would be made of the terms and conditions of the publications, distribution, and other material aspects of the continuity book series program, including the fact that the book series was only planned and might not actually be published.

3. If the decision were made not to publish the book series, notice was to be given to persons who subscribed within a reasonable time after the date of first mailing the solicitation for subscriptions. Four months or less was suggested as reasonable, "unless extenuating circumstances existed." If the decision to publish the book series were not made within that time, persons who expressed a desire to subscribe should be notified of this fact and should be given an opportunity to cancel their orders.

4. There were to be no substitutions of any other books for those that were ordered.

Obviously, this opinion refers to a continuity book series only, and the FTC's position could be changed or modified at any time. Therefore, while dry-testing is still legal and is in general a wise decision from an economic standpoint, the legal aspects of any dry-testing should be investigated thoroughly with a lawyer before proceeding. Also, if you do dry-test you should keep in mind the 30-day rule mentioned previously. You must have a reasonable basis for assuming you can meet the date you state in your advertisement or 30 days after the receipt of an order from your customer.

STATE TAXATION

Interstate Taxation

There are two types of state taxation with which you may be concerned—use tax and sales tax. Basically, use tax is paid when your place of business is located in the state whose tax you're paying. Sales tax is generally paid by the buyer on purchases made within the state levying the tax. The problem is that each of the 50 states has a different concept of what "place of business" means. As a result, all states are trying, to some extent, to impose some sort of taxation on direct marketers, whether or not the place of business is located in that state. This can lead to some real problems for the mail order operator who is dealing or selling goods by mail in a state that insists on controlling a direct marketer's business and taxing it, even though he or she may not be located in that state.

Senator Charles Mathias of Maryland has been instrumental in seeking to introduce legislation to clarify the interstate taxation situation. In 1977 and 1979 he introduced bills that called for federal judicial review of the application of jurisdictional guidelines for the state taxation of interstate commerce and for the apportionment of interstate income among the states. His legislation would prohibit a state's taxation of a company unless the company had a place of business in the state. In this case, "place of business" is defined as having employees in the state, renting or owning property in the state, or maintaining inventory on a regular basis in the state. However, this legislation has not yet passed.

Meanwhile the situation is confused. The *Direct Marketing Manual,* which is published by the Direct Marketing Association and covers a wide number of mail order and direct marketing issues including ethical, legal, and regulatory subjects, recommends the following:

All states are now trying to impose jurisdictional nexus over direct mail marketers. If the states cannot prevent out-of-state sales, then they will protect local merchants and revenues by imposing the collection liability on direct mailers. Limiting your contact with a state to common carrier or the United States mail will help to relieve you of this obligation.

LOTTERIES AND GAMBLING

According to postal regulations, lotteries are synonymous with gambling and are forbidden through mail. You should be especially aware of this in dealing in direct marketing since the use of a sweepstakes, which is a legal technique that will add greatly to your response to an offer with which it is linked, may be termed a lottery if not handled correctly. According to the U.S. Postal Service regulations, a sweepstakes is legally considered a lottery if it contains three elements: prize, chance, and consideration. If any one of these elements is not present, a lottery does not exist. The usual and legal way of getting around this in promotional sweepstakes in mail order is to omit the element of consideration, making the sweepstakes technique legal. What do we mean by "consideration?" Consideration means that anyone may enter the sweepstakes, regardless of whether he or she orders the product, service, or item being promoted in conjunction with the sweepstakes. Therefore, there is no charge of any kind for entering the sweepstakes.

However, if you do intend to run a sweepstakes to promote a product or service, you should be aware that some states have laws concerning sweepstakes, which may range from outright prohibition to having to post a bond to guarantee that the prize does, in fact, exist. Therefore, if you intend to run a nationwide sweepstakes, you should definitely consult your attorney and a consultant specializing in sweepstakes promotions. You should also obtain a copy of the book, *Planning for Chance Promotionals*, by Frank T. Dierson, who is general counsel for the Promotion Marketing Association of America. The book is published by the Promotion Marketing Association of America, Inc., 420 Lexington Avenue, New York, New York 10017, and currently sells for $25 plus $5 for an update.

PORNOGRAPHY

Pornography is a confused area at best, since very few people can agree on what's obscene and pornographic, and the definition has varied so much over the years that people have gone to jail for selling what is very common today. I do not recommend dealing in this area. It is a case, again, of having to look in the mirror every morning when you get up and every evening when you go to bed. However, if you do intend to deal in some fashion with a product or service that may, by even the most remote definition, be considered pornographic or obscene, my advice is to see a competent attorney before you do so.

CHAIN LETTERS

A chain letter is a variation on a theme that has existed for perhaps a hundred years or more, in which you are invited to make money in the same way as the promoter. Usually there is a list of names and you put your name at the bottom of the list. When your name reaches the top of the list, according to the promotion, you will be wealthy. One current

COULD YOU FIGHT INFLATION IF YOU HAD ½ MILLION DOLLARS (OR MORE) WITHIN 60-90 DAYS ?

Dear Inflation Fighter,

How many times have most of us said, "If only I had the money to buy that piece of property...that business..that gold...that stock...etc.,I would be financially independent by now."

To be financially independent is to be free; free to make the financial choices that really matter in our lives: "Shall I go into business or buy that investment or take that trip?" We no longer have to think in terms of "If only..."

Yet very few of us reach financial independence because either the opportunities never come along or, worse yet, when they do come along, we simply ignore them.

You can make $500,000 or more by following our simple marketing program. It's perfectly legal, affordable, practical, and, what really matters, IT WORKS!

The saying "He who hesitates is lost" has never been more applicable. Don't be so busy SEEKING an opportunity to let this one slip by!

The way it all works is as follows: You purchase a $5 report entitled "How to Fight Inflation," and then, in a very short period of time, you will be selling this report to thousands of others at $5 per copy. (The report you purchase can be duplicated for about 3¢ per copy!) Remember, only 5% (One out of twenty people) need to participate and you will reach your ½ million dollar goal.

Do not confuse this multi-level marketing program with the run-of-the-mill "Pie in the Sky" chain letter. We offer a product for every dollar that will be exchanged. This program conforms to all current postal regulations and is perfectly legal.

In fact, multi-level marketing has been around for a long time and has been used from time to time (quite successfully by the way) by major American companies. This marketing technique was examined by Dan Rather of "60 Minutes" and was found to be a tremendous success!

(OVER)

(a)

Figure 3-3.   Chain letters.

Then,

using your home or office typewriter, neatly retype the list of Advertisers below on ‑lain white paper. Eliminate the person in the #1 position to whom you have just sent $. Then, simply add YOUR NAME and ADDRESS to the bottom of the list in the #5 position. W.‑h scissors or razor blade, cut out your revised Advertisers' list and paste it into the Advertisers Section.

Now you are ready to take the letter to an offset printer (listed in the Yellow Pages); tell him to ‑un off 200 copies (or more if you wish). Do not make any other changes of this letter as you may harm its "pulling power."

You then send out 200 (or more) copies of this revised letter to friends, relatives, smart business people in your local telephone directory or you can order names of opportunity seekers and small businesses from name brokers.

We recommend that if you purchase a name list that you use one of the following because of their up-to-date lists, quick service and low price. Ask for "opportunity seekers and small business buyers." Send cash or money orders (personal checks will delay your order two weeks). They have new names each week that really pull.

Or look in the yellow pages of your phone book under list brokers.

EXAMPLE: (FOR ONLY A 5% PARTICIPATION)

	You send	200 copies with your name in the #5 position - 5% respond =	10
Those	10 people send	200 copies with your name in the #4 position - 5% respond =	100
Those	100 people send	200 copies with your name in the #3 position - 5% respond =	1,000
Those	1,000 people send	200 copies with your name in the #2 position - 5% respond =	10,000
Those	10,000 people send	200 copies with your name in the #1 position - 5% respond =	100,000

At $5 Each and at Only a 5% Participation You Would Receive $500,000.

Your name simply moves up the list and multiplies as it reaches the #1 position. As you can see from the example . . . up to 100,000 people (or more) could be sending you $5 for your copies of the report or up to $500,000 in cash. Not at all shabby for a minimal investment.

Financial success is not reserved for just a few "smart" people. Take a look around your neighborhood; you'll see a lot of people who are less intelligent than you are. . . who don't work any harder than you do . . . but . . . for some reason, they are earning a lot more money. These people look for opportunity, and when the right one comes along, they act on it! Here's your opportunity to help assure your well being, and that of your family's. This offer will not be repeated; therefore, I urge that you take action, today!

Sincerely,

Your #5 Advertiser

ADVERTISERS

(b)

Figure 3-3. (Continued)

variation is for you to sell a money-making plan that is sold to you as you join the chain and that, according to the promotional letter, makes the promotion legal. However, this is not true. Chain letters are always illegal, and if you are caught dealing in one, you will not only probably lose your money but also be liable for prosecution. A typical chain letter is shown in Figure 3-3. Remember, this scheme is illegal and definitely *not* recommended by the author or any other reputable consultant or writer in mail order.

DRUGS

Drugs fall into a special category because they are administered by the Food and Drug Administration (FDA). Be careful of new drugs that are not standard and accepted medical remedies. You cannot sell new drugs that fall into this category without special permission from the FDA. Naturally, this permission is not granted overnight or without extensive testing. Therefore, even if you have discovered a miracle drug that you personally know will cure what you claim it will, you cannot advertise it without permission from the FDA; furthermore, you should expect to spend a great deal of money proving the truth of your claim.

USE OF FICTITIOUS NAMES

In the last chapter we discussed some of the aspects of obtaining proper fictitious name registration. As I noted then, it is illegal to use words that imply you are something you are not. For example, do not use words such as *university, institute,* and *bureau,* which suggest nonprofit organizations of various types, if, in fact, you are not. Do not use words such as *laboratory* or *manufacturing company* if, in fact, you are not a laboratory and do no manufacturing. Remember that there are two diferent laws here that come into play. One is the law requiring a fictitious name registration for any name other than your own that you use for your business. The other law prohibits attempting to deceive the public by using a name that misrepresents the business functions in which you are actually engaged.

FRAUD

Fraud means taking money from your customer under false pretenses. Unfortunately, mail order rip-off artists have been doing this almost since mail order began. Julian L. Simon, in his excellent book, *How to Start and Operate a Mail Order Business,* has collected a number of obvious mail order frauds from various sources. Here are a few (from *How to Start and Operate a Mail Order Business* by Julian L. Simon, copyright © 1981, 1976, 1965 by McGraw-Hill, Inc. Used with permission of McGraw-Hill Book Company):

1. An ad offering a steel engraving of George Washington for 50¢. The copy beneath the headline described the excellence of the engraving, the beautiful, deep, rich color used, and the fact that the paper

was deckled on all four edges. For 50¢ the buyer received a 2¢ postage stamp.

2. A patented potato bug killer for $1. The buyer was to receive sufficient equipment to kill all the potato bugs in a 10-acre field. For $1 the buyer received two slabs of wood, which were sent with instructions telling the purchaser exactly how to pick the bugs off vines, lay them between the slabs, and press one slab firmly down on the other.

3. *"$3.95 for This Five-Piece Wicker Set"* was a headline for an illustration showing a handsome, sturdy table, settee, two straight-back wicker chairs, and a rocker. The copy included a guarantee that the set would be exactly like the illustration. When the set arrived, it *was* exactly like the illustration—not only in appearance, but also in size.

Modern frauds are just as vicious in taking an unsuspecting mail order buyer. There is envelope stuffing with various variations, for example. An advertisement reads, "Learn to stuff envelopes, work at home, make a thousand dollars a month. Free details." The potential customer receives a more detailed promotional asking for from $15 to $35. For the money, one buyer received 200 brochures that promoted envelope-stuffing schemes, a chain letter type of scheme. Sometimes the buyer receives a few pages encouraging him or her to enter the mail order business.

Another modern fraud is that of unclaimed merchandise. You receive a letter in which the writer claims to represent the Bureau of Unclaimed Merchandise. In this form letter you are told that, by filling out an enclosed card and remitting, say, $10, you will be shipped Parcel No. 740, which is awaiting claim. In return for your money you receive nothing.

One firm with which we are familiar sells phony job recommendations for any position you wish in a variety of dummy companies it has established across the United States and on Pacific islands. For a fixed sum you can obtain a letter of recommendation certifying that you performed outstanding work as an engineer, technician, technical writer, or whatever, and a statement indicating that the dummy company would be happy to hire you if you chose to return to their employ.

Another currently practiced deception that I believe is on the borderline of legality, is catalogs or sales leaflets that are imprinted with your name and address. The promotional materials are described as ready to mail, and you are advised that you need not carry any inventory or stock of products since all items are stocked by the company that is selling you the catalogs. They offer to drop-ship direct to the customer for you and you keep somewhere between 40 and 50% of the revenue.

For many new mail order dealers this may appear to be a great way to get into the mail order business, primarily because catalogs are so expensive to develop on your own and because of the attraction of not having to carry any inventory. Sometimes these companies will even offer to sell you names of mail order buyers. In fact, you can make little money with a deal like this unless you can mail these catalogs along with an item you are already successfully selling. What many of these companies are really selling to you is the printing, not the proposed service of catalog development and drop-shipping the merchandise. Although these schemes are undoubtedly a form of fraud, they have not yet been stopped by the authorities. But they have cost thousands of would-be mail order entrepreneurs money. I mention these here not only because you should avoid operating such a scheme yourself, but also so you can avoid investing your money in one.

E. J. Kahn, Jr. in his book *Fraud,* indicates that a recent list drawn up by the U.S. Postal Service included such fraud mail order schemes as "advanced fees, check kiting, unordered COD parcels, falsified contest entries, phony coupon redemption plans, credit card frauds, delinquent debtors schemes, fictitious classified directories, endless chain referral selling plans, alleged business opportunities, chain letters, missing heir swindles, false financial statements, numbers rackets and lucky charms, home improvement frauds, investments, supposed job opportunities, mortgage loan and debt consolidation schemes, phony manuscript and song publishing companies, matrimonial swindles, numismatic and philatelic swindles, real estate (improved and unimproved), shady correspondence schools and diploma mills, fake charity solicitations and dubious work-at-home schemes."

The penalties for wrongdoing can be severe and are mainly in the hands of the U.S. Postal Service or the Federal Trade Commission.

You may not know it, but the Postal Inspection Service Division of the U.S. Postal Service is the oldest law enforcement agency in the country. It is incredibly effective: On a yearly basis, 98% of the criminal cases it brings to trial result in conviction, compared with an average for the FBI of about 96%. Not bad, you might say! What can the Postal Service do? The Postal Service can arrest you, it can put you out of business, and it can apply stamps to your mail that read "Fraudulent," "Refused," and "Out of Business" and return them to your customer. If you weren't out of business before the stamps were applied, you certainly would be thereafter.

The Federal Trade Commission is not without teeth either. The FTC may give you a chance to state your case and appeal it, but after that it can order you to cease what it considers to be an illegal practice and can stick you with walloping fines.

Other government agencies such as the Food and Drug Administration can also have at you if you violate government regulations. They can also stop you, fine you, or send you to jail. Lest you think only the "feds" can do you in should you decide to take the wrong route in mail order, you should know that most states have state fraud commissions with various powers that sometimes exceed those of the federal agencies to punish you for your wrongdoing.

In judging whether a contemplated mail order promotion is legal or illegal, consider the following:

1. Be honest with yourself. Are you trying to deceive or cheat a potential customer in some way? If you are, don't do it. When looking at yourself in the mirror, if you get a bad feeling, don't do it.
2. Consult the U.S. Postal Service and ask whether in that office's opinion the project you are thinking about will be illegal.
3. Consult the FTC and get an opinion as to whether a contemplated promotion is legal.
4. Consult the Better Business Bureau in your area and ask whether there have been complaints about similar operations.
5. Finally, you can and should consult an attorney in any questionable situation.

FIVE GUIDELINES TO AVOIDING LEGAL PROBLEMS

Here are five things you should do to minimize running afoul of mail order law.

1. If you're going to be late, give the buyer the choice of having his or her money refunded, and let him or her know about the delay as soon as you do.
2. Always give your customer maximum value for his or her money. While it is true that the price usually must be three to four times your cost for you to make any money selling through the mail, the value received should be perceived to be worth the price paid for any merchandise or service. Mail order expert Hubert K. Simon, author of *Out of the Rat Race and into the Chips,* recommends always giving your customers an additional and unexpected value when you fulfill their orders.
3. Do not try to cheat your customer. If you do, your business will not succeed in the long run, even if you escape fines or imprisonment.
4. Don't lie in advertising. The same result will occur as above, even if you aren't found guilty of some legal fault. Your credibility will

suffer, and since mail order is a back-end business with much of your profits made with subsequent sales, your business will ultimately fail. Even if all your profits are up front in your first sale, if your advertising is untruthful, your project will fail because of returned products.

5.   Finally, if you have any questions pertaining to legal issues, pay the money and consult an attorney. It will save you money in the long run.

As a consultant, I am frequently asked, "Why, if such and such is true and the FTC opposes it and the Postal Service can send you to jail, has such-and-such advertiser been using the same apparently fraudulent promotions for over a year?" I cannot honestly answer this question. I suppose some people have always gotten away with murder and will continue to do so. Some unscrupulous individuals always operate on the borderline of what is legal and what is not. They know from experience exactly what they can and cannot do. Maybe their firms are large enough to pay the legal fees or fines if they are perceived to have stepped over the line into illegality. You are not in this position. Further, you don't know that the individual's case has not been under study for some time and perhaps soon the individual will be arrested, tried, and fined or sent to jail. Therefore, even if you see a scheme that obviously violates the laws of the land but the individual is apparently getting away with it—*don't do it!*

The following books may be useful as references in deciding whether your anticipated promotion is legal and for other aspects of legalities of mail order and direct mail marketing.

1.   *The Law of Advertising,* in two volumes, by George Rosden and Peter Rosden. Mathew Bender, 235 East 45th Street, New York, New York 10017.

2.   *Applying for Chance Promotions,* cited earlier in the text, by Frank T. Dierson.

3.   *Postal Laws Transmittal Letter No. 24,* December 12, 1974. Available from the Superintendent of Documents, U.S. Government Printing Office, Washington, D.C. 20402.

4.   *The Law and Direct Marketing.* Publication Division of the Direct Mail Association, 6 East 43rd Street, New York, New York 10017.

5.   *Law for Advertising and Marketing,* by Morton J. Simon. Norton Company, New York, New York 10017.

6.   *Mail Fraud,* by the U.S. Chief Postal Inspector. U.S. Government Printing Office, Washington, D.C. 20042.

7. *Do's and Don't's in Advertising Copy,* by the Council of Better Business Bureaus, 11507 17th Street NW, Washington, D.C. 20036.
8. *A Primer on the Law of Deceptive Practices,* by Earl W. Kintner. Macmillan Publishing Co., Inc., 866 Third Avenue, New York, New York 10022.
9. *The Direct Marketer's Legal Advisor,* by Robert J. Posch. McGraw-Hill Book Company, 1221 Avenue of the Americas, New York, New York 10020.

SUMMARY

In this chapter we have covered the legal problems you may encounter as a mail order operator and some basic ethics of the profession.

1. Never offer anything in an advertisement in which the promotion is not clear and honest.
2. Be careful of deceptive pricing.
3. Obey the 30-day rule for delivery of mail order merchandise.
4. Remember the rules of endorsements and testimonials, that they must be real, and how they should be used.
5. Dry-testing is still legal, but be aware of changes that might take place at any time.
6. Under certain circumstances you must pay state taxes.
7. Lotteries and gambling are the same. They are illegal. Sweepstakes are legal as a promotional technique when used properly.
8. In general, stay away from pornography and obscene literature.
9. Chain letters are always illegal.
10. Drugs are watched over by the Food and Drug Administration. Do not get involved in selling drugs without being aware of the FDA's regulations and without FDA approval.
11. Be careful of the use of fictitious names that are not representative of your actual business.
12. Beware of fraud. Don't be deceived yourself, and don't engage in deception under any circumstances.

Finally, in this chapter we reviewed the penalties for wrongdoing, general guidelines as to what you should and should not do, and the fact that you should never assume that something is legal simply because some other mail order operator is doing it now.

4

How to Find Profitable Products to Sell by Mail

The basic principle of finding and then selling products successfully by mail is always to look at the market first and decide what the market wants before you zero in on a specific product to sell. This rule is altered only slightly if you already have an established product or service you are selling profitably through other means. In this case, you must evaluate your established product or service to see whether it can be sold profitably through the mail. In all cases, test before you sink huge sums of money into your product.

There are numerous examples of fortunes that have been made by following these principles. Robert Collier and Joe Karbo both recognized the need for a book to show people how to lead successful lives before they wrote them. Joe Sugarman noted that there was a tremendous demand for high-technological electronic items and that this demand could be met readily through a mail order operation. Brainerd Mellinger discovered an immense market, not only for items that he could import from foreign countries, but for assisting individuals who wanted to get into importing and exporting themselves.

In looking at the market first, concentrate on what your potential consumers are currently buying, as well as on economic conditions, the state of technology, culture, the political environment, the laws, and competition. Look at any factor you feel may affect your ability to sell the product. These factors are known as environmental variables, and each is crucial to your success in the mail order business.

Consider, for example, what your potential customers are currently buying. If there is no demand for a product that you want to sell, it is extremely difficult to try to build a demand, no matter how exciting your copy. You'll be far better off finding a product that already fills a demonstrated need in the marketplace and for which demand already exists, as proved by what your potential customers are already buying. In the same fashion, you cannot sell a product that is illegal, no matter what the demand. Joe Cossman tells of a fabulous product he found on one of this trips to Thailand. Troubled by insect bites, the druggist gave him a product known as Tigerspaw, which instantly relieved the pain from his insect bites and stings. Thinking what a wonderful mail order product this would make in the states, Joe asked the FDA about Tigerspaw, only to discover that many people had tried to bring this product into the United States to sell. There was one problem: The main ingredient of Tigerspaw was morphine.

You can think of many products that might be successful in one culture but not in another, or in one political environment but not in another, or products such as the electronic devices sold by Joe Sugarman, which are very, very successful in a high-technology country such as the United States, but would not be in a country that gained widespread use of electricity only yesterday.

Consideration of competition is awfully important and I suppose this is as good a time as any to mention the copycat principle, which some mail order books advise as the only real way to mail order success.

According to the copycat principle, you simply copy someone else's success in mail order as closely as you can; that is, since mail order advertising is open to everyone, you simply observe what is successful by watching advertising in magazines or in your own mail. If a particular proposition is repeated over a long period of time, you know it is successful and you simply introduce an identical proposition or one that is as close to the original as possible without running afoul of copyright or other laws. This procedure is supposed to guarantee success.

I take issue with the copycat principle for selecting new products, depending upon how it is presented. I won't even go into ethics here: That is for every individual to decide on his or her own. But look at it this way: If you copy another mail order operator's product, medium, and so on almost exactly, what market are you going to go after? Obviously, the identical market. This means that the market must be split between you and the original dealer. Now any market, no matter for what product, is only so large. Further, unfortunately, the mail order business is full of rip-off artists who constantly, and without much thinking, attempt to follow the copycat principle exactly. This means that in a very, very short time, unless the originator has total control over his or her product or service, numerous imitators will have jumped in and split the market to such an extent that there is little profit for anyone.

A second problem with following the copycat principle is that you may not know the whole story—that is, you are privy only to the advertising of your competition, not to his or her marketing plan. Since mail order is a back-end business, you don't know whether any profit is being made up front. Julian Simon, author of *How to Start and Operate a Mail Order Business*, tells a story of a copycat who copied another mail order success exactly and went broke at the end of the year. Eventually meeting with the originator, he said, "I can't understand it. I followed you exactly and I lost money on every single sale that I made." The eminently successful originator of the product smiled and said, "Of course; so do I, but I make great profits on those products I sell to the customer after the initial sale."

A third problem with the copycat principle is that your competitor may already have established himself or herself in the marketplace so that an imitator can no longer break in. I think this is the reason that many imitators of Joe Karbo are unsuccessful with advertisements of books and manuals that attempt to imitate *The Lazy Man's Way to Riches*. Joe is so well established in the marketplace that any copier simply doesn't have the stature, or the financial resources, to affect Joe's market significantly.

Because of these facts, I do not recommend your ripping off someone else's product. However, there is one way of using this principle successfully, and that is not to copy the product, medium, and so forth of the originator, but to give someone else's concept an entirely new twist. A good way of doing this successfully is illustrated by Melvin Powers, president of Wilshire Book Company. Noting that diet and weight control books were on the top of every list of best-sellers, and that a book called *How to Flatten Your Stomach* by Coach Jim Everroad had reached number one on the best-seller list with more than 200,000 copies sold, Powers created a tremendous spoof called *How to Flatten Your Tush*, by Coach Marge Reardon, in less than a day. As Melvin described it in *How to Get Rich in Mail Order*, he sold 25,000 copies to major bookstore chains immediately and went back later and sold them another 25,000. He soon promoted a Miss Tush contest and got extensive national coverage through the press and on television. The *New York Times* called the book one of the year's funniest books and Melvin, continuing the spoof, printed across the outside cover, "Soon to Be a Major Motion Picture." He was amazed to receive letters from satisfied readers who wanted to know who was to produce the film. Powers's book was a fabulous success and an outstanding example of how to use the copycat principle properly, by giving an old concept a new twist.

HOW TO SELL YOUR PRODUCT BY MAIL ORDER—AN
IMPORTANT CONSIDERATION IN PRODUCT SELECTION

There are several different ways of selling your product through mail order, and the one you choose will affect your selection of new products. These methods are one-shot, inquiry and follow-up, repeat, and catalog. Let's look at each one individually.

One-Shot

The one-shot product is probably every would-be mail order operator's dream. This is where you simply advertise a product in a display or classified advertisement or in a letter direct to your customer. Your customer sends you the money, you send the product, and that ends the deal. You make your profit immediately. While you obviously have your list of customers, you do not have a line of similar products to sell them. Examples of the one-shot were Joe Karbo's book *The Lazy Man's Way to Riches,* or Joe Sugarman's electronic devices. Each product is sold separately and individually. Usually the one-shot is defined by two characteristics; first, that you sell on a single, first advertisement, whether it is by letter or by display or by classified advertisement, and, second, that you have no other product to follow up and sell to your customer after selling your initial product. *One-shot* can refer to a product, the method of selling, or both. By the way, both Karbo and Sugarman now have follow up products, and Sugarman has a catalog.

While many people feel that the one-shot *is* mail order, the fact of the matter is that a one-shot operation has a number of significant disadvantages, and while it can clearly be successful (as evidenced by Karbo, Sugarman, and others), it is far easier to be successful in some sort of repeat business. Mail order is a back-end profit business because of the high cost of advertising to obtain your customer's name. For example, in very simple terms, if you have a product that costs $2 and you sell it for $10, the cost of the product, plus the packaging, plus the postage, plus the advertising costs, is deducted from your profit. If the advertising, packaging, and postage cost a total of $8.50 (say, $7.50 for the advertising and $1 for the postage and packaging), the total cost to you for the first sale is $10.50. So for every single sale, you lose 50¢. On the second sale, or any additional sales you make of the same product, the cost is still $2, but now

First Sale to Customer		All Back-End Sales to Customer	
Product cost	$ 2.00	Product cost	$2.00
Postage and packaging	1.00	Postage and packaging	1.00
Advertising cost	7.50	Advertising cost	.00
Total	$10.50	Total	$3.00
Profit	$10 − $10.50 = −50¢	Profit	$10.00 − $3 = $7
50¢ loss!		$7 profit on each sale!	

Figure 4-1. Mail order is a back-end profit business.

your advertising is very close to zero because you already have your customer's name. Your packaging and postage remain at $1. So the total cost to you is $3. Since the sales price is $10, minus $3, your net profit is $7. Of course, in this simple example, as shown in Figure 4-1, we have eliminated factors such as overhead to illustrate the point.

Except for direct mail, another disadvantage of a one-shot is the relatively limited space you have to tell your story and make a sale. This is why selling direct from classified ads is so difficult. You just haven't got the words available to convince your potential customer to buy your product.

To summarize the one-shot, it is possible to be successful this way, but it is harder than if you sell a line of products to be the same customer or if you use inquiry and follow-up.

Inquiry and Follow-up

This is a method that can be used with either one-shot or repeat products. The basic difference between it and the basic one-shot method is the fact that, regardless of what you sell, your initial advertisement merely serves to bring in an inquiry for a more expensive follow-up to interested potential customers. The initial advertisement may be a space or classified advertisement, a postcard through direct mail, or a letter through direct mail. All have been used. Brainerd Mellinger is famous for very large full-page space advertisements that have a coupon at the bottom in which you write only to receive additional information about his proposition. Can you believe that these are advertisements that can cost $40,000 a page or more? That should make clear not only how expensive advertising is but also just how much profit there must be on the back-end of the mail order business. Otherwise, neither Brainerd Mellinger nor anyone else could afford to spend this kind of money just to acquire a potential customer's name.

Last month I used this same technique of inquiry and follow-up to sell $20,000 worth of research by mail. The first mailing was a direct mail let-

ter to a number of senior aerospace executives. It outlined the general research I wanted to sell and provided a tear-out coupon to request the full
proposal for the research. Those executives who responded with this
coupon were mailed the expensive proposal, which contained all of the
follow-up information and allowed me more space to sell the product.

Repeat Methods

Repeat methods of selling are the most profitable in mail order. After you
sell an initial product to your customer, you continue to sell the same or
similar products to him or her. Examples of repeat methods are film de-
velopers who give you a special bargain or even free film so that you can
continually buy from them in the future, and book-of-the-month-type
clubs, where a special bargain brings you in the door and thereafter you
are given the opportunity to buy books at reduced prices for as long as
you retain your membership. Brainerd Mellinger's business also uses repeat methods, since after selling his course on mail order import or export, he sells products, seminars, newsletters, and other similar or related
items to his initial customers. There are no disadvantages to repeat business except that when you sell your first product to your customer, you
must have something else, a line of products, or a service, or something,
ready to sell right away. In fact, with the very act of fulfillment of the initial item you sell, you can put in an advertisement for follow-up products
or services. This, by the way, is known as a "bounce-back." Even if you
sell by the one-shot method, having a repeat product to sell will greatly
increase your profitability and chance for immediate success.

Catalog Sales

Catalog sales are a type of repeat business since the object is to persuade
your customer to order again and again. It is very difficult for a beginner
to make money with catalogs, although it has been done. Witness
Gerardo Joffe with Haverhills, and now Henniker's. However, putting together a catalog takes a huge initial investment and a great deal of talent
regarding product selection, locating sources, controlling them, and so
forth. This is usually not for the beginner. As was discussed in chapter 3,
some companies make a business of selling preprinted catalogs, which
they will imprint with your own name. I strongly recommend against
purchase of these catalogs. While, in theory, you save the cost of putting
your own catalog together and the cost of inventory, since these companies are ready to drop-ship the items to your customers, the fact is that
the markup on these products is so slight that you cannot make a profit

from them, even if you find customers who are willing to buy from this type of catalog. Further, few customers will buy from a catalog they recognize as not coming from the original source. In fact, many of these potential customers may receive more than one identical catalog with different names on them. Save yourself some money—don't buy ready-made catalogs.

So many companies have made it big with catalog sales—starting with Sears and Montgomery Ward, and going through the Horchow Collection, Sunset House, Spiegel, and many, many others—that it is clear that mail order can be very profitable when practiced in this fashion. However, you would be well advised to begin with a small product line and expand the size of your catalog slowly as you obtain experience and financial resources for investment. Roger Horchow, president of the Horchow Collection, says in his book, *Elephants in Your Mail Box*, that he planned on losing $1 million the first year with one of his first catalogs. He actually lost $2 million in both his first and second years.

These, then, are the basic methods you can use to sell a product through the mail. We will talk about more advanced methods in a later chapter. As you select your product for your first mail order venture, keep in mind this methodology of selling, since one or more of these methods will be your key to mail order success.

SELLING THROUGH THE MAIL IF YOU ALREADY HAVE A PRODUCT OR SERVICE

Many readers may already have a company in which they are selling products or services through means other than the mail and are wondering whether they can sell their established product through this channel of distribution. In considering whether you can do this, picture selling your product through the methods described above. Also consider the following factors.

1. Do you have competitors who are selling through the mail?
2. Do you have customers you know about who buy by mail right now?
3. Is your product lightweight and relatively easy to package for mail order selling?
4. Does your product have a high markup? Remember that, in general, if a product is to be profitable, you must be able to sell it at three to four times the mail cost to you. There are exceptions to

this, which are mentioned elsewhere in this book, but this is the general rule.

5. Is your product easily obtainable in stores? Generally, if it is, there is no reason for an individual to buy it through the mail.

6. Can you communicate sales appeal for your product on paper? This is pretty important, because if you are going to sell by mail, that is exactly what you are going to have to do.

If the answer to every question except number five is yes, you have a good chance for success in selling your product through the mail.

THE RULES OF PRODUCT SELECTION

There are many rules of product selection. I have three general principles that I try to follow in selection of a new product, and I recommend these to clients, friends, and everyone else interested in mail order selling. Rule number one is to work with a product that you like to handle. Your main objective may be to make money; however, if you don't like the product or service, it'll be much more difficult for you to work with it. Conversely, if you really like your product, it really isn't work to sell it—it's fun. You'll work harder and have fun doing it. So find a product you like and your chances of success increase.

Rule number two is to handle a product you know something about. Now obviously, if you are going to sell a large number of different products, you will eventually sell products at some time or other about which you know very little. However, at the beginning, you need everything possible going for you. Selecting products you know something about will be a real asset. Many people make mistakes in this area, including yours truly. When I first started dealing in mail order, I selected a jewelry product about which I knew absolutely nothing. I didn't make money—I lost it. I began to be successful in mail order when I selected products I knew something about. In my case, this was the selling of information about writing for publication. If you want to maximize your chances for success right up front, select a product or service about which you are knowledgeable.

The third rule, and perhaps the most important, is to handle a product you respect. I mentioned in the last chapter that it may be possible to skirt the line of legality and sell a product that is technically legal but ethically questionable. If you want to be truly happy and successful with your mail order business, handle a product that you and other people can respect.

Jim Kobs, author of *Profitable Direct Marketing,* developed a four-plus-one formula for product selection that he recommends for help in evaluating a new product. Here it is.*

1. *Broad Appeal.* Kobs says always to look for something that virtually every man, woman, or household can use and that has broad appeal to certain specific market segments, which you can reach at low cost and high profit.

2. *Unusual Features.* Look for a product that has unusual features. This is good for mail orders, says Kobs, because little salesmanship is left at the retail level today. Therefore, a product selling by retail that has unusual features is usually not discoverable by the potential customer. As a direct marketer, you can highlight these unusual features and make a sale by emphasizing them.

3. *A Product That Is Not Readily Available in Stores.* This goes back to the reason and rationale for individuals' buying through the mail and has been mentioned previously. It is a fact that if you can't find it in stores or won't find it in stores at the price you are selling it for, or if it is not available in the way you are selling it as a complete package in stores, your chances of success are much better.

4. *Proper Price and Proper Margins.* According to Kobs, the starting point for any product or service being sold by mail is the right price. It is important to understand that the right price may not necessarily be the lowest price, as we will get into later in our full discussion on pricing.

Okay, those are Kobs' "four." What is his "plus?" It's what he calls the *dream element,* or the *story element.* The dream element is using your imagination to give the item a new twist that no one else has thought of before. The pet rock certainly falls into this category. The story element is the telling of an interesting or appealing story behind the product. Look at John Caples' ad, "They Laughed When I Sat Down at the Piano," shown in Figure 4-2. Is that an interesting story or not?

Bob Stone is the chairman of Stone and Adler, Inc., one of the country's leading mail order advertising agencies, and the author of one of the most successful books on direct marketing ever written, *Successful Direct Marketing Methods.* Bob Stone has developed a four-step method for

* From Jim Kobs, *Profitable Direct Marketing,* Crain Books (a division of Crain Communications, Inc.), 1979. Reprinted by permission of Jim Kobs.

"Can he really play?" a girl whispered. "Heavens, no!" Arthur exclaimed. "He never played a note in his life."

They Laughed When I Sat Down
At the Piano
But When I Started to Play!—

ARTHUR had just played "The Rosary." The room rang with applause. I decided that this would be a dramatic moment for me to make my debut. To the amazement of all my friends I strode confidently over to the piano and sat down.

"Jack is up to his old tricks," somebody chuckled. The crowd laughed. They were all certain that I couldn't play a single note.

"Can he really play?" I heard a girl whisper to Arthur. "Heavens, no!" Arthur exclaimed. "He never played a note in all his life . But just you watch him. This is going to be good."

I decided to make the most of the situation. With mock dignity I drew out a silk handkerchief and lightly dusted off the keys. Then I rose and gave the revolving piano stool a quarter of a turn, just as I had seen an imitator of Paderewski do in a vaudeville sketch.

"What do you think of his execution?" called a voice from the rear.

"We're in favor of it!" came back the answer, and the crowd rocked with laughter.

Then I Started to Play

Instantly a tense silence fell on the guests. The laughter died on their lips as if by magic. I played through the first bars of Liszt's immortal Liebestraume. I heard gasps of amazement. My friends sat breathless—spellbound.

I played on and as I played I forgot the people around me. I forgot the hour, the place, the breathless listeners. The little world I lived in seemed to fade—seemed to grow dim—unreal. Only the music was real. Only the music and the visions it brought me. Visions as beautiful and as changing as the wind-blown clouds and drifting moonlight, that long ago inspired the master composer. It seemed as if the master musician himself were speaking to me—speaking through the medium of music—not in words but in chords. Not in sentences but in exquisite melodies.

A Complete Triumph!

As the last notes of the Liebestraume died away, the room resounded with a sudden roar of applause. I found myself surrounded by excited faces. How my friends carried on! Men shook my hand—wildly congratulated me—pounded me on the back in their enthusiasm! Everybody was exclaiming with delight—plying me with rapid questions.... "Jack! Why didn't you tell us you could play like that?"

"Where did you learn?"—"How long have you studied?"—"Who was your teacher?"

"I have never even seen my teacher," I replied. "And just a short while ago I couldn't play a note."

"Quit your kidding," laughed Arthur, himself an accomplished pianist. "You've been studying for years. I can tell."

"I have been studying only a short while," I insisted. "I decided to keep it a secret so that I could surprise all you folks."

Then I told them the whole story.

"Have you ever heard of the U. S. School of Music?" I asked. A few of my friends nodded. "That's a correspondence school, isn't it?" they exclaimed.

"Exactly," I replied. "They have a new simplified method that can teach you to play any instrument by note in just a few months."

How I Learned to Play Without a Teacher

And then I explained how for years I had longed to play the piano.

"It seems just a short while ago," I continued, "that I saw an interesting ad of the U. S. School of Music mentioning a new method of learning to play which only cost a few cents a day. The ad told how a woman had mastered the piano in her spare time at home—and without a teacher! Best of all, the wonderful new method she used required no laborious scales—no heartless exercises—no tiresome practising. It sounded so convincing that I filled out the coupon requesting the Free Demonstration Lesson.

"The free book arrived promptly and I started in that very night to study the Demonstration Lesson. I was amazed to see how easy it was to play this new way. Then I sent for the course.

"When the course arrived I found it was just as the ad said—as easy as A. B. C.! And as the lessons continued they got easier and easier. Before I knew it I was playing all the pieces I liked best. Nothing stopped me. I could play ballads or classical numbers or jazz, all with equal ease. And I never did have any special talent for music."

* * * *

Play Any Instrument

You, too, can now teach yourself to be an accomplished musician—right at home—in half the usual time. You can't go wrong with this simple new method which has already shown almost half a million people how to play their favorite instruments by note. Forget that old-fashioned idea that you need special "talent." Just read the list of instruments in the panel, decide which one you want to play and the U. S. School will do the rest. And bear in mind no matter which instrument you choose, the cost in each case will be the same—just a few cents a day. No matter whether you are a mere beginner or already a good performer, you will be interested in learning about this new and wonderful method.

Send for Our Free Booklet and Demonstration Lesson

Thousands of successful students never dreamed they possessed musical ability until it was revealed to them by a remarkable "Musical Ability Test" which we send entirely without cost with our interesting free booklet.

If you are in earnest about wanting to play your favorite instrument—if you really want to gain happiness and increase your popularity—send at once for the free booklet and Demonstration Lesson. No cost—no obligation. Sign and send the convenient coupon now. Instruments supplied when needed, cash or credit. U. S. School of Music, 812 Brunswick Bldg., New York City.

"They Laughed When I Sat Down at the Piano"

Figure 4-2. John Caple's famous ad. The emphasis here is on telling a good story.

74

evaluating new products. He recommends asking yourself the following to estimate potential marketability.

1. Does the product or service have a reason for being? Is there a perceived need or can it be created?
2. Does the product suit your prospect's taste, life-style, and the price he or she may be willing to pay?
3. Does the product have a perceived beauty, utility, or value for the individual prospect?
4. Will it appeal to the majority of your prospects?

Win Barnes, president of Kross, Inc., and former general manager of the mail order division of Shell Oil, a man who has selected literally thousands of mail order products of all types and sold over five and a half million items by mail, recommends that the mail order marketer ask 19 questions before making the decision to market the product by mail:

1. Is it available in retail stores?
2. Can everyone use the item or is it limited?
3. Has it a perceived value at least equal to offer?
4. Is it easy to use?
5. Does it solve a recognizable problem?
6. Will it photograph well?
7. Is it easy to describe?
8. Is it just another version of a readily available product?
9. Can installation be made by a novice?
10. Does it need to be put together upon arrival?
11. Is it unisex in nature?
12. Does it provide something of benefit for the buyer ... savings, safety, security, fun, satisfaction, pleasure?
13. Is it needed immediately?
14. Are there choices that have to be made, that is, color, size?
15. Can it be offered at a competitive price with sufficient margin?
16. Is the time right for it?
17. Does it fit the media to be used in selling ... telephone, mail, space, television, catalog?
18. Does a market have to be created for the product?
19. Is the supplier reliable?

THE MAIL ORDER PRODUCT EVALUATION FORM

The mail order product evaluation form is one that I myself have developed over the years from a number of different sources. It is shown in Figure 4-3. I have formulated relative weightings I consider most important for overall mail order suitability. Under certain circumstances this relative weighting might change, and in this case, you must adapt the mail order product evaluation form to your own circumstances. Using it is simple. Simply multiply the relative weighting times from zero through four points. Use four points if the question gets a rating of *excellent* for your product. Three points indicates *very good*. Two points is for *good*. One point is for *fair*, and zero is for *poor*. Add up all the points after multiplying by the weighting. You should consider those products with the most points as candidates for your mail order product.

Here are 17 great sources of new mail order products:

1. Start with the concept of currently successful products, but be careful. Don't copy everything about your competitor's product. If you do, you will not win; you will lose because of the reasons I have stated earlier; however, if you change the basic concept, as Mel Powers did with his book, *How to Flatten Your Tush*, you can find a successful product that can make you a fortune.

2. Attend inventor shows. Many inventors are not good marketers, and, in fact, most inventions that are patented are never actually produced in quantity. At inventor shows you will see hundreds of new products that the inventors would like to license to you for a royalty or perhaps sell outright. To find out when an inventor show will be in your local area, contact your local chamber of commerce.

3. Consider foreign products. Foreign products not available in the United States can frequently be outstanding products for sale by mail. One additional factor that can help you is that every country would like to see the number of its exports increased. Therefore, one primary source of foreign products is the commercial attaché of foreign consulates and embassies. Find the telephone numbers in the telephone book of any large city and ask for the commercial attaché. One particular product I know about was available for licensing and hadn't yet been introduced in the United States; further, the government of this foreign country spent thousands of dollars assisting the entrepreneur in selling the item in the United States simply to better its trade position through exporting. If you do not live close to a large city where a foreign consulate or em-

MAIL ORDER PRODUCT EVALUATION FORM

Instructions: Give each evaluation item
          4 points for an evaluation of excellent
          3 points for an evaluation of very good
          2 points for an evaluation of good
          1 point for an evaluation of fair
          0 point for an evaluation of poor

Multiply the evaluation points times the importance weighting. Only pick new products that have a high point total.

	Importance Weighting	Evaluation Points	Total
I. Market ability			
1. How large is the potential market?	.03	× _____	= ____
2. How important is the need that the product fills?	.08	× _____	= ____
3. Can the customer buy the product easily in a store?	.03	× _____	= ____
II. Profitability			
1. What is the total and yearly profitability estimate?	.08	× _____	= ____
2. Can the item be sold at 3 to 4 times your cost?	.08	× _____	= ____
3. Does the product lend itself to repeat business?	.07	× _____	= ____
4. What is the ratio of total profit to total investment?	.03	× _____	= ____
III. Investment			
1. How much investment will the project require?	.05	× _____	= ____
2. How many units must be sold until the investment is recouped?	.04	× _____	= ____
IV. Legal Consideration			
1. Is the product strictly legal?	.15	× _____	= ____
2. Is the product completely safe?	.09	× _____	= ____
3. Can there be any legal repercussion through use or misuse of the product?	.08	× _____	= ____
V. Mailing			
1. Can the product be shipped and mailed easily?	.06	× _____	= ____
2. Is the product breakable?	.06	× _____	= ____
3. Can the product be shipped at low cost?	.07	× _____	= ____
		Grand total	_____

Figure 4-3. The mail order product evaluation form should help you decide which products to try to sell.

bassy is located, get a copy of *Business America,* published by the U.S. Department of Commerce. This magazine contains a license opportunity section in which many foreign-made products available for licensing in the United States are listed. To get a copy, contact the Department of Commerce's local field office, which you should also find in your telephone book. Other books are available that will be of help if you are looking for products to be imported. One is the *American Register of Exporters and Importers,* published by the American Register of Exporters and Importers Corporation, 38 Park Row, New York, New York 10038. Another is *Directory of New York Importers,* published by Commerce Industry Association Institute, Inc., 65 Liberty Street, New York, New York 10005. Finally, for almost every country there is at least one directory of importers and exporters, usually published annually. Frequently your local library will have one or more of these directories from each of the major countries of the world. These books are valuable for product selection because they list not only importers and exporters, but also product manufacturers.

4. Read the business opportunity section of your local newspaper, as well as such publications as the *Wall Street Journal.* Very frequently individuals who have a product to sell will advertise in one or more of these publications. You can contact them to negotiate the best deal possible for a product that may be very successful in mail order.

5. Call local manufacturers. Every manufacturer has created a product at one time or another that was not successful for his or her particular line of work but might be very, very successful for a mail order product. This was one of Joe Cossman's secrets for finding successful mail order products. Joe would go to the Yellow Pages and look up plastic manufacturing companies and ask to speak with the president. The question to the president was always the same: "Do you have any tooling for discontinued products from your line?" This really has a twofold advantage because tooling for plastic products is generally very expensive. I know, from my experience as head of research and development for a plastics company, that very frequently we would sell tooling for which we had paid $40,000 or more for $300 or less, just to get if off the premises because the product had failed or been discontinued. Cossman used this technique to buy tooling for a few hundred dollars for such successful products as the potato spud gun. Cossman sold 1,585,000 spud guns, for which he had paid $600 for the tooling.

6. Repackage information from books printed by the U.S. government. Books published by the U.S. government generally are in the public domain and are copyright free (unless they contain copyrighted material from another source). This means that you can use the material and reprint it anyway you wish. It is a fact that several books on the best-seller list have been created by merely repackaging, retitling, and perhaps reorganizing material from U.S. government books that are already in print. You can do the same thing. If you live in a large city, there may be a U.S. government book store near you. If that's the case, you can see for yourself exactly what is available. You can obtain the latest catalog of books available from the government by writing the Superintendent of Documents, U.S. Government Printing Office, Washington, D.C. 20402, and asking for it.

7. Write or contact major corporations in the United States. Almost every large corporation that has a research and development division will, on occasion, develop products for which it has no use, by-products of the mainstream of its commercial interests. As a result, most major corporations have established special offices to market the licensing of their patents to individuals outside their companies. The titles of these special offices vary. However, you can usually get in touch with them by contacting a company or corporation that is large enough to have a research and development division and asking for the director of patent licensing. You should give this individual some general idea of the types of patent or product you would be interested in.

8. Consider distress merchandise. Many retailers have been in situations in which certain merchandise could not be sold. What do they do? They reduce the price greatly and attempt to sell it at bargain rates. This is distress merchandise. I do not recommend that you buy this merchandise for resale, because as soon as all of the products are sold, you will be out of a mail order product. Instead, if you see distress merchandise, which is identified as such because it has been greatly reduced in price by the retailer, and if you feel this might make an excellent mail order product, look at the item and see if it contains a patent number. If it does, you can locate the inventor by writing to the patent office and purchasing a copy of the patent, which currently sells for 50¢. Or if you live close to a depository for patents, you can look at the patent at no cost at all. Every U.S. patent contains the name and address of the inventor. As I mentioned earlier, inventors are usually poor marketers, and the fact that this is distress merchandise indicates that if the inventor still controls the patent, he or she may well be interested in either an outright sale of the patent or the licensing of the manufacture of the item to you. The address of the patent office is: U.S. Patent Office, Washington, D.C. 20231.

9. Another source of mail order products is expired patents. In the United States, a patent is good for only 17 years. The only exception is an ornamental design patent, which is good for three and a half, seven, or 14 years. Remembering that many patents are never even put into production, expired patents, which are over 17 years old and are now in the public domain, are a ready source of new product ideas for mail order. In addition, you can look at the entire technology of any general product area by writing to the patent office and asking for a list of all patent numbers falling into your product area. The patent office will charge you a small amount for each patent number. Once you have the list of numbers, if you are close to a major library, check to see if it is a patent depository. This will be the case most frequently in large cities, such as Los Angeles and New York. If the library is a depository, every patent that has been granted is on microfilm there. All you need do is look up the number and you can get information about every patent in the product area you selected. Every patent is a source of ideas for you. You may approach the inventor about licensing the patent, or the idea itself may get you thinking about new ideas that don't violate the inventor's patent. Of course, if the patent has expired, you can do whatever you want with the invention.

10. Overseas trade publications, such as *Made in Europe, Hong Kong Enterprise,* and others, are excellent sources for importing new products into the United States. Here is a list of typical foreign publications and their addresses. Write and ask for a sample copy of their magazine.

Hong Kong Enterprises, 3rd Floor, Connaught Center, Connaught Road Central, Hong Kong

Made in Europe, P.O. Box 174027, D-6, Frankfurt-am-Main, West Germany.

Canada Commerce, Department of Industry, Trade and Commerce, Ottawa, Ontario, Canada, K1A0H5.

Commerce in France, At the Chamber; 21 Avenue George V, Paris 8^e, France.

Other foreign trade magazines can be found in your local library and will contain many potential mail order products.

11. Attend Trade shows. Like inventor shows, trade shows will have hundreds of products, some of which will be outstanding for mail order. To find out about trade shows, contact your local chamber of commerce.

12. Rework items from old magazines. If a product was a great mail order seller, 10, 15, 20, or more years ago, it may well make a great mail order seller today. When Joe Cossman sold more than a million potato spud guns this product was in its fiftieth year and had had frequent resurrections. You can find old magazines containing mail order products at your local library. also, old catalogs—such as Sears and Montgomery Ward—are currently being reprinted to contain items that may even now be of interest to the mail order market. Get these old magazines and catalogs, read them, and use your imagination.

13. Personalize items. People like to see items with their names on them, and this device has been used again and again to sell products of all sorts, from card cases to briefcases to wallets to address labels and paperweights. Do some research. If you can figure out a new twist or way to personalize an item, you have a good possibility for a winner.

14. Write a book or a correspondence course. Many of the successful mail order entrepreneuers I mentioned in chapter 1 succeeded because of their ability to write and sell information. Information meets many of the outstanding criteria of a mail order product, including low cost, light weight, and relative indestructibility in the mail, and, as we'll see shortly in discussing controlling your product, printed products you write yourself are relatively easy to control at low cost. Look in the classified section of any magazine containing many mail order products, such as *Mechanics Illustrated* or *House and Garden,* and you will find individuals either advertising directly or using the two-step inquiry and follow-up method of selling information, books, booklets, and correspondence courses through the mail.

15. Go to the library and look at manufacturers' directories, such as *Thomas' Register of Manufacturers.* You will find not only names and addresses, but also products and the individual to contact about obtaining them. Every page is a potential source of a new mail order product.

16. Sell instructional tape cassettes. Learning by listening to a tape at home, or even in a car while driving to work is very popular today. If you have special knowledge of anything, you may be able to tape it on a cassette and sell the information in this way at from $5.95 to $9.95 or more per tape. You can obtain duplicate

tapes for $1.00 or so depending on the quantity, so the markup is quite good. Many cities have companies offering this service today, but if you want you can deal with a company that duplicates your master tape by mail. Write to Dove Enterprises, 907 Portage Trail, Cuyahoga Falls, Ohio 44221, and ask for their catalogue.

17. Get a copy of *The Wholesale by Mail Catalog* by the Print Project and published by St. Martin's Press. This book lists over 350 companies selling all sorts of products wholesale by mail. The discounts offered are 30 to 90% off retail for single items, but you should be able to negotiate much larger discounts, in quantity buys for resale. Some may also offer a drop-ship arrangement whereby they will ship each item individually directly to your customer. Your profits will be much less if you use drop-shipping, but you can fill out your product line in this way, and of course it has the definite advantage that you need carry no inventory of that particular product.

WHY YOU MUST CONTROL YOUR PRODUCT AND HOW TO DO IT

Controlling the product is of utmost importance in any mail order sales, and you should consider it right from the start. What do I mean by controlling your product? I mean that no one else can sell your product except you. This is so important because when you advertise in mail order, your competitor not only sees your proposition, but can determine that you are successful, if you continue to advertise. Your competitor knows that you must be successful or you would not be spending the money for advertising. This is one of the dilemmas of the beginner in mail order. If one is successful, every copycat competitor in the world will jump in to rip off the product by selling the same one. Since many will have much greater financial resources than you, they will be able to undersell you and take your market away from you if you do not control your product. How can you control the product? There are six basic methods: a patent, a copyright, an exclusive, a secret formula, a proprietary methodology, and a trademark. Let's look at each in turn.

The Patent

A patent is a grant issued by the government that gives you, as the inventor, the right to exclude all others from making, using, or selling your invention within the United States, its territories, and possessions. It is important here to understand that we are talking about the United States only. Each country has its own patent laws and there is no such thing currently as an international patent. If you wanted patent protection all over the world, it would cost you thousands and thousands of dollars to obtain. Therefore, individuals will obtain a patent only in those countries in which they feel the item might be made, used, or sold.

The patent law is for your protection if you invent or discover a new and useful process or improvement.

Most individuals misunderstand exactly the type of protection provided by a patent in the United States. First, the U.S. government does not protect your patent, and this is why the patent itself, even after you obtain it, is frequently referred to as "a license to sue." If someone violates your patent, it is up to you to sue them to obtain redress. This you do with your own money. Further, and unfortunately, the mere fact that you have a patent does not guarantee that your patent cannot be invalidated by the court when you do sue. Thus, if the individual who is violating your patent is able to show prior use, even though you have the initial patent on a device, your patent can be invalidated and, despite the fact that you may have spent thousands of dollars on patenting the items and on court costs, you will receive nothing in return.

There are two further disadvantages you should consider regarding this type of protection for your product. One is that patents can sometimes be designed so that, while your patent is not violated, the essential result of your patent is copied. For example, an individual who had a patent on a slide fastener or zipper for putting two sections of a suit together would not be violated by Velcro tape or a button, either of which performs the identical function. Another disadvantage has to do with the cost. Usually, a patent in the United States costs several thousand dollars. It is worth the money only if you have something totally unique, which is difficult to design around and which has not seen prior use. How the patent is written—the claims it makes and so forth—can determine whether you will be able to protect your patent successfully.

However, it is possible to patent something yourself legally. If you want to know more about this, read *Patent It Yourself,* by David Pressman, published by McGraw-Hill. Pressman is an electrical engineer and has had more than 18 years of experience as a patent examiner for the U.S. Patent and Trademark Office, as a corporate patent attorney, and currently as a patent attorney in private practice.

The Copyright

The copyright is the right of an author to control the reproduction of an intellectual creation, and it protects your original and creative works from unauthorized reproduction by others. In effect, you get a complete monopoly over whatever you have copyrighted. Your copyright work

APPLICATION FOR COPYRIGHT REGISTRATION
for a
Nondramatic Literary Work

HOW TO APPLY FOR COPYRIGHT REGISTRATION:

- *First:* Read the information on this page to make sure Form TX is the correct application for your work.

- *Second:* Open out the form by pulling this page to the left. Read through the detailed instructions before starting to complete the form.

- *Third:* Complete spaces 1-4 of the application, then turn the entire form over and, after reading the instructions for spaces 5-11, complete the rest of your application. Use typewriter or print in dark ink. Be sure to sign the form at space 10.

- *Fourth:* Detach your completed application from these instructions and send it with the necessary deposit of the work (see below) to: Register of Copyrights, Library of Congress, Washington, D.C. 20559. Unless you have a Deposit Account in the Copyright Office, your application and deposit must be accompanied by a check or money order for $10, payable to: *Register of Copyrights.*

WHEN TO USE FORM TX: Form TX is the appropriate application to use for copyright registration covering nondramatic literary works, whether published or unpublished.

WHAT IS A "NONDRAMATIC LITERARY WORK"? The category of "nondramatic literary works" (Class TX) is very broad. Except for dramatic works and certain kinds of audiovisual works, Class TX includes all types of works written in words (or other verbal or numerical symbols). A few of the many examples of "nondramatic literary works" include fiction, nonfiction, poetry, periodicals, textbooks, reference works, directories, catalogs, advertising copy, and compilations of information.

DEPOSIT TO ACCOMPANY APPLICATION: An application for copyright registration must be accompanied by a deposit representing the entire work for which registration is to be made. The following are the general deposit requirements as set forth in the statute:

Unpublished work: Deposit one complete copy (or phonorecord).

Published work: Deposit two complete copies (or phonorecords) of the best edition.

Work first published outside the United States: Deposit one complete copy (or phonorecord) of the first foreign edition.

Contribution to a collective work: Deposit one complete copy (or phonorecord) of the best edition of the collective work.

These general deposit requirements may vary in particular situations. For further information about copyright deposit, write to the Copyright Office.

THE COPYRIGHT NOTICE: For published works, the law provides that a copyright notice in a specified form "shall be placed on all publicly distributed copies from which the work can be visually perceived." Use of the copyright notice is the responsibility of the copyright owner and does not require advance permission from the Copyright Office. The required form of the notice for copies generally consists of three elements: (1) the symbol "©", or the word "Copyright", or the abbreviation "Copr."; (2) the year of first publication; and (3) the name of the owner of copyright. For example: "© 1978 Constance Porter". The notice is to be affixed to the copies "in such manner and location as to give reasonable notice of the claim of copyright." Unlike the law in effect before 1978, the new copyright statute provides procedures for correcting errors in the copyright notice, and even for curing the omission of the notice. However, a failure to comply with the notice requirements may still result in the loss of some copyright protection and, unless corrected within five years, in the complete loss of copyright. For further information about the copyright notice and the procedures for correcting errors or omissions, write to the Copyright Office.

DURATION OF COPYRIGHT: For works that were created after the effective date of the new statute (January 1, 1978), the basic copyright term will be the life of the author and fifty years after the author's death. For works made for hire, and for certain anonymous and pseudonymous works, the duration of copyright will be 75 years from publication or 100 years from creation, whichever is shorter. These same terms of copyright will generally apply to works that had been created before 1978 but had not been published or copyrighted before that date. For further information about the duration of copyright, including the terms of copyrights already in existence before 1978, write for Circular R15a.

Figure 4-4. The copyright application and certificate form.

FORM TX

UNITED STATES COPYRIGHT OFFICE

REGISTRATION NUMBER		
	TX	TXU
EFFECTIVE DATE OF REGISTRATION		
(Month)	(Day)	(Year)

DO NOT WRITE ABOVE THIS LINE. IF YOU NEED MORE SPACE, USE CONTINUATION SHEET (FORM TX/CON)

(1) Title

TITLE OF THIS WORK:

PREVIOUS OR ALTERNATIVE TITLES:

If a periodical or serial give Vol...... No...... Issue Date ....

PUBLICATION AS A CONTRIBUTION: (If this work was published as a contribution to a periodical, serial, or collection, give information about the collective work in which the contribution appeared.)

Title of Collective Work .... Vol....... No....... Date .... Pages ....

(2) Author(s)

IMPORTANT: Under the law, the "author" of a "work made for hire" is generally the employer, not the employee (see instructions). If any part of this work was "made for hire" check "Yes" in the space provided, give the employer (or other person for whom the work was prepared) as "Author" of that part, and leave the space for dates blank.

1

NAME OF AUTHOR:

DATES OF BIRTH AND DEATH:
Born .... Died ....
(Year) (Year)

Was this author's contribution to the work a "work made for hire"? Yes...... No......

AUTHOR'S NATIONALITY OR DOMICILE:
Citizen of .... } or { Domiciled in ....
(Name of Country) (Name of Country)

WAS THIS AUTHOR'S CONTRIBUTION TO THE WORK:
Anonymous? Yes...... No......
Pseudonymous? Yes...... No......
If the answer to either of these questions is "Yes," see detailed instructions attached.

AUTHOR OF: (Briefly describe nature of this author's contribution)

2

NAME OF AUTHOR:

DATES OF BIRTH AND DEATH:
Born .... Died ....
(Year) (Year)

Was this author's contribution to the work a "work made for hire"? Yes...... No......

AUTHOR'S NATIONALITY OR DOMICILE:
Citizen of .... } or { Domiciled in ....
(Name of Country) (Name of Country)

WAS THIS AUTHOR'S CONTRIBUTION TO THE WORK:
Anonymous? Yes...... No......
Pseudonymous? Yes...... No......
If the answer to either of these questions is "Yes," see detailed instructions attached.

AUTHOR OF: (Briefly describe nature of this author's contribution)

3

NAME OF AUTHOR:

DATES OF BIRTH AND DEATH:
Born .... Died ....
(Year) (Year)

Was this author's contribution to the work a "work made for hire"? Yes...... No......

AUTHOR'S NATIONALITY OR DOMICILE:
Citizen of .... } or { Domiciled in ....
(Name of Country) (Name of Country)

WAS THIS AUTHOR'S CONTRIBUTION TO THE WORK:
Anonymous? Yes...... No......
Pseudonymous? Yes...... No......
If the answer to either of these questions is "Yes," see detailed instructions attached.

AUTHOR OF: (Briefly describe nature of this author's contribution)

(3) Creation and Publication

YEAR IN WHICH CREATION OF THIS WORK WAS COMPLETED:

Year ....

(This information must be given in all cases.)

DATE AND NATION OF FIRST PUBLICATION:

Date ....
(Month) (Day) (Year)
Nation ....
(Name of Country)

(Complete this block ONLY if this work has been published.)

(4) Claimant(s)

NAME(S) AND ADDRESS(ES) OF COPYRIGHT CLAIMANT(S):

TRANSFER: (If the copyright claimant(s) named here in space 4 are different from the author(s) named in space 2, give a brief statement of how the claimant(s) obtained ownership of the copyright.)

• Complete all applicable spaces (numbers 5-11) on the reverse side of this page
• Follow detailed instructions attached • Sign the form at line 10

DO NOT WRITE HERE
Page 1 of .... pages

Figure 4-4. (Continued)

HOW TO FILL OUT FORM TX

Specific Instructions for Spaces 1-4

- The line-by-line instructions on this page are keyed to the spaces on the first page of Form TX, printed opposite.
- Please read through these instructions before you start filling out your application, and refer to the specific instructions for each space as you go along.

SPACE 1: TITLE

- **Title of this Work:** Every work submitted for copyright registration must be given a title that is capable of identifying that particular work. If the copies or phonorecords of the work bear a title (or an identifying phrase that could serve as a title), transcribe its wording completely and exactly on the application. Remember that indexing of the registration and future identification of the work will depend on the information you give here.

- **Periodical or Serial Issue:** Periodicals and other serials are publications issued at intervals under a general title, such as newspapers, magazines, journals, newsletters, and annuals. If the work being registered is an entire issue of a periodical or serial, give the over-all title of the periodical or serial in the space headed "Title of this Work," and add the specific information about the issue in the spaces provided. If the work being registered is a contribution to a periodical or serial issue, follow the instructions for "Publication as a Contribution."

- **Previous or Alternative Titles:** Complete this space if there are any additional titles for the work under which someone searching for the registration might be likely to look, or under which a document pertaining to the work might be recorded.

- **Publication as a Contribution:** If the work being registered has been published as a contribution to a periodical, serial, or collection, give the title of the contribution in the space headed "Title of this Work." Then, in the line headed "Publication as a Contribution," give information about the larger work in which the contribution appeared.

SPACE 2: AUTHORS

- **General Instructions:** First decide, after reading these instructions, who are the "authors" of this work for copyright purposes. Then, unless the work is a "collective work" (see below), give the requested information about every "author" who contributed any appreciable amount of copyrightable matter to this version of the work. If you need further space, use the attached Continuation Sheet and, if necessary, request additional Continuation Sheets (Form TX/CON).

- **Who is the "Author"?** Unless the work was "made for hire," the individual who actually created the work is its "author." In the case of a work made for hire, the statute provides that "the employer or other person for whom the work was prepared is considered the author."

- **What is a "Work Made for Hire"?** A "work made for hire" is defined as: (1) "a work prepared by an employee within the scope of his or her employment"; or (2) "a work specially ordered or commissioned" for certain uses specified in the statute, but only if there is a written agreement to consider it a "work made for hire."

- **Collective Work:** In the case of a collective work, such as a periodical issue, anthology, collection of essays, or encyclopedia, it is sufficient to give information about the author of the collective work as a whole.

- **Author's Identity Not Revealed:** If an author's contribution is "anonymous" or "pseudonymous," it is not necessary to give the name and dates for that author. However, the citizenship or domicile of the author must be given in all cases, and information about the nature of that author's contribution to the work should be included.

- **Name of Author:** The fullest form of the author's name should be given. If you have checked "Yes" to indicate that the work was "made for hire," give the full legal name of the employer (or other person for whom the work was prepared). You may also include the name of the employee (for example, "Elster Publishing Co., employer for hire of John Ferguson"). If the work is "anonymous" you may: (1) leave the line blank, or (2) state "Anonymous" in the line, or (3) reveal the author's identity. If the work is "pseudonymous" you may (1) leave the line blank, or (2) give the pseudonym and identify it as such (for example: "Huntley Haverstock, pseudonym"), or (3) reveal the author's name, making clear which is the real name and which is the pseudonym (for example, "Judith Barton, whose pseudonym is Madeleine Elster").

- **Dates of Birth and Death:** If the author is dead, the statute requires that the year of death be included in the application unless the work is anonymous or pseudonymous. The author's birth date is optional, but is useful as a form of identification. Leave this space blank if the author's contribution was a "work made for hire."

- **"Anonymous" or "Pseudonymous" Work:** An author's contribution to a work is "anonymous" if that author is not identified on the copies or phonorecords of the work. An author's contribution to a work is "pseudonymous" if that author is identified on the copies or phonorecords under a fictitious name.

- **Author's Nationality or Domicile:** Give the country of which the author is a citizen, or the country in which the author is domiciled. The statute requires that either nationality or domicile be given in all cases.

- **Nature of Authorship:** After the words "Author of" give a brief general statement of the nature of this particular author's contribution to the work. Examples: "Entire text"; "Co-author of entire text"; "Chapters 11-14"; "Editorial revisions"; "Compilation and English translation"; "Illustrations."

SPACE 3: CREATION AND PUBLICATION

- **General Instructions:** Do not confuse "creation" with "publication." Every application for copyright registration must state "the year in which creation of the work was completed." Give the date and nation of first publication only if the work has been published.

- **Creation:** Under the statute, a work is "created" when it is fixed in a copy or phonorecord for the first time. Where a work has been prepared over a period of time, the part of the work existing in fixed form on a particular date constitutes the created work on that date. The date you give here should be the year in which the author completed the particular version for which registration is now being sought, even if other versions exist or if further changes or additions are planned.

- **Publication:** The statute defines "publication" as "the distribution of copies or phonorecords of a work to the public by sale or other transfer of ownership, or by rental, lease, or lending"; a work is also "published" if there has been an "offering to distribute copies or phonorecords to a group of persons for purposes of further distribution, public performance, or public display." Give the full date (month, day, year) when, and the country where, publication first occurred. If first publication took place simultaneously in the United States and other countries, it is sufficient to state "U.S.A."

SPACE 4: CLAIMANT(S)

- **Name(s) and Address(es) of Copyright Claimant(s):** Give the name(s) and address(es) of the copyright claimant(s) in this work. The statute provides that copyright belongs to the author of the work (including, in the case of a work made for hire, the employer or other person for whom the work was prepared). The copyright claimant is either the author of the work or a person or organization that has obtained ownership of the copyright initially belonging to the author.

- **Transfer:** The statute provides that, if the copyright claimant is not the author, the application for registration must contain "a brief statement of how the claimant obtained ownership of the copyright." If any copyright claimant named in space 4 is not an author named in space 2, give a brief, general statement summarizing the means by which that claimant obtained ownership of the copyright.

Figure 4-4. (Continued)

86

CONTINUATION SHEET FOR FORM TX

FORM TX/CON

UNITED STATES COPYRIGHT OFFICE

- If at all possible, try to fit the information called for into the spaces provided on Form TX.
- If you do not have space enough for all of the information you need to give on Form TX, use this continuation sheet and submit it with Form TX.
- If you submit this continuation sheet, leave it attached to Form TX. Or, if it becomes detached, clip (do not tape or staple) and fold the two together before submitting them.
- PART A of this sheet is intended to identify the basic application. PART B is a continuation of Space 2 PART C is for the continuation of Spaces 1, 4, 6, or 7. The other spaces on Form TX call for specific items of information, and should not need continuation.

REGISTRATION NUMBER	
TX	TXU
EFFECTIVE DATE OF REGISTRATION		
(Month)	(Day)	(Year)
CONTINUATION SHEET RECEIVED	
Page _____ of _____ pages	

DO NOT WRITE ABOVE THIS LINE: FOR COPYRIGHT OFFICE USE ONLY

(A)
Identification of Application

IDENTIFICATION OF CONTINUATION SHEET: This sheet is a continuation of the application for copyright registration on Form TX, submitted for the following work:

- TITLE: (Give the title as given under the heading "Title of this Work" in Space 1 of Form TX)

- NAME(S) AND ADDRESS(ES) OF COPYRIGHT CLAIMANT(S): (Give the name and address of at least one copyright claimant as given in Space 4 of Form TX)

(B)
Continuation of Space 2

NAME OF AUTHOR:

Was this author's contribution to the work a "work made for hire"?   Yes   No

DATES OF BIRTH AND DEATH:
Born _____ (Year)   Died _____ (Year)

AUTHOR'S NATIONALITY OR DOMICILE:
Citizen of _____ (Name of Country) or Domiciled in _____ (Name of Country)

AUTHOR OF: (Briefly describe nature of this author's contribution)

WAS THIS AUTHOR'S CONTRIBUTION TO THE WORK:
Anonymous?   Yes   No
Pseudonymous?   Yes   No
If the answer to either of these questions is "Yes," see detailed instructions attached

NAME OF AUTHOR:

Was this author's contribution to the work a "work made for hire"?   Yes   No

DATES OF BIRTH AND DEATH:
Born _____ (Year)   Died _____ (Year)

AUTHOR'S NATIONALITY OR DOMICILE:
Citizen of _____ (Name of Country) or Domiciled in _____ (Name of Country)

AUTHOR OF: (Briefly describe nature of this author's contribution)

WAS THIS AUTHOR'S CONTRIBUTION TO THE WORK:
Anonymous?   Yes   No
Pseudonymous?   Yes   No
If the answer to either of these questions is "Yes," see detailed instructions attached

NAME OF AUTHOR:

Was this author's contribution to the work a "work made for hire"?   Yes   No

DATES OF BIRTH AND DEATH:
Born _____ (Year)   Died _____ (Year)

AUTHOR'S NATIONALITY OR DOMICILE:
Citizen of _____ (Name of Country) or Domiciled in _____ (Name of Country)

AUTHOR OF: (Briefly describe nature of this author's contribution)

WAS THIS AUTHOR'S CONTRIBUTION TO THE WORK:
Anonymous?   Yes   No
Pseudonymous?   Yes   No
If the answer to either of these questions is "Yes," see detailed instructions attached

---

(C)
Continuation of Other Spaces

CONTINUATION OF (Check which)   ☐ Space 1   ☐ Space 4   ☐ Space 6   ☐ Space 7

Figure 4-4.   (Continued)

87

EXAMINED BY:	APPLICATION RECEIVED:	FOR
CHECKED BY:		COPYRIGHT
CORRESPONDENCE: ☐ Yes	DEPOSIT RECEIVED:	OFFICE USE
DEPOSIT ACCOUNT FUNDS USED: ☐	REMITTANCE NUMBER AND DATE:	ONLY

DO NOT WRITE ABOVE THIS LINE. IF YOU NEED ADDITIONAL SPACE, USE CONTINUATION SHEET (FORM TX/CON)

PREVIOUS REGISTRATION:

- Has registration for this work, or for an earlier version of this work, already been made in the Copyright Office?   Yes ...... No ......
- If your answer is "Yes," why is another registration being sought? (Check appropriate box)
  - ☐ This is the first published edition of a work previously registered in unpublished form
  - ☐ This is the first application submitted by this author as copyright claimant
  - ☐ This is a changed version of the work, as shown by line 6 of this application
- If your answer is "Yes," give: Previous Registration Number ....   Year of Registration ....

⑤ Previous Registration

COMPILATION OR DERIVATIVE WORK: (See instructions)

PREEXISTING MATERIAL (Identify any preexisting work or works that this work is based on or incorporates.)

{

MATERIAL ADDED TO THIS WORK (Give a brief, general statement of the material that has been added to this work and in which copyright is claimed.)

{

⑥ Compilation or Derivative Work

MANUFACTURERS AND LOCATIONS: (If this is a published work consisting preponderantly of nondramatic literary material in English, the law may require that the copies be manufactured in the United States or Canada for full protection. If so, the names of the manufacturers who performed certain processes, and the places where these processes were performed must be given See instructions for details.)

NAMES OF MANUFACTURERS	PLACES OF MANUFACTURE

⑦ Manufacturing

REPRODUCTION FOR USE OF BLIND OR PHYSICALLY-HANDICAPPED PERSONS: (See instructions)

- Signature of this form at space 10, and a check in one of the boxes here in space 8, constitutes a non exclusive grant of permission to the Library of Congress to reproduce and distribute solely for the blind and physically handicapped and under the conditions and limitations prescribed by the regulations of the Copyright Office   (1) copies of the work identified in space 1 of this application in Braille (or similar tactile symbols), or (2) phonorecords embodying a fixation of a reading of that work; or (3) both

  a ☐ Copies and phonorecords   b ☐ Copies Only   c ☐ Phonorecords Only

⑧ License For Handicapped

DEPOSIT ACCOUNT: (If the registration fee is to be charged to a Deposit Account established in the Copyright Office, give name and number of Account.)	**CORRESPONDENCE:** (Give name and address to which correspondence about this application should be sent.)
Name	Name ....
Account Number	Address .... (Apt.)
	(City) (State) (ZIP)

⑨ Fee and Correspondence

CERTIFICATION: ✳ I, the undersigned, hereby certify that I am the: (Check one)

☐ author ☐ other copyright claimant ☐ owner of exclusive right(s) ☐ authorized agent of ....

(Name of author or other copyright claimant, or owner of exclusive right(s))

of the work identified in this application and that the statements made by me in this application are correct to the best of my knowledge.

Handwritten signature: (X) ....

Typed or printed name ....   Date ....

⑩ Certification (Application must be signed)

MAIL CERTIFICATE TO	**⑪ Address For Return of Certificate**
.... (Name)	
.... (Number, Street and Apartment Number)	
(City) (State) (ZIP code)	
(Certificate will be mailed in window envelope)	

✳ 17 U S C § 506(e) Any person who knowingly makes a false representation of a material fact in the application for copyright registration provided for by section 409, or in any written statement filed in connection with the application, shall be fined not more than $2,500

✳ U.S. GOVERNMENT PRINTING OFFICE: 1980 341 278/1

Nov. 1980 – 500,000

Figure 4-4.   (Continued)

INSTRUCTIONS FOR SPACES 5-9

SPACE 5: PREVIOUS REGISTRATION

• **General Instructions:** The questions in space 5 are intended to find out whether an earlier registration has been made for this work and, if so, whether there is any basis for a new registration. As a general rule, only one basic copyright registration can be made for the same version of a particular work.

• **Same Version:** If this version is substantially the same as the work covered by a previous registration, a second registration is not generally possible unless (1) the work has been registered in unpublished form and a second registration is now being sought to cover the first published edition, or (2) someone other than the author is identified as copyright claimant in the earlier registration, and the author is now seeking registration in his or her own name. If either of these two exceptions apply, check the appropriate box and give the earlier registration number and date. Otherwise, do not submit Form VA; instead, write the Copyright Office for information about supplementary registration or recordation of transfer of copyright ownership.

• **Changed Version:** If the work has been changed, and you are now seeking registration to cover the additions or revisions, check the third box in space 5, give the earlier registration number and date, and complete both parts of space 6.

• **Previous Registration Number and Date:** If more than one previous registration has been made for the work, give the number and date of the latest registration.

SPACE 6: COMPILATION OR DERIVATIVE WORK

• **General Instructions:** Complete both parts of space 6 if this work is a "compilation," or "derivative work," or both, and if it is based on or incorporates one or more "preexisting works" that are not eligible for registration for one reason or another works that have already been published or registered, or works that have fallen into the public domain. A "compilation" is defined as "a work formed by the collection and assembling of preexisting materials or of data that are selected, coordinated, or arranged in such a way that the resulting work as a whole constitutes an original work of authorship." A "derivative work" is "a work based on one or more preexisting works." In addition to various forms in which works may be "recast, transformed or adapted," derivative works include works "consisting of editorial revisions, annotations, elaborations, or other modifications" if these changes, as a whole, represent an original work of authorship.

• **Preexisting Material:** If the work is a compilation, give a brief, general statement describing the nature of the material that has been compiled. Example: "Compilation of 19th Century political cartoons". In the case of a derivative work, identify the preexisting work that has been recast, transformed, or adapted. Examples: "Grunewald Altarpiece", "19th Century quilt design".

• **Material Added to this Work:** The statute requires a "brief, general statement of the additional material covered by the copyright claim being registered." This statement should describe all of the material in this particular version of the work that (1) represents an original work of authorship (2) has not fallen into public domain, (3) has not been previously published, and (4) has not been previously registered for copyright in unpublished form. Examples: "Adaptation of design and additional artistic work", "Reproduction of painting by photolithography", "Additional cartographic material", "Compilation of photographs".

SPACES 7, 8, 9: FEE, CORRESPONDENCE, CERTIFICATION, RETURN ADDRESS

• **Deposit Account and Mailing Instructions (Space 7):** If you maintain a Deposit Account in the Copyright Office, identify it in space 7. Otherwise you will need to send the registration fee of $10 with your application. The space headed "Correspondence" should contain the name and address of the person to be consulted if correspondence about this application becomes necessary.

• **Certification (Space 8):** The application is not acceptable unless it bears the handwritten signature of the author or other copyright claimant, or of the owner of exclusive right(s), or of the duly authorized agent of such author, claimant, or owner.

• **Address for Return of Certificate (Space 9):** The address box must be completed legibly, since the certificate will be returned in a window envelope.

MORE INFORMATION

THE COPYRIGHT NOTICE: For published works, the law provides that a copyright notice in a specified form "shall be placed on all publicly distributed copies from which the work can be visually perceived." Use of the copyright notice is the responsibility of the copyright owner, and does not require advance permission from the Copyright Office.

• **Form of the Notice:** The required form of the notice for copies generally consists of three elements: (1) the symbol "©", or the word "Copyright", or the abbreviation "Copr."; (2) the year of first publication; and (3) the name of the owner of copyright in the work, or an abbreviation by which the name can be recognized, or a generally known alternative designation of the owner. Example: "© 1978 Samuel Marlove." Under the statute, the year date may be omitted from the notice in cases "where a pictorial, graphic, or sculptural work, with accompanying text matter, if any, is reproduced in or on greeting cards, postcards, stationery, jewelry, dolls, toys, or any useful articles".

• **Position of the Notice:** The notice is to be affixed to the copies "in such manner and location as to give reasonable notice of the claim of copyright".

• **Errors or Omissions:** Unlike the law in effect before 1978, the new copyright statute provides procedures for correcting errors in the copyright notice, and even for curing the omission of the notice. However, a failure to comply with the notice requirements may still result in the loss of some copyright protection and, unless corrected within five years, in the complete loss of copyright. For further information about the copyright notice and the procedures for correcting errors or omissions, write to the Copyright Office.

FORM OF DEPOSIT FOR WORKS OF THE VISUAL ARTS

Exceptions to General Deposit Requirements: As explained on the reverse side of this page, the statutory deposit requirements (generally one copy for unpublished works and two copies for published works) will vary for particular kinds of works of the visual arts. The copyright law authorizes the Register of Copyrights to issue regulations specifying "the administrative classes into which works are to be placed for purposes of deposit and registration, and the nature of the copies or phonorecords to be deposited in the various classes specified." For particular classes, the regulations may require or permit "the deposit of identifying material instead of copies or phonorecords," or "the deposit of only one copy or phonorecord where two would normally be required".

What Should You Deposit? The detailed requirements with respect to the kind of deposit to accompany an application on Form VA are contained in the Copyright Office Regulations. The following does not cover all of the deposit requirements, but is intended to give you some general guidance.

• For an unpublished work, the material deposited should represent the entire copyrightable content of the work for which registration is being sought.

• For a published work, the material deposited should generally consist of two complete copies of the best edition. Exceptions:

– For certain types of works, one complete copy may be deposited instead of two. These include greeting cards, postcards, stationery, labels, advertisements, scientific drawings, and globes.

– For most three-dimensional sculptural works, and for certain two-dimensional works, the Copyright Office Regulations require the deposit of identifying material (photographs or drawings in a specified form) rather than copies.

– Under certain circumstances, for works published in five copies or less or in limited, numbered editions, the deposit may consist of one copy or of identifying reproductions

Figure 4-4. (Continued)

may not be printed, published, dramatized, translated, adapted, broadcasted, or reproduced in any other way without your consent.

The copyright has important advantages over a patent. It costs only $10, is extremely easy to register, and does not require an attorney. For the correct forms, write to the Register of Copyrights, Copyright Office, the Library of Congress, Washington, D.C. 20559. Form A, reproduced in Figure 4-4, is generally for a written document in book form. There are other forms for journal articles, and so on.

Another advantage over the patent is that there is an international convention of copyrights, and with the indicia ©, the date, and your name, you are protected in every country that is a member of the convention. Generally, in the United States, in addition to the indicia, date, and name, you also write the words *copyrighted by*. But it is the indicia that protects you internationally.

Under current regulations, a copyright protects for the life of the author plus 50 years, as compared with the patent, which runs out in 17 years and cannot be renewed. Items that can be copyrighted include books, periodicals, speeches prepared for oral delivery, dramatic composition, usable compositions, maps, works of art, models or designs, reproductions of works of art, drawings, plastic works of scientific or technical character, photographs, prints and pictorial illustrations, commercial prints and labels, photoplays, motion pictures, nondrammatic films, music for mechanical instruments, and sound recordings.

The Exclusive

The exclusive is another way of controlling the item or product you are going to sell by mail. An exclusive usually means obtaining an agreement from the manufacturer, located either in the United States or abroad, that you alone can sell his or her product in a certain area. Since we are talking about the mail order business, obviously, this area should include the entire United States. Many times foreign exporters of manufacturers located in other countries will grant you an exclusive if they are convinced that you can sell large quantities of their product. You can convince them by a track record of success with prior products, your professional conduct and professional stationery in correspondence with the manufacturer, and your statement that to market this item in large quantities, you must have an exclusive for this product.

Secret Formula

Although formulas can be patented because of the nature of the patent law, it is sometimes difficult to patent a formula and still have it protected. But as long as you can keep the formula secret, you can control the product. This can be much longer than 17 years. An example is Coca-Cola, for which the exact formula for manufacturing is over 100 years old and has never been patented. It is said that the formula is known only to the chairman of the board and the president of the company at any one time, and that these two individuals never fly on the same airplane.

Sometimes it is definitely in your interests *not* to patent an item, but rather to keep it as a secret formula. One example is the paper used to correct typewritten mistakes, currently sold in any stationery store. Had this product been kept a secret and not patented, the inventor would control it to this day. However, the patent office refused to grant a patent unless the exact percentage of formula impregnation in the paper was provided, even though a correction would occur or the material could be used for correcting typewriting over a large range of impregnation. As a result, the inventor selected the optimum formula and patented it. His competitors purchased his formula for 50¢, and by a slight modification, they were able to go around the patent without violating it. The result was that instead of one brand of correction paper on the market today, there are half a dozen or more. Keeping the formula secret might have saved this inventor's control over the product. A secret formula can be a very effective way of protecting and controlling your mail order product when a patent is ineffective.

Proprietary Methodology

Proprietary methodology is similar to the secret formula and has to do with how you put something together. Again, this may be patentable. But before patenting it, you should consider whether the patent is easy to design around. If it is, you should consider keeping this methodology proprietary, rather than using the patent office to attempt to control and protect your process.

Trademark

A trademark is a word, name, symbol, design, or combination of these that identifies a product with the owner of the trademark.

A trademark is somewhat different in that it should be registered only if you contemplate long-term use, and it is important to protect it from copying. Unlike a patent, the trademark must be used in commerce for some time prior to your registering it, and evidence of this use must be filed with the trademark application. Like patents, trademarks are filed with the U.S. Patent Office and a search is necessary to make certain that the mark you are submitting does not conflict with other trademarks that someone else may be using. In general, if you are going to file for a trade-mark, consult a patent attorney.

A trademark does not protect your product per se, but only the name. If you have a product whose name is important to you and it cannot be protected by copyright, this method of protecting and controlling it may be essential for you.

PRODUCTS THAT MADE THEIR PROMOTERS A MILLION

Joe Cossman lists the following products as having made a fortune for their creators: the fountain pen, zipper, roller skates, disposable diapers, chip soap, frozen food, dancing lessons, prepared dog food, bandages, the cash register, cellophane, the kiddie car, gelatin capsules, sanitary nap-kins, schools by mail, Dixie cups, Good Humors, book clubs, home hair wave, bottle caps, deodorant, snap fasteners, Scotch tape, the teddy bear, chewing gum, shorthand system, the pink hairpin, the paperclip, the rub-ber heel, ready-made bows, tea bags, corn plasters, vacuum cleaners, and alarm clocks.

ITEMS THAT ARE SELLING BIG

Standard Rate and Data Service, which publishes a number of important directories we will talk about in a later chapter, has developed sales sta-tistics on mail order items, which Benjamin Suarez analyzed to deter-mine the current best-selling products in mail order. Here they are, with their current annual sales in dollars.

1. Books, 21.4 million
2. Wearing apparel, 9.9 million
3. Hobby and craft items, 8.9 million
4. Housewares, 8.1 million
5. Agriculture, 7.4 million
6. Automobiles, 6.4 million
7. Cosmetics, 5.9 million
8. Health and comfort items, 5.8 million
9. Foods, 5.5 million
10. Entertainment, 4.2 million
11. Sports and outdoor equipment, 3.7 million

12. Greeting cards and stationery, 2.7 million
13. Devices and gadgets, 2.2 million
14. Collectors' items, 1.5 million
15. Child-care and nursery items, 1.1 million

In a recent survey, *Better Homes and Gardens* asked its readers about items they had bought or inquired about in 1979. The percentage breakdowns for these different classifications of mail order products were as follows: collectibles, 14%; books, 37.9%; clothing, 57.6%; food items, 14.3%; fund-raising contributions, 3.5%; garden/nursery, 25.7%; gift merchandise, 38.1%; health foods, 3.7%; home study courses, 1.6%; insurance, 2.3%; photofinishing, 10.0%; records, tapes, and cassettes, 18.0%; self-improvement, 1.4%; none of the above, 8.4%; and no answer, .9%.

The Maxwell Stroge Company, a major consulting and research company for the mail order industry, picked the top 10 mail order product categories and published them in a recent *Maxwell Stroge Co. Mail Order Industry Annual Report.*

1.	Insurance	$4,000,000,000
2.	General merchandise/home furnishings/ housewares/gifts	$2,700,000,000
3.	Magazine subscriptions	$1,900,000,000
4.	Books	$1,388,000,000
5.	Ready-to-wear	$1,340,000,000
6.	Collectibles	$ 920,000,000
7.	Sporting goods	$ 780,000,000
8.	Crafts	$ 550,000,000
9.	Foods	$ 500,000,000
10.	Records and tapes	$ 478,000,000

As a beginner, follow these guidelines to maximize your chances of success right from the start:

1. Control your product. If you do not, someone else will steal your justly deserved success from you.
2. Stay away from things that can commonly be bought at the store.
3. Don't start with a fad item. You don't know where the product is in its life cycle. You can lose as much money as you can make.
4. Stay away from low-quality goods. Your goods don't need to be the

top of the line. However, if they are really cheap, you are going to get lots of returns and start with a bad reputation.

5. Unless you are thoroughly familiar with the business, stay away from products closely regulated by the government, such as drugs.

6. Again, unless you are already in the business, do not get involved initially with perishable goods, such as foods.

Finally, to quote Joe Karbo, "The best product is between your ears." By this, Joe means that it is not the product or service itself that will sell to your market and become a profitable mail order product, but rather your own ingenuity, imagination, and perception of the product and how you communicate this to your potential customers.

SUMMARY

In this chapter we have learned that the basic principle of success for product selection is to look at the marketplace first and then decide what the market wants before selecting a product. Next we considered the different methods of selling in mail order and how selection of our product depended on what methods we decided to choose. Then we looked at general rules of product selection and I gave you 17 sources of mail order products. We then turned to the methods of controlling your product—patent, copyright, exclusive, a secret formula, proprietary methodology, or a trademark. And finally, we talked about which products are selling best and which have made and continue to make fortunes for their promoters.

5

The Critical Importance of the Mail Order Offer and How to Develop It

The mail order offer is certainly one of the most critical factors you must consider in selling by mail. It has been said that success in direct mail and mail order operations for any given project is due one-third to the offer, one-third to the medium, and one-third to your creative package, which includes copy and graphics.

Smith-Hemmings-Gosden, a leading direct-response advertising firm in California, says that no less than 40% of success in any effort is due to the offer. Regardless of the exact percentage, it is clear that with a poor offer you will fail. In fact, differences in response for a given promotion have been as much as 25, 50, or 100%, or even more, depending only upon the offer for the same product that was presented to the market.

What are we speaking of when we speak of the offer? Basically, we are talking about the proposition presented to the customer for consideration. Let's consider an item we are offering called a widget. Ordinarily each widget costs $1, but we are trying to build up our customer list and so we're offering a special: we're going to give two widgets for $1. How can we best present this to our potential customers?

Well, one way is simply to state that we will offer two widgets for the price of one, or two for $1. But there are other ways. We could say we are going to offer our widget for $1, which is the standard price, and those who purchase within a certain time will get an additional widget free. Or we could say we are going to offer one widget for 99¢ and the buyer can purchase a second widget for 1¢. Or we could offer two widgets free and merely require the potential customer to send us $1 for postage and handling.

Look at all these different offers again and you will see that they are identical. All result in the customer's receiving two widgets for $1, but the differences are in the presentation of the offer. This is what we are talking about when we speak of the offer, and this is what can make such a tremendous difference in whether a project is successful.

Bob Stone relates three ways in which the same offer was stated. The first was "half-price." The second was "buy one, get one free." The third was "50% off." Each statement conveyed exactly the same offer, but they did not elicit identical responses. The second offer pulled 40% better than either the first or third. Clearly, customers felt that "buy one, get one free" was the most attractive of the three.

How do you decide which offer is best? There is only one way, and I stress it throughout this book: Test. You must always test to find out which offer is actually better than another. However, certain psychological principles come into play here, and there are reasons that consumers tend to perceive certain offers to be better than others. It only makes sense to consider the needs and desires of our customers when we structure and decide on the components of the offer before we invest our money to advertise it to our potential customers.

Dr. Abraham Maslow of Brandeis University developed a theory of human motivation that is directly applicable to mail order. Maslow's theory, which has been substantiated by much research, is that people are motivated by their own needs. He classified these needs into various levels of importance: Level one includes our physiological needs, those for food, rest, exercise, and so forth; level two includes our safety or security needs—protection against danger, threat, and deprivation; level three, our social needs, includes the need for belonging, association, acceptance, and giving and receiving love and friendship; level four, ego needs, includes the need for self-confidence, independence, achievement, knowledge, status, recognition, appreciation, and respect for others; and level five, our self-fulfillment needs, includes the need to realize one's own potential, to experience development, and to be creative.

Two important points about Maslow's hierarchy of needs are most important for our purposes. The first is that once a need is satisfied, it no longer motivates the individual's behavior; the second is that if a need is frustrated at any level, it is of extreme importance. For example, if an individual's safety or security needs are totally satisfied in a totally safe environment, it would be ridiculous to structure an offer to appeal to these needs. You are not going to be able to sell a burglar alarm to someone who lives in an area in which there are no burglaries.

Two basic offers have withstood the test of time, and you must offer them to your potential customers for a successful mail order appeal: the money-back guarantee and the free trial. Both appeal mainly to security needs.

The money-back guarantee is one of the oldest offers known to mail order. It appeals to your potential customers' safety and security needs in that they are sending their money to an unknown source for a product they've never seen before and so are taking a considerable risk. There-fore, you give them the strongest guarantee you can possibly make, so that they are confident that if, for any reason, they are dissatisfied with a product or service you offer, they may get their money back easily and with no problems or questions. Some media in which you may want to advertise will insist that you offer a money-back guarantee for any prod-uct or service that you advertise. The publication itself may state that all advertisers have agreed to a money-back guarantee. Never mind whether this is said by the medium you are advertising in; you should restate this guarantee in the strongest terms you possible can in your own ad: "Iron-Clad Guarantee," "No-Questions-Asked Guarantee," and so forth.

The second basic offer, which is essential in mail order, is the free trial. The free trial allows your customer to use the product for a specified pe-riod and then return it without question, even though it is used, and re-ceive his or her money back if dissatisfied. Traditionally, this period has been from 10 days to two weeks, and both of these free trial periods are still used successfully by many mail order operators. However, many in-novations to increase the response of potential mail order buyers are tak-ing place. These have included the 31-day free trial period, combined with the money-back guarantee. Joe Karbo's advertising that he would hold a check in escrow for 31 days before cashing it to allow for the free trial period is one of these innovations. More recently, several adver-tisers, including Melvin Powers and Joe Sugarman, have offered no less than a money-back guarantee for a one-year period. Whether this experi-ment will work will be decided over the coming years. Clearly, the re-sponse will increase, but will it increase sufficiently to make up for the increased returns sure to occur with such a long trial period for the mer-chandise?

You may wonder whether offering a free trial period won't allow someone to copy your merchandise, if it is printed, or to use it and then return it for a refund. Of course, such things are possible—and there are people in this world who will take advantage of you. However, generally, for a satisfactory product or service, your returns will not exceed 15%, even including those customers who are rip-off artists. The 15% is sort of a working figure that many mail order operators use to decide whether there is something wrong with their product or service. If the return is less than 15%, everything is all right; if it's more than 15%, something is wrong. At one point, Joe Karbo's book, *The Lazy Man's Way to Riches,* had a return of about 7%, a pretty good rate!

Tabulate your returns carefully and use these tabulations as a guide to whether there is something wrong with your offer, product, or advertising. If you are getting more than 15% returns, you should consider changing your product, dropping it, or looking at your advertising appeal to see if it is in some way overstating the case and raising the expectations of your potential customers to such a degree that they are tremendously disappointed when they receive the product.

In any case, remember that these two basic offers—the money-back guarantee and the free trial period—are essential to success in direct mail operations.

Ray W. Jutkins of Nelson-Panullo-Jutkins Direct Marketing states that the offer must be outstanding and must make the individual want to buy through a promise or an offer that he or she cannot refuse. He lists nine basic appeals the offer can make. Note how well these basic appeals fit in with Maslow's hierarchy of needs. Make an offer to make the purchaser feel: (1) more important; (2) happier; (3) more comfortable; (4) more prosperous; (5) that his or her work is easier; (6) a greater sense of security; (7) more attractive or able to have a better life; or (8) some distinction. Finally, (9) convince the purchaser that you're offering a bargain.

DEVELOPING THE COMPONENTS OF YOUR OFFER AND STRUCTURING THEM

There are two parts to the offer—the components, which include the price, product, packaging, and so forth, and the *structure,* which means how the components are put together. In considering both the components and structure of your offer, you should consider the effect the offer will have on your objective for this project. Bob Stone says that one question is the key in the design of any offer: "How will this offer help to accomplish my objective?" Therefore, before deciding how to structure or develop the components of your offer, decide what the primary objective of that offer is.* Consider the following alternatives: (1) Is your objective to make an immediate profit on this offer and not consider back-end profits? (2) Is your objective to make back-end profits so that repeat business is the factor critical to profitability? (3) Are you breaking

---

* From Jim Kobs, *Profitable Direct Marketing,* Crain Books (a division of Crain Communications, Inc.), 1979. Reprinted by permission of Jim Kobs.

in or penetrating into a new market and so your objective is to get the maximum number of new customers for your product or service as quickly as possible?

Jim Kobs, who is president of Kobs & Brady Advertising in Chicago, developed a list of no less than 99 proved direct-response offers, which he describes in his book, *Profitable Direct Marketing*. Here is Jim's list. *Basic offers:* (1) right price, (2) free trial, (3) money-back guarantee, (4) cash with order, (5) bill me later, (6) installment terms, (7) charge card privileges, (8) C.O.D. *Free gift offers:* (9) free gift for an inquiry, (10) free gift for a trial order, (11) free gift for buying, (12) multiple free gifts with a single order, (13) your choice of free gifts, (14) free gifts based on size of order, (15) two-step gift offer, (16) continually incentive gifts, (17) mystery gift offer. *Other free offers:* (18) free information, (19) free catalog, (20) free booklet, (21) free fact kit, (22) send me a salesman, (23) free demonstration, (24) free survey of your needs, (25) free cost estimate, (26) free dinner, (27) free film offer, (28) free house organ subscription, (29) free talent contest, (30) gift shipment service. *Discount offers:* (31) cash discount, (32) short-term introductory offer, (33) refund certificate, (34) introductory order discount, (35) trade discount, (36) early-bird discount, (37) quantity discount, (38) sliding scale discount, (39) selected sales, (41) reason why sales, (42) price increase notice, (43) auction by mail. *Sample offers:* (44) free sample, (45) nominal-charge sample, (46) sample offer with tentative commitment, (47) quantity sample offer, (48) free sample lesson. *Time limit offers;* (49) limited time offers, (50) enrollment periods, (51) prepublication offer, (52) charter membership or subscription offer, (53) limited edition offer. *Guarantee offers:* (54) extended guarantee, (55) double-your-money-back guarantee, (56) guarantee buy-back agreement, (57) guaranteed acceptance offer, *Build-up-the-sales offers:* (59) piggyback offers, (60) deluxe offer, (61) good, better, best offers, (62) add-on offer, (63) write your own ticket offer, (64) bounce-back offer, (65) increase and extension offer. *Sweepstakes offers:* (66) drawing-type sweepstakes, (67) lucky number sweepstakes, (68) everybody-wins sweepstakes, (69) involvement sweepstakes, 70) talent contests. *Club and continuity offers:* (71) positive option, (72) negative option, (73) automatic shipment, (74) continuity loadup offer, (75) front-end loadup offer, (76) open-end commitment, (77) no-strings-attached commitment, (78) lifetime membership fee, (79) annual membership fee. *Specialized offers:* (80) the philanthropic privilege, (81) blank check offer, (82) executive preview charge, (83) yes/no offers, (84) self-qualification offer, (85) exclusive rights for your trading area, (86) a super dramatic offer, (87) trade-in offer, (88) third-party referral offer, (89) member-get-a-member offer, (90) name-getter offer, (91) purchase with purchase offer, (92) delayed billing offer, (93) reduced down payment, (94) stripped-down products, (95) secret bonus gift,

(96) rush shipping service, (97) competitive offer, (98) nominal reimbursement offer, and (99) established value offer.

As Jim himself says, "When you sit down to make a list of direct response offers and their variations, it's amazing how many you can come up with." Let's look at some of the most important of these types of offers and some examples of how companies engaged in mail order are using them profitably. Remember as we look at these examples that there is nothing stopping you from developing your own variation of the basic offer that can be even more profitable.

Basic Offers

These are used to overcome the reluctance of a potential customer to order a product sight unseen by mail, and they also include different payment options.

Right Price.   The price is, of course, one of the critical components of the offer. "Right" might be higher or lower than what your competition is charging. Basically, you must consider what your market will pay as well as what the competition may be charging for similar products or products that do the same thing. But at the same time, you must make certain that you have charged a high enough price that the offer is profitable. Remember that the general rule in mail order is that you must sell your product for at least three to four times your in-the-mail cost of the product.

Free Trial.   This is the offer we discussed earlier. Remember that it is not an option—it is a must. You must offer a free trial period to your customer under almost all circumstances in mail order to be successful. To decide what time to offer for a trial period, you should look at your competition as guidelines. Later, when you are an experienced mail order operator you may become innovative like Joe Karbo, Melvin Powers, or Joe Sugarman.

Money-Back Guarantee.   This was also discussed earlier, but is so important that it is worth repeating. And for success in mail order, you must make this offer for most products. If a customer is dissatisfied, he or she can return the product to you for a full refund. To a certain degree, inertia is on your side, because it is some trouble to send a product back. Tabulate your returns and use the 15% rule. As long as your product has less than 15% returns, your product or service is probably all right, and your advertising claims are probably being met.

Cash with Order. This is a normal, perhaps the basic, payment alternative. Your customer sends the money with the order for your product. "Cash" here can also mean a check or money order.

Bill Me Later. This is another payment option and is considered the basic one if a free trial offer is used in lieu of the money-back guarantee. This will sometimes occur in selling books by mail. The bill is enclosed with the merchandise or sent a few days after the merchandise is delivered. Response, as you might expect, is usually much greater than if you required cash with the order. However, it is a fact that in some cases, you will not receive the payment or the returned merchandise. This is a cost of doing business, and as long as this "cost" does not stop you from being profitable, it should not stop you from making the offer.

Installment Terms. This is where you offer a payment option in which your customer pays over a period of time, rather than all in one lump sum. Some sort of installment plan is generally needed when a "big-ticket" or high-priced item is sold. It will increase response, although, again, in many cases you will not receive full payment. Even with collection agencies, most mail order firms that sell through this offer ultimately collect only from 60 to 70% of the customers who order.

Charge Card Privileges. Charge cards offer advantages similar to installment plans since there is a built-in installment plan with the charge card. The advantages here are that you don't have to assume the risk of nonpayment. However, when using charge cards, you will be charged a certain percentage—4% or more—by the company involved.

C.O.D. C.O.D. stands for *cash on delivery* and is a service offered by the U.S. Postal Service. The mail carrier collects your money when your product is delivered to the customer. Sounds too good to be true? Well, there are some problems. First, this service is expensive. And, not infrequently, your potential customer's interest in your product has cooled by the time the mail carrier appears with the item in hand. Then you must pay not only for the item to be delivered to the potential customer, but also for its return to you. If you do decide to use C.O.D., it is usually better to ask for a certain percentage of the money with the order, so that the customer has already made a commitment toward purchasing the item, and it is harder for him or her to refuse payment. Also, ship as soon as possible after the order is received, so there is less time for your customer's interest to wane.

Free Gift Offers

Free gift offers are used to encourage the potential customer to do something else that you want him or her to do—usually buy another product. However, there are some important cautionary notes here. A gift should have something to do with the product or service that you want the prospective customer to buy. Otherwise, the folks that order your free gift may not be the same kind of folks who are interested in buying your product in the future. There is also a decision to be made as to which item is to be sold and which is to be the free gift. Clearly, this is another decision that you must make in structuring your offer.

Free Gift for an Inquiry.   In this case, you will offer the free gift merely for requesting more information about the product or service you are selling. This will obviously increase your response for inquiries at the same time. However, it will also increase the cost of the response because many of the respondents will be merely curious and will not be as interested in buying your product as those who might inquire without the offer of a free gift. The same rule applies regarding the connection between your free gift and what you are selling. Notice Brainerd Mellinger's advertisement in Figure 5-1 and how the free sample import is tied in with his product. This and similar advertisements have brought in millions of dollars.

Free Gift for a Trial Order.   This is where you offer a free gift if the potential customer will merely place the order for what you are trying to sell on a trial basis. For example, I once sold three books called *The Writer's Guide to Publication and Profit*. With the order, the respondent got a free book on punctuation. Further, he or she was to keep this whether or not the other books were returned. Figure 5-2 is certainly an unusual free offer. You buy four filet mignon steaks and get two steaks free!

Other Free Gifts

This classification by Kobs includes a number of different free gifts for different markets. There is an important principle at work here regarding all free gifts, and that is that as you offer more free gifts and more valuable free gifts, you will increase the quantity of your responses. However, the quality of the responses will not be so great, since many curiosity seekers will respond. On the other hand, if you offer a relatively inexpensive free gift, the quantity of your responses will be less than that if

Figure 5-1. Brainerd Mellinger's ad. The customer gets a free sample just for requesting information.

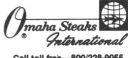
Figure 5-2. If you order four steaks, you get two free—a gift for a trial order.

you offered more, but their quality will be greater. In other words, even though not as many responded to your free offer, these respondents will order more. It is part of your job to pick the offer that is most profitable for you.

Free Information. This is where you offer additional information for merely responding to your offer. When selling my writer's book, I once advertised in classified ads, "Write for profit. Complete details free." This was free information offered to get inquiries that I could then use to present my full-paying proposition.

Free Catalog. A free catalog is useful for a number of different businesses and as a way of selling your mail order products. I'll be talking about catalogs in detail later on.

Free Booklet. A free booklet can be of great assistance in selling either your product or service, even though the book may or may not mention the product or service explicitly. For example, a company I know of sells business insurance. It offers a free booklet, *25 Things You Should Know about Purchasing Business Insurance Before You Do So.* Such a booklet establishes your company as an expert in that product or service and, of course, puts your name immediately before your potential customer for ordering that product or service. Figure 5-3 offers a free booklet, but with a twist. You get the booklet only if you respond to three cards out of a number that have been sent to you in a packet describing other similar mail order offers. Note also that Figure 5-3 is actually printed on an envelope.

Free Fact Kit. A fact kit can contain a number of different items, all of which may help to sell your product or service. It may include reprints of articles, free booklets such as I described above, samples, and so forth. Free fact kits enable your prospective customer to visualize exactly what you are selling, and they may contain a number of different types of sales approach, all of which can add up to a sale. Of course, a fact kit costs you something to put together, so as always, you should watch not only the number of responses but also profitability.

Free Film Offer. This is used by many companies processing film through the mail. The customer gets a new roll of film when one is sent in for processing, or sometimes an initial roll is offered free in return for a promise to send the film in for processing after the pictures have been taken.

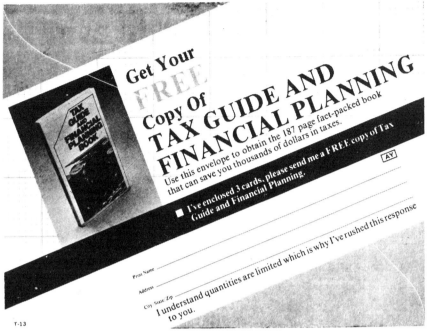

Figure 5-3.   A free booklet offer.

Free House Organ Subscription.   Newsletters are booming throughout the country, and many of them contain helpful information for customers and prospective customers. An offer might be for a year's free subscription or for a free sample issue, or you might offer the subscription free as long as your customer continues to buy from you.

Free Talent Test.   Many home correspondence courses have used this offer. A test of writing or drawing ability, for example, has been used for years. However, the FTC has tightened up on these talent tests: They must measure real ability, rather than be only an opener to sell the product or service. But you are not prohibited from making the offer, as long as the test measures what it is supposed to.

Discount Offers

Discount offers appeal to the bargain instinct of your prospective buyers. But you must be careful that your discounting doesn't affect the image you want to project of the product. We'll talk about the effect of discounting and price on image later.

Cash Discount. This is where you offer a price discount or a discount certificate for the product. This offer is an alternative to one of the free gift offers we discussed earlier. Figure 5-4 offers a discount on a "Bullworker," an exercise device that has been sold very successfully through the mail.

Short-Term Introductory Offer. This is where you offer a discount, but only for a short period. You have probably received a mailing like this from an insurance company, stating that your insurance is only 25¢. Sometimes subscriptions are offered for a short trial period at a reduced price in the same fashion. The key here is whether you can convert enough short-term buyers into long-term buyers. If you can't, this offer will do nothing but cost you a great deal of money.

Refund Certificate. This is a rebate or delay type of discount. An order for a catalog for $1 may include a discount certificate for the same amount, or you may offer the rebate after the customer tries the product. Brainerd Mellinger, in his import-export courses, sometimes uses a discount certificate in the form of a "check" to induce individuals to "buy now."

Introductory Offer Discount. This is a discount offer only to new customers, to get them to place an initial order. The problem with the introductory offer discount is that you may upset your old customers. Further, some old customers will also place the order for the introductory offer. You must be very careful about testing here and watch your results to make certain this offer is profitable. Figure 5-5 shows a successful introductory offer discount by the RCA music service.

Trade Discount. This is a discount offered to members of certain types of institutions or businesses merely because of their membership. For example, the Direct Marketing Association offers a special membership discount to college or university professors.

Early-Bird Discount. This is a discount that attempts to get potential customers to order before the normal buying season or period. It is frequently used to sell books; a so-called prepublication price is offered before the book is actually published. It has also been used for Christmas cards, gifts, pre-school buying, and in many similar situations.

BULLWORKER

BULLWORKER SERVICE, 201 LINCOLN BLVD., MIDDLESEX, N.J. 08846
A DIVISION OF MARGRACE CORP.

Save $11.00 off regular price on Bullworker Demonstration Models

Dear Friend,

We have a certain number of Bullworkers which we have used as demonstration models. We are prepared to sell these to the first customers who request them for only $31.50 - a reduction of over 25% off the normal price.

These Bullworkers are in perfect condition. Each comes to you with the same five-year guarantee as a brand new Bullworker.

This offer is made on a first come first served basis. We cannot tell how long we shall be able to hold open this generous offer, so if you would like to obtain one at this advantageous price, we suggest you send your order off to us this very day.

Yours sincerely,

Bill Anderson

Bill Anderson,
Chief Sales Executive

P.S. If not thoroughly satisfied with the demonstration model, return it to us within two weeks and you will owe nothing, be under no obligation.

Figure 5-4. An example of a discount offer.

Figure 5-5. An introductory discount offer from the RCA Music Service.

Quantity Discount. "Buy more and you get a discount" is not unique to mail order, but it is used frequently to sell magazine subscriptions and many other types of products and services.

Sliding Scale Discount. In the sliding scale discount, the discount itself is variable—2, 5, or 10%—and may be linked to the amount of the order. Or the discount can be tied to when the payment is made—that is, a 2% discount if payment is made before 10 days, full amount thereafter.

Selected Discounts. These are discounts made on certain selected products, usually in catalogs. Discounts are given on certain products to push their sale harder or to give the appearance of a general sale, or sometimes simply to close out on merchandise that hasn't sold.

Sale Offers

A sale and a discount may be the same thing described in a different way. This group of offers is classified this way because the sale itself, rather than a discount, is emphasized in the offer.

Seasonal Sale. This may be a post- or pre-Christmas sale, a back-to-school sale, a summer vacation sale, and so forth. It is usually related to a certain time or season and is generally repeated every year at the same time.

Reason Why Sale. In this type of sale, a reason must be given for the sale's occurring. It could be a fire, clearance, going out of business, inventory reduction, or some other reason. But in every case, you give a reason for the sale's taking place. This makes the sale more credible in the prospective customer's mind. Figure 5-6 shows an inventory reduction sale by Barnes and Noble.

Price Increase Notice. This type of sale is being held because at the future date indicated in the offer, the price will be increased. Therefore, the customer gets a last chance to order at the old price and has an incentive to order right away. Notice how Mellinger does this effectively in Figure 5-7.

Random Drawing Sale. This type of sale is used when there is a limited amount of merchandise—that is, you are using the sale only to bring names in. Because you will probably have more orders than products to fill the orders, only a certain number of your customers can buy at the

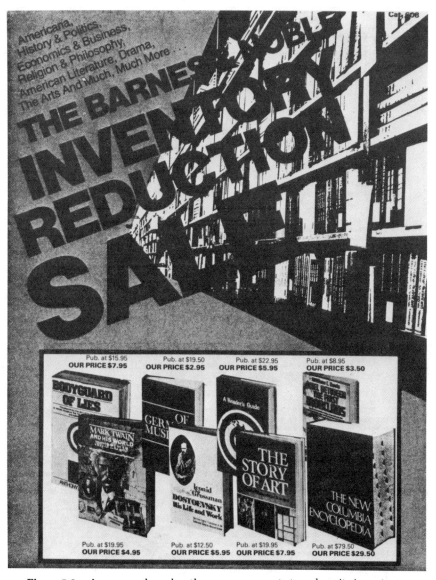

Figure 5-6. A reason why sale—the company wants to reduce its inventory.

LOS ANGELES BANK
BANK OF AMERICA

MEMBER
●
FOREIGN TRADE ASSN. OF SO. CALIFORNIA

The Mellinger Co. *Exporters – Importers*

TELEPHONE (213) 984-4400 ● CABLE: OVRHAUL
6100 VARIEL AVENUE ● WOODLAND HILLS, CALIFORNIA, U.S.A. 91367

LAST CHANCE TO GET MY PLAN AT OLD LOW PRICE!

Dear Ambitious Friend...

Regretfully...I have found it absolutely necessary to raise the price of my Mellinger Mail Order World Trade/Home Business Plan!

BUT WITH ONE BIG DIFFERENCE!

Because you wrote before price went up...I am offering you...for a short time only...the opportunity to enjoy all benefits of the Mellinger Plan at old original low price. I have authorized the enclosed order form for your personal use only...this offer is not transferable to anyone else!

Price simply had to go up. Costs for everything here at International Traders Headquarters have gone through the roof. Salaries of our staff, our foreign travel expenses, supplies, all have gone up and up, just as your own daily personal expenses have moved up with the times. New applicants for my Mellinger Plan now pay new higher price. This is why my special offer to you covers only a very limited time.

EXTRA! Did you catch the extra benefit as you looked over the enclosed order form. You're right! New I.T. Members joining at the new price will enjoy a TWO YEAR membership in International Traders. But even though you will be ordering at the old low price, you will still receive a full TWO YEAR I.T. Membership. That's just like finding an extra $10!

This is the perfect time to get started. I.T. Members I talk with at my Mellinger Seminars around the country tell me their home businesses are booming... thanks to exciting new import products discovered on my recent foreign travel. Even more exciting Imports are coming! With my help and the Mellinger Plan to guide you...opportunities for profit are far better today than when I started my own business in a rented garage and less than $100 to work with!

Save while you still can! This must be your last opportunity to save on the Mellinger Plan and start your big profit future as an International Trader. Check payment Plan 1 or Plan 2 on the enclosed special Inspection Request—and mail it to me today! Either payment plan entitles you to my positive home inspection money-back guarantee! Mail your order to me today.

P.S. Profits on imports are often five times cost! The money you save will buy enough imports to more than pay for entire Plan. Order today!

BLM:jk
9203

Sincerely,

Brainerd L. Mellinger
President

Figure 5-7. A price increase notice. The idea is to convince the reader that the price will never be lower.

price advertised. Therefore, a random drawing is used to pick those customers who will receive the product at the sale price advertised. Of course, you must let your customers know, in your advertising literature and offer, that you have limited merchandise. Meanwhile, you get the names of all those customers who respond, whether they were those fortunate enough to be picked by the random drawing or not. Of course, you return the money of those whose orders you could not fill.

Sample Offers

A sample offer is good when you believe that simply getting your product in the hands of the customer will result in future sales. It is clearly not good for a marginal product in which you think the customer will not be fully satisfied, and here again, you will lose a lot of samples to the ever-present curiosity seekers.

Free Sample.   A free sample is an outstanding method if your product really can sell itself once the customer uses it. Clearly, you have to be careful here that this criterion is met and also that the project will ultimately be profitable even though you are giving away free samples.

Nominal-Charge Sample.   Through charging a small sum of money, you share the cost of the sample with your customer. This small price also helps to qualify and weed out those who would order anything that is free but nothing that they must pay for. The main disadvantage is that you will have a much lower response than if you charged nothing.

Time Limit Offers.

As I said before, in mail order, the idea is always to get your potential customer to act at once and not to delay, for it has been shown and proved time after time that people who delay are far less likely to order. Therefore, a time limit helps to hype the order and get the individual to order at once.

Limited Time Offer.   In this instance, you make your offer good only for a certain time. Here you have a choice: You can say that the offer is good for two weeks or you can indicate a specific cut-off date, such as the first of June. The theoretical advantage in use of a time period rather than a date is that since you won't know exactly when the letter will arrive, you won't compromise your offer if it arrives a little late. Also this will allow you to use the same advertising piece over a greater period of time. How-

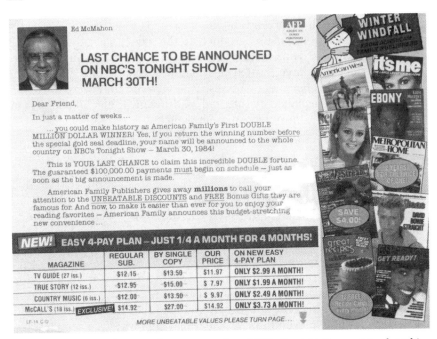

Figure 5-8.   Last chance to be announced on NBC's Tonight Show—March 30th!

ever, the fact is that research has shown that people respond much better to a specific date than to a time period. Figure 5-8 makes it clear March 30 ends the offer.

Prepublication Offer.   This is really a type of early-bird discount, as mentioned earlier, and it allows individuals to order something, usually a book, at a prepublication price lower than the price that will be charged later.

Charter Membership or Subscription Offer.   *Charter* implies that you are offering something new. This type of offer is used for new clubs, magazines, and other types of associations. It usually includes a special introductory price or some other incentive, such as a special charter member's certificate, which appeals both to people who like to be innovators and to those who like to be joiners.

Limited Edition Offer.   This offer implies that there will be only so much of the product available and no more. It therefore appeals very much to people who collect things and it is used to help sell books, plates, coins, works of art, and many other types of collectibles. Figure 5-9 is a limited edition offer by the Calhoun's Collectors Society.

PRIORITY RESERVATION CERTIFICATE

The Royal International Gold Collection of Official British Commonwealth
First Day Covers Bearing Authentic Proof-Quality Specimens
MADE WITH 18 KARAT GOLD

SEND NO MONEY NOW – MAIL YOUR PRIORITY RESERVATION WITHIN 21 DAYS

SIGNATURE X (required) _____

Edition Limit:
7,500 Subscribers

International Postal Collectors League
A division of Calhoun's Collectors Society
Calhoun Center, Minneapolis, Minnesota 55435

Telephone Number ( )
(Your number will be held confidential and used only by our representatives to contact members.)

If you wish each shipment to be charged to your VISA or Master Charge when it is ready, please complete this section:
☐ VISA   ☐ Master Charge
Acct. # (all digits)

☐ YES. Please enter my subscription to the Royal International Gold Collection of First Day Covers bearing authentic specimens of British Commonwealth commemorative stamp designs made with 18 Karat Gold.
   I need send no money now. I will be billed when Shipment No. 1 is ready. Future shipments of the series will then be billed and sent to me automatically at the rate of two First Day Covers per month approximately. The cost is just $14 each ($28* plus $1 postage and handling per shipment of two Covers). This price is firmly guaranteed me for at least 12 consecutive shipments.
   I understand that this special low subscription price includes a deluxe collector's album that will be sent after the third shipment each year at no extra charge. And when IPCL's advisors spot especially unusual and choice new issues, I will receive a bonus set with my Cover — also at no extra charge.
   I RISK NOTHING. Should Shipment No. 1 fail to please, I may simply return everything in it within 15 days for a refund of the purchase price or a charge card credit, whichever applies, and nothing further will be sent.
   Even thereafter I am protected, for I may cancel at any time simply upon 30 days written notice to IPCL.
   See important time limit information on reverse side.

*Minnesota residents, please add 4% ($1.12) sales tax.

Exp. date _____

**This Certificate is Non-Transferable
without permission of the person named hereon**

So that we may serve you better, please correct
any errors in your name and address as shown

PLEASE FOLD AND MAIL ENTIRE CARD IN THE ENCLOSED POSTPAID ENVELOPE

Figure 5-9. A limited edition offer, this one for philatelists.

Guarantee Offers

I mentioned earlier that the money-back guarantee is a requirement in mail order because it helps the customer overcome his or her considerable reluctance to order an unknown product from an unknown firm. The more strongly you can word your guarantee and the more generous you can make it, the greater will be your response for any particular offer.

Extended Guarantee.   I mentioned earlier that the period of the money-back guarantee had been lengthened now to include a year or so. I have also seen offers for products such as knives in which the money-back guarantee for breakage has been increased to a lifetime. Such a guarantee has a tremendous effect on overcoming the resistance of a potential customer to order. The reality is that few of the types of products used with this guarantee are ever returned after a year or so—it's difficult for most people to retain even the seller's address that long!

Double-Your-Money-Back Guarantee. This type of offer really intends to demonstrate your confidence in a product. However, it has two disadvantages. One is that you could lose your credibility if an individual believes that you are not as likely to return double the money as you would be simply to return just the money invested. Second, unless your product is really good, you can really lose your shirt by paying double money back for a product with which your customer didn't really fall in love at first sight.

Guaranteed Buy-back Agreement. This is, of course, a type of extended guarantee, but it is very effective with certain types of collectibles that mail order buyers—and especially investors—may purchase. Basically, what you do is offer to buy the item back for the purchase price up to a certain specified period, or indefinitely. This proposition does a lot to convince the potential buyer of your belief in the present and future worth of the item.

Build-Up-the-Sale Offers

These are offers that increase the size of the average order, certainly a goal any mail order operator can and should subscribe to.

Multiproduct Offers. This is where you offer two or more products or services in the same advertisement. You must be careful in offering more than one product that you do not confuse the customer. Remember that confusion leads to delay, which could cost you the sale. There is something of a paradox here, for clearly, one very successful multiproduct or multiservice medium is none other than the catalog. However, it is a fact that if you have offered two or more products in the same advertisement, your total response may be lower than if you have offered only one product. It is okay to offer the customer different colors, sizes, and styles, or, where the opportunity exists, to trade up for a more expensive version of the same product: A good example is a watch in which the stainless steel version is priced at $39.95, while a gold version is offered in smaller print for $49.95. However, if you confuse the customer with a number of different watches you risk losing the sale rather than increasing your chances of making a sale. So, as a general rule, save multiproduct offers for the catalog.

Piggyback Offers. This is really a multi-product offer, but the ad or offer features one main item, and then, tucked away somewhere in the corner or at the bottom of the advertisement, complementary products are offered.

The Deluxe Offer. This is where you give the opportunity for the customer to trade up after you have already sold him or her. A deluxe version of a book with a much better binding and with letters in gold sells for a higher price than the standard version.

Good, Better, Best Offer. This is a variation of the deluxe offer, except that instead of one or two choices, you offer three. That's where the "good, better, best" comes from. One book seller we know of offered a standard edition, a deluxe edition, and then a grand edition. I needn't add that the price went up with the description of the edition being offered.

Add-on Offer. This is where you attempt to get the prospective customer to buy something else after you have sold him or her the main item. For example, you might sell a knife for $9.95 and then, for $2.50, offer a sheath to go with it.

Bounce-back Offer. This is where you simply add on to the original sale by promoting another product when you fulfill the original product order. This is really a tremendously profitable situation, and I don't know why every mail order operator doesn't take advantage of it. You not only save the money of obtaining the customer's name, but you even save the postage. Besides, what better time to sell to your customer than when he or she is delighted by receiving the first product ordered!

Increase and Extension Offers. This is another type of offer that builds on the original sales made to your customers. Again, the object here is to sell them while they're hot from their first purchase. With the magazine subscription, an extended subscription may be offered with some sort of reduced price. Or perhaps additional accessories might be offered to the buyer of the knife and sheath, such as a matching belt, a pocketknife, and so forth.

Sweepstakes Offers

Sweepstakes offers have really come into their own over the last 10 years, even though they are now highly controlled by the federal government and many states. Recall from chapter 3 that you must have a contest in which all prizes are awarded, and the respondent must be able to participate in the sweepstakes whether he or she places an order with you or not. However, when you consider that responses increase as much as 400% when sweepstakes are used over when they are not, it clearly makes sense to use a sweepstakes type of offer in conjunction with some types of mail order promotions.

Figure 5-10.   A personalized sweepstakes form.

Lucky Number Sweepstakes.   This is where the winning numbers are preselected even before they are mailed to your prospective customers. In this case, your copy emphasizes this fact to your prospective customer: "You May Already Have Won," or "You May Already Be A Winner." Figure 5-10 shows my "Lucky Numbers" from a *Consumers Digest* sweepstakes.

Involvement Sweepstakes.   Involvement means that the potential customer becomes involved in some way in entering the sweepstakes. He or she must play a game, match a number against an eligible number list, or perform some other task to determine the prize. Involvement of the potential customer has been shown to be clearly effective in increasing responses not only to the sweepstakes but also to any other type of promotion that can be linked to potential customer involvement. Figure 5-11 is from a Foster's House sweepstakes. Notice the involvement required in the instructions.

Talent Contests.   This isn't really a sweepstakes in the strictest sense of the word, but it requires the prospective customer to do something involving talent—write a story, draw a picture—and the winner is offered a free scholarship or some other type of prize.

Club and Continuity Offers

These are the offers of the book clubs, record clubs, and others that sell repeat products over a period of time. They were developed back in 1920

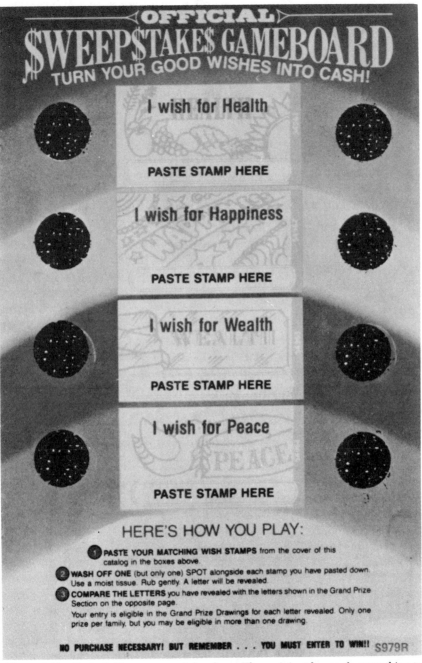

Figure 5-11. Foster's House sweepstakes form. The recipient has to do something to win.

by Maxwell Sackheim and Harry Scherman, when they founded the Book-of-the-Month Club.

Positive Option. This is where you are in a certain type of club and are notified every month of the monthly selection. However, to order you must take some positive action and thereby request the order.

Negative Option. This is generally much more effective than positive option. You are notified in advance of the new selection, but under the terms you agreed to when you joined the club, this selection is shipped to you unless you return a card or something else that rejects the offer by a certain date. This works better because you have human inertia going for you. Figure 5-12 explains the operations of the Popular Science Book Club.

Specialized Offers

This group of offers includes those that can't be grouped easily into the other categories.

How Popular Science Book Club Works

Just mail the postpaid card to get your $24.50 4-VOLUME CARPENTERS AND BUILDERS LIBRARY. Send no money now. We'll bill you later for only $3.95 plus delivery and handling.

Then, about every four weeks (15 times a year), you'll receive a Club bulletin describing the coming main selection and alternate books also available, all at Club discounts. If you want the main selection only, do nothing. It will be sent automatically. If you don't want the main selection, or want alternate books, or no books, please make sure to indicate your wishes on the Instruction Form and return it to us by the date shown. Club mailings are carefully scheduled to assure you of at least 10 days in which to do this. But in the unlikely event that you don't have 10 days, and you receive an unwanted selection, you may return it at our expense.

After receiving your joining shipment, your only obligation is to buy two more regular selections or alternates in the next year. After that, membership may be cancelled at any time, by either you or the Club.

Club books are comparable in every way — paper, printing, binding, jacket — to original publishers' editions, yet you may save up to 50% and sometimes more on hundreds of special books offered each year in the club. To become eligible for these bargains, mail the card today!

Figure 5-12. How the Popular Science Book Club works. The negative option is described in the second paragraph.

Yes/No Offers. Your potential customer is asked to indicate in some special way whether he or she is ordering or not ordering. Obviously, a "no" order is not of much value to you. However, it has been found that forcing an immediate decision actually increases the number of "yes" responses over what you would otherwise have ended up with. Figure 5-13 is a yes/no offer for the Bullworker exerciser described earlier, while Figure 5-14 is a yes/no offer for a sampler of cigars from the Thompson Cigar Company.

The Super-Dramatic Offer. This is an offer that contains some sort of dramatic appeal. For example, one old mail order offer selling revolvers advised potential customers to "hammer the hammer." The hammer containing the firing pin was to be struck with a carpenter's hammer to prove that the gun would not fire without pulling the trigger. Another ad I recall for a hunting knife invited the would-be buyer to try to break the blade.

Trade-in Offer. This is where you get your prospective customer to return something for which you give a discount. Several years ago a credit card firm offered a discount on its prestige credit card by encouraging the prospective customer to cut up and send in old credit cards from competing firms. This accomplished two things at once: It sold the customer the new credit card service at a discount and eliminated the competition at the same time.

Third-Party-Referral Offer. A third party is used to recommend your product or service. It is important here that the third party have credentials that are respected by your prospective customers or this offer will not be very effective. Also, remember the applicable laws on testimonials covered in chapter 3.

Member-Get-a-Member Offer. You make this offer to a member or customer who is currently buying from you. You offer him or her something free if he or she gets another member to join. This is an offer frequently used by book clubs. Members who sign another member up receive free books in return.

Reduced Down Payment. This is for big-ticket items in which some sort of installment plan must be used for purchase. If the initial purchase is not made and a customer does not respond to your offer, you offer a reduced down payment. There are many ways of doing this. One is the "damaged merchandise" offer. If you're selling an item such as a course

BULLWORKER

MARGRACE CORP. 201 LINCOLN BLVD., MIDDLESEX, N.J. 08846

WE ARE STILL RESERVING A DEMONSTRATION
MODEL BULLWORKER IN YOUR NAME AT $11
off the regular price.

With ever more men taking a greater
interest in fitness every day, orders
for the BULLWORKER are coming in faster
than we can ship them. To enable us to
serve as many really fitness-conscious
men as quickly as possible, we'd
appreciate it if, after reading the
letter below, you'd affix one of these
stamps on the enclosed special discount
certificate and mail it back to us.

Dear Friend,

A few weeks ago, we wrote to you regarding a very special
discount sale on BULLWORKER demonstration models.

We made our offer at that time only to those people who had
already expressed interest in developing their physical well-
being . . . and BULLWORKER is the extraordinary new invention
that helps you keep fit and trim without hard exercise.

Since we haven't heard from you, we were going to offer the
discount model, reserved in your name, to someone else. But,
before doing so, we want to be sure that you are really willing
to give up this opportunity to get back in shape fast -- and at
a special reduced price.

If you do not wish to take advantage of our 14-DAY FREE HOME
TRIAL offer, we will release your BULLWORKER to another man.
But if you have made the decision to get back in shape fast --
then please paste the YES stamp on the card and we'll dispatch
your BULLWORKER to you right away to try in your own home,
without cost or purchase obligation.

Don't delay -- MAIL THE CERTIFICATE TODAY. There is no risk,
no obligation to buy. You have absolutely nothing to lose ...
but possibly years of happy, healthy, vigorous life to gain.
Act now!

Sincerely yours,

Bill Anderson

Bill Anderson

Figure 5-13. Yes/no offer for a Bullworker.

122

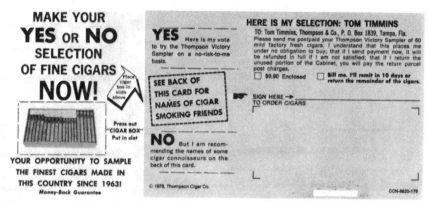

Figure 5-14. Yes/no for Thompson cigars. Note that the "no" option still invites the reader to participate.

of instruction, you can offer a reduced down payment for "slightly damaged merchandise," such as a slightly torn book cover. The damage is "very minor and even hard to locate" but still "cannot be sold as new."

The Nominal Reimbursement Offer. This is where you offer some nominal reimbursement in return for some services rendered by the respondent. A research survey fits this criterion. You must have the highest percentage of response to ensure the accuracy and completeness of the survey. Last year I received a survey with a brand new, crisp $1 bill attached to the letter that asked me to respond. You may think that the average person would keep the dollar bill and still not respond, but the fact of the matter is that the dollar not only acts as an inducement, but it works on the guilt feelings of the respondents. I responded to the survey.

Established Value Offer. If you are offering a special deal, such as an item at a reduced price or a free gift, you can show the value of this offer to your potential customers by offering to send an extra one of your products to them for a friend or a member of their family at the regular going retail price. This does two things for you. First, it helps to establish the value of your free or reduced price offer. Second, you will pick up a few additional sales.

SUMMARY

In this chapter, we have discussed the importance of the offer and why it is so critical to your promoting your product or service successfully. To maxi mize your response, your offer should be constructed in such a way as to motivate your potential customer to order. Remember Abraham Maslow's hierarchy of needs: physiological, safety and security, social, ego, and fulfillment needs.

Structure your offer in accordance with the objective you are seeking to attain—whether it is to break even or make a profit up front, to get repeat business, or to obtain a maximum number of new customers through penetration of a new market.

Finally, consider Kob's checklist of 99 proved direct response offers and our discussion of those that are most important. Select those offers that are applicable to the business proposition to your customer and use them to increase response—or create your own variations.

Do not forget that it is essential to do two things if at all possible: Offer the strongest money-back guarantee that you possibly can, and allow a free trial of your product or service.

6

Essential Cost and Profit Calculations for Your Business Made Easy

Many of us don't care very much for mathematics. You may think math is dull when compared with the fun of preparing copy or graphics, or the excitement of locating new products, or the truly incredible thrill of opening envelopes stuffed with checks and dollars. Or you may just be turned off by math because you feel it is complicated and difficult to understand. Whatever your reason, let me assure you that math is essential for operating a mail order business profitably and an important part of your mail order business plan. You don't need to be a mastermind to master it. I'm going to show you how in this chapter. Once you get your financial calculations together, you will know where you are headed and what you must do, and you will be able to devise ways of doing it to achieve your profit goals and objectives. If you don't do these calculations you will be constantly adrift and unable to control your business. With these calculations, you will know:

Whether your project is financially successful or not

How much improvement is needed to make your project profitable

Where the best opportunities for improving your project are

So, if you want to make it big in mail order—if you really want to succeed—please don't skip this important chapter.

THE BREAKEVEN ANALYSIS

The breakeven analysis is an excellent technique for determining the ultimate success of your mail order project even before you start it. The breakeven analysis will tell you

How many units you must sell to start making money

How much profit you will make at any given level of sales

How changing your price will affect profitability

How expense reductions of different types will affect profitability

To do a breakeven analysis, you must first separate the costs associated with a project into two kinds—fixed and variable costs.

Fixed costs are those expenses associated with a project that you would have to pay whether you sold one unit or 10,000 units, or for that matter, sold none at all. For example, if you rented a garage to be used in your business, and the owner charged you $600 to rent this garage for a period of one year, this would be a fixed cost for that year. It would stay the same whether you sold any product or not. Or, maybe you are going to develop your own proprietary mail order product for this project. Let's say that you estimate it will cost $2000 to develop this product. This development cost would also be considered a fixed cost, since the $2000 does not vary with the number of units you will eventually sell—it is the same whether you sell 100 units or 100,000. Because many fixed costs, such as space rental, are tied to a time period (in this case, $600 a year for the garage), you need to estimate the time you are talking about to come up with the total fixed cost. The fixed cost for two years for the garage would be $600 times 2, or $1200, assuming you could rent the garage for that period.

Variable costs vary directly with the number of units sold. For example, if the manufacturer of the product charges you $1.80 per unit, that $1.80 is a variable cost. In the same way, if postage for mailing your product to the customer is 50¢, that 50¢ is a variable cost. If you sell 10 units, postage costs will be $5. If you sell 100 units, your total variable costs for postage will be 50¢ times 100, or $50.

For some costs it is more difficult to decide whether the cost should be considered a fixed or variable cost, and frequently there is no "right" answer—it is your decision as president and manager of your own company. The general guideline is this: if you can see a relationship between cost and number of units sold, consider the cost variable; if you can find no relationship, consider it a fixed cost.

The total cost of any project always equals total fixed costs plus total variable costs. For example, let's say that we are going to sell red widgets by mail. you looked at this red widget project and decided that your fixed costs included the following: utilities, $100 a month; office supplies, $50 a month; depreciation on part of your home for an office, office furniture, and telephone, $200 a year; developing the item, $1000; and patenting it, another $2500. We will say that you estimate that you will be selling the product for three years. Let's say that you have also identified the following variable costs:

Cost to produce	$1.00
Cost of postage and packaging	0.50

Finally, you have decided that you are going to sell this item only through space advertising. Based on prior experience, you estimate that it will cost you $3 in advertising per red widget sold. Here is the way our costs stack up.

Fixed Costs

Utility expense at $100/month, 36 months	$3600
Telephone at $200/year, 3 years	600
Product development	1000
Patenting expense	2500
Total fixed cost	$7700

Variable Costs

Cost	$1.00 per unit
Cost of postage of packaging	0.50 per unit
Cost of advertising	3.00 per unit
Total variable cost	$4.50 per unit

Now, how in the world can we add them together to arrive at our grand total of costs for red widgets unless we know how many units we are going to sell? The answer is, we can't—but this is how the whole concept of breakeven comes together.

To calculate breakeven we start with profit. What is profit? Profit is the number of units sold multiplied times the price at which we are selling them. We then subtract the number of units sold multiplied times the total variable cost minus the total fixed cost. Or, if you like equations, here is what it looks like. Where P = profit, p = price, U = number of units sold, V = variable cost, and F = fixed cost,

$$P = (U \times p) - (U \times V) - F$$

or we can simplify this equation so that we have

$$P = [U \times (p - V)] - F$$

Now let's try our profit formula out. If we sell 1000 units and our selling price is $10 per unit, what is our profit? Well, we already know that fixed costs are $7700 and that variable costs are $4.50 per unit, so we come out with

$$
\begin{aligned}
P &= [1000 \times (\$10 - \$4.50)] - \$7700 \\
&= \$5500 - \$7700 \\
&= -\$2200
\end{aligned}
$$

Whoops! That's a minus number. That means that instead of making a profit, we lost money—$2200, to be exact. Well now, how many red widgets do we need to sell to make money? That is, how many units do we need to sell just to break even, the point at which we won't make any money, but we won't lose any either?

Let's go back to our profit formula. At breakeven, profit is equal to zero, because there is no profit. So, we know what profit equals. What we don't know is U, the number of units we need to sell to break even. Okay,

$$P = [U \times (p - V)] - F, \text{ and } p = 0$$

That means $[U \times (p - V)] - F = 0$, and now

$$U = \frac{F}{p - V}$$

Now, we know that $F = \$7700$, $P = \$10$, and $V = \$4.50$. Therefore,

$$U = \frac{\$7700}{\$10 - \$4.50} = 1400$$

So, if we don't change price or reduce our expenses in any way, we need to sell 1400 red widgets before we start making any money. So remember:

$$P = [U \times p (- V)] - F$$

and

$$U = \frac{F}{p - V}$$

These two formulas can tell you a lot about your project before you even start.

There is a way of calculating all of this graphically without using the formulas. A *breakeven chart* has a major advantage over the breakeven and profit formulas: It shows pictorially the relationship of fixed variable and total expenses to sales at all volumes of sales. That means that you can calculate profits at any level of sales right away. Here is how to construct a breakeven chart.

Step 1.   Get some graph paper and label the horizontal line on the bottom *Units Sold.* Label the vertical line at the left of the graph *Dollars* (*Sales and Expenses*). Divide each line into equal parts of dollars and units and label it appropriately.

Step 2.   Analyze all of your costs for the project and decide whether each is fixed or variable. Decide on the period of sales for your project. Total up your fixed and variable costs.

Step 3.   Draw a horizontal line to intersect the proper point on the vertical line to represent fixed costs, as at A in Figure 6-1.

Step 4.   Calculate the dollar value of sales for any unit number. For example, if we sell 2000 units, how much is this in sales dollars? For red widgets, total sales volume could be 2000 × $10, or $20,000. Plot this point at 2000 units and $20,000 on the chart as point a. Put one end of a ruler at the 0 point in the lower left corner of the chart and the other end at the point you just plotted. This is the total sales line B in Figure 6-1.

Step 5.   Calculate the dollar value for variable cost for any unit number. For example, for red widgets, variable cost is $4.50 per unit. At, say, 2000 units, total variable cost is 2000 × $4.50, or $9000. Add $9000 to the fixed cost (in this case, $7700) to come up with $16,700. Plot this on the chart (b in Figure 6-1). Lay one end of the ruler at the point where the fixed cost line B intersects the vertical dollar scale and the other at the point you just plotted. Draw a line to form the variable cost line C in Figure 6-1.

Now your breakeven chart is complete. The point at which the total sales line and variable cost line intersect is the breakeven point, which

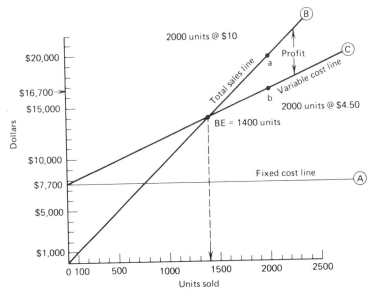

Figure 6-1.   A breakeven chart.

you read on the horizontal unit scale at the bottom of the chart. In Figure 6-1, breakeven is 1400 units, as we calculated before using our formula.

To calculate profit for any number of units you want, simply subtract the dollar value read at opposite the proper point on the variable cost line C from the dollar value read opposite the proper point on the total sales line B. For example, to calculate the profit if you sell 2000 red widgets, read right up from 2000 units on the unit scale to point b on the variable cost line. Read straight across from point b to $16,700 on the vertical dollar scale. Now read straight up from 2000 units on the unit scale to point a on the total sales line. Read straight across from point a to $20,000 on the vertical dollar scale: $20,000 minus $16,700 equals $3300 if you sell 2000 units. Do the same thing for any number of units to calculate profit.

Use breakeven analysis any time you want to calculate profit or how many units you must sell before you begin to make money.

COST AND PROFIT CALCULATIONS WITH INQUIRY FOLLOW-UP

We now know how to apply breakeven analysis to a straightforward mail order or direct mail proposition in which the costs are pretty much up front—we place the classified or display (space) advertisement or send out our advertisement in a direct mail piece to the customer. The customer orders, and that's it. Now we're going to complicate our cost and profit calculation a little by using a slightly different method of mail order operation—the inquiry/follow-up, or two-step promotion, that we discussed in the last chapter.

The complication is that we don't ask for the money right away. Instead, we invite our potential customer to write to us for additional information, and it is with the additional information that we make the sale. The inquiry/follow-up can be initiated with a classified ad, a display ad, or a direct mail piece. It is generally an essential method when trying to sell a high-priced item. For example, when I sold a set of booklets called the *Writer's Guide to Publication and Profit,* the first step was a small classified ad reading, "Write for profit. Free details." To all those who wrote, I sent a complete sales package that described my proposition in more detail—and about 15% of those inquiring ordered. How you do cost calculations for this type of offer is what we are going to talk about now.

Let's look at my breakeven calculation for the sale of my writer's booklet through the two-step operation. In one magazine, one classified advertisement for free details of my full proposition cost $45. The in-the-mail cost of my four brochures was $2 and my selling price was $19.95. The in-the-mail cost of the sales literature sent to inquiries received as a result of my classified advertisement was 50¢ per package. Now our breakeven equation is

$$BE = \text{fixed costs/selling price} - \text{variable costs}$$

If we want to calculate the number of inquiries we need to break even for this project, disregarding overhead costs such as salary, the $45 is a fixed cost because it does not vary with the number of sets of booklets we sell. It remains the same whether we sell one set or 1000. The in-the-mail cost of $2 for the brochures would be a variable cost, since, if we sell one set the cost is $2, but if we sell 1000, this cost is $2000.

Now comes the problem. Clearly the 50¢ per sales literature package is a variable cost, but how do we calculate it for each set of brochures sold? We lack one very important bit of information. We do not know the conversion rate—that is, we want to know what percentage of inquiries we are able to convert to paying customers. What we need to do here is assume various conversion rates and calculate a breakeven point for each. Let's take conversion rates of 5, 10, 15, and 20%. If we convert 5% of our inquiries to customers, that means we get five customers (100 × .05) for every 100 inquiries, or one customer out of every 20 sales literature packages sent. Therefore, the cost in packages for one sale is 20 × .50, or = $10. For a conversion rate of 10%, cost is $5 for 15%, $3.33; for 20%, $2.50.

We add this variable cost to the variable cost of $2 for the in-the-mail cost of the booklets. This gives us the following:

Conversion rate	50%	10%	15%	20%
Total variable cost	$12.00	$7.00	$5.33	$4.50

We can now calculate the number of inquiries needed to break even for each potential conversion rate

If we can convert 5% of the inquiries into customers,

$$BE = \frac{\$45.00}{\$19.95 - \$12.00} = 5.7, \text{ or 6 inquiries}$$

For 10% conversion,

$$BE = \frac{\$45.00}{\$19.95 - \$7.00} = 3.5, \text{ or 4 inquiries}$$

For 15% conversion,

$$BE = \frac{\$45.00}{\$19.95 - \$5.33} = 3.1, \text{ or 4 inquiries}$$

For 20% conversion,

$$BE = \frac{\$45.00}{19.95 - 4.50} = 2.9, \text{ or 3 inquiries}$$

To compute profit with the two-step type of mail order sale you must assume a certain conversion rate. If you want to calculate profit at 60 inquiries for your ad at a conversion rate of 10%, your number of sales would be 60 × .10, or 6. Your fixed cost would still be $45. Your variable cost would be 6 times $2 for the set of booklets plus 60 × .50 for the sales literature. That's a total of $42 variable cost. Because of the two-step operation and the complication of the number of inquiries versus number of sales, it is easier to state our original profit equation this way:

Profit = gross revenue − variable costs − fixed costs
Gross revenue = 6 × $19.95 = $119.70
Profit, therefore, = $119.70 − $42.00 − $45.00, or $32.70

Now what about calculating the number of inquiries we must convert to break even once we know the total number of inquiries? Let's say that at the end of the first month we have 26 inquiries and we project these returns to be a total of 52 inquiries (we'll learn how to project returns this way in a later chapter). Okay, with 52 inquiries, the cost for the sales literature will be 52 × .50, or $26. In this way, we'll treat the number of inquiries as a fixed cost, not a variable cost, since once the mailing to the inquiries has been made, it will remain the same whether we sell one set of booklets or 1000. Our equation is

$$BE = \frac{\$45 + \$26}{\$19.95 - \$2} = 3.95, \text{ or 4 sales}$$

$$\frac{4 \text{ sales}}{52 \text{ inquiries}} = \begin{array}{l} \text{a conversion rate} \\ \text{of 7.7\% for breakeven} \end{array}$$

BACK-END PROFITS

The name may not be very elegant, but the back-end profit concept is the key to big money and success in mail order. The concept is simple: Rather than concentrating on making your money on the initial proposition to a prospective customer, you use this initial proposition mainly to get the customer to order. If you break even, that's great. But even if you don't, you now have the name of an individual who has demonstrated an interest in your products or service in the best possible way—by actually placing an order. You can now make huge profits by selling similar items to your customers over and over again. Now comes the big question: Since you aren't making your money with the first order, how do you know whether your magazine advertisement, direct mail piece, or two-step sale is profitable or not?

Let's assume the following as facts for a minute. For each unit of product we sell on our first deal, we will sustain a loss of $1. However, in fulfilling this first customer order, we enclose a bounce-back offer that advertises a similar product with the order. Let's say that 4% of our customers reorder on the bounce-back, which has a selling price of $50 and a variable cost of $20.00 per unit. Now, if the first order came from a magazine advertisement costing $5000, what we would like to know is how many orders we must get from the advertisement to break even. Here's how we figure it out. Our breakeven equation is

$$BE = \frac{\text{fixed costs}}{\text{selling price} - \text{variable costs}}$$

In this case, the only fixed cost is the $5000 for the magazine advertise-ment. Variable costs include the $1 we lose on each first order plus 40% of the $2 per unit cost of the bounce-back. Similarly, we use 40% of the $5 per unit selling price on the bounce-back. Now our breakeven equation looks like this:

$$BE = \frac{5000}{(.04)(50.00) - .04(20.00) - 1.00}$$

$$= \frac{5000}{2.00 - .80 - 1.00}$$

$$= \frac{5000}{.20} = 25,000 \text{ units}$$

Now let's say that, to each customer who orders on the first bounce-back, you send a second bounce-back, and that 2% order. Will this affect the breakeven on your ad? Most certainly! If the selling price of $50.00 and the in-the-mail variable cost of $20.00 remain the same, we have one ad-ditional selling price of .02 ($50.00) and one additional variable cost of .02 ($20.00). Now breakeven for the advertisement is:

$$BE = \frac{5000}{(.04)(50.00) + (.02)(50.00) - (.04)(20.00) - (.02)(20.00) - 1.00} =$$

$$\frac{5000}{.80} = 6250 \text{ units}$$

Once you know how many of your customers reorder on each offer, the average amount of reorder, and your average cost, you can easily calcu-late your breakeven number of orders or inquiries for each advertisement in this same way. Later I will show you how to estimate your response from any advertisement. Using response estimates and this equation, you will know at once whether an ad is going to be profitable—and whether to continue to use the ad or to drop it.

HOW TO TELL WHETHER YOU ARE WINNING OR LOSING

There is a basic question that will help you analyze your results to show whether you are winning or losing in your mail order business. This equation is return on investment, frequently referred to as ROI.

"It takes money to make money" is an old saying that emphasizes the fact that any business requires an investment, whether the investment is your own money or money borrowed from someone else. If you have invested your money in the bank, you are earning interest, or profit, on your investment. For example, if you have $5000 in your bank account and it is paying 7% interest per annum, your annual ROI is 7%. You can calculate ROI for any investment you have by the simple equation

$$ROI = \frac{net\ profit}{total\ investment}$$

ROI is the most popular measurement of business success in use today. Not only business people, but also bankers, accountants, investors, and all types of financial analysts calculate ROI for individual companies or divisions of companies to determine how they are doing. Based on their analyses, firms receive loans or do not, are bought and sold, or even expanded or liquidated. ROI is used in big firms and small, and you can use it too as an indication of whether your profits are what they should be.

What ROI can you expect from your mail order business? Bob Stone says a 15% ROI is not unusual, and, in fact, for large companies a 15% ROI is not bad. But your operation, with a much lower overhead, should do even better. Let's look at the ROI equation again.

$$ROI = \frac{net\ profit}{total\ investment}$$

Net profit is fairly straightforward. The figure that goes here is the net profit we realize for the year after taxes. The total investment figure is a bit more complicated. Some mail order beginners tend to leave out all investments that don't consist of cold, hard cash they must put out. This is wrong. Total investment includes any negotiable commodity. It could be money, but it might also be an automobile, or part of an automobile, the labor that goes into your business—both yours and that of others—or costs associated with the use of part of your home as an office. Whether or not you pay yourself a salary, or use your personal car on company business but don't charge your company, investments are being made in your business operation. If you don't calculate them in computing your ROI, they haven't gone away: The result will be a less-than-accurate ROI. So be certain to calculate all your expenses as part of your total investment, and if some of these expenses don't have an established value because you haven't started paying yourself a salary from your business yet, you should still figure an hourly rate for your labor and include it as part of total investment. You will see the importance of this in a minute.

To help ensure that you don't forget expenses as a part of your total investment, I have included a list of potential mail order expenses at the end of this chapter.

Let us say that new profit for the year was $5000, for a total investment of $25,000. Remember, this $25,000 must include everything, including an hourly or daily rate tacked onto the hours of time we invested in the business, even if we didn't take out a salary. ROI will equal 5000/25,000, or 20%. That's not bad, but can it be better? It can if we can increase the profit of $5000 without increasing the total investment, or if we can reduce the total investment without decreasing the net profit. So we analyze both, and here's why it's important that such things as your labor be documented as part of total investment. Maybe we can increase ROI by reducing your labor. Maybe you're paying yourself $10 an hour for such things as stuffing envelopes, when you can pay some kid to do the same thing after school at less than half your labor rate. The net savings will increase your ROI, and that illustrates one of the main reasons for your calculating ROI—you should always analyze it to see if you can do better by more efficient selling or a more efficient investment.

SHOULD YOU DO IT OR NOT?
A MATHEMATICAL GUIDE TO INVESTMENT DECISIONS

At some time in your career as a mail order businessperson, you will come face-to-face with an opportunity that, if taken, will require a major business investment. Many of your business decisions will be made on the basis of an educated guess. You make the decision based on your judgment, your experience, and what you have learned from other sources, such as this book. However, a really big investment should not be made without consideration of a major quantitative factor that we haven't talked about up to now. This factor is the time value of money. It refers to the fact that there are alternative choices for the use of the money required for your investment, and that this fact must be taken into consideration when making any major investment decision.

Let's look at an example. Let's say that you are considering an investment of $10,000 for a new addressing machine. The terms of payment are $5000 down and $2500 a year for two years. The machine will last 10 years, and after that you can sell it for scrap for $500. Why buy the machine? Well, because if you don't have the machine, you are paying to have your mailings addressed by hand, which is costing you $1300 a year. So if we didn't consider the time value of money, our calculations would look like this:

Costs		Savings
$5000	down payment	$1300 per year
$5000	at $2500 per year	for 10 years
− $ 500	salvage value after 10 years	= $13,000
$9500		

$13,000 − $9500 = $3500

This calculation says we should definitely buy the machine. But wait. We said there was a time value to money. This means we could do something else with the money. Maybe we could put it in the bank and get 7% interest per year, compounded yearly. This is the adjustment we must make for our basic calculations. These calculations are capital budgeting, and they can be of considerable importance if the investment we are considering is large enough.

Let's look at our example again and at Figures 6-2 and 6-3. Figure 6-2 gives the present value of $1 received at the end of any number of years, up to 50. Figure 6-3 shows the present value of $1 received annually at the end of each year for any number of years we care to choose, up to 50. In both figures, the horizontal line across the top of the page represents different interest percentages, from 1 to 50% at various intervals.

Now our basic task in order to make a comparison, considering the fact that there are alternative uses for our money that will pay us interest, is to bring all calculations to the present.

Let's look at costs first. The $5000 down payment is already in the present, so there is nothing to do here. Next we have $2500 to be paid for the next two years. Look at Figure 6-2 for the end of year 1 under the 7% column and we see .9346. Under year 2 and 7%, we see .8734. Further, there is a salvage value for our machine of $500 after 10 years. Looking at year 10 and 7%, we copy down the number .5083. Now we add our costs up as follows:

Costs

Down payment	$5000.00
$2500 at end of year 1 = ($2,500)(.9346)	+2,336.50
$2500 at end of year 2 = ($2,500)(.8734)	+2,183.50
$500 salvage value after 10 years = ($500)(.5083)	− 254.15
	$9265.85

For our savings of $1300 per year for 10 years, we use Figure 6-3. At year 10 and 7%, we read 7.0236.

n/r	1%	2%	3%	4%	5%	6%	7%	8%	9%	10%	11%	12%	13%	14%	15%
1	.9901	.9804	.9709	.9615	.9524	.9434	.9346	.9259	.9174	.9091	.9009	.8929	.8850	.8772	.8696
2	.9803	.9612	.9426	.9246	.9070	.8900	.8734	.8573	.8417	.8264	.8116	.7972	.7831	.7695	.7561
3	.9706	.9423	.9151	.8890	.8638	.8396	.8163	.7938	.7722	.7513	.7312	.7118	.6931	.6750	.6575
4	.9610	.9238	.8885	.8548	.8227	.7921	.7629	.7350	.7084	.6830	.6587	.6355	.6133	.5921	.5718
5	.9515	.9057	.8626	.8219	.7835	.7473	.7130	.6806	.6499	.6209	.5935	.5674	.5428	.5194	.4972
6	.9420	.8880	.8375	.7903	.7462	.7050	.6663	.6302	.5963	.5645	.5346	.5066	.4803	.4556	.4323
7	.9327	.8706	.8131	.7599	.7107	.6651	.6227	.5835	.5470	.5132	.4817	.4523	.4251	.3996	.3759
8	.9235	.8535	.7894	.7307	.6768	.6274	.5820	.5403	.5019	.4665	.4339	.4039	.3762	.3506	.3269
9	.9143	.8368	.7664	.7026	.6446	.5919	.5439	.5002	.4604	.4241	.3909	.3606	.3329	.3075	.2843
10	.9053	.8203	.7441	.6756	.6139	.5584	.5083	.4632	.4224	.3855	.3522	.3220	.2946	.2697	.2472
11	.8963	.8043	.7224	.6496	.5847	.5268	.4751	.4289	.3875	.3505	.3173	.2875	.2607	.2366	.2149
12	.8874	.7885	.7014	.6246	.5568	.4970	.4440	.3971	.3555	.3186	.2858	.2567	.2307	.2076	.1869
13	.8787	.7730	.6810	.6006	.5303	.4688	.4150	.3677	.3262	.2897	.2575	.2292	.2042	.1821	.1625
14	.8700	.7579	.6611	.5775	.5051	.4423	.3878	.3405	.2992	.2633	.2320	.2046	.1807	.1597	.1413
15	.8613	.7430	.6419	.5553	.4810	.4173	.3624	.3152	.2745	.2394	.2090	.1827	.1599	.1401	.1229
16	.8528	.7284	.6232	.5339	.4581	.3936	.3387	.2919	.2519	.2176	.1883	.1631	.1415	.1229	.1069
17	.8444	.7142	.6050	.5134	.4363	.3714	.3166	.2703	.2311	.1978	.1696	.1456	.1252	.1078	.0929
18	.8360	.7002	.5874	.4936	.4155	.3503	.2959	.2502	.2120	.1799	.1528	.1300	.1108	.0946	.0808
19	.8277	.6864	.5703	.4746	.3957	.3305	.2765	.2317	.1945	.1635	.1377	.1161	.0981	.0829	.0703
20	.8195	.6730	.5537	.4564	.3769	.3118	.2584	.2145	.1784	.1486	.1240	.1037	.0868	.0728	.0611
21	.8114	.6598	.5375	.4388	.3589	.2942	.2415	.1987	.1637	.1351	.1117	.0926	.0768	.0638	.0531
22	.8034	.6468	.5219	.4220	.3418	.2775	.2257	.1839	.1502	.1228	.1007	.0826	.0680	.0560	.0462
23	.7954	.6342	.5067	.4057	.3256	.2618	.2109	.1703	.1378	.1117	.0907	.0738	.0601	.0491	.0402
24	.7876	.6217	.4919	.3901	.3101	.2470	.1971	.1577	.1264	.1015	.0817	.0659	.0532	.0431	.0349
25	.7798	.6095	.4776	.3751	.2953	.2330	.1842	.1460	.1160	.0923	.0736	.0588	.0471	.0378	.0304
26	.7720	.5976	.4637	.3607	.2812	.2198	.1722	.1352	.1064	.0839	.0663	.0525	.0417	.0331	.0264
27	.7644	.5859	.4502	.3468	.2678	.2074	.1609	.1252	.0976	.0763	.0597	.0469	.0369	.0291	.0230
28	.7568	.5744	.4371	.3335	.2551	.1956	.1504	.1159	.0895	.0693	.0538	.0419	.0326	.0255	.0200
29	.7493	.5631	.4243	.3207	.2429	.1846	.1406	.1073	.0822	.0630	.0485	.0374	.0289	.0224	.0174
30	.7419	.5521	.4120	.3083	.2314	.1741	.1314	.0994	.0754	.0573	.0437	.0334	.0256	.0196	.0151
35	.7059	.5000	.3554	.2534	.1813	.1301	.0937	.0676	.0490	.0356	.0259	.0189	.0139	.0102	.0075
40	.6717	.4529	.3066	.2083	.1420	.0972	.0668	.0460	.0318	.0221	.0154	.0107	.0075	.0053	.0037
45	.6391	.410	.2644	.1713	.1112	.0727	.0476	.0313	.0207	.0137	.0091	.0061	.0041	.0027	.0019
50	.6080	.3715	.2281	.1407	.0872	.0543	.0339	.0213	.0134	.0085	.0054	.0035	.0022	.0014	.0009

n/r	16%	18%	20%	22%	24%	26%	28%	30%	32%	34%	36%	38%	40%	45%	50%
1	.8621	.8475	.8333	.8197	.8065	.7937	.7813	.7692	.7576	.7463	.7353	.7246	.7143	.6897	.6667
2	.7432	.7182	.6944	.6719	.6504	.6299	.6104	.5917	.5739	.5569	.5407	.5251	.5102	.4756	.4444
3	.6407	.6086	.5787	.5507	.5245	.4999	.4768	.4552	.4348	.4155	.3975	.3805	.3644	.3280	.2963
4	.5523	.5158	.4823	.4514	.4230	.3968	.3725	.3501	.3294	.3102	.2923	.2757	.2603	.2262	.1975
5	.4761	.4371	.4019	.3700	.3411	.3149	.2910	.2693	.2495	.2315	.2149	.1998	.1859	.1560	.1317
6	.4104	.3704	.3349	.3033	.2751	.2499	.2274	.2072	.1890	.1727	.1580	.1448	.1328	.1076	.0878
7	.3538	.3139	.2791	.2486	.2218	.1983	.1776	.1594	.1432	.1289	.1162	.1049	.0949	.0742	.0585
8	.3050	.2660	.2326	.2038	.1789	.1574	.1388	.1226	.1085	.0962	.0854	.0760	.0678	.0512	.0390
9	.2630	.2255	.1938	.1670	.1443	.1249	.1084	.0943	.0822	.0718	.0628	.0551	.0484	.0353	.0260
10	.2267	.1911	.1615	.1369	.1164	.0992	.0847	.0725	.0623	.0536	.0462	.0399	.0346	.0243	.0173
11	.1954	.1619	.1346	.1122	.0938	.0787	.0662	.0558	.0472	.0400	.0340	.0289	.0247	.0168	.0116
12	.1685	.1372	.1122	.0920	.0757	.0625	.0517	.0429	.0357	.0298	.0250	.0210	.0176	.0116	.0077
13	.1452	.1163	.0935	.0754	.0610	.0496	.0404	.0330	.0271	.0223	.0184	.0152	.0126	.0080	.0051
14	.1252	.0985	.0779	.0618	.0492	.0393	.0316	.0253	.0205	.0166	.0135	.0110	.0090	.0055	.0034
15	.1079	.0835	.0649	.0507	.0397	.0312	.0247	.0195	.0155	.0124	.0099	.0080	.0064	.0038	.0023
16	.0930	.0708	.0541	.0415	.0320	.0248	.0193	.0150	.0118	.0093	.0073	.0058	.0046	.0026	.0015
17	.0802	.0600	.0451	.0340	.0258	.0197	.0150	.0116	.0089	.0069	.0054	.0042	.0033	.0018	.0010
18	.0691	.0508	.0376	.0279	.0208	.0156	.0118	.0089	.0068	.0052	.0039	.0030	.0023	.0012	.0007
19	.0596	.0431	.0313	.0229	.0168	.0124	.0092	.0068	.0051	.0038	.0029	.0022	.0017	.0009	.0005
20	.0514	.0365	.0261	.0187	.0135	.0098	.0072	.0053	.0039	.0029	.0021	.0016	.0012	.0006	.0003
21	.0443	.0309	.0217	.0154	.0109	.0078	.0056	.0040	.0029	.0021	.0016	.0012	.0009	.0004	.0002
22	.0382	.0262	.0181	.0126	.0088	.0062	.0044	.0031	.0022	.0016	.0012	.0008	.0006	.0003	.0001
23	.0329	.0222	.0151	.0103	.0071	.0049	.0034	.0024	.0017	.0012	.0008	.0006	.0004	.0002	.0001
24	.0284	.0188	.0126	.0085	.0057	.0039	.0027	.0018	.0013	.0009	.0006	.0004	.0003	.0001	.0001
25	.0245	.0160	.0105	.0069	.0046	.0031	.0021	.0014	.0010	.0007	.0005	.0003	.0002	.0001	.0000
26	.0211	.0135	.0087	.0057	.0037	.0025	.0016	.0011	.0007	.0005	.0003	.0002	.0002	.0001	
27	.0182	.0115	.0073	.0047	.0030	.0019	.0013	.0008	.0006	.0004	.0002	.0002	.0001	.0000	
28	.0157	.0097	.0061	.0038	.0024	.0015	.0010	.0006	.0004	.0003	.0002	.0001	.0001		
29	.0135	.0082	.0051	.0031	.0020	.0012	.0008	.0005	.0003	.0002	.0001	.0001	.0001		
30	.0116	.0070	.0042	.0026	.0016	.0010	.0006	.0004	.0002	.0002	.0001	.0001	.0000		
35	.0055	.0030	.0017	.0009	.0005	.0003	.0002	.0001	.0001	.0000	.0000	.0000			
40	.0026	.0013	.0007	.0004	.0002	.0001	.0001	.0000	.0000						
45	.0013	.0006	.0003	.0001	.0001	.0000									
50	.0006	.0003	.0001	.0000	.0000										

Figure 6-2. Present value of $1 received at end of *n* number of years.

n/r	1%	2%	3%	4%	5%	6%	7%	8%	9%	10%	11%	12%	13%	14%	15%
1	.9901	.9804	.9709	.9615	.9524	.9434	.9346	.9259	.9174	.9091	.9009	.8929	.8850	.8772	.8696
2	1.9704	1.9416	1.9135	1.8861	1.8594	1.8334	1.8080	1.7833	1.7591	1.7355	1.7125	1.6901	1.6681	1.6467	1.6257
3	2.9410	2.8839	2.8286	2.7751	2.7232	2.6730	2.6243	2.5771	2.5313	2.4869	2.4437	2.4018	2.3612	2.3216	2.2832
4	3.9020	3.8077	3.7171	3.6299	3.5459	3.4651	3.3872	3.3121	3.2397	3.1699	3.1024	3.0373	2.9745	2.9137	2.8550
5	4.8534	4.7135	4.5797	4.4518	4.3295	4.2124	4.1002	3.9927	3.8897	3.7908	3.6959	3.6048	3.5172	3.4331	3.3522
6	5.7955	5.6014	5.4172	5.2421	5.0757	4.9173	4.7665	4.6229	4.4859	4.3553	4.2305	4.1114	3.9975	3.8887	3.7845
7	6.7282	6.4720	6.2303	6.0020	5.7864	5.5824	5.3893	5.2064	5.0330	4.8684	4.7122	4.5638	4.4226	4.2883	4.1604
8	7.6517	7.3255	7.0197	6.7327	6.4632	6.2098	5.9713	5.7466	5.5348	5.3349	5.1461	4.9676	4.7988	4.6389	4.4873
9	8.5660	8.1622	7.7861	7.4353	7.1078	6.8017	6.5152	6.2469	5.9952	5.7590	5.5370	5.3282	5.1317	4.9464	4.7716
10	9.4713	8.9826	8.5302	8.1109	7.7217	7.3601	7.0236	6.7101	6.4177	6.1446	5.8892	5.6502	5.4262	5.2161	5.0188
11	10.3676	9.7868	9.2526	8.7605	8.3064	7.8869	7.4987	7.1390	6.8051	6.4951	6.2065	5.9377	5.6869	5.4527	5.2337
12	11.2551	10.5753	9.9540	9.3851	8.8632	8.3838	7.9427	7.5361	7.1607	6.8137	6.4924	6.1944	5.9176	5.6603	5.4206
13	12.1337	11.3484	10.6350	9.9856	9.3936	8.8527	8.3577	7.9038	7.4869	7.1034	6.7499	6.4235	6.1218	5.8424	5.5831
14	13.0037	12.1062	11.2961	10.5631	9.8986	9.2950	8.7455	8.2442	7.7862	7.3667	6.9819	6.6282	6.3025	6.0021	5.7245
15	13.8650	12.8493	11.9379	11.1184	10.3797	9.7122	9.1079	8.5595	8.0607	7.6061	7.1909	6.8109	6.4624	6.1422	5.8474
16	14.7179	13.5777	12.5611	11.6523	10.8378	10.1059	9.4466	8.8514	8.3126	7.8237	7.3792	6.9740	6.6039	6.2651	5.9542
17	15.5622	14.2919	13.1661	12.1657	11.2741	10.4773	9.7632	9.1216	8.5436	8.0216	7.5488	7.1196	6.7291	6.3729	6.0472
18	16.3983	14.9920	13.7535	12.6593	11.6896	10.8276	10.0591	9.3719	8.7556	8.2014	7.7016	7.2497	6.8399	6.4674	6.1280
19	17.2260	15.6785	14.3238	13.1339	12.0853	11.1581	10.3356	9.6036	8.9501	8.3649	7.8393	7.3658	6.9380	6.5504	6.1982
20	18.0455	16.3514	14.8775	13.5903	12.4622	11.4699	10.5940	9.8181	9.1285	8.5136	7.9633	7.4694	7.0248	6.6231	6.2593
21	18.8570	17.0112	15.4150	14.0292	12.8211	11.7641	10.8355	10.0168	9.2922	8.6487	8.0751	7.5620	7.1015	6.6870	6.3125
22	19.6604	17.6580	15.9369	14.4511	13.1630	12.0416	11.0612	10.2007	9.4424	8.7715	8.1757	7.6446	7.1695	6.7429	6.3587
23	20.4558	18.2922	16.4436	14.8568	13.4886	12.3034	11.2722	10.3711	9.5802	8.8832	8.2664	7.7184	7.2297	6.7921	6.3988
24	21.2434	18.9139	16.9355	15.2470	13.7986	12.5504	11.4693	10.5288	9.7066	8.9847	8.3481	7.7843	7.2829	6.8351	6.4338
25	22.0232	19.5235	17.4131	15.6221	14.0939	12.7834	11.6536	10.6748	9.8226	9.0770	8.4217	7.8431	7.3300	6.8729	6.4641
26	22.7952	20.1210	17.8768	15.9828	14.3752	13.0032	11.8258	10.8100	9.9290	9.1609	8.4881	7.8957	7.3717	6.9061	6.4906
27	23.5596	20.7069	18.3270	16.3296	14.6430	13.2105	11.9867	10.9352	10.0266	9.2372	8.5478	7.9426	7.4086	6.9352	6.5135
28	24.3164	21.2813	18.7641	16.6631	14.8981	13.4062	12.1371	11.0511	10.1161	9.3066	8.6016	7.9844	7.4412	6.9607	6.5335
29	25.0658	21.8444	19.1884	16.9837	15.1411	13.5907	12.2777	11.1584	10.1983	9.3696	8.6501	8.0218	7.4701	6.9830	6.5509
30	25.8077	22.3965	19.6004	17.2920	15.3724	13.7648	12.4090	11.2578	10.2737	9.4269	8.6938	8.0552	7.4957	7.0027	6.5660
31	26.5423	22.9377	20.0004	17.5885	15.5928	13.9291	12.5318	11.3498	10.3428	9.4790	8.7331	8.0850	7.5183	7.0199	6.5791
32	27.2696	23.4683	20.3888	17.8735	15.8027	14.0840	12.6466	11.4350	10.4062	9.5264	8.7686	8.1116	7.5383	7.0350	6.5905
33	27.9897	23.9886	20.7658	18.1476	16.0025	14.2302	12.7538	11.5139	10.4644	9.5694	8.8005	8.1354	7.5560	7.0482	6.6005
34	28.7027	24.4986	21.1318	18.4112	16.1929	14.3681	12.8540	11.5869	10.5178	9.6086	8.8293	8.1566	7.5717	7.0599	6.6091
35	29.4086	24.9986	21.4872	18.6646	16.3742	14.4982	12.9477	11.6546	10.5668	9.6442	8.8552	8.1755	7.5856	7.0700	6.6166
40	32.8347	27.3555	23.1148	19.7928	17.1591	15.0463	13.3317	11.9246	10.7574	9.7791	8.9511	8.2438	7.6344	7.1050	6.6418
45	36.0945	29.4902	24.5187	20.7200	17.7741	15.4558	13.6055	12.1084	10.8812	9.8628	9.0079	8.2825	7.6609	7.1232	6.6543
50	39.1961	31.4236	25.7298	21.4822	18.2559	15.7619	13.8007	12.2335	10.9617	9.9148	9.0417	8.3045	7.6752	7.1327	6.6605

n/r	16%	18%	20%	22%	24%	26%	28%	30%	32%	34%	36%	38%	40%	45%	50%
1	.8621	.8475	.8333	.8197	.8065	.7937	.7813	.7692	.7576	.7463	.7353	.7246	.7143	.6897	.6667
2	1.6052	1.5656	1.5278	1.4915	1.4568	1.4235	1.3916	1.3609	1.3315	1.3032	1.2760	1.2497	1.2245	1.1653	1.1111
3	2.2459	2.1743	2.1065	2.0422	1.9813	1.9234	1.8684	1.8161	1.7663	1.7188	1.6735	1.6302	1.5889	1.4933	1.4074
4	2.7982	2.6901	2.5887	2.4936	2.4043	2.3202	2.2410	2.1662	2.0957	2.0290	1.9658	1.9060	1.8492	1.7195	1.6049
5	3.2743	3.1272	2.9906	2.8636	2.7454	2.6351	2.5320	2.4356	2.3452	2.2604	2.1807	2.1058	2.0352	1.8755	1.7366
6	3.6847	3.4976	3.3255	3.1669	3.0205	2.8850	2.7594	2.6427	2.5342	2.4331	2.3388	2.2506	2.1680	1.9831	1.8244
7	4.0386	3.8115	3.6046	3.4155	3.2423	3.0833	2.9370	2.8021	2.6775	2.5620	2.4550	2.3555	2.2628	2.0573	1.8829
8	4.3436	4.0776	3.8372	3.6193	3.4212	3.2407	3.0758	2.9247	2.7860	2.6582	2.5404	2.4315	2.3306	2.1085	1.9220
9	4.6065	4.3030	4.0310	3.7863	3.5655	3.3657	3.1842	3.0190	2.8681	2.7300	2.6033	2.4866	2.3790	2.1438	1.9480
10	4.8332	4.4941	4.1925	3.9232	3.6819	3.4648	3.2689	3.0915	2.9304	2.7836	2.6495	2.5265	2.4136	2.1681	1.9053
11	5.0286	4.6560	4.3271	4.0354	3.7757	3.5435	3.3351	3.1473	2.9776	2.8236	2.6834	2.5555	2.4383	2.1849	1.9769
12	5.1971	4.7932	4.4392	4.1274	3.8514	3.6059	3.3868	3.1903	3.0133	2.8534	2.7084	2.5764	2.4559	2.1965	1.9845
13	5.3423	4.9095	4.5327	4.2028	3.9124	3.6555	3.4272	3.2233	3.0404	2.8757	2.7268	2.5916	2.4685	2.2045	1.9897
14	5.4675	5.0081	4.6106	4.2646	3.9616	3.6949	3.4587	3.2487	3.0609	2.8923	2.7403	2.6026	2.4775	2.2100	1.9931
15	5.5755	5.0916	4.6755	4.3152	4.0013	3.7261	3.4834	3.2682	3.0764	2.9047	2.7502	2.6106	2.4839	2.2138	1.9954
16	5.6685	5.1624	4.7296	4.3567	4.0333	3.7509	3.5026	3.2832	3.0882	2.9140	2.7575	2.6164	2.4885	2.2164	1.9970
17	5.7487	5.2223	4.7746	4.3908	4.0591	3.7705	3.5177	3.2948	3.0971	2.9209	2.7629	2.6206	2.4918	2.2182	1.9980
18	5.8178	5.2732	4.8122	4.4187	4.0799	3.7861	3.5294	3.3037	3.1039	2.9260	2.7668	2.6236	2.4941	2.2195	1.9986
19	5.8775	5.3162	4.8435	4.4415	4.0967	3.7985	3.5386	3.3105	3.1090	2.9299	2.7697	2.6258	2.4958	2.2203	1.9991
20	5.9288	5.3527	4.8696	4.4603	4.1103	3.8083	3.5458	3.3158	3.1129	2.9327	2.7718	2.6274	2.4970	2.2209	1.9994
21	5.9731	5.3837	4.8913	4.4756	4.1212	3.8161	3.5514	3.3198	3.1158	2.9349	2.7734	2.6285	2.4979	2.2213	1.9996
22	6.0113	5.4099	4.9094	4.4882	4.1300	3.8223	3.5558	3.3230	3.1180	2.9365	2.7746	2.6294	2.4985	2.2216	1.9997
23	6.0442	5.4321	4.9245	4.4985	4.1371	3.8273	3.5592	3.3253	3.1197	2.9377	2.7754	2.6300	2.4989	2.2218	1.9998
24	6.0726	5.4509	4.9371	4.5070	4.1428	3.8312	3.5619	3.3272	3.1210	2.9386	2.7760	2.6304	2.4992	2.2219	1.9999
25	6.0971	5.4669	4.9476	4.5139	4.1474	3.8342	3.5640	3.3286	3.1220	2.9392	2.7765	2.6307	2.4994	2.2220	1.9999
26	6.1182	5.4804	4.9563	4.5196	4.1511	3.8367	3.5656	3.3297	3.1227	2.9397	2.7768	2.6310	2.4996	2.2221	1.9999
27	6.1364	5.4919	4.9636	4.5243	4.1542	3.8387	3.5669	3.3305	3.1233	2.9401	2.7771	2.6311	2.4997	2.2221	2.0000
28	6.1520	5.5016	4.9697	4.5281	4.1566	3.8402	3.5679	3.3312	3.1237	2.9404	2.7773	2.6313	2.4998	2.2222	2.0000
29	6.1656	5.5098	4.9747	4.5312	4.1585	3.8414	3.5687	3.3316	3.1240	2.9406	2.7774	2.6313	2.4999	2.2222	2.0000
30	6.1772	5.5168	4.9789	4.5338	4.1601	3.8424	3.5693	3.3321	3.1242	2.9407	2.7775	2.6314	2.4999	2.2222	2.0000
31	6.1872	5.5227	4.9824	4.5359	4.1614	3.8432	3.5697	3.3324	3.1244	2.9408	2.7776	2.6315	2.4999	2.2222	2.0000
32	6.1959	5.5277	4.9854	4.5376	4.1624	3.8438	3.5701	3.3326	3.1246	2.9409	2.7776	2.6315	2.4999	2.2222	2.0000
33	6.2034	5.5320	4.9878	4.5390	4.1632	3.8443	3.5704	3.3328	3.1247	2.9410	2.7777	2.6315	2.5000	2.2222	2.0000
34	6.2098	5.5356	4.9898	4.5402	4.1639	3.8447	3.5706	3.3329	3.1248	2.9410	2.7777	2.6315	2.5000	2.2222	2.0000
35	6.2153	5.5386	4.9915	4.5411	4.1644	3.8450	3.5708	3.3330	3.1248	2.9411	2.7777	2.6315	2.5000	2.2222	2.0000
40	6.2335	5.5482	4.9966	4.5439	4.1659	3.8458	3.5712	3.3332	3.1250	2.9412	2.7778	2.6316	2.5000	2.2222	2.0000
45	6.2421	5.5523	4.9986	4.5449	4.1664	3.8460	3.5714	3.3333	3.1250	2.9412	2.7778	2.6316	2.5000	2.2222	2.0000
50	6.2463	5.5541	4.9995	4.5452	4.1666	3.8461	3.5714	3.3333	3.1250	2.9412	2.7778	2.6316	2.5000	2.2222	2.0000

Figure 6-3. Present value of $1 received annually at end of year for n years.

Savings

Labor savings = ($1300)(7.0236) $9130.68

Note the difference. Since $9130.68 in savings is less than our costs of $9265.85, even considering the salvage value, we should not buy the machine, after all. In this example, the difference changed from a savings of $3500 in buying the machine to a loss of $135.17. Larger investments or different percentages of interest considered would show even greater differences. For example, instead of putting your money in the bank at 7% interest, what if you put it into advertising and your ROI is 15%? Instead of the 7% column, you would use the one that reads 15%. You might want to do this using 15% as an exercise, just to make sure you understand how to do it. If you do, you will find that your costs less salvage are $8940.65, while your savings of $1300 per year brought to the present are only $6524.44. This means that you would really be losing $2416.21 ($8940.65 − $6424.44) if you made this investment. So keep this capital budgeting concept in mind before you make any major investment, and use Figures 6-2 and 6-3 to help you make the right decision.

MAIL ORDER BUSINESS EXPENSES

Here is a list of expenses common to the mail order business. Use it in your business planning before you start, and also to help you include all of your investments when calculating your ROI.

Product Costs
1. Amount paid to supplier for product
2. Manufacturing costs if you make product yourself
3. Printing costs if product is a course, manual, or book
4. Packaging costs
5. Shipping costs for raw materials or the product to be shipped to you from supplier
6. Postage cost to your customers
7. Allowance for damage or return by customer (I usually start with a 5% figure here until I can calculate my costs for this product from actual experience)
8. Allowance for bad checks (I usually start by assuming I'll have about 5% in bad checks and then correct my figures based on actual experience)
9. Storage costs

Typical Overhead Expenses

1. Automobile
2. Insurance
3. Licenses
4. Office rent
5. Office supplies, including stationery
6. Professional services (accountant, attorney, etc.)
7. Salaries
8. Taxes
9. Telephone
10. Utilities, including gas, water, and electricity

Advertising Expenses

1. Advertising agency
2. Addressing and stuffing envelopes
3. Copyrighting
4. Mailing list rental
5. Media advertising
6. Photography and artwork
7. Postage
8. Printing
9. Typesetting

You may not have all of these expenses. You may not want to use the services of an advertising agency. In fact, later in the book I will show you how to save 15% on all of your advertising by setting up your own in-house advertising agency. But these lists include many expenses you might overlook, and you should consider them before proceeding.

SUMMARY

In this chapter we've gone into some very important calculations that can affect the profitability and success or failure of your business. These included:

Breakeven both for your business and on a project basis
Calculating breakeven graphically
Breakeven for the two-step offer
The profitability formula

Calculating number of replies to breakeven on an ad, considering back-end profits

The ROI concept and how to calculate ROI

How to do capital budgeting when making major investment decisions

All of these concepts and calculations are important. Come back to this chapter and refer to it whenever you need to make profit or cost calculations in your business.

7

How to Develop a Marketing Plan That Works

A marketing plan can be extremely important in your mail order business for any new product or project you are about to start. Yet many mail order operators neglect the marketing plan, or, at best, formulate a half-baked one that does not consider all the various aspects that are important for success. Some indication of how important marketing plans are is the fact that if you were to have someone else create the marketing plan that I am going to show you how to develop in this chapter, it would cost you somewhere between $500 and $5000. In fact, one firm with which we are familiar does nothing but develop marketing plans for small companies. It does them by mail and receives incredible sums for every plan it develops for its clients.

A marketing plan is very important because it does some very important things for you.

1. It acts as a road map.
2. It assists you with management control.
3. It helps you in briefing new employees and other personnel.
4. It helps you to obtain financing.

Let's look at each of these in turn. A marketing plan acts as a road map in getting you from where you are now to where you want to be: successful, profitable, and making lots of money from the product you are thinking of introducing. Now, if you were traveling from your home to somewhere you had never been before, it could be very difficult for you to find the place if you didn't consult a road map. This is exactly what the marketing plan does for you. Regardless of how long you have been in business, you have never been to exactly this place, where you want to go with the new product. The marketing plan acts as your road map and guide, and it takes you step by step until you finally reach your goal.

MANAGEMENT CONTROL

Along with being a road map, the marketing plan acts as a tool that allows you, as a manager, to control your progress. It is a fact that nothing will go exactly as planned. However, the fact that you have a complete plan laid out and documented will allow you to see the exact differences between what is happening and what you have planned and intended to happen to reach your goal. But more than that, the marketing plan will assist you in returning to the proper course to reach the goal you have decided upon.

BRIEFING NEW EMPLOYEES AND OTHER PERSONNEL

As a small businessperson, you may work alone, with a small number of other people, or with many other people. Regardless, at some point in your progress toward your ultimate goal of success with this mail order product, you will want to brief someone else about what you are doing and those tasks you wish him or her to do or become involved with. If you have everything documented in a marketing plan, this is a relatively easy task. You can brief suppliers, new employees, or even a spouse as to not only where you are going, but how you plan to get there and how you want them to help.

OBTAINING FINANCING

As was mentioned earlier, you may need financing at some point in the growth and development of your mail order company. If so, a full business plan will assist you greatly in getting it, whether it be from the Small Business Administration, a bank, or a venture capitalist. A marketing plan is the heart of a good business plan and with some additions, as noted in Appendix C, you can use your marketing plan as the basis of your business plan to help you in acquiring the capital that you will need.

Not long ago, Roy Abrams spoke to a group of professional mail order people who were taking New York University's Extension Course in Direct Marketing. Roy Abrams had held senior positions in a variety of large direct mail and mail order companies, including such positions as senior vice president of the Longines Symphonette, director of merchandising at American Express, and vice president of merchandising at Columbia House. Here's what Roy Abrams said about the marketing plan: "Whether in a small com pany or a large company, the marketing plan is important because in today's business environment, every profitable dollar must be squeezed out of every market and every medium. The road to doing this is to develop a full marketing plan."

THE MARKETING PLAN'S STRUCTURE

Now let's take a look at the structure of a marketing plan. What are the secrets that would require you to spend $500, $5000, or more if you were to pay someone else to develop your plan? Look at Figure 7-1. This is a complete outline of a full marketing plan for a mail order direct mail business. If you complete every one of the four sections, you will have gone a

---

I.   General situation and background for project
    A. Demand
        1. Need for product
        2. Extent of need
    B. Target market
    C. Competition
    D. Unique advantages over your competition
    E. Legal restrictions
    F. Problems and opportunities
    G. Other important situational variables

II. Strategy
    A. Objectives
    B. Product strategy
    C. Price strategy
    D. Distribution strategy
    E. Promotional strategy
        1. Offer
        2. Media
        3. Creativity (graphics and copy)

III. Financial plans

IV. Strategy implementation time schedule

Figure 7-1. An outline of a mail order marketing plan.

long way toward insuring your success with the new product or product line you are introducing.

In the first section, *General situation and background for the project,* are several factors you must analyze: demand, your target market, competition, unique advantages, legal restrictions, if any, problems, opportunities, and other situational variables that you feel are important.

Demand

Under *Demand,* you should note how strong the need is for this new product and also what need the product is satisfying. Remember that products satisfy psychological needs, as conceptualized by Maslow, and are not necessarily purchased for the obvious use of the product. I recently bought a brass case for carrying my business cards from an ad I saw in the *Wall Street Journal.* The manufacturer engraved my initials on the side of the case at no extra charge. Did I buy the case only to carry my business cards, or does my need for status fit in here somewhere? You should also note, under *Demand,* the extent of this need. This means both how strong the need is that will be fulfilled by your product, and also whether it will be satisfied again and again by repeated purchases of your product or a follow-up product, and whether the demand is a short-lived fad or a long-term need that will enable your product to have a long life cycle.

Target Market

Usually, the larger your market potential target is, the better. But there are several strategies you might follow, and it may be advantageous to offer your product only to a certain segment of the total potential market. This is called market segmentation, and it offers you a major advantage. You can concentrate all your resources against this specific segment and be stronger against it than your competition can be if it spreads its advertisements through publications read by every single potential customer who may be even remotely interested in your proposition. An example was a book I wrote called *The Executive's Guide to Finding a Superior Job,* which was published byAMACOM in 1978. This book was segmented in two ways. First, it is a book on job finding and is therefore not of interest to everyone, but only to people who are looking for a job. Secondly, because I used the word *executive* in the title, I segmented my market again to concentrate only on the target market of people who considered themselves to be in decision-making roles. Now, you may think that this segmentation could have an adverse effect since it reduced the total growth size of the market to which I was appealing. However, *The Executive's Guide to Finding a Superior Job* was a tremendous success with this segmentation strategy. Within three years, the book went into four printings and recently came out in a new edition. So consider the target market to which you are offering your product and describe it fully in your marketing plan. The selection of a target market in itself can help your product to be successful.

Competition

Regardless of the product you offer, you will always have competition, even if the competition does not offer exactly the same product or service, but sells a product that fills the same need. Look at the ordinary bicycle. If you sell bicycles, your competition may be not only other bicycle manufacturers or sellers or distributors, but also, since it is in part a recreational vehicle, firms that provide other forms of recreation. In the same way, when hand-held calculators came out in the early 1970s, priced at approximately $200, and had relatively limited functions, their competition was not only other manufacturers of these new electronic calculating devices, but also the manufacturers of the traditional slide rules, which were then selling for as much as $100. Even though the products were not identical, for some people, they filled the same need.

When you consider your competition, you should also consider the fact that your competition will not remain static. If you introduce a new product into the marketplace that competes with a product that is already there, you can bet that if you are successful, you will not be ignored. Your competition will then initiate some other strategy to try to overcome your success. If you introduce a successful new product that competes against a similar product already in the marketplace, you might expect your competition to do something with the price, to change the offer, or perhaps to change its advertising in some way. So when you formulate the portion of your marketing plan having to do with competition, think ahead, just as a chess or checkers player must plan ahead. Think about what your competition is going to do next, and what you might have to do in response.

Unique Advantages You Have

Your firm is not the same as my firm or any other mail order firm in existence. You, as an individual, and therefore your firm, as well, have certain unique advantages. These may be knowledge of a certain industry, a price break you are able to offer because you are obtaining the product more cheaply than your competition can or because you are producing the product yourself, engineering knowledge, certain financial knowledge, certain unique connections. These advantages may be any of a thousand different things, and they will add greatly to your chances of success with your product. It is important to write these advantages down in your marketing plan to make certain that you do not overlook them and that you exploit them to the maximum. Spend some time thinking about this particular part of the marketing plan because many advantages you may take for granted are, in fact, not enjoyed by anyone else in your marketplace. If you ignore these advantages, it will be as if they did not exist. But if you use them, you may have something that your competition does not have and is unable to get.

Legal Restrictions

Legal restrictions do not always exist. But when they do, it is important to consider them, esecially if you are dealing with a product related to drugs or one controlled by a federal regulatory agency. If you have such a product, be certain to contact the agency, find out about possible license requirements and restrictions, and write these restrictions into your plan.

Problems and Opportunities

Problems and opportunities are different sides of the same coin. Very frequently when you note a problem, you will also see that within this problem lies an opportunity for success. Listerine mouthwash has a rather harsh taste—in the words of the competition, "mediciney." However, Listerine has managed to make this "problem" into an "opportunity" because the company realized that many people feel that if mouthwash does have a harsh taste, it may be harsher on germs, whereas a mouthwash that tastes sweet or, in the words in one advertisement, "like soda pop," may not be killing germs as well. List every problem, as well as the opportunity the problem may present.

Situational Variables

The final part of the first section should include other important situational variables unique to your particular product. They may relate to the fact that the product is seasonal, good only for the Christmas or Thanksgiving holidays, or perhaps during the summer heat wave. Or, they may include the fact that current business conditions favor or do not favor the introduction of the product. In any case, you should not stop with the variables I have listed in Figure 7-1 but should proceed to list and analyze other important variables that have an impact on your introducing this new product or service.

STRATEGY

The next section listed in Figure 7-1 is *Strategy,* under which we have objectives, product strategy, price strategy, promotional strategy, and distribution strategy.

Objectives

Objectives are very important because, remembering that your marketing plan is a road map, the road map must be focused on reaching a specific destination. The destination is the objectives listed under this part of the strategy section of your plan. These include the volume you wish to sell over the lifetime of the product, the volume you forecast selling on a yearly basis, and profit goals you may desire to reach. There may be other goals you intend to achieve by the introduction of this product. For example, if the product is totally unique and offers something in fulfilling the psychological need that cannot be fulfilled by any other product, perhaps you are going to try to capture the majority share of the market. If so, you should specify that here under *Objectives.* Your objectives for testing should also be listed.

Product Strategy

Product strategy is obviously very important. There are three basic things you can do with any product: introduce it, drop it, or change it. Each of these possibilities has an important impact on profitability, and you might consider each for inclusion in your marketing plan. However, we are going to focus here on your product introduction. I suppose this is as good a spot as any to point out that estimates of new product failure run as high as 90%: That means that nine out of every 10 new products introduced into the marketplace fail. They fail for a variety of reasons, including lack of knowledge by the introducer, failure to develop a marketing plan, and failure to do many of the things found in this chapter and elsewhere in this book. The bottom line is that many new products fail even with the best intent and wishes of those who introduce them.

Now, since most new products fail, you may wonder why you should bother to introduce a new product at all. Why can't you find one product or a couple of products that are successful, stay with them, and make your money with them in the future? In some cases this is possible. But in most cases, it is not, because of what is called the product life cycle, shown in Figure 7-2.

According to this concept, every product goes through a number of stages, which may be named differently, but which all mean essentially the same thing. First, a product goes through an introduction and growth stage. Then it becomes mature and the market becomes saturated. Finally, the product goes into decline. In Figure 7-2, you will see two curves. One shows profit margins. You can see that, as the product progresses from introduction into growth and maturity, the profit margins increase. But then, sometime in the maturity stage, profit margins begin to decline. The sales volume curve, however, does not follow the profit margin curve exactly. The sales volume continues to rise, even as profit margins begin to go down. This happens because, even though sales are increasing, competition is entering the market and the product is becoming obsolete. There may be considerable price competition as the market becomes saturated with the product. What this means is that if you want your firm to continue to be profitable, you must continue to introduce new products. You cannot be satisfied with one profitable "winner."

Another useful product strategy you can employ is called product differentiation. Using this product strategy, while you continue to satisfy the needs of your customers with a product similar to that offered by your competitors, you differentiate your product from theirs by its unique advantages. These advantages may be almost anything. They may have to do with the fact that your product is personalized with the buyer's name, initials, or picture and your competitor's product is not personalized. Or they may have to do with the performance of your product, your product's quality or reliability. Whatever advantages you

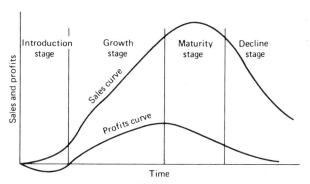

Figure 7-2. The product life cycle.

choose to promote, differentiating your product from that of your competition can work very effectively to increase your sales and profits.

Another product strategy you can adopt for an older product is a product extension strategy. In other words, you already have—and have had for some time—a product in the marketplace, and it has begun to go into the saturation and decline stage of the product life cycle. The product extension strategy can breathe new life into it as if it were a new product in the introduction stage. To employ a product extension strategy, you must find some way of extending its life. One way is to find a completely new use for the product, which can mean an entirely different market. An example is Arm and Hammer baking soda. For years people used baking soda for baking only (that's what it's made for, isn't it?), but some years ago Arm and Hammer got a fantastic idea for extending the product life cycle. The company advertised the use of baking soda to absorb odors in refrigerators. Did this extend the life of this product? You bet it did. A good example of product extension in mail order products is that done by *Moneysworth,* that incredibly successful newsletter in newspaper format published by Ralph Ginzburg. Ginzburg has a column called "The Steal of the Month." And the steal is usually a book that has been published by one of the larger publishers, which Ginzburg has obtained at closeout prices because the product is in the decline stage of it's life cycle. Ginzburg describes the book in his column in brand new terms, listing advantages that appeal to the totally new market represented by *Moneysworth.* Further, he offers these books at a tremendous discount. You can bet that Ginzburg sells lots of books through this product extension strategy. As a result, this successful formula has been copied in Ginzburg's other publications, *American Business* and *Better Living,* as well as by many imitators.

Price Strategy

Development of a price strategy should never be overlooked in mail order, and naturally, it too goes into your marketing plan. Basically, you can price high or low or you can meet the competition's price. Pricing strategy has to be considered carefully because the price that you select has an important effect on the image of the product or service that you are offering. This image helps to determine your market and whether your product will be successful. High price is frequently called a price-skimming strategy. It is very effective because if you are first to the marketplace with your new product, you can charge high because you have no competition. As competition enters the marketplace at a lower price, you reduce your price to meet your competition and use the increased financial resources you have to expand your advertising and maintain your share of the marketplace. Or, in some cases, you can actually raise your price, positioning your product as "top of the line" over your competitor's product.

A low price is basically a penetration strategy and is usually effective when your competition is already established in the marketplace, and your product isn't very different from your competitor's product. To get in and take part of your competition's business away, you must give your potential customers a reason to buy from you. One reason is low price. However, there are some problems with low price, and one of them is that if your competition has followed a skimming strategy, it now has the financial resources to turn around and do to you what I said you could do to it if you were first in the marketplace.

A "meet the competition" price is simply going in at the same price as your competition with a similar or identical product or service. If you do this you must follow a product differentiation strategy or offer something unique. Otherwise, why should customers turn from the competition and buy from you? There is no reason to when either the customer is already buying successfully from your competition, or your competition has already established a name in the marketplace. I believe this to be one of the main reasons that Joe Karbo's competitors generally have not been successful with a very similar product. Joe had already established himself in the marketplace, and at the same or a similar price, a potential customer would rather buy from the original.

I have said this to you before, and I will continue to say it throughout this book: *Testing is the heart of mail order.* This is especially true of price, regardless of what basic strategy you have decided to use. Some years ago I introduced a price of $19.95 for a set of four books on how to write for publication. At $19.95, the product was reasonably successful. Thinking to increase the number of sales, I tested other prices, $14.95 and lower. To my amazement, I discovered that as I reduced the price, the number of sales actually went down! Wouldn't you have thought that I would sell more books at a lower price? I quickly returned to my successful $19.95 price. In analyzing these tests, I decided that the reason for the phenomenon was the fact that there were many courses in writing for publication selling for $50 or more, but none between $19.95 and $50. On the other hand, below my price of $19.95, the next competitor's price was $10 for a short booklet. I believe that at $19.95 my books were perceived as a bargain, compared with the $50 to $200 courses. However, at $14.95 or less, my product was compared with the booklet offered at $10 and it was considered a very expensive $10 item.

Promotional Strategy

Promotional strategy includes three of the four essentials for mail order, discussed earlier: The product, the offer, the medium, and the creative package. Remember that the offer has to do with how you present your deal to the prospective customer. Two for $1, one for $1 and one free, one for 99¢ and the second for 1¢—all are the same deal presented in a different way. In this section you should list the different offers that you anticipate trying, along with the different prices you are going to test according to the price strategy you decided on earlier.

Magazines, television, and radio are all examples of advertising media. Which magazines, television channels, or radio stations to choose comprises the second part of medium selection. The order of selection is also part of our strategy. See chapter 9 for more details on how we will pyramid our advertising logically, greatly enhancing our chances of success.

The third part of our promotional strategy has to do with creativity, which includes the graphics and the copy we are going to use to advertise our mail order or direct mail product. At the time of developing the marketing plan, we may or may not have the graphics and copy already prepared. However, we should at least indicate the general style of graphics and copy that will be used, or, if it is a direct mail package, exactly what the elements of that direct mail package will be. We will get into this in later chapters.

Distribution Strategy

You may think that a distribution strategy is unnecessary. We're going to distribute through mail order, aren't we? However, there are many possibilities here.

If we manufacture the product ourselves, we may send the product right from our own home. If we have bought the product wholesale, in quantity, we could do the same thing. If someoone else makes the product, we could have them drop-ship for us, which means we send them the name of the customer along with the wholesale price we have agreed upon, and the manufacturer sends the product to the customer. Or maybe we don't want to sell direct to the final customer, but want to wholesale or drop-ship ourselves. Or we could sell through agents. Or we could sell through some combination of these methods. All can work to make you rich. There is no one best distribution strategy. Brainerd Mellinger has sold direct, drop-shipped, and wholesaled to customers all over the world; Joe Sugarman sells his electronic products direct; Joe Cossman sold millions of ant farms, imitation shrunken heads, Potato Spud Guns, and a host of other unusual products mainly through wholesaling to mail order houses. Whatever your method of distribution strategy, this is the time to think it through and document it in your marketing plan.

FINANCIAL PLANNING

Section 3 of the marketing plan is *Financial plans,* and in Figure 7-3, you will see actual forms you may use for your own marketing plan for this section. Basically, what we are doing in the *Financial plans* section is noting every single action and task we must accomplish to introduce our

PROJECTED INCOME STATEMENT

Months after Starting Business

	1	2	3	4	5	6	7	8	9	10	11	12
Total net sales												
Cost of sales												
Gross profit												
Expenses (controllable)												
Salaries												
Payroll taxes												
Advertising												
Automobile												
Dues and subscriptions												
Enterainment												
Legal and accounting												
Office supplies												
Telephone												
Utilities												
Miscellaneous												
Total												
Expenses (fixed)												
Depreciation												
Insurance												
Rent												
Taxes and licenses												
Loan payments												
Total												
NET PROFIT (OR LOSS) (before taxes)												

Figure 7-3.   Financial forms for your marketing plan.

CASH FLOW PROJECTIONS

Months after Starting Business

	Start-up or prior to loan	1	2	3	4	5	6	7	8	9	10	11	12	TOTAL
Cash (beginning of month)														
Cash on hand														
Cash in bank														
Cash in investments														
Total cash														
Income (during month)														
Cash sales														
Credit sales payments														
Investment income														
Loans														
Other cash income														
Total Income														
TOTAL CASH AND INCOME														
Expenses (during month)														
Inventory or new material														
Wages (including owner's)														
Taxes														
Equipment expense														
Overhead														
Selling expense														
Transportation														
Loan repayment														
Other cash expenses														
TOTAL EXPENSES														
CASH FLOW EXCESS (end of month)														
CASH FLOW CUMULATIVE (monthly)														

Figure 7-3. (Continued)

157

BALANCE SHEET
(Project at Start-up and After One Year)

	YEAR 1	YEAR 2
Current assets		
Cash	$ _____	$ _____
Accounts receivable	_____	_____
Inventory	_____	_____
Fixed assets		
Real estate	_____	_____
Fixtures and equipment	_____	_____
Vehicles	_____	_____
Other assets		
License	_____	_____
Good will	_____	_____
TOTAL ASSETS	$ _____	$ _____
Current liabilities		
Notes payable (due within 1 year)	$ _____	$ _____
Accounts payable	_____	_____
Accrued expenses	_____	_____
Taxes owed	_____	_____
Long-term liabilities		
Notes payable (due after 1 year)	_____	_____
Other	_____	_____
TOTAL LIABILITIES	$ _____	$ _____
NET WORTH (ASSETS minus LIABILITIES)	$ _____	$ _____

TOTAL LIABILITIES plus NET WORTH should equal ASSETS

Figure 7-3.   (Continued)

new product into the marketplace and make it profitable, and what each action and task will cost, along with what we anticipate it will bring in sales. We may also include a breakeven analysis in this section, as illustrated in an earlier chapter, and use some of the techniques described to calculate breakeven or profitability for a particular magazine advertisement or series of advertisements.

STRATEGY IMPLEMENTATION TIME SCHEDULE

Section IV of the marketing plan is *Strategy implementation time schedule.* An outline is shown in Figure 7-4. The strategy implementation time schedule is extremely important, so that you will know when you are supposed to do what. Writing down every action and task you must do as a part of your plan will help you remember everything essential and will

Weeks After Project Initiation

TASK	1	2	3	4	5	6	7	8	9	10	11	12	13	14	15	16	17	18	19	20	21	22	23	24	25	26	27
Prepare classified copy	↑																										
Place first ad		↑																									
Order product for test		↑																									
Prepare and order follow-on material			↑																								
Product inventory received					↑																						
Follow-on material received					↑																						
First ad appears								↑																			
Send follow-on material									↑																		
Profitability forecast											↑																
Additional ads placed													↑														
Additional product inventory ordered													↑														
Additional follow-on material ordered													↑														
Product inventory received															↑												
Follow-on material received															↑												
Additional ads appear																				↑							
Send follow-on material																											↑

Figure 7-4. Strategy implementation time schedule.

159

also act as a reminder as to when to do it. Figure 7-4 is an example only. Use the same general outline for your plan, and write down exactly which action the plan will require, month by month.

SUMMARY

The marketing plan is very important for your success in this business. With it, you will enhance your chances of succeeding because

1. You will have a road map to tell you exactly where to go and when you should be at each point along the road.
2. You will be able to check constantly to see how you are progressing against what you have planned to do. If there are problems, you can then take the necessry action to solve them and still proceed toward your goal.
3. When you must brief and talk to other people regarding what you are doing in your mail order business, you will be able to use your marketing plan or parts of it. In this way it will be clear in their minds how the part they play fits into your overall picture.

Appendix C contains a sample marketing plan that will help you in developing your own.

8

How to Make Money with Classified Ads

Classified ads are found in thousands of newspapers and magazines. They represent a great medium for the beginner as well as the experienced professional in mail order. But a classified ad cannot be used for all products or in every situation, and in this chapter we are going to examine both when to use a classified ad and when not to, along with the advantages and disadvantages or using them. I am also going to tell you how to use a classified ad for maximum effectiveness, as well as how to construct a classified ad, how to write one, how to pick the right medium to place it in, how to classify the ad, how to minimize your costs and maximize your profits through a sound strategy of pyramiding, and how to make additional money through the inquiries received in your classified ads. I am going to give you 10 proved ways to increase your classified ad results dynamically. Finally, I am going to share with you the full details of a classified ad strategy used by the author. To understand when and when not to use classified advertising in your business, it is necessary to look at the advantages and disadvantages of using a classified ad. Let's look at the advantages first.

ADVANTAGES

Low Cost

The cost of classified advertising is extremely low when compared with that of direct mail, space advertising or electronic media. A classified advertisement in *Specialty Salesmen and Business Opportunities,* a magazine read by what are known as "opportunity seekers," currently costs $2.10 a word, as opposed to up to several thousand dollars for a display advertisement in the same magazine. This cost difference between classified and display or space advertising is typical for all other magazines used by mail order dealers. In fact, classified advertising today is perhaps the only method of mail order advertising in which an advertiser can advertise his or her product or service for much less than $100 in just about any mail order magazine.

Highest Profitability

Classified advertising usually offers a mail order dealer the highest profitability potential of any form of mail order advertising. This means that, for every dollar spent, classifieds will bring far more profit in return than dollars spent in display advertising or for direct mail or other media utilized. Ron Playle, who has used classified advertising almost exclusively in the sale of several self-published booklets, including one entitled *Thirty Thousand Dollars Worth of Classified Results,* says, "Dollar for dollar, they will produce more inquiries and sales than any other method." If this is true, you may wonder why you should not use classified advertising exclusively. The answer, which I will explain in detail in this chapter, has to do with the limitation of the size of your market if you use only classified. But for practicality, classified is the unchallenged winner!

A Good Way to Start Your Business

Classified advertising, because it does offer such a high profitability potential at low investment, is a good place to start your business in mail order. Melvin Powers says that classified is "one of the lowest and least expensive ways of getting started." Eric Weinstein, who built a million-dollar mail order business in less than eight months at the age of 23, says this about classified ads: "You don't have to be a brilliant copywriter and you are not risking thousands of dollars every time you advertise."

You may wonder whether any large companies started in this way. *Popular Mechanics,* a magazine that has a great many classified mail order ads, publishes a small booklet called *Profits from Classified Advertising,* which mentions an ad that appeared way back in 1913 in *Popular Mechanics* under the heading of *Agents.* It read as follows: "We are the largest manufacturers of Twisted Wire Brushes in America, highest grade goods, best service, highest profit. Write for our new catalog. You are sure to win." Who placed this small classified advertisement in 1913? None other than the Fuller Brush Company, which went on to sell millions of dollars worth of brushes through salespeople. But the company started with this small classified advertisement.

No Need for Layout or Artwork

With display or space advertisement and in direct mail, professionally prepared artwork and layout are essential. This means additional cost and additional delay in planning and getting ready for your promotional campaign. The allocation of these resources and the delay are unnecessary in classified. You can easily write the ad yourself, and a professional artist or other specialist is not required to prepare the ad for you.

A Good Medium for Test

Because of classified advertising's low costs, it is a very good medium in which to test a new product or service, either directly or through use of the two-step inquiry and follow-up method. You can do your tests for just a few dollars and, if profitable, not only expand the number of magazines in which you place your classified ad, but also expand into display, direct, or other more expensive mail order advertising media for additional profits.

Building Up Your Inquiry List

Lists of potential customers are critical for a mail order business. Your house list, which consists of those people who have responded to your ads, is very important for your company, both for your use as a list of individuals interested in the type of product or service you have to offer, and also, as we will talk about later, for you to rent to others and make significant profits from this rental. Classified advertising offers a good, quick way to build up your list of names of house customers.

Useful Adjunct to Display Advertising

Even those firms that have already "arrived" and are doing millions and millions of dollars worth of business in mail order still advertise in classified. Why is this? Well, one reason is that it is a useful adjunct to a display ad. Classified attracts people who are looking for a specific item under a specific classification, as opposed to a display ad, which attracts the usual passers-by. As a result, a classified advertisement, placed precisely under a certain heading, will draw people who are sometimes missed by your display ad. Many advertisers use a classified advertisement to refer to their larger display ad: "Look for our display ad on page 20." For just a few dollars more, your display advertisement is made much more effective.

Hot Prospects

Because your customers must actually be looking for your type of ad, not just stumble across it as is the case for a display or a space advertisement, or be targeted as in a direct mail campaign, the inquiries you receive from a classified advertisement are frequently of higher quality. These are people who are actually interested in the product or service you are advertising. You can believe that people who read the classified section under the heading *Hypnotism* are actually interested in that subject.

Lower Drop-off

As you advertise in any medium month after month, there is a drop-off as your ad is seen by more of the readers of that particular magazine. However, with classified ads, the drop-off is lower, and the reason relates to the fact that a much smaller percentage of total readership sees your ad in any one month than is the case with a display advertisement.

DISADVANTAGES

Though you can make good money with classified advertising, there are disadvantages to using it, and recognizing these disadvantages before you start your campaign can save you money.

Not Every Product Can Be Sold

In the first place, you cannot sell every type of product that can be sold by mail through a classified advertisement. Classified advertising does not give you very much space to describe your product, so your potential customer must already be familiar with the sort of product it is before he or she sees the ad. This is the main reason that if any product is sold directly from classified advertising, it usually consists of information.

You cannot sell expensive items directly through classified advertisements. Many beginners make this mistake. They hear of the huge profit potential in classified advertisements and so they attempt to sell a relatively high-priced item in just a few words through a classified ad. A little reflection will indicate just how impossible this is. One of the most successful ads ever written was Joe Karbo's advertisement for his book, *The Lazy Man's Way to Riches*. Yet it takes somewhere between one-third and a full page to tell Joe Karbo's story and to sell this $10 book. The same goes for Mark O. Haroldsen's $10 book and other books selling for similar amounts. Now, if it takes Joe Karbo or Mark O. Haroldsen a third of a page or more to tell his story and sell a $10 item, and these two ads are among the most successful ads ever written for this type of mail order product, how can you possibly sell your product, costing $10 or so, in just a few words? The answer is, you cannot. In fact, you will probably be unsuccessful in selling a product directly from any classified advertisement. Therefore, I recommend that you use the two-step method, which I've discussed earlier and which I will talk about a little later in this chapter.

Limited to Low Volume

I mentioned this earlier when I talked about the profitability of classified advertising. Yes, you get more bang for the buck, more return on your invested dollar than any other means of mail order advertising, but the problem is that you just cannot reach your entire market by using classified. Ron Playle, a successful classified advertiser who advertised a single product intensively for five years, from 1972 to 1977, was able to locate only 35 magazines that could carry his product, even though he spent $30,000 in advertising. We will talk a little more about Ron Playle's experience in a moment. Now I just want you to realize that here was a successful advertiser who spent sufficient money and was making good profit, but 35 magazines were all he could find to carry his ad profitably.

Limited Space to Tell Your Story and Sell

One thing that you should always remember when you're talking about mail order is that it is selling, just as if it were face to face or through any other means. To sell, you must be able to communicate your story so that your prospective customer wants to buy. Usually a classified advertisement is not sufficient for this purpose.

THE PROFESSIONAL AND CORRECT WAY
TO USE CLASSIFIED ADVERTISING

In the old days, one might have been able to sell a product directly through a classified ad and, though the dollars received were few, the ad was profitable because the breakeven point was so low. For example, once upon a time you could reach one million potential buyers with a classified ad for only $1 a word. So for $20 you got a 20-word ad. If your product sold for $1 and cost only a few cents, your breakeven was very low, considering the number of potential customers who looked at your ad. Even if you made a profit of only a few dollars on each ad, multiply this times the number of ads in different magazines and the 12 months of the year, and with a number of different products, you had a pretty profitable little business. The problem today is that costs have gone up tremendously. To reach one million prospective buyers, except in a newspaper, may cost you three or four times this amount or even more. You can't really consider the newspaper, because a newspaper usually isn't very good for a classified mail order ad. That means your breakeven is much, much higher. Furthermore, other costs, such as printing, makes your product costs higher. To add insult to injury, postage costs have gone up 10 times or more since the good old days when selling a product direct from classified was frequently possible. The 1¢ stamp for first class is now an 18¢ stamp. If you have a heavy product to send, it costs much more than 18¢. Well, you say, why can't you simply increase the price of the product? Instead of selling the product for $1, we will sell the product for $5 or $10. Good thought. But we are back to the other problem again: You haven't got sufficient space to tell your story to sell a $10 product in classified. The fact is that there is an upper limit to what people will pay for a product advertised in a classified ad. It has been estimated currently to be a maximum of $5. Until such time as our money becomes less valuable because of inflation, I would consider $5 the extreme upper limit if you are going to attempt to sell direct from a classified advertisement.

However, you can make reasonably good money with a classified ad by using the two-step method of operation, where you get inquiries from your classified ad and then mail a sales package to each inquiry. Do inquiries from a two-step classified advertisement lead to sales? Well, Cahners Publishing Company does a series of advertising research reports that they make available to interested parties at no cost. Cahners did one study designed to determine the actions taken by inquirers after they receive the requested information. Three separate studies were conducted and a combined total of 9200 inquiries was analyzed. Based on replies they received from their survey, Cahners determined that more than 12% of the inquirers either bought the product or saw that it was bought if the respondent was an industrial customer. This method has been used by all the experts, and I used it myself in selling my booklet, *The Writer's Guide to Publication and Profit*. If you are interested in obtaining the full series write: CARR Reports, Cahners Publishing Company, 5 South Wabash Avenue, Chicago, Illinois 60603.

Ron Playle used this method, as described in his booklet, *Thirty Thou-*

sand *Dollars Worth of Classified Ad Results,* published by R & D Services, P.O. Box 644, Des Moines, Iowa 50303. It is highly recommended for someone who wants to build a classified advertising business. Ron ran a single classified advertisement in the five-year period 1972 to 1977, and spent approximately $30,000 for his ads. Of course, they were profitable or he would not have continued to advertise. Ron's ad read, "Never won anything? Anyone can win sweepstakes contests. Free details. Services, Box 644, Des Moines, Iowa 50303." Those individuals responding to Ron's classified ad were sent a package that contained a sales letter, a circular with a coupon, and a self-addressed reply envelope. What was the product? A booklet called *Anyone Can Win Sweepstakes,* and Ron sold it profitably through the two-step method, first at $3 and later at $3.95. The little booklet was only 22 pages long and cost Ron only a few cents. Ron Playle draws this conclusion from his experience: "This is not a get-rich-quick scheme, but you can make a nice profit if you are prepared to work hard and can learn as you earn."

Another book that is useful if you are going to sell through classified advertising is called *Dollars in Your Mailbox,* by Ernest P. Weckesser, published by the Green Tree Press, 10576 Temple Road, Dunkirk, New York 14048. This book also concentrates on selling information as opposed to other types of products by mail, but it's useful for anyone interested in selling through classified advertising.

THE FOUR ESSENTIAL ELEMENTS OF A CLASSIFIED AD

In any classified ad, there are four elements that are essential for success: the attention-getter, the promise, the call to action, and the key plus address. The attention-getter is a one- to two-word headline written to grab the attention of the reader looking through the classified advertising section. Some good attention-getters are "Free," "Write for Profit," "Play Piano Instantly," "Big Money." The promise may be combined with the attention-getter. For example, "$1000 per Week Is Possible" is a promise, but it may also be what draws the attention of your prospective customer. Or how about "Lose 10 Pounds in One Week." This too is both a promise and an attention-getter. If you can combine both elements, you will save money in your ad, since combining these elements will result in fewer words.

The call to action is what you use to tell the reader what you want him or her to do. "Send $2" is a call to action if you are selling direct from the classified ad. Or the simple words "Write" or "Free details" followed by your address are calls to action.

The last element in any classified ad is the key plus the address. The key is necessary so that you can tell from what magazine the response came and also from which issue. We'll talk more about keying in just a moment. First I want to show you how to write a classified advertisement.

HOW TO WRITE YOUR CLASSIFIED ADVERTISEMENT

The first step in writing your classified advertisement is to look at your competitors and see how they are advertising similar products or services. As a starting point, I would recommend going to the library and looking at their selection of magazines. Look for magazines that are likely to advertise the type of product or service you want to advertise. Once you locate your competitors' advertising in certain magazines, make copies of these ads and also make note of the magazines that they are advertising in. The more classified advertisements, the better the mail order medium, in general. The more classified advertisements for your product, the better for the product or service you have to offer because your ad will have more readers—don't concern yourself about the competitors just yet. If your library has collections of magazines going back several years, try to find ads that have been repeated over many months, or a year, or even over several years. If the ad wording has changed little in this time, this is fairly a successful ad. This is good for your purposes for two reasons:

1. It tells you that there is a viable market for the product or service you intend to offer.
2. It gives you some guidelines as to what is selling or bringing in the inquiries by the way the copy is written.

In Figure 8-1, I have shown a number of classified advertisements, taken from a number of magazines, containing various headings under which your product might fall. You can refer to these as a starting point and look for competition ads under these headings. However, it is a starting point only and no substitute for your own thorough examination of many different magazines.

The second step in preparing your classified advertisement is to write a letter to your potential customer as if you had no word limitation. Tell your potential customer your proposal and what you want him or her to do at this point—either purchase the product outright or send for additional information. Let's look at the classified advertisement for the *Writer's Guide to Publication and Profit* as an example. Figure 8-2 is the

MONEY MAKING OPPORTUNITIES

END MONEY WORRIES FOREVER! I MADE $77,000 last year. Paid hardly any taxes. You can too. Free proof! Sterne, 8361-A, Vickers, San Diego, Ca 92111.

PASS ANY CREDIT INVESTIGATION. Secret techniques, procedures and guidelines, plus special loan application. No Gimmicks! National Company, free Details. Loan Department 03-E2, 1145 Reservoir Avenue, Cranston, Rhode Island 02920

FREE MAILERS KIT—POSTAGE, BROCHURES Names, included . to our subscribers Offer—Details, Rush Stamped self-addressed envelope. Universal-SO, X16180, Fort Lauderdale, Florida 33318

WE BUY NEWSPAPER CLIPPINGS OF Wedding Announcements for $1.00 each. Instructions $1.00 Clippings. Box 491SO, Gatesville, Texas 76528

CASH BY PHONE. TELEPHONE YOUR WAY TO WEALTH Millions of dollars paid already. World's easiest money. Spare time. Free details. Kashbuilder, PO Box 1132-SO, Indianapolis, In 46206

SENSATIONAL BARGAINS!!! GET WORLD'S BIGGEST Wholesale Import Catalog. Write: Worldwideco, Medina, Wa 98039

SELL LAS VEGAS FUNPACKS—400% PROFIT Drop shipments available. LucPacs, PO Box 370, Henderson, NV 89015

COLOR PHOTOGRAPHIC BLOWUPS SELL FROM home! Mailorder! Free Samples. Postermatic-CE, East Providence, R.I. 02914

BEAT THE RACES! FREE BOOKLET! UNLIMITED LIFE-time income from Thoroughbreds—Harness. Elias, Box 47GG, Brooklyn, New York 11219

$45,000 IN THREE WEEKS! GUARANTEED! GENE Sanders, 1316SO Lyric, Fort Worth, Texas 76134

MAILORDER SUCCESS! INTERESTED? FREE EXPOSE TWP-N, Box 6226, Toledo, Ohio 43614

BIG MONEY! INTERESTED? FREE DISCLOSURE FEBRE-N, Box 6073, Toledo, Ohio 43614. (419) 865-5667

MIRACLE CHRIST PICTURE Wherein His eyes change from Closed to Open! Story of Miracle with each picture (8½x11). Perfect Fund Raiser. Sells everywhere. $20 per 100. 5 samples $3.00. Free Details. Money back guarantee. Mansfield's, Dept. 0-6, 2524 East 7th, Long Beach, Ca 90804

MAIL ORDER-$10 ORDERS WITH $9 PROFITS. FREE Details. MacMillan, 3401A Barr, Columbus, Ohio 43224

MAKE BIG MONEY IN MAILORDER! DETAILS Free! Beaco-S, Box 192, Lincolnton, NC 28092

MAKE 50%. WINTER'S HERE. CHIMNEY KLEAR CLEANS. Chimneys easy. Write for details. Sample $2.00, refundable. Blue Chip Brands, 2006 Detroit Ave. El Paso, Tx 79902

BIG PROFITS IN BECOMING A SUPPLIER TO MAJOR industry through electroplating small parts and metalizing nonmetallics. Write for free particulars. Mason, Room MC-48-JA, 1512 Jarvis, Chicago, Ill 60626.

HOW TO MAKE MONEY AS A COMMISSION circular mailer. Complete program. Rush $2.00. Baskera, 1500 Chestnut St. Kulpmont, Pa. 17834.

$205.80 GUARANTEED FOR 5 HOURS WORK at home. Write Hollingsworth, 309 N.E. 4th St. Linton, Ind. 47441

BECOME THE NEXT MAIL ORDER MILLIONAIRE! New Money Making book by leading expert. Proven Methods. Only $10.00 (90 day guarantee). Send Today! East Coast Pub. Box 82, Island Hgts., NJ 08732.

MAKE BIG MONEY. PUBLISHING 75 POPULAR REPORTS. Rights included. RR1, Box 4381G, Pensacola, Fla. 32507

HOW TO EARN $2,000 WITHOUT HARDLY WORKING at all! Free Details. Miyamoto (7A), 1020 Auahi Street, Honolulu, Hawaii 96814.

STEEL TORNADO SHELTERS—SOLD PROFITABLE FOR 15 years. Inventory investment $1,500. References and Details FREE. Write, Shelters, Box 362-0, Chanute, Ks. 66720.

ADVERTISE IN 30 DIFFERENT RURAL-SUBURBAN Weekly Newspapers At Same Time. Total cost under $25.00 4 Best Mailing Lists that pull cash orders Fast. Only $25.00 per thousand names. Free Details. Budget-Ads, P.O. Box 68-SO, Park Ridge, Ill. 60068.

EARN UP-TO $50,000 CASH IN YOUR Spare Time. Copyrighted Report list common household articles which may be worth hundreds of dollars. 15 days Money Back Guaranteed. Time is Money—Get Yours now . $1.98. J.P. REPORT, Dept 03, URB, SAN FELIPE, CALLE 1-A 31 Arecibo, P.R. 00612.

LIKE TO SELL 7 MILLION? SECRETS REVEALED in "Big Money" Report! Treasure-118SA, Colorado 80465

0 to $250,000 LESS THAN 2 Years!! . Free Information!!! Real Investments, P.O. Box 147-SO1, Robbinsville, NJ 08691.

PRODUCT CATALOG. CONFIDENTIAL PRICE LIST. Send $2.00 to Jackson's Gifts, R.F.D. 2, Box 458, Clayton, Indiana 46118.

$3000 PER WEEK FLOODS HIS MAIL- box! How About yours? Free Booklet. Hermanson, Box 4277-SO, Modesto, Ca 95352

$3,000 MONTHLY SELLING INFORMATION by mail. Write: Robbie, 2205 Windchime Dr. Grand Prairie, Texas 75051.

MAKE 3 TIMES YOUR COST ON 2500 GIFT items, novelties, toys, household items, watches and jewelry. $3.00 brings giant catalog, refundable on first order. Pierson Company, Box 18471, Phila, Pa 19120, Dept. S2.

ENERGY SAVING

ALUMINUM STORM WINDOWS. Install yourself. Free information. Send S.A.S.E. to B.E.C., 1417 SSE Loop 323, #99, Tyler, Texas 75701

EARTH SHELTER DIGEST — A magazine devoted solely to earth sheltered housing. Articles, color photos and plans for underground homes. Subscription $15. Sample $3. WEBCO Publishing, Dept. MI, 479 Fort Road, St. Paul, MN 55102

COMFORTABLE, WARM AIR NEAR FLOOR LEVEL, if you have heat on the ceiling. Make it yourself: $60.00. Pat. Pend. Proven. Portable. Simple. Complete plans and instructions. $10.95 ppd. USA. Conserv-A-Temp, Box M1513, Lawton, Okla. 73502.

AGENTS WANTED

GET CASH Commission With Each Order from friends, neighbors, for America's finest shoes. Easy & profitable. No Investment. Instant income. Free sales kit. Mason Shoes, K-546, Chippewa Falls, WI 54729.

SPARE TIME CASH. Sell famous Hanover Shoes. Samples, sales kit free. No experience needed. No age limit. Big commissions. Hanover Shoe, Dept. 2661, Hanover, Pa. 17331.

TURN SPARE TIME INTO BIG EARNINGS without investment! Hundreds of National Companies seek men and women for part-time, spare-time, weekend work. Their offers are detailed in 5 issues of Opportunity Magazine and they're yours free! Write Opportunity, Dept. 544, 6 N. Michigan, Chicago 60602.

PROFITABLE OCCUPATIONS

BECOME A MORTGAGE Broker. Highly respected, interesting, lucrative, prestige business. For complete information write United, Box 6284-H, Marietta, Ga. 30060.

BUY IT WHOLESALE

400,000 BARGAINS BELOW Wholesale! Many Free! Liquidations . Closeouts . Job Lots. Single Samples. Free Details. Bargainhunters Opportunities, Box 730-MMK, Holland, Mich. 49423.

BELTS AND BUCKLES. Complete line fast sellers including truckers, motorcycles, CB's, westerns etc. Big Profits. Complete dealer set up. Catalog, details free. Anchor Specialties, Box 3958-BMM, No. Providence, R.I. 02911.

WORLDWIDE WHOLESALE BARGAINS. Imports . Closeouts . Surplus . Samples . Mar-nees, Box 1717, Highland, Ind. 46322-MM.

MAKE TWO TO Three times your cost on hundreds of products. Gift Items, Novelties, Toys, Carded Merchandise, 1001 Others. $2.00 brings giant catalog, refundable on first order. My company is Lamont Specialty Gift World, Dept. M-1, 50 Knightsbridge Rd., Great Neck, NY 11021.

SELL DEHYDRATED FOODS Wholesale. No investment. Zion, Fayette Rd., Gordo, AL 35466.

HEALTH

SKINNY FORMULA Interested in facilitating weight loss Nature's Way? Now available . a unique formula of 11 pure herbs designed to help you do just that. The herbs in our SKINNY FORMULA have amazing qualities . they dissolve fat reduce the appetite activate the elimination of excessive water, aid digestion, help eliminate toxic materials from the body and much more! Complete description of all eleven herbs included with 100 SKINNY FORMULA CAPSULES for ONLY $9.50, postage included. SKINNY FORMULA, 7164 Melrose Avenue, Suite 203, Los Angeles, CA 90046

SERVICES

WORDSMITHS. Ghost writers unexcelled. Books, studies, papers. Confidential. Professional. Box 5882h, Chicago, IL 60680

WRITING, EDITING, RESEARCH All disciplines. Original Professional team. Confidential. Superior library facilities—Library of Congress. WRITERS UNLIMITED, Box #4391, Washington, D.C. 20012. (202) 723-1715. Mastercharge Visa

RESEARCH, WRITING, STATISTICS — all subjects confidential. Professional team. FREE details! INTELLEX, Lockbox 10,000, Dayton, Washington 99328. (509) 382-2545

WRITING, RESEARCH. All disciplines. Quality guaranteed. Prompt, confidential. Mastercharge-Visa accepted. (213) 473-3729. Box 25097E. Los Angeles, CA 90025

FAMILY TREES professionally traced. GENEALOGICAL RESEARCH ASSOCIATES, 10 So. Maine 314-F, SLC, Utah 84101 (801) 355-1662

(a)

Figure 8-1. Classified advertisements for various products and services.

TOOLS, MACHINERY & SUPPLIES

AIR TOOLS! Free Wholesale Catalogue. Hoosier Distributing, 3009 W. Sample, South Bend, Indiana 46619

DRILL SETS - High Quality-American Made - With Folding Steel Case. 13 Piece 1/16"-1 4" $10.75. 21 Piece 1/16"-3/8" $25.65. Satisfaction Guaranteed. Send Check. Mastercard - Visa Number. GAT Supply, 2520C' Morgan Ave. Evansville, IN 47711

LATHES - UNIMAT - Maximat - Sherline - Machines. Catalog $1.00 Shop Supplies $1.00. Campbell's, 2100 Selma Road, Springfield. Ohio 45505

RUN THREE phase motors with single phase power. MP-7 wiring diagram and instructions $5.00. Advance Research, 3232 Shawnee, Fort Worth, Texas 76135

4" METAL Cutting Lathe $72.65. Taig, 15048 Proctor, Industry, CA 91746

ENGINES MAJOR Brands to 16HP for Mowers, Tillers, Riders, Hobby, etc. Tremendous Discounts Illustrations. Prices $2.00 Refundable Ashland Small Engines, Ashland, MO. 65010

MAGNETIZE YOUR own screwdriver. I'll show you how. Send $1.00 to N. H. Wyatt, 6633 Hoadley Road, Manassas, VA 22110 Guaranteed Answer.

EDUCATION & INSTRUCTION

INSTANT MEMORY . . . NEW WAY TO REMEMBER. No memorization, Release "photographic" memory. Forget nothing! Liberates - extraordinary knowledge, talents, ESP. Immediate results! Free information. Institute of Advanced Thinking, 845MX ViaLapaz, Pacific Palisades, California 90272.

USED COURSES! Books! List 25c Smith's, 124 Marlborough, Salem, Massachusetts 01970

VETERINARY ASSISTANT - Train at home for exciting animal-care career. Send for Free "Career Kit". North American School of Animal Sciences, Dept. PAC40, Newport Beach, CA 92660.

COLLEGE STUDENTS! Improve your grades. Send $1.00 for your term-paper catalog. 10,250 available. Box 25916X, Los Angeles, California, 90025. (213)477-8226.

GUN REPAIR! Train at home! Career or home business. Learn gun repair, customizing, ballistics, ammo-making, buying, selling — more. Get free facts. Firearms School, Dept. PAC60, 4500 Campus, Newport Beach, CA 92660

LEARN JET-GAS TURBINES Train now in the privacy of your own home - in your spare time! Theory, Construction, Inspection, Maintenance, All Systems, Overhaul, Technical Skills - Aircraft, Nonaircraft, Trucks, Marine, Power Generation and more! Write for complete details - American Jet School, Dept. MI-4B, Darby, Montana 59829

PRINTING PRESSES, RUBBER STAMP OUTFITS

RUBBER STAMP supplies catalog. Jackson, Brownsville Rd., S-120, Mt. Vernon, IL 62864

PRINT YOUR OWN——Printing Presses, type, supplies, direct from factory. Send 25c for catalog and samples to: Kelsey Co., DI, Meriden, Conn. 06450.

RUBBER STAMPS & MARKING DEVICES

RUBBER STAMPS. Free catalog. Jackson's, Brownsville Rd. G-102, Mt. Vernon, IL 62864

CUSTOM AND STOCK rubber stamps. Free catalog. Magnetic Research Box 299 Boonton, NJ 07005

3 LINE Rubber Stamps $5.00. Additional Lines 50c. Mid-Ill. Stamps. Box 371, Litchfield, Il. 62056

WORK AT HOME

MAKE MONEY WITH ART, CRAFTS, HOBBIES. FREE Details Box 296. Avalon, California 90704

MONEY MAKERS SURPRISE PACKAGE. YOU WON'T believe what $5 will bring Guaranteed Credit Cards accepted 203 Metropole, Avalon, Ca 90704

MONEY MAKING REPORT
How to Make Big Money In Your Spare Time - Send $2 and self-addressed stamped envelope to J D and Associates, P.O. Box 250-S. Dupo, Illinois 62239

REFUNDING - EASY. REWARDING - FACTS. $1.00 Guzzo. S-5019 Carpenter Road, Hamburg NY 14075

AUTOS—ACCESSORIES

PLASTICGUARD CAR POLISH WRITE THE MANUFACTURER 6511E Caminodelos Ranchos, Scottsdale, Arizona 85254

NEW CAR EVERY YEAR - COST FREE? How? Details Supercar Box 28101-C1 St. Louis, Mo 63119

DISTRIBUTORS

SAFE WORM REMEDY FOR HORSES CHEAP WORM poisons not always the solution to expensive worm problems in horses Write. Westward Products, Box 1032. Studio City, Ca 91604

DISTRIBUTORS WANTED FOR $1,000 VEGAS FUNPAKS Resorts. Box 8089, Lumberton, Texas 77711 (713-385-6673)

FREE DETAILS, AUTOMATIC FISHHOOKS. PROfitable Samples $3.00 (Refundable) Aronmarine, 61-B. Mastic Beach, New York 11951

COMPUTERIZED CONTROL OF AIR CONDITIONING and heat in motels and offices. Low Cost Remote Control No wiring. Non-technical Territories available Viking, 2499 Rice, St. Paul, Mn 55113

$1,000 WEEK DISTRIBUTING BACTERIOSTATIC water purifiers (Details - $1.00) Safewater, Box 39195, Phoenix, Arizona 85069

SHARE SHAKLEE SUCCESS' QUALITY PRODUCTS Earn Bonuses. Car. Lynn. 661 San Bruno, Brisbane, Ca 94005

RECORDS & TAPES

OLD RADIO programs on cassettes. Free catalog. Nostalgic, Box 16365-MI, St. Louis, MO. 63125.

OLDIES-Original Hit 45's. Catalog $2.00, C&S Record Sales, Box 22C, Wampsville, New York 13163

RECORD - TAPES! Discounts to 73%; all labels; no purchase obligations; newsletters; discount dividend certificates; 100% guarantees. Free details. Discount Music Club. 650 Main St., Dept. 2-0880, New Rochelle, New York 10810.

HYPNOTISM

FREE HYPNOTISM. Self-Hypnosis Sleep-learning Catalog! Drawer M-400, Ruidoso, New Mexico 88345.

SLEEP-LEARNING — Hypnotism! Strange catalog free! Autosuggestions. Box 24-MM, Olympia, Washington 98507

FREE FASCINATING Hypnosis Information! Startling! DLM, Box 487, Anaheim, California 92805.

HYPNOTIZE YOURSELF And Others Successfully! "Instantaneous"- "One Word" - "Against Will" methods exposed! Complete illustrated course $4.95. Dr. Fowler, Box 4399, Woodbury, N.J. 08096

HYPNOTIZE OTHERS without their knowing it. $3.00 - HTM, Box 1659, Bristol, CT. 06010

GREATEST SKILL you can develop takes just minutes a day! Hypnosis Cassettes. Brochure. HRA, 1170-M Beacon, Brookline, MA 02146.

WINEMAKING & OTHER RECIPES

BEERMAKERS-WINEMAKERS Free catalog. Yeast, equipment Continental, Box 68016-MI, Indianapolis, Ind 46268

FREE ENCYCLOPEDIA Winemaking, Beermaking, Supplies, Equipment, Ingredients. Vynox, Box C-7498, Rochester, N.Y. 14615.

HOW TO MAKE FLOUR TORTILLAS. Send $3.00. John Bargas, P.O. Box 2854, Merced, Calif. 95340

BEERMAKERS - FINEST equipment. supplies Lowest prices. Free catalog **BEERGEAR,** Box 25093-1, Lansing, Michigan 48905

MAKE WINE, beer, liqueurs. Free catalogue. Bacchanalia, Box 51, MI Central Village, Mass. 02790

WINEMAKER-BEERMAKERS - Free Catalog - Fast Service - Large Selection. Kraus, Box 7850-T, Independence, Missouri 64053.

BEER. WINE Making Supplies. Catalog. Jim Dandy Sales Box 30377M Cincinnati, Ohio 45230

COLLEGES & UNIVERSITIES

EXTERNAL DEGREES. Internationally accredited. Experience recognized Personal educational guidance $5.00 U.S. UNIVERSITY OF AMERICA. 927-15th St., N.W., Washington, D.C. 20005

LAW STUDY thru correspondence. Registered Law School. Qualify CA. Bar Exam. Toll-free 800-423-4530. CA residents (213) 795-5558. Southland Law School, 69 N. Catalina, Dept. B2. Pasadena, CA 91106

GOVERNMENT SURPLUS

SURPLUS JEEPS — $19 30' — CARS — $13 50' — 650,000 ITEMS' — Government Surplus - Most Comprehensive Directory available tells how, where to buy — Your area — $2- Moneyback Guarantee — GOVERNMENT INFORMATION SERVICES. Department GE 44, Box 99254, San Francisco California 94109

GOVERNMENT SURPLUS DIRECTORY - Buy 500,000 items (including Jeeps) - low as 2c on dollar! Most complete information available — $2.00 Surplus Disposal Box 19107 EX, Washington, DC 20036

(b)

Figure 8-1. (Continued)

Tells exactly how to write and sell articles to magazines.
Is not an academic course; no time wasted on theory.
Shows how to organize and write ideas for maximum impact.
Details how to sell articles step by step.
Is complete in every respect.
Lists and describes more than 200 ideas for subjects.
Tells how to find subjects.
Shows how to change an outline into an article.
Shows how to illustrate article at little or no cost.
Comprises four volumes of material.
Tells how to get free copies of sample magazines.
Is sold only through mail order.
Includes a money back guarantee.
Tells how to obtain free instructions about writing for certain magazines.
Tells how to sell your article to more than one magazine.
Tells how to get an editor to buy your article before you write it.
Tells how to sell your rejects.
Tells how to avoid legal problems

Figure 8-2. The complete story of the *Writer's Guide to Publication and Profit.*

entire story of the *Writer's Guide to Publication and Profit*, the story I want to put in the classified advertisement to secure an inquiry from my potential customer.

The next step is to write the headline for your classified. Remember that the headline must be brief and dramatic. It must also capture the reader's attention. In this case, you already have a person who is looking through the classified section under the very heading you chose for your advertisement. However, there may be hundreds of other advertisements for the same or similar products under this single heading, so your advertisement must stand out if it is going to be read. In the case of the classified for the *Writer's Guide to Publication and Profit*, I considered several different headlines: "Write Profitably Now," "Get Published Immediately," "Write for Big Money," "Huge Profits in Writing," "Dollars through Writing," and "Profitable Writing." I finally settled on "How to Write for Profit."

The next step is to trim your letter until it looks like a telegram. Take out every word that is unnecessary to accomplish your objective. But be careful here; tests have shown that the longer your ad is, the more sales or inquiries your classified ad will bring in. On the other hand, since every word costs money, you cannot measure profitability simply by the number of inquiries or sales. You must measure it by the profits. You must weigh the increased number of returns or respondents against the increased cost of the ad. Usually, you can drop indefinite and definite articles or any word automatically understood by your prospective customer. The results of an initial trimming are shown in Figure 8-3.

In refining your classified ads, you should be sure to use simple words

---

HOW TO WRITE FOR PROFIT. You can get complete details free by writing to Global Associates, P.O. Box 575, Dept. 1-A, Sierra, California 91079.

Figure 8-3. A classified ad in the initial trimming stages. There are 24 words to be paid for.

that are easily understood and be specific in what you say. What do I mean by "simple words"? Use *doctor*, not *physician*. Use *lawyer*, not *attorney*. Use *arrest*, not *apprehend*. Use a short word like *grouping*, not a long, complicated word such as *apportionment*, which means the same thing. By specific, I mean exact figures or exact things. Instead of "big profit," it's much better to say "make $500 profit." It's better to say "learn in 30 days" than "learn quickly."

You should now check to make certain that you have a phrase that calls the prospective customer to action, and you should also check to make sure you have your address and a key in your advertisement. As I mentioned before, it is essential to key your advertisement so that you know what the "pull," or response rate, is from each magazine and each issue. It is necessary to know and separate these figures so that you can forecast your response from any given magazine within 30 days after receiving the first response. In this way, you will know whether to continue this advertisement or to stop and reconsider. Even a successful classified ad may not be profitable in every magazine you test or in certain months of the year. One way to key your advertisement is with the words *department, room,* or *drawer,* followed by the key. For example, you may have numbers 1 through 24 represent 24 different magazines in which you are advertising—1, *Mechanix Illustrated;* 2, *Popular Mechanics;* 3, *Popular Science* and so forth. You can then use letters to represent the months of the year—A for January, B for February, C for March, and so forth. In any case, your system should identify both the magazine and the month of advertising. Now there is one problem with using *drawer* or *room* or *suite* or *department.* Many experienced mail order buyers recognize this as a key and to save a couple of seconds they simply do not put this part of the address in their response, defeating the entire purpose of a key. One way of getting around this problem is with use of your initials. By using different initials in front of my name—A. A. Cohen, B. A. Cohen, C. A. Cohen, and so forth—I can represent different magazines and their months of publication. Some people do this by spelling their names in different ways, such as Cohen, Cohn, or Kohn. Another possible way of keying that works fairly well if you have a post office box number is to add two letters to the box number after a hypen. If your post office box number is 575, you can add a dash and then add a letter and number combination such as A1 or B2. The letter would stand for the magazine, the

---

WRITE FOR PROFIT. Free details. Global-1A, Box 575, Sierra, California 91079.

Figure 8-4. The classified ad in final form. The same information is given as in Figure 8-3, but you pay for only 11 words.

number for the month of publication, so that a mailing address of Box 575-A1 might indicate the January issue of *Popular Mechanics*. You should probably check with your postmaster on this to ensure that the mail will be delivered even though it has additional figures after the hyphen, but usually there will be no problem. One method I hit upon and I eventually used in my advertisement for the *Writer's Guide to Publication and Profit* was shortening my company's name, Global Associates, to one word, Global, and then adding figures after this word to form my key. The advertisement read, "Global-1A" or "Global-2C." In this way, I accomplished two things. First, I saved one word since I did not have to use *department, suite, room,* or some other word to designate my key. Also, since this word was combined with the company name, respondents did not omit it when responding to the ad. All of these methods of keying your ad work. Pick the one that works best for you. You can see the final results of all this work in Figure 8-4.

HOW TO PICK THE MAGAZINES TO ADVERTISE IN

When you are first picking magazines to advertise in, you should know all the magazines that are potential carriers for your advertisement. The *Standard Rate and Data Service* (SRDS) has published several volumes, including some that deal with lists, other media such as television and radio, and two that have to do with magazine advertising. The first of these covers business publications and the second, consumer and form publications. Go through the SRDS and list all those magazines that might be potential vehicles for your classified advertisement. Write to these publishers and ask for a sample copy of their magazine and a rate card. This information will be useful later for display advertisement.

Always look at your competition and advertise where they do. Now, this does not say that you do not have to be innovative, but only that until you are successful enough to afford to assume more risk, it is wise to go where the tried, true, and proved advertisers go and not to strike off on your own. Joe Karbo was the first to learn how to advertise with a mail order ad in the classified section of the newspaper, even though his is not a typical classified ad because it is much larger than usual. Joe not only developed this technique—he has made millions with it. However, before

Joe ever did this, he was already making several hundred thousand dollars a year in mail order. Mark O. Haroldsen once took a full-page ad in *Time*. *Time* is not known as an especially good medium for either his type of product or their type of mail order ad. The ad failed, and Mark did not advertise in *Time* again. (How do I know the ad failed without talking to Mark? It was never repeated!) Haroldsen could afford to drop $45,000 for such a test ad. Most beginners cannot, and so it's far better to use the fact that other people are advertising with similar ads in the same medium, rather than to try new territory before you have some experience under your belt.

Newspapers usually just don't work for the average classified ad for a mail order product, though there are some exceptions—*The Wall Street Journal, National Enquirer,* and other such newspapers. But the average hometown newspaper is simply not a good mail order medium for the average product, although I guess every mail order person has tried the newspaper at least once with some idea or another, as I have done myself.

Once, several years ago while on my first jury duty, I discovered that the greater part of a day in the life of a prospective juror is spent in waiting. I had about 30 days of waiting to be selected as a member of a jury, and only about 10 days of actually working as a juror. Most prospective jurors spent their waiting hours reading, talking, playing checkers, watching television, or whiling away the time in some other way. The year before, I had written my first book, *The Executive's Guide to Finding a Superior Job,* and it had been very well received by top managers seeking a career change. I decided to sit down and write down some of my job-finding ideas in an explicit and concise form for anyone looking for a new job. I thought that perhaps I could find some way to sell these ideas by mail. At the end of my jury duty, I had completed about 5000 words of closely typed material that I thought I could market through a classified ad for about $2. Since, in quantity, the printed material cost only a few cents, I had sufficient markup so that I really didn't need to sell many copies to break even. My idea was to advertise in the weekend classified section of major newspapers. I decided to run my test ad in the *Los Angeles Times* and, if successful, expand to classified ads in Sunday newspapers throughout the country. One of the first things I discovered is that you cannot place an advertisement under the column headed *Employment Opportunities* unless you have an actual employment opportunity, so I was forced to put a separate ad under *Employment Opportunities* saying "See our ad under *Announcements*" and then run the actual ad under the *Announcements* heading in the classified ad section. At any rate, the Sunday issue of the *Los Angeles Times* came out, and my breakeven was computed at something like 20 respondents. Since breakeven was so low, I was pretty certain that the project would be successful and I was all set to expand the operation throughout the country and make my fortune at once. I had already consulted SRDS and I was ready to roll out as soon as those dollars started rolling in. Well, the *Los Angeles Times* has a circulation of 120,000. I don't know how many actually read my ad, but I do know how many ordered. At the fantastic price of $2 with a full money-back guarantee, I got exactly one buyer.

Joe Karbo maintains that any medium can be used for mail order once you learn how. Unfortunately, not many mail order operators have found how to use the classified sections of newspapers yet.

After finding a magazine in which classified mail order advertisements appear and in which the competition is advertising, the third thing to look for is volume. We want to reach the largest number of readers for a particular advertisement right at the start. This does not mean we don't advertise in magazines that have a lower volume of readers, but that we go to those with higher circulations first. Why does it make a difference? First, you must test your ad before you can make really big profits with it. But who says you can't make money with a test ad? You have a better chance of doing so if you reach a bigger market. Secondly, since you are going to have people trying to copy you if you are successful, it's better that you get to more people first, which you can do by advertising in larger circulation magazines first.

HOW TO CLASSIFY YOUR AD
IN THE CLASSIFIED SECTION

Once we locate the initial magazines for our tests, we are faced with an array of different classification headings—*Salesmen Wanted, Distributors Wanted, Advertising Specialty Salesmen Wanted, Agents Wanted, Money-Making Opportunities, Business Opportunities*—the headings go on and on. Under which of these classifications do we advertise, since, in many cases, we will find several headings under which our ad could fit? The standard rule—look for the competition—holds. If a competitor is advertising the same or a similar product successfully, chances are that the ad's heading is where our ad belongs as well. But what if we have an item so new or so different that the competition isn't there yet? In that case, look for as similar an item as you can possibly find. If you had wanted to sell electronic calculators to engineers back in the days when these calculators were just introduced, you would have selected a heading under which slide rules could be found. Why? Because a slide rule was the existing product that performed the same function as electronic calculators.

Now, what if there are no similar items? In that case, look for those classified headings that would be of interest to a group of people who would also be interested in your item. The same people who are interested in purchasing government surplus may also be interested in bargains and close-outs, for example.

Finally, if there is no heading, do not be afraid to ask for one. If you look at almost any classified columns in magazines, you will find some headings with only a single advertisement underneath. Very frequently, it is a case of the advertiser's not finding a heading for his or her product. The advertiser simply asked the magazine to provide a separate heading. This has an additional advantage: With only one ad under a certain heading, the chance of your ad being read is much greater, so never be afraid to ask for one. You may not get one, but it's always worthwhile to ask.

In many cases, and since your product or service will fit under more than one classified heading, you can advertise under more than one heading. You may want to do this at the outset to determine which heading is more successful. Or, after you have determined that your test is successful with a single ad under one heading, you may advertise under two different headings. Now, if you do advertise under more than one heading, do not expect to double your number of responses. But who cares? As long as your response rate is profitable for each heading, you will increase your total profits.

HOW TO INSERT YOUR AD IN A MAGAZINE

Inserting a classified advertisement is very easy to do. Since no artwork or graphics are required, you simply type the ad exactly as you would like it to appear and state under what classification you want it to run. If you are a first-time advertiser, you must usually include a check or money order for the full amount of the ad. Be careful of the closing date of the magazine, which is the final date on which the magazine will accept advertising for the specific issue in which you wish to advertise. It is not unusual for the closing date to be six weeks prior to the date on the cover of the magazine. If you want a weekly magazine with a quicker response, you may consider the *National Enquirer* or *Grit* or the *Wall Street Journal,* whose lead times are usually less.

Many magazines will require a sample of what you are selling or are going to send in response to an inquiry you receive from your ad. By policing itself, the industry attempts to keep unethical or dishonest mail order dealers from advertising in their magazine.

SAVING MONEY WITH YOUR CLASSIFIED ADS

There are several ways to save money when you place your classified ads. In many publications, it is possible to save 2% on your advertising by paying within a specific period, usually 10 days. This discount will be indicated on the rate card you receive from the magazine upon request.

Another way you can save money when you place a classified ad is by having your own in-house advertising agency. Advertising agencies make money by getting a 15% discount for any ads they place with a publication. So if you have your own advertising agency (see chapter 9), you can save 15%. Most publications say they do not give discounts to in-house agencies. But most publications *will* give you a discount if the fact that you are an in-house agency isn't made so obvious that they must reject it so as not to displease their regular advertising agency customers.

Another way to save money in your classified ad campaign is called "till forbid." Many magazines will offer you a discount if you give them a till forbid order, which means they will continue to run your ad until you tell them to stop. This saves money in several ways. First, there is the discount, usually for three insertions or more of the same ad. You also save labor and postage in writing every month to request the ad be repeated. However, you should be cautious about use of till forbid. Many advertisements cannot be placed every month in every magazine. Also, you should not run till forbid until your testing is complete. But once it is, all you need to do is inform the magazine of your key so it can automatically be changed with each new issue.

THE STRATEGY FOR PYRAMIDING YOUR PROFITS
IN CLASSIFIED ADVERTISING

To pyramid your money in classified advertising, you start with one test and one magazine. If the test is successful, then and only then do you proceed. You continue to advertise in that magazine and start testing in another magazine of the same category, as defined by SRDS. For example, there are shelter magazines, such as *Better Homes and Gardens,* and *Good Housekeeping;* then there are opportunity magazines, such as *Salesman's Opportunity, Specialty Salesman,* and *Money-Making Opportunities;* there are the hunting and fishing magazines, such as *Field and Stream, Hunting and Fishing,* and *Outdoor Life.* Every magazine can be grouped in this fashion. Well, after you have tested successfully in two magazines in each group, you can assume, with a slight degree of risk, that your classified ad will work in all the other magazines in a group. So after testing several magazines in one group, move on to another group and start testing in one magazine in that group. If you are successful, continue to advertise in the magazine. If you are unsuccessful, stop, take note, and move on to something else. In this way you can expand from group to group, repeating the process in every group and making increasing profits as you find more groups that are profitable for your classified ad.

In doing this testing, you will discover that some months are better for your ad than others, especially with seasonal products: a Christmas item naturally sells best in the Christmas season, and some summer products, such as suntan oil and beach towels, would not sell at all during the winter. Many surveys have been done to show when advertising works best. They are useful as a starting point for testing if you do not have a seasonal product. You will find such a rating of months in chapter 9. January is usually considered the best month for the average mail order product. (January will be the month in which your ad actually appears, *not* the month printed on the magazine cover, which may precede the actual month in which the magazine appears by several weeks or a month.) Remember that any listing such as the one in chapter 9 is an average only, and you must work with your particular product to discover which months are best for you. You may find that in some very good months it pays to increase your advertising, whereas in particularly bad months, it pays not to advertise at all.

Being able to forecast future returns based on early returns from your ad will help you pyramid your profits quickly. It has been found that 50% of the responses you will ever receive from a classified ad in a monthly magazine will occur about a month after you receive the very first order inquiry. So it's easy to forecast returns accurately. As soon as you get an inquiry or order, write down this particular date, using the records systems I will show you later on in the book. One month after this date, you will have received 50% of the responses you will ever receive. Multiply this number by two and you will have accounted for 100% of your responses. The forecast is different with a weekly magazine or newspaper. You will receive 50% of the orders or inquiries you will ever receive about two weeks after receipt of the first order or inquiry. You can make your decision much more rapidly with this technique than if you waited until all your orders were received, which, for a monthly magazine, would be about a year. You can't afford to wait this long to make decisions in mail order because your competition will inevitably strike if your advertisement is successful. It's up to you to do what you can to capture as much of the market as you possibly can before that happens. Using your forecasting figure, you can make a decision as to the ad's profitability and whether to proceed or stop running it in that magazine.

THE SECRET OF MAKING MUCH MORE MONEY WITH YOUR CLASSIFIED ADVERTISEMENTS

There is one important way in which you can make a lot more money with your classified advertisements, and that is to rent the names you receive from the response to your ads. Those names are very important in mail order, because people who respond have qualified themselves as mail order buyers. If they will buy your product by mail, they will buy other mail order dealers' products, so their names are valuable. In fact, some mail order businesses make as much as 25% of their annual sales simply from renting the names of respondents. Now, here's how it works in classified. Let's say that in your first year of operations, you receive 10,000 names. A typical rental fee is $30 per thousand, so 10 times $30 is $300. However, we are not through. It is a fact that some companies rent their names as many as 24 times a year or more, so you could make several thousand dollars just from renting your 10,000 names. Do not overlook this additional source of income.

SUMMARY

Here are 10 proved ways to increase your results from classified advertising.

1. Get your prospect's attention. This is the first and most important job your classified ad must do, from the very first word.

2. Since you are paying for classifieds by the *word*, you can make your advertisement look longer by avoiding abbreviations that don't save you words. For example, do not use "CA" for California. Spell it out. Similarly, do not abbreviate your city. Your ad will look bigger without adding one penny to its cost.

3. Do use abbreviations that save you money: "$1" compared to "one dollar" saves you an additional word. Each word saved is money in your pocket.

4. Once you have a successful ad in a magazine, try to run an identical ad simultaneously under a different classified heading. In this way you can overcome the limitation of the number of magazines in which you will be able to advertise.

5. If you can use a street address rather than a box number, do so. A street address lends credibility to your company and to your advertisement.

6. Form your key with a one-word company name. "Global-1A" instead of "Global Associates, Department 1A" saves several words and a lot of money.

7. Test before you leap. Start with one ad and one magazine. The chances of your competition's reacting to one ad are just about nil. Your competition is like you: It is going to look for repeated ads in many magazines as a sign of success, and only then attempt to get into your market. Don't assume success before you have proved it by testing. You can have more failures than successes and still make a million dollars by exploiting your winner.

8. The two-step inquiry and follow-up is much preferred in classified over attempting to sell a product directly from your classified ad. If you do sell direct, it is better to use even dollar figures, rather than $1.98 or $2.99, because most people will send cash rather than checks for these small amounts, and 98¢ or 99¢ is hard to mail in an envelope.

9. Always be aware of what your competitors are doing. Consider the magazines in which they advertise as a place to start. Look at the classifications your competition is using as starting places for you. Follow your competition when you are a newcomer and you will save a lot of money and have a much better chance of succeeding.

10. Be as brief as possible in your classified ad, but make certain that you have included the words necessary to obtain the inquiry or the sale.

Many companies have started with classified ads and gone on to other media. Other companies are successful using only classified ads. Still other companies use classified ads as an adjunct to their business. So don't neglect use of the classified ad in your mail order business: The ad may be small, but its size belies its ability to contribute significantly to your business.

9

How to Develop and Use Display Ads Profitably

To many people, display advertising is synonymous with mail order. And no wonder, when display ads can run as long as 40 years, as did the ad in Figure 9-1, "Do You Make These Mistakes in English?" This ad, which was written by Maxwell Sackheim, continuously outpulled ads written by many of the country's top mail order copywriters from the time it was written in 1915 until the mid-1950s. How many orders for Sherwin Cody's course in English do you think this ad brought in during this 40-year period? It had to be in the tens of millions! Back in Figure 4-2 is another great mail order ad that ran for years: "They Laughed When I Sat Down at the Piano . . . but When I Started to Play!" This ad for the U.S. School of Music was written by ad genius John Caples. Not every display ad can bring in millions of orders as these two ads did, but you don't need millions of orders from one display ad to make a good living from mail order, which is what you are going to learn to do in this chapter.

WHAT IS A DISPLAY AD?

A display ad is space in a medium such as a magazine or newspaper in which advertising is placed. For this reason, *display* and *space* are two words that are frequently used interchangeably in mail order. Both mean the same thing. Figure 9-1 shows a full-page display ad. However, a display ad can range from a single inch in height by one column in width to an entire page. Why do people use display ads when they are far more expensive than classified advertising? Well, as I mentioned earlier, for many people, display advertising *is* mail order. A full-page display ad is placed to offer a product that can be ordered immediately by a potential

Do You Make These Mistakes in English?

Sherwin Cody's remarkable invention has enabled more than 100,000 people to correct their mistakes in English. Only 15 minutes a day required to improve your speech and writing.

MANY persons use such expressions as "Leave them lay there" and "Mary was invited us well as myself." Still others say "between you and I" instead of "between you and me." It is astonishing how often "who" is used for "whom" and how frequently we hear such glaring mispronunciations as "for MID able," "ave NOO," and "KEW pon." Few know whether to spell certain words with one or two "c's" or "m's" or "r's" or with "ie" or "ei," and when to use commas in order to make their meaning absolutely clear. Most persons use only common words—colorless, flat, ordinary. Their speech and their letters are lifeless, monotonous, humdrum.

Why Most People Make Mistakes

What is the reason so many of us are deficient in the use of English and find our careers stunted in consequence? Why is it some cannot spell correctly and others cannot punctuate? Why do so many find themselves at a loss for words to express their meaning adequately? The reason for the deficiency is clear. Sherwin Cody discovered it in scientific tests which he gave thousands of times. *Most persons do not write or speak good English simply because they never formed the habit of doing so.*

What Cody Did at Gary

The formation of any habit comes only from constant practice. Shakespeare, you may be sure, never studied rules. No one who writes and speaks correctly thinks of *rules* when he is doing so.

Here is our mother-tongue, a language that has built up our civilization, and without which we should all still be muttering savages! Yet our schools, have made it a study to be avoided —the hardest of tasks instead of the most fascinating of games! For years it has been a crying disgrace.

In that point lies the real difference between Sherwin Cody and the schools! Here is an illustration: Some years ago Mr. Cody was invited by the author of the famous Gary System of Education to teach

SHERWIN CODY

English to all upper-grade pupils in Gary, Indiana. By means of unique practice exercises *Mr. Cody secured more improvement in these pupils in five weeks than previously had been obtained by similar pupils in two years under old methods.* There was no guesswork about these results. They wer proved by scientific comparisons. Amazing as this improvement was, more interesting still was the fact that the children were "wild" about the study. It was like playing a game!

The basic principle of Mr. Cody's new method is habit-forming. Anyone can learn to write and speak correctly by constantly using the correct forms. But how is one to know in each case what is correct? Mr. Cody solves this problem in a simple, unique, sensible way.

100% Self-Correcting Device

Suppose he himself were standing forever at your elbow. Every time you' mispronounced or misspelled a word, every time you violated correct grammatical usage, every time you used the wrong word to express what you meant, suppose you could hear him whisper: "That is wrong, it should be thus and so." In a short time you would habitually use the correct form and the right words in speaking and writing.

If you continued to make the same mistakes over and over again, each time patiently he would tell you what was right. He would, as it were, be an everlasting mentor beside you—a mentor who would not laugh at you, but who would, on the contrary, support and help you. The 100% Self-Correcting Device does exactly this thing. It is Mr. Cody's silent voice behind you, ready to speak out whenever you commit an error. It finds your mistakes and concentrates on them. You do not need to study anything you already know. There are no rules to memorize.

Only 15 Minutes a Day

Nor is there very much to learn. In Mr. Cody's years of experimenting he brought to light some highly astonishing facts about English.

For instance, statistics show that a list of sixty-nine words (with their repetitions) *make up more than half of all our speech and letter-writing.* Obviously, if one could learn to spell, use, and pronounce these words correctly, one would go far toward eliminating incorrect spelling and pronunciation.

Similarly, Mr. Cody proved that there were no more than one dozen fundamental principles of punctuation. If we mastered these principles, there would be no bugbear of punctuation to handicap us in our writing.

Finally he discovered that twenty-five typical errors in grammar constitute nine-tenths of our everyday mistakes. When one has learned to avoid these twenty-five pitfalls, how readily one can obtain the facility of speech which denotes the person of breeding and education!

When the study of English is made so simple, it becomes clear that progress can be made in a very short time. *No more than fifteen minutes a day is required.* Fifteen minutes, not of study, but of fascinating practice! Mr. Cody's students do their work in any spare moment they can snatch. They do it riding to work or at home. They take fifteen minutes from the time usually spent in profitless reading or amusement. The results really are phenomenal.

Sherwin Cody has placed an excellent command of the English language within the grasp of everyone. Those who take advantage of his method gain something so priceless that it cannot be measured in terms of money. They gain a mark of breeding that cannot be erased as long as they live. They gain a facility in speech that marks them as educated people in whatever society they find themselves. They gain the self-confidence and self-respect which this ability inspires. As for material reward, certainly the importance of good English in the race for success cannot be overestimated. Surely, no one can advance far without it.

FREE — Book on English

It is impossible, in this brief review, to give more than a suggestion of the range of subjects covered by Mr. Cody's new method and of what his practice exercises consist. But those who are interested can find a detailed description in a fascinating little book called "How You Can Master Good English in 15 Minutes a Day." This is published by the Sherwin Cody School of English in Rochester. It can be had by anyone, free upon request. There is no obligation involved in writing for it. The book is more than a prospectus. Unquestionably, it tells one of the most interesting stories about education in English ever written.

If you are interested in learning more in detail of what Sherwin Cody can do for you, send for the book "How You Can Master Good English in 15 Minutes a Day."

Merely mail the coupon, a letter or postal card for it now. No agent will call. SHERWIN CODY SCHOOL OF ENGLISH, 8811 B. & O. Building, Rochester 4, N. Y.

SHERWIN CODY SCHOOL OF ENGLISH
8811 B. & O. Building, Rochester 4, N. Y.

Please send me, without obligation on my part, your new free book "How You Can Master Good English in 15 Minutes a Day." No agent will call.

Name

Address

City   Zone No.   State
☐ If 18 years or under, check here for Booklet A

"Do You Make These Mistakes in English?"

Figure 9-1. Maxwell Sackheim's successful display ad for an instruction book.

buyer through use of a coupon. The potential buyer sends in money and receives your product in return. But notice that neither of the two ads in Figures 9-1 and 4-2 attempts to sell the product directly from the advertisement itself; rather, they invite the potential customer to fill out a coupon, requesting additional information. Both are attempts to sell through the two-step method. The same technique is used in the Mellinger advertisement in Figure 5-1 (a similar ad is running currently).

Okay, so to many people, display advertising *is* mail order. But why use it if classified advertising is far more profitable in that the per order cost of advertising with classified is a lot less than that of display advertising? Here are the reasons.

1. It is a good way to build a volume business that cannot be built with classified ads.
2. For many products and services, you can reach more readers or more potential customers more cheaply than you can through a direct mail campaign.
3. It is a good way of getting the names of many potential customers fast.

Let's look at each of these reasons in detail. If you are going to make big money in mail order, you must have a volume business, and you cannot build volume business through classified advertisements. This means there is a limit to the total profits you can make with a classified ad campaign because not enough people look at classified advertising. Further, there is a limit to the number of magazines and newspapers that carry classified advertisements. No such limits exist with display ads. So even though it may cost more per inquiry or order received, a display ad produces potential profits far greater than a classified ad, and it is only through display advertising that you can build a volume business.

Display advertising is also cheaper than direct mail for many types of products you may want to sell. Why is it cheaper? Well, let's look first at reaching 1000 potential customers who are interested in entrepreneurial products through a direct mail campaign. First, you must rent the names, which will cost you $50 or $60 per thousand. Next, you have your mailing package, which includes a sales letter, a brochure, a self-addressed envelope, a guarantee, and other essential items that will be explained in chapter 10. Let's say that this costs us another 25¢ per unit, or $250 per thousand. Next, we have postage at bulk rate, which is currently 10.9¢ per letter and probably 12.8¢ very shortly. The total cost to reach potential customers interested in our entrepreneurial type of product will be almost $400 per thousand.

Now, if we can find a magazine read by individuals interested in entrepreneurial products, we can reach a much larger readership at a much lower cost. Is there such a magazine? Of course, there are many, and we can find such a list in one of the Standard Rate and Data Service publications. Let's look at the magazine *Entrepreneur*, published by Chase Revelle, Inc. A full-page advertisement appearing one time in this magazine currently costs approximately $2500. It reaches approximately 64,000 potential customers. What's our cost per thousand potential customers here? Only about $39. That's a ten-fold difference in reaching our potential customer through a display advertisement, compared to direct mail in this case! Since we can identify a magazine that would carry a space or display advertisement that would interest potential customers of this particular product, we could advertise here at about one-tenth of the cost of direct mail.

The third main reason we may want to use display advertisements to build our business is to get as many customer names as we can, fast. Now, this goes along with the fact that mail order is a back-end business and that we can make additional revenue by renting the names we receive. The more names we get, the more revenue we can get through these two methods. But there is another reason for getting customers' names as rapidly as we can: our competition. If our product or service is successful, as proved by the fact that we continue to advertise it, we will have imitators, who will attempt to jump into the same market with a similar product and similar ad. Of course, we will protect ourselves if possible through the protection devices discussed in an earlier chapter. However, in many cases, perfect protection is impossible. Therefore, our strategy must be to capture a major share of the market as rapidly as we can by selling our product and getting a list of customers' names before our competition does. This we can do very effectively through display ads.

WHAT YOU NEED TO KNOW
TO MAKE IT WITH DISPLAY ADS

There are 13 questions you must understand and be able to answer to make money using display advertisements.

1. How do you create an effective display ad?
2. Where do you advertise?
3. When and how do you advertise?
4. How frequently do you advertise?
5. What size should your advertisements be, and should they be black and white or in color?
6. Where in the magazine should your advertisement appear?

7. How do you place your advertisements?

8. How do you buy display advertising at less than the standard rates?

9. How can you get free advertisements for your products?

10. What results should you expect from display advertising, and how quickly should you expect them?

11. How do you do media planning strategy, and pyramid your profits?

12. Should you use an advertising agency, and how do you find one?

13. What can you do to multiply your display advertising success?

HOW TO CREATE AN EFFECTIVE DISPLAY AD

Before considering whether to create an effective display ad on your own, perhaps you should consider the alternative—having someone else create it for you. Most advertising agencies will make a commission of 15% on the cost of your ad, so if the cost of the display advertisement is $2500, the agency will get a $375 commission. This commission comes out of the total cost of the advertisement and is not an additional cost to you, so it may sound like an immediate good deal. However, there are some factors about using a mail order advertising agency that you should be aware of, not the least of which is the fact that many advertising agencies will not want to deal with you until you are a fairly large advertiser.

Are there other alternatives you could choose? Certainly. There are many free-lance copywriters and artists around. For a fee, they can create the entire advertisement for you. Here are several sources of copywriters and creative designers.

1. *Your Telephone Book.* Look in the Yellow Pages under *Writers, Copywriters, Advertising Agencies, Artists,* or *Creative Designers.* Contact these experts and explain your needs to them. Show them examples of the type of advertisement you want and let them go to work. Remember that the copywriter is the one who writes the words and the creative graphic designer does the artwork. Sometimes you can get this done under one roof and sometimes not. Check with whomever you are speaking with to find out if they do both. Remember that these are two different specialties and that it would be rare to find a single individual capable of doing both, although you may find both specialists working in one firm.

2. *Your Local College or University.* Call the department of journalism, art, or advertising.

3. *Mail Order Magazines.* Get a copy of *Direct Marketing Magazine,* 224 Seventh Street, Garden City, New York 11530, or *Zip Magazine,* North American Publishing Company, 401 North Broad Street, Philadelphia, Pennsylvania 19108. These are the two major professional magazines of the mail order industry. In their classified sections you will find both types of specialists.

If you decide to create your own advertisements, be aware that a learning process is involved, and while you may be fortunate enough to create great advertisements right from the start, the chances are that you will not. The best advice I can give you is to glance through magazines and pick out advertisements for similar products that have been running for a reasonably long period. Copy not the ad, but the concept, in the sense that you try to create an ad that follows the same winning principles as the successful ad you see and admire.

In creating a full-page display ad, there is a one-third, one-third, and one-third rule. As with any rule, it is frequently violated. However, as a basis for starting, it should be considered. This rule says that one-third of your display ad should be devoted to headlines, one-third to graphics, and one-third to copy. Look at the display ads in Figures 9-1, 4-2, and 5-1, and you will see how this rule is sometimes applied.

Of course, there are many effective display advertisements without any illustrations at all. Karbo's ad is, again, the leading example. If you do decide to use an illustration, make it serve some definite purpose. In the Mellinger ad in Figure 5-1, the purpose is not only to show a picture of Brainerd Mellinger, which says that this man does exist and that his business is import/export and mail order, but also to show some of the many thousands of products he mentions in the advertisement. John Caples's ad in Figure 4-2 shows a line drawing of the incident described in the headline. The purpose here is to reinforce the benefit implied in the headline and throughout the copy. Do you recognize this benefit? It is the triumph of the writer who played the piano successfully after his friends had laughed because they thought he could not play. Maxwell Sackheim's ad in Figure 9-1 shows the author of the course, Sherwin Cody. A picture of this type is almost always used for credibility purposes. It shows the reader that this is a real man, a real individual who actually exists, not a figment of someone's imagination.

When constructing or deciding upon the illustration for your display advertisement, you should keep two questions uppermost in your mind: (1) Why am I putting this illustration in the ad? and (2) What purpose will this illustration serve? Putting an illustration in your ad just to have one there is counterproductive. It wastes space that could be used for hard-selling copy. What if Joe Karbo had used several square inches of his ad to show a picture of his book? Do you think this illustration would help the reader to make his mind up to purchase the product more than the copy that Karbo carries in his advertisement? Probably not. Everyone knows what a book looks like. If you aren't showing a picture for credibility, the purpose of the illustration should be to show the benefit of the product, which is usually done best by showing the product in use. In the case of Karbo's book, the benefit is success, a difficult concept to portray visually in a display advertisement usually carried in the classified section of the Sunday newspaper.

HOW TO APPLY THIS CONCEPT TO OTHER PRODUCTS

Let's say you are selling a pair of earrings. The picture of the earrings themselves may or may not elicit interest. But what if you showed a picture of a woman wearing such earrings, with several women and men admiring them? This shows satisfaction of the need—the benefit of the product. Always stress and show the benefit of a product by showing the buyer receiving the benefit.

SHOULD YOUR ILLUSTRATION BE A PHOTOGRAPH OR A LINE DRAWING?

Many people say photography is always superior. Others argue for illustrations, and still other mail order dealers use a combination of both. Gerardo Joffe, author of *How You Too Can Make At Least One Million Dollars (but Probably Much More) in the Mail Order Business* and the founder of Haverhills and Henniken's mail order houses, says that photography is probably suitable in many cases and that you should probably stick with it until you find a really good illustrator or artist. Joffe also feels that such products as clothing and food are probably better shown by photography. However, according to Joffe, in gadgets, equipment, and many other inanimate products, a good draftsman can often do things a camera cannot quite bring out. The draftsman can subtly emphasize points, bring out highlights, show attractive features, and suppress distracting details that cannot be readily accomplished with photography except by extensive and fairly expensive retouching. Do a little experimenting with both until you are satisfied with the results. Once you are successful, it's probably better to stick with your final choice to establish your own image.

HOW YOUR AD WILL BE REPRODUCED

There are three basic methods of printing, and depending on the type of printing used by the medium in which you are going to place your display advertisement, different materials must be furnished. These three types are offset, rotogravure, and letterpress.

Offset. Today most magazines and newspapers are printed by offset. The printing is done with a flat plate, which has been treated to make the ink adhere to portions of the plate that will be printed, while no ink will adhere to those portions of the plate not intended to be printed. The process gets its name because the ink from this plate is transferred to another cylinder that offsets it to the paper. As an advertiser, you must furnish "camera-ready artwork" to the magazine or newspaper. Camera-ready artwork is a paste-up of the artwork and copy display you want or a good, photographic positive copy of it. This positive copy is also called a reproduction proof. Your artist can prepare either for you.

Rotogravure. Rotogravure is used for Sunday supplements and similar publications. The areas to be printed are depressed and ink is deposited in these depressions. Again, all you need to furnish is camera-ready artwork or a reproduction proof. The publication itself will make its own plate from the material you send.

Letterpress. In a letterpress process, the printing is done with regular metal plates. Many magazines that strive for expert and fine reproductions use the letterpress process. Here your cost is going to be higher because camera-ready copy is not enough. You must supply the plates to the publication yourself, or you will have to pay to have a special plate made for you.

WHERE TO ADVERTISE

To decide where to advertise, the first step, as with other aspects of mail order, is to go where your competition goes. Therefore, if you know your competition is advertising heavily in certain magazines, they are as good a place as any to start. However, at some point, you must learn to use the publications from SRDS, Standard Rate and Data Service, Inc., 5201 Old Orchard Road, Skokie, Illinois 60077. SRDS produces a series of subscription publications throughout the year that are extremely useful to everyone in the mail order industry. For display advertising, the particular SRDS publications include *Community Publication Rates and Data,* which comes out semiannually, *Consumer Magazine and Farm Publication Rates and Data, Newspaper Rates and Data,* and *Business Publication Rates and Data,* which come out monthly.

To use SRDS, turn first to the classification groupings section of the publication. In *Consumer Magazine and Farm Publication Rates and Data* you will find approximately 50 different classifications. In a recent issue these were *Airline Inflight; Almanacs and Directories; Art and Antiques; Automotive; Aviation; Babies; Boating and Yachting; Brides and Bridal; Business and Finance; Campers, Recreational Vehicles, Mobile Homes, and Trailers; Camping and Outdoor Recreation, Children's; College and Alumni; Comics and Comic Technique; Crafts, Games, Hobbies and Models; Dancing; Dogs and Pets; Dressmaking and Needlework; Editorial and Classified Advertising; Education and Teacher; Entertainment Guides and Programs; Entertainment and Performing Arts; Epicurean; Fishing and Hunting; Fraternal, Professional Groups, Service Clubs, Veteran's Organizations, and Associations; Gardening; Gay Publications; General Editorial; General Editorial/Contemporary; General Merchandise Catalogs; Health; History; Home Service and Home; Horses, Riding, and Breeding; Humanities and Contemporary Topics; Labor-Trade Union; Lifestyle Service; Literary, Book Reviews, and Writing Techniques; Mechanics and Science; Media/Personalities; Men's; Metropolitan; Military and Naval; Motorcycle; Music; Mystery, Adventure and Science Fiction; Nature and Ecology; News Weeklies; News Biweeklies, Semimonthlies; Newspaper-Distributed Magazine; Photography; Physical Sciences; Political and Social Topics; Religious and Denominational; Romance; Science; Senior Citizens; Sex; Snowmobiling; Society; Sports; Travel; TV and Radio/Communications and Electronics; Women's; Women's Fashions, Beauty, and Grooming;* and *Youth.* That's quite a collection. How do you pick the right classification?

Begin by selecting those classifications of publications whose readers are most likely to be interested in your product or service. For example, under the *Youth* classification the following magazines are listed: *Boys' Life, Campus Life, The 18 Almanac, Exploring, Junior Scholastic,* Laufer Youth Publications, Scholastic Magazine Groups, *16 Magazine, Teen Beat, For Seniors Only, National 4-H News, New York News For Kids, Scholastic Newstime, School Guide, Vica,* and *Young Miss.*

Now look up the number assigned to this classification under the general classification listings. See Figure 9-2. For *Youth,* the proper classification number is 50. In the general classification section, you will see all of the magazines listed, including extensive information on each magazine, as in Figure 9-3. This information includes the local representatives and branch offices with addresses, the commission and cash discount, the general rate policy, the black/white rates, the combination rates, dis-

Classification Groupings—Consumer Magazines—Continued

Consumer Magazine and Farm Publication Rates and Data

Figure 9-2. SRDS classification groupings of consumer magazines.

190

Figure 9-3. SRDS information listing for advertising in The *American Legion Maga-*
zine.

counts, color rates, covers, inserts, bleed, special position rates, classified
and reading notices, split run and special issue rates and data, geographical and/or demographic additions, contract and copy regulations, mechanical requirements, issue and closing dates, special services,
circulation, distribution, print order, and other pertinent information. In
short, you will find everything you need to know to advertise in every
major magazine you might be interested in.

The next step is to write to every magazine that is a potential publication for your promotion and ask for a sample copy and a rate card. The
rate card should have information identical to that contained in the section describing that magazine in SRDS. However, since it is coming from
the publisher, it may have additional details and may be slightly more
current, even though *Consumer Magazine and Farm Publication Rates
and Data* is published monthly. A typical rate card is shown in Figure 9-4.

WHEN SHOULD YOU ADVERTISE
AND HOW FREQUENTLY?

As I've said before, the month in which you advertise your product or
service can have a great impact on your results. For general guidelines,
you will find the following to be true.

1. Some products can be advertised all year. Some can be advertised
   and sold only during certain seasons.
2. Major events can affect the results of your promotion. Ordinarily,
   November is a good month for your products, but it may not be
   good, depending upon what product you are selling in an election
   year, since an election is a major event. Similarly, a war, the death
   of an important person, or other major events will affect your results in a mail order promotion.
3. Whatever your product, some months are better than others. You
   can only find out what months these are for your product by testing. As a starting point, here is a list of months from best to worst,
   as compiled from various sources: January, February, October, November, March, September, August, April, December, July, May,
   and June.

If you start your testing in a "good" month, recognize that your results
may be much better than had you tested in an average or poor mail order
month. In the same way, if your test ad appears in a "bad" month for a
general mail order product and the results you achieve are only marginal,

RATE CARD

NUMBER
37

Effective with October 1980 Issue

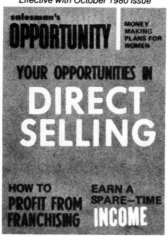

MONTHLY MAGAZINE FOR SALESPEOPLE, FRANCHISE AND BUSINESS OPPORTUNITY SEEKERS.

A. ADVERTISING RATES
B. COMMISSIONS, DISCOUNTS
   & CREDIT
C. MECHANICAL REQUIREMENTS
D. CLOSING DATES
E. ADVERTISING CONDITIONS
F. CHARACTER OF CIRCULATION

published by:

OPPORTUNITY PRESS, INC.

GENERAL ADVERTISING OFFICE
Suite 1405, 6 North Michigan Avenue
Chicago, Illinois 60602
312-346-4790
Cable / Salesopp Chicago
Telex / 25-6138

Figure 9-4. A typical rate card, this one for *Salesman's Opportunity.*

A. ADVERTISING RATES

DISPLAY RATES SPACE IN AGATE LINES (14 Agate lines equal 1 inch deep by a column $2^3/_8$ inches wide)	Wide × Deep	FREQUENCY DISCOUNT (Within 12 Month Period)		
		1 Issue	6 Issues	12 Issues
14-69	per line	$ 9.90	$ 9.40	$ 8.91
70	(1/6 pg.) $^1/_2$ Column $2^3/_8'' \times 5''$	651.00	618.80	585.90
71-142	per line	9.30	8.84	8.37
143	($^1/_3$ pg.) 1 Full Column $2^3/_8'' \times 10^1/_4''$ or 71 lines on 2 columns $5'' \times 5^1/_8''$	1.310.00	1.244.50	1.179.00
144-213	per line	9.10	8.65	8.19
214	($^1/_2$ pg.) Standard $5'' \times 7^5/_8''$ 107 lines on 2 columns	1.660.00	1.577.00	1.494.00
214	($^1/_2$ pg.) Special Vertical· $3^5/_8'' \times 10^1/_4''$ full depth of page	1.730.00	1.647.00	1.564.00
214	($^1/_2$ pg.) Horizontal $7^1/_2'' \times 5''$ 71 lines on 3 columns	1.730.00	1.647.00	1.564.00
215-285	per line	8.30	7.89	7.47
286	($^2/_3$ pg.) $5'' \times 10^1/_4''$ 143 lines on 2 columns	1.990.00	1.890.50	1.791.00
287-428	per line	6.90	6.55	6.21
429	(1 pg.) black on white $7^1/_2'' \times 10^1/_4''$	2.620.00	2.489.00	2.358.00
429	(1 pg.) Black and Red	2.835.00	2.704.00	2.573.00
429	(1 pg.) Black and Special Color	2.895.00	2.764.00	2.633.00
Over 429	per line	6.10	5.80	5.49
858	(2 pgs.) Facing Black on White	4.900.00	4.655.00	4.410.00
PREFERRED POSITIONS·				
429	2nd or 3rd Cover in Black (Color Extra)	2.800.00	2.660.00	2.520.00
429	4th Cover in Black (Color Extra)	2.900.00	2.755.00	2.610.00
858	Center Spread in Black (Color Extra)	5.000.00	4.750.00	4.500.00

COLOR & SPECIAL DIMENSION EXTRAS
(No frequency discount)

Standard Red per page or less $215.00
Special Color per page or less· $275.00
4 Colors· 725.00
Ad layouts across 3 columns
   of less than full page space· 70.00
·When available

SPECIAL 3-TIME CONSECUTIVE INSERTION DISCOUNT
First 2 consecutive insertions at '1 issue' rate. 3rd consecutive insertion only at 10°° discount. (If display advertising appears in 6 or more
issues within a one year period, the advertiser will qualify for the higher
discount, less the amount deducted.)

CLASSIFIED ADVERTISING RATES
Per Word . . . . $ 2.60
Line of Bold Face or White Space $26.00
Minimum of 12 words $31.20

10°° off for three or more consecutive insertions

Name and address, number groups and initials count as words.
Standard setting, first line upper case, balance upper and lower case.

Figure 9-4. (Continued)

194

B. COMMISSIONS, DISCOUNTS & CREDIT

1. Agency commission to recognized advertising agencies only — 15°₀.

2. Payment with order on all accounts whose credit has not been established with the publication.

3. Billing date is on or before the 5th of month preceding month of issue. (Example: July issue advertising will be billed by 5th of June.)

4. Cash discount. 2°₀ on display advertising only, if paid by 15th of month prior to month of issue. (Example: July issue advertising discountable if paid by June 15th.)

5. Account past due on 1st of month of issue. (Example: July issue advertising past due on 1st of July.)

6. Frequency rates apply only to advertisements by advertiser (or wholly-owned subsidiary) within a 12 consecutive month period and in different issues.

7. Billing involving frequency discount will be payable at the "1 issue" rate until the number of insertions required for discount have been placed. Upon placement of required number of insertions, discount applicable to all previous advertising due to frequency of insertion will be credited or refunded.
   Example: Place 6 or more advertisements in 12 months and earn retroactive 6 time rates on sixth insertion. Six time frequency discount totals 5°₀ credit on space charges, exclusive of color costs. Consecutive insertions in 12 issues will qualify for retroactive 12 time rates upon completion of schedule. Twelve time advertisers will earn 10°₀ discount from single insertion rate on space charges, exclusive of color costs.

8. Minimum display space accepted and required to maintain frequency rate — 14 lines (1 inch).

C. MECHANICAL REQUIREMENTS

1. Widths: Single column . . . . $2^3{}_8''$
   Double column . . . . 5''
   Type page . . . . $7^1{}_2''$ × $10^1{}_4''$ deep
   Trim size . . . . $8^1{}_8''$ × $10^7{}_8''$ deep

2. Type page — 429 agate lines consisting of 3 columns of 143 agate lines deep each.

3. Printing process: Web offset.

4. Binding method: Saddle stitched.

5. Bleed: $8^1{}_4''$ × $11^1{}_8''$, minimum of 5/16'' between live matter and trim.

6. Preferred material: Right reading negatives emulsion side down, positives, reproduction proofs.

7. Acceptable material: Negatives, positives, reproduction proofs, scotchprints. For halftone reproduction in scotchprints or reproduction proofs, forward Black and White glossy photos.

8. Recommended screens and densities:
   a. B/W and/or 2c screen: recom. 100
   b. B/W and/or 2c density: max. 160°₀; 2nd color not to exceed 100°₀. Only one color may be solid.
   c. 4c screen: recom. 120; max. 133
   d. 4c density: max. 260°₀.

9. AAAA/MPA/ABP offset standards apply.

10. Rotation of colors: Y, R, B, Blk.
    (Contact Chicago office for 4-color mechanical requirements and offset standards).

Figure 9-4. (Continued)

D. CLOSING DATES

1. Cover and center spread forms close 15th of second month preceding issue month. (Example: July issue covers and center spread close on May 15th.)
2. Body of magazine except center spread — final forms close 26th of second preceding month. (Example: July issue closes May 26th.)
3. No proofs furnished for correction or changes after 25th of second preceding month. (Example: July issue proof changes not accepted after May 25th.)
4. Cover, center spread and insert cancellations not accepted after 1st of second preceding month. (Example: No cover, center spread or insert cancellations accepted for July issue after May 1st.)
5. No body of magazine cancellation of advertising or changes in submitted copy accepted after 16th of second preceding month. (Example: No inside of magazine cancellations or changes accepted for July issue after 16th of May.)

E. ADVERTISING CONDITIONS

1. Artwork required by advertisement as indicated in layout, billed at cost plus 15%.
2. Orders demanding positions other than covers and center spreads not accepted.
3. We assume no responsibility for film, art or cuts uncalled for six months after date of insertion.
4. Companies unknown to publisher must send full particulars of proposition and credit information.
5. No order accepted until approved by Opportunity Press, Inc.
6. Opportunity Press, Inc. reserves right to refuse any advertising for any reason and to omit accepted advertising which interferes with production schedule due to tardiness of receipt or special demands of advertiser.
7. We assume no responsibility for errors in ad keys.
8. Cost of changes in approved copy after advertisement is in proof form will be billed to the advertiser.
9. No blind advertisement will be accepted until full information on specific purpose and proposition is submitted to Opportunity Press, Inc.
10. Advertisements with box numbered addresses or no street addresses not accepted, unless Opportunity Press, Inc. is supplied with full address and phone number. This information maintained in confidence on request.
11. Advertisers and advertising agencies assume liability for all contents of advertisements printed, and for any claims on OPPORTUNITY PRESS, INC. arising therefrom.
12. Advertisers and advertising agencies agree that OPPORTUNITY PRESS, INC. shall be under no liability whatsoever by reason of any error or omission for which Salesman's OPPORTUNITY may be responsible in any advertisement beyond the cost of space actually occupied by the error.
13. Mailing Instructions: Send all orders, copy, layouts, positives, proofs and other materials to OPPORTUNITY PRESS, INC., Suite 1405, 6 North Michigan Avenue, Chicago, Illinois 60602.

F. CHARACTER OF CIRCULATION

1. Direct to consumer salesmen, saleswomen, house-to-house agents, both full time and part time, including party plan operators, crew managers, route men, wagon jobbers. Also potential franchisees, independent salesmen, business opportunity seekers, distributors selling to stores and retail outlets for resale. Salesmen servicing big users such as industries, institutions, schools, hospitals, hotels.
2. Locality of Circulation: National, throughout the United States and possessions and Canada.
3. Subscriptions and highly qualified controlled mailing.
4. In circulation last week of month preceding date of issue.
5. Established 1923.
6. Single copy price, $1.25, subscription price per year $8.00, Canada $9.00, Foreign $12.00.
7. Average monthly circulation 190,000, including paid subscription and controlled.

Figure 9-4. (Continued)

196

you should recognize that you may achieve much better results in other months.

When first starting off with your new product or service, start with the logical months, considering your product and the season of the year. If you are successful, depending upon the strength of your response, you can consider additional months of the year for your advertising. For example, if the strength of your response from your selection was extremely strong, you can consider advertising this product quite frequently. Brainerd Mellinger runs his ads for his import/export and mail order courses continuously and has for years. If the strength of your response is only moderately strong, but still profitable, you should advertise less frequently—perhaps every other month or even once a quarter, or only during certain months. Finally, if you are profitable but the response is weak during a good mail order month, you may be able to advertise this particular product or service only infrequently during the year.

Again, the only way to discover when to advertise is through testing.

Jerry Buchanan of Vancouver, who has made a fortune selling his *Writer's Utopia Formula Report* and the *Towers Club Newsletter,* has found that he can safely shut down his operation two months out of the year and not publish his newsletter at all. He uses this time for vacation. Jerry has also discovered that certain months don't pay for him to advertise at all, despite the fact that both his newsletter and report are fabulously successful. Lesson: You can be very successful and take a two-month vacation to boot without year-round advertising.

WHAT SIZE SHOULD YOUR AD BE?

There is a basic trade-off between the space you need to tell your story and the cost of this ad space. In other words, a large ad in which you can tell your entire story will cost more money than a small ad in which you don't have as much space to say everything that will convince a prospective customer to buy.

There are also standard sizes for magazines and newspapers, and when considering the construction of your ad you must also consider what size is available. For a typical magazine, the standard page is seven by 10 inches. Each page is divided into three columns. Each column on the page is 140 lines deep or 14 lines per inch. Of this area, a full page is always available. You can also obtain two-thirds of a page, which is two columns wide; one-third of a page, which is one column wide; or a third of a page that is one-third of the page square and is 14 columns wide. You can also obtain one-sixth of a page, which is half a column wide; and one-twelfth of a page, which is one-quarter of a column wide.

Sometimes you can buy magazine space by the number of lines you need. Consult the SRDS publications or the rate card of the magazine in question.

There are also standard sizes for newspapers: Most have advertising columns 1⅞ inches wide. But these sizes vary, and you can choose depending upon the column width. There are other standards for the Sunday supplement, *TV Guide*, and so forth.

Here are the facts you must consider in your decision about the size of your ad. First, consider cost per order per inquiry: Given a certain size, how much money does each inquiry cost you? You must test to find this figure. Take the total number of inquiries or orders you generate from your ad and divide by the cost of the advertisement.

The second consideration is speed in establishing yourself in the marketplace. Remember that everything you do in mail order is seen by everyone else, including all your competitors. One successful strategy for beating the competition is getting established in the marketplace before your competition can do so. A large ad helps in doing this by appearing before a large number of people in a relatively short time.

The third aspect to consider is the size of the market reached. A classified advertisement is seen by only a small portion of the readership of any particular publication. To reach a larger market, you need a larger ad. Therefore, in many cases, even though the cost per inquiry or order may be much higher with a large advertisement, it still makes sense to pay the higher price to reach a much larger market.

The fourth factor to consider is the nature of the product or service you are selling. Some types of product demand a very large advertisement—one with which the public is unfamiliar, for example. You need more time and space to describe and sell this product since you must describe and sell not only its unique features but also the advantages of the product as a generic type. Another example might be an intangible or informational kind of product, such as those sold by Karbo, Haroldsen, Suarez, and Buchanan. Finally, you will need more space to sell a more expensive, or "big-ticket," product than a cheaper one.

There are some other guidelines to help you decide whether your product requires a large or small ad. Let's be honest: Sometimes the size of your ad, although not optional, will be dictated by your budget. If you have determined that you cannot sell your product or service effectively through a small advertisement, you should consider borrowing money (see chapter 2). The old saying that you can't squeeze blood out of a stone holds here. Your product may be the type that can be totally successful through a large advertisement but cannot be successful at all in a smaller one. If you are in this situation, borrow the money you need for a proper campaign or wait until you have the money to do the job right. Once again, look at your successful competition for similar products or services. If your competition sells with a large ad and it is successful, chances are you will have to do the same. If your competition is successful, this means it has already been in business for some time and has probably tested smaller ads as well and found that the larger ad is the one best suited for this particular product or service. Conversely, if your successful competition is using smaller ads, this means the exact opposite.

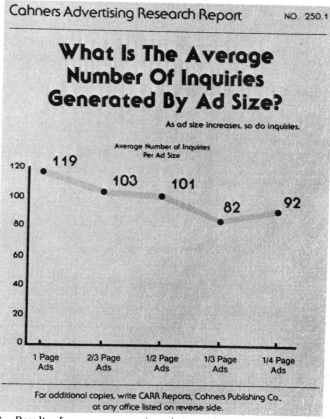

Figure 9-5. Results of a survey comparing ad size and number of inquiries. The larger the ad, the more inquiries.

Finally, consider the strategy and tactics you have decided upon to introduce your product. Are you selling direct from the ad or through a two-
step method? Sometimes the inquiry and follow-up can be done with a
smaller ad. Sometimes, of course, it is still more effective to use a larger
ad, as Brainerd Mellinger does so successfully.

Cahners Publishing Company did two studies that are important to
your ad size decision. One study analyzed how the readership was influenced by ad size as the size of the ad increased. Cahners sorted 2353
advertisements by size classification and response. An average response
was calculated and assigned an index number, an arbitrary number used
for the convenience of the researcher. This index number for the average
response was 100. Against this number, ads had index scores as follows: a
quarter-page ad had an index score of 55, a little over half the average; a
half-page ad had an index score of 91; and a full-page ad had an index
score of 124. Note here that doubling the ad size did not result in doubling
the index score. Cahners concluded that as the size of the ad increased,
reader influence, as measured by response, increased, but not in direct
proportion.

In a second study, Cahners measured the average number of inquiries
generated by advertisement size. In this survey, Cahners analyzed 500,-
000 inquiries generated by several industrial magazines, as shown in Figure 9-5. As ad size increased, more inquiries were generated. However,
again, the increase in the average number of inquiries was not in direct
proportion to the size, indicating that cost per inquiry is probably less for
smaller ads than for larger ones.

SHOULD YOU USE COLOR OR BLACK AND WHITE
FOR YOUR ADVERTISEMENT?

Color, of course, costs more money than does black and white. To make
up this additional cost, you will generally need a 20% greater response.
Does color bring in a 20% greater response? The answer is "yes" when it
is appropriate, and that depends upon your product. Bob Stone reports an
increase of 30 to 60% in response to color ads for appropriate products.
What is meant by appropriate products? If your product is the kind that
must be seen to be appreciated, where the colors are vivid and make an
impact on the potential buyer, color is worth considering. But if color
does not have this anticipated effect on your potential buyer, it should not
be used, or its use should be delayed until you have a successful black
and white test completed.

WHERE IN EACH PUBLICATION SHOULD YOU ADVERTISE?

You may be surprised to learn that, depending upon the location in the magazine or newspaper, the identical ad will result in different numbers of responses.

There are two major rules to follow regarding ad positioning. The first is that the better visibility your advertisement has, the better results you will get. The second general rule is that the front of the magazine produces better results than the back. A major exception to this rule is the back cover, which produces excellent results.

There are other general rules. The upper part of the magazine appears to do better than the lower part. The outside of a page does better than the inside of a page. It is usually better to be near editorial matter—that is, appearing close to the regular copy of the magazine, rather than away from it. Finally, it is usually a little better to be in front of the editorial matter than after it. If you think about it, you'll see that all of these results are due to visibility.

How important can positioning be? Let's look at an example. Let's assume that the standard cost of advertising in a magazine is $2000 for a full-page ad. Now, most magazines recognize the fact that some positions are much better than others. So, we'll say that we want to advertise on the back cover. A full-page ad on the back cover will cost 50% more, or $3000. Which position is more profitable for us? Well, if our $2000 ad appears at one of the less favored positions in the magazine, it may bring in only half the response of the back cover. Therefore, let's assume that our normal response is 1.5 times the cost of the ad in sales—that is, our $2000 ad cost will bring us $3000 in sales for our product. If we subtract the $2000 ad cost and, let's say, $500 for the cost of the product, that leaves a $500 profit. Now, let's look at the back cover. This ad will cost us $3000. Since our response is twice that of the other location, this ad would bring in $6000. From this, we subtract the $3000 cost of the advertisement and $1000 cost of product and fulfillment, leaving $2000 in profit. That's a big difference in profits. The location of the ad is very important.

How can you control the location of the ad? You can pay a premium, as in our example. However, sometimes locations are not recognized by the publication as being better or worse. If special rates aren't mentioned for particular locations in the SRDS publication or the rate card, good positions are not recognized by the magazine, and you can ask for a favorable location. Sometimes the magazine will grant it. However, if you are a new advertiser with a small budget, you will probably have little luck with your request until you are a bigger advertiser, spending more money. But if your ad appears in a poor location and fails to do well, ask the publication if it will rerun it in a better location at no extra charge. Sometimes it will, since it recognizes that the mail order advertiser must make money with his or her ad or not advertise at all. Of course, a magazine won't always do this for you, and how much advertising you are currently doing there will probably affect its decision. But it never hurts to ask.

HOW TO PLACE YOUR AD

If you are placing your own advertisement without going through an agency, all you have to do is follow the instructions in the SRDS publication or on the rate card. For example, Figure 9-3 is an extract from the SRDS instructions for advertising in *The American Legion Magazine*. One of the important items to remember is the issue and closing dates for your advertisement. In paragraph 16 of Figure 9-3, *Issue and Closing Dates,* it is stated that the magazine is published monthly and issued the first day of the publication month. This paragraph also states a firm order closing date for black and white and two-color forms: the tenth of the second month preceding month of issue. So if the month of issue is December, you must submit your order and advertisement by October 10. Paragraph 16 further states that the firm order closing for four-color forms is the twelfth of the third month preceding the month of issue. These lead times vary from one magazine to another. Since the month of your ad appearance can be very important, make certain that you read this section of the SRDS or the rate card very closely.

Your letter to the publication should state that you intend to advertise and include the details regarding the size, color, special locations of your ad, and so forth, and should include whatever copy is required. Some magazines will require that you submit a sample of your product or the sales package with which you will respond to inquiries. Be certain to include this material if it is requested. Otherwise, the magazine may not run your ad.

HOW TO BUY DISPLAY ADVERTISING
AT MUCH LESS THAN THE STANDARD RATE

The pros in the business buy advertising at a lot less than the price paid by most beginners. These differences are significant and can spell the difference between profitability and failure with your advertisement, so please don't skip this section.

Here are 12 methods of saving money with space advertising, each of which can save you hundreds, or even thousands, of dollars:

1. Mail order discounts
2. PI (per inquiries) deals
3. Frequency discounts
4. Standby rates
5. Help if necessary
6. Remnants in regional editions
7. Barter
8. Bulk buyers
9. Seasonal discounts
10. Spread discounts
11. Your own advertising agency
12. Cost discounts

Mail Order Discounts

Magazines know that, as a mail order advertiser, you must make money directly from your ad or you will not advertise again. Further, unlike an institutional advertiser, you will know immediately exactly how well your ad did and whether it is making money for you. So many magazines give special discounts, up to 40%, to mail order advertisers. That means that a $100 ad will cost you only $60. That is certainly nothing to sneeze at and can easily spell the difference between a failure and a very profitable promotion.

PI Deals

A PI deal is one in which you agree to pay the publication only for those inquiries or sales that the ad attracts. In return for this agreement, the magazine runs your advertisement at no charge to you. Sometimes the mail is sent directly to you. At other times the publication will insist that the mail be sent to it. Of course, the ad must be keyed and, if the mail is sent to you, you must keep accurate records and send the money owed to the publication at fixed periods agreed to between you and the magazine. If the orders go to the publication, it will send you the names of those who order so that you can send the product to the customer. It will also send you the money owed for each product. For a PI deal, most magazines will require something like 50% of the price of the product you are selling in return for running your advertisement with no money up front.

Sometimes it's difficult to locate PI deals, and you should talk to the salesperson representing the magazine. Few magazines would like their other advertisers to know that PI deals are accepted, so, don't expect to see them advertised on the rate card and don't expect every magazine to offer them.

Melvin Powers, the dean of mail order book publishers, says, "I have several PI deals that are resulting in thousands of orders every week for my books."

Frequency Discounts

Most magazines will offer a discount for frequency. For example, if you advertise every month, you can expect to get a substantial discount. If you advertise six times, four times, or three times a year, you can also expect a discount. The one cautionary note about frequency discounts is that you should not arrange to advertise in a medium at a fixed frequency until you do the proper testing. If your ad is not working, advertising frequency is no bargain, no matter what the discount.

Standby Rates

A magazine or newspaper is committed to publication on a regular basis. At certain times, all the available advertising space may not be sold out at the last minute. The magazine, therefore, has a choice: sell this advertising space at a greatly reduced amount or put in editorial content, which does not generate additional profits. To get the standby rate, you must first let magazines know that you are interested in this type of deal. Of course, these magazines must be able to get hold of you quickly by telephone. Usually the standby rate is available only after you have advertised in a magazine for some time. Then the people at the magazine know you and trust you. This is important since the magazine is offering to run your ad based on a telephone conversation with no money from you in advance. But asking for the standby rate is well worth it. You may pay as little as 40 or 50% of the normal cost of the advertising. That's quite a bargain and can mean big profits for you.

Help If Necessary

You cannot always get "help if necessary," but again, many magazines will give you help when they recognize that they are dealing with a mail order advertiser. What this means is that, although you agree to pay for the ad in advance, if the advertisement runs and is not profitable, the publication agrees to run the ad again and repeat it if necessary until you at least break even. You may not make any additional money with a "help if necessary" arrangement, but you sure can prevent yourself from losing a lot. And, as in every business situation, avoidance of losing your valuable financial resources can be as important as reaching your profit goals immediately. Why? Because retaining your financial clout means you can change your ad, offer, or product to win out eventually.

Remnants for Regional Editions

Today, many national magazines will allow you to buy space only in certain regions, rather than providing space for advertising nationally. This situation reduces your advertising cost and is ideal for testing, especially when you want to test one copy in one region and one copy in another, or only to advertise in certain regions that may be profitable to you. The result for many regions, however, is remnant space—space left over much as in the standby situation we talked about before. Again, you find out about this by asking the salespeople or publishers whether they have regional remnant space available and having them contact you. Typical discounts for remnant space are as much as 50%.

Barter

If you have something to trade, a publisher may allow you to trade for something he or she wants and run your ad for nothing or at a reduced cost. This occurs where the publisher has interests other than publishing the magazine and can make money from the product or service you are offering. Or, if you are a publisher yourself, sometimes you can trade or barter advertising space with other publications. Barter has an advantage in addition to getting advertisements at a greatly reduced or net cost: It builds up sales of the product you are bartering. Although you may agree to barter at wholesale, usually you make money on it anyway, since your production costs are lower than the wholesale costs you charge.

Bulk Buyers

Bulk buyers buy huge amounts of space from a magazine at reduced cost. The bulk buyer fulfills the contract by either running the advertisement for his or her own products or services or selling off unused space to other advertisers. The price you pay with a bulk buyer will vary greatly and is negotiable. You may be able to get as much as a 50% discount from what you would normally pay.

You may have a problem locating bulk buyers. There are not a whole lot of them. One way is to keep your eyes open in magazines such as *Zip* and *Direct Marketing*, the two leading professional magazines of the mail order industry. Look in the classified section. Another way is to have a mail order consultant locate a bulk buyer for you. Consultants can also be found in these magazines.

Seasonal Discounts

Some magazines whose advertising decreases in certain seasons will offer a discount to a mail order advertiser who will advertise then. Again, if this information is not on the rate card, ask for it and see whether the magazine offers a seasonal discount. The one thing you must be careful of here is that your product is profitable to advertise during this magazine's off season. As we talked about earlier, profitability will vary by season, depending on the product you are selling. However, it may be that your product fits perfectly into the season for which you can get a discount. If so, it's your lucky day and you can save a lot of money this way.

Spread Discounts

If you are a really big advertiser and advertise on two or more pages in one issue of a particular magazine, you may be able to get a spread discount. Here again, this may not be on the rate card so you should ask about it. A spread discount can run as high as 50% of the total cost of your advertisement.

Your Own Advertising Agency

Advertising agencies get an automatic 15% discount from any medium in which they place your ad. As a result, many mail order dealers have established their own in-house advertising agencies. They then place their own ads with the magazines through their in-house agencies and get automatic 15% discounts. Most magazines say that they will not deal with in-house agencies and will not accept advertisements from them at the 15% discount. But the fact is, most will. They say this only to protect the advertising agencies who are their regular customers. However, you should not make it obvious that you are an in-house agency when you place your ad. This means:

1. Your in-house advertising agency should have a name different from your company's.
2. You should have special stationery printed up with the in-house advertising agency's name.
3. You should not volunteer the fact that you are an in-house agency. Merely indicate that you are placing the ad for the company indicated and give other instructions in accordance with the rate card or SRDS publication.

Cash Discounts

Many people dealing in mail order advertising overlook the fact that most media will give a 2% discount for payment of cash within 10 days. However, if you do not take this discount, very few magazines will automatically return your money. So look for this information in the rate card or in the SRDS publication and, if you do pay for the ad with cash or check within 10 days of billing or follow whatever other instructions are required, take the discount offered. If you are a giant advertiser like Joe Karbo, Brainerd Mellinger, or Joe Sugarman, 2% can amount to $20,000, $30,000, $40,000, $50,000, or even more.

HOW TO GET FREE "ADVERTISING"

Every magazine is constantly looking for new ideas, new news, and new information to tell its readers, so whenever you have a new product or service, magazines will be happy to publicize this for you at no charge if it thinks it's readers will be interested. This free "advertising" has the advantage, in addition to not costing anything, of appearing to be a recommendation by a very credible, impartial source—the editor or writer of the magazine in which this material appears. You should understand that not every new idea or product will be run by every magazine you approach. Therefore, you must conduct a mini–direct mail campaign to locate magazines that will be interested. Your campaign package should consist of three basic elements.

1. A cover letter.
2. Suggested editorial material about your new product or service. This is called a publicity release.
3. Either the new product itself or a four-by-five-inch glossy photograph of the product. Sending the product itself does not necessar-

ily enhance your chances of getting this free advertising, so send a photograph except for those products a photograph of which would not in any way add to a reader's or editor's understanding of what the product is. For example, if you are selling a book or booklet, the product itself may do be better than the photograph.

Figure 9-6 is a letter to the editor for free promotion for a body armor product I sold several years ago. Follow this general format when asking for free promotion in a letter. Do not mention that you may become a paid advertiser later. If you are sending money to the magazine for a paid display advertisement, do not send it with the letter to the editor requesting free editorial mention.

Figure 9-7 shows a typical publicity release that might accompany a letter such as the one shown in Figure 9-6. Figure 9-8 shows a photograph of the product. While you can have publicity information as listed in Fig-

---

Mr. A.B. Jones
Editor
World Military Gazette
101 New State Drive
New York NY   10065

Dear Mr. Jones:

I am writing to you because my company, Global Associates, has just developed a new product which will have a tremendous effect on casualty reduction in military operations. This new product is a personal protective body armor which is half the weight of current models but gives slightly more than double the level of protection.

This amazing armor is called "KPC Composite," and it is soft and flexible although it has five times the tensile strength of steel. A special patented carrier has been developed for the KPC Composite material. The whole unit is called "The Commando MK III Armor Jacket."

I know that your readers will be interested in knowing not only of the existence of this life-saving garment, but also that individual soldiers can order their own Commando MK III Armor Jackets directly from Global Associates at $300 per unit, insurance and postage costs included. I have enclosed a publicity release along with a photograph for your use if desired.

                                        Sincerely,

                                        President
                                        GLOBAL ASSOCIATES

Figure 9-6.   A letter to a magazine editor to try to obtain coverage—in other words, free advertising.

PUBLICITY RELEASE

New Body Armor Announced

Global Associates, a body armor company, announced the development of a new personal protective body armor today. The new armor, known as KPC Composite, is half the weight of current body armor, but offers twice the level of protection. The armor also has the unusual properties of being soft and flexible although it displays five times the tensile strength of steel.

The armor has defeated projectiles travelling as fast as 2000 feet per second. It has also been tested against and has stopped various small-arm ammunition, including .38 caliber, .45 caliber, .22 magnum, 9mm, .41 magnum, and .44 magnum.

A special patented carrier has been designed for the armor and designated the Commando MK III Armor Jacket. This garment itself has many unusual features. It is worn like a jacket, with a closure in the front. This permits increased ventilation during use and allows the armor to be donned or doffed without removing the helmet or other headgear.

In addition, a special lockstrap suspension system has been developed. Although the straps cannot be pulled apart, under emergency conditions the armor can be completely jettisoned in less than three seconds. For normal armor closure, a protected slide fastener is provided.

The entire ensemble comes in three sizes—small, medium, and large. It weighs just 4½ pounds.

Interested buyers can purchase the Commando MK III Armor Jacket by sending $300 to Global Associates, P.O. Box 1975, Sierra, California 91076.

Figure 9-7. Publicity release to accompany the letter shown in Figure 9-6.

ure 9-7 reproduced in quantity, the letter to the editor works better if individually typed. Photographs can also be reproduced in quantity cheaply, although usually not by your standard photographer. For example, four-by-five-inch glossies in quantities of 100 can be obtained for as little as 15¢ a copy by a duplicate photo service; check your Yellow Pages. Here is one I have used and found satisfactory: Duplicate Photo Laboratories, Inc., P.O. Box 2670, 1522 North Highland Avenue, Hollywood, California 90028.

RESULTS TO EXPECT AND HOW QUICKLY TO EXPECT THEM

An advertisement itself may be profitable and yet you can still lose money because of overhead. Also, since mail order is a back-end profit business, you must also consider this factor when you talk about the profitability of an ad. So reread the chapter on mail order profit calculations. As a rough rule, a space advertisement should bring a return on

Figure 9-8.   Photograph of the product, included in the publicity packet sent to a magazine editor.

your investment of at least 30% to be profitable. Let's say that the advertisement cost is $8000; 30% of $8000 is $2400. Since you want a return of your investment of $2400, you must add this to your investment, making a total of $10,400.

From this figure we can calculate how many responses are needed. If the price of your product is $10 and the product cost plus the fulfillment cost (that is, postage, package, etc.) is $1, your gross profit is $9 for each unit you sell. Take the $10,400 and divide this by $9: we must sell about 1156 units for the ad to give us a 30% return on our advertising investment. If we sell this many, the ad is profitable and worth repeating. If you want to know the total sales required, just multiply 1156 times the sale price of $10: $11,560.

Now we must deal with another problem. The results from your advertisement will come in over a year or more. How can we estimate these returns quickly so we can decide whether to increase our advertising?

Responses to advertisements seem to come after about the same time, regardless of which monthly magazine you are advertising in. One week after your first response, you will probably receive 5% of the responses you will ever receive. After two weeks for a monthly magazine, you will probably receive 20% of your total returns. After one month, you will probably receive 50%, and after one year, you will probably receive very close to 100%. (I must tell you that on several occasions I have received responses more than four years after the advertisement appeared in a particular issue of a particular magazine, but these are unusual cases.) Therefore, by simply multiplying the number of responses you have received after one month by two, you will know the total number of responses you can expect from this particular ad. In the case of the example we used earlier, where 1156 responses were required, if after one month we received 600 responses, we would multiply times two, giving 1200 responses. Since 1200 is greater than 1156, it would be worth repeating this advertisement. If, however, only 500 responses were received, 500 times two is 1000, which is less than 1156, so we probably would not repeat the ad without making some changes.

The response period for weekly magazines and newspapers is not identical to that of monthly magazines, so you must adjust the formula somewhat. With weekly magazines, in general, 50% of your total responses will be received two weeks after the first response; and with newspapers, 90% of the total responses will be received by the end of the second week. Take these calculations into consideration when you decide whether to repeat the ad.

Once you start your advertising, keep your own records since some differences may occur, depending upon the type of weekly magazine or newspaper and your product. Sometimes conditions such as improved mail delivery may change these patterns.

MEDIA PLANNING STRATEGY AND PYRAMIDING

Before you submit your first advertisement, you should anticipate ahead of time that if you are successful you will want to expand your advertising rapidly. This procedure is called media planning strategy and it is especially important if you have a limited budget. You must develop your media planning strategy and pyramid your advertising rapidly because if you are successful, you will invariably have imitators who will attempt to copy your product, your service and your advertisements, and even the magazines you advertise in. Therefore, the trade-off is the money you must risk versus the competition that will attempt to split your market. The general principle to follow is to pick the various categories or groupings discussed earlier in this chapter in which the readers may be interested in what you have to sell and advertise first in one of these. If successful, expand your advertisement into another category, at the same time repeating your ad in the successful magazine as well as an additional magazine in the same category. Now, you are advertising simultaneously in two categories. If the second magazine of the first category you advertised in is successful, you can then assume that the entire category of magazines will be successful for that ad and for that product. You should then advertise in as many of the magazines in that first category as possible, considering your budget. Now look at the second category. Was it successful? If so, repeat that ad and run it in a second magazine in that category, and meanwhile expand into a third category with one advertisement. Once you really have a winner, you can roll out and begin to take some increased risks. But the important principle here is to walk before you run. Do not assume that because a magazine in one category is successful, all magazines in that category will be successful until you have tested at least two of them.

SHOULD YOU USE AN ADVERTISING AGENCY?

Many beginners feel that they must have an advertising agency to be successful; others feel equally strongly that they should never use an agency. Either approach may be correct, depending on the situation. It is very difficult to get an advertising agency to work with you at the beginning because they usually work on commission. If you are doing a very small amount of advertising, and this is usually true of the beginner, the agency can't make enough money from you to make a business relationship worthwhile. On the other hand, if you do not use an advertising agency, you will have to do much of the legwork yourself, including finding and engaging the necessary freelance copywriters and creative people. One major advantage of using an agency is that you can get professional and expert help all at one stop. If you decide to use an agency, you can contact one through your Yellow Pages. But be absolutely certain that they have mail order experience, and do not be bashful about asking for samples from mail order experience they have had. Ask for some client references in the mail order field, then contact them to find out their experiences with this particular agency. Many agencies like to think that they have had mail order experience, although, in fact, they've really been concerned mainly with non-direct response ads. You will find a list of advertising agencies that deal primarily in mail order or direct mail in Appendix E of this book.

I believe that if you can do without an advertising agency at the beginning, it's a good way to learn a lot of the things that you should know when dealing with them. Once you have started to make big money, it makes more sense economically to contact an advertising agency to perform as many professional services as you would like. And since you have done a lot of work yourself previously, you can approach their recommendations on a much more professional basis.

From Ron Ball, manager of marketing services of Pentel of America, Ltd., and reader of the first edition of *Building a Mail Order Business*, comes the following story, which illustrates well how to put it all together to develop a successful space advertising campaign.

How to Take a Product that Won't Fly and Make it Soar like an Eagle

In May of 1981, Pentel, manufacturers and marketeers of some of the most innovative writing instruments in the world, proudly introduced its unique, laser cut, Ceramicron pen to the marketplace. It never took off the ground.

Why? Several reasons. First, Pentel relies heavily on the wholesale trade to move products to the retail level. This means the product benefits have to be communicated to the Pentel sales force, to the wholesale buyer, to the wholesaler sales rep, to the retail buyer, retail sales clerk and finally the consumer. Too many variables to effectly communicate what the product is and does.

Second, the marketing department felt this was a specialized pen for people who need very fine writing. It's not a general writing instrument. It required a rifle shot instead of a shotgun blast. Third, it was a totally new type of pen, utilizing new technology which had to be communicated.

Enter direct marketing. For the previous two years, I had pushed the idea of direct marketing specific products. Persistence paid off because the Pentel Ceramicron pen was a product Pentel had put a lot of research and development in. The CEO said it had to move.

So I went to work and quickly put together a direct marketing subsidiary called Omnex to test the idea. Pentel wanted to market the pen through a company with a different name because they were concerned they'd get complaints from wholesalers and retailers about selling directly to consumers. The results later proved the ads we ran did the reverse—they created greater product awareness and increased the wholesaler and retailer business. People who buy by mail order purchased their pen through Omnex. Customers who buy retail walked into stores with the ad in their hand.

I had been studying direct marketing for five years and felt confident I had the variety of skills necessary to make the program work.

COMPUTER AGE PEN WRITES, DRAWS MICRO LINES

This may be the most important breakthrough in pen technology since the ball-point was invented over 40 years ago.

Laslo Biro was a talented Hungarian journalist, sculptor and hypnotist. In 1938 he tried something new. He invented the ballpoint pen. It won instant success when introduced at Gimbels in New York. Even at the unheard of price of $12.50. In fact, over 10,000 pens sold before closing time. Now over 40 years later, another revolutionary pen has come of age.

Writes in Tiny Spaces

The Pentel® Ceramicron™ pen is a technical masterpiece. It has a patented ceramic point that writes and draws micro-precision 0.3mm lines. So you can squeeze writing into tiny spaces other pens can't. Yet your writing stays neat and easy to read. You'll be amazed how such a sharp point writes so smooth too. All with such a light, easy touch.

The Ceramicron pen makes a welcome pocket companion for doctors, lawyers, business executives, sales people, accountants, architects, engineers, designers, art directors, editors, writers, librarians, computer programmers and scientists. Anyone who needs very fine writing, letters or numbers.

It's perfect for notebooks, pocket calendars, journals and ledger books. Superb for computer work too. Use the pen for editing memos, reports or manuscripts. And, if you favor a special pen for correspondence, the Ceramicron pen gives you expressive, hair-line signatures that command attention.

Consistent Line Quality

You'll also want to use it for drawing. Whether you're a graphics pro or someone who occasionally does forms, graphs and charts. The Ceramicron pen draws black, micro-precision lines. Consistently! The last line you draw is as dark and sharp as the first. Another feature — the pen has a long 4mm steel sleeve that serves as a guide for line work.

If you require a technical pen, think of the Ceramicron pen as an alternative. It's durable and reliable. And uses convenient refill cartridges. No tips to clean. No ink spills to worry about. Just snap on the leak-proof, airtight cap. And back in your pocket it goes. Ready to use any time, anyplace.

High-Tech Styling

The Pentel Ceramicron pen is also extremely good looking. The non-corrosive, brushed stainless steel barrel is made to last. And it looks sleek, high-tech, futuristic. It's a pen that gets noticed.

Innovative Ceramic Tip

The Ceramicron pen has a point different from any other pen. Picture this. A ceramic porcelain pipe, small as a straight pin, shielded by a 4mm steel sleeve. (Ceramic porcelain because it's second to a diamond in hardness.) Inside the pipe, a filament "pumps" ink to the tip by capillary action and regulates ink flow. What you end up with is a precise point that's also very strong and durable.

Quick Drying Ink

The ink in the Ceramicron pen is a specially formulated water based ink. It penetrates into paper and dries quickly. You won't have problems like skipping, globbing, beading and smearing. Some of the things that happen with oil based ink pens. Write or draw over 4000 feet before you need a new ink refill. As far as almost 4500 sheets of paper lined end to end for 3/4 of a mile. You'll find refill cartridges in the most popular ink colors — black, blue, red and green.

Consistent Line Quality Dark, micro-precision lines. Ink flows instantly, evenly. Excellent for graphics.

Figure 9-9. Omnex ad in the *Wall Street Journal.*

214

As I mentioned to you when we met, Dr. Cohen, your book, "Building a Mail Order Business," has been an important educational tool for me. I've got about 15 good books at home on mail order and direct marketing. Your book is the best and the first book I'd recommend anyone to buy.

Even though I have never written a direct marketing space ad before in my life, I literally put together everything from A to Z concerning concept, copy and management. Within five weeks we went from nothing to a company with an ad in the *Wall Street Journal*.

Don Malucky, our art director, was my partner in preparing the visual elements of the ad, literature and packaging. [The actual ad is shown in Figure 9-9.]

I came up with the name Omnex because I wanted a short, easy-to-remember, high-tech-sounding name. And, it took me about a week to come up with a name no other company was using.

I set up the banking and credit cards. We use the National Communications Center in Shingle Springs, California for our toll-free service and Motivational Packaging and Fulfillment in Commerce, California for our cashiering and fulfillment. [The results were as shown in Figures 9-10, 9-11, and 9-12.]

What I Think the Omnex Program Proves—

1. A company can take a good product, lagging in sales through regular channels of distribution, and turn it into a sales winner using direct marketing techniques to effectively communicate product benefits.
2. A company can use direct marketing ads to generate a self-perpetuating advertising budget and increase the retail awareness of the product.
3. A person who is a self-starter, persistent, has attention to detail, entrepreneurial skills, and a willingness to study everything he or she can find about direct marketing can build a mail order business.

To me, the most exciting thing about this program was being able to blend all my creative and management skills together and put everything into action in a short period of time and on a tight budget and see it all work. I'm an entrepreneur at heart. And I've always been fortunate enough to work in companies where I have tremendous freedom and total responsibility.

I've done a lot of things in my career. For three years, I produced radio special programs and interviewed over 150 recording artists. Everybody from Paul Anka to Stevie Wonder. I also spent three years at Vivitar Corporation writing everything from ads to booklets on all kinds of photography. At Pentel, I've been able to use all my marketing communication skills. But nothing I've ever done feels as great as the first order that somebody sent in at Omnex. There is nothing that compares to it. Self-esteem fireworks go off.

Publication	Type	Date	Orders pulled	Ranking
Wall Street Journal Eastern Edition	daily	2/2/83	378	4
Wall Street Journal Midwest Edition	daily	2/2/83	418	5
Wall Street Journal Western Edition	daily	2/2/83	268	6
Wall Street Journal Southwest Edition	daily	2/2/83	136	8
American Medical News	weekly	2/4/83	557	1
Journal of Accountancy	monthly	2/83	378	3
Wall Street Journal Midwest Edition	daily	5/6/83	385	7
American Medical News	weekly	5/6/83	317	2

Figure 9-10. Omnex media testing.

Offer	Ceramicron Pen Offer	Bounce-backtx Total	Total
Sales revenues (As of January 31, 1983)	$72,313	$12,691	$85,004
Unit sales	4837 ea.	1414 ea.	6255 ea.
New profit	$9.987	$5,885	$15,872
Total investment	—	—	$29,192
Return on investment (ROI)	34%	20%	54%

Figure 9-11. Omnex sales results.

	Number of orders	Percentage
By toll-free number and credit cards	2000	41%
By mail and credit card	709	15%
By mail and check	2128	44%
WCustomer who bought pen and bounce-back offer	1418	29%
Returns from customers	15	.3%

Figure 9-12. How people bought.

SUMMARY

In this chapter, you have learned important facts and techniques for running profitable display ads. In review, keep in mind these important points.

You will use display ads because you can build a bigger volume business in this way, reach more readers less expensively than by other methods such as direct mail, and get many names for the back-end part of your business.

You can create an effective space ad by yourself or through the help of an agency. If you create a display ad on your own, you locate the copywriters and creative people yourself . . . or you write the copy yourself.

You will advertise in those magazines that are better for advertising your particular product or service.

Some months and some seasons are better for advertising than others. The frequency of advertising depends on the product and the success you had with your initial ad.

The appearance of your ad is important. How large the ad is can determine success, as well as proper use of color and black and white.

Different responses can be expected depending upon whether your ad appears on the back cover, near editorial matter, away from editorial matter, in the upper part of the magazine, on the outside, and so forth. Usually the key is visibility.

When placing your ad, allow sufficient lead time, as indicated on the rate card.

Twelve different ways were given in which you might greatly reduce the cost of your display advertising from standard rates. These were use of mail order discounts, PI deals, frequency discounts, standby rates, help if necessary, remnant space in regional editions, barter, bulk buyers, seasonal discounts, spread discounts, use of your own in-house advertising agency, and cash discounts.

You can get free promotion in magazines, and this can greatly increase sales of your product.

To know how to expand, you must first know the results you can expect from a display advertisement and how quickly to expect them. Basically, for a monthly magazine, 50% of your total returns will arrive after one month. To predict the returns you will get, multiply that number by two.

Finally, we discussed the advertising agency, how to find one, and whether you need one.

Display advertisements can cause your business to skyrocket in profits. Don't neglect them!

10

There Is Big Money in Direct Mail

Direct mail involves sending your sales material directly to your prospective customer without the preliminary step of gathering names through some type of advertisement, as in the two-step method for classified or display. It is made possible by the rental of lists of names from others or by special mailings to your own house list of customers. For the professional mail order dealer, direct mail is an important and powerful strategy. It has major advantages over other strategies of mail order selling.

THE IMPORTANT ADVANTAGES OF DIRECT MAIL

Direct mail has five important advantages over other mail order processes.

1. Selectivity
2. Personalized approach
3. Speed in getting to the market
4. Concealment of test information
5. More sales copy possible

Let's look at each of these in turn. Direct mail means selectivity. It is the rifle approach as compared to the shotgun. With this rifle, you can aim very precisely at your target market through the rental of the name list you use. Are you interested in selling to women executives? List manager Ed Burnett offers breakdowns in the category of women executives by age, income, and job functions; whether divorced, single, widowed, or married; special classifications of women executives such as Catholics, Jews, womens college graduates, executives of major corporations, women golfers and country club members, high school graduates, investors, lawyers, and so on. You do not reach this degree of precise market segmentation accuracy when advertising through classified ads or with display advertisements in magazines or newspapers. Because of this accuracy, many mail order firms do virtually all of their business by direct mail. Paul McDonald, president of Procurement Associates, Inc., which gives seminars around the world, promotes to its potential attendees entirely through direct mail. McDonald has reached more than 20,000 seminar attendees this way, and his business exceeds $2 million a year.

Personalized contact is possible through the use of direct mail. When you deal with direct mail, you are dealing with a one-on-one situation— you are speaking directly to your potential customer. Furthermore, your letter can be personalized through use of the computer in a way that is absolutely impossible for other mail order methods. For example, look at the cover of the catalog in Figure 10-1. Would you believe that every one of the millions of recipients of this catalog received it with his or her own name and address, just as the one shown? This personalization greatly increases your chances of success. One of the most successful techniques in my book *The Executive's Guide to Finding a Superior Job,* is a direct mail campaign to individuals who may be interested in hiring you, and this letter goes out with the potential employer's name and title on each and every letter. This direct mail strategy yields phenomenal results in getting interviews and job offers. Yet space advertising that promotes an individual seeking a job is usually unsuccessful. It is this personalized feature of direct mail that helps to make it a winner. And it works equally well whether you are selling a product, a service, or yourself.

As I told you in the last chapter, the lead time with many magazines for placing an advertisement can be six weeks or more; and then after that, you must wait a full year before you receive most of the responses you will ultimately receive. Not so with direct mail. You can mail whenever you are ready. With direct mail, you will receive half your response only one week after the first inquiry! This means you will know at once whether your proposition is profitable or not. If it is, you can expand your promotion immediately with little lead time. Furthermore, you will receive all your responses six months after receiving the first inquiry and you will have 95% after only two months. If mail order has the potential of being a fast way to riches, the direct mail method has the potential of being super fast.

Maintaining confidentiality of your operations to the maximum extent possible is very important in mail order because it is easy for potential competitors to see what you are doing. With display advertising or even

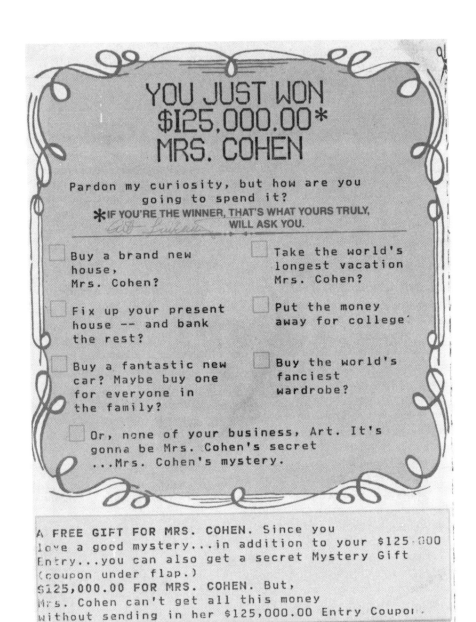

Figure 10-1. Lure of big winnings.

classified, it's impossible to conceal success. Your success can be spotted easily by your repeated advertising. Direct mail is also open to your competitors since many names on a list will be individuals who are interested or engaged in mail order operations. However, it is much harder for your competition to track what you are doing since it is unlikely that any one competitor will see more than a small portion of your mailings to different lists. Because you're being able to keep much of your advertising confidential except to the individuals who receive the ads, it is also easier to test various prices with little chance of confusing or irritating your potential customers. Although not a major problem, it is true that if you take a full-page display ad that indicates one price, it is difficult to show the same display ad in another magazine at another price without creating some confusion and question in the minds of your prospective customers. With direct mail, you can test many different prices with a reduced chance that the same potential customer will see many of your different prices being tested.

Advertising in media such as magazines and newspapers allow you to use sales copy from a few words in a classified ad up to many hundreds of words in a full-page display ad. However, this cannot compare at all with direct mail, in which you can tailor the advertising copy to achieve maximum profitability. You are not limited to one full page. In fact, your letter to a customer may go from four to six pages by itself, and letters are usually not the only element of the direct mail package. As a consequence, you have a much greater chance of making the sale than if less copy was necessitated by limitations of space and cost in a magazine.

With all these good things, you must realize that, like any other business or any other method of dealing in direct response, it is not a guaranteed success, and in some cases your other mail order strategies will be more profitable. Your product may not be suited to a direct mail campaign and your ads may work better with space advertising or classified. Also, direct mail is relatively expensive as far as reaching total numbers of potential customers is concerned. As was pointed out in chapter 9, costs per potential customer reached by space advertising are a lot less than those required by direct mail, if you consider the numbers of readers as representing potential customers. So don't assume that any direct mail campaign will automatically be successful.

WHEN TO USE DIRECT MAIL

You should use direct mail when you have a clearly defined product with a clearly defined market segment to which it appeals. When Ed McLean developed a very successful campaign for selling Mercedes-Benz cars with diesel engines by direct mail, his specialized product was introduced to a clearly defined market segment, consisting of individuals who not only were interested in expensive foreign cars, but who had the income to purchase them. Correct use of direct mail was extremely successful and won for Ed McLean the Golden Mailbox Award of the Direct Mail/Marketing Association. AMACOM, a division of the American Management Association, sold more than 20,000 copies of my book *The Executive's Guide to Finding a Superior Job* through direct mail because it was a specialized product offered to a clearly defined market segment of executives who were members of the American Management Association or who had bought similar products from this organization previously. Chase Revel in Los Angeles built his product, an information newsletter on new businesses to individuals who were interested in starting new businesses, from a simple eight-page letter to a multimillion-dollar business with a slick magazine called *Entrepreneur* and two large organizations, the International Entrepreneur's Association and the American Entrepreneur's Association. Each of these organizations does a multimillion-dollar business annually in selling booklets, business plans, the magazine *Entrepreneur,* seminars, and other information to individuals interested in small business. Once again, this was made possible because Chase Revelle sold a clearly defined product to a clearly defined market segment.

Even if you meet the criteria of a clearly defined market segment and a specialized product that appeals to it, you must still test first to see whether your product and offer will work using this strategy. The principle is to test first, and then, if you have a winner, expand with more direct mailings fast. The term used is *roll-out,* and the implication is a much larger mailing mailed as soon as possible. Even such giants as Ben Suarez, author of *Seven Steps to Freedom,* and Joe Sugarman, with his multimillion-dollar electronics business operating mainly through space advertising, at first stumbled with products when using direct mail.

49 WAYS TO USE DIRECT MAIL

Richard S. Hodgson, in his encyclopedic, *Direct Mail and Mail Order Handbook,* lists 49 different ways to use direct mail. This list was assembled by the Direct Marketing Association when it was still known as the Direct Mail Advertising Association. But don't think that because the list is old the different ways are no longer used. On the contrary, each and every way listed is still bringing in millions of dollars every year.

If you already have a non-mail order business, direct mail can help:

1. Build morale of employees
2. Secure data from employees
3. Stimulate salespeople to greater efforts
4. Pave the way for salespeople
5. Secure inquiries for salespeople
6. Teach salespeople how to sell
7. Sell stockholders and others interested in your company
8. Keep contact with customers between sales calls
9. Further sell prospective customers after a demonstration of sales call
10. Acknowledge orders or payments
11. Welcome new customers
12. Collect accounts

If you want to build new business, direct mail can help:

13. Secure new dealers
14. Secure direct orders
15. Build weak territories
16. Win back inactive customers
17. Develop sales in areas not covered by salespeople
18. Develop sales among specified groups
19. Follow inquiries received from direct or other forms of advertising
20. Drive home sales arguments
21. Sell other items in line
22. Get product prescribed or specified
23. Sell new type of buyer

Direct mail can assist present dealers by:

24. Bringing buyer to showroom
25. Helping present dealers sell more
26. Merchandising your plans
27. Educating dealers on superiorities of your product or service
28. Educating retail clerks in the selling of a product
29. Securing information from dealers or dealers' clerks
30. Referring inquiries from consumer advertising to local dealers

Direct mail can assist in gaining customers by:

31. Creating a need or demand for a product
32. Increasing consumption of a product among present users
33. Bringing customers into a store to buy
34. Opening new charge accounts
35. Capitalizing on special events

Some additional uses are:

36. Building good will
37. Capitalizing on other advertising
38. As a leader or hook in other forms of advertising
39. Breaking down resistance to a product or service
40. Stimulating interests in forthcoming events
41. Distribution of samples
42. Announcing a new product, new policy, or new addition
43. Announcing a new address or change in telephone number
44. Keeping a concern or product in mind
45. Research for new ideas and suggestions
46. Correcting present mailing lists
47. Securing names for lists
48. Protecting patents or special processes
49. Raising funds

Probably no business in the world can use all 49 ways of using direct mail, but in looking through this list you can see the wide variety of things you can do with it and use to help you build your business profitably.

THE FIVE SUCCESS STEPS IN DIRECT MAIL

There are five success steps for direct mail. If you follow these five steps, you will build a successful business through the use of this amazing tool.

1. Identify your market.
2. Prepare your package.
3. Pick your list.

4. Test.

5. Roll out if successful.

Let's look at each of these in turn.

Identify Your Market

Identifying your target market means identifying those people who probably have the greatest interest in buying your product or service. You may say that everyone in the United States is a potential candidate to buy the product you are offering. However, in reality, certain people have a much greater potential than others, and it is better to concentrate on that segment. So it is important to stop right here and think who exactly is going to buy what you are offering. Try to picture them in your mind. What are their interests? Where are they located? How much money are they earning? This process is called market segmentation and you can segment a market in a number of different ways by introducing different variables into your thinking and seeing which offers you the best opportunities for selling your product.

The major variables for market segmentation are geographic, demographic, psychographic, and behavioristic. Geographic variables have to do with location. Certain products, for example, can be offered only to those potential customers living in a climate such as Southern California or Florida. On the other hand, if you have a product that has to do with snow removal, this would not be the geographical area that would be interested. Demographics have to do with many factors, including age, sex, family size, family life cycle (that is, young; single; married; married, no children; retired; etc.), income, occupation, education, religion, race, and nationality. All of these demographic factors will affect the purchase of the product or service you are offering. Psychographic factors include breakdown by social class, life style, and personality of potential buyers. Finally, we have behavioristic variables, which include reason for the purchase, whether it is a regular or special occasion, benefit sought, whether the user is a first-time user, a nonuser, or an exuser of the type of product, the rate of use, whether the potential customers are already informed about the types of product you are selling or are totally unaware that such a type of product exists, sensitivity to price, quality, service, and so forth.

You may think there is an awful lot of time to be spent in identifying the market segment to which you will sell your goods when "almost anyone would be interested." Believe me when I tell you that the time spent in identifying your market will pay dividends later on and will help to make your product successful and profitable, whereas if you jump in and try to sell to everyone, your campaign may well fail.

Prepare Your Package

Having identified the target market you are after, you must prepare your mail package, considering all of the above factors. Typically, a direct mail package will include an outside envelope, sales letter, guarantee, order blank, self-addressed and stamped envelope, publisher's letter, and testimonials.

The outside envelope is critical for the direct mail package and you have some major decisions to make here. Unless the recipient opens your direct mail package, he or she will never see the offer that is inside. There are different approaches to this problem. One is to use an envelope with nothing on it but the customer's address. The theory is that the individual will open it out of curiosity; he or she does not know who is writing and whether it is important. Another solution is to offer a teaser on the outside of the envelope that will encourage your potential customer to open it. Figures 10-2 through 10-9 show different examples of outside envelopes used as teasers. Some mail order advertisers try to give their envelopes the appearance of an official letter—from the government or a lawyer or doctor—in hopes that the respondent will be sure to open it, believing it to be of some importance. I do not agree with this tactic at all, although I do believe that it serves its purpose of getting the respondent to open the letter. The problem here is one of credibility. If you take this approach, you are trying to fool your potential customer, and once he or she realizes that he or she has been fooled, your proposition will be much less credi-

Figure 10-2. Lure of a great deal.

Figure 10-3. Lure of a free gift.

ble. Of course, the same is also true with the teaser if it promises something that is not delivered inside. The bottom line is that you lose credibility, which will definitely hurt your response rate. You should also be
careful of the use of the words *personal* and *confidential* on envelopes.
Many industrial sales letters use them to attempt to circumvent the secretary, who is sometimes instructed to screen out all "unimportant mail."
The problem here is that this is so overused that it is a dead giveaway for
some sort of sales package. Furthermore, it also affects credibility if, in

Figure 10-4. A free watch.

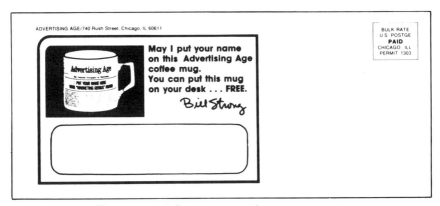

Figure 10-5.   A free mug . . . with your name on it.

fact, there is no reason that the contents should be personal or confidential.

The Sales Letter.   The sales letter is an extremely important component of your overall direct mail package. As its name implies, its job is to sell your product or your service. One common myth is that the sales letter should be short. This is not necessarily true. For consumer sales letters, the sales letter should be four pages or more. In some cases they are from eight to 10 pages and are extremely successful. Sales letters selling industrial products should be somewhat shorter—one to three pages; but they must still sell and not just be a cover sheet that says "See brochure enclosed." I am going to tell you how to write copy for sales letters in a later chapter. For now, I want you to look at some really outstanding examples of sales letters. Look at the letters in Figures 10-10 and 10-11. Note how they get the reader's interest and attention immediately. Note also that both letters use a P.S. Why is that? Did the writer of the letter really forget something after spending so long writing it? Nonsense. The P.S. is always included in a good sales letter because a P.S. is always read. The sales letter is the centerpiece of your direct mail package. One offering, selling a $10,000 product, consisted of a seven-page sales letter and nothing else. It resulted in $600,000 in sales in one mailing. If done correctly, your sales letter can do similar things for you.

The Flier.   The flier is a brochure, separate from the sales letter, that contains additional information and frequently an illustration to capture the reader's attention and convince him or her to buy. The fliers done by large companies are frequently multicolored, printed on very thick paper,

Figure 10-6. "Incredible savings."

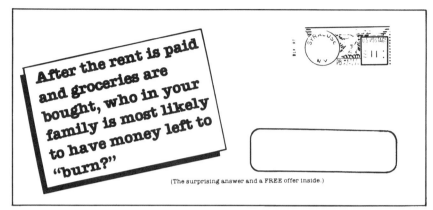

Figure 10-7. A tantalizing question; "Surprising answer and a free gift inside."

Figure 10-8. Lure of improved health.

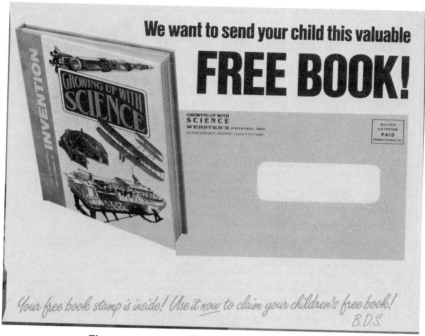

We want to send your child this valuable

FREE BOOK!

GROWING UP WITH
SCIENCE
WEBSTER'S UNIFIED, INC.

Your free book stamp is inside! Use it now to claim your children's free book!

B.D.S.

Figure 10-9.   "Valuable free book" for your child.

and extremely expensive. However, their high cost is justified because they bring in additional sales and help convince the buyer to purchase. Such a flier is shown in Figure 10-12. The flier restates many of the terms and information contained in the letter, but it acts as a visualizer to enable the prospective customer to picture the product better. A less expensive flier is shown in Figure 10-13. It is not printed on glossy paper, but it serves the same purpose and reinforces the sales presentation started by the sales letter.

Sometimes the envelope, sales letter, and brochure are combined into one, with additional components of the mailing packages stapled in. A very successful package of this type is the Harvey Brody direct mail piece selling his course on how to become wealthy, shown in Figure 10-14. It consists of a booklet explaining his program, inside of which is a self-addressed envelope, a letter, questions and answers, a list and description of bonuses, a page of testimonials, and an additional brochure highlighting the main points. The entire package is held together by a single staple.

Accept this amazing offer now and wear this handsome Jet Plane Swiss Movement Calendar Watch as a FREE GIFT from me!

TELLS DATE TOO

Save $40.00 Too!

Dear Friend:

World Trade is a rolling snowball! It is an avalanche of profit ready to be pocketed by those who take advantage of opportunities that are offered today. See how this beautiful Jet Plane Calendar Watch helps you start quickly.

Wear it proudly...and take easy big-profit orders from friends, stores, everyone who sees this beautiful Calendar Watch. It is just one example of hundreds of products we set up for you to order direct from overseas suppliers. Many suppliers will drop ship direct to your customers, so you pocket profits in advance--even before ordering merchandise.

The future of World Trade is greater than ever. Profits are waiting. Import or Export one "right" product and you can make a fortune as other World Traders have!

Are you going to become a part of the big import boom? Are you going to start your own profitable import business just 10 days from today? The enclosed article from a leading national magazine tells you how others following my Plan cash in on World Trade. And you can too!

But their success is nothing compared to opportunities ahead! The really big boom--with our government's program behind it--is right now. Start today!

TIME IS ON YOUR SIDE--IF YOU ACT NOW

My Plan helps beginners start now--it shows you how to ride the crest of this new import boom--it shows you how to line your pockets with good cash profits. And it starts you fast--the very first day you are ready.

Here is how I start beginners in World Trade. First I send my 5-Volume World Trade Plan at my risk--to inspect and examine in the privacy of your home. Second, I put you in touch with overseas suppliers who send products direct from overseas. Third, I make it so easy to start your own Import business at home, that you are shown how to make good profits on the very first order.

When you accept my special offer that saves $40.00, here's what happens! You receive, with International Traders membership, all the other extras--8 Sample Imports including the World Trader Jet Plan Calendar Watch, Portfolio of Sample Business Forms, Drop Ship Directory, Membership Card and World Trade Certificate plus the special Trade Agreements. These Trade Agreements put you in good standing with overseas suppliers, trusted merchants we know will take good care of you. You should be treated with respect and consideration whether you order a single sample product or whether you send big quantity orders.

One of the Trade Agreements which I personally arranged for, is a complete line of beautiful, carved Teakwood Trays at amazing low prices. I found this supplier when I was in Bangkok, Thailand. I can assure you of the fine quality of this merchandise. But I don't ask you to take this proof alone. To help you start im-

(Please turn page)

Figure 10-10. Sales letter offering free watch.

DISCOVER

IS LOOKING FOR A FEW MORE BRIGHT PEOPLE WHO WANT TO KNOW EXACTLY WHAT'S GOING ON IN THE WORLD AND THE UNIVERSE ALL AROUND US.

■ ■ ■

THAT'S WHY *YOU* WERE CHOSEN FOR THIS INTRODUCTORY SUBSCRIPTION FREE GIFT OFFER

Dear Science Enthusiast,

    An incredible new kind of science magazine, called DISCOVER, has been launched by the publishers of TIME and LIFE.

    And you are one of an elite circle of people chosen for our exciting introductory subscription offer.

    DISCOVER is a special kind of magazine for special people. And from the indications we have about you, you're a literate, well-educated, and intellectually very curious person.

    If that sounds like a fair description, then DISCOVER is the magazine you've been waiting for; because it's "the science magazine for intelligent non-scientists."

<u>DISCOVER IS ALL ABOUT YOUR WORLD</u>
<u>... AND WHAT MAKES IT TICK</u>!

    We're living in the middle of an "age of discovery" unlike any era since the dawn of civilization. And DISCOVER has been created to help you cope with these far-reaching discoveries and use them to enrich your life style.

                            (over, please)

Figure 10-11.   Another outstanding sales letter.

233

In just a few months you will have a superb stamp collection.

Each month, you will receive a shipment of beautiful stamps.

We shall send you these stamps at the special price for friends of the Margrace Stamp Service, which means an overall reduction of at least

25% on the Stanley Gibbons catalog for the whole collection

If you join the **Margrace Stamp Service**, you automatically become a privileged collector.

For, unlike the independent collector, you will not have to spend several years building an acceptable collection. You will only have to wait a few months to acquire a remarkable collection of very beautiful stamps. You will not have to send for, or swap stamps, you need not even stir from your house.

We make it easy: every month, or thereabouts, stamp selections will be delivered to your door, every one enlarging and enhancing your collection.

You get everything you need to begin building a fascinating and educational stamp collection. Together with your first set of 55 stamps, you get all this

FREE!

- Collector's Album
- Collector's Manual
- National Emblems
- Flags of the World
- 1,000 Stamp Hinges
- Magnifying Glass
- Tweezers
- Perforation Gauge
- Map of the World
- Country Identification Manual

Stamps sent may differ from those illustrated.

55 STAMPS IN EACH SELECTION!

Each selection we send you will include 55 stamps from different countries and themes. Among these stamps, approximately thirty will form a set on a specific theme: cars, birds, railways, sports, religion, etc. These stamps will be in a small envelope inside your selection.

Also, each selection is protected by a specially designed folder so that the stamps are not damaged in the mail. On this folder you will find details of the general composition of the selection, points to note about certian stamps, and their geographic origins.

How do we do it?

It's simple: we buy in bulk and this means we obtain excellent terms. In fact, we are in touch with the top international dealers, and we know about the best terms and the most worthwhile stamps. Also, the selections are compiled by our Committee of Philatelic Experts, which guarantees the validity of your collection.

© 1984 Margrace Corp.

Figure 10-12. Example of a flier.

YOURS FREE
With Your Charter Subscription to Tax Avoidance Digest

Free Bonus #1:

35 Frequently Overlooked Tax Deductions

Here are some of the most inge-
nious tax reduction techniques
we've been able to find after years of
researching tax publications. We've
gathered them all into this special
report that is **sure** to shave dollars
off your tax bill. Here you'll find
simple methods for deferring income into future years, while increasing your deductions **this** year
. . . how a cooperative doctor can
vastly increase your medical deductions . . . **legitimate** ways to bury
personal expenses in your business
. . . using the stock market to create
paper losses . . . and much more!

Free Bonus #2:

How to Survive A Tax Audit

The prospect of an IRS audit
frightens most people, yet they
haven't planned what they will do if
they actually **are** audited. Then,
when the IRS calls, they are un-
prepared and immediately make
fatal mistakes. This report will tell
you exactly how to respond . . .
what your rights are . . . what you
must show the IRS, what you don't
have to . . . should you get a lawyer?
. . . plus: some aggressive tactics
that **don't** work.

5 Free Bonus Reports That Can Cut Your Taxes By Thousands of Dollars!

Free Bonus #3:

Tax Advantages to Starting Your Own Business

Every year, thousands of Americans
go into business for themselves. In
fact, 80% of the country's new jobs
come from small businesses. When
you read this special report, you'll
understand why. The federal government has literally **showered** tax
benefits on the small business—it is
truly **the ultimate tax shelter!** In this
report you'll learn: How to invest in
stocks, gold and other assets while
paying almost **no taxes** . . . how to
shift income and expenses back
and forth between you and your
business . . . the pros and cons of
incorporating . . . lend yourself
interest-free money . . . shelter vast
sums in retirement plans . . . enjoy
cars, health clubs, life insurance,
even free lunches with nontaxable
income!

Free Bonus #4:

Tips on Planning Your Estate

Many people never turn to estate
planning simply because they link it
with death and find the subject
unpleasant. What they **don't** know is
that estate planning has a lot to do
with reducing your tax bite while
you're still among the living! The
new tax law changes the picture
substantially. Some people needn't
fear estate taxes. Others will still
have to hustle to make sure their
possessions go to their loved ones
instead of the federal government.
This brief compendium of estate
planning ideas will point you in the
right direction.

Free Bonus #5:

A Checklist for Screening Tax Shelters Before You Invest

There are hundreds of legitimate tax
shelter deals that not only slice your
taxes—they are also good, solid
investments. You **should** invest in
them, if you can afford it. But **never**
take a prospectus or a general partner's promises at face value. Check
them out yourself, using the techniques you'll learn in this report:
How to do a character check on your
partners . . . the importance of
visiting the site yourself . . .
enlisting an outside expert . . . and
more.

All 5 of these valuable reports will be sent to you FREE just for trying Tax Avoidance Digest.

Tax Avoidance Digest • P.O. Box 6638 • Silver Spring • Maryland • 20906

Figure 10-13. Five free bonuses offered with charter subscription.

235

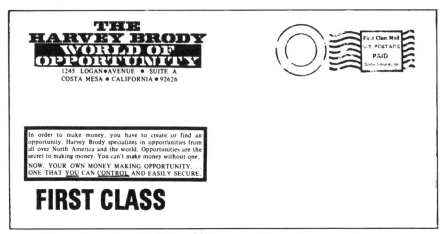

Figure 10-14.   Outside of Harvey Brody booklet and direct mail package.

The Guarantee.   The guarantee is important because it has an impact on your credibility. It must be stated in the strongest possible terms. To emphasize its importance, a separate guarantee is frequently included in direct mail packages. This guarantee, printed on a special paper, separated from the rest of the package, is frequently embossed with fancy artwork and contains big headlines that proclaim the guarantee is "ironclad." The potential customer cannot possibly miss it. It reinforces the idea that the potential buyer risks nothing by ordering by mail, and that whatever is purchased may be returned for a full refund. The guarantee helps to sell the item being sold. Figures 10-15, 10-16, and 10-17 shows examples of the direct mail guarantee.

The Order Blank.   You always want to make it as easy as possible for your potential customer to purchase from you, so an order blank is frequently used. It serves several purposes:

1.   As with every other element of the direct mail package, it is a sales device and frequently restates the proposition in favorable terms so that it again reinforces the purchase idea in the customer.
2.   It makes it easier for your customer to order since he or she does not have to write a separate letter to you.
3.   It ensures that the customer does not forget to include his or her name and address, something that happens more frequently than you might think.

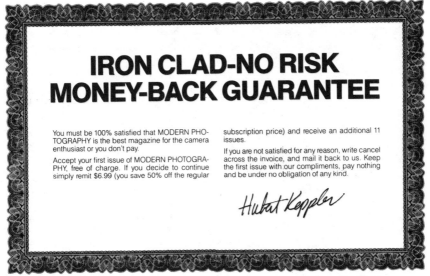

IRON CLAD-NO RISK MONEY-BACK GUARANTEE

You must be 100% satisfied that MODERN PHOTOGRAPHY is the best magazine for the camera enthusiast or you don't pay.

Accept your first issue of MODERN PHOTOGRAPHY, free of charge. If you decide to continue simply remit $6.99 (you save 50% off the regular subscription price) and receive an additional 11 issues.

If you are not satisfied for any reason, write cancel across the invoice, and mail it back to us. Keep the first issue with our compliments, pay nothing and be under no obligation of any kind.

Hubert Keppler

Figure 10-15. Example of a money-back guarantee (Hubert Keppler).

If you are selling on a time payment plan, the order blank can also be constructed so it is, in effect, a contract for time payments. The most successful example I have seen of this is Mellinger's "inspection request" in Figure 10-18. What a beautiful way to ease the psychological trauma of having to obligate yourself for time payment for a high-cost item.

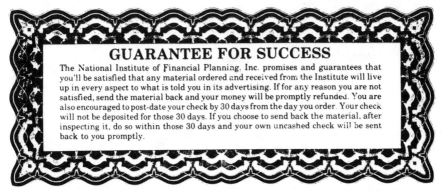

GUARANTEE FOR SUCCESS

The National Institute of Financial Planning, Inc. promises and guarantees that you'll be satisfied that any material ordered and received from the Institute will live up in every aspect to what is told you in its advertising. If for any reason you are not satisfied, send the material back and your money will be promptly refunded. You are also encouraged to post-date your check by 30 days from the day you order. Your check will not be deposited for those 30 days. If you choose to send back the material, after inspecting it, do so within those 30 days and your own uncashed check will be sent back to you promptly.

Figure 10-16. Another guarantee. Buyer is encouraged to postdate check.

You get a BONUS in...the *reusable* Picnic Cooler!

The insulated cooler your Omaha Steaks arrive in is a bonus gift you can use in many ways.

With its tight-fitting lid and recessed handles, it makes a great picnic cooler — which keeps cold foods cold, or hot foods hot. Take it along for picnics, vacations, camping, tailgate parties and other outings. Keep the reusable cooler handy for party use. Fill it with ice and add soft drinks, beer, bottles of wine — or whatever. Great for the patio and party room.

To order, call anytime
TOLL FREE 1-800-228-9055.
(In Nebraska, call collect 0-402-391-3660.)

You must be pleased
Guarantee...
If you are not pleased for any reason, we will replace your order or refund your money, whichever you prefer.

Omaha Steaks 🔲
International®
4400 South 96th Street • P.O. Box 3300
Omaha, Nebraska 68103

G2378-0283

Figure 10-17. You must be pleased GUARANTEE . . .

Inspection Request

$9 ONLY **BRINGS YOU 20 SECTION PLAN, SUPPLEMENT AND 11-PIECE VISUALIZER KIT.** *Your money back if not satisfied.*

POSITIVE MONEY-BACK
Agreement

Order your Mellinger World Trade Plan with the understanding that you can examine it in your home for 7 days after it has been delivered. If within that time you decide for some reason — any reason — that you do not wish to keep the Plan, simply mail it back to us by insured parcel post and we will refund your remittance in full. THE MELLINGER CO.

Important, record below exactly how you have given us your name. Please show it the same way each time you write to us.
Enter it here_____

Both payment plan and cash plan are covered by Positive Money-Back Agreement. Please read the information below. It explains the time payment arrangements when you use the Inspection Request to examine the offer of the World Trade Plan of 20 Sections, the Supplement and 11-piece Visualizer Kit on Plan No. 1.

Cash Price $146. 110
Less Cash Down Payment 9. 9
Amount financed $136. 101
Finance Charge 9. 9
Total of Payments $145. 110
Deferred Payment Price $155. 119
Annual Percentage Rate 35% 17%

You may examine the Plan for 7 days in your own home. If you keep the Plan after 7 days you agree to pay the Mellinger Co. at their offices shown above the TOTAL OF PAYMENTS shown above in 15 monthly installments of $10. 11

SEE OTHER SIDE FOR PARTIAL LIST OF WHAT YOU RECEIVE
1225

TEAR OFF HERE AND KEEP OUR MONEY-BACK CERTIFICATE

THE MELLINGER CO.
6100 Variel Avenue, Woodland Hills, CA 91367   Date_____

I want to examine the World Trade Plan of 20 Sections, the supplement and 11-piece Visualizer Kit. Ship to me by prepaid, insured parcel post with the understanding that I may mail it back within 7 days after I receive it for a full refund of my money if I am not satisfied.

It is agreed that I am to have consultation service. When paid in full, I am to receive my 2-year International Traders membership, 8 sample Imports, 6 Trade Agreements, Drop Ship Directory, Trade Opportunities magazine for 24 months, with bulletins on Mail Order methods and sample portfolio of business forms. I will follow the Plan carefully and restrict use of materials to myself. I I keep the Plan longer than 7 days, I will pay as I have checked below.

☐ **PLAN NO. 1** I enclose $9 inspection deposit. If I keep the Plan, I will pay $10 every 30 days until a total of $150 has been paid. 119

☐ **PLAN NO. 2** I enclose $146 Cash price. (I save $10) 110

Use your Master Charge, Visa, or Chargex on Plan No. 2 if you prefer. (See back of this form)

• Send Check or Money Order. Register currency. If under 21 have guarantor sign name, relationship and address on margin. Accounts overdue 30 days subject to 1½% monthly service charge on overdue amount. *Both plans are covered by positive money-back agreement.*

Check One ☐ Mr. ☐ Mrs. ☐ Miss   Phone:_____
                                                    Area   Number

NAME IN FULL _____ AGE____
                    (Please write in ink. Do not print.)

ADDRESS_____

CITY_____ STATE_____ ZIP_____
        Please correct any address error below. Don't mark top number.

I'll show you how to make big money. B. L. Mellinger, President.

Figure 10-18. The Mellinger Company's "inspection request," an effective order blank.

Self-Addressed Envelope.   Going back to the basic principle of making it as easy as possible for your prospective customer to order, a self-addressed envelope should always be included so that all that the prospective customer has to do is insert the order blank, enclose a check, put a stamp on it, seal it, and send it. One decision you have to make is whether to stamp this envelope or not. If you decide to have the envelope postage paid, you do not use regular postage stamps, since those who do not order will not use the envelope and that would waste your money. Instead, what you do is get a permit from the post office that gives you permission to have your printer print an envelope such as the one shown in Figure 10-19. Your printer knows how to do this for you—all he or she needs is the city and your permit number. The advantage of using an envelope like this is that, while you pay a premium for each envelope you receive, you pay none for envelopes that you send out that are not used. Now there is a disadvantage here that you should think about. In dealing in mail order you will run into a lot of nice people as customers. You will also run into some real nuts. Joe Karbo once received one of his self-addressed, stamped envelopes back with a sheet of lead inside. That lead cost Joe a couple of dollars in postage. I have received all sorts of strange things in stamped envelopes—from sheets of blank paper I had to pay for to things such as a sheet sent by a clearly unbalanced person who had written, over and over again in very tiny letters on both sides of the paper, in response to my sales package for the *Writer's Guide to Publication and Profit*: "I want to write for profit. I want to write for profit." You must pay the postmaster the required postage for whatever comes back with your name on it. Using a postage paid envelope will definitely

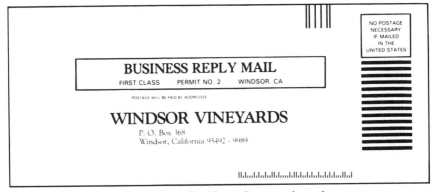

Figure 10-19.   A self-addressed, stamped envelope.

increase your response. You must compute whether you are still profitable in paying not only for the legitimate responses, but also for those that come back with nothing inside, a blank sheet of paper, lead, or whatever.

Publisher's Letter.   The publisher's letter is a more recent innovation. Its use began within the last 10 years or so and it has proved to be a very good idea indeed. The publisher's letter says something on the outside like, "Do not read this unless you intend not to order" (see Figure 10-20). When you open the letter, it usually starts with a sentence reading something like, "Frankly, I'm puzzled" (see Figure 10-21). The writer of the letter states that he or she doesn't understand why you would hesitate to order since this is such an unusually good offer. The letter then goes on to restate the offer and generally restate the fact that there is absolutely no risk involved and so forth. If getting something free simply for trying a product is part of the deal, the "no-risk" aspect is really emphasized. The publisher's letter is, of course, an additional expense to you. But, in many cases, it has proved to be worth its weight in gold: It brings in many more returns than a direct mail package without the publisher's letter.

Testimonials.   As in a display advertisement, testimonials can be crucial in helping you to make sales because they affect the credibility of what

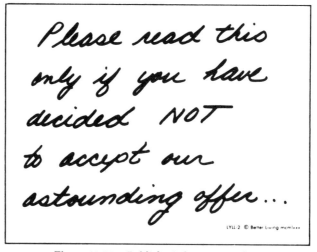

Figure 10-20.   Publisher's letter (outside).

Dear Reader,

Frankly, I'm puzzled. I can't understand your decision not to accept our offer of a LIFETIME subscription to Better Living FOR ONLY $4.95!! Better Living is one of the nation's most highly regarded, supremely useful, authoritative, enriching, indispensable service monthlies. And its $4.95 price for a LIFETIME subscription is less than most magazines nowadays charge for just a single year!

Would you please take a moment right now to jot down a note telling me why you've decided not to accept this unprecedented LIFETIME offer? I enclose a postage-free reply envelope.

We're presenting you with the most munificent subscription offer in history!

In case you're unfamiliar with Better Living, let me explain that it is America's most comprehensive service periodical. It covers home design and decor, food, fishing, camping, the outdoors, health, fitness, travel, photography, gardening, cars, sports, boating, beauty, crafts, hobbies, product ratings, personal finance, and other consumer interests and leisure-time activities.

To get your LIFETIME subscription to Better Living, just fill out and mail the enclosed subscription order form. If you like, we'll bill your credit card. And remember, your Lifetime Subscription is sold with this astounding money-back guarantee: If, after receiving Better Living for six months, you find you don't like it, you may cancel your subscription for a FULL REFUND, not just the partial refund issued by most magazines. Thus, you will have enjoyed a half year of Better Living ABSOLUTELY FREE! How can you lose?

Can you afford NOT to accept this offer? Whatever your decision, please let me hear from you.

With thanks for your help, and with all good wishes, I am

Cordially,

R. Clifford Webster

R. Clifford Webster, Associate Publisher

Figure 10-21. Publisher's letter (inside).

you say. It's one thing for you to boost your own product in your sales letter, your flier, and on your order blank or guarantee. It's quite another thing when some previous buyer says something nice about your product or service. What the buyer says is much more believable than what you say. If you give the full name and address or the full name and at least the city and state, along with what is said about your product or service, this is the most credible form of testimonial. But to do so you must have the explicit permission, *in writing*, of the individual who has written to you with the testimonial. You cannot publish the testimonial simply because you received a letter congratulating you on your product. A considerable step down is merely a set of initials along with the city and state. Here, again, these must be real compliments for your product or service. The only difference is that if you use initials instead of the name, you need not have permission to publish and use the remarks. The problem is that initials just aren't as credible as real names. One way around this, used by Ben Suarez and mentioned in his book, *Seven Steps to Freedom*, is to use real testimonials but fictitious names. His argument is that he is obeying both the spirit and the letter of the law, even though the names used are made up. If you decide to go this route, you should definitely check with a lawyer before doing so. Remember the rules we discussed in the chapter on legal and illegal aspects of mail order. It is important that you obey them so as not to run afoul of the FTC.

Since testimonials are very useful for your mail order promotions, I am going to tell you here and now how to acquire them so that you may use them not only in your direct mail packages, but also in your advertising. First, you should understand that even if you have a great product, only a relatively few testimonials come without asking for them. Further, even those that do come unsolicited may not come as soon as you might wish. Therefore, it is far wiser to begin planning ahead to get testimonials before you advertise your product.

One good way of getting testimonials for a new product is to send samples to your present customer list along with a letter asking them to describe their impressions of the product and what good they have received from using it. Your cover letter should include a friendly note stating that you are sending this product to a select list of your own customers so that you may discover what their opinion of it is and that you are eager to hear from them. After your questions, always have a sentence that allows your customer to check "yes" or "no" as to whether you may use his or her statement as a part of your advertising campaign. And, of course, have your potential customer sign the response. Even though it may be expensive for you to get testimonials in this fashion, they will more than pay for your expense once you begin using them in your advertising.

Another way of getting testimonials is to include a product evaluation sheet in every unit you send out. It should also include a little note to the effect that you want to know what your customers think of your product and that you would like to use their information for improving it, as well as advertising it. Again, be certain to insert a sentence that indicates whether your customer will allow you to use his or her name. Usually I send a little gift to all those who respond. Figure 10-22 shows a product evaluation sheet you can use.

TO OUR CUSTOMER . . .

We really appreciate your order. We would also like to know what you think about our product. Maybe it's perfect the way it is. Maybe some features should be kept the same, but others should be changed. In any case, we would like to know.

Date_____

1. Overall I think this product is:
   a. excellent   b. good   c. fair   d. poor   e. very poor

2. The things I like best about the product are:

3. Features I think should be changed are:

4. Other comments I would like to make are:

Other potential buyers of our products would like to know what you think. May we quote you in our future advertising?
   a. yes   b. no

Signature_____

Figure 10-22. An evaluation sheet for obtaining product testimonials.

There are other sales devices you may consider putting inside your direct mail package, but the ones I have described are the major components and the ones that you should think about using first. Every component of the direct mail package costs money. If this component brings in enough additional sales, the component is worth adding. If a component does not bring in additional profits that more than make up for the cost, you should drop it after testing.

Pick Your List

To pick your list, it is again hard to compete with Standard Rate and Data Service. SRDS publishes a special two-volume *Direct Mail List Rates and Data,* consumer lists, and business lists. The editorial objective of *Direct Mail List Rates and Data* is to compile, organize, classify, and arrange in sequential order all known available opportunities for using the mail for advertising. Because the listing is free, *Direct Mail List Rates and Data* probably contains most lists you may wish to use. Further, if you can't find the exact list you are seeking, SRDS will help you locate it. However, you should know that a subscription to *Direct Mail List Rates and Data* is not cheap. Currently, the subscription runs $153 a year and is published bi-monthly. If you are interested, write Standard Rate and Data Service, Inc., 5201 Old Orchard Road, Skokie, Illinois 60077. We will be talking more on how to use *Direct Mail List Rates and Data* in the next chapter.

You can also get your lists through list brokers, list managers, and list compilers. List brokers, as you might have guessed from the name, put the user of a list and a seller of a list together. Actually, the term *seller* is inaccurate since rarely do you "purchase," a list but rather rent it for one-time use.

A list manager is usually someone with a computer who is managing someone else's list. List managers may also act as list brokers, but they differ from list brokers in that they usually have exclusive authority to manage a specific list for rental purposes.

Finally, we have a list compiler, who actually compiles lists of various types. The compiled list is usually a demographic list or a list of people who have some factor in common. A compiler might compile a list of engineers by buying the membership list for various engineering organizations. Or a list compiler could compile a list of seminar attendees.

Bob Stone says that no one succeeds in direct marketing without working with competent list brokers and compilers. To this we may add list managers.

Since you can go to SRDS yourself to pick lists, why do you, as a list renter and mail order dealer, need a list broker, manager, or compiler? The reason is for the expert consulting that you receive. At no extra charge whatsoever, these individuals will act as your own personal list consultants and advise you in your mailing, and in which lists to use. This costs you nothing because they get their money from the individual who owns the list. Their fees are typically 20% of the price of the rental fee. But you cannot save this money by dealing directly with the list owner. The price will be the same. The owner will simply pocket the 20%. If you are successful, you will reorder lists from the individual broker, compiler, or manager you have dealt with. Therefore, this individual wants you to be successful and will do everything to make it so.

You will find a list of brokers, managers, and compilers in Appendix D to this book. Most of them publish a directory or a list of their offerings in the form of a catalog. A page from the Ed Burnett Consultants, Inc., catalog is shown in Figure 10-23.

MISC. BUSINESS SERVICES

SIC CODE		NATIONAL QUANTITY
7372	Computer Programming & Software Services	510
7374	Data Processing Services	26,070
7374A	Computer Services & Stores	10,180
7391	Research & Development Laboratories	4,830
7392	Management, Consulting & Pub Relations	50,730
7392A	Business Management Consultants	21,120
7392B	City & Town Planners	2,230
7392C	Communications Consultants	2,800
7392D	Educational Consultants	2,930
7392F	Foreign Trade Consultants	330
7392H	Industrial Consultants	1,650
7392I	Market Research & Analysis Services	3,670
7392J	Marketing Consultants	2,500
7392L	Personnel & Labor Relations Consultants	5,370
7392M	Public Relations & Publicity Services	6,270
7392N	Sales Promotion Services	2,310
7393	Detective Agencies & Protective Services	9,000
7393A	Detective Agencies	6,350
7393B	Guard & Patrol Services	3,440
7393C	Armored Car Services	510
7394	Equipment Rental & Leasing Services	43,650
7394A	Aircraft Charter & Leasing Services	4,580
7394B	Carpet & Upholstery Cleaning Equipment Rentals	8,800
7394C	Contractors Equipment & Supplies Rentals	10,390
7394D	Equipment Rental Services	12,870
7394E	Furniture & Carpet Rentals	4,380
7394F	Industrial Truck Rentals	570
7394G	Leasing Services	4,910
7394H	Recreation & Party Equipment Rentals	1,900
7394I	Television Rentals	3,580
7394J	Tool Rentals	2,890
7395	Photofinishing Laboratories	17,530
7397	Commercial Testing Laboratories	4,450
7399	Business Services, n.e.c.	79,960
7399A	Appraisers	15,130
7399B	Auctioneers & Liquidators	9,260
7399C	Business Brokers	3,010
7399D	Draftsmen Services	3,150
7399E	Interior Designers	27,090
7399G	Messenger Services	2,500
7399H	Microfilm Services	2,320
7399J	Recording Services—Sound & Video	4,610
7399K	Telephone Answering Services	6,420
7399L	Translators & Interpreters	1,080
7399M	Water Softening Services	6,000
7399N	Field Warehouses	310

AUTOMOTIVE SERVICES

SIC CODE		NATIONAL QUANTITY
7512	Automobile Rental & Leasing Services	23,620
7513	Truck Rental & Leasing Services	17,070
7519	Utility Trailer & Recreational Vehicle Rentals	9,930
7519A	Mobile Homes—Renting & Leasing	1,330
7519B	Trailer Renting & Leasing	8,550
7523	Parking Lots	40
7525	Parking Lots & Structures	40
7531	Top & Body Repair Shops—Automotive	72,360

SIC CODE		NATIONAL QUANTITY
7531A	Body Repair Shops	58,530
7531B	Customizing Shops	3,240
7531C	Seat Cover, Top & Upholstery Svc.	8,530
7531D	Undercoating & Rust Proofing Svc.	4,060
7534	Tire Retreading & Repair Shops	9,470
7535	Paint Shops	5,090
7535A	Truck Painting & Lettering Shops	4,390
7538	Repair Shops—General Automotive	182,520
7538A	Truck Repair Services	18,150
7538B	Auto Machine Shops	8,690
7539	Automotive Repair Shops, n.e.c.	87,440
7539A	Brake Services	29,210
7539B	Carburetor Repair Shops	2,620
7539C	Electrical Equipment Services	10,990
7539D	Glass Repair Shops	3,600
7539E	Muffler Repair Shops	15,140
7539F	Radiator Repair Services	9,570
7539G	Transmission Repair Shops	16,980
7539H	Wheel Alignment, Frame & Axle	20,000
7542	Car Washes	11,840
7549	Automotive Services—(Except Repair)	39,280
7549A	Towing Services	39,000

ELECTRICAL REPAIR SERVICES

SIC CODE		NATIONAL QUANTITY
7622	Radio, TV & Sound System Repair	32,540
7622A	Radio & TV Repair Services	29,050
7622B	Sound System & Equipment Repairing	4,420
7623	Refrigeration & Air Conditioning Repair	22,660
7623A	Air Conditioning Repair Services	10,970
7623B	Refrigeration Repair Services	14,100
7629	Electrical & Electronic Repair Shops	29,800
7629A	Appliance Repair Services	8,860
7629D	Electric Tool Repair Services	1,150
7629E	Vacuum Cleaner Repair Services	6,900
7629F	Washing Machine & Dryer Repair Services	10,990
7629G	Electronic Equipment & Supplies Repair	3,900
7631	Watch, Clock & Jewelry Repair Services	15,370
7631A	Watch & Clock Repair Services	11,310
7631B	Jewelry Repair Services	5,830

MISC. REPAIR SERVICES

SIC CODE		NATIONAL QUANTITY
7641	Reupholstery & Furniture Repair	39,100
7641A	Antique Repairing & Restoring Services	5,780
7641B	Furniture Cleaning Services	6,320
7641C	Furniture Repairing & Refinishing	9,810
7641D	Upholsterers	23,090
7692	Welding Repair Services	28,300
7694	Motor Repair Shops—Electric	7,840
7699	Repair Services, n.e.c.	92,200
7699A	Compressor & Pump Repair Services	5,880
7699B	Bicycle Repair Services	3,190
7699C	China & Glassware Repair Services	110
7699D	Doll Repair Services	360
7699E	Fix-It Shops	590
7699F	Gas Appliance Services	6,600
7699G	Lawn Mower Sharpening & Repair	7,820
7699H	Leather Goods Cleaning & Repair	4,900
7699I	Locksmiths	11,590
7699J	Piano & Organ Tuning & Repair	6,000
7699K	Sewing Machine Repair Services	4,460
7699L	Silverware Repairing & Replating	160

TOLL-FREE 800-223-7777
(IN N.Y. STATE CALL 212-679-0630)

43

Figure 10-23. A page from Ed Burnett Consultants, Inc., catalog.

Testing Your List

I am going to tell you exactly how to test a list later in the book. But, for now, you should know that after picking your list, you want to test a certain percentage of the names on it. There are many rules for this. Basically, you need to obtain enough responses to have statistic validity, which lowers the risk of your investment—you don't invest big unless your test is successful. In practical terms, this usually means testing 10% of the list.

Since you will probably be testing more than one list simultaneously, just as we keyed our advertisements for space or classified ads, we must also key or code our advertisements when using direct mail. Since you may be testing other things, your code may have to be more extensive than the simple two-figure code we developed for advertising in magazines or newspapers. You can develop a code with the help of computers that will take care of all the variables in direct mail. For example, you may design a five-digit code as follows: The first digit would be whatever list you are using; the second would be the date of the mailing; the third, the year; the fourth, the particular package you used; and the fifth, the particular offer. Once you have established your code, it is essential that you ensure that the individuals ordering your product or service respond with an order blank that contains this code. For this reason, many mail order dealers using direct mail ensure that the code goes not only on the outside of the envelope but also on the order blank. This has the additional advantage of ensuring that you receive the name and address of your customer and that it is written so that you can read it. You will probably be surprised as to just how many of your customers write illegibly. Finally, this method does not depend on your customer's writing in the code on the order blank for you since the code already appears. A variation is to use a type of pressure-sensitive label for the customer's name and address on the outside envelope that can be detached and put on the order blank. This saves the cost of an additional label.

Since only one week after receiving your first response from your mailing you will have received 50% of your total number, you can tell the total number after this short period by multiplying by two. You then make the calculation as to whether this particular list is profitable. If it is, you roll out your promotion to the remainder of the list, and at the same time, you start looking for new lists. You test them in the same fashion. In this way you can make huge profits in a short time, and you have also minimized your risks.

The list is not the only element you test in a direct mail package. However, you should never test frivolously.

Roll-out

Roll-out is the last success step in dealing in direct mail. It is really the action step of the old saying, "Be sure you're right; then go ahead." In direct mail, you find out whether you are right during your testing. Once you have decided that you are right, you roll out and mail to the remainder of that list. Some cautionary words here.

1. Be certain that you do an Nth name test. We will talk about this and other tests in the chapter on testing. What it means essentially is that the names you order from the total number of names on any list are developed by taking every Nth name from this list. For example, if the total list is 100,000 and you are going to test 10,000, an Nth name test would mean that you received every tenth name on the list. In this way you can be sure that these names are not all bunched around one geographical location or certain alphabetical letters.

2. Be very careful that the names tested are no more recent than the other names on the list. We Americans are a very mobile people. Addresses and names change very rapidly, as much as 20% a year. You can see that if your test consists of this year's names and the remainder of the list is last year's, you are going to get very different results when you roll out after your test.

3. Be cautious in the use of very large lists. You must test sufficient statistical examples. Again, we will talk about this when we talk about lists and testing in coming chapters.

WHEN TO REMAIL

After your initial mailing, you may wonder when to remail, or when you can remail the same or a similar offer to the same list. Well, you have two situations here: One is where you have your own customer list, and the second is is where you are using a rented list. For your own customer list, the rule is simple. You can mail as often as you have something to sell. Sunset House may mail out 12 or more catalogs a year to its customers. Publishers Central Bureau, which sells books, mails even more often. It's all up to you, and you should test to see how many mailings are most profitable. Ed Burnett says as a rule of thumb, response to remailings to the same list segment after a short interval can be expected to drop off from 33 to 50%. But the basic rule is that if you have something to sell, mail to your customers.

The rented list presents a somewhat different situation. If the list worked well for you with the product, it may work well again even though some of the individuals on the list have already ordered. But you should wait awhile, usually several months. And, again, you should test to find out what happens in the case of your particular product in this particular situation.

WHAT THE COMPUTER HAS BROUGHT TO DIRECT MAIL

Massive use of the computer in direct mail is fairly recent, only in the last 10 years or so, and it has caused major changes and has made many of the old methods of addressing and keeping customer lists obsolete. In addition, through the computer we can do printing, individual addressing, management of your customer list, mailing to certain selected geographical zones or zip code zones, and so on. Further, the computer permits you to use one of the most powerful tools ever developed for use of your customer list—the Recency Frequency Monetary formula, which we will discuss in chapter 11. The name refers to your customer list: how recently they have ordered, how frequently they have ordered, and how much money they have spent with each order. Close monitoring of these facts can maximize the profitability of mailing to any customer list.

Ed Burnett developed a list a 11 major pitfalls in direct mail and how to avoid them. Any direct marketer can profit from reading this list. So here it is exactly as Ed wrote it:

How to Avoid Pitfalls and Disasters (in Direct (Mail) Response, by Ed Burnett

Probably the first thing to get straight is the title. *Response* (through any medium) is the "name of the game"—and direct mail is just one of the players.

With a typical in-person sales call now costing well over $175, the price tag on a direct mail piece—15¢ to 20¢ per unit—looks very attractive. But there is mail which works, and the mail which doesn't, and mail may not be the way to go.

So, *RULE #1 is determine your objective first*—then find out whether direct mail is the best, or only, or just one of the ways to reach the objective.

RULE #2 is lean on the experts. You can find out enough in a few phone calls to knowledgeable specialists to tell whether you are equipped to run a direct response operation without the help of a consultant or not. If a lot is involved, buy the best consultant you can locate. If the world doesn't rest on the result of a given test, you may wish, for cost considerations, to wing it for yourself. (But if it involves direct mail, at least *talk* to experts in the list business. They can improve by a significant multiplier, almost any result you can obtain by yourself.)

PITFALL #1

In direct mail you are in the *order margin business,* not the "markup" business. A book or booklet costing $1 and selling for $5 has a highly favorable markup—500%—but an order margin ($4/unit) which is a guarantee of disaster in the mails, where the cost in the mail may be $300/M.

PITFALL #2

Too high expectations. About twice a year a young administrative aide from some major management association comes to us to start his own seminar business. "You select the lists, and I will run the show—and if we hit 1%, we'll both make out like bandits." As gently as we know how, we point out that if seminars at $350 could achieve 1% (10 orders per 1,-000—or $3,500 per 1,000 pieces in the mail—$10 for every dollar expended) everybody and his brother would be in the seminar business! It so happens the usual response to this type of offer is under 1/10th of 1% (less than 1 per 1,000 pieces mailed) and without non-profit status, profit is very hard to realize.

PITFALL #3

Gauging results on "A continuous series of *one* experiment." A great deal of mail, particularly mail sent by one business to another, consists of *one* offer couched in one grouping of words, wrapped in in *one* package, and sent out at *one* time, to *one* list. What you know about such mail is what one offer did with one list. That's a pretty unsafe and unsatisfying way to go.

PITFALL #4

Buying the best copy, employing the best art department to lay out the piece, using the best graphics, worrying over the typography, selecting a top grade paper and a fine printer—and *then* sending your secretary or the mail clerk out to get the mailing list. *Response is affected more by list selection than by all other components of a mailing list put together.* It is therefore better to send a poor mailing to a good list, than a good mailing to a poor list. Lists are *markets.* You need to know markets to choose lists. And you need to know list marketers to help you choose lists intelligently.

PITFALL #5

The belief that direct response is "easy"—anybody can make a success of it. In truth, each form of direct response has its own unique problems, and relatively few (out of thousands) who start do a really good job of it. Some die due to the cost to buy customers .. . some die because they lack staying power . . . some die because they have not understood the iron rule of mathematics in this business . . . some die because they cannot handle the "back-end" (all the operations necessary once an order is received). This business, to paraphrase a well-known book, "never promises you a rose garden."

PITFALL #6

Very few direct response campaigns to cold prospects make a "profit" on an initial sale. Most mailers "buy" customers at a loss. This is true of magazines seeking subscribers, and fund raisers seeking donors—as well as establishments offering products or services for sale. If you are planning to use a mail request offer for one product—one sale—be very careful, or every dollar you spend will be lost.

PITFALL #7

Owners of lists of direct response customers rarely mail to them often enough. Customers *like* to receive mail from the firms they buy from. For every company concerned that it may be mailing to its customers too often, there are 99 where the list is not mailed often enough.

It is a hard lesson to learn—but your customers are not your exclusive property. Your mail order or mail-response individual can usually be found on a number of other mail-responsive lists . . . and they are asking him or her for help.

And a customer file is not truly homogeneous. It consists of current customers, old customers, former customers, dead customers . . . in effect cells of customers with distinctly different characteristics. You need to differentiate between them—and cultivate them differently.

PITFALL #8

In the building of a customer file in the business field, only the rare mailer is foresighted enough to recognize the need to code every customer by classification (S.I.C., or Standard Industrial Classification—the U.S. Government classification system)—and by size (number of employees, if possible, or net worth rating). Those that do can measure penetration by classification—and go where the sales are easier to make. Those that do not, are destined to repeat the same waste in prospecting over and over again—or experience the cost of finding out. Some time ago a penetration analysis by S.I.C. of computers in use which we did for a major publication, found some "raisins in the rice pudding of lists" at a ratio of 1 to 1, while others were at a ratio as high as 1 in 10,000.

PITFALL #9

In the building of a customer file in the consumer field, too few mailers really believe it is important to record the 6 keys of response—**"RFU$ISM"**—which stands for:

—Recency
—Frequency
—Dollars (US $)
—Item (or class)
—Source, and
—Method of payment (check, credit card, etc.)

A firm like Montgomery Ward or Sears or J.C. Penny, will create up to 200 separate cells from "RFU$ISM"—each with its own distinct response rate to any given offer. Such segmentation is the art of direct response customer "massaging." Without it—it's like flying blind in a storm without instruments.

PITFALL #10

There are five acronyms which spell out the major problems most mailers encounter when it comes to computing a list of customers. They are:

KISS— *Keep it simple stupid!*—for never before has man had at his command a tool—the computer—which can make so many mistakes so fast!

GIGO— *Garbage in, garbage out.* You enter mish-mash, and that's exactly what the machine presents back.

DIDO— *Duplication in, duplication out.* Unless you can identify and tag duplicate records, your list is destined to suffer from a chronic case of "duplicatitus."

NINO— *Not in, not out*—undoubtedly the most important phrase in the computer lexicon. If you don't put it in, in the first place—you cannot retrieve it. If you bury two or three separate kinds of business under one code, there is no way you can break out one of the segments laer on. Remember NINO—and keep it sacred!

RAFO— *Research and find out.* If you leave something out, and have to go back and "research and find out"—the resulting cost can be horrendous. One year, this firm compiled a million-name business file, and in our wisdom decided to save a few thousand dollars and leave off coding for counties. We had Zip, didn't we? Then along came a good customer who said, flatly, that he would not rent or buy any part of the list unless and until it was county coded. It cost *12 times more* to RAFO and made good on the NINO, then it would if it had been done at the compiling stage!

PITFALL #11

"The usual response in direct mail is 2%." This is nothing but errant nonsense! Five major factors influence response. They are:

- *COPY*   The words you use.
- *PACKAGE*   The "dress" or packaging your copy comes in.
- *OFFER*   The theme your copy and package attempt to convey.
- *TIMING*   The time of year in which your mail will be received.
- *LIST*   The market or market segment you are seeking to reach with your message.

2% can be fabulous for one offer, and close to disaster on another. Offers can vary by 300%; lists by 1,000% ... which underlines two answers to *every* direct response question:

1) "It depends."
2) "Test—and find out" ... because for every mailer who tests too much, there are 999 who do not test enough.

SUMMARY

In this chapter we have discussed the great potential of direct mail for your business. Remember the following points:

1. There are important advantages in direct mail. These include selectivity and personalization, speed in getting to your market and concealing test information from your competitors, and being able to provide much more sales copy than you can in any other type of advertising.
2. Use direct mail when you have a clearly defined market segment to which you can appeal.
3. There is more than one way to use direct mail in your business. I gave you 49 different ways to use direct mail for profits.
4. There are five success steps of direct mail: Identify your market, prepare your package, pick your lists, test, and roll out.
5. When do you remail? Your customer list is used whenever you have something to sell. For a rented list, try remailing after several months.
6. A computer can do remarkable things for you today in direct mail. This tool is so powerful that, while you may not be able to afford a computer yourself until you become a multimillion-dollar business, you can find competent direct mail computer services that can assist you in getting rid of duplicate names, doing a zip code or geographical analysis, or incorporating a Recency Frequency Monetary analysis of your customer list.

11

How to Maximize Your Direct Mail Success with Lists

WHAT IS A LIST AND WHY IS IT CRITICAL FOR DIRECT MAIL?

A list for direct mail is no more than a collection of names and addresses that have something in common that is tied in with your product and greatly increases your chances of making a sale. Lists are critical to your success because of the marketing concept that says that, for successful marketing, the emphasis should be on your potential customer rather than on the product or service you want to sell. This implies that you want potential customers on your list—people who will want your product, who will have money to buy your product, and who will buy by mail. The bottom line is that the lists you select can be twice as important as your offer and five times as important as your direct mail package.

To give you some example of the importance of the list and its emphasis on the marketing aspects of the buyer, you need only consider the Yellow Pages or the telephone book as a list source. Now here is a list of thousands of names. Why won't the telephone book work for a product that you might sell by mail? First, only a small portion of people in the telephone book will actually want to buy your product. Secondly, only a small portion may have the money to buy your product. And finally, only a small portion of the listees in a telephone book actually buy by mail.

Here's another example that will help you to understand the considerable importance of the list. Let us say you are selling a baby product. You have two direct mail packages. One package contains great copy and tremendous graphics to advertise your baby product. But there is one problem: The only list available is one of garage mechanics. The other direct mail package isn't very good at all. It describes the baby product you are selling but the graphics and copy are both poor. However, when you mail this package, you are able to obtain a list of expectant mothers. In a situation like this, even though you have poor copy and poor graphics, this package will pull much better to the list of expectant mothers than the great copy and great graphics to the list of garage mechanics. Obviously, expectant mothers are far more likely to order a baby product than are garage mechanics.

TYPES OF LISTS

There are many ways to categorize different types of lists for use in direct mail—mail order response lists, in-house lists of mail order buyers versus lists of mail order buyers from other firms, compiled lists, and business versus consumer lists. Each has its proper time and place for use. Let's take a closer look.

Mail Order Response List

The mail order response list is a list of people who have responded to mail order ads. It can be broken down further into two other categories: categorized inquiries and actual orders; and your own mail order buyer's list versus someone else's.

Inquiry lists are lists containing individuals who made an inquiry in response to a space, classified, or direct mail ad, or an ad in some other medium, but did not necessarily place an order. Inquiry lists can be useful in that they list individuals who have at least expressed an interest in the type of product or service that was advertised. On the other hand, buyer lists actually qualify the individual as a mail order buyer and specifically for the type of mail order purchase that was made; be it a product, a seminar, a magazine subscription, or whatever, the customer actually sent in cold, hard cash. This is certainly a cut above a simple expression of interest. As you might expect, a list of individuals who actually order by mail is far more valuable than a list of people who only inquire about a product or service.

In-House Lists and Lists from Other Firms

We can also break down a mail order response list according to your own responses versus other dealers' responses. You might guess that your own customer list will be more valuable than some other dealer's customer list, because your own customers have already dealt with you and, assuming that you have been reliable and honest, they trust you. On the other hand, someone who has ordered a mail order product of a similar type from another company will trust that firm but may not trust your promotion quite so much. As a result, you will not get as many orders from such a list as you will from a mailing to your own customers.

There is another important factor about a mail order buyer list that I would like to emphasize here. Mail order purchase in itself is sometimes better than any other factor for determining whether a particular list will work for you. This is true because even today, with mail order growing at the very rapid rate it has experienced over the last few years, not everyone buys by mail. In fact, the majority of people do not. Therefore, even great interest in a product or a service in itself may not result in a sale. But mild interest *in a mail order buyer* may generate a sale. What I am saying here is that the deciding factor in a sale may be whether the individual on the list is a mail order buyer.

Let me give you an example. A company in Illinois was introducing a new miniature television set into the American market. Large television sets have not been sold sufficiently by mail to generate sizable lists for this single product. However, lists of purchasers of regular television sets from stores are available. A mailing to this list of television buyers from retail stores failed miserably. A similar mailing with the identical package to a list of mail order buyers of electronic goods succeeded. During testing, the company was then motivated to try a list of non-mail order buyers who had bought special electronic goods similar to those of the mail order buyer's list. In other words, these individuals had bought special electronic goods but had not purchased them through the mail. This promotion also failed, illustrating the fact that it is frequently more important for an individual to be a mail order buyer than a non-mail order buyer of the identical or very similar product you are offering by mail.

Compiled List

Compiled lists come from previously printed sources. A list may be compiled from the telephone directory, a trade directory, the membership of an association, registration at a seminar, owners of automobiles, credit references, government reports, and so forth. A compiled list can also be compiled to order, but such a list will cost you much more than one that is already available.

List compiler and consultant Ed Burnett has found more than 40 different kinds of lists that are available from compilers. All but three of these are essentially developed by compilers. The three exceptions are contributors, mail respondents/business, and mail respondents/consumer. Here is Ed Burnett's complete tabulation of more than 40 different lists available from compilers.

Advertisers
Alumni
Business executives
Businesses
Canadian
Churches
"Clusters" around known groups
Homemakers
Contributors
Credit cards
Data qualified by field research or questionnaires
Editors
Education
Engineers
Ethnic
Financial
Foreign
Government
Influentials and opinion leaders
Institutional executives
Institutions (except churches and government)
Insurance
Investment and stock ownership
Libraries
Magazine subscribers and recipients
Mail respondents/business
Mail respondents/consumer
Membership
New businesses
Newly established households
Newly promoted executives
Occupant

Owners of products
Professionals
Retail
Scientists
Senior citizens
Stratified lists by demographic characteristics
Students—high school and college
Teenagers
Trade show registrants

Business Lists versus Consumer Lists

A consumer list contains the names of those who are the ultimate users of a product or service, while a business list contains the names of those who are in business and will somehow use the product or service in the resale of this product or another product or service to someone else. This distinction is crucial in all types of mail order and direct mail operations. For example, seminars are given to dispense needed information to businesses as well as consumers. The seminar operations, depending on whether they are given to a consumer or a businessperson, are entirely different. When a seminar is given to a business or employees of a business, it is held on a weekday, so that the employee is paid at normal salary while attending the seminar. Further, the pricing for a professional seminar to a business can be $250 per day per person or more. However, a seminar given to a consumer is entirely different. Let us say it is a seminar on how to start your own business to individuals who are not in business at that time. The seminar is on a weekend, because the attendee will not be compensated while attending the seminar. Furthermore, since the company is not paying for the seminar, $250 a day is usually considered too high. Frequently the seminar is priced at under $100 per day. Because of the considerable differences in all types of products and services, SRDS publishes one volume for consumer lists and one for business lists. Many list compilers, managers, and brokers specialize in either one or the other.

HOW TO PICK A LIST THAT WILL BE SUCCESSFUL FOR YOU

I mentioned in the previous chapter that free consulting was available from list managers, compilers, and brokers because it is in their interest to help you succeed so that you will continue to do business with them. If this is true, why not always use these free consulting resources and not even attempt to pick a list yourself? There are several reasons why you must know how to pick your own list, even if you do use the services of one of these three experts in the direct mail business.

1. You know your business better than anyone else possibly can. Therefore, you can sometimes suggest and find lists that even an expert consultant, compiler, manager, or broker may not think of using.

2. You can help one of these experts. Your list expert will be doing the best possible job to help you. The more you know about list selection, the better you can make suggestions to be followed up in trying to find outstanding lists for you.

3. As in any other type of business, there are experts who are good and experts who are not. There are experts who have been in the business for years, have had experience, and have proved themselves many times over. There are also experts who started yesterday on the off chance that they might be able to succeed at being a list compiler, broker, or manager. There are also fly-by-nighters who are totally dishonest. To protect yourself, you must know how to avoid being misled, which means knowing how to pick a list yourself so that you know whether what is being recommended makes sense.

SRDS AND *DIRECT MAIL LIST RATES AND DATA*

Congratulations! You are living in the age of SRDS. The publications I mentioned earlier are of immense help in the mail order business, but the two volumes of consumer lists and business lists, *Direct Mail List Rates and Data,* are fairly recent. They have had a tremendous and positive effect on the industry. *Direct Mail List Rates and Data* is a two-volume catalog of mail list names that are readily available from thousands of different sources. Both volumes are released twice a year, in January and July, but monthly updates are also furnished.

What *Direct Mail List Rates and Data* does is to invite every single list owner, manager, broker, or whatever, to request listing questionnaires through which listing in *Direct Mail List Rates and Data* can be made. SRDS advertises and otherwise actively searches for individuals who are presumed to offer lists for rent. The bottom line is that SRDS leaves no stone unturned to get every single new list listed in its massive publications just as soon as it becomes available. Because listing is free, it is very likely that most lists available on the market are included in these two volumes. However, SRDS itself records nine reasons that mailing lists are withheld by the list owner and not submitted for publication. These reasons run the gamut, but generally boil down to the fact that some list owners do not want to rent, do not want to rent to everyone, or do not want to rent now. Every serious direct mailer should be familiar with SRDS. And if you can't afford to subscribe, you should check with your local business library; many of these subscribe to these publications.

HOW TO USE *DIRECT MAIL LIST RATES AND DATA* TO FIND AND SELECT POTENTIAL MAILING LISTS

The starting point for using *Direct Mail List Rates and Data* is the subject market classification index shown in Figure 11-1. All lists that pertain to a specific market are grouped together here and listed in alphabetical order. In some cases, several classifications contain similar items. When this happens, the subject market classification index tells you what the other different classifications are. After each subject market listed, you will find a number. This number pertains to SRDS's own number and title classification system, shown in Figure 11-2. Note that the number system goes to 351 for business lists, from 502 to 612 for consumer lists, and finally from 700 to 718 for farm lists. Looking at the numbers in Figure 11-1, you can see that we are in the business list section. Let's look at an example. Assume that we want to look at the business list for the fur trade. Looking alphabetically, we'll see *Fur Trade, Fur Farming, Trapping,* and so on, Class 125, in Figure 11-1.

We now turn to the business section of *Direct Mail List Rates and Data* under the appropriate number, 125, shown in Figure 11-3. Under 125, the first list shown is *American Furriers,* which has the media code 312523509.00. Note that each separate list described contains a series of numbered paragraphs. To the right of Figure 11-3, look at the list entitled *Furniture Design and Manufacturing Magazine Active Subscribers,* containing a total of 11 paragraphs. All listings in *Direct Mail List Rates and Data* are organized in exactly the same way to make it easier to use and to compare lists. For example, a description of the list is always contained in paragraph 2, and the rates are always contained in paragraph 4. A complete description of all 11 paragraphs is shown in Figure 11-4. Not all 11 paragraphs are contained under every listing in the book because a list renter may not provide certain information to SRDS. But clearly, much of the information listed is extremely important. Therefore, it is worthwhile to become familiar with Figure 11-4 so as to look for the essential infor-

Subject	Class.

G

Direct Mail—Master Index Section

Figure 11-1. Subject market classification index from *Direct Mail List Rates and Data.*

Classifications Numbers & Titles

BUSINESS LISTS

3—Advertising & Marketing
5—Air Conditioning, Plumbing & Heating, Sheet Metal & Ventilating
7—Amusements
9—Appliances
11—Architecture
13—Arts
15—Automatic Data Systems
17—Automotive, Automobiles, Tires, Batteries, Accessories, Service Stations, Garages
19—Aviation & Aerospace
21—Baking
23—Banking & Financial
25—Barbers
27—Beauty & Hairdressing
29—Boating
31—Books & Book Trade
33—Bottling
35—Brewing, Distilling & Beverages
37—Brick, Tile, Building Materials
39—Brushes
41—Building
43—Building Management & Real Estate
45—Business Executives
46—Business Firms
47—Camps & Camping
49—Cemetery, Monuments & Funeral Suppliers
51—Ceramics
52—Certified Public Accountants and Accountants
53—Chain Stores
55—Chemical & Chemical Process Industries
57—China & Glassware
61—Clothing & Furnishing Goods (Men's)
63—Clothing & Furnishing Goods (Women's)
65—Coal Merchandising
67—Coin-Operated and Vending Machines
69—Confectionery
71—Control & Instrumentation Systems
73—Corsets, Brassieres & Undergarments
75—Cosmetics
77—Dairy Products
79—Dental
81—Department, General Merchandise and Specialty Stores
83—Discount Marketing
85—Display
87—Draperies & Curtains
89—Drugs, Pharmaceutics
91—Educational
93—Electrical
95—Electronic Engineering
97—Engineering & Construction
99—Engineers
101—Farm Implements & Supplies
105—Fashion Accessories
107—Feed, Grain and Milling
109—Fertilizer and Agricultural Chemicals
113—Fire Protection
115—Fishing Commercial
117—Floor Coverings
119—Florists & Floriculture
121—Food — Processing and Distribution
123—Funeral Directors
125—Fur Trade, Fur Farming, Trapping, Etc.
127—Furniture & Upholstery
129—Gas
133—Giftware, Antiques, Art Goods, Decorative Accessories, Greeting Cards, Etc.
135—Glass
137—Golf
139—Government Administrative Services & Public Works — Municipal, Township, County, State, Federal
141—Grocery
143—Hardware & Housewares

145—Home Economics
147—Home Furnishings
149—Hospitals & Hospital Administration
151—Hotels, Motels, Clubs & Resorts
161—Industrial Distribution
163—Industrial Purchasing
165—Infants', Children's & Teen Age Goods
167—Institutions
169—Insurance
171—Interior Design & Decorating
173—International Trade
175—Jewelry & Watchmaking
177—Journalism
179—Landscape, Garden Supplies, Seed and Nursery Trade
181—Laundry and Dry Cleaning
183—Leather, Boots & Shoes
185—Legal
187—Lighting & Lighting Fixtures
189—Linens & Domestic
191—Luggage & Leather Goods
193—Lumber & Forest Industries
195—Maintenance
197—Maritime, Marine, Shipbuilding, Repair & Operating
201—Materials Handling & Distribution
203—Meats & Provisions
205—Medical & Surgical
207—Metal, Metalworking & Machinery
213—Mining (Coal, Metal & Non-metallic)
215—Motion, Talk, Sound, Commercial Pictures, Etc.
217—Motor Trucks & Accessories
219—Motorcycle & Bicycle
221—Moving & Storage
223—Music & Music Trades
225—Notions & Fancy Goods
229—Nursing & Health
233—Ocean Science and Engineering
235—Office Equipment & Stationery
236—Office Mail Order Buyers
237—Office Methods & Management
239—Oils (Vegetable)
241—Optical & Optometric
245—Packaging (Mfrs.) Paperboard
247—Packaging (Users)
249—Paint, Painting & Decorating
251—Paper
253—Parks, Public
255—Petroleum & Oil
257—Pets & Pet Supplies
259—Photographic
261—Plant & Manufacturing Executives
263—Plastics & Composition Products
265—Plumbing
267—Police, Detective & Sheriff
269—Pollution Control, Environment, Ecology, Energy
271—Poultry & Poultry Products
273—Power & Power Plants
275—Printing & Printing Processes
277—Produce (Fruits & Vegetables)
279—Product Design Engineering
281—Public Transportation
283—Radio & Television
285—Railroad
287—Refrigeration
289—Religious
291—Rental and Leasing Equipment
293—Reproduction — Inplant & Commercial
295—Restaurants and Food Service
297—Roads, Streets, Etc.
299—Roofing
301—Rubber
303—Safety, Accident Prevention
305—Sales Management
309—Schools & School Administration
311—Science, Research and Development
315—Selling & Salesmanship
317—Sporting Goods
319—Stone Products, Etc.
321—Sugar & Sugar Beets
323—Swimming Pools
325—Tea, Coffee, Spices

327—Telephone & Telegraph
329—Textiles and Knit Goods
331—Tobacco
333—Toys, Hobbies and Novelties
335—Trailers & Accessories
337—Transportation, Traffic, Shipping & Shipping Room Supplies
339—Travel
341—Venetian Blinds/Storm Windows
343—Veterinary
345—Water Supply & Sewage Disposal
347—Welding
349—Wire & Wire Products
351—Woodworking

CONSUMER LISTS

502—Almanacs & Directories
506—Art & Antiques
508—Automotive
510—Aviation
512—Babies
514—Boating & Yachting
516—Brides
518—Business Leaders
520—Children's
520A—Collectibles
521—College & Alumni
522—Contributors (Philanthropic)
524—Crafts, Hobbies & Models
525—Credit Card Holders
526—Dancing
528—Dogs & Pets
530—Dressmaking & Needlework
532—Education & Self Improvement
536—Epicurean & Specialty Foods
538—Ethnic
544—Fashions
546—Fishing & Hunting
548—Fraternal, Professional Groups, Service Clubs & Associations
549—Game Buyers, Contest and Puzzle Participants
550—Gardening (Home)
552—General
553—General Merchandise Mail Order Buyers
554—Gifts — Gift Buyers
556—Health
558—Home & Family Service
559—Horses, Riding & Breeding
560—Insurance Buyers
561—Investors
562—Labor — Trade Unions
563—Land Investors
564—Literature & Book Buyers
566—Mechanics & Science
568—Men's
572—Military, Naval & Veterans
578—Music & Record Buyers
584—Occult, Astrological & Metaphysical
586—Occupant & Resident
588—Opportunity Seekers
590—Photography
592—Political & Social Topics
593—Premium & Catalog Buyers
594—Professional
596—Religious & Denominational
598—Senior Citizens
600—Society
602—Sports
604—Teenagers
606—Travel
612—Women's

FARM LISTS

700—Dairy & Dairy Breeds
702—Diversified Farming & Farm Home
704—Farm Education & Vocations
710—Field Crops & Soil Management
714—Land Use & Conservation
716—Livestock & Breed
718—Poultry

Direct Mail List Rates and Data

Figure 11-2. SRDS number and title classification system.

125—FUR TRADE, FUR FARMING, TRAPPING, ETC.

AMERICAN FURRIERS
Media Code 3 125 2350 5.00
Customized Mailing Lists, Inc., 158-23 Grand Central Parkway, Jamaica Estates, N. Y. 11432. Phone 212-969-8800.
For basic information on listing segments 1, 3, 5, 6, 7, 9, 10, 11 see Customized Mailing Lists, Inc. listing in Classification 45.
2. DESCRIPTION
Furriers.
ZIP Coded in numerical sequence 100%.
4. QUANTITY AND RENTAL RATES
Rec'd May, 1980.

	Total Number	Price per/M
Furriers & fur salons	1,700	35.00
Fur manufacturing	800	*60.00

(*) Price for total list.
Selections: state, title addressing, 2.50/M extra; SCF, 5.00/M extra; key coding, 1.00/M extra.

FUR MANUFACTURERS
Media Code 3 125 4700 3.00
Ever Ready Mailers, Inc., 4021 Austin Blvd., Island Park, L. I., N. Y. 11558. Phone 516-432-0754.
For basic information on listing segments 1, 5, 6, 7, 9, 10, 11 see listing for Ever Ready Mailers, Inc. in Classification 45.
2. DESCRIPTION
Fur manufacturers.
ZIP Coded in numerical sequence 100%; by state 100%.
4. QUANTITY AND RENTAL RATES
Rec'd May, 1980.

	Total Number	Price per/M
Total list	1,000	19.50

FUR TRADE
Media Code 3 125 4837 3.00
Member: D M.M.A.
Market Data Retrieval, Inc., Ketchum Pl., Westport Conn. 06880. Phones: 203-226-8941; 212-582-3311.
For basic information on listing segments 1, 2, 3, 4, 5, 6, 7, 8, 9, 10, 11 see Market Data Retrieval, Inc. listing in Classification 46.
3. LIST SOURCE
Classified telephone directories and trade directories.
4. QUANTITY AND RENTAL RATES
Rec'd May, 1980.

SIC Code:	Total Number	Price per/M
2371—Fur goods mfrs.	507	35.00
5681—Furriers & fur shops	2,042	"

NATIONAL BUSINESS LISTS FUR TRADE, FUR FARMING, TRAPPING, ETC. LISTS
Media Code 3 125 4875 1.00
Member: D M.M.A.
National Business Lists, Inc., 162 N. Franklin, Chicago, Ill. 60606. Phone 312-236-0350.
For basic information on listing segments 1, 2 & 3 (symbols preceding SIC's), 5, 6, 7, 8, 9, 10, 11, see listing for National Business Lists in Classification 46.
4. QUANTITY AND RENTAL RATES
Rec'd May, 1980.

SIC Code:	Total Number	Price per/M
x2371 Fur goods manufacturers	516	*45.00
†5681 Furriers & fur shops	1,651	45.00

(*) Price for total list.

ZELLER & LETICA FUR RETAILERS & MANUFACTURERS
Media Code 3 125 6500 5.00
Member: D M.M.A.
Zeller & Letica, Inc., 15 East 26th St., New York, N. Y. 10010. Phone 212-685-7512. Toll free 800-221-4112.
For basic information on listing segments 1, 3, 5, 6, 7, 10, 11, see Zeller & Letica, Inc. listing in Mailing List Compilers Section.
4. QUANTITY AND RENTAL RATES
Rec'd May, 1980.

	Total Number	Price per/M
Fur retailers and fur mfrs.	2,300	35.00
Fur cleaning	950	*35.00

(*) Total list.
Minimum 75.00.

127—FURNITURE & UPHOLSTERY
(Also see Floor Coverings, Home Furnishings, Interior Design & Decorating)

AMERICAN FURNITURE INDUSTRY
Media Code 3 127 2175 5.00
Customized Mailing Lists, Inc., 158-23 Grand Central Parkway, Jamaica Estates, N. Y. 11432. Phone 212-969-8800.
For basic information on listing segments 1, 3, 5, 6, 7, 9, 10, 11 see Customized Mailing Lists, Inc. listing in Classification 45.
2. DESCRIPTION
Furniture industry.
ZIP Coded in numerical sequence 100%.

---

4. QUANTITY AND RENTAL RATES
Rec'd May, 1980.

	Total Number	Price per/M
Manufacturing—all	10,000	30.00
Manufacturing—larger—presidents by name	6,200	"
Manufacturing—larger—executives	16,000	"
Wholesale	9,000	"
Upholster & slipcovers	20,900	"
Stores & showrooms	64,000	"
Antique stores	25,000	"
Repairing & cleaning	7,800	"

Selections: state, title addressing, 2.50/M extra; SCF, 5.00/M extra; key coding, 1.00/M extra.
Minimum 3,000.

FURNITURE
Media Code 3 127 4350 3.00
Addresses Unlimited, 14621 Titus St., Van Nuys, Calif. 91402. Phone 213-873-6114.
For basic information on listing segments 1, 3, 5, 6, 7, 8, 10, 11 see Addresses Unlimited listing in Classification 45.
2. DESCRIPTION
Retail furniture stores—U.S.A.
ZIP Coded in numerical sequence 100%.
4. QUANTITY AND RENTAL RATES
Rec'd November, 1978.

	Total Number	Price per/M
Total list	35,000	25.00
California only	2,500	"

FURNITURE DEALERS
Media Code 3 127 4825 4.00
American Business Lists, Inc., 5639 S. 86th Circle, P. O. Box 27347, Ralston, Neb. 68127. Phone 402-331-7169.
For basic information on listing segments 1, 3, 4, 5, 6, 7, 8, 9, 10, 11 see American Business Lists, Inc. listing in Classification 46.
2. DESCRIPTION
List includes name, address, city, county name, ZIP Code, area code phone number and franchise information (if available).
ZIP Coded in numerical sequence 100%; numerically by state 100%; by state 100%; alpha-geo 100%; random 100%.
List is computerized.
Selections available: 3 digit ZIP Code-sectional centers, state.
4. QUANTITY AND RENTAL RATES
Rec'd May, 1980.

	Total Number	Price per/M
Total list	34,845	35.00

FURNITURE DEALERS
Media Code 3 127 5300 7.00
Member: D.M.M.A.
Research Projects Corp., Executive Plaza, 50 Clinton St. Hempstead, N. Y. 11550. Phone: 516-481-4410; 212-895-1048; toll free 800-645-2980.
For basic information on listing segments 1, 5, 6, 7, 8, 9, 10, 11 see Research Projects Corp. listing in Classification 45.
2. DESCRIPTION
Furniture dealers.
4. QUANTITY AND RENTAL RATES
Rec'd May, 1980.

	Total Number	Price per/M
Stores—new	60,000	30.00
Second hand furniture	11,000	"

Furniture Design & Manufacturing Magazine Active Subscribers
Media Code 3 127 5425 2.00
Delta Communications Inc., 400 N. Michigan Ave., Chicago, Ill. 60611. Phone 312-222-2000.
1. PERSONNEL
Publisher—S. L. (Sandy) Berliner.
Circulation Manager—Chuck Taylor.
Broker and/or Authorized Agent
All recognized brokers.
2. DESCRIPTION
Subscribers to Furniture Design & Manufacturing Magazine.
ZIP Coded in numerical sequence 100%.
3. LIST SOURCE
Circulation list.
Derived thru mail 98%.
4. QUANTITY AND RENTAL RATES
Rec'd May, 1980.

	Total Number	Price per/M
Total list	25,184	50.00

5. COMMISSION, CREDIT POLICY
20% commission to recognized brokers.
6. METHOD OF ADDRESSING
4-up Cheshire labels.
Magnetic tape available (9 track, 1600 BPI).
7. DELIVERY SCHEDULE
15 days after receipt of order.
8. RESTRICTIONS
Advertisers must order from list owner direct.
Other mailers must order through broker.
Sample mailing piece must be submitted for approval.
9. TEST ARRANGEMENT
Minimum order 250.00.
10. LETTER SHOP SERVICES
Labels will be sent.
11. MAINTENANCE
Updated regularly with subscription mail returns and corrections.

FURNITURE MANUFACTURERS
Media Code 3 127 5500 2.00
Addresses Unlimited, 14621 Titus St., Van Nuys, Calif. 91402. Phone 213-873-6114.
For basic information on the following numbered listing segments: 1, 3, 5, 6, 7, 8, 10, 11, see Addresses Unlimited listing in Classification 45.
2. DESCRIPTION
Furniture manufacturers.
4. QUANTITY AND RENTAL RATES
Rec'd November, 1978.

	Total Number	Price Per/M
Total list	4,500	30.00

FURNITURE MARKETPLACE
Media Code 3 127 6175 2.00
Ed Burnett Consultants, Inc., 2 Park Ave., New York, N. Y. 10016. Phone 212-679-0630. Toll free 800-223-7777.
For basic information on listing segments 1, 5, 6, 7, 8, 9, 10 see Ed Burnett Consultants, Inc. listing in Mailing List Compilers section.
3. LIST SOURCE
Classified telephone directories, trade directories, credit reference directories.
4. QUANTITY AND RENTAL RATES
Rec'd May, 1980.

Pricing:	Price per/M
Under 10,000	35.00
10,000 to 49,999	33.00
50,000 to 99,999	30.00
100,000 to 249,999	25.00
250,000 to 499,999	21.00
500,000 to 999,999	18.00
Over 1,000,000	15.00

Minimum order 4,000.

(This listing continued on next page)

Figure 11-3. A sample listing from *Direct Mail List Rates and Data.*

1. PERSONNEL
Names of individuals in selling or service function
Branch office identification—brokers, authorized agents or list managers

2. DESCRIPTION
Description of characteristics
Type & kind of pattern
Special features
Response & characteristics
List arrangement
Average unit of sale
ZIP Coding sequence
Identification if list is computerized

SELECTIONS AVAILABLE
Describes special selection capabilities

3. LIST SOURCE
When, where and how developed or derived
Sources of names:
For a published source, date and name
For a response source, date and description
For roster source, date and description

4. QUANTITY AND RENTAL RATES
Effective date, received by SRDS date
For total list and list parts:
Total names
Price per thousand
Combination rates—discounts
Special selection rates
Minimum order requirement

5. COMMISSION, CREDIT POLICY
Agency commission, broker's commission
Cash discount policy
Deposits, if any, with amounts and conditions
Credit conditions

6. METHOD OF ADDRESSING
Complete and detailed information concerning addressing methods, impression selections and rate differential, if any

7. DELIVERY SCHEDULE
Availability
Time lag or delivery
Guarantees and/or special considerations

8. RESTRICTIONS
Conditions of availability
Conditions regarding re-use or security

9. TEST ARRANGEMENT
Rates
Premiums
Minimum number requirement
Conditions

10. LETTER SHOP SERVICES
Services performed
Mailing instructions
Returned material

11. MAINTENANCE
Updating procedures
Guarantee, if any, on delivery
Refund conditions
Duplication considerations

Advertising Executives

Media Code 3 003 2258 3.00
Member: D.M.M.A
Standard Rate & Data Service, Inc., 5201 Old Orchard Rd., Skokie, Ill. 60076. Phone 312-966-8500.

1. PERSONNEL
Assistant List Manager—Margaret L. Waren.
Broker and/or Authorized Agent
All recognized brokers.
Branch Offices
Atlanta 30305—3224 Peachtree Rd., N E. Phone 404-233-6493.
New York 10017—20 E 46th St Phone 212-682-0677
Chicago 60601—333 N. Michigan Ave Phone 312-726-5741
Los Angeles 90048—6300 Wilshire Blvd Phone 213-651-5990.

2. DESCRIPTION
Names of executives employed by both advertising agencies and companies who do national advertising. Names have been selected on the basis of job responsibility. Each has a far above average income; most have college degrees, are married and have a family.
ZIP Coded in numerical sequence 100%.
List is computerized.
Selections available: 3 digit ZIP Code, state, Nth name.

3. LIST SOURCE
SRDS subscription files, latest advertising directories, company communications, trade press items, conference attendees.
Derived thru mail 25%; compilation 75%.

4. QUANTITY AND RENTAL RATES
Rec'd November, 1976.

	Total Number	Price per/M
Advertising managers-national advertisers	4,900	30.00
Advertising managers—total list	16,000	25.00
Advertising agencies—president—largest	2,300	"
Advertising agencies—all	10,000	"
Advertising agency:		
Treasurer & controller	1,139	35.00
Creative or copy director	2,300	30.00
Time & space buyers	2,700	"
Art directors	2,300	35.00
Production managers	1,300	"
Senior acc'ts, exec's & supervs.	6,400	30.00
Public relation & adv. dir.	550	*35.00
Sales promotion & advertising managers—electronics industry	1,000	*35.00
Public relations firms	4,600	25.00
Public relations Soc. of Amer.—members	6,700	"
Exec's of public relations depts.	4,200	"
Corporate public relations directors	1,600	35.00
Lettershops	3,200	25.00
Direct mail ad agencies	1,200	50.00

(*) Price for total list.

5. COMMISSION, CREDIT POLICY
20% commission to recognized mailing list brokers on list rentals only. Brokers must guarantee payment within 30 days. Non-rated firms must send payment in advance. All postage and postage fees must be paid in advance.

6. METHOD OF ADDRESSING
4-up labels will be sent.

7. DELIVERY SCHEDULE
Lists are run on the 20th of each month. Orders must be in before the 7th of the month to be included in the 20th of the month run. Delivery dates requested sooner than the 20th of the month group run will be handled subject to a 75.00 service charge.

8. RESTRICTIONS
Right of refusal reserved. Sample mailing piece requested.
Cash in advance plus 4.50 shipping charge; political, home improvement or land development solicitations. Right reserved to require cash in advance (all solicitations).

9. TEST ARRANGEMENT
Entire list must be rented.

10. LETTER SHOP SERVICES
Complete lettershop and printing facilities available.

11. MAINTENANCE
Continuously maintained and updated by our own mailings approximately 12 times a year.

Figure 11-4. Complete description of paragraphs from *Direct Mail List Rates and Data.*

mation in which you may be interested right away. For example, it is worth knowing that in the description of the list, you will find not only the characteristics of the list, but the type and pattern of buying, special features, special selection capability, response characteristics, list arrangement, the average unit of sale, zip coding sequence, and whether the list is computerized. Of course, the name, address, and telephone number of the owner are always stated.

USING LIST CATALOGS

Catalogs are frequently available from list managers, owners, and compilers. In general, they offer information similar to that contained n *Direct Mail List Rates and Data*. The advantage they offer is that they bring a number of different lists of a similar type together. Also, they may provide more information about certain lists than is available in the SRDS publications. Finally, you can't beat the price: they are usually free. In general, you would use the catalog much as you did the *Direct Mail List Rates and Data*, except that usually you would write or call to request additional information about the list or perhaps a data card, as shown in Figures 11-5, 11-6, and 11-7. Like the information obtained in *Direct Mail*

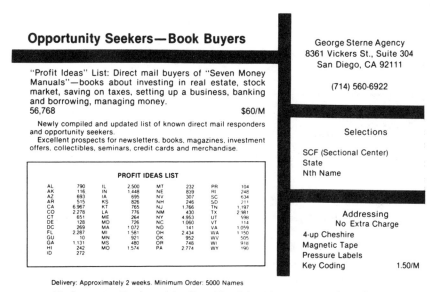

Figure 11-5. Data card for list of book buyers, opportunity seekers.

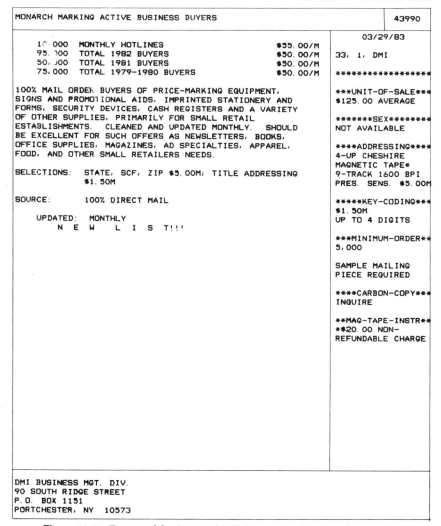

Figure 11-6. Data card for Monarch Marking active business buyers list.

List Rates and Data, the information on the data card will tell you what is available, how much it costs, what the delivery time is, and other important information.

However, a list catalog sometimes does not use the same classification system as do the SRDS books. A typical catalog publisher will probably arrange their lists alphabetically by class, perhaps separately for those that are mail response lists as opposed to compiled lists, and then very frequently by SIC number.

INVESTORS BY INCOME

235,703 Annual income exceeds $20,000................. $35/M
208,536 Annual income exceeds $30,000................. $45/M
103,798 Annual income exceeds $40,000................. $60/M
 42,928 Annual income exceeds $50,000................. $80/M

All records available with home phone number $20/M

Affluent individuals who have invested in one or more of the following: oil & gas participations, real estate, livestock, commodity options, and stocks. Median income is a very conservative figure and assures you of reaching those investors whose actual annual income is extremely high.
Very responsive for fund raising appeals, travel & merchandise, newsletters, books & magazines as well as investments of all types.

Sample mail piece required for direct mail programs.

DELIVERY: Approximately 2 weeks   MINIMUM ORDER: 5,000 names

SOURCE: Over 15 individual sources of information were used to compile this file including public records and customer files.

AMERICAN DIRECT MARKETING SERVICES, INC.

2536 Walnut Hill Lane, Suite 337
Dallas, Texas 75229

CALL TOLL FREE
1-800-527-5080
(In Texas call 214-358-4626)

SELECTIONS

Zip Code	$2.50/M
SCF	$2.50/M
State	$2.50/M
Area Code	$2.50/M
Nth Name	N/C

ADDRESSING

4-up Chesire	N/C
Magnetic Tape	N/C
P/S Labels	$5.00/M
3 - 5 Cards	$15.00/M
Key Coding	$1.00/M

Call Mike Casson or Marianne Ferro for complete details or contact your list broker.

WE BELIEVE THE INFORMATION CONCERNING THIS LIST TO BE ACCURATE, BUT WE CANNOT GUARANTEE ITS ACCURACY OR THE OUTCOME OF THE MAILING.

Figure 11-7.   Data card for list of potential investors.

HOW TO USE THE SIC NUMBER

SIC stands for Standard Industrial Classification, which is an index developed and sponsored by the Department of Commerce. This classification system provides a four-digit number to identify the function of every business, profession, or industry in the United States, as well as a specified product manufactured. In the SIC system, the first two numbers are used to define the 10 major fields of endeavor as follows: 01 to 09, agriculture, forestry, and fisheries; 10 to 14, mining; 15 to 17, contracting; 20 to 39, manufacturing; 40 to 47, transportation; 48 to 49, communication and utilities; 50 to 51, wholesaling; 52 to 59, retailing; 60 to 65, finance; 70 to 95, services. Each digit within the range of each of the 10 different classifications is used to define further a specialized kind of the endeavor noted. For example, the number 23 falls within the manufacturing classification, which is 20 to 39. The second two digits are used to show a specific line of activity of the company. Let's look at 2311: 2311 to 2399 happen to be reserved for apparel manufacturers and textile products made from fabrics and similar materials. The last two digits, 11, are reserved for suits, coats, and overcoats for boys and men. Thus, 2311 describes apparel manufacturers of suits, coats, and overcoats for men and boys. A complete SIC index can be obtained by writing the U.S. Government Printing Office, Washington, D.C. An abbreviated SIC index is contained in Figure 11-8.

01. Agricultural production
07. Agricultural services and hunting and trapping
08. Forestry
09. Fisheries
10. Metal mining
11. Anthracite mining
12. Bituminous coal and lignite mining
13. Crude petroleum and natural gas
14. Mining and quarrying of nonmetallic minerals, except fuels
15. Building construction—general contractors
16. Construction other than building construction—general contractors
17. Construction—special trade contractors
19. Ordnance and accessories
20. Food and kindred products
21. Tobacco manufactures
22. Textile mill products
23. Apparel and other finished products made from fabrics and similar material
24. Lumber and wood products, except furniture
25. Furniture and fixtures
26. Paper and allied products
27. Printing, publishing, and allied industries
28. Chemicals and allied products
29. Petroleum refining and related industries
30. Rubber and miscellaneous plastics products
31. Leather and leather products
32. Stone, clay and glass products
33. Primary metal industries
34. Fabricated metal products, except ordnance, machinery, and transportation equipment
35. Machinery, except electrical
36. Electrical machinery, equipment, and supplies
37. Transportation equipment
38. Professional, scientific, and controlling instruments; photographic and optical goods; watches and clocks
39. Miscellaneous manufacturing industries
40. Railroad transportation
41. Local and suburban transit and interurban passenger transportation
42. Motor freight transportation and warehousing
44. Water transportation
45. Transportation by air
46. Pipe line transportation
47. Transportation services
48. Communication
49. Electric, gas, and sanitary services
50. Wholesale trade
52. Retail trade—building materials, hardware, and farm equipment
53. Retail trade—general merchandise
54. Retail trade—food
55. Automotive dealers and gasoline service stations
56. Retail trade—apparel and accessories
57. Retail trade—furniture, home furnishings, and equipment
58. Retail trade—eating and drinking places
59. Retail trade—miscellaneous retail stores
60. Banking
61. Credit agencies other than banks
62. Security and commodity brokers, dealers, exchanges, and services
63. Insurance carries
64. Insurance agents, brokers, and service
65. Real estate
66. Combinations of real estate, insurance, loans, law offices
67. Holding and other investment companies
70. Hotels, rooming houses, camps, and other lodging places
72. Personal services
73. Miscellaneous business services
75. Automobile repair, automobile services, and garages
76. Miscellaneous repair services
78. Motion pictures
79. Amusement and recreation services, except motion pictures
80. Medical and other health services
81. Legal services
82. Educational services
84. Museums, art galleries, botanical and zoological gardens
86. Nonprofit membership organizations
88. Private households
89. Miscellaneous services
91. Federal government
92. State government
93. Local government
94. International government
99. Nonclassifiable establishments

Figure 11-8. An abbreviated SIC index.

The SIC code can be used to segment a larger list as well as to identify potential lists in the catalogs of those specialists in the mail order field who handle lists. Ed Burnett provides fifth-digit SIC which adds 3000 separate classification breakdowns to the approximately 900 published by the U.S. government.

HOW TO HANDLE LIST DUPLICATION

If you are going to become really successful, you will eventually use more than one list in your direct mail business at the same time. What do you do about duplicate names on various lists that you're using? There is always the possibility of renting the same names on different compiled lists or even different mail order lists, since one individual may be a member and register in more than one thing or may buy a mail order product from more than one company. One way of handling this problem is to do a "merge-purge." In other words, you take the lists you're going to mail and, using a computer, merge the names. Those that are duplicated are eliminated by the computer.

A second way of attacking the problem of potential duplication of names on different lists is spaced mailings. Don't mail to all your lists at the same time. Mail to one first and wait before mailing to another list. This means that even though duplicate mailings will be made, the individual will receive them at different times. In effect, this increases the chance for a sale since the first letter may not be opened, or the individual may not be ready to buy at the time the first mailing is received. Of course, you can have a third, fourth, or even more separate mailings this way. There is a disadvantage here, and that is if you are going to test one list against another, you must mail at the same time because a spaced mailing will not give accurate results for your test.

Finally, there is one other thing you can do about the problem of list duplication: Simply live with the fact that you will have duplication on your lists, and in your forecasting of results recognize that duplication may cause some reduction in results if the mailings are done simultaneously and the duplication is sufficiently large.

DEMOGRAPHICS AND PSYCHOGRAPHICS: WHAT THEY ARE AND HOW TO USE THEM TO YOUR ADVANTAGE

Demographics is measurable statistics of population and how it is actually distributed, including age, income, occupation, size of family, and so forth. Psychographics is a newer system of classification. It is measurable statistics of how members of a population behave.

To make maximum use of demographics, you must picture your customer in your own mind and make a list of different attributes you think your customer has: Is he or she of a certain ethnic background, certain age, or in a certain occupation, does he or she make a certain income, live at one residence for a certain period of time, have a certain educational level, is in a household with or without children, and live in certain kinds of communities in certain states?

In the same way, if you are dealing with a business customer, you should sit down and work out a picture of what this customer looks like. You might, for example, list the SIC number, the number of employees, the business's sales volume or its net worth, and so forth.

This demographic picture of your customer is one way in which you enter the catalog or the *Direct Mail List Rates and Data* when you go to select a list. It is also your clue for finding likely lists in other locations.

Psychographics means how your potential customer thinks and therefore behaves. The mailings you receive addressed to "Resident" are based on psychographics. How so? Because they make the assumption that even if you have moved, another individual moving into your house will be interested in the same product or service you might have been. Research has shown this assumption to be accurate. It is for this reason that I recommend to my clients that in their mailings for business seminars they not use a particular individual's name, or if they do, that they do not request forwarding postage to locate that individual. Why? A vice-president of engineering who attends engineering seminars will be replaced by another vice-president of engineering, who will also be interested in attending engineering seminars. Please note that this does *not* mean that you should never address your mailings by name. Quite the contrary. In most cases, personalization will increase your results. But, as is evident by this example, there are exceptions.

Let us say that you have invented a new product to be used by someone interested in the outdoors, yet this product is so new that no list exists for selling it, or even a similar product, through the mail. In that case you must use psychographics. Someone who is interested in the outdoors is a potential buyer of your product. For example, a buyer of a book on camping, hunting, or fishing, or an individual who is buying hunting, fishing, or camping equipment, may be interested.

Here is another example. Let's say that you are selling classical records through the mail and have exhausted all possible sources and all lists currently available. What lists might you try next? According to psychographics, a list of someone whose purchasing behavior in general would indicate an interest in classical records. How about buyers of art?

You can probably think of a number of cases where people who hold one interest also hold another. A purchaser of health foods may also be interested in exercise equipmei t, or vice versa. Someone who contributes to a museum may also contribute to a college or university. A member of a book club may also be interested in joining a record club.

A combination of demographics and psychographics can add greatly to profitability when you select your intial list and afterwards, when you have a successful product and really want to roll out to additional lists for giant profits.

USE OF GEOGRAPHICS

Sometimes a particular area is of great value to you for a particular product or service that you are selling. Yet, the basic list as described may not give the number of names available for any particular state or locality. Fortunately you can estimate this on your own if you know the total number of names on a particular list. Here's how you do it. A strong correlation exists between the geographic distribution of most lists and the geographic distribution of either total U.S. population, all U.S. manufacturing firms, or U.S. retail sales. Figure 11-9 is a chart showing the percentage distribution of population, manufacturing firms, and retail sales by states. For consumer lists, use the population distribution. For lists of manufacturers and wholesalers, use the manufacturing firm's distribution. For retailer service, financial institutions, and so on, use the retail sale's distribution. Look at the state you are interested in, multiply the percentage by the total number of names available on the list, divide this by 100, and you'll have a fairly good idea of the number of names available in this state. Research has shown that a state count is accurate to approximately plus or minus 10%. If you are looking for the number of names available on a list in a region, add up the percentages of each state and then multiply by the total quantity of the list before you divide by 100. Use of this technique can show you whether a particular list will be of any use to you, considering the geographic area in which you want to do a precise mailing.

One cautionary note, however: Certain industries—including mining, agriculture, communication services, and government—tend to be clustered in specific geographical areas. Do not use this technique for mailing in these industries.

State	Population (%)	Manfacturing Firms (%)	Retail Sales (%)
Puerto Rico	.01	0.01	0.01
Virgin Islands	.01	0.01	0.01
)tx Massachusetts	2.77	3.60	2.70
Rhode Island	0.47	0.81	0.45
New Hampshire	0.35	0.40	0.36
Maine	0.48	0.45	0.45
Vermont	0.22	0.22	0.22
Connecticut	1.49	1.86	1.59
New Jersey	3.54	4.63	3.57
New York	8.91	12.24	8.12
Pennsylvania	5.74	6.08	5.20
Delaware	0.27	0.16	0.32
Dist. of Col.	0.37	0.18	0.56
Maryland	1.93	1.17	1.95
Virginia	2.28	1.26	2.19
West Virginia	0.84	0.48	0.70
North Carolina	2.50	2.34	2.24
South Carolina	1.28	0.93	1.06
Georgia	2.27	1.19	2.20
Florida	3.40	3.01	4.47
Alabama	1.69	1.25	1.33
Tennessee	1.94	1.61	1.90
Mississippi	1.10	0.77	0.82
Kentucky	1.58	0.97	1.35
Ohio	5.23	5.19	5.14
Indiana	2.55	2.30	2.65
Michigan	4.38	4.61	4.47
Iowa	1.38	1.15	1.65
Wisconsin	2.15	2.38	2.14
Minnesota	1.86	1.84	1.84
South Dakota	0.32	0.21	0.31
North Dakota	0.30	0.16	0.31
Montana	0.34	0.26	0.35
Illinois	5.45	6.33	5.72
Missouri	2.31	2.11	2.41
Kansas	1.11	1.03	1.23
Nebraska	0.73	0.81	0.76
Louisiana	1.80	1.11	1.42
Arkansas	0.95	0.80	0.84
Oklahoma	1.26	1.10	1.16
Texas	5.56	5.12	5.73
Colorado	1.10	0.98	1.29
Wyoming	0.10	0.12	0.15
Idaho	0.35	0.31	0.42
Utah	0.52	0.47	0.51
Arizona	0.88	0.64	0.99
New Mexico	0.50	0.28	0.51
Nevada	0.24	0.14	0.33
California	9.87	11.24	10.33
Hawaii	0.39	0.29	0.36
Oregon	1.04	1.30	1.17
Washington	1.68	1.50	1.76
Alaska	0.15	0.09	1.13

Figure 11-9. Percentage distribution of population, manufacturing firms, and retail sales by states.

HOW THE LIST YOU ORDER
WILL BE FURNISHED TO YOU

Lists can be furnished to you in the following ways, and each has its own advantages, depending upon your business and the type of list you're mailing to.

1. Perforated labels
2. Pressure-sensitive labels
3. Cheshire labels
4. Sheet listing
5. Index cards
6. Magnetic tape

Gummed Perforated Labels

Gummed perforated labels need to be moistened, just as would a postage stamp. Each label is 3.44 by 1 inches and the print area is 30 characters. Usually you will be charged a small additional fee of something under $5 per thousand for receiving your names on gummed perforated labels.

Pressure-Sensitive Labels

Pressure-sensitive labels peel off a waxed paper backing and then are stuck on. The dimensions are 3.2 by .92 inches. They are much easier to affix than gummed labels since they do not have to be licked. They're ideal for small runs. However, the cost is slightly higher, approximately $8 to $10 per thousand over the cost of rental.

Cheshire Labels

Cheshire labels require a special Cheshire machine to be used to affix the labels. They come in columns of four across and 44 to a page and are neither gummed nor perforated. The size and number of characters are identical to those of gummed perforated labels. Usually Cheshire labels are furnished at no additional charge.

Sheet Listing

Sheet listing is simply a list of names, but in addition to the standard name and address, you will usually receive other information such as SIC sales volume, number of employees, and so forth, if such information is available. A sheet listing rental may cost you an additional $15 to $20 per thousand names.

Index Cards

Index cards are the standard three-by-five-inch cards. Each has the information as contained in the sheet listing above plus additional information as available. Index cards may also cost you an additional $15 to $20 per thousand names.

Magnetic Tape

Magnetic tape is usually nine-track, 800 BPI, IBM mode, although other formats can be obtained. These can be rented for one-time use or purchased for unlimited use during the course of the year for compiled lists. Actually, use of the tape implies availability of your own computer. There is also an additional cost here, which can vary widely depending on the type of tape and length.

Regardless of the format in which you order your list, remember that you are renting names only for one-time use unless specified otherwise, such as names from a compiled source. You generally do not have the right to use these names repeatedly without permission of the list owner or those who control the list.

COST OF LISTS

List costs vary from less than $25 to more than $100 per thousand, depending upon the type of list. Obviously a compiled list that is easily obtained, such as those from a telephone book in a certain geographic area, is of least value. A highly specialized mail order list in a certain limited product area may cost you a great deal simply because the entire set of names is so limited and so difficult to obtain. There are usually no great bargains in this industry, and if you are paying much less for your names, it may mean that they are easily compiled or that they are old and have not been updated for some time and so are worthless. If you are paying more, you can expect the names to be more current and highly selective. Deal with a reputable list broker, compiler, or manager.

One final word on the process of renting lists: Be absolutely certain that you allow time for delivery of the list prior to mailing. Delivery time will vary from list to list, since the individual from whom you are ordering may have to get the list from some other source. This and reproducing the list take time. Sometimes you must submit a sample of your direct mail package before the rental can be approved. Think in terms of ordering a list one month prior to your mailing date to be safe.

THE RFM FORMULA FOR SELECTING A LIST

Every professional today in the direct mail business uses the RFM formula to help select his or her list. What does RFM stand for? R stands for recency, which is how recently a mail order buyer has actually purchased. Someone who has purchased within the last month or so is a much hotter prospect for your proposition than someone who purchased a year or more ago. F stands for frequency, which refers to how many times the individual on the list has purchased. A mail order buyer may have purchased an item one time, been dissatisfied, and never ordered this type of product or through the mail again. However, someone who has ordered more than once has shown desire to purchase through the mail. Multiple buyers will always pull better than a one-time mail order buyers' list. M stands for money, which refers to how much in dollars the individual buyer purchased. It's no good trying to sell a $200 item to a list of buyers, mail order or not, who purchase only $5 to $10 items, and the opposite is also true.

You can use the RFM formula when mailing to your own in-house list and when deciding whether to keep mailing to someone on it. One way of doing this is to work out a special formula based on RFM. Assign points or weightings to each factor in the formula. Such a use of RFM is shown in Figure 11-10. Points have been assigned to recency as follows: order in the current quarter, 10 points; order within the last six months, 5 points; order within the last year, 3 points; order before last year, 1 point. For frequency, multiply the number of points by 5. For money, use 10% of the average order maintained on a continuing basis.

Through the use of this formula, you can see who your hottest customers are or you can quickly analyze some other lists that may be available for your product or service. Naturally, the points and weightings are up to you. The example shown in Figure 11-10 is only that. You should work out your own weightings and point system depending upon how important different factors are in your particular situation, product, or industry. Keep accurate records and you can develop a formula that will work for your company only. Best of all, because the point weightings are yours, unique to your products, industry, and company, no one can ever steal this formula from you because it will be of no use to anyone else.

Recency

Customer ordered _____ months ago.		Months	Points
		3	25
		6	20
		12	15
		18	10
	more than	18	0

Frequency

Customer ordered on the average once every _____ months.			
		1	50
		2	45
		3	40
		4–6	30
		7–9	20
		10–12	15
	more than	12	10

Money

Size of average order was _____.		
more than $300		25
250–299		20
200–249		17
150–199		15
100–149		14
75–99		13
50–74		12
25–49		11
10–25		10
less than $ 10.		5

The best customers are those with the highest point count.

Figure 11-10.   An example of an RFM weighting formula.

A METHOD OF COMPILING A LIST THAT IS EVEN BETTER THAN RFM

As good as RFM is, it has some limitations that can be improved upon by a more effective method. RFM only considers three characteristics of your buyers: How recently they have bought, how frequently, and how much money they've spent. Yet other variables may also be of importance in deciding on your best prospects. These may include categories of merchandise purchased, where the buyers' name originated (what magazine or what list), geographic location, type of promotion responded to, and so on. Also, RFM may not be as important as some of these other variables under all conditions.

Borrowing from statistical analytical methods, direct marketing experts have begun to adopt and use a research technique known as multiple regression analysis. With multiple regression analysis, you find the combination of different variables that best predicts response in your particular situation. You don't even need to know what these variables are in advance. What you do need to do is to keep your customer file so as to have available as much data as possible. Thus, in addition to name and address, you definitely want to keep information on RFM, what medium the customer responded to, what type of promotion, whether any type of credit was used, the category of product, and so on. Be careful not to overlook anything that you feel might in some way influence future response to a promotion. In the old days, keeping and accessing this data was quite difficult. But today, with the magic of personal computers, it can be very easy.

Paul Cohen (no relation), director of research at Garden Way Marketing Associates and an expert in this field, says that you can perform a valid analysis with as few as 300 buyers on your in-house list. If you own a personal computer, software is available for you to do your own multiple regression analysis. If not, contact a company that does computing for small business. They'll help you set up to get it done right.

The output of your multiple regression analysis should be a list of the best names on your list for any particular mailing, along with an average predicted response based on those variables that made a difference on similar mailings for you in the past. You can actually get a list of names ranked according to likelihood of purchase. Thus, if you need a 1% response to break even for a particular mailing, you can mail only to those names that on the average are predicted to give you a 1% response or better. If there are insufficient names in the category of a 1% response to make the project worthwhile, at least you'll know this before you invest your money and do the actual mailing.

Naturally, you should keep tabs on the results and monitor how closely the predicted response matches the response actually received . . . and you should repeat the regression analysis as environmental changes occur that would cause the multiple regression equation that you develop to deviate from reality in the marketplace.

HOW TO ORDER A LIST

Craig Huey, president of Infomat, Inc., a full-service agency, has prepared a special list-ordering checklist for his clients. With Craig's permission, this checklist has been reproduced in Figure 11-11 so that you can use it too. "Clearance" refers to the fact that some owners of response lists want clearance approval authority before they will permit you to rent their in-house lists. This is so that your mailings will not compete directly with theirs. "Mail date protection" will ensure exclusive use of the list for the time of your mailing. It may or may not always be

1.	Clearance (mail date)	_____
2.	Clearance (sample)	_____
3.	Mail date protected?	_____
4.	Delivery date versus mail date	_____
5.	Mode of delivery (UPS blue)	_____
6.	85% net name available	_____
7.	Label format specified	_____
8.	All instructions written and sent to list broker	_____
9.	Split test?	_____
10.	Key coding?	_____
11.	Special selection? (hotline, etc.)	_____
12.	State select?	_____
13.	Nth select?	_____
14.	Omitting any previous orders?	_____
15.	Check acknowledgment from broker	_____

Figure 11-11. Infomat's list-ordering checklist

available as an option. "Mode of delivery" (such as UPS) refers to the
method that you want the list delivered to you. "85% net name available"
has to do with a merge-purge of two or more lists that you are renting. As
noted earlier a merge-purge saves you from duplicating your mailings because a prospect is on two or more lists. 85% net means that you pay only
85% of the rental fee of lists (plus a percentage of the computer running
fee to do the merge-purge) even though you start with 100% of each list.

SUMMARY

In this chapter we've learned about how to maximize your success with
direct mail through the correct use of mailing lists. We learned about the
different types of mailing lists and which are best. We learned how to
pick a list using *Direct Mail List Rates and Data* and independent list
compilers, brokers, or managers. We also learned how to select a list using
demographics and psychographics, and how to estimate current list geographical percentages in the areas in which we are interested. Finally, I
showed you the RFM formula and the multiple regression analysis technique for using and judging others' lists as well as your own.

12

Other Important Methods of Mail Order Marketing

In this chapter, we are going to look at three major methods of direct-response marketing with which you may not be familiar, which may be a dramatic means of increasing your mail order sales. These three methods are radio, television, and the telephone.

Television and radio together are known as broadcast media, and we will talk about them first. Then we will talk about the remarkable growth of telephone marketing and how, combining them with mail order techniques, you can make a fortune using these methods.

MAIL ORDER MARKETING THROUGH RADIO

Radio advertising has been around since 1922, and though it has declined somewhat with the introduction of television, it is still a tremendous medium for mail order sales. In fact, it was through the medium of radio mail order that Joe Cossman sold no less than 1,810,000 sets of 100 toy soldiers. Others have been similarly successful.

There are differences between space advertising and direct mail advertising in letters and buying advertising through time when using broadcast media. In space, we specify the magazine, the size of the ad, the date, and the position. If we are sending a direct mail package out, we develop the contents of this package and then decide when we will mail it. However, when we are buying time, no schedule is available in advance. In fact, program and spot positions are not known until the time of your purchase. This makes it a little bit more difficult for planning, although again, as with the other media we discussed in earlier chapters, SRDS has several publications available that can help us: *Spot Radio Rates and Data, Spot Television Rates and Data,* and *Network Rates and Data.* The last of these covers both radio and television.

The two broadcast media have something else in common. In both cases we can seek help from the stations in preparing our advertising. For example, stations can produce and provide programming service, write our ads, give us publicity and promotion, give us merchandising assistance and research guidance, and let us use their specialized broadcasting equipment for preparing our advertising.

THE ADVANTAGES OF RADIO ADVERTISING

Even today, there are reasons for using radio versus television advertising in many circumstances. Let's look at radio advertising first. Here are the advantages.

1. Relatively low cost per thousand listeners
2. Outstanding segmentation of the market, geographically and demographically, much more than television
3. Rapid change of schedule or copy
4. Frequency of advertisement to our potential customers
5. Quick response
6. A wide range of stations

Radio advertising costs much less than television to reach potential customers on a per-thousand basis. Further, because of this low cost, we can reach the listener with the same message far more frequently than we can through television. Also, since most radio copy is simply spoken or taped on a cassette, it is relatively easy to change and the schedule change can be made rapidly as well. Although stations may officially require two weeks' notice to cancel an ad, frequently they may let you do so instantly if your ad is not profitable. A quick response is possible because the lead time is far less than that of print media, such as magazines, and there is no mail time as in direct mail. Those who respond to a radio ad respond immediately. There is a wide range of stations throughout the country, which allows many, many possibilities for advertising your product. In fact, to advertise everywhere and take advantage of the full range of possibilities is more than the average mail order operator can afford. But perhaps the most important of the above advantages is the segmentation that radio permits. Current popular formats of radio programs may include talk, news, classical music, country and western music, popular music, rock music, and ethnic minority formats, sometimes even in a foreign language. This variety allows for incredibly precise segmentation of your market.

DISADVANTAGES OF USING RADIO

There are three basic disadvantages of using the radio medium. The first is called reach, which refers to the proportion of the total market you are able to get to with your message. Regardless of how much radio advertising you do, the maximum reach or amount of market that you can have your message heard by is 60%, partly because not everyone listens to the radio for long periods.

The second disadvantage of using radio advertising is that, like television advertising, it is difficult to monitor. Even if you are a prime-time buyer, you yourself will find it difficult to sit down and watch the television or listen to the radio during the periods in which your ad is going to appear to ensure that it appears as advertised, with no mistakes and not cut short. Thus, if your sales begin to fall off for one reason or another, or your inquiries begin to drop, you do not know whether it is a genuine drop that you must take immediate note of and act upon, or whether it was an error in the reading of your advertisement at a particular time.

The third basic disadvantage is time. You do not have the time to say everything you might wish as you have in most forms of print advertising. We'll talk more about this later.

HOW TO BUY RADIO ADVERTISING

The first step in the buying of radio advertising is to identify your market. Write out the demographics and geographics of your customer—where he or she lives, how old he or she is, whether he or she is male or female, what type of music, talk shows, or radio format he or she likes. Your next step in identifying this market is to compare your formulation with various surveys available in the industry. One such survey is done for both radio and television by the American Research Bureau and is called *Arbitron*. *Arbitron* collects information through panels of consumers. These detailed surveys cover who is watching or listening to what programs. Two surveys based on telephones have been started recently. One is called *Audits and Surveys Tract 7,* and the other, *The Burke Marketing Research.*

As with print media, name, address, telephone, and other information can be obtained from SRDS publications, in this case *Spot Radio Rates and Data* and *Network Rates and Data.*

Once you have matched your demographics and geographics with the station and program format, you must consider other variables.

The first radio variable to consider is network, spot, or program. We can pretty much eliminate program, which is where you sponsor an entire radio program and get your commercials during the program break. This is only for major advertisers. It's very expensive and is not generally for most direct response or mail order advertisers. Spot radio is radio at a particular time and by a particular station. Turn to the SRDS *Spot Radio Rates and Data* for detailed information. And finally, network is where you obtain national advertising through one of the major networks. Then the publication to look at is SRDS *Network Rates and Data.*

Having decided on the use of network or local spot advertisements, your next choice is station and program. Having matched up the demographics with one of the studies mentioned previously, you have a selection of these and you can start advertising on one or two stations. Since repetition is very important in this type of advertising, it is far better to advertise several times on one station than one time on several different stations. At this time you should also select the particular programs on which you would like your advertisements or commercials to appear.

As with print advertisements, the seasonality of your product is very important. You wouldn't want to try to sell a Christmas product during the summer or a swimming pool product in the middle of the winter. There is also an off-season for radio, which as I will point out later, can affect the cost. The radio-off season is January, February, and, to a certain extent, July and August. Although this is off-season for radio, it may not be off-season for mail order radio *ads.* So you may obtain a very good deal as a mail order advertiser during one of these periods.

The length of time of your commercial is another radio variable. You can buy a 10-second advertisement, which is almost totally useless for mail order. You can also buy a 30- or a 60-second advertisement. For your purposes, a 60-second ad is probably the best. In fact, in many cases, a 30-second ad is priced at approximately 75% that of a 60-second ad anyway.

Frequency is another important factor. As mentioned earlier, repetition is key in mail order advertising through this medium. One of the advantages of radio is the fact that you can hit your potential customers frequently with the same ad. How frequently depends upon your budget and what you are trying to achieve.

Finally, the last variable is spot time, meaning at what period during the broadcast day you want your ad to appear. The radio day is broken up basically into five periods. From 6:00 to 10:00 a.m. is called morning driving time, and from 3:00 to 7:00 p.m. is known as evening driving time. These are both expensive times for radio. There are also the periods from 10:00 a.m. to 3:00 p.m., 7:00 p.m. to midnight, and from midnight to 6:00 a.m. There are two principles to keep in mind when considering spot time. First, you'll pay more for the prime times. Second, for mail order–type advertising, sometimes a non–prime time is far better. Now it is a well-known fact that during prime time you will have more listeners. However, for mail order advertising by radio or by television, there is no direct relationship in many cases between the number of orders received and the size of the audience. This is an important factor to keep in mind when selecting your spot time and also when considering your cost options.

COST OPTIONS IN RADIO

As with various types of print media, you are going to have various options available in which you can pay more or less for your radio advertisements. Your advertising options for radio advertisements are prime rate, TAP, or total audience plan, ROS, or run of station, off-season rates, and various rates depending upon spot time.

The prime rate is the top of the line. You pay the rate as per the rate card, but you get to specify when the ad goes on the air and your ad cannot be bumped.

In TAP, or total audience plan, spots are scheduled for each of the day parts. You don't have quite as much choice, but you are guaranteed that you have a spot in each day part specified.

ROS, or run of station, is a lot less money. But your ad runs at the station's choice. It's much like the remnant space in print advertising. Your ad will be run when the station is able to run it for lack of paid prime time or TAP time advertisers.

During the off-season, you pay less than you would during the rest of the year.

Spot time means that you pay according to the time spot in which your advertisement appears. For example, your ad, running in the late evening during the period from 7:00 p.m. to midnight, may cost only 50% as much as it would during the prime driving time.

PI, or per inquiry, is the same as described for print advertising earlier in the book. You pay nothing up front but work out a joint venture with the station so that you pay a certain amount for each order received. Again, per inquiry can be a terrific deal because you have no investment for your advertising and don't pay anything until your orders actually start to come in. But it's as difficult to locate stations for a PI deal as it is to locate magazines willing to do the same thing. Again, never be afraid to ask. If you are dealing through an agency or a media buyer and seek per inquiry–type advertising, be sure to ask about it.

HOW TO PREPARE A RADIO COMMERCIAL

In preparing a radio commercial, your first task it to list the objectives. Remember that, just as with a print ad, there are various tactics you can use to make the sale. For example, the basic objectives may be to sell directly from your radio advertisement; to use a two-step method where all you're seeking are inquiries to which you will send a further sales package through the mail; or to support a direct mail campaign by radio advertising.

If your objective is a support campaign, be certain and test first through your primary method of selling. By testing your primary method first (say, a display advertisement), you can see the change that the support advertising coming through radio either accomplishes or does not accomplish.

Once you have decided on your objectives, you have several alternatives regarding how your advertisement is presented to your potential customer. One is straight reading by the announcer or yourself or a professional actor on tape. Another is a dialogue, sort of a conversational situation between two or more individuals. You've probably heard these witty dialogue situational advertisements on the radio selling everything from Time to Blue Nun wine. Finally, the third option is that of a jingle, something sung. This may or may not be applicable to the direct mail proposition you envision.

You should definitely ask the advice of the representative of the radio station with which you intend to advertise when you begin to prepare your radio commercial. The radio station can help, as indicated earlier, with the various technical and research facilities at its disposal. In addition, radio representatives may be able to get you sample cassettes that have spot commercials for you to listen to and from which you can get ideas. These are obtained through your radio station or from the Radio Advertising Bureau. In addition to the cassettes, the station may provide you with results and how these commercials were used. It is permissible for you to copy the concept, but not the word-for-word presentation. In other words, you cannot simply substitute your name and your product for those in the cassette. But you can use the same idea, approach, or concept for your advertisement.

HOW TO PREPARE YOUR RADIO COMMERCIAL

First, I should say to you *do not prepare anything yourself.* The radio station can actually prepare the entire commercial for you. If you decide to go this route, find out exactly when it is being done so that you can be there while your commercial is being prepared. If changes are necessary you can make them immediately and do not have to waste money or time by going through the full cycle of having the commercial aired before you listen to it and are dissatisfied.

If you decide to prepare the commercial yourself, use the copywriting techniques outlined in chapter 14. However, you must limit yourself greatly in your copy. A 60-second radio advertisement contains only 150 to 170 words, far less than the full-page copy in a print advertisement. As some basis for comparison, a successful Joe Sugarman ad for JS&A Sales runs to over 2000 words. You should also be certain that the address or phone number or wherever the response is to be sent and the order instructions are repeated several times. These instructions should be extremely simple. Remember that, in most cases, your potential customer is not sitting there with paper and pencil in hand waiting to hear your ad. Once your ad is written out, you should practice reading it yourself to see at what speed you must read to complete it within the required time. You will find that if you get much above 170 words, it will be impossible for you to articulate the words properly without sounding like a high-speed jet, so watch this point very carefully.

After you have the copy completed, type it out, double-spaced, in capital letters.

At the same time, if you decide that background music or a noise is needed in your ad, indicate when this noise is to occur. The way to do this is through elapsed time. In other words, if you want automobile noises to begin during a conversational situation in your advertisement, you could indicate that automobile noises occur at 10 seconds, a honking horn at 15, or whatever, depending on the situation. Whatever your noise or music description and its timing, it must be coordinated with your copy.

RUNNING YOUR RADIO ADVERTISING CAMPAIGN

As with print advertising or direct mail, you must walk before you run. You cannot assume a success merely because you are advertising or even because the product has been successful in the past with some other medium. Therefore, start with one or two stations and expand slowly. In every case you should compare your cost per order for different stations and different times and do testing as if it were print testing. Keep very close records of these costs per order. You may be able to use them later to negotiate a lower cost or better spot with the station, or if you can't get either to improve your response, drop the station entirely from your advertising.

TELEVISION ADVERTISING

There's been an incredible growth in television advertising for mail order operators in recent years. According to Bob Stone, during a four-year period, mail order television advertising increased no less than 469%. It's little wonder when we consider the fact that there are 73,000,000 homes with televisions today in the United States, and that the average viewing period per day is six hours per person. Naturally, there are some distinctive reasons for this tremendous increase in mail order television advertising, and these have to do with the advantages of advertising in this medium. They are the following.

1. The fact that you can see as well as hear the advertisement
2. The tremendous reach of television
3. The quick response, which equals that of radio
4. The fact that you can demonstrate the product in action
5. The wide range of television stations across the United States
6. The fact that television is relatively inexpensive for testing
7. The synergism among audio, visual, and motion effects
8. The capacity for repeats because of video recorders and taping by potential customers

Let's look at these advantages. The fact that you can see as well as hear the advertisement is going to increase your response. The only question is: Will it increase it enough to justify the additional cost? Because television has passed radio as the major broadcast medium, there is a tremendous reach in this market. You can get to almost your entire potential customer market through the use of television, whereas the reach of radio at maximum is only 60%. As noted, television is no slower than radio in response, and it has the additional advantage that you can actually demonstrate your product in action, which is extremely important for such products as a special knife that has various kitchen household uses, a jogging board that allows you to count the number of steps you've taken in your exercise program, special frying pans and pots to which food cannot adhere, and so forth. Finally, as with radio, there's a wide range of stations throughout the United States.

Many people think television's cost is prohibitive. It *is* more expensive than radio, and if you are just starting out you may have difficulty using this medium. However, according to Jim Kobs, author of *Profitable Direct Marketing,* you can advertise your product or service through television, including creating the spot, producing the advertisement, getting the talent necessary, and buying the time, for less than $10,000.

Synergism means that the sum total of parts is greater than each separate component. Here we're talking about the synergism among the audio, visual, and motion portions of the ad. When the sound (audio), sight (visual), and movement come together, they make for a tremendously effective method of communicating your message to your potential customer.

Finally, video recorders are becoming ever more popular, and though it is possible to eliminate the commercials when using a video recorder, many people do not. This means that, while in radio the life of the ad is only that short time it is actually being heard by the potential customer, television ads may "live" much longer through taping.

DISADVANTAGES OF TELEVISION ADVERTISING

The disadvantages of television advertising are similar to those in radio, except for cost.

1. *Cost.* Television, of course, costs more than radio and so may be difficult for a new mail order dealer to use.
2. *Time.* As with radio, the amount of copy is severely limited because of time. A full-page advertisement in print may be 2000 words. A two-minute advertisement spot in television may be only a little more than 10% of that figure.
3. *No Life.* Except for those instances when the advertisement is recorded on a video recorder, the ad has no life.
4. *Little Control.* As with radio, you cannot view every single ad spot in the medium to ensure that it has come out exactly as you intended it to, or that no mistake was made in the advertisement.

THE USES OF TELEVISION ADVERTISING

The uses of television advertising are basically the same as those of radio: to sell directly from your ad; to use the two-step method—that is, to send additional information on receipt of an inquiry and to sell the potential customer through this material; to support a mail order campaign conducted primarily through some other means.

If you are considering use of television as support for another type of ad campaign, you should keep in mind that such a plan is workable only if you can saturate the identical market covered by television. If you have a direct mail campaign, the area and potential customers on which that campaign is focused must cover the same market being reached by television. It has been estimated that use of television to support a direct marketing or print advertising campaign in mail order may cost an additional 10% of your advertising budget. On the other hand, if the support campaign is successful, it can add 30% or more to your sales.

THE PARADOXES OF TELEVISION ADVERTISING

There are several paradoxes in television advertising, not the least of which is the fact that, as in radio, prime time may not be the best for your advertising. If you have watched the late, late show, you are more likely to see television mail order ads then than during prime time.

Another paradox of television advertising is the fact that low ratings may actually be good for you. How can this be? Well, for one thing, a program that has a low rating also has lower ad rates. In addition to that, certain types of programs that have low ratings are much more responsive to mail order offers. Why is this so? There are perhaps several reasons. One is that during a prime time program, a viewer may be much less likely or willing to go for a pencil and paper because he or she might miss something important. On the other hand, an old movie is much less likely to cause the viewer to be afraid to leave the screen. Further, perhaps because of these factors, as mail order ads begin to gather around certain periods of time, the viewer is more likely to be thinking about responding to mail order ads. Certain periods of television viewing are becoming much like the classified ads in magazines. Individuals looking at television at these times may already be looking for a certain type of product or something to buy. What's more, they are thus more likely to purchase through mail order.

RATINGS AND WHAT THEY ACTUALLY MEAN

Ratings are actually a measurement of household viewing. One rating point is equal to 1% of the households in the market. If a particular program has a 10 rating, 10% of all households are thought to be viewing that program. Total advertising is calculated in gross rating points, or GRPs.

GRPs are the total of the ratings attributed to each of the programs or time periods. Therefore, let's say that you have two different advertisements, one appearing on a program with a 20 rating and another appearing on a program with a 30 rating. Added together that's 50%, or 50 GRPs. You could also add up various combinations to achieve 100 GRPs, in which case you would reach the equivalent of 100% of the households in that market.

HOW THE TELEVISION DAY IS DIVIDED

Just as a radio day is divided into time periods, so is the television day. The television day is in four parts: daytime, early fringe, prime time, and late fringe. Daytime is from sign-on in the morning until 4:00 p.m. Early fringe is from 4:00 to 8:00 p.m. on weekdays and all day on weekends. Prime time, the most expensive, is from 8:00 to 11:00 p.m. And finally, late fringe is from 11:00 p.m. until sign-off in the early morning hours.

Television advertising costs vary greatly, but as noted earlier, more highly rated programs will cost much more for ad time. Prime-time advertising is far more expensive than that at other times. Yet, as I said before, neither prime time nor highly rated shows may be desirable for the mail order advertiser. Keep this in mind. It is a very important principle.

According to the *DMMA Fact Book, 1980 Update,* most buyers of television advertising deal directly with the station and can get from 15 to 45% off the regular rate for direct response advertising.

HOW TO BUY TELEVISION ADVERTISING

Television advertising must be purchased by first identifying the market you're going after. The breakdown isn't quite the same as in radio, but you can get information on viewers and what they are watching, just as with radio. Again, use the American Research Bureau's *Arbitron.* The Nielsen Company also provides research information, which usually includes the population being surveyed, the number of households owning television sets, program times and their names, and the number of households, men, women, children, and adults who are estimated to be watching each of the programs listed. And don't forget the SRDS booklets.

Because television is not so segmented by market as radio and does not have as many specialized stations dealing with special interest groups, you will not be able to advertise to as precise a segment of your market as you can in radio.

TELEVISION VARIABLES YOU MUST CONSIDER
FOR YOUR ADVERTISING

Just as certain important variables exist for radio advertising, others exist for television. These include network, spot, or cable television ad; the station or program; the length of time; the seasonality; and the spot you select.

Use of nationwide network or spot advertising is very similar to radio. However, cable television is growing greatly and represents yet another advertising opportunity for those potential customers who are watching current movies shown through the cable television network. Station program decisions can be made through the use of the research services already mentioned. The length of time is again a variable and an important one you must consider. Your options in time for television advertising are 30, 60, and 90 seconds, and two minutes, although all of these options may not be available with every single station. Thirty seconds is not very good for direct response advertising; 60 seconds is by far the most popular; 90 seconds is a compromise between 60 and the increased cost of a two-minute advertisement. One of the longer advertisements might be necessary for a product that needs a considerable amount of demonstration or is a big-ticket item. Again, seasonality plays its part, because television also has its off season: you can expect to pay higher costs during the period of October through April. There are certain special periods when television ads will cost much less—immediately after Christmas until about January 15, from January 16 through March 1, from July through August 31, and then from September 1 until the new fall programming season starts. As noted earlier, the spot you select for your advertisement will cause the cost of the ad to vary. For example, an advertisement that costs $100 at 6:00 a.m. may cost $1000 during prime time.

COST PRICING OPTIONS FOR TELEVISION ADVERTISING

As with radio and the print media, you have various options regarding the price you pay for your ads.

1. In prime rate, you specify the exact time you want your spot to run. You cannot be bumped.
2. One level down from this is the TAP, or total audience plan. Here you schedule your spots to run in each of the day periods, but you can be rescheduled by the station if they find a fully paid advertiser.

3. Below this is the ROS, or run of station. A run of station plan is much less specific. You buy a certain number of spots per week and the station can run them whenever it gets a chance, whenever the time slot is open. This is the least expensive.

4. PI deals are also possible in television, but very difficult to obtain. PI in television works just as it does in radio or with print advertising.

5. The bonus to pay out is another option you may find with a local station. It is also very difficult to work out, but worthwhile if you can. In this case, you negotiate the cost as well as a certain number of orders or inquiries. The station continues to run your ad until it fulfills its contract and you obtain the number of orders or the number of inquiries stipulated in your contract.

PREPARING A TELEVISION COMMERCIAL

As with the preparation of a radio commercial, your first step is to list your objectives and decide on the strategy or tactics you want to follow to bring in the order. Once you decide this, the next step is to prepare your copy.

Television copy should be short, simple, and direct, just as the radio copy. Remember that your time is very limited. In general, have a simple theme and message, and repeat your order instructions several times. Don't forget that you have another dimension with television. The viewer, your potential customer, can see as well as hear. So when you list the order information, have it *shown,* as well as having the announcer repeat the information.

One good way to prepare your television commercial is by use of a storyboard, as shown in Figure 12-1. As you write your dialogue, indicate the sound effects where required as you did with radio. You'll also draw a little sketch of what is being shown or what the viewer would see at that time.

The basic options in preparation of your television advertisement are a film, a videotape, or slides. Again, the station can give you a lot of help in preparing your commercial.

TACTICS TO FOLLOW IN TELEVISION ADVERTISING

If at all possible, try to use print advertising as a basis for your television advertising campaign. Finding out what works and what doesn't and who

Video 1. Sketch of Visual and number of seconds	Video 2. Second Sketch and seconds	Video 3. Third Sketch and seconds	Video 4. Fourth Sketch and seconds
Audio 1 (Copy 1)	Audio 2 (Copy 2)	Audio 3 (Copy 3)	Audio 4 (Copy 4)
Video 5. Fifth Sketch and seconds	Video 6. Sixth Sketch and seconds	Video 7. Seventh Sketch and seconds	Video 8. Eighth Sketch and seconds
Audio 5 (Copy 5)	Audio 6 (Copy 6)	Audio 7 (Copy 7)	Audio 8 (Copy 8)
Video 9. Ninth Sketch and seconds	Video 10. Tenth Sketch and seconds	Video 11. Eleventh Sketch and seconds	Video 12. Twelfth Sketch and seconds
Audio 9 (Copy 9)	Audio 10 (Copy 10)	Audio 11 (Copy 11)	Audio 12 (Copy 12)

Figure 12-1. A storyboard for a television commercial.

is ordering your product will be very helpful. Definitely start in a less expensive medium before you go into television.

Start your ad initially by running it a couple of times in one week on a very limited number of stations. As with radio, expand slowly only after proved success. Bob Stone suggests watching your television advertisement very closely, and when the responses begin to decline, stop advertising right then and there. Don't try to wrench every single possible order out of that particular advertisement. The reason, again, is the high cost. According to Stone, two series of advertisements a year is maximum for most offers.

Again, after advertising is completed, you should compare the results you obtain on a cost per order basis for the various stations and ads. Think again about whether to change your copy, whether your advertising costs must be lowered, or whether you should change your positioning during the day, time of advertising, and so forth. And again, this is good information to use in negotiating with the station for further advertising later. If you need a certain price to break even or to make money, since you are a mail order advertiser, you may be able to negotiate this lower cost of advertising and become profitable on an ad that otherwise might be marginal.

GIANT PROFITS THROUGH TELEPHONE
MAIL ORDER ADVERTISING

The advent of the WATS line, which stands for *wide area telephone service* and reaches nationwide, has been one of the main motivating forces in an explosion of telephone advertising over the last 10 years. In fact, telephone advertisers are currently making a little less than three billion calls a year to sell products and services over the telephone, which the customer then receives by mail.

There are decided advantages to telephone advertising.

1. Quick response, equal to that of television or radio
2. The feedback that you can get from the potential customer while selling
3. The usually much higher response rate through telephone over direct mail, print advertising, or broadcast media

Quick response is greater in telephone advertising and is, of course, an advantage over print advertising or direct mail. But the verbal feedback is possible with no other medium used for mail order. The telephone is very similar to a face-to-face selling situation, and the higher response rate can be termed truly incredible. One campaign, reported by Jim Kobs for an industrial product, produced 10.1% immediate orders, 46.2% future orders, and finally, 8.8% leads for salespeople. In other words, the success rate for the telephone calls exceeded 65%!

Murray Roman, who wrote *Telephone Marketing: How to Build Your Business by Telephone* and pioneered the use of taped messages by phone, once described a membership campaign that failed through direct mail but led to a preorder rate of better than 80% through the use of telephone mail order marketing.

BASIC USES OF TELEPHONE MAIL ORDER MARKETING

The three basic uses for telephone mail order marketing are order generation, either directly or through the two-step method; obtaining sales leads; and support for other campaigns being conducted by broadcast media or print media.

The basic tactics to be considered are two. One is delivery: Should the delivery of the telephone message be done totally live or partially live and partially by tape? Both totally live and live by tape delivery have proved extremely effective. The use of tape is particularly useful when a celebrity is involved, or someone who is of importance to the individual being telephoned. In this case, the individual making the telephone call can ask whether the recipient of the call could stand by for a message from, for example, Ronald Reagan. Assuming the answer is yes, a short, taped message, asking, say, for a contribution of funds, is played. The live voice then comes back on to make the close and solicit the donation.

The second tactic is timing, which is very important when the telephone is used as a support medium. Is the telephone call made prior to the potential customer's receiving a direct mail package or being exposed to broadcast or print media, or should it be done after he or she has already received the package, or should it be done simultaneously? Each has its advantages and disadvantages. If you are calling before, you are prepping the individual to receive the other message through the other medium, and you depend then on the other medium to make the close. If you are calling afterward, you are trying to mop up those customers who have not already ordered and make the close through direct person-to-person contact by telephone. If you call simultaneously when the individual is to receive the direct mail package or be exposed to other media, you are looking for an overwhelming effect in which the combination will serve to get the individual to order.

COST OF A TELEPHONE MARKETING CAMPAIGN

The cost of a telephone marketing campaign is not low. According to the Direct Marketing Association, the estimated cost per 1000 calls is from $750 to $5000, several times the cost of a direct mail campaign. On the other hand, for items costing from $7 to $2000, the response has been 3% to 40%. If you recall that a direct mail campaign response rate for breakeven is usually much lower, you can see just how successful telephone marketing can really be.

HOW TO BE SUCCESSFUL WITH
TELEPHONE MAIL ORDER MARKETING

Success in telephone direct marketing rests on three major points: the ability to sell face to face (or in this case voice to voice), calls per time period, and ability to deal with rejection.

Since telephoning is a sales situation in which you're involved with person-to-person contact, the individual making the call must be a salesperson. One salesperson estimated that it is twice as difficult to sell by voice it is face to face. On the other hand, you can reach 10 times as many people by telephone as you can through running around and seeing them on a face-to-face, person-to-person basis.

If the individual who's making the call talks too fast, he or she is apt to be distrusted and may not be understood. On the other hand, if he or she talks too slowly, it is annoying to the individual who is being sold and it also means that the salesperson will make fewer calls per time period.

I mentioned that a friend of mine has a seminar company and is extremely happy with a return on direct mailing of .25%. With that return he has built up a $2 million-a-year business, and he isn't despondent at all about the fact that 99.75% of the invitations he sends to people are rejected. On the other hand, the telephone, which has a much higher acceptance rate, will involve a personal rejection on a daily basis, day in and day out, and the ability of the individual who's making these calls to take this rejection will, to a large degree, determine your success.

SHOULD YOU DO A DIRECT TELEPHONE CAMPAIGN YOURSELF?

It is possible for you to do a telephone mail order campaign yourself, but it is not easy. It depends on the consideration of a number of different things including:

1. *Your Own Training.* Are you the sales type and can you take rejection? If you have done a great deal of face-to-face selling and you have the time, it's possible for you to be your own direct caller and make a fortune through telephone calls combined with mail order.

2. *A WATS Line.* A WATS line costs money to rent. Can you afford to maintain one during the period of your campaign?

3. *Legal Requirements.* There are various legal requirements to be met in each state regarding calls made directly into a person's home or business and selling through the telephone. You must be aware of all of them because you will be responsible.

4. *Time.* Is making these direct calls yourself the best expenditure of your time? Or is it better for you to be planning, preparing copy, or just plain thinking? If you decide that you want someone else to handle telephone marketing for you, you can locate a telephone marketing operation through your telephone book, through the classified advertising pages of *ZIP* or *Direct Mail Marketing,* or through your local direct marketing organization listed in Appendix D.

SUMMARY

In this chapter, we have discussed in detail three very important means of mail order marketing other than print advertising—radio, television, and telephone. The important points to remember are these:

1. The advantages and disadvantages of each of these media, and when to use each
2. How to buy broadcast media, how to identify your market, and how to locate those stations that are likely to be received by your market
3. Those variables in television and radio that will affect both the response you receive and the cost you pay for advertising
4. The cost options you have in both radio and television, and how to negotiate the best deal
5. How to prepare a radio commercial
6. How to prepare a television commercial
7. How to run both radio and television campaigns
8. What you have to do to run a successful telephone campaign
9. Whether you should run a telephone campaign yourself or have someone else run it

Do not overlook the points in this chapter even if you decide to start with print media. If you are successful, at some point in your career you will want to expand and use these other media for dramatically increased profits.

13

How to Write Copy
That Creates Sales

MUST YOU BE ABLE TO WRITE COPY?

Several months ago a well-known expert in mail order was speaking to my class at the university about copywriting, and he was asked, "What if you can't write good copy yourself?" He answered, "If you can't write good copy, you don't belong in the business." I most emphatically disagree. The fact is that most large mail order businesses are run without the owner writing the copy. Certainly in most of the companies that are huge conglomerates, members of the *Fortune* 500 group, the manager of the mail order division does not write copy.

However, even if you decide that you are not qualified to write copy nor do you have the desire to do so, please don't skip this chapter. You must understand the basic principles to know what the copywriters working for you are doing, and whether what they propose in your advertisements has any chance of working. Let me give you a specific example here. At one point in my life I was attempting to get leads for military body armor that would protect the soldier against various types of projectiles through a space advertisement in a magazine called *International Defense Review*. At that time I'd written some copy, but not a great deal of mail order copy. Accordingly, I gave the idea and product to an agency and asked them to come up with a concept. After several weeks of activity, they presented me with an ad headlined, "What the Well-Dressed Soldier Wears." The body of the copy discussed various specifications of the body armor having to do with its size and the projectiles it would stop. Because I had taken the time to study the basic principles of copywriting, I knew this was wrong because the discussion centered not on benefits, but on a description of the product. I rejected this ad and wrote my own, which was highly successful, headed, "Body Armor Wins Battles." As you might imagine, the copy itself focused not on a mere description of what the body armor would do, but on how it benefited the wearer.

WHAT IS COPY AND CAN IT MAKE A DIFFERENCE?

Copy is the words used to communicate your message or offer to your prospective customers in a classified ad, a display ad, direct mail, or through some other medium. It can make an incredible difference in whether your proposition is successful or unsuccessful. World-famous copywriter John Caples, in his book *Tested Advertising Methods,* speaks of two ads in which the size was the same, the publications were identical, and both ads used identical photo illustrations; only the copy differed. One ad sold 19½ times as much goods as the other. Stop now and think what this means. This is not only the difference between success and failure, but the difference between failure and making an immediate fortune. So the copy used in your ad is not just something you must consider somewhere along the way. It, by itself, can make you a mail order millionaire.

IS COPYWRITING POSSIBLE TO LEARN?

Copywriting can be learned by anyone who is reading this book and can write. It is simply a method of communicating with your customer. It is sales in writing.

Some years ago, Dr. George W. Crane, in his *Psychology Applied,* described how Professor S. N. Stevens of Northwestern University had a debate with some professional advertisers. Professor Stevens felt that he could identify which ads had been successful, based upon psychological principles. Eventually he challenged the professional advertisers to give him 10 advertisements whose results they already knew. His job would be to rank them in their order of merit, from best to worst, according to the response these advertisements had generated. Professor Stevens asked only the target market and the purpose of the advertiser in each advertisement. He then picked up his pencil and pad and ranked them in order of by their actual pulling power. Out of 10 advertisements handed to him, he erred only in the last and two weakest samples submitted, which he transposed. He identified the first through the eighth correctly. This shows that while copywriting may be mysterious, there are known psychological principles that are used and that work.

HOW TO LEARN COPYWRITING

To learn copywriting, there are four steps that you must take. They are not always easy, but if you follow them faithfully you will be able to write good copy with confidence.

1. *Read Books on Copywriting.* I'm going to recommend three books right now because they are written by three great copywriters. The first is _Tested Advertising Methods,_ by John Caples, published by Prentice-Hall, Englewood Cliffs, New Jersey 07632. The second is _My First Sixty Years in Advertising, by_ Maxwell Sackheim, published by Prentice-Hall, Englewood Cliffs, New Jersey 07632. The third is _How to Write a Good Advertisement: A Short Course in Copywriting,_ by Victor O. Schwab, published by Harper and Row, 10 E 53rd St., New York 10022, and by Wilshire Book Company, 12015 Sherman Road, North Hollywood, California 91605.

2. *Collect and Read Successful Ads.* You will find them in magazines, through the mail, and so forth. You know the advertisement is successful if you see it repeated over a long period. I have a file of hundreds of advertisements and letters I have received. I read and reread all of them. In some cases I can tell you the copywriter simply by reading the copy. After a while, you will be able to do the same. More importantly, in many cases you will be able to pick up a magazine or a direct mail piece you have received and tell instantly whether the product has a chance for success, simply by reading the copy.

3. *Learn the Basic Principles.* We will discuss these principles in this chapter.

4. *Practice.* You can read books, you can read copy, and you can learn the principles and still not become a copywriter unless you practice writing copy frequently. One way to do this is to take an advertisement you feel to be a poor one and rewrite it, using the principles of good copywriting. Do at least one ad a week. Don't be satisfied with just rewriting the advertisement once. Try several different appeals and several different ways to reach your customer. Show your efforts to friends and ask them to pick which ad

they would be most likely to respond to. (Retype the advertisement which appears in the magazine or in a letter so they cannot tell the difference.) When your ad is picked more often as the best ad, you will know that you are becoming an individual who can write good mail order copy.

HOW TO STRUCTURE THE COPY IN YOUR AD OR LETTER

There are many different formulas around for structuring copy. In fact, there are so many that some copywriters recommend that you not try any formula at all, but simply try "to communicate." My belief is that you should start out with a definite structure. Learn this structure and write your advertisements in this way initially. Once you know that you can write good mail order copy, you can experiment and try the more philosophical concept of communicating without reference to a formula.

The basic structure I recommend is as follows:

1. Get attention.
2. Develop interest.
3. Show the benefits and advantages of your product or service.
4. Build up and maintain credibility.
5. Deliver a call to action.

THE HEADLINE IS YOUR ATTENTION GETTER

The most important aspect of your ad and copy is the headline. Yet, many copywriters who will spend hours and hours slaving over the copy in the body of the ad will spend just a few minutes on the headline. David Ogilvy, chairman of Ogilvy Mather International, one of the world's best-known advertising agencies, says in his *Confessions of an Advertising Man*, "The headline is the most important element in most advertisements."

The weekly magazine *Advertising Age* once told how Maxwell Sackheim sold 500,000 copies of a book by changing the title slightly. The book was originally published as *Five Acres*. While it enjoyed reasonable sales, it was not a best seller and was about to go on the inactive list when Maxwell Sackheim got involved. Sackheim believes that the title of a book should be good enough to be used as the headline of an advertisement. So he changed the title from *Five Acres* to *Five Acres and Indepen-*

dence. This small change caused sales to double and triple previous records, and within six years, 500,000 copies of the book were sold.

Want more proof about headlines? Book publisher E. Haldeman-Julius sold tens of millions of *Little Blue Books* through newspaper and magazine advertisements. These books were small paperbacks that sold for only 5¢ and 10¢ each. In the advertising, they were designated only by their titles, with no other description or copy. In his book, *The First Hundred Million*, Haldeman-Julius tells how he frequently rescued books about to be dropped from his line because they were not selling well by changing the titles. The right change brought a dramatic increase in sales. Dr. George W. Crane began using Haldeman-Julius's results in his lectures. The idea was for the subject to imagine himself or herself a publisher selling books to the general public. The subject was asked to pick which of a pair of book titles he or she would select to sell the greater number of volumes. Remember that *Little Blue Books* were sold with no description whatsoever other than the title. This test was administered in conventions and society meetings to over 50,000 editors, physicians, dentists, lawyers, engineers, advertisers, salespeople, merchants, and teachers. Other individuals also gave the identical test to over 75,000 adults. Would you like to take this test? I have prepared a similar test from the results published in Haldeman-Julius' book, shown in Figure 13-1. Mark which one of the pair of titles you think would sell the most books. The answers are found in Figure 13-2, which shows both the old and new titles and the number of books sold with each. The more right answers, the better your understanding of headline writing.

Okay, you say, so titles of books can actually have a tremendous impact on selling them, and titles of books can also be used as the headlines for advertisements, and someone may buy a book based solely on the title. But will someone read copy in an advertisement based solely on a headline? Victor Schwab, in his book, *How to Write a Good Advertisement,* describes a story about Max Hart of Hart, Schaffner, and Marx, and his advertising manager, George L. Dyer. The story goes that they were arguing about long copy and Dyer said, "I'll bet you $10 I can write a newspaper page of solid type and you would read every word of it." Mr. Hart was ready to bet and said that he didn't have to read a line of copy to know that he would never read an entire page of solid type. But Mr. Dyer responded, "I'll only have to give you the headline. The headline would be, 'This Page Is All about Max Hart.' "

John Caples devotes more than one-fifth of the entire book to headlines, and he says, "This is not too much space to devote to this vital subject."

The Tallow Ball_____	The Truth About Patent Medicine_____
or	or
A French Prostitute's Sacrifice_____	Patent Medicine and Public Health_____
Privateersman_____	Art of Controvery_____
or	or
The Battles of a Seaman_____	How to Argue Logically_____
Fleece of Gold_____	Life of Barnum_____
or	or
The Quest for a Blonde Mistress_____	P.T. Barnum and His Circus_____
Honey and Gall_____	Casanova, History's Greatest Lover_____
or	or
Studies in Mystic Materialism_____	Casanova and His Loves_____
A Book of Intellectual Rowdies_____	When You Were a Tadpole and I Was a Fish_____
or	or
Cupbearers of Wine and Hellebore_____	Poems of Evolution_____
The Mystery of the Man in the Iron Mask_____	An Introduction to Einstein_____
or	or
The Mystery of the Iron Mask_____	Einstein's Theory of Relativity Explained_____
The King Enjoys Himself_____	Markheim_____
or	or
The Lustful King Enjoys Himself_____	Markheim's Murder_____
None Beneath the King Shall Enjoy This Woman___ ___	Ten O'Clock_____
or	or
None Beneath the King_____	What Art Should Mean to You_____
Terse Truths About the Riddles of Life_____	The Man Who Apes Nobility_____
or	or
Apothegms_____	The Show-Off_____
Pen, Pencil and Poison_____	The Love Sonnets of an Artist_____
or	or
The Story of a Notorious Criminal_____	The Sonnets of a Portrait Painter_____

Figure 13-1. Which *Little Blue Book* title do you think sold best? (From Little Blue Book Company, by permission of E. Haldeman-Julius Publications.)

HOW TO WRITE HEADLINES

All good headlines have certain things in common. First, a good headline appeals to the reader's self-interest and stresses the most important benefit of the product or service. If the copywriter can arouse the curiosity of the reader or present startling news or suggest a quick and easy way that the reader might obtain a certain benefit in which he or she is interested, this will enhance the stopping power of the headline. That is what you as a copywriter are trying to do—stop the reader as he or she glances over

	Yearly Sales
The Tallow Ball	15,000
A French Prostitute's Sacrifice	54,700
Privateersman	less than 6000
The Battles of a Seaman	10,000
Fleece of Gold	6000
The Quest for a Blonde Mistress	50,000
Honey and Gall	almost 0
Studies in Mystic Materialism	15,000
A Book of Intellectual Rowdies	11,000
Cupbearers of Wine and Hellebore	almost 0
The Mystery of the Man in the Iron Mask	30,000
The Mystery of the Iron Mask	11,000
The King Enjoys Himself	8000
The Lustful King Enjoys Himself	38,000
None Beneath the King Shall Enjoy This Woman	34,000
None Beneath the King	6000
Terse Truths About the Riddles of Life	9000
Apothegms	2000
Pen, Pencil, and Poison	5000
The Story of a Notorious Criminal	15,800
The Truth About Patent Medicine	10,000
Patent Medicine and Public Health	3000
Art of Controversy	almost 0
How to Argue Logically	30,000
Life of Barnum	4000
P.T. Barnum and His Circus	8000
Casanova, History's Greatest Lover	28,000
Casanova and His Loves	8000
When You Were a Tadpole and I Was a Fish	7000
Poems of Evolution	2000
An Introduction to Einstein	15,000
Einstein's Theory of Relativity Explained	42,000
Markheim	almost 0
Markheim's Murder	7000
Ten O'Clock	2000
What Art Should Mean to You	9000
The Man Who Apes Nobility	almost 0
The Show-Off	10,000
The Love Sonnets of an Artist	6000
The Sonnets of a Portrait Painter	almost 0

Figure 13-2. These *Little Blue Book* titles sold best. (From Little Blue Book Company, by permission of E. Haldeman-Julius Publications.)

the hundreds of advertisements in a magazine and get your copy read.

Look at this headline: "How to Wake Up the Financial Genius within You." This headline is from Mark O. Haroldsen's book, which has sold several hundred thousand copies over the last few years. Notice how this headline appeals to self-interest and states a very strong benefit. It also arouses the curiosity of the reader. How do you wake up the financial genius within you? The headline promises that, by reading the copy that follows, you will learn how.

Now look at this headline: "How to Form Your Own Corporation without a Lawyer for under $50." This is the ad Ted Nicholas used to sell more than 100,000 copies of his book. Again, self-interest is stressed. It is a news item. It arouses curiosity. And notice how the headline promises the benefit of a quick, easy, and inexpensive way of forming a corporation without even using a lawyer.

Or look at this headline: "Language Translator—Communicate in Any Language without Saying a Word or Learn a New Language with the World's First Computerized Language Translator." Again, this headline appeals to self-interest. It stresses the important benefit of communicating in any language without saying a word and the benefit of learning a new language by the use of what is being sold. This is one of Joe Sugarman's famous ads that has helped him to build a $50 million-dollar-a-year business starting from his garage.

The second thing that good headlines have in common is certain key words that are psychologically powerful in attracting potential customers and getting them to continue to read. David Ogilvy says that the most important of these key words are free and new, but there are other powerful words you can use to work in your appeal. Here is a list of some words psychologists have discovered to be powerful in stopping your readers and getting them to read your entire copy:

advice to	how to
amazing	hurry
announcing	important
at last	improvement
bargain	introducing
challenge	it's here
compare	just arrived
easy	last chance
found	magic
free	miracle
how	new

now	startling
power	success
powerful	suddenly
quick	wanted
remarkable	who else
revolutionary	why
secret	which
sensational	when

Another way to use key words in your headline is to find those words that are so startling and unusual that they stop the reader cold and urge him or her to read on: "lazy man," "98-pound weakling," "quit work." All of these phrases are unusual enough that they stop the reader, which is the first thing you must do to get your potential customer to read further.

To write a winning headline implies winning out over others. Therefore, the key is to write more than one headline against each of several different appeals. These appeals should relate to Maslow's hierarchy of human needs, discussed earlier.

OTHER IMPORTANT ADVICE CONCERNING HEADLINES

Here are some other factors to consider when you write your headline.

1. Be specific. Being specific helps to lend credibility and makes your headline more believable. Don't just say, "Make a Lot of Money," say, "Make One Million Dollars," or whatever the amount is. Or don't just say, "Do It Fast"; say, "Do It in 30 Days or Less."

2. Do not put negatives in your headline. Salespeople have found that the positive sells better than the negative. Therefore, avoid the negative and accentuate the positive side in your headlines.

3. Make certain there is a clear connection between your headline and the copy. I have occasionally seen headlines that say something like, "Make 10 Million Dollars Today," and the copy goes on to say that what is promised in the headline is impossible and was used only to trick the reader into reading. I have never seen such copy work. No one likes to be tricked. Further, if you have tricked your customer once, he or she has every reason to believe you may do so again. Don't even hint to something like this. Make certain that what you say in the headline relates directly to what is said in the copy.

HEADLINES THAT MADE MILLIONS FOR THEIR ADVERTISERS

Let's look at some winning headlines. Victor O. Schwab, in his book, *How to Write a Good Advertisement,* lists 100 good headlines that were profitable for those who used them.*

1. THE SECRET OF MAKING PEOPLE LIKE YOU
2. A LITTLE MISTAKE THAT COST A FARMER $3000 A YEAR
3. ADVICE TO WIVES WHOSE HUSBANDS DON'T SAVE MONEY—BY A WIFE
4. THE CHILD WHO WON THE HEARTS OF ALL
5. ARE YOU EVER TONGUE-TIED AT A PARTY?
6. HOW A NEW DISCOVERY MADE A PLAIN GIRL BEAUTIFUL
7. HOW TO WIN FRIENDS AND INFLUENCE PEOPLE
8. THE LAST 2 HOURS ARE THE LONGEST—AND THOSE ARE THE 2 HOURS YOU SAVE
9. WHO ELSE WANTS A SCREEN STAR FIGURE?
10. DO YOU MAKE THESE MISTAKES IN ENGLISH?
11. WHY SOME FOODS "EXPLODE" IN YOUR STOMACH
12. HANDS THAT LOOK LOVELIER IN 24 HOURS—OR YOUR MONEY BACK
13. YOU CAN LAUGH AT MONEY WORRIES—IF YOU FOLLOW THIS SIMPLE PLAN
14. WHY SOME PEOPLE ALMOST ALWAYS MAKE MONEY IN THE STOCK MARKET
15. WHEN DOCTORS "FEEL ROTTEN" THIS IS WHAT THEY DO
16. IT SEEMS INCREDIBLE THAT YOU CAN OFFER THESE SIGNED ORIGINAL ETCHINGS—FOR ONLY $5 EACH!
17. FIVE FAMILIAR SKIN TROUBLES—-WHICH DO YOU WANT TO OVERCOME?
18. WHICH OF THESE $2.50-TO-$5 BEST SELLERS DO YOU WANT—FOR ONLY $1 EACH?
19. WHO EVER HEARD OF A WOMAN LOSING WEIGHT—AND ENJOYING 3 DELICIOUS MEALS AT THE SAME TIME?
20. HOW I IMPROVED MY MEMORY IN ONE EVENING

* From *How to Write a Good Advertisement,* by Victor O. Schwab, copyright © 1962 by Victor O. Schwab. By permission of Harper and Row, Publishers, Inc.

21. DISCOVER THE FORTUNE THAT LIES HIDDEN IN YOUR SALARY

22. DOCTORS PROVE 2 OUT OF 3 WOMEN CAN HAVE MORE BEAUTIFUL SKIN IN 14 DAYS

23. HOW I MADE A FORTUNE WITH A "FOOL IDEA"

24. HOW OFTEN DO YOU HEAR YOURSELF SAYING: "NO, I HAVEN'T READ IT; I'VE BEEN MEANING TO!"

25. THOUSANDS HAVE THIS PRICELESS GIFT—BUT NEVER DISCOVER IT!

26. WHOSE FAULT WHEN CHILDREN DISOBEY?

27. HOW A "FOOL STUNT" MADE ME A STAR SALESMAN

28. HAVE YOU THESE SYMPTOMS OF NERVE EXHAUSTION?

29. GUARANTEED TO GO THROUGH ICE, MUD, OR SNOW— OR WE PAY THE TOW!

30. HAVE YOU A "WORRY" STOCK?

31. HOW A NEW KIND OF CLAY IMPROVED MY COMPLEXION IN 30 MINUTES

32. 161 NEW WAYS TO A MAN'S HEART—IN THIS FASCINAT- ING BOOK FOR COOKS

33. PROFITS THAT LIE HIDDEN IN YOUR FARM

34. IS THE LIFE OF A CHILD WORTH $1 TO YOU?

35. EVERYWHERE WOMEN ARE RAVING ABOUT THIS AMAZING NEW SHAMPOO!

36. DO YOU DO ANY OF THESE TEN EMBARRASSING THINGS?

37. SIX TYPES OF INVESTORS—WHICH GROUP ARE YOU IN?

38. HOW TO TAKE OUT STAINS ... USE [product name] AND FOLLOW THESE EASY DIRECTIONS

39. TODAY ... ADD $10,000 TO YOUR ESTATE—FOR THE PRICE OF A NEW HAT

40. DOES YOUR CHILD EVER EMBARRASS YOU?

41. IS YOUR HOME PICTURE-POOR?

42. HOW TO GIVE YOUR CHILDREN EXTRA IRON—THESE 3 DELICIOUS WAYS

43. TO PEOPLE WHO WANT TO WRITE—BUT CAN'T GET STARTED

44. THIS ALMOST-MAGICAL LAMP LIGHTS HIGHWAY TURNS BEFORE YOU MAKE THEM

45. THE CRIMES WE COMMIT AGAINST OUR STOMACHS

46. THE MAN WITH THE "GRASSHOPPER MIND"

47. THEY LAUGHED WHEN I SAT DOWN AT THE PIANO—
    BUT WHEN I STARTED TO PLAY!—

48. THROW AWAY YOUR OARS!

49. HOW TO DO WONDERS WITH A LITTLE LAND!

50. WHO ELSE WANTS LIGHTER CAKE—IN HALF THE MIX-
    ING TIME?

51. LITTLE LEAKS THAT KEEP MEN POOR

52. PIERCED BY 301 NAILS . . . RETAINS FULL AIR PRESSURE

53. NO MORE BACK-BREAKING GARDEN CHORES FOR ME—
    YET OURS IS NOW THE SHOWPLACE OF THE NEIGHBOR-
    HOOD

54. OFTEN A BRIDESMAID, NEVER A BRIDE

55. HOW MUCH IS "WORKER TENSION" COSTING YOUR
    COMPANY?

56. TO MEN WHO WANT TO QUIT WORK SOMEDAY

57. HOW TO PLAN YOUR HOUSE TO SUIT YOURSELF

58. BUY NO DESK . . . UNTIL YOU'VE SEEN THIS SENSATION
    OF THE BUSINESS SHOW

59. CALL BACK THESE GREAT MOMENTS AT THE OPERA

60. "I LOST MY BULGES . . . AND SAVED MONEY TOO"

61. WHY [brand name] BULBS GIVE MORE LIGHT THIS YEAR

62. RIGHT AND WRONG FARMING METHODS—AND LITTLE
    POINTERS THAT WILL INCREASE YOUR PROFITS

63. NEW CAKE-IMPROVER GETS YOU COMPLIMENTS GA-
    LORE!

64. IMAGINE ME . . . HOLDING AN AUDIENCE SPELLBOUND
    FOR 30 MINUTES!

65. THIS IS MARIE ANTOINETTE—RIDING TO HER DEATH

66. DID YOU EVER SEE A "TELEGRAM" FROM YOUR HEART?

67. NOW ANY AUTO REPAIR JOB CAN BE "DUCK SOUP" FOR
    YOU

68. NEW SHAMPOO LEAVES YOUR HAIR SMOOTHER—EAS-
    IER TO MANAGE

69. IT'S A SHAME FOR YOU NOT TO MAKE GOOD MONEY—
    WHEN THESE MEN DO IT SO EASILY

70. YOU NEVER SAW SUCH LETTERS AS HARRY AND I GOT
    ABOUT OUR PEARS

71. THOUSANDS NOW PLAY WHO NEVER THOUGHT THEY COULD

72. GREAT NEW DISCOVERY KILLS KITCHEN ODORS QUICK!—MAKES INDOOR AIR "COUNTRY-FRESH"

73. MAKE THIS 1-MINUTE TEST—OF AN AMAZING NEW KIND OF SHAVING CREAM

74. ANNOUNCING ... THE NEW EDITION OF THE ENCYCLOPEDIA THAT MAKES IT FUN TO LEARN THINGS

75. AGAIN SHE ORDERS ... "A CHICKEN SALAD, PLEASE"

76. FOR THE WOMAN WHO IS OLDER THAN SHE LOOKS

77. WHERE YOU CAN GO IN A GOOD USED CAR

78. CHECK THE KIND OF BODY YOU WANT

79. "YOU KILL THAT STORY—OR I'LL RUN YOU OUT OF THE STATE!"

80. HERE'S A QUICK WAY TO BREAK UP A COLD

81. THERE'S ANOTHER WOMAN WAITING FOR EVERY MAN—AND SHE'S TOO SMART TO HAVE "MORNING MOUTH"

82. THIS PEN "BURPS" BEFORE IT DRINKS—BUT NEVER AFTERWARDS!

83. IF YOU WERE GIVEN $200,000 TO SPEND—ISN'T THIS THE KIND OF [type of product, but not brand name] YOU WOULD BUILD?

84. "LAST FRIDAY ... WAS I SCARED!—MY BOSS ALMOST FIRED ME!"

85. 67 REASONS WHY IT WOULD HAVE PAID YOU TO ANSWER OUR AD A FEW MONTHS AGO

86. SUPPOSE THIS HAPPENED ON YOUR WEDDING DAY!

87. DON'T LET ATHLETE'S FOOT "LAY YOU UP"

88. ARE THEY BEING PROMOTED RIGHT OVER YOUR HEAD?

89. ARE WE A NATION OF LOW-BROWS?

90. A WONDERFUL TWO YEARS' TRIP AT FULL PAY—BUT ONLY MEN WITH IMAGINATION CAN TAKE IT

91. WHAT EVERYBODY OUGHT TO KNOW ... ABOUT THIS STOCK AND BOND BUSINESS

92. MONEY-SAVING BARGAINS FROM AMERICA'S OLDEST DIAMOND DISCOUNT HOUSE

93. FORMER BARBER EARNS $8000 IN 4 MONTHS AS A REAL ESTATE SPECIALIST

94. FREE BOOK—TELLS YOU 12 SECRETS OF BETTER LAWN CARE

95. GREATEST GOLD-MINE OF EASY "THINGS-TO-MAKE" EVER CRAMMED INTO ONE BIG BOOK

96. $80,000 IN PRIZES! HELP US FIND THE NAME FOR THESE NEW KITCHENS

97. NOW! OWN FLORIDA LAND THIS EASY WAY ... $10 DOWN AND $10 A MONTH

98. TAKE ANY 3 OF THESE KITCHEN APPLIANCES—FOR ONLY $8.95 (VALUES UP TO $15.45)

99. SAVE 20¢ ON 2 CANS OF CRANBERRY SAUCE—LIMITED OFFER

100. ONE PLACE-SETTING FREE FOR EVERY THREE YOU BUY!

MORE OUTSTANDING HEADLINES

In their book, *Eighty Years of Best Sellers—1895 to 1975*, Alice Payne Hackett and James Henry Burke listed a compilation of both hardcover and paperback titles that sold in the millions. Here are some of the top selling headliners from the list compiled by Hackett and Burke.

Pocket Book of Baby and Child Care, by Dr. Benjamin Spock, sold approximately 23 million copies; *Joy of Cooking*, by Irma S. Rombauer and Marian Rombauer Becker, sold 9 million; *Everything You Always Wanted to Know about Sex but Were Afraid to Ask*, by David Reuben, sold 8 million; *How to Win Friends and Influence People*, by Dale Carnegie, sold 6.6 million; *Thirty Days to a More Powerful Vocabulary*, by Wilfred J. Funk and Norman Lewis, sold 6.3 million; *Doctor's Quick Weight Loss Diet*, by Irving Stillman and S. S. Baker, sold 5.6 million; *The Power of Positive Thinking*, by Norman Vincent Peale, sold 5.2 million; *Let's Eat Right to Keep Fit*, by Adelle Davis, sold 4.4 million; *The Greatest Story Ever Told*, by Fulton Oursler, sold 3.9 million.

Note in the above list how the titles fit in with our general rules of selecting good headlines.

Here are some of the successful headlines used by mail order operators over the last 10 years. Note how they too appeal to self-interest and stress important benefits to the potential customer at the same time that they arouse curiosity, sometimes give actual news information, and show a quick and easy way of reaching a benefit sought by a customer.

THE LAZY MAN'S WAY TO RICHES—MOST PEOPLE ARE TOO BUSY EARNING A LIVING TO MAKE ANY MONEY; OHIO MAN DIS-

COVERS THE SECRET OF HOW TO ESCAPE THE AMERICAN RAT RACE; USING A LAWYER MAY BE DANGEROUS TO YOUR WEALTH; THE SECRET OF HAVING GOOD LUCK; NEWEST DISCOVERY BY IAA MAY BE BIGGEST IN THE HISTORY OF ASTROLOGY; HOW YOUR HOROSCOPE CAN BRING YOU WEALTH, LOVE, SUCCESS, AND HAPPINESS; THE AMAZING DIET SECRET OF A DESPERATE HOUSEWIFE; ELECTRONIC INVENTION TURNS HOUSE WIRES INTO GIANT TV ANTENNA; NOW MEASURE DISTANCES QUICKLY AND ACCURATELY WITH RANGER; WITH NO PREVIOUS EXPERIENCE YOU CAN LEARN AT HOME IN SPARE TIME; LOSE TEN TO TWENTY POUNDS OR MORE; EXTRA INCOME EVERY WEEK; HOW TO BE YOUR OWN BOSS IN THE FABULOUS MAIL ORDER BUSINESS WITHOUT STOCKING, PACKING, OR SHIPPING; SEND FOR IT, IT'S FREE; HOW TO MASTER THE ART OF SELLING ANYTHING; DO YOU HAVE WHAT IT TAKES TO SUCCEED IN THE 1980's—TAKE THIS SIMPLE TEST AND FIND OUT; HEWLETT-PACKARD PRESENTS THE WORLD'S FIRST POCKET CALCULATOR THAT CHALLENGES A COMPUTER; AT 4½, SHE'S READING THIRD GRADE BOOKS; FREE MONEY; STEAL THESE BOOKS.

HOW TO GAIN INTEREST FOR YOUR ADVERTISEMENT OR YOUR DIRECT MAIL LETTER

Now that you've stopped your potential customer and gotten him or her to begin to read, you must gain interest immediately. There are four basic ways in which to do this: a story; a startling, shocking, or unusual statement; a quotation; or news.

A Story

Perhaps the most effective use of a story is shown in Figure 4-2, "They Laughed When I Sat Down at the Piano, but When I Started to Play ... !" This ad, written by John Caples, ran for 40 years. Notice how it grabs your interest: "Arthur had just played *The Rosary*. The room rang with applause. I decided that this would be a dramatic moment for me to make my debut. To the amazement of my friends, I strode confidently over to the piano and sat down."

We've talked about Joe Karbo's ad, "The Lazy Man's Way to Riches," throughout this book. It too is a story. Look at the ad, in Figure 13-3. The title is, "The Lazy Man's Way to Riches," and the subtitle is "Most People

The Lazy Man's Way to Riches
'Most People Are Too Busy Earning a Living to Make Any Money'

I used to work hard. The 18-hour days The 7-day weeks.

But I didn't start making big money until I did less - a lot less.

For example, this ad took about 2 hours to write. With a little luck, it should earn me 50, maybe a hundred thousand dollars.

What's more, I'm going to ask you to send me 10 dollars for something that'll cost me no more than 50 cents. And I'll try to make it so irresistible that you'd be a darned fool not to do it.

After all, why should you care if I make $9.50 profit if I can show you how to make a lot more?

What if I'm so sure that you will make money my Lazy Man's Way that I'll make you a most unusual guarantee?

And here it is: I won't even cash your check or money order for 31 days after I've sent you my material.

That'll give you plenty of time to get it, look it over, try it out.

If you don't agree that it's worth at least a hundred times what you invested, send it back. Your uncashed check or money order will be put in the return mail.

The only reason I won't send it to you and bill you or send it C.O.D. is because both these methods involve more time and money.

And I'm already going to give you the biggest bargain of your life.

Because I'm going to tell you what it took me 11 years to perfect: How to make money the Lazy Man's Way.

O.K.—now I have to brag a little. I don't mind it. And it's necessary—to prove that sending me the 10 dollars . . . which I'll keep "in escrow" until you're satisfied . . . is the smartest thing you ever did.

I live in a home that's worth $250,000. I know it is, because I turned down an offer for that much. My mortgage is less than half that, and the only reason I haven't paid it off is because my Tax Accountant says I'd be an idiot.

My "office," about a mile and a half from my home, is right on the beach. My view is so breathtaking that most people comment that they don't see how I get any work done. But I do enough. About 6 hours a day, 8 or 9 months a year.

The rest of the time we spend at our mountain "cabin." I paid $30,000 for it—cash.

I have 2 boats and a Cadillac. All paid for.

We have stocks, bonds, investments, cash in the bank. But the most important thing I have is priceless: time with my family.

And I'll show you just how I did it—the Lazy Man's Way—a secret that I've shared with just a few friends 'til now.

It doesn't require "education." I'm a high school graduate.

It doesn't require "capital." When I started out, I was so deep in debt that a lawyer friend advised bankruptcy as the only way out. He was wrong. We paid off our debts, and, outside of the mortgage, don't owe a cent to any man.

It doesn't require "luck." I've had more than my share, but I'm not promising you that you'll make as much money as I have. And you may do better; I personally know one man who used these principles, worked hard, and made 11 million dollars in 8 years. But money isn't everything.

It doesn't require "talent." Just enough brains to know what to look for. And I'll tell you that.

It doesn't require "youth." One woman I worked with is over 70. She's travelled the world over, making all the money she needs, doing only what I taught her.

It doesn't require "experience." A widow in Chicago has been averaging $25,000 a

". . . I didn't have a job and I was worse than broke. I owed more than $50,000 and my only assets were my wife and 8 children. We were renting an old house in a decaying neighborhood, driving a 5-year old car that was falling apart, and had maybe a couple of hundred dollars in the bank.

Within one month, after using the principles of the Lazy Man's Way to Riches, things started to change — to put it mildly.
- *We worked out a plan we could afford to pay off our debts — and stopped our creditors from hounding us.*
- *We were driving a brand-new Thunderbird that a car dealer had given to us!*
- *Our bank account had multiplied tenfold!*
- *All within the first 30 days!*
And today:
- *I live in a home that's worth over $250,000.*
- *I own my "office". It's about a mile and a half from my home and is right on the beach.*
- *I own a lakefront "cabin" in Washington. (That's where we spend the whole summer — loafing, fishing, swimming and sailing.)*
- *I own two oceanfront condominiums. One is on a sunny beach in Mexico and one is snuggled right on the best beach of the best island in Hawaii.*
- *I have two boats and a Cadillac. All paid for.*
- *I have a net worth of over a Million Dollars. But I still don't have a job . . ."*

year for the past 5 years, using my methods.

What does it require? Belief. Enough to take a chance. Enough to absorb what I'll send you. Enough to put the principles into action. If you do just—nothing more, nothing less—the results will be hard to believe. Remember—I guarantee it.

You don't have to give up your job. But you may soon be making so much money that you'll be able to. Once again—I guarantee it.

The wisest man I ever knew told me something I never forgot: "Most people are too busy earning a living to make any money."

Don't take as long as I did to find out he was right.

Here are some comments from other people. I'm sure that, like you, they didn't believe me either. Guess they figured that, since I wasn't going to deposit their check for 31 days, they had nothing to lose.

They were right. And here's what they gained:

$260,000 in eleven months
"Two years ago, I mailed you ten dollars in sheer desperation for a better life. One year ago, just out of the blue sky, a man called and offered me a partnership . . . I grossed over $260,000 cash business in eleven months. You are a God sent miracle to me."

B. F., Pascagoula, Miss.

Made $16,901.92 first time out
"The third day I applied myself totally to what you had shown me. I made $16,901.92. That's great results for my first time out."

J. J. M., Watertown, N.Y.

'I'm a half-millionaire'
"Thanks to your method, I'm a half-millionaire . . . would you believe last year at this time I was a slave working for peanuts?"

G. C., Toronto, Canada

$7,000 in five days
"Last Monday I used what I learned on page 83 to make $7,000. It took me all week to do it, but that's not bad for five day's work."

M. D., Topeka, Kansas

Can't believe success
"I can't believe how successful I have become . . . Three months ago, I was a telephone order taker for a fastener company in Chicago, Illinois. I was driving a beat-up 1959 Rambler and had about

$600 in my savings account. Today, I am the outside salesman for the same fastener company. I'm driving a company car . . . I am sitting in my own office and have about $3,000 in my savings account."

G. M., Des Plaines, Ill.

I know you're skeptical. After all, what I'm saying is probably contrary to what you've heard from your friends, your family, your teachers and maybe everyone else you know. I can only ask you one question.

How many of them are millionaires? So it's up to you.

A month from today, you can be nothing more than 30 days older . . . or you can be on your way to getting rich. You decide.

Figure 13-3. A good example of an ad that tells a story.

312

Are Too Busy Earning a Living to Make Any Money." Then Joe gets into his story. "I used to work hard. The 18-hour days, the 7-day weeks, but I didn't start making big money until I did less, a lot less."

A Startling, Shocking, or Unusual Statement

I've talked about the ad "How to Wake Up the Financial Genius within You" before. This is Mark O. Haroldsen's ad, and his lead-in reads, "Millionaires are not 100 or even 10 times smarter than you, but it is a fact that millionaires are making 10 to 50 and even 100 times more than you." This ad sold 250,000 copies of Mark's book in one year. Another ad with copy using this technique is headlined, "New $20 Projector Turns Any Size TV Set into a Giant 7-Foot Screen." Then the first paragraph reads as follows: "Yours absolutely free on a 30-day home trial and I won't collect even 1¢ from you until you've had a full month to enjoy and sell for only $20 my new TV projector kit that enlarges theater-size pictures from any television set." The third example is shown in Figure 13-4. The headline reads, "Yours Free, My Gift To You! The Treasure of Alan Shawn Feinstein!" The lead-off paragraph reads, "Dear Friend, what you're about to read is the most exciting opportunity to increase your income and enrich your life you may ever see. I'm going to prove it to you absolutely free, yes, no cost, no obligation to you whatsoever."

Using a Quote

Using a quote is an excellent way of gaining your reader's interest. Duraclean, which provides dealerships under a franchise for cleaning furniture, carpets, and so forth, uses this technique very successfully. The headline reads, "I Wanted a Business Where I Could Work Part-Time, with a Small Investment, Something I Could Do Myself, a Quality Product in Great Demand, with Stability in Hard Times, with Good Profit Potential—I Found It All with Duraclean." Then the first paragraph is a quote: "This is by far the best deal I have ever had. I only regret I didn't find this 25 years ago." Ms. Magazine uses this technique in a headline that reads, "What Is Ms. Magazine and Why Is It Saying All These Terrible Things?" Then the lead-in begins with the quote, "I'm never too thin to feel fat." An ad that sells a course on vinyl repair starts out with a quote: "Repaired 63 chairs for a VA nursing home. The job paid $190, could have charged more. The nursing home previously paid an upholsterer $22,700 for repairing the same number of chairs." Note how effectively quotes can be used to make your copy interesting and to lead in to the rest of your advertisement or direct mail letter.

YOURS FREE—My Gift To YOU!

A fascinating new way to make money and enrich your life . . . Yours absolutely free to prove it!

"The Treasure of Alan Shawn Feinstein!"

Dear Friend:

What you're about to read is the most exciting opportunity to increase your income and enrich your life you may ever see. I'm going to prove it to you absolutely free—yes, no cost, no obligation to you whatsoever.

I write a syndicated financial column. For it I examine all kinds of money-making opportunities, seeking out the few really good ones from among the many . . .

Then, suddenly, something unlike *anything* I had ever seen before . . .

What I'm about to reveal to you is shocking . . . Please read this carefully:

DID THE JAPANESE ACTUALLY PLAN TO FORCE US TO USE THIS AFTER THEY "TOOK OVER" AMERICA?

It began like any other April morning. Little did I know I was about come upon the most exciting opportunity for my readers I had ever seen . . .

The mail arrived. In it a communique from the East about something made by the Japanese government during World War II. According to my source, *every single* American would have been forced to use these had the Japanese won the war!

Bizarre . . . Fascinating . . .

I reported this to some of my readers. And told them where they could get some of these.*

Then a strange thing happened. Readers who got them began writing me excitedly, some of them being offered *ten* and *twenty* times over their cost for these . . . Yes, TEN and TWENTY TIMES more . . .

The letters came pouring in . . .

"WOW! Have you ever got something here! I have already put $35,000 where my mouth is. I look forward to the day when I can thank you personally.'

David Black, Canada

"Fantastic. Easiest way to make money I know of. Anyone can make money with this."

J.H. Leonard, Oh.

"Every item you have advised buying has been extremely profitable to me. These have to be the jackpot."

F. Wardwell, New York.

I immediately decided to write a report revealing everything about these . . .

Now I invite YOU to read this startling Report to see for yourself how valuable these can be to you . . .

Yes, whether you want an exciting new future or just some extra money week after week, I think you're about to find this *the greatest opportunity you've ever seen!*

Here's why:

● **No skills or training needed to profit from this.** That's right. You can start profiting from this immediately. Whatever you do now.

Wherever you are . . .

● **It will enrich your life AS WELL as your pocketbook.** This is more than just a way to make some easy money. It will open up a whole new world to you. With rewards you never imagined before . . .

● It should get more profitable for you AUTOMATICALLY. As word spreads about this, the more profitable it should become to you. Yes, *automatically!* You'll see why when you read this Report.

WANT PROOF?

In this Report I'll reveal to you someone right in your own area who can prove the value of this to you. Yes, a reference right near you—whom you can call the very day you receive this!

Have you ever heard of anything like that before?

● Think about it for a moment—a reference you can call right near you, no matter where in the world you live . . . Who can prove the value of this to you . . .

If I can make such an incredible guarantee—and send you this Report absolutely free to boot—isn't this something you owe to yourself to see?

No, I can't promise you'll make a fortune from this or even as much money as others are. But I can tell you this: No matter where you are, no matter what you now do — I think you're about to find this the *best* way to enrich your life you will ever see . . .

Here's all you have to do:

1. Send for this shocking Report today Remember, it's yours absolutely free.

2. Read it as soon as it arrives. See how easily you can profit from it.

3. If you have any questions, call any person whose name and telephone number appears in this Report. See what he or she tells you about this.

4. Then, put it to work for YOU!

It's as simple as that.

A prominent publisher said this dynamite 10 page Report was so valuable I should sell it for $20.00. But, as I promised, it's yours free. That's right, no cost, no obligation whatsoever.

WHY AM I SENDING YOU THIS ABSOLUTELY FREE?

Because once you read this and see for yourself how valuable this is, I think you'll want to get anything I ever write again.

But more than that . . . For fifteen years I've been writing my financial column, hearing people say I uncover the best new ways to make money they've ever seen. Now, this discovery, I believe, will prove it. That's why I'm sending you this startling Report free —*to prove it!*

There are dozens of books you can buy telling you how to make money—costing $10, $20, even more. But I believe you'll find this One Report more valuable than any of them. That's right, more valuable than anything you can buy . . .

And I promise you: You will never be asked to pay one cent for this—now or ever.

Your copy is waiting here for you.

Wait until you see it. I think it will change your life.

The rest, my friend, is up to you.

Sincerely yours,

Alan Shawn Feinstein

Alan Shawn Feinstein's financial column, *The Treasure Chest*, is syndicated in newspapers in Europe, Africa and Asia as well as throughout the U.S. He is listed in "Who's Who in the East" and "International Men of Achievement." A new laboratory at a leading university has recently been named 'The Alan Shawn Feinstein Laboratory' after him.

IMPORTANT—We've received word that the Japanese are now trying to buy up all of these they can find! We urge you to get this Report as soon as possible.

Figure 13-4. An unusual and provocative headline for a good story ad.

News

News can be used in two different ways to lead into your story. One way is simply a short statement that says something of news value. For example, a recent advertisement started with the simple statement, "The U.S. Mint stopped production of these commemorative coins after 1976." Or how about this one? "Break-ins are at an all-time high." Or this one: "Forty-six million small engines are in service today." The second type is an ad written entirely as if it were a news story. A good example of this is Ben Suarez's ad, "Ohio Man Discovers the Secret of How to Escape the American Rat Race," shown in Figure 13-5. Note how this ad leads off: "The secret to making a quick fortune in America has been reduced to a simple 7-step system by an entrepreneur from Canton, Ohio. It requires little or no money, a minimum of time and no elaborate plant or equipment. In fact, you can do it in your home or anywhere."

Each of these methods of leading into your copy has its advantage for your particular product in your particular situation. Very frequently you may be able to try all four of these different types of lead-in and test them against one another to see how each does.

SHOWING BENEFITS AND ADVANTAGES

Now that we have established interest on the part of our prospective customer, we must immediately demonstrate the benefits and advantages of ordering. In doing so, you must tell the customer why he or she should buy. How do you do this? Refer to Maslow again and consider the motivations for human beings to do anything. State the advantages and benefits of your product or service in such a way as to satisfy these needs described by Maslow.

When you state these needs, state them in such a way that they are irresistible, in as strong terms as possible, while still being truthful and credible. Joe Karbo says that you must state the benefits and advantages of your product or service so strongly that the reader must conclude afterward that he or she would be a fool not to respond to your advertisement. In fact, in "The Lazy Man's Way to Riches" ad in Figure 13-3, Karbo actually says in the fourth paragraph, "What's more, I'm going to ask you to send me $10 for something that'll cost me no more than 50¢ and I'll try to make it so irresistible that you'd be a darn fool not to do it."

If you read further in Karbo's ad, you will see that he shows the benefits and advantages that appeal to human needs. Look at how Karbo describes his material goods—a home worth $250,000, an office a mile and a

Ohio Man Discovers The Secret of How to Escape The American Rat Race

7 Simple Rules Net This Working Man With No Money or Experience $145,000 in First Year

By John Whitehead,
Special Features Writer

(Canton, OH) The secret to making a quick fortune in America has been reduced to a simple 7 step system by an entrepreneur from Canton, Ohio. It requires little or no money, a minimum of time and no elaborate plant or equipment. In fact, you can do it in your home or anywhere.

There are hundreds of rags to riches stories each year in America. However, this one is very unique.

Most successful get rich ventures were spin-offs of something else, or somebody was in the right place at the right time. This venture was accomplished by a working man with no money or experience and was accomplished in a very short period of time.

The man who did it is Ben Swarez from Canton, Ohio, the Pro Football Hall of Fame city.

His neighbors here in Canton call it a movie script. One of the neighbors interviewed had this to say: *"It was unbelievable. One day he's driving around in a rusted out '68 Pontiac station wagon, living in an uncarpeted house that didn't even have a color T.V., and struggling to make ends meet like the rest of us. The next day he's driving in a brand new Lincoln Mark, a brand new Mercury station wagon, a $35,000 GMC motorhome, his house is fixed up like a palace, and he's traveling all over the country."*

So, how was all this accomplished. For that answer I went right to the horse's mouth, my main interview with the creator of the system, Ben Swarez.

QUESTION: OK, Ben, so how in the world did this all start?

ANSWER: I was typical of a good majority of Americans — working at a job for 10 years that I hated, worrying about layoffs, living from pay to pay with no money to do anything except buy the bare essentials. Work held little chance for advancement. Big companies are immoveable and impersonal. I found out quick that moving up had little to do with talent and hard work and more to do with politics, lodge membership, being a friend or relative of a high executive, or riding onto the coattails of an executive and hoping he ascends the organization. I wanted out but I saw no way to escape the proverbial rat race.

Then one day in April the last straw came. An invention of mine was shelved by my company because it had "shown up" the research division. My first thought was to get another job. But, then it hit me. You don't HAVE to work for someone else in this country. This is the land of free enterprise. At that point I said, "I don't know what I'm going to do, or how I'm going to do it, but I'm going into something for myself."

Says You Can Do It Anywhere. He Does It While Traveling In His Motor Home

"My system is geared to the working man who is in the same situation I was: living from pay to pay, no savings or assets, working an 8 hour a day job for a big company, no experience, no rich relatives, nothing."

OFF ON ANOTHER TRIP. "We never had the money for a vacation before, so we're making up for it by traveling off and on 4 months out of the year. We've been just about everywhere." Swarez does his system in his motor home while his wife, Nancy, drives and his two daughters, Sharon and Michele, play and sight-see. That's the family's pet shetland sheepdog on a favorite perch.

Swarez on the spacious wooded grounds of his second home which he uses as a retreat and a guest house.

Doing what he likes to do best on certain weekdays. "I especially like to loaf on Mondays because I hated that day so much when I worked for a big corporation."

QUESTION: Excellent point. Is this when you developed your system?

ANSWER: No, that came a little later — after some hard knocks trying to do things the orthodox way. I tried to start the standard types of businesses that require buying buildings, equipment, hiring people, etc. But, since I had no money I had to try to borrow to do this. I soon found out that banks don't lend you money for new businesses or buying established businesses for that matter. The only time banks lend you money is when you don't need it. The fact is that no one is going to

lend you money to start a business. I finally did manage to start a standard type business through renting and getting credit. To make a long story short, I ended up losing a lot of money I didn't have trying to do things this orthodox way.

Then I started to buy the "get rich books". I quickly found out that these are nothing but franchise schemes, selling jobs or stupid real estate deals that take you forever to make money.

Then another thing spurred me on. I read an article by the Social Security Administration.

(Over)

C-09

Figure 13-5.   An ad that looks like news.

It related, "out of every 100 persons reaching 65 years old: 50 are flat broke, 30 are dead, 15 have a little money and only 5 are rich". I wasn't going to work 40 years and end up in a "home", flat broke.

QUESTION: So this is when you came up with the big system?
ANSWER: Yes, but there is a little more to it. I pondered and researched how to do it for months always running into stone walls. They say your subconscious does all your heavy creative work. It does. One night of all times when I was lifting weights in my basement the solution rolled out of my mind like a computer print out. It was the simplest, fastest and most direct way to make a lot of money. I quickly wrote it down and after analyzing it, the system boiled down to a few simple rules or steps.

You use these steps to assemble what I call a Net Profit Generator System or N.P.G.S. for short. That night I stayed up late and assembled N.P.G.S.-1.

To make a very long story short, the first N.P.G.S. failed miserably and I lost even more money. But, I could see that my N.P.G.S. concept was sound. It just needed to be perfected. After going to the limit of my creditors and being $70,000 in debt, I came up with what I felt was a perfected system, N.P.G.S.-4. It was time to test it. If N.P.G.S.-4 failed, it was the end of the line.

QUESTION: That must have been a tense moment waiting for the results to come in?
ANSWER: It was real life drama at its highest intensity.

It was a muggy mid-August morning when I waited for the results to come in. I would know that day if it worked or not.

The phone rang with the results. I stood there with sweaty palms and my heart in my mouth. The news? N.P.G.S.-4 was a smashing success!

The first rollout paid off all my debts with money left over.

QUESTION: Incredible. When did you start making your first big money for yourself?
ANSWER: Very shortly afterward. I projected a way to do big rollouts without having to put up any money. My second rollout of N.P.G.S.-4 netted my first big payday. I made $80,000 clear!

QUESTION: I can't even imagine getting that much money all at once. What was it like?
ANSWER: It's almost impossible to verbalize. My wife and I just stared at the check for a long time. We had a two day celebration with a dinner and party. It's a fantastic experience to go into work and tell them you quit. I had a little fun doing it. The chance to say what you truly feel to people who have had you under their thumb for 10 years is truly a pleasant release of frustration.

The first thing I did was pay off all my bills. Then I paid off my house. I took the money to the savings and loan company who held the mortgage personally to see the looks on their faces. The teller did a double take. The manager came out and smiled insincerely and said *"We don't get too many people paying off a $20,000 mortgage all at one time."* Then we had a "burn the mortgage" party. Then I went to the showroom of the local Lincoln-Mercury dealer and laid down the cash for a brand new Mark. I never had a new car in my life. I never even had the experience of a new car even as a kid at home.

Then my wife and I went on a shopping spree for clothes. We had been making do with old clothes for so long they had become worn out. She always had to shop for clothes with very little money. I always joked with her that "If I gave you $5,000 to spend on clothes could

you do it in one day?" She used to say "I could do it in a couple hours." So that's what I did. I gave her $5,000 to go out and buy clothes. It ended up taking all day and she said she relished every minute.

We then took a long trip. In New York I bought her a large diamond at Tiffany's — another thing we always dreamed about.

But I'll tell you the money was not the most important benefit in this. What money really does is give you precious time. Time to be with your wife and children before they grow up before you know it — and time to do things you really want to do. Another priceless thing you gain is your self respect. No more crawling and kneeling because you're dependent. The words of Frank Sinatra's song "My Way" says it all.

QUESTION: This definitely could be a movie script. How did things go after that?
ANSWER: Excellent. The first year I assembled two more systems and made a total of $145,000.

QUESTION: You've been at it for 3½ years now. Were the succeeding years as good?
ANSWER: Better. Here are the results by year: The 1st year as mentioned I made $145,000; the 2nd year I made $205,000; and 3rd year $309,000. And already in the first half of this year I have made $200,000. I have audited financial statements from certified public accountants and income tax returns to verify this to any agency or investigator of any kind who wishes to challenge me on this.

QUESTION: That's quite a system. I understand you're now ready to tell everyone how you did it.
ANSWER: I have put it all into a book, but I may limit the number I will sell.

QUESTION: What can you tell me about the book?
ANSWER: It's called "7 Steps to Freedom, How to Escape the American Rat Race". It contains the complete step-by-step details on how to assemble an N.P.G.S. system which I finally reduced to just 7 simple steps. Here are some highlights of the system:

- The system requires a minimum of time and money to start.
- You don't need special experience or skills to do it.
- You don't need to buy or rent buildings, buy or rent equipment and you don't have to hire people.
- You can do it anywhere in your house, while you travel or at a favorite vacation spot or retreat.
- With the system you can earn $10,000 to $500,000 in a matter of months and even within two days depending on which system you assemble.
- The money you make is all earned income which is subject to one of the lowest tax bites.

QUESTION: Did you say you can make big money within days?
ANSWER: No, that's an understatement. You can actually do it within hours in some cases. You can compile a system in an afternoon one day and start having spendable money in your hands produced by the system the very next morning!

QUESTION: How much money do you average on a system?
ANSWER: I'd say the average is $200,000. That's the type I usually stick to. I'll tell you this, doing a system to make $10,000 to $20,000 is literally duck soup. I have these available all the time but don't even use them

QUESTION: You said you need no special talent or experience. Who all can do it?
ANSWER: You only need to follow directions. All you need is common sense, a sense of pride in your work and the ability to see a job through to completion. This system is also perfect for people who are confined at home, such as housewives.

QUESTION: O.K. So, why do you want to reveal your system to other people when it's obvious you're making loads of money with it?
ANSWER: There are several reasons. First, the old proverb is true. Everyone likes to brag when they accomplish something; and, I'm no different. Second, I am in the position now to completely retire. I have put all my money into a diversified portfolio of blue chip investments that no one can touch, including myself. So, I'm protected from losing my money myself or someone taking it away from me. These investments generate a comfortable guaranteed income for life for my family and me.

Also, I think I can keep everyone from knowing my secret by only making the book available on a limited, controlled basis. The book is not in book stores.

QUESTION: I shudder to ask, how much does a book cost?
ANSWER: If it was priced at what it's worth, few people could afford it. There's at least a million dollars' worth of knowledge in this book. I'm not exaggerating when I say I don't know of any other book in which a person stands to gain and benefit so much. But, I will make it a very reasonable price of $20.00. This book is being distributed for me under my control by the Publishing Corporation of America.

A most interesting interview and I would have to call this the book of the century. For those who want a copy of the book from this present press run, the following information is provided:

The book contains over 286 8½" x 11" pages containing detailed, illustrated instructions on how to set up a Net Profit Generator System (N.P.G.S.) complete with all necessary forms. It is written in clear, easy to understand language. Also included is a diary of how the system was developed with some very interesting behind the scenes tales. The amount of knowledge you pick up about human nature is staggering in this diary.

To order: 1) Get a blank piece of paper; 2) At the top of the paper, print the words "7 Steps to Freedom, How to Escape the American Rat Race", 3) Print your name and address; 4) Mail this along with $20.00 in cash, check or money order to Publishing Corporation of America; Dept.   ; 4626 Cleveland Avenue N.; Canton, Ohio 44767.

Or, if you want us to start processing your order immediately, phone in your order as follows: 1) Dial this TOLL FREE number, 1-800-321-0888 (Ohio residents dial 1-800-362-0636) and ask for operator   ; 2) Say the words "7 Steps to Freedom"; 3) Give your name and address; 4) Give the operator one of your following credit card numbers: Master Charge or Visa (also include your Interbank number). Or, if you don't want to use a credit card, tell the operator you want it mailed C.O.D. Operators are on duty right now and around the clock.

Direct any inquiries to (216) 494-4282. Please do not dial the toll free number for information. The operators are not permitted or qualified to answer questions.

This offer carries a full money-back guarantee.

C-09X

Figure 13-5. (Continued)

half from his home right on the beach, a cabin in the mountains, two boats and a Cadillac, stocks, bonds, investments—you could go right down Maslow's list to see what these appeal to, everything from safety and security needs to needs to belong, needs for love, esteem, recognition, status, and self-actualization. Further, note the other benefits, as stated by Joe Karbo: It does not require education or capital or luck or talent or youth or experience. Joe practically guarantees your fortune and all this for how much? A mere $10. Isn't his ad irresistible, and wouldn't you feel like a fool not to risk $10 to achieve these benefits?

CREDIBILITY

Credibility is most important in making your copy effective and getting your potential customers to order because, regardless of what you say about the benefits or advantages of your product, if your potential customer does not believe what you say, he or she will not order your product or service. It is for this reason that, for many years, Joe Karbo did not state in his ads that he owned a Rolls-Royce, or that his homes had actually been valued at far more than the figures stated. Even though he did own a Rolls-Royce and more expensive homes, he knew these facts were less believable than that he owned a Cadillac (which Karbo did own) or a $250,000 house. Credibility also explains why Joe Sugerman takes such pains to explain the intricate details of his fabulous electronic products, along with providing good, clear photographs.

In my own use of a direct mail campaign for job finding and as recommended in my book, *The Executive's Guide to Finding a Superior Job,* I state that in a direct sales letter a paragraph must be included that states the specific area of study and name of the college or university that a job seeker attended. Why? Because anything else is merely unsupported claims. To give credibility, you must include a known quantity, a quantity that can be checked—in this cse, noting your university or school by name.

USE OF TESTIMONIALS

But the listing of courses and names of universities will not work in an ad. What will work? Testimonials. And testimonials are crucial for giving the credibility necessary for your potential customer to order. Look at how the successful advertisements in this chapter have used testimonials. Why are testimonials so effective? Because they mean that someone else is complimenting you, rather than you tooting your own horn. If you are able to list the entire name—if you have the permission of the individual whose testimonial you have on file—that gives even more credibility because a person can actually check to verify that the testimonial is accurate.

Look at Karbo's ad again. At the end of the ad you'll find a box in which is contained a sworn statement: "On the basis of my professional relationship as his accountant, I certify that Mr. Karbo's net worth is more than $1 million. (signed) Stuart A. Cogan." This was one of the many innovations initiated by Joe Karbo. Like the testimonial, it is a powerful instrument of credibility. Since its first appearance, it has been copied by a lawyer, accountants, and others. Many ads contain not only the words "sworn statement" but also the actual imprint and signature seal of a notary public. These definitely add credibility.

Other means of achieving credibility are stating a bank, accountant, or attorney reference, or even showing the picture of a building your company owns. An imposing structure in itself will add credibility.

Clearly, every method of establishing credibility has not been exhausted; there are other ways which have yet to be thought of or become apparent that can assist greatly in accomplishing this most necessary of tasks in your advertisement. You are not limited to testimonials or statements by your accountant. Using your imagination, you can think of totally new ways to add credibility to your proposition.

ACTION

A face-to-face salesperson must ask for an order. This is a basic law of sales. And just as face-to-face salespeople do this, so must you, as a mail order salesperson selling through an advertisement, ask for the order. You do this by calling your customer to immediate action. In other words, you don't want your customer to wait and think it over for several days. You don't want him or her to cut out the coupon at the bottom of your advertisement and put it away for another day, or to wait until he or she is in the proper frame of mind. You want to compel your customer to order now, immediately.

Why is immediate action so necessary? Because mail order buying from advertisements in magazines or even ordering for information in a two-step offer is an impulse kind of purchase or action. Delay is fatal. Even with the best intent, if your potential customer clips the coupon with the intent of ordering, not now, but later, research has proved conclusively that in most instances he or she will not place this order. How do you accomplish this call to action? Here are three specific methods you can use to get your customer to order right now: limited time offer, limited quantity offer, or a special.

Limited time means that your offer is limited to a specific period. For example, if your ad appears in a magazine you might say, "Good for 30 days only." Or you can list a specific date after which the offer is no longer good. Limited quantity means that the quantity of whatever it is you are supplying is limited. This is a valid statement since it is always true. If you are able to state the precise limitations of your product, so much the better. A special means a special proposition, good for this ad only. For example, you may offer an additional premium to the first 100 customers who place an order. Or you may offer something free only to those who respond to this one ad.

Here are some examples of how good copy encourages immediate action from prospective customers. In Figure 13-4, "Yours Free, My Gift to You," in smaller letters at the bottom is the statement, "Important: we've received word that the Japanese are now trying to buy up all of these they can find. We urge you to get this report *as soon as possible*." If you read through the advertisement, you will discover that even though the Japanese may be trying to "buy all of these they can find," you don't know what they are trying to buy. That's not important. The important thing is that the advertisement urges the potential respondent to act immediately. In Figure 13-3, Joe Karbo has done the same thing a little more subtly by saying, "A month from today you can be nothing more than 30 days older, or you can be on your way to getting rich. You decide."

THE COUPON

I may conclude here that most display or space advertisements have a coupon, and that research has shown that a coupon works better and will outpull noncoupon ads in most instances. And this is true even of those coupons that are so small that it is almost impossible to write your name and address in the space provided. The exception is advertisements that appear to be news articles, such as Figure 13-5.

HOW TO WRITE OUTSTANDING COPY

Once you have attracted the attention of your reader, you want him or her to continue to read. So your copy must be not only structured, as described above, but also interesting and fun and easy to read. There are three basic principles that successful copywriters have found to work best.

1. Use short words, short sentences, and short paragraphs.
2. Write conversationally.
3. Keep your copy moving; don't let it bog down.

Along these lines, I would like to recommend a book that is extremely valuable in helping you to become a successful copywriter. This book is called *The Art of Readable Writing,* by Dr. Rudolf Flesch. In this stimulating guide, Dr. Flesch uses special graphs for calculating whether copy has human interest and reading ease. The human interest graph designed by Dr. Flesch is shown in Figure 13-6, while the reading ease graph is shown in Figure 13-7. The combination of these charts produces Dr. Flesch's readability formula. Here is how to use these graphs and compute the readability formula of any copy for an advertisement or a direct mail letter.

Step 1. Take samples from the advertisement, for example, every third or fourth paragraph. Each sample should start at the beginning of a paragraph. Let's analyze the advertisement, "Do You Make These Mistakes in English?" shown in Figure 9-1, for readability.

Step 2. Count the number of words in each sample up to 100 words. Count contractions and hyphenated words as one word. Count numbers and letters as words if written numerically or abbreviated (e.g., 1981 would count as one word, as would $5, etc., or C.O.D.). Now, in "Do You Make These Mistakes in English?" there are 17 paragraphs, excluding the testimonials, headlines, and coupon. I will take as our sample the fourth, eighth, twelfth, and sixteenth paragraphs. The fourth paragraph contains 55 words, the eighth 101 words, the twelfth 41 words, and the sixteenth paragraph 32 words.

Step 3. Find the average sentence length for your sample. In other words, take all your samples, count the number of sentences, and divide by the number of words in those sentences. In doing so, follow the units of thought, not the punctuation: Whereas sentences are marked at the end by periods, sometimes the units of thought are marked by a colon or a semicolon; count each separate unit of thought as a separate sentence. In the sample advertisement, I find four sentences in paragraph 4, eight in paragraph 8, two in paragraph 12, and one in paragraph 16, for a total of

HOW INTERESTING?

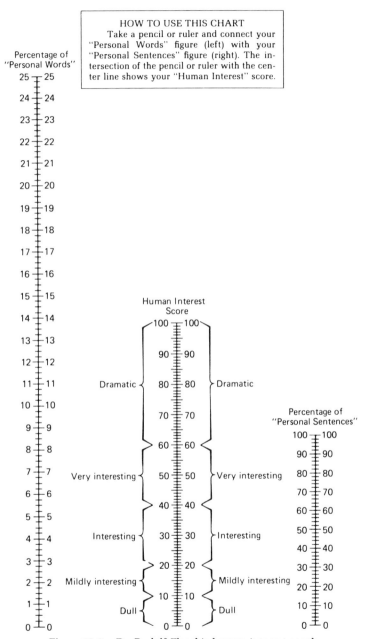

Figure 13-6. Dr. Rudolf Flesch's human interest graph.

HOW EASY?

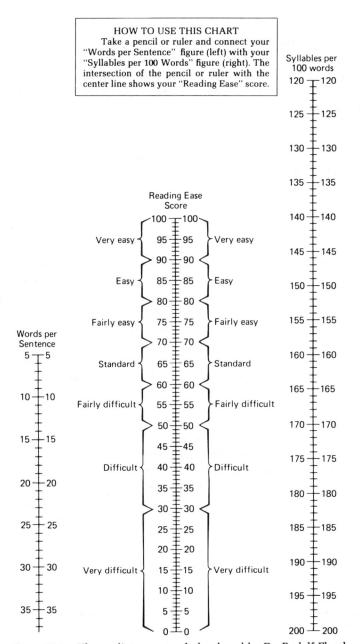

Figure 13-7. The reading ease graph developed by Dr. Rudolf Flesch.

15 sentences; there are 229 words, so the average sentence length is 15.26 words.

Step 4. Count the syllables in your samples, divide the total number of syllables by the total number of words, and multiply by 100. This will result in the total number of syllables per 100 words in the copy in the advertisement. In the four sample paragraphs there are 328 syllables. Dividing 328 by 229 and multiplying times 100 gives 143.23 syllables per 100 words. When you do this count, count the syllables as you pronounce the word, so that "$5" would be "5," one syllable, and "dollars," two more, or a total of three syllables. On the other hand, if you have a great number of figures in the samples that you are using, do not include the figures as part of your syllable count.

Step 5. Count the personal words in your sample. Personal words are all first-, second- and third-person pronouns except neuter pronouns such as *it, its,* and *itself,* and plurals such as *they, them, theirs, themselves,* if referring to things rather than people. Personal words also include words that can be assigned either to the masculine or the feminine gender, such as one's name or *father, brother, mother, sister, postman,* and so forth. Do not count those words that have a single word for either gender, such as *doctor, lawyer, teacher,* and so forth. Finally, you can also count as personal words those group words such as *people* and *folks.* In total, there are 27 personal words in all the samples combined. Twenty-seven divided by 229 and multiplied by 100 is 12.66 personal words per 100 words.

Step 6. Count the personal sentences in your samples. Personal sentences are spoken sentences marked by quotation marks; lead-in words such as "he said"; questions, requests, or directions aimed directly at the reader; explanations; exclamations; or grammatically incomplete sentences whose complete meanings must be inferred from the context in which they appear. If a particular sentence fits into more than one of these definitions, you should count it only once. As in steps 4 and 5, count the total number of personal sentences, divide by the total number of sentences, and multiply by 100 to find the number of personal sentences per 100 sentences. There are nine personal sentences in our samples. Nine divided by 15 sentences, times 100, is 60 personal sentences per 100 sentences.

Step 7. Now it is time to find your reading ease score, using Figure 13-7. To do this, take the average sentence length that we got in step 3, and the number of syllables per 100 words that we got in step 4. From step 3 we got 15.26 words per sentence, which we round off to 15, and in step 4, 143.23 syllables per 100 words, which we round off to 143. In Figure 13-7, we connect the words per sentence, which is the left-hand vertical column, with the syllables per 100 words on the right. In the center, under reading ease score, we read the score; ours is 71, which means that it is fairly easy to read, on a scale of from 0, very difficult, all the way up to 100, very easy.

Step 8. Now let's find our human interest score. Use the number of personal words per 100 words that we found in step 5, and the number of personal sentences per 100 sentences from step 6. In the same fashion as with the reading ease score, compute our human interest score. In step 5 we found 12.66, or 13, personal words per 100 words. In step 6 we found 60 personal sentences per 100 sentences, so we come up with a human interest score of 74, which is between *very interesting* and *dramatic*. Is it any wonder this ad ran for 40 years?

As an exercise, you might want to take a more modern ad and compute the readability score.

One additional tip in writing your copy and putting it into the skeleton or structure that we discussed earlier: Use lots of subheads for your paragraphs.

HOW DOES DIRECT MAIL COPYWRITING DIFFER FROM SPACE ADVERTISING COPYWRITING?

The basics of direct mail copywriting and space advertising copywriting are almost identical. The same structure should be followed, and the keys to success are the same. The biggest difference is that you have more space in which to sell and explain your proposition and your offer. There are also some differences depending upon whether you are selling to a consumer or an industrial customer. Figure 13-8 is a letter to a consumer customer. Such letters can run to more than four pages. Figure 13-9 is a direct mail piece to an industrial customer. Usually the industrial customer has less time and will spend less time reading your letter. Therefore, an industrial customer letter should normally be from one to three pages long. Note than an industrial customer here means any customer who is not using your end product directly, but is using it in some fashion to assist him or her in selling to the final consumer. Figure 13-10 is a direct mail letter I wrote and used to help sell research at the university. This direct mail letter had better than a 30% response rate. Note that in all

Have You Ever Wished You Had A Better Memory?

Now An Outstanding Home Study Course Can Help You Make That Wish Come True

My name is Don Bolander.

Quickly, cover that first sentence with your hand. Can you remember my name? Probably you had no trouble at all. Holding a name or a telephone number in your mind for a few seconds or a few minutes is called "short-term memory." But will you remember it tomorrow? Next week . . . or next year?

You, of course, don't really have any reason to remember my name. But what about all of those endless facts, figures and important details that are a necessary part of your everyday social or business life? Do you easily and quickly remember them when you need them?

The average person has a poor ability to remember. Without an address book, note pad or ever present lists, most of us would be lost. The busy executive relies on his secretary to remind him of his daily appointments. The housewife in a supermarket would be in a sad situation without her grocery list.

And think of all the times you've been embarrassed by not remembering the name attached to a familiar face. Or your mother-in-law's birthday. Even your own wedding anniversary. Remember the time the boss asked you for a run-down on some figures you had been working on? Perhaps, your mind went blank.

These uncomfortable memory lapses are only too common in most people's lives. Sometimes they are merely annoying; occasionally they can be serious.

Memory & Concentration Studies 1500 Cardinal Drive, Little Falls, N.J. 07424

MC-L1-1178 78201118

Figure 13-8. A direct mail piece to a consumer customer.

326

You Can Do Something About Your Memory

Maybe you have shrugged your shoulders and said, "Oh well, it's human nature to forget." That may be true -- but it needn't be true of YOU! There is absolutely no need to let another day go by, dotted with irritating, embarrassing moments of forgetfulness. There IS something you can do about it NOW!

The Furst Method of Memory Control

YOU CAN REMEMBER was developed by Dr. Bruno Furst, a world-famous memory expert. No special education or background is required to learn this amazing method. All you must have is a sincere desire to improve your own memory and be willing to stay at it for about 15 to 30 minutes a day.

The Bruno Furst Program has been used in schools, colleges and universities, by the government and by branches of the military all over the world. Now its highly-praised methods of memory mastery may be learned by businessmen and women, lawyers and doctors, students, office and factory workers, housewives, entertainers . . . not in a classroom, but at home.

How Does the Furst Method Work?

It may sound like magic, and to other people it often looks like magic, but it's not. The Furst Method is a down-to-earth, practical way of exercising your mind -- just like a muscle -- and getting it in shape to do what you want.

The Furst Method consists of certain basic rules. They involve association, concentration and classification. Your "recall powers" are strengthened, then channeled into efficient memory banks.

You learn to remember faces by classifying facial types and features. Names are remembered by a simple six-step method. Numbers are recalled by using an effective and logical word code.

The course shows you how to think in mental pictures. You learn how to train your mind to come up with whatever information you need, when you need it. Not just dates, facts and names -- but whole paragraphs and entire pages of printed matter!

Figure 13-8. (Continued)

What This Memory Course Can Do For You

I have in my files records of amazing, almost unbelievable feats of memory that have been accomplished by men and women who have completed the YOU CAN REMEMBER Program. For example, there's the General Electric executive who took the Course and can now recall the catalog numbers, specifications and list prices of 20,000 items in current production!

Get ahead faster in your job. A good memory is almost certain to help you work more efficiently. And your command of details and facts is very likely to impress the people you work with.

Remember names! We teach you how to recall the names of an entire roomful of strangers after a single introduction!

Gain self-confidence! Remember anything you want to remember -- an article you read, an ancedote you heard, a recipe, an address, a phone number, a poem, a person's name . . . the possibilities are endless.

Twelve Steps To Memory Power

By experience, we know that the majority of people who try the course will continue with it. That's why we want you to see and determine for yourself how quickly you can build the kind of memory of which you can be more than proud.

When you try the program under our approval plan, here's what you will receive:

* 12 easy-to-understand lessons each bound in booklet form. Charts, cartoons, drawings and photographs graphically illustrate the text.

* A 60-page book of Questions and Answers with simple instructions for charting your progress.

* Dr. Furst's handy vest-pocket Number Dictionary with 96 pages of word entries.

* A deluxe library slipcase for displaying the course on your desk or bookshelf.

* A free copy of the Instant Quotation Dictionary. This book is yours to keep as our gift to you even if you return the program at the end of the approval

Figure 13-8. (Continued)

328

Why wait another day? Why go on being aggravated by a poor memory? I can promise you that if you devote just a little time and effort you will develop your memory into a brilliant, sharp-honed tool and you will have fun doing it!

The YOU CAN REMEMBER Program is a challenging, exciting game. The prize you win is new pride in your own abilities . . . and a wide-open future. The future is whatever you want to make of it! Once you have "memory power", you can move full-speed ahead, armed with the confidence that only a strong reliable memory can give you.

The Biggest "Plus" of All -- A Better Brain

A psychologist at a Canadian university said recently, "The brain responds to exercise." In other words, the more you use it, the better it gets. Scientists tell us that as far as they know, there is no limit to the mind's capacity. The trouble is, we are all a bit lazy about exercising our mental abilities. Most people really don't know how to fully use their mental powers.

Dr. Furst's Course, YOU CAN REMEMBER, shows you the way . . . not just to a better memory, but to a better mind. Today is the day you can take the first important step toward a more powerful memory.

10-Day On-Approval Offer

Based on past experience, I know that the Memory Program, YOU CAN REMEMBER, can prove to be of immense and lasting value to you. I am so confident of this that I would like to make an offer that I hope you will accept:

Just fill in the enclosed membership application and mail it to me today with a small deposit. I will send you the complete Course at once for your approval.

Examine the Course, read it thoroughly, try it -- for 10 full days. If it is not all I have said and everything you want, just send it back. Your money will be refunded in full.

Sincerely yours,

Don Bolander, Director
MEMORY & CONCENTRATION STUDIES

P.S. Send full payment with order -- save shipping charges -- same money back guarantee.

Figure 13-8. (Continued)

J.W. ⁄⁄URDOCK

INDUSTRIAL PRODUCTS GUIDE
2403 Waukegan Rd. • Deerfield, Ill. 60015
(312) 948-8940

Now you can end messy,
time-consuming packaging problems
forever with super-adhesive,
wear and tear resistant
PVC sealing tape!

*And here's a free Deluxe Tape Dispenser
to prove it! A $14⁹⁵ value —
FREE with your order!*

Dear Friend,

Please take a look at the sample of PVC Sealing Tape that
came with this letter. It looks like an ordinary piece of
packaging tape, right? But now test it, pull on it . . .
try to remove it. You'll find it won't come off . . . now
just think how tightly it will hold your packages!

    PVC Sealing Tape uses a powerful new adhesive
    that gives it up to 90 lbs. tensile strength.
    It's tough. It's rugged. It holds up under
    weather, wear, tear, even impact. And what's
    more, PVC Tape won't peel, frazzle or get
    ragged with age--it holds and holds and even
    gets stronger the longer it's on!

With PVC Tape you can say goodbye to packaging problems
forever! That's why we hope you'll send in the Order Form
for this fast-acting, super-adhesive tape, and to persuade
you we'll send you a Free Deluxe Tape Dispenser--a $14.95
value--yours free with any size order of PVC Tape!

PVC Tape is pressure sensitive--it needs no messy glue that
gets on your clothes--you just place the Dispenser on the
carton you want to seal and smoothly glide it across the
surface. The Dispenser automatically gives just the right
pressure to seal your package. What's more, efficient,
fast-packaging PVC tape eliminates the need for costly

                   (over, please)

Figure 13-9. A direct mail piece to an industrial customer.

packaging machines. With your Deluxe Dispenser you can seal
any size, any shape carton with a single easy motion--it
even cuts the tape for you.

It's safe, it's sure. PVC Tape meets all OSHA
standards for safety. There's no need to bother
with dangerous straps or staples. Plus, PVC
Tape can be used to give your packages a weather-
resistant, water-proof seal that discourages
pilfering and ensures that your package won't
accidentally open in transit. And it meets all
postal requirements, so you can use it on all
your outgoing mail.

If you send today for your PVC Tape (minimum order 12 rolls),
we'll rush you both the Tape and your Free Deluxe Dispenser.
Then, when you get them, try them out on the next big package
you have to ship. You'll be amazed how fast and accurately
the Dispenser works. And you'll see how PVC forms a strong
bond on any size, any odd-shaped, bulky package.

Please take advantage of this special offer, right away.
Send in the enclosed Form to order your super-adhesive PVC
Tape and get your free Deluxe Tape Dispenser as our gift.
Do it now!

                                        Cordially,

TB:Dl   *Tom Brice*

                                        Tom Brice
                                        Vice President

Figure 13-9. (Continued)

three letters illustrated, the principles discussed above in copywriting apply.

YOUR COPYWRITING CHECKLIST

I have developed a special checklist that I use to check all of my copy. You may ask why a checklist is necessary after all the principles discussed above. The answer is that you can easily leave some important factor out of your copy, even after you have worked at it and polished it. I'm ashamed to admit that one beautiful piece of copy and layout I completed for a seminar left one important factor out: where the seminar was being held. So there are some very good reasons for using a checklist. The one that follows is compiled from dozens of different sources and information. It enables me to check my copy to ensure that the headline is correct, that the offer is as I want it, that the copy context is as I want it, and that the copy quality is at its very highest. Use this checklist when you first begin to write your copy or construct your advertisements for di-

CALIFORNIA STATE UNIVERSITY • LOS ANGELES

5151 STATE UNIVERSITY DRIVE LOS ANGELES, CALIFORNIA 90032

SCHOOL OF BUSINESS AND ECONOMICS
OFFICE OF THE DEAN (213) 224-3876

April 4, 1980

Dear

Quality of proposal not the main key to winning? Low price not of primary importance? These statements certainly didn't sound right, and I would have never believed them until I looked at the results of some preliminary research conducted on 51 small R & D contracts bid to the Government.

The focus on this research was on preproposal marketing and the number of contacts, type of contact, and quality of contact that project engineers make, or should make before the arrival of the RFP or before developing and submitting unsolicited proposals for small R & D contracts. The primary purpose of the research was to determine what influence preproposal marketing might have on winning these small contracts, valued at under $2 million each.

As you probably expected, it was definitely confirmed that preproposal marketing did have a significant influence on winning or losing. Frankly, even though some proposals were not very good, and were even priced higher than competitive proposals, the number of contacts made with the customer influenced the results of the competition to an extraordinary degree. To be specific, for a total of 1,787 different contacts made on 51 contract bids, the average number of contacts for a win was 40.6 -- more than twice the average number of contacts (18.5) which resulted in a loss.

Fine, this was something we all more or less expected. However, we found out other things which were more surprising. For example, we learned that certain kinds of contacts with the customer are more important to winning than others. We found out when quality of contact is more important to winning than quantity of contacts. We looked at figures that told us whether the probability of winning increased with the number of contacts, and whether there is an optimal number of contacts for winning. We quantified how important it is that you bring the customer to your facilities, and we discovered much, much more.

Can this information be of any practical value to you, a Government contractor? Let me answer by asking you some questions:

THE CALIFORNIA STATE UNIVERSITY AND COLLEGES

Figure 13-10. A direct mail letter for university research.

2

1. You are on a fixed budget. Is it more important for winning to visit the customer at his facilities, or to meet him at a symposium?

2. A very competent engineer doesn't relate well to the customer, but no one else is available to meet with the customer. Do you cancel the meeting or hold it anyway?

3. Should you ever bid a contract without making contacts, and if so when?

4. Who is it more important for your customer to meet: The project engineer? The proposal manager? All engineers at the working level? Senior and top company management of the company? Marketing personnel?

5. What minimum number of preproposal contacts must you have in order to win?

6. What difference is there in preproposal marketing contacts between the various government agencies?

7. To what extent can a phone call substitute for face-to-face meetings?

8. What is the relative importance in contacts with the customer by engineering personnel, management personnel, and marketing personnel assigned to field representative duties?

9. To what extent can preproposal marketing compensate for the lack of quality in technical proposals and/or competitive pricing?

10. Does contact after receipt of an RFP hurt you or help you?

If the answers to these questions can be used by you, then the result of this research is important to you and to the competitive position of your company in the research and development field. Unfortunately, the study completed was too small a sampling for conclusions upon which you should base decisions. Further, it was also too small a sampling to allow for segmentation by different Government agencies.

The Bureau of Business and Economic Research at California State University, Los Angeles, however, is now embarking on a considerably larger research program dedicated to investigation of preproposal marketing activities of small Government R & D projects. We are inviting a limited number of the leading companies in industry to participate.

All industrial participants will receive progress reports and detailed technical reports containing graphs, tables, and explicit conclusions from the research which you can put to immediate use. The distribution of this information will be limited to participating firms. In addition, segmentation of results for your

Figure 13-10   (Continued)

333

firm will be provided to you only. In this way, proprietary information of all participating firms will be fully protected.

Since participation in this program is a service to the community, all companies assisting in the funding of this research will receive a certificate of apprecia- tion from the Bureau of Business and Economic Research at California State Univer- sity Los Angeles.

I know you are busy. Therefore, if you are interested in receiving a copy of our proposal for the research, there is no need to write a formal letter -- just sign below and enclose your business card -- we'll see that you get a copy.

Sincerely,

William A. Cohen, Director
Bureau of Business & Economic Research

WC:ba

P.S. Because time is critical in coordinating the research of proposal activities for several firms simultaneously, and I know that this letter may find you traveling, I have taken the liberty of sending copies to your vice presidents of marketing and engineering/research and development. We will also respond to their requests for our proposal.

ATTN: William A. Cohen, Director
       Bureau of Business and Economic Research

Yes, I feel this research can be of importance to my firm. Please send a copy of your research proposal to the following address:

(Name) _____

(Address) _____

_____

_____

Figure 13-10 (Continued)

rect mail letters. After you are more experienced, you may find certain elements that are particularly useful in your work. If so, include them and eventually develop your own personalized checklist. Here is mine.

I. *Headline*
   A. Does the headline appeal to self-interest, offer exciting news, or arouse interest?
   B. Is the headline positive, rather than negative?
   C. Does the headline suggest that the reader can obtain something easily and quickly?
   D. Does the headline make use of the powerful words of mail order advertising?
   E. Does the headline stress the most important benefit of the product?
   F. Does the headline stop the reader and cause him or her to read further?
   G. Is the headline believable?
   H. Does the headline tie in with the copy?

II. *The Offer*

   A. Are all the elements of the offer present in the copy?
      1. Product
      2. Price
      3. Terms
      4. Guarantee
      5. Options
      6. Additional inducements to buy
      7. Dates
      8. Places

III. *Copy Content*
   A. Do you gain interest at once by use of a story, a startling or unusual statement, a quote, or news?
   B. Do you show benefits and advantages that appeal to emotional needs to such an extent that your offer is irresistible, and the reader would "have to be a fool not to order"?
   C. Do you establish credibility with your reader through the use of testimonials, statements by your accountant, or some other means?
   D. Do you demand immediate action on the part of your reader and give your reader reason to order *now* (limited quantities, time limit on offer, etc.)?

IV. *Copy Quality*
   A. Is the copy written in a conversational tone?
   B. Does your copy move right along?
   C. Do you use short words, short sentences, and short paragraphs?
   D. Do you use lots of subheads throughout your copy?
   E. Do you have a high Flesch reading ease score?
   F. Do you have a high Flesch human interest score?

SUMMARY

In this chapter, you've learned some very important things: why the emphasis on copy is so important, how to structure your advertisement or direct mail letter, how to get attention with a headline, how to gain and maintain interest with your copy, how to show benefits and advantages, how to write outstanding copy, how to gain credibility in your advertisement or direct mail letter, how to get your customer to order now, as well as the differences between space advertising copywriting and direct mail copywriting. Finally, I gave you a copywriting checklist to use every time you write copy.

Master the techniques of copywriting contained in this chapter and your future in the direct mail order business will be assured.

14

How to Prepare Your Own Artwork and Graphics at Low Cost

THE IMPORTANCE OF ARTWORK IN MAIL ORDER SELLING

While it is true that copy is one of the primary factors in selling through direct mail or mail order, it is equally true that the proper artwork and graphics go hand in hand with good copy and can greatly enhance your chances of making the sale. Just as with copy, you don't have to do your own work: anything and everything you need can be obtained from a variety of sources. On the other hand, if you are talented in preparing art or doing layout work or just want to do the thing yourself in order to keep your cost to a minimum, you can do so.

WHAT YOU WILL LEARN IN THIS CHAPTER

In this chapter, you will learn a number of money-making and money-saving ideas that will not only enable you to create or obtain quality artwork at low cost, but will also provide you with a number of options. Specifically, you will learn sources of free ideas for artwork and graphics, sources of low-cost artwork and photography, how to do a layout, typography, and illustrations, and finally, how to prepare what is known as camera-ready copy, which you give to your printer or publisher for reproduction.

SOURCES OF FREE IDEAS FOR YOUR ART

Even the most creative person in the world needs a place to begin for a source of new ideas. Here are four major sources of ideas that cost you absolutely nothing. It is not intended that you copy these things exactly. Rather, they are ideas from which you can begin and from which you can get concepts for illustration.

One of the primary sources of free ideas is work done by other mail order operators, which has been published in magazines or which you have received in direct mail pieces. Although mail order is growing every year, it is really a very old form of selling. Therefore, you have more than 100 years of artwork to look at, more than 100 years during which people who sell or once sold products either identical or very similar to yours have commissioned or done artwork on their own and had it published. Under the copyright law in effect when much of this material was published, the material is in the public domain if it's more than 56 years old, and you can actually copy it exactly as it is. More recent material is available to you every day in the form of advertisements you see in magazines or newspapers or your own mail. As with copy, I would recommend maintaining a file of good artwork—artwork you feel is appealing, that has proved to be successful, and that is applicable to the particular type of products you are selling. The idea is not to copy artwork, but to use the idea or concept as a starting point, for your own.

Another source of free ideas is professionals in the field—printers, painters, designers, and so forth. All art professionals will have samples of artwork, different styles of type, of paper, and of just about everything you might think of to give you good ideas as to how to proceed and what type of graphics you might want for your ad. If you are considering having one of these professionals help you prepare your art for pay, you will definitely want to see their samples. During the process of gathering information, talking with them, and considering the possibilities, you will be exposed to many different ideas, which will help you refine your own concepts for your advertisement.

Government and corporate pamphlets, booklets, and other publications are a tremendous source of ideas you can incorporate into your advertisement. Large corporations spend thousands and thousands of dollars a year for artwork to illustrate their products in pamphlets, brochures, and annual reports. Frequently, you can get permission to use their artwork at no charge whatsoever. The U.S. government spends even more—millions of dollars, perhaps—to obtain high-quality artwork that is usually available to you, not only to help you generate ideas, but, in most cases, to use, free of charge. Anything published by the government is in the public domain, and you may use this material without having to secure permission. Government material has no copyright unless the material itself comes from a copyrighted source.

SOURCES OF LOW-COST ART

There are many different sources of art. Let's proceed from the most expensive to the most inexpensive. The most expensive way of getting high-quality art is maintaining your own staff. And should your mail order operation ever become the size of Neiman-Marcus, perhaps this expensive option is really the most economical, since it gives you the greatest amount of control. The art staffs of agencies or studios are relatively high-priced sources that can assist you in preparing your advertisements. However, you can expect to have top-of-the-line illustrations for your advertisements if you are dealing with experienced mail order people. Free-lance artists typically work by the hour. They are usually less expensive than art studios or agency art staffs. An experienced free-lance artist can be extremely economical while providing you with quality work and creative ideas. Printers specializing in the mail order business also frequently maintain an art staff and can provide you with a good job at a reasonable price. Since they're experienced in direct mail and mail order operations, you need not explain many of the peculiarities pertaining to mail order illustrations, such as why your layout must contain so much copy. They already know.

The art departments of colleges and universities represent a fantastic source of quality art, usually at very low cost. These are artists in the learning stage, but the learning stage does not necessarily mean a lowering of quality. And art students who need the money are frequently grateful for work you can give them. One prominent mail order dealer I know uses nothing but student art. In fact, he even holds competitions in which all entering art becomes his property and the winners receive cash prizes. This source of art for mail order advertisements has been much overlooked by many of the larger companies simply because they can afford to pay higher prices. But for quality art at relatively low cost, look into this source. It's good for you and it's good for the art students as well.

Yes! We do cartoons and we do them exceptionally well - in many contemporary styles such as those you see here. All in simple black-and-white line, camera ready, easily and effectively reproduced. All this and more in the original "Clip Books" at an average cost of only $2.50 per week. Nearly 1,000 new illustrations each year. Four new books (a total of 40 pages) and four matching index folders every month.

EAGER BEAVER   LITHO IN U.S.A.

Figure 14-1.   Examples of clip art.

Clip art is a type of syndicated art. It is done by artists, reproduced in great quantities, and sold to anyone who wants to use it. It is usually printed on heavy white stock and you merely clip it out with a pair of scissors and paste it in as necessary. Examples of clip art are shown in Figure 14-1. This is from a free sample clip book of line art provided by Volk, of Pleasantville, New Jersey 08232. Another prominent dealer of clip art is Dynamic Graphics, Inc., 6707 North Sheridan Road, Box 1901, Peoria, Illinois 61656. Either of these companies will be happy to send you samples and price lists of the work. Clip art is usually furnished in booklets chock-full of hundreds of illustrations that you can cut out and use once you have purchased the booklet.

Outdated art—art on which the copyright has already expired and which is now in the public domain—is an incredibly good source of material for your advertisements. An example is shown in Figure 14-2. You can find old books of outdated art at your library. Or, you can buy an entire book of outdated art. Two good books you can clip for your use are *Attention Getters,* compiled by Robert Sietsema, Hart Publishing Company, New York, New York 10012, and the *Complete Encyclopedia of Illustration* by J. G. Heck, Park Lane, a Division of Crown Publishers, One Park Avenue, New York, New York 10016. You can obtain an entire catalog of books containing outdated art from Dover Publications, 180 Varick Street, New York, New York 10014.

Figure 14-2.   Example of outdated art in the public domain.

DEALING WITH ARTISTS

Before engaging an artist to work for you, you should meet with him or her and discuss the work he or she is doing now, as well as the work you want. You should see samples of work done for other clients. You should then tell the artist as much as possible about the artwork and advertising campaign you're planning to conduct. Sometimes it's very helpful, as well as time-saving, to work up rough sketches, using stick figures of your own concepts or ideas. From these figures, the artist can do a professional job while still following the general outline and broad principles you want to incorporate into your advertisement. The artwork shown in Figure 14-3 was created by an artist from my instructions in Figure 14-4. Be certain to get an estimate from the artist before you request work from him or her, and be absolutely certain that the artist is given a firm deadline.

Figure 14-3. An original cartoon created by an artist from a rough sketch.

Figure 14-4. Rough sketch for cartoon in Figure 14-3.

SOURCES OF PHOTOGRAPHS

You can, of course, commission a photographer to make a special photograph of a product or situation for your advertisement. If you intend to show your product in the advertisement, this will be absolutely necessary unless you can obtain a glossy photograph from the manufacturer of the item itself. If special photography is necessary, do not attempt it yourself unless you are fully experienced in photography of this type. Also, when selecting a photographer, be certain that he or she is proficient in product photography and is not simply a portrait photographer. There is a tremendous difference, and you may not get satisfactory results if you attempt to get product photography through a commercial photographer who is experienced only with portraits. Again, asking is not enough; you should ask to see samples of the photographer's work. When I first started in mail order, I made this mistake myself. I spent $30 for a product photograph that was absolutely worthless. The photographer was experienced, but in commercial photography only. Don't make this mistake! It will cost you both time and money. Compupix Rental (21822 Sherman Way, Canoga Park, California 91303 (213) 888-9270) will search its bank of 6,000,000 photographs and find a photograph for you at no charge (the photographer pays them a commission).

There are several other ways of getting photographs for your advertisements, some that will cost you a small amount and others that won't cost you a cent. Stock photographs are available from many sources throughout the country. These are photographs that have been collected and are kept on file. You merely look in a catalog and pick out the photograph you wish to use in your advertisement. You then buy a copy of the photograph from the owner. One major source of firms that have large files of stock photographs is the Yellow Pages of your telephone directory. If you are unable to locate a source of stock photographs locally, try Webb Photos, 1999 Shepard Road, St. Paul, Minnesota 55116, who would be delighted to have your business. Simply write and ask for a catalog.

Free Photographs

There are four basic sources of free photographs: corporations and public relations firms, government agencies, trade organizations, and local newspapers. Be certain when you request the photograph that you get permission to use the photograph in your advertisement.

Usually any company will be more than happy to give you pictures of their product. Frequently they maintain photos of subjects somewhat removed from their product as well. To locate these companies, look up the subject by type of business in your local telephone book. If you want a photograph of a tractor in use, find a firm that manufactures tractors, or for a photograph of an airplane, write to a company that makes them. If you live in a small town and the company you want to write to is located elsewhere, call the local number and get the address of the main office. If there is no local number, you can use other directories, such as the Thomas Register of Manufacturers, or one of the directories published by Dun and Bradstreet, for locating these companies. Write a letter to the public relations office of the company you think may have the photograph you want, and don't forget to ask for permission to use the photograph in your ad.

Government Agencies

Just about every government agency has a photograph file, including the Department of Defense, the Department of Agriculture, and state and local government agencies. Just write a letter to the agency you think may have photographs of the subjects you want.

Trade Organizations

Trade organizations are manufacturers' organizations, professional associations, and so forth. You can also find a list of them in your telephone book under *Associations, Clubs,* or *Organizations.* Call or write those that are likely to have photographs of the subject you want. Here again, the photographs will probably be provided at little or no cost.

Local Newspapers

Local newspapers maintain a file of photographs, but there is likely to be some charge for each photograph provided.

One final word about photographs: If you are using a photographer, do not request more than one glossy copy of each photograph. If you require more than one glossy copy, it is easy to go to a duplicate photograph service, as described earlier, and have many, many copies made at a lower cost than the photographer's. You should be able to find a photograph duplicating service by consulting the Yellow Pages of your telephone book. However, if you are in an area where such a service is not available, I can recommend Duplicate Photo Laboratory, Inc., 1522 North Highland, Los Angeles, California 90028.

LAYOUT

Layout refers to the arrangement that makes up your advertisement— whether it appears in print media or is a brochure or flier included with your direct mail package.

You always start your layout with a rough sketch that includes the headline, outlines of illustrations, and some rough ideas or room for the copy you are going to use in the advertisement. How you put these elements together is called composition.

THE SEVEN PRINCIPLES OF COMPOSITION

In general, there are seven principles to consider in laying out your advertisement: unity, clarity, simplicity, rhythm, balance, proportion, and movement.

Unity

Unity refers to the fact that your entire advertisement should be laid out in such a fashion that it presents a unified whole, and that no single element seems to be outside the whole.

Clarity

Clarity means being clear, and the underlying message and point of your ad should come through very clearly without being confused by varying typeface sizes or too many different styles of typeface, or mixing photographs and line drawings indiscriminately, all of which will make your ad layout confusing to the reader.

Simplicity

When designing your layout, you should always remember "KIS," which means "keep it simple." Simplicity adds to the sharpness and distinctiveness of your layout. It means that your potential customer will grasp the message of your advertisement, whatever it is, without straining or having to look or read twice. To ensure simplicity after you complete the initial rough sketch of your layout, you should try to eliminate elements that do not add to the central message. The more elements, the more complex your ad will be. If the element adds something to the central message you're trying to get across, that's fine. But if not, the element will make your ad more complex at no benefit. Get rid of it.

Rhythm

Rhythm is typically obtained by two subcomponents—progression and repetition. A good example of progression and repetition is shown in Joe

Karbo's "The Lazy Man's Way to Riches" and similar ads, which, paragraph after paragraph, give you strong reasons for placing an order for the product being offered. Each reason or "sales close" is separate, and yet each progresses logically until the call to action to order the item. This is rhythm raised to its highest state in advertising.

Balance

Balance conjures up the image of scales, one side balanced against the other. In art, it refers to the perception of the eye, not necessarily what the ruler itself measures, but where the eye or what the eye sees of the different elements you have brought together in your layout. A balance may be symmetrical, in which the layout seems to balance or weigh equally from side to side, or asymmetrical, in which one side of your advertisement has more material than the other side. Both types of balance can be correct, provided they are in the right proportions. Balance is very important for two reasons: First, a properly balanced ad will act as an attention getter and will assist your headline in performing this function; secondly, proper balance will assist in maintaining interest after the headline of your ad has been read.

Proportion

Proportion acts with balance to attract and maintain interest. It is concerned with how the different elements of your layout—headline, copy, illustrations—relate to one another and to the advertisement as a whole. There is a golden rule of proportion, which reads as follows: If you divide your composition into two parts, then the ratio of the smaller part to the larger part should be equal to the ratio of the larger part to the entire composition. This can be illustrated by drawing a line and dividing it such that if a smaller part of the line is .382 and the larger part of the line is .618, the ratio of the smaller part to the larger is equal to the ratio of the larger part of the entire line as follows: .382 is to .618 as .618 is to 1. But forget the numbers. The eye must be the basic guide in determining how you break up your advertisement so that the proportions encourage the interest of your reader.

Movement

Movement is extremely important in mail order advertising. Movement across a layout may be in any direction. As a normal rule it's clockwise. In other words, a reader begins in the upper left-hand corner and ends at the lower right-hand corner. Anything in between the upper left-hand corner and the lower right that strikes the fancy of the reader may stop him or her to read. But your ultimate goal is to lead your potential customer all the way around in this direction. This is why in full-page advertisements, coupons are frequently found in the lower right-hand corner. Now, allowing for movement, there are two different theories of mail order advertisements and you should allow for both of them. The first one, the down-the-chute theory, is emphasized in many ads, including those by Ben Suarez. This theory says you begin to read the ad and progress all the way through it, never stopping so long as interest is maintained. Ben Suarez says you can tell whether your ad has proper movement by following the eyes of someone reading the ad. The eyes should continue down the page through the entire advertisement. But if he or she stops, there is some problem with either your layout or copy that has caused a snag. This theory is referred to as "down-the-chute" because once the reader begins reading, he or she goes all the way down and around until the reading is completed at the end of your advertisement. The other theory, which is also applicable in many cases in mail order, is that the reader does not go down a chute at all, but rather, once struck by your headline and beginning to read your ad, is attracted by various components or subparagraphs of the advertisement. Therefore, your potential customer may read a little here, read a little there, read a little somewhere else, as he or she progresses from upper left to lower right of the advertisement. To the best of my knowledge, extensive research has not been done on these theories. I believe both to be applicable, depending upon what the layout and copywriter of the advertisement intend. Both can and do work successfully. But you must consider from the beginning which you intend to follow and construct your ad appropriately. In either case, movement is important, and you must lead your reader to the final portion in the lower right part of your advertisement where the final close of the sale is made.

In accomplishing layout for mail order ads, remember that the ultimate purpose is not beauty, but rather to make the sale. Therefore, if your ad sells, it is a good advertisement. If it does not result in sales, it is not good, regardless of its appearance.

TYPOGRAPHY

Typography refers to the kind of type that is available for your ad. All kinds of typefaces are available in all sizes. In fact, there are over 1000 different recognized type styles. Trying to cope with so many styles is made somewhat easier in that most styles can be classified as either serif

Executive Fitness

A Proven Way To

Figure 14-5.   Examples of serif and sans serif type styles.

or sans serif. Two exceptions are text and script. The basic difference between serif and sans serif type styles is that serif styles have little cross-strokes at the tops and bottoms of the letters and sans serif styles do not. Both are shown in Figure 14–5.

If you are doing your own typesetting, you have several different options you might consider: paste-up or rub-on type; VariTyper machine; a typewriter such as an IBM; cutouts, printed material, or clip art; or typesetting.

Paste-up or Rub-on Type

These are letters printed individually on paper or on clear acetate with an adhesive back. With one type you merely paste these letters on your layout sheet, and with the other you simply lay the sheet over and rub out the letter, which adheres to the sheet on which you are working.

VariTyper Machine

A VariTyper is a reasonably economical method that uses a special machine for composing your headlines or other type work. It offers a variety of different type sizes and styles, including italics, and is relatively easy to use.

A Typewriter

Certain typewriters can be used for your typography, such as an IBM with which a variety of typeface styles is available. For example, because of the changeable type now available with many typewriters, there are over a 100 different ball elements and "butterfly wheels" that fit IBM and other typewriters. If you are going to use an electric or electronic typewriter for your typography, make certain that the type is clean and that you use only carbon ribbon, which gives a very clear impression.

Cutouts, Printed Material, or Clip Art

Material that has already been printed is also a source of material for your typography. Clip art generally refers to illustrations, but it also includes headlines and phrases. However, printed art, which you do not purchase but which has already been printed by someone else, is usable so long as you do not use more than one or two words and thus get yourself in trouble with copyright law. Make sure that the printed material you use is clean. Generally a white background is best.

Typesetting

Finally, we have a typesetting machine. These machines are not inexpensive, so this is a professional service you will have to pay for. The work is of high quality and offers an unlimited selection of all the various type sizes and styles.

Whatever method you use for reproducing the copy and headline in your layout, the type can be reduced or enlarged to any dimensions you desire in keeping with the overall layout and composition of your advertisement. One word of caution is appropriate here: Any enlargements of type will show up many errors that were concealed by small size. Therefore, extensive enlargement of typography produced by a typewriter should be very carefully tested before you commit yourself to an advertisement using this technique.

ILLUSTRATIONS

Illustrations consist of both drawings and photographs. In addition, illustrations for advertisements are broken down into two other groups. First are photographs and pencil drawings that have general shadings of tone, and second, line drawings that have no shadings. Illustrations that have general shading of tone are known as continuous tone or half-tone copy because they have no absolute separation into stark black and stark white. The difficulty with continuous tone or half-tone illustrations is that they contain various shades and tones of gray through black and white that can't be produced as you see them with only one ink color, no matter what method of printing is used. To get around this problem, an optical illusion is employed to enable use of only one ink color in the printer, but it is done in such a fashion that the photograph, pencil drawing, or whatever, appears to have many different tonal shades. This illusion is accomplished by breaking the image into hundreds and hundreds of small dots, done photographically through a special process. The original drawing or photograph is photographed again with a screen placed between the lens of the camera and its film. This screen, which looks much like the screen of a screen door, has extremely fine lines. It breaks the image photographed into an overall pattern of thousands of microscopic dots on the negative. These dots will vary in size according to the intensity of the tone in the photograph or illustration being reproduced. When the photograph is light, the dots are relatively small. When the photograph is darker, the dots become larger and may even join together on the negative. When this negative is reproduced through the printing process, the relative size of these dots create an illusion of tones and shades. Figure 14-6 shows two ads, the bottom one illustrated with line copy, the top one illustrated with a photograph that has been reproduced. If you look very closely at the photograph or examine it with a magnifying glass, you will see that even though it appears to be tonal in quality, these tones come from the very small dots I just spoke about.

You can also reproduce continuous and half-tone illustrations that have been printed previously. Since these have already been through the screening process, it is not necessary to repeat it. However, if you reproduce a photograph or illustration that has already been printed, you lose some of the quality of the original.

As with type, the size of your illustration can vary, depending upon your desires and how it fits into the composition and layout you have designed. If you want to reduce or enlarge it, you can. Again, you must be very careful that in enlarging you do not expose errors that were not visible at its smaller size. Another important fact is that when you photographically enlarge or reduce an illustration, the enlargement or reduction occurs in all directions. Thus, an illustration that is reduced 50% in size will be only 25% the size of the original because each side has been reduced proportionally. This is shown in Figure 14-7, and it applies to your type and illustrations. However, it is easy to determine the proper reduction or enlargement of an illustration or copy by the diagonal line method. First, determine the dimensions of the illustration or piece of copy you intend to reduce or enlarge. Draw these dimensions on a separate piece of paper. Now, simply draw a line in the box outline of the illustration from left to right, as shown in Figure 14-8. Draw a horizontal line or a vertical line in the box illustration you have just drawn to the dimension to which your illustration must be either reduced or enlarged. For example, if the original size of your illustration was four by five inches and it is necessary that the five-inch side be reduced to three inches to fit into your layout, you can find the length that the other side of the illustration will appear by measuring three inches from point A in

Figure 14-6. Top ad is illustrated with a photograph; bottom ad is illustratred with line copy.

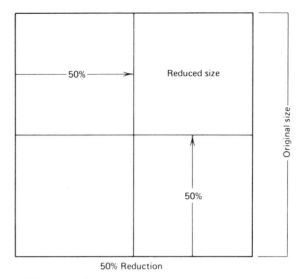

Figure 14-7. An illustration that is reduced 50% in size will be only 25% the size of the original.

Figure 14-8, which gets you to point B. Draw a vertical line up from point B to point C. This is the length to which the other side of your illustration will be reduced. By using this method, you can see to what dimensions your illustrations must be reduced or enlarged without making an error that will cause you to have to repeat the attempt at arriving at the correct size.

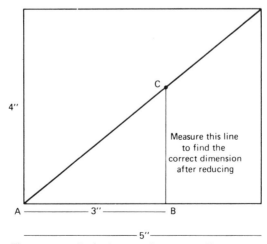

Figure 14-8. Reducing or enlarging an illustration.

PREPARING CAMERA-READY COPY

Camera-ready copy is the final artwork, including everything that goes into your advertisement—headline, illustration, and copy—exactly as you wish to see it printed. This paste-up, or mechanical, as it is called, is photographed, and the negative is used to make a master to create your advertisement. You can have someone prepare your camera-ready copy for you professionally, or if you have the necessary tools and want to do it yourself, I will show you how.

If you intend to create your own camera-ready copy, you should get the following tools together. First, blue pencils are necessary to make any comments to the photographer or printer that will not be reproduced in your advertisement. A drawing board—some flat board or table with a smooth surface—is required to do your work without a lot of trouble and many mistakes. India ink is jet black, a professional ink used by artists when preparing camera-ready copy. It is used to make corrections in copy that has been printed with minor mistakes so that a light area appears. Unwanted light areas are blackened with the India ink. Liquid whitener, also known as white opaque, is also used to correct errors, in this case by whiting the error out. Masking tape is necessary to hold the camera-ready copy page steady on the drawing board. Rubber cement is used to paste the type or artwork onto the paper. Rubber cement is very important, and it has major advantages over paste. First, it allows you to make corrections while you work, since the cement does not dry instantly, and excess cement creeping around the edge of what you are pasting is easily removed. Further, if you do make a mistake after the cement dries, you can easily separate the material you have pasted, make your correction, and re-paste with a little additional rubber cement. Finally, you will need scissors for cutting and drawing triangles and a ruler for getting proper dimensions.

The steps in preparation of your camera-ready copy are as follows.

1. Carefully proofread all copy. This is very important because once the master plate is made, some expense is required to re-photograph the artwork. Further, once your advertisement goes to press, any typographical or other errors will be very expensive for you to redo since they must be reprinted.

2. Make certain that all illustrations, headlines, and copy are the correct size. Do this before you start using your rubber cement. It will save you much time and effort.

3. Use rubber cement to paste on the illustrations, headlines, and so forth, on clean, heavy, white paper or cardboard, which is the background for your camera-ready copy.

4. Use yor ruler and the triangles to insure that positioning is absolutely accurate and precise.

After positioning and rubber cementing to the heavy cardboard or white
paper, check each portion of the artwork to ensure that every line drawn
is completely inked in. If it is not, use the India ink.

Now go over your artwork once again and remove any unwanted
marking with the white opaque liquid. Be very careful; the white opaque
runs easily. After completely finishing your camera-ready copy, protect it
with either a protective sheet of plastic acetate or light plastic wrap. Remember that the plate made for your advertisement cannot be any
cleaner or better than the camera-ready copy from which it is started, so
keep your camera-ready copy as clean as you can.

SUMMARY

In this chapter you've learned how to prepare or obtain your artwork and
graphics at low cost. You now know free sources of ideas for your art,
sources of low-cost art and photographs, how to accomplish your layout
for your artwork, how to do your typography, what you must do to prepare your illustrations properly, and finally, how to prepare your own
camera-ready copy. Use of these techniques can save you literally thousands of dollars while still enabling you to turn out really professional
work.

15

How to Save and Make Money with Your Printing

PRINTING IS ESSENTIAL TO YOUR MAIL ORDER BUSINESS

You will need printing for your stationery, your advertisements, brochures, sales letters, envelopes, and even invoice forms. The right printing is important to you because it represents your business just as a store and its atmosphere represent a retail business, or the appearance of a restaurant affects how the food tastes to customers. In the mail order business, your customers do not visit you at your place of business. Therefore, next to your products and the service you perform, the quality of the printing in your direct mail packages and other literature and stationery represents you and gives clues to your customer as to the quality of your business—whether it is a high-class or low-class business, whether you are trustworthy or untrustworthy, literate or illiterate. The right kind of printing actually makes money for you. At the same time, the right kind of printing at the right price can save you a lot of money. In this chapter we are going to talk about both stimulating sales and saving money through buying the correct printing for your business and your project.

WHO SHOULD YOU GO TO FOR YOUR PRINTING?

The price of any printing job that you might want—from a simple self-addressed return envelope to a complex multicolor brochure with many illustrations—will vary greatly from printer to printer, not because of any dishonesty on the part of printers or the printing trade, but because printers specialize in different types of printing operations. They have different equipment, they may specialize in different run sizes, the quality they offer may be different, the quantity suitable for their equipment may be different, and their experience and ability to buy paper and other materials differ. You should always get bids from at least five different printers for any extensive printing job. Do this until you begin doing business on a regular basis with one or more printers for certain different types of tasks. Some experienced mail order operators would advise always getting bids, even after you are established. However, once you develop a relationship with certain printers for certain types of printing, you will discover that other factors may become more important than price—reliability, for example, and the fact that if you are a regular customer you will probably get priority at difficult times when one press is down, paper is short, or your printer has other problems.

PRINTING METHODS

I'll tell you exactly how to go about getting these bids in a minute. First, let's look at the basic types of printing done in the mail order business in which you will probably be interested. Three different printing methods are most often used in mail order operations: letterpress, offset lithography, and gravure.

Letterpress

Letterpress is the oldest printing process. Until fairly recently, it was the process most often used by operators in the mail order business. Even today letterpress is considered by many people to be the most versatile process, and it is still used for many newspapers, books, and magazines, as well as commercial work for mail order advertisers. With letterpress, the printing is accomplished by means of raised type, line, and dot surfaces for photographic plates, which are inked and then pressed onto the paper to make the printed copy. The type characters and other illustrations used for letterpress are always in reverse, so that when they print the image on the paper the image will be seen and read correctly. The elements of type are locked together to form words and the words locked together to form sentences. The versatility of a letterpress operation lies in the fact that parts of the printing surface can be changed without changing the entire page to be printed.

The advantages of letterpress printing are flexibility, in that you may change parts of the job easily; higher quality at much faster speeds than possible with other types of printing; a closer combination of colors than otherwise can be achieved; a wide range of accessory equipment available with the letterpress operation; and the additional operations possible on the same press, such as cutting and perforating, all done simultaneously at the time of printing.

The major disadvantage of letterpress is that it is expensive when compared with the available alternatives.

There are many different presses used for letterpress printing. We may classify these many different presses into three basic types: platen, flatbed cylinder, and rotary.

Platen. Platen is the original form of letterpress printing. The raised type surfaces and paper are carried on two opposing flat surfaces. The raised type surface plane is known as the bed. The flat surface that contains the paper is known as the platen. The raised type is inked with the platen press in an open position, then the bed and platen are brought together under pressure, as much as 600 pounds per square inch. The press is then brought to the open position and the printed paper removed. With a platen press, there is a general limitation as to the size of the printed matter, usually 14 by 22 inches. Operating speed is limited as well, usually to around 5000 impressions an hour. For this reason, the platen press is generally used only for short runs, or for combination jobs where different cutting, perforating, or other special operations can be combined with the printing.

Flatbed Cylinder. With the flatbed cylinder press a flat printing form of the raised letters or illustration is used. However, instead of being pressed against another surface in a plane-to-plane contact, the paper is on a cylinder form. As the cylinder turns, the paper is forced between the cylinder and the raised impression from the press. The cylinder itself applies the necessary pressure to print on the paper. The printing form containing the impression to be printed moves in a lateral fashion. After the impression is completed, it returns to its original position and the cylinder is raised, allowing the printed sheet to be released and the type form to be re-inked, and the process is then repeated. The speed of the flatbed cylinder is relatively slow, but many printing jobs for use in mail order can be produced on such a press, including brochures, catalogs, and other printed forms.

Rotary Press. Rotary presses, unlike the flatbed press, require a curved printing surface. The rotary press is based on a cylinder-to-cylinder principle. The two cylinders turn in opposite directions at high speed, and as a result, this method of letterpress operation is the most efficient and fastest of the three types discussed. Rotaries are used typically for long runs such as newspapers, large-circulation magazines, and very-high-volume direct mail. Newspapers can be produced through the rotary press method at the rate of 70,000 newspapers an hour. Because of the expense, a minimum run is usually 25,000 impressions. And the disadvantage here, because of the need for curved plates, which are more expensive, is cost. Another advantage is that many attachments are available to be put on the rotary press and allow folding, cutting, perforating, and so forth, at the same time the other high-speed operation takes place.

Offset Lithography

Whereas once letterpress was the most used printing process in mail order, the honor today goes to offset. Of the three major printing processes noted here, offset has had the greatest growth. It passed letterpress in dollar volume around 1965. Quality was once a problem with offset printing in comparison to letterpress, but not today. Today you can obtain quality equal to the letterpress operation, although quality does differ from printer to printer.

The offset process is based on photography. A special plate is made from a photograph of camera-ready copy and the offset image is transferred from the inked plate to a rubber blanket and then printed onto the paper. This printing from the blanket to the paper, or offsetting, is where the process gets its name. It is distinguished from other methods of printing such as letterpress or gravure in that both the printing and nonprinting areas of the plate are in the same plane: The printing surfaces are neither raised from nor indented into the plate. Another unique fact that makes the offset process possible is that the ink used has a grease base and will not mix with water, so raised impressions are not required for printing. The plate is used in such a way that those portions to be printed attract this greasy ink, whereas those portions not to be printed attract water, which is applied to the plate before the ink is applied. Since water and the greasy ink will not mix, the ink remains only on the area to be printed.

For mail order, there are two main methods of offset printing that you should know about and consider—sheet-fed offset and web offset. In sheet-fed offset, the sheets of paper to be printed are placed in the press one at a time. In web offset, a continuous roll of paper is used and the paper cut during or after printing operation, permitting extremely high speeds. The distinctions between the two methods in the past have been that sheet-fed offset has permitted better quality in printing and that the web press has had a cost advantage in large quantities while having restrictions on paper size that could be used. Today, however, these two methods are very competitive for a number of operations once limited to one or the other, and both should be considered, depending upon the type of press your printer has and the particulars of your job.

The advantages of offset printing include cost savings over letterpress because of labor involved in typesetting and much cheaper plates. Also, the setup time for the press is generally much lower than that of letterpress, and you can obtain duplicate plates very inexpensively, compared to letterpress. Finally, it is easy to make reprints once you have an original using the offset method. For example, a book publisher who is publishing a new edition of a book need not reset type or make up new plates, but can make inexpensive offset plates from the original edition.

Gravure

The gravure method of printing is similar to letterpress in the sense that contact is made directly between the inked plate and the paper to be printed. However, gravure is the opposite to letterpress in that rather than a raised surface's being printed, a depressed surface is used for ink transference. The design to be printed is actually etched into the plate, forming small cavities that contain the ink. Like letterpress, the entire image is reversed. Gravure gives the highest quality reproductions of continuous tone art in all illustrations, including photographs. During the printing process, the etched plate is inked by ink roll or by a spray. But before it comes in contact with the paper to make the impression, excess ink is scraped from the surface by a sharp, flexible piece of metal or blade. Thus, only the ink remaining in the cavity on the plate is transferred to the paper to make the impression. Naturally, this process is expensive, so a typical run for the gravure process is long—250,000 and up.

COMPUTER LETTERS

Although letterpress, offset, and gravure are the three basic processes of printing used in mail order, a new printing process has caught on recently and been used to increase mail order sales at reduced cost. As was mentioned in previous chapters, whenever you can personalize anything in mail order, the product sells better. This is the story of computer letters, in which an individual can be addressed directly by name because it is printed by a computer. Each letter appears to be typed individually and you can bet that such a letter will pull far better than a letter that is not

Figure 15-1. A computer letter.

and that opens, merely, "Dear Friend," or even a form letter in which the name and address have simply been inserted. Such a computer letter sent to me is shown in Figure 15-1. You may not be able to get computer letters printed from a printer in your home town. But you can locate people who do this type of printing in the classified sections of the magazines *Direct Marketing* and *ZIP*. Here are two printers of computer letters. Write to either for samples of their work and information about cost: Response Graphics, 1480 Renaissance Drive, Park Ridge, Illinois 60068, and Scan Forms, Inc., 181 Rittenhouse Circle, Bristol, Pennsylvania 19007.

In conjunction with computer letters, a number of different technological developments have led to personalization through nonimpact printing. Such printing is possible through the ink jet (the spraying of small dots of ink at high speed to form letters), lasers, and other unique processes. Along with a computer, these developments allow personalized messages to be printed using variable sizes of type, anywhere on the page, and oriented toward any direction. They permit a degree of creativity in personalization previously not economically feasible.

PREPARING A PRINTING PLAN AND FINDING A PRINTER

So much depends upon your printing that you should actually work up a formalized plan to ensure that the printing you need can be obtained when you need it and at the most cost-effective price. I have broken this process down into six steps.

Step 1. See a number of printers, at least five. I also recommend that you do this as soon as you have completed your overall project marketing plan. In this visit, you should tell the printer exactly what you want and ask for samples of similar material he or she has printed. Your specifications should include paper. You can see a number of different types of paper and decide on exactly what you want. Also explain the kind of illustrations you want, the quality of work you're looking for, the binding if this is important, the size and number of pages, the quality of the material, and the color or colors. Ask a bid for different quantity runs, but make sure your printer knows the quantity you are most likely to order. Finally, make sure that he or she understands when you need the material so that he or she knows whether other jobs may interfere with your project.

Be certain that you document exactly what it is you want and that you get prices and a time commitment in writing. Also, don't forget to ask how the price can be decreased. Is glossy paper really needed, considering how much you can save by not using it? You can save a lot of money by just asking the question. Finally, I would make sure that the printer you have contacted understands that he or she is in competition. If the quantity of material you're having printed is large enough, the printer may be willing to lower the price to beat out the competition. On the other hand, if this is an initial run for a small test, and you haven't done this before and do not have a regular printer, I would emphasize only that you would like to check this price against some others before making the final decision. Don't expect any major reductions in price because of competition for a limited job. Your job may just not be worth it. However, you can make sure that he or she understands that while you're just getting started now and need a small-quantity run, other runs are anticipated in larger quantities, and that once you have someone you are satisfied with you will probably tend to continue to work with that person for most of your printing.

In addition to considering printers locally, I would also consider printers who operate through mail order. Sometimes printing bought this way can save you a lot of money. On one offset job ordered through mail order, my local printer told me that he could not even purchase the paper for the amount the mail order offset printer was going to charge me. However, there is a trade-off. While you can frequently save money by dealing through the mail with certain firms, you lose a lot of control over the work. So, if you're going to deal through the mail in getting your printing, make certain that everything is exactly the way you want it before you order. It is very difficult to make changes in the original order by mail. Also, make certain that you order the printed material well ahead of time. Even then you may still have problems and need to make phone calls trying to get various details straightened out or to encourage the printer to get your work done faster. Remember, if you are dealing by mail, you will not be able to see your printer face-to-face and you may not be as persuasive on the telephone. If you're interested in low-cost mail order printing and you want to make a comparison, here are three such offset printers who do black and white work through the mail. Write for their catalogs and ask for additional information: Champion Printing Company, Box 148, Ross, Ohio 45061; Dinner and Klein, 2030 Westlake Avenue, P.O. Box 21188, Seattle, Washington 98111; and Speedy Offset Printers, 23800 Aurora Road, Bedford Heights, Ohio 444146.

Before making a commitment with one or another of the printers you have consulted, make certain you write down exactly what you want so that when you're comparing these printers, you are comparing apples with apples and not apples with oranges.

Step 2. Get the actual bids in writing, including what is to be done and the prices from each printer. Again I caution you to make certain that you know exactly what each printer is going to supply so that you're making an accurate comparison among the five or more printers that you have solicited.

Step 3. Make the comparison. Here you have to consider those factors that are most important to you in your unique situation. Is quality very important? Then you should consider the samples supplied by the individuals you have solicited very carefully. If quality is not so important, you must think about that too. You should also consider whether it is important to be geographically close to the printer, which gives you more control, or whether you are willing to give up some control for potential cost savings. And, of course, you should consider price. If it is not your first time and you have worked with some printers with whom you are happy, you might want to give a lot of consideration to reliability.

Step 4. Prepare or have someone prepare your camera-ready copy if you are using offset. You should check it very carefully to make sure there are no errors. Keep in mind that from this step on, every single error will cost you additional money and it is best to catch errors before you submit the work to the printer. If you aren't using offset, you're giving the printer a detailed layout and manuscript. Do your job and make certain it is error free.

Step 5.   Take the camera-ready copy to your printer and he or she will supply you with brown lines or proofs, which you can and should check over very carefully. This is your last chance to correct before going to press. It is more expensive to correct these brown lines or initial proofs than it was to correct your camera-ready copy. However, it is still far cheaper than going to press and having something important left out or being incorrect—typographical errors, error in address, address left off, and so forth. Have someone other than yourself check the proof before you tell the printer your work is ready for printing. If you aren't using offset, and with offset for an expensive run, you may get to check a single printed copy.

Step 6.   This is the final step, where you give your printer the okay to go ahead. It takes but a few minutes to read about this whole process, but please keep in mind that it takes a considerable time, and as one famous mail order man said about printers, the only thing consistent about them is that they are always late. So do not forget to allow yourself enough time when you start to complete the job on time.

This knowledge about the basics of printing is essential for your success. If you conduct your mail order business correctly with regard to the printing aspect, not only will you save money but your printing will make additional money for you.

SUMMARY

In this chapter we have discussed why printing costs are different from printer to printer and why it is important to get multiple bids every time you have a major printing project to do. We've also discussed the three basic mail order printing methods—letterpress, offset lithography, and gravure—and the advantages and disadvantages of each method. Finally, we discussed a six-step printing plan you should follow every time you need to have printing done. If you follow this plan, it will ensure that your costs are minimized for the correct printing for your job.

16

Testing

TESTING: WHY DO IT?

The quality of testing that is possible in mail order is a major advantage over any other business. Every successful mail order operator tests, so it's not just theory. It's a real part of mail order and vital to your success.

In earlier chapters in this book, I introduced you to some methods of testing. In this chapter we're going to look at testing much more thoroughly. But first, let's consider some basic questions. Why test? Let us say that you are about to embark on a promotion for a new product. Your ads have been prepared. All the material for your direct mail packages has been developed and everything is ready to go. In the initial stages of the promotion you anticipate spending between $10,000 and $20,000. You have already researched the market thoroughly and picked a product. You know in your heart of hearts that this product cannot fail and your campaign will be a sure winner. Why not just jump in and spent your $10,000 to $20,000 and make the money as soon as possible?

Before I tell you what a test will do, let me say one thing that a test probably will not do: It will not make you money. If it does, that's all well and good, but that is not the objective. The purpose of the test is to save you from losing your $10,000 to $20,000 needlessly. The fact is that, despite preliminary research and good preparation, most new products fail in the marketplace. So how can you make money? The mail order operator makes money because of testing. Because even though the majority of his or her campaigns may be unsuccessful, he or she finds out that they're unsuccessful at the very beginning through testing. The successful mail order person spends maybe $500 or $1000 on this test, and only if he or she is successful is the next step taken to spend the larger sums of money required. This means that even though an operator has loss after loss, when he or she finally does win, it's a big win. One success more than makes up for all the relatively small amounts of money spent on many tests for unsuccessful campaigns.

But that's not the only reason for testing. Even a successful product and offer can be tested for various features of the promotion, as we have talked about previously. Some copy may pull 500% or better than other copy for the same product. Surely it is worth a relatively small sum of money to find this out inasmuch as the return of this investment is so great both over the long run and in the immediate future.

We said that testing does cost money. Think of testing as buying intelligence or buying market research. It is far better to pay the small price to learn whether you can succeed with your proposition, or to learn which proposition is more profitable than another. The alternative is to jump in and make your mistakes, and possibly lose thousands of dollars in the process without any chance of recouping it. That makes mail order too much of a gamble. There is risk in mail order—after all, it is a business. But it is not gambling.

WHAT TO TEST

There are some major things that we test, including the following:

1. Profitability
2. One ad against the other (different copy, different graphics, or both, and positioning of ad)
3. One medium against another or one magazine against another
4. Price
5. The offer
6. One list against another
7. A direct mail package
8. Elements of the direct mail package, including copy, graphics, the sales letter, the flier, self-addressed stamped envelope, wording of the guarantee, length of the period in which the money is refundable, and so forth
9. Terms of payment
10. Use of color
11. Letterhead and stationery

Testing for Profitability

Testing for profitability is perhaps the basic reason for testing. Some propositions are so inherently unprofitable that it is little use to try to modify your copy or the medium in which you're advertising to make them work. It just can't be done. It is better to know this up front, so that if necessary, you can drop a project that is unprofitable and move on to another, where the money is. Therefore, initial testing of any proposition we try in mail order is for the purpose of determining whether we can make a profit.

Testing One Ad against Another

In testing one ad against another, there are many things that we can test. I mentioned copy before. Sometimes just the copy change makes a tremendous difference. We can change the graphics, including the picture or illustration. Sometimes neither the copy nor the graphics by itself will make much difference: You must change both to get good results. The position of the ad in the magazine carrying it can be tremendously important. But to get special positioning in a magazine or newspaper frequently costs additional money. The question is whether this additional money is worth it. We must consider not only the number of responses received and the profitability for the first product sold, but more importantly, profitability over the entire period that the customer continues to buy from us.

Testing One Medium against Another
or One Magazine, Newspaper, Radio Station,
or Television Station against Another

Certain media in which we advertise will be more effective than others in producing orders and customers. We discover not only whether they are profitable, but also their relative effectiveness from testing. Why is this important? If we had all the money we could possibly use in every single promotional campaign, we could advertise and continue to advertise. As long as we were creating a profit, as long as it was profitable to continue advertising in every medium, we would do so. However, you will never have unlimited financial resources, no matter how big you get. Therefore, some newspapers or magazines will be more profitable than others. Also, certain types of advertising may be more effective than others—television may be better than radio or vice versa. We do these tests first, to find out whether the medium being tested is profitable at all. Once this testing is complete, we want to know the relative profitability of each. Only in this way will we know how to allocate our limited financial resources, not only between different advertising media for one project or product, but over several different projects simultaneously.

Testing Price

Earlier I discussed price and we looked at just how important price really is in its projection of image and its psychological impact on whether your customer will purchase. Also, I showed you an example with my own *Writer's Guide to Publication and Profit* of how lowering the price not only did not increase profits through greatly increased sales, but actually reduced sales. For certain products there is a selective ideal price perceived by your potential customers. Economists tell us that the normal demand curve slopes downward, as in Figure 16-1. As we reduce the price, more of whatever we are selling is bought by our customers. However, this simple downward-sloping demand curve is not the case for all products. By testing various prices, we come up with the demand curve shown in Figure 16-2, which is that for my *Writer's Guide to Publication and Profit*. The shape of this curve is different, of course, depending upon your particular product and various other factors associated with your proposition. But it is important to know exactly what this demand curve is so that we can calculate the price we wish to charge for our item,

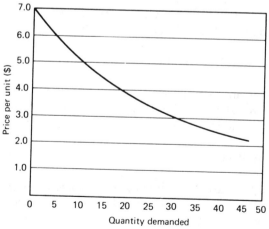

Figure 16-1. The normal downward-sloping demand curve. As price is reduced, quantity demand increases. As price is raised, quantity demand decreases.

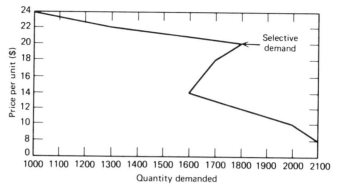

Figure 16-2. The demand curve for the *Writer's Guide to Publication and Profit,* showing selective demand at a certain price.

keeping in mind that not only the first order, but also long-range profit-ability in the back-end part of the mail order business is important.

The Offer

I've mentioned it earlier in the book, but it doesn't hurt at all to say again that the offer can have a tremendous effect on purchase by your cus-tomer. Sometimes a simple change will have many times the profitability of the baseline offer with which you started. There are many ways of making a presentation to your customer, but one generally works best, and finding out which one this is can mean the difference in thousands and thousands of dollars every time you come up with a new product or service that you offer through the mail.

Testing One List against Another

A single list can run to millions of names. Therefore, without having to mail to the entire list, you definitely want to know which list is better and more profitable than the others. Testing will supply this answer.

The Direct Mail Package

There are two theories about direct mail package testing. One says that every time you test you should test the entire package, including the copy, graphics, direct mail letter, return envelope, guarantee, and so forth, and that the direct mail package must be viewed as a single entity, not as separate elements, because the elements interact. According to this approach, you must test the entire direct mail package against another entirely different package to see which is best.

Elements of the Direct Mail Package

The alternative to testing the entire direct mail package is to test several of the important elements of this package—the sales letter, flier, publisher's letter and whether to include it, copy and graphics, how you word your guarantee and what kind of guarantee you give, whether you enclose a self-addressed, stamped envelope or only a self-addressed envelope, and the period for which the money is refundable. All of these elements will have a bearing on your orders and also on your profitability, so each element must be checked individually. For example, a short period for which the money is refundable—let's say, two weeks—may result in fewer orders than if you gave a full year or lifetime guarantee on an item. On the other hand, if the product for which you are conducting your promotional campaign is likely to have many, many returns after a certain period for one reason or another, maybe the shorter period for guarantee or money-back refund is best, even though it generates fewer orders. Along these lines, many mail order operators find that, regardless of their product, if they offer a very long or lifetime guarantee, they receive returns much later, even though their customers were clearly satisfied with their product initially.

What should you do—test the entire package, or each of the major elements? My advice is to tune your major elements first, and only after you have attained the maximum profitability should you begin testing the entire package against another package with different elements.

Terms of Payment

Terms of payment can have quite an effect on your customers' ordering of your product or service. If you offer to sell C.O.D. (cash on delivery), you will undoubtedly get many more orders than if you do not offer it. However, many of the people who order C.O.D. will choose not to pay the letter carrier and not to take delivery of the item. As a result, you pay the postage both ways and still don't make a sale. If you decide to offer C.O.D., you should test it. In the same way, many mail order operators allow time payments. If you do, you should recognize that, even under the best conditions and after many dunning letters to your customers who owe you money, you will probably receive full payment from only 60% of your customers. This is the reality of selling on credit, and you have to recognize it. However, you will certainly sell more if you do offer credit and a time payment plan. Now, if you are profitable, despite the drawbacks, and don't mind the paperwork, it's worthwhile for you to offer time payment. On the other hand, if it is not profitable or you don't want the bother, don't offer it. In every case you must calculate for profitability, and these calculations must include the fact that you have other items to sell to your customer after the initial order.

Use of Color

Testing the use of color is important because color will increase the number of your orders in almost every case. However, use of multicolor brochures and of color in ads costs a lot of money. Is it worth the extra money to bring in these extra orders? You can find out by testing.

Letterheads and Stationery

You might think that letterheads and stationery have very little bearing on whether an individual will order from you, but this is not the case. The appearance of your outside envelope will even determine whether your customer opens it. Does the letterhead match the type of product that you're offering? You can lose credibility if your envelope appears to be from a lawyer or the U.S. government when you are selling a product that has no connection to either. You can tell the effect of your letterhead and stationery only by testing.

BASIC TEST PROCEDURES AND DECISIONS

Testing is never done haphazardly, and there are certain procedures and decisions that you must take into account as you enter into the process. When you start out, you must decide how confident you want to be in the results—how much risk you are prepared to assume in believing the results. If you want no risk whatsoever, then, of course, you must mail to the entire list of perhaps millions of names—not a very wise or practical approach. More realistically, a 95% confidence factor is usually acceptable. We will use the table shown in Figure 16-3 for doing the calculations associated with our testing. You must also decide how much error you are willing to accept as chance and what is unacceptable to you. If you are doing testing concerning direct mail, you must decide what your expected return will be before deciding on sample size. A different sample size is required, depending on your expected return. In fact, one basic procedure here that is hard for many beginners to understand is that sample size is dependent upon expected return, not on the total size of your list.

After these basic decisions are made, you will use the table shown in Figure 16-3 to pick the correct sample size, which is most important. There used to be an old rule in mail order: Check 10% of any list. Even today, many mail order or direct mail operators do very rough testing by simply testing lists by equal numbers, say, 5000 of one list, 5000 of another list, and 5000 of yet another. The problems with this approach are several. One obvious drawback is that the numbers you are testing may be larger than necessary. In that case, you are wasting money because you didn't have to test that many. On the other hand, this number may be too few names, in which case, your results may be totally misleading. You may get good results with your test and then spend large amounts of money in mailing to what you thought was a successful list, only to lose a lot of money when you roll out and mail to the other names on the list. Or you could drop a list that would really pay off in general mailing if the test results on numbers too small to be truly representative of the rest of the list were poor.

After you have decided on the sample size, you mail to the sample size or, in the case of an ad campaign, you place your ads. When the results come in, you can use the table in Figure 16-3 to analyze your results. With this test, you're trying to answer two questions. First, you want to know if the results show a significant difference if you are testing one thing against another. In some cases, even though there is some difference in numbers of responses, the difference is not statistically significant. It could have happened by accident and have no real meaning. We'll talk about that in a minute. The second thing you want to know is how much error or deviation from the results you can possibly expect if you go ahead and mail to the remainder of the list—in other words, your confidence level, and the reason for your continuing to mail to the list.

USING THE TABLES FOR TESTING

Let's look at several different cases for each of the reasons you might use the tables. The first is determining sample size. Here, you want to know how many names you need to mail to in order to have a statistically representative sample of the list you are testing.

The first step is to decide on a confidence level. I have chosen the 95% confidence level table in Figure 16-3, which means that you can be 95% confident that the results you get are repeatable on subsequent similar samples. Some people in mail order use a 99% table. However, with a 99%

Percent Response	Limits of Error														
	.02	.04	.06	.08	.10	.12	.14	.16	.18	.20	.30	.40	.50	.60	.70
.1	95944.	23986.	10660.	5996.	3838.	2665.	1958.	1499.	1184.	959.	426.	240.	154.	107.	78.
.2	191696.	47924.	21300.	11981.	7668.	5325.	3912.	2995.	2367.	1917.	852.	479.	307.	213.	156.
.3	287256.	71814.	31917.	17953.	11490.	7979.	5862.	4488.	3546.	2873.	1277.	718.	460.	319.	234.
.4	382623.	95656.	42514.	23914.	15305.	10628.	7809.	5978.	4724.	3826.	1701.	957.	612.	425.	312.
.5	477799.	119450.	53089.	29862.	19112.	13272.	9751.	7466.	5899.	4778.	2124.	1194.	764.	531.	390.
.6	572783.	143196.	63643.	35799.	22911.	15911.	11689.	8950.	7071.	5728.	2546.	1432.	916.	636.	468.
.7	667574.	166894.	74175.	41723.	26703.	18544.	13624.	10431.	8242.	6676.	2967.	1669.	1068.	742.	545.
.8	762173.	190543.	84686.	47636.	30487.	21171.	15555.	11909.	9410.	7622.	3387.	1905.	1219.	847.	622.
.9	856581.	214145.	95176.	53536.	34263.	23794.	17481.	13384.	10575.	8566.	3807.	2141.	1371.	952.	699.
1.0	950796.	237699.	105644.	59425.	38032.	26411.	19404.	14856.	11738.	9508.	4226.	2377.	1521.	1056.	776.
1.1	1044819.	261205.	116091.	65301.	41793.	29023.	21323.	16325.	12899.	10448.	4644.	2612.	1672.	1161.	853.
1.2	1138650.	284663.	126517.	71166.	45546.	31629.	23238.	17791.	14057.	11387.	5061.	2847.	1822.	1265.	930.
1.3	1232289.	308072.	136921.	77018.	49292.	34230.	25149.	19255.	15213.	12323.	5477.	3081.	1972.	1369.	1006.
1.4	1325736.	331434.	147304.	82859.	53029.	36826.	27056.	20715.	16367.	13257.	5892.	3314.	2121.	1473.	1082.
1.5	1418991.	354748.	157666.	88687.	56760.	39416.	28959.	22172.	17518.	14190.	6307.	3547.	2270.	1577.	1158.
1.6	1512054.	378013.	168006.	94503.	60482.	42001.	30858.	23626.	18667.	15121.	6720.	3780.	2419.	1680.	1234.
1.7	1604924.	401231.	178325.	100308.	64197.	44581.	32754.	25077.	19814.	16049.	7133.	4012.	2568.	1783.	1310.
1.8	1697603.	424401.	188623.	106100.	67904.	47156.	34645.	26525.	20958.	16976.	7545.	4244.	2716.	1886.	1388.
1.9	1790090.	447522.	198899.	111881.	71604.	49725.	36532.	27970.	22100.	17901.	7956.	4475.	2864.	1989.	1461.
2.0	1882384.	470596.	209154.	117649.	75295.	52288.	38416.	29412.	23239.	18824.	8366.	4706.	3012.	2092.	1537.
2.1	1974486.	493622.	219887.	123405.	78979.	54847.	40296.	30851.	24376.	19745.	8775.	4936.	3159.	2194.	1612.
2.2	2066397.	516599.	229600.	129150.	82656.	57400.	42171.	32287.	25511.	20664.	9184.	5166.	3306.	2296.	1687.
2.3	2158115.	539529.	239791.	134882.	86325.	59948.	44043.	33721.	26643.	21581.	9592.	5395.	3453.	2398.	1762.
2.4	2249641.	562410.	249960.	140603.	89986.	62490.	45911.	35151.	27773.	22496.	9998.	5624.	3599.	2500.	1836.
2.5	2340975.	585244.	260108.	146311.	93639.	65027.	47775.	36578.	28901.	23410.	10404.	5852.	3746.	2601.	1911.
2.6	2432117.	608029.	270235.	152007.	97285.	67559.	49635.	38002.	30026.	24321.	10809.	6080.	3891.	2702.	1985.
2.7	2523067.	630767.	280341.	157692.	100923.	70085.	51491.	39423.	31149.	25231.	11214.	6303.	4037.	2803.	2060.
2.8	2623825.	653456.	290425.	163364.	104553.	72606.	53343.	40841.	32269.	26138.	11617.	6535.	4182.	2904.	2134.
2.9	2704390.	676098.	300488.	169024.	108176.	75122.	55192.	42256.	33388.	27044.	12020.	6761.	4327.	3005.	2208.

3.0	2794764.	698691.	310529.	174673.	111791.	77632.	57036.	43668.	34503.	27948.	12421.	6987.	4472.	3105.	2281.
3.1	2884946.	721236.	320550.	180309.	115398.	80137.	58876.	45077.	35617.	28849.	12822.	7212.	4616.	3205.	2355.
3.2	2974935.	743734.	330548.	185933.	118997.	82637.	60713.	46433.	36728.	29749.	13222.	7437.	4760.	3305.	2429.
3.3	3064732.	766183.	340526.	191546.	122589.	85131.	62546.	47886.	37836.	30647.	13621.	7662.	4904.	3405.	2502.
3.4	3154338.	788584.	350482.	197146.	126174.	87620.	64374.	49287.	38942.	31543.	14019.	7886.	5047.	3505.	2575.
3.5	3243751.	810938.	360417.	202734.	129750.	90104.	66199.	50684.	40046.	32438.	14417.	8109.	5190.	3604.	2648.
3.6	3332972.	833243.	370330.	208311.	133319.	92583.	68020.	52078.	41148.	33330.	14813.	8332.	5333.	3703.	2721.
3.7	3422001.	855500.	380222.	213875.	136880.	95056.	69837.	53469.	42247.	34220.	15209.	8555.	5475.	3802.	2793.
3.8	3510838.	877710.	390093.	219427.	140434.	97523.	71650.	54857.	43344.	35108.	15604.	8777.	5617.	3901.	2866.
3.9	3599483.	899871.	399943.	224968.	143979.	99986.	73459.	56242.	44438.	35995.	15998.	8999.	5759.	3999.	2938.
4.0	3687936.	921984.	409771.	230496.	147517.	102443.	75264.	57624.	45530.	36879.	16391.	9220.	5901.	4098.	3011.
4.1	3776197.	944049.	419577.	236012.	151048.	104894.	77065.	59003.	46620.	37762.	16783.	9440.	6042.	4196.	3083.
4.2	3864265.	966066.	429363.	241517.	154571.	107341.	78863.	60379.	47707.	38643.	17175.	9661.	6183.	4294.	3155.
4.3	3952142.	988036.	439127.	247009.	158086.	109782.	80656.	61752.	48792.	39521.	17565.	9880.	6323.	4391.	3226.
4.4	4039827.	1009957.	448870.	252489.	161593.	112217.	82445.	63122.	49874.	40398.	17955.	10100.	6464.	4489.	3298.
4.5	4127319.	1031830.	458591.	257957.	165093.	114648.	84231.	64489.	50955.	41273.	18344.	10318.	6604.	4586.	3369.
4.6	4214619.	1053655.	468291.	263414.	168585.	117073.	86013.	65853.	52032.	42146.	18732.	10537.	6743.	4683.	3441.
4.7	4301728.	1075432.	477970.	268858.	172069.	119492.	87790.	67214.	53108.	43017.	19119.	10754.	6883.	4780.	3512.
4.8	4388644.	1097161.	487627.	274290.	175546.	121907.	89564.	68573.	54181.	43886.	19505.	10972.	7022.	4876.	3583.
4.9	4475368.	1118842.	497263.	279710.	179015.	124316.	91334.	69928.	55251.	44754.	19891.	11188.	7161.	4973.	3658.
5.0	4561900.	1140475.	506878.	285119.	182476.	126719.	93100.	71280.	56320.	45619.	20275.	11405.	7299.	5069.	3724.
5.1	4648240.	1162060.	516471.	290515.	185930.	129118.	94862.	72629.	57386.	46482.	20659.	11621.	7437.	5165.	3794.
5.2	4734388.	1183597.	526043.	295899.	189376.	131511.	96620.	73975.	58449.	47344.	21042.	11836.	7575.	5260.	3865.
5.3	4820344.	1205086.	535594.	301271.	192314.	133898.	98374.	75318.	59510.	48203.	21424.	12051.	7713.	5356.	3935.
5.4	4906107.	1226527.	545123.	306632.	196244.	136281.	100125.	76658.	60569.	49061.	21805.	12265.	7850.	5451.	4005.
5.5	4991679.	1247920.	554631.	311980.	199667.	138658.	101871.	77995.	61626.	49917.	22185.	12479.	7987.	5546.	4075.
5.6	5077059.	1269265.	564118.	317316.	203082.	141029.	103613.	79329.	62680.	50771.	22565.	12693.	8123.	5641.	4145.
5.7	5162246.	1290562.	573583.	322640.	206490.	143396.	105352.	80660.	63731.	51622.	22943.	12906.	8260.	5736.	4214.
5.8	5247241.	1311810.	583027.	327953.	209890.	145757.	107087.	81988.	64781.	52472.	23321.	13118.	8396.	5830.	4283.
5.9	5332045.	1333011.	592449.	333253.	213282.	148112.	108817.	83313.	65828.	53320.	23698.	13330.	8531.	5924.	4353.
6.0	5416656.	1354164.	601851.	338541.	216666.	150463.	110544.	84635.	66872.	54167.	24074.	13542.	8667.	6019.	4422.

Figure 16-3. Test sample table for mailing response levels and a 95% confidence level.

table, you would need a much larger sample size than with a 95% confidence level table. Other mail order operators use a 90% table, meaning much greater risk, even though the sample size required is lower. I feel that a 95% confidence level is about the right one and I recommend that you use it.

The next step, if you are testing sample size for a list, is to calculate your expected return. Now, it is important that when you calculate your expected return or expected response it is not wishful thinking. Of course, you should always "wish" big. You could wish that every single recipient of your direct mail package would respond. Then you would get a 100% response. But, of course, that's totally unrealistic. Some people have very profitable businesses at less than a 1% response. If you don't have prior records to go on, start with assuming a 1% response. Or you could calculate the response you need to break even and add a minimum profit and use that. Let's assume in our example that we expect to get a 1% return.

Our next step is to decide by how much we can miss our expected return and still have an acceptable lower response limit. For example, we assumed that we would get a 1% return. How low can we get and still be okay? Some people would say breakeven. Some people would say something else. In this case, let's assume that we can live with a .2% difference. A .8% return will still be all right—we will still make money. Okay. We now refer to Figure 16-3. First, look at the response column all the way to the left and read down until you see the figure 1.0, which stands for 1% response. Go horizontally to the right and look under the .20 limits of error column. This means the .2% difference we decided we could live with in this particular situation. Read right across from the 1% response at the left, and under .20, we read the figure 9508. This is the minimum sample size we should use, rounded off to 9500 or 10,000.

HOW TO ANALYZE THE RESULTS

Let's assume that we mailed 10,000 packages each to two different lists. In one list we got a 1% response. In the second we got a 1.5% response. Now, if we look at these percentages by themselves, we would say the second list is better. But is it? Is this difference statistically significant? This is an important question because, if it is not statistically significant, we should treat the lists equally. One may really not be better than the other, even though from the percentage of responses received, one list appears to be better. To find this out we again enter with a 1% response. Move horizontally to the right until you find the number nearest 10,000. In this case we find the number we had before, 9508. Then read up to .20. This means that if the difference is within .20, the number is not statistically significant. In this case the number is 1.0—1% we got on one list, minus 1.5% we got on the other, or a .5% difference; since .5% is greater than the .2% we just calculated, this number is statistically significant and list 2 is greater than list 1. However, if the two lists had been 1% and 1.2%, respectively, there would have been no actual difference in quality between the two lists. They would have been considered the same in responsiveness and we would have treated them the same in our future operations . . . unless subsequent retestings proved the difference to be significant.

Now let's see how we test for permissible error in future mailings. Let's say that we mailed 30,000 pieces and got a 3% response. We enter our table again with 3% and read right across to the number closest to 30,000. This is 27,948. Again we read right up to .20. This means that the results we actually received were 3% plus or minus .2%. Furthermore, in returns you can expect in the future from this mailing, the percentage can vary from 2.8, which is 3.0 minus .2%, to 3.2%, which is 3.0 plus .2%.

HOW TO TEST ADS

Testing ads requires somewhat special techniques because of certain inherent problems. It doesn't make much sense to test one ad in one issue and a different ad in a different issue of the same magazine. Why not? In the first place, one issue may attract buyers or pull better than others. Perhaps one issue contains an exposé and is therefore read by more potential customers. If you advertise in different issues, the position of the ad in the magazine may well be different unless a special position is purchased. Some national, local, or even international event that occurs at the time of publication of one issue can affect results. When a really hot news item, such as the return of the hostages from Iran, takes place, certain magazines will be much more closely read and bought at much higher levels than is the norm. At certain times the event itself may affect mail order purchase, such as when President Kennedy was assassinated. Products identified with President Kennedy were purchased at much higher levels than normally even though most mail order offers in the mail at that time suffered grievously. Also, in certain issues of the magazine, competition may be evident or not, or may be more severe than in others. For all these reasons, it seems that the obvious approach to testing different ads in different issues of the same magazine isn't a very good solution. What is a good solution, then?

Well, one way to do this type of test is to use different geographical areas of distribution of the same magazine, so that in the same month you can have a different ad in each geographical area. However, there are some problems here as well. Circulation levels are different in different geographical areas of the country. Also, certain types of offer may not pull the same in different areas of the country, depending upon the climate, attitude of the people, and many other factors. You may be able to sell a heavy wool coat through a direct mail ad along the eastern seaboard in the middle of the winter. In California or Florida or Hawaii, it would be highly unlikely.

A better solution is a so-called split run. A split run means that you run two different ads in a single issue of the magazine, but every other magazine leaving the production plant has one ad, while the other issue has the other ad. These two different ads are keyed differently so that you can measure the results easily. Also, in every geographical area, both ads appear in equal numbers. Now, there are some drawbacks with this approach too. You can expect to pay additional costs for a split run. And, not all magazines offer the split-run feature. If you want to advertise with a split run, you should see the appropriate volume of SRDS or the rate card. Either will tell you whether the split run is available and the cost. Then you can make your decision.

Telescopic testing is a variation of the split run. With the use of telescopic testing, you can test many more than two ads at the same time. In fact, the name comes from actually telescoping a year's work into a single test. Let's say that you have ads A, B, C, and D, and you want to test them simultaneously. In one geographical region of the magazine you test A versus B. In the second region you test A versus C. In the third, A versus D, and so forth. Regardless of the results achieved with ad A, we assign it a numerical weighting of 100. We then compare the results of each other ad against ad A and assign every other ad proportional numerical values. Then we rank the ads accordingly. Let's see how this works out. Let us say in region 1 ad A pulled 3000 inquiries and ad B got 2000. In region 2, ad A pulled 3200 and ad C, 5000. In region 3, ad A pulled 500 inquiries and ad D, 1000. From looking at these raw data, all we can see is that in region 1 ad A was better than ad B; in region 2 ad C was better than ad A; and in region 3 ad D was better than ad A. But which of these ads is best and how do they rank? Well, we let the results of ad A equal 100. To calculate B, we divide B's returns by A's and multiply times 100, so the results for ad B are 67. In the same way, C equals 156 and D, 200. Therefore, the best ad is ad D, the second best ad is ad C, the third, ad A, and the worst, ad B. Of course, telescopic testing also costs more and a split-run capability is necessary.

Another technique that is effective and doesn't cost quite as much as split runs or telescopic testing is called crisscross testing. If you are testing two different ads, do the crisscross by testing two different magazines or newspapers. The first month you test one ad in, say, *Hunting and Fishing* magazine and the second ad in *Outdoor Life*. Then, the second month, you crisscross: The second ad goes in *Hunting and Fishing* and the first ad in *Outdoor Life*. You then compare the results to see which ad is better.

Another technique along the same lines is to alternate your ads in the same magazine every other month. This technique takes a long time to work, up to six months or more. And remembering what I said earlier about the competition coming in and copying a successful campaign, you certainly wouldn't want to expose yourself by testing in this fashion right at the start. However, at some point after you are established in the marketplace, it can be a fully acceptable way of testing two good ads against one another.

What do the results mean when you're testing one ad against the other, or one ad in three different magazines? Let's say that you're running one ad in three different magazines. In one month, magazine A brings you 500 orders, magazine B brings 300 orders, and magazine C results in 100 orders. In their raw form, these figures mean very little. However, when combined with the cost of advertising, they will tell you not only whether you are profitable, but also what your profitability is. If advertisement A costs $3000, you are paying $6 per order. If advertisement B costs $1500, this ad cost you $5 per order. And if advertisement C costs you $300, it cost $3 per order. If the combined cost of fulfillment, overhead, advertising, and so forth was $4, then you lost $2 per order in advertising in magazine A, you made $1 advertising in B, and you made $2 per order in advertising in C. Okay. So we eliminate magazine A because you are losing money. However, in magazine B, even though you made only $1 per order you made $300 because there were 300 orders. In magazine C, even though we made $2 per order, we made only $200 total. Therefore, profitability was greater in magazine C, but magazine B was more profitable. Of course, as always, we must consider back-end profits and profitability to get the true picture. If we consider everything together, perhaps even magazine A is worth advertising in.

DIRECT MAIL TESTING

You must be extremely careful in testing direct mail lists in that you must be sure that you have a fair sample in terms of sample size. It has been the practice for some time to request an Nth name list, as described in an earlier chapter. However, even the Nth name is not completely statistically correct because Nth names are not random names. Many mail order experts today are recommending geographical selections as being more correct statistically and netting better results for the test versus the results received later when the full list is used. A geographical name split can be done fairly easily using several zip code numbers. A method that provides a more representative selection of names can be worked out with your list broker, manager, or compiler. Frequently you can arrive at a better sampling methodology than the Nth name selection.

You should also test your largest good list first. If one list has a total of 500,000 names and another has only 20,000, it's far better to start testing the larger list first, because if it is successful, it allows you a much better population base to mail to than would the smaller list. However, you should use the largest "good" list. "Goodness" is a measure of quality, and you must remember that the most recent mail order buyers' names are much better than those whose purchase was made at an earlier date. It has been calculated that lists lose their effectiveness at the rate of as high as 20% a year; thus even a few months can make big differences in results.

YOU CAN TEST MORE THAN ONE THING AT A TIME

For many years, some mail order experts were fond of saying that you could test only one thing at a time. In fact, by the use of what is called *matrix testing*, you can test several different items at the same time. The advantage is not only that you receive the results much more quickly, but also that you can save a lot of money. Here's how. First, as shown earlier, you must arrive at the correct sample size necessary considering your confidence level, acceptable error limits, and expected response. Let's assume a sample size of 10,000. You want to test two different copy appeals, which means 10,000 names against 10,000 names, for a total of 20,000. Further, if you wanted to test two different headlines against each other, you would need an additional 10,000 names against 10,000 names. If you wanted to check copy 1 against copy 2, and headline 1 against headline 2, in a sample of 10,000, you would need an additional 10,000, plus 10,000, plus 10,000, or 40,000 names. An example of matrix testing is shown in Figure 16-4. You can still have 20,000 names per test as required, but instead of a 40,000 total, your total required sample mailing is to only 20,000 names. How is this done? Simply set up your mailing in four equal segments of 5000 each. One segment receives copy 1 and headline 1; 5000 receive copy 1 and headline 2; 5000 receive copy 2 and headline 1; and 5000 receive copy 2 and headline 2. Naturally, you can also use the same tech-

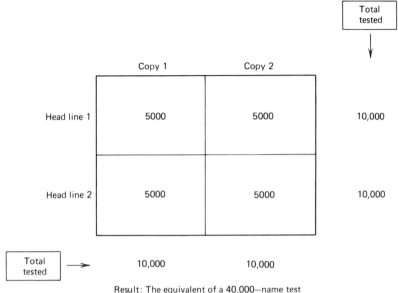

Result: The equivalent of a 40,000–name test
at the cost of a 20,000–name test.

Figure 16-4. An example of matrix testing.

nique to test three things at once, as long as your matrix has the same number of boxes on each side.

There is one small problem with this technique. Look at Figure 16-5, which shows the results you might get from a matrix test, testing two headlines and two different copies. Now the question is, do you choose the best combination of headline and copy, or the best of each and then

Figure 16-5. A problem with matrix testing.

combine? If you get results like those shown when using matrix testing, you must exercise some judgment as to whether the most important factor is the interaction between the copy and the headline, in which case you would choose a combination, or whether the headline or copy by itself is most important, in which case you would choose the best of each and then combine.

CAUTIONARY NOTES IN TESTING

There are some important cautions you should observe when you do your testing in mail order.

1. Sometimes observed differences are not real, and if retested, they will disappear. This is especially noticeable if the percentage differences are not very large. For example, Dick Hodgson reports in his book, *Direct Mail and Mail Order Handbook,* that a number of leading direct mail advertisers have sent identical mailing pieces to different large lists and observed differences as large as 10 to 25%. The solution to this problem is that if you do not observe great differences in testing two or more items, be sure to retest at least once to confirm your initial results.

2. Don't jump the gun when your results start coming in, but wait until the full results of your test are known. On the other hand, use the projection techniques discussed earlier to project the remainder of the results after a reasonable period of time—say, 30 days.

3. Don't make unwarranted assumptions in your test. For example, when I sold the *Writer's Guide to Publication and Profit,* at one point my classified ad tested the use of "free details" versus "free instructions." "Free instructions" pulled considerably more inquiries than "free details." However, remember that I was selling this on a two-step basis. And despite the fact that "free instructions" drew more inquiries, "free details" brought in more *orders.* Why was this so? I believe it was because "instructions" encouraged the respondent to believe he or she was getting a great deal more than a sales package, and so the credibility of my promotion suffered. The result was fewer orders.

4. Don't test insignificant things such as the type of stamp, small differences in envelope size, print size, and the like. Test the big things we talked about earlier in this chapter. However, I want to point out here that some factors that appear to be insignificant on the surface may, in fact, be very important. One such item is the

signature. For a typical sales letter, it has been found that a signature printed in blue pulls much better than one printed in black, even though the cursive is obviously printed, not handwritten. A handwritten signature pulls better than a printed signature, regardless of color. But you must calculate the cost of hand signing your mailing.

5. Don't forget to calculate the sample size necessary to make your test valid. It is foolish to think that you are saving money by testing a sample so small that your results will not be applicable to a larger population. The difference in sample size does make a significant difference. Also remember that it is not the number you mail to, but the number of returns you receive that is important for your test. Therefore, your sample mailing size must always be calculated on your expected returns.

6. Finally, to have a valid test for direct mail, you must mail all your test pieces at the same time, since even a day can make a tremendous difference in the results and therefore invalidate your test. In the same way, if you do magazine or newspaper tests, or tests with other media, you must use some technique to overcome the fact that one identical ad in two different magazines of the same month or two different ads in the same magazine in two different months cannot be compared accurately. You must find some way to ensure that the majority of the conditions you can control are identical, such as crisscross testing, alternating ads in different months, or split run.

SUMMARY

In this chapter, we've discussed the basics of testing. Your ability to test successfully will be one of the great determinants as to whether you will succeed or fail with your mail order promotions. Our discussion centered not only on what testing is, but also on why it is necessary. We talked about what to test and what not to test, as well as the steps of testing and how to use the table provided to obtain a proper sample, to determine the importance of differences you note in the results of your test, and the variance that might normally occur even though your results are accurate.

While it is not true that every mailing or advertisement you ever do should be a test, it is true that you should keep accurate records for every promotional activity you do in mail order. By carefully comparing these and monitoring changes that may occur, you will be able to judge how your product is doing as it proceeds through its life cycle, what your competition is doing, and how changes in the marketplace affect your promotion.

Do not be afraid to refer to this chapter again and again as you begin your mail order business, start placing advertisements, start on your direct mail campaigns and observe measurable results. The information in this chapter will help you achieve your greatest goals in mail order.

17

Profitable Fulfillment Operations and How to Accomplish Them

FULFILLMENT: WHAT IT IS AND WHY IT'S IMPORTANT

Fulfillment means carrying out your part of the bargain with your customer. You've received money from your customer; now you must furnish the product or service in return. Fulfillment is important because without good fulfillment operations you will not have a satisfied customer. In mail order, a satisfied customer is crucial because a satisfied customer is a repeat customer, and repeat means back-end profits and a profitable mail order business.

Let me give you an example of how poor fulfillment can ruin an otherwise good mail order operation. Several months ago I received a unique catalog of special tools that I could not purchase at the hardware store. One of the offerings was a set of three dental picks, which have a number of different applications for a hobbyist. Since I had never dealt with this company before, I placed a single order for less than $10 for a set of the dental tools advertised in their catalog. A month went by and I heard nothing. But I did get my canceled check back. I sent a letter to the company with a copy of the original canceled check, asking what had happened to the merchandise I had ordered. Again I waited several weeks but heard and received nothing. Finally I called the company on the telephone. The office manager answered and I explained the problem. While this individual was apologetic, she disclaimed responsibility, saying there were just too many orders coming in and if a mistake was made it was almost impossible to fix unless someone called by telephone—that complaint letters were routinely not answered. While the matter at hand was settled and I got my merchandise and money for the telephone call, I believe that if this company continues to maintain its current fulfillment policy, it won't have to worry about so many orders in the future. As you might imagine, I have never placed another order with this company—although their expensive and colorful catalog is frequently mailed to my address, and I frequently see things I would be interested in buying.

Fulfillment is especially important because the more successful you become, the more important good fulfillment practice becomes to sustain your success. Sloppy fulfillment will soon terminate any initial success that you might have.

When you first get into the mail order business, fulfillment isn't too difficult because the relatively small number of orders you receive is easily handled. Also, there is an alternative to carrying a heavy product inventory. This is the drop-ship method by which another firm will agree to stock the product and send it directly to your customer for you. Once you receive the order and money, you merely send the percentage of the sales prices agreed upon beforehand to the company that has agreed to drop-ship, usually the manufacturer. This firm then fulfills the order to your customer. Of course, it is very expensive for a manufacturer to fill orders one by one and you can expect to pay much more than if you had ordered a quantity of the product for you to fulfill on your own. There are other drawbacks to the drop-ship method, some of which I've discussed previously. If you decide to do your fulfillment by drop-shipping, you should try to get an exclusive, so that only you have the right to sell this product by mail. Or you should use a drop-ship product to fill out your own line of products, because if you depend upon a single product or several over which you have no control because of drop-shipment, others will soon be able to copy your success. If they have greater financial resources, they will even be able to shut you completely out of the marketplace for a product you may have been the first to promote successfully.

Also initially, you can do dry-testing, described earlier, in which you don't maintain an inventory at all until you find out whether the product is going to be successful. Of course, if you are going to dry-test, you must not forget about the 30-day rule and obey every aspect of it (see chapter 3).

However, even early in your career you will probably begin to do actual fulfillment yourself because dry-testing is just that, and as soon as the product is successful you must begin to fulfill it. My initial advice about fulfillment is to keep a watchful eye on your overhead. Do not hire additional people or rent buildings that do not contribute immediately to your mail order profits. As a matter of fact, I would look first at hiring individuals part-time rather than full-time, and use as many members of the family as you can to help you out. High school students represent a good source of part-time labor. Be sure you aren't violating any local laws if you do hire people part-time, however. Also, instead of large stocks of inventory in a separate rented building or warehouse facility, you should store as much inventory as you can in your home or garage and perhaps do your fulfillment operations on a workbench or on your kitchen table. Anything you can do to keep your expenses down at this early growth stage is good. Anything that costs money you need not spend is bad.

However, at some point in your mail order career, the money is going to start rolling in, and then you're going to have to get more sophisticated if you are going to maintain your success. You will have outgrown the garage and the kitchen table, and part-time labor will no longer fill the bill. Now you should look at each step of fulfillment and ensure that you are doing it in the most efficient manner possible, at the same time taking care that each time you fulfill an order you have a satisfied customer on the other end of the line.

THE FULFILLMENT STEPS

Here are the fulfillment steps necessary to maintain your hard-won success.

1. Estimating required inventory before mailing
2. Adjusting your required inventory after initial response
3. Ordering
4. Receiving
5. Warehousing
6. Mail opening, reading, and sorting
7. Responding
8. Location controlling
9. Inventory withdrawing
10. Packing
11. Metering and shipping

Estimating Required Inventory before Mailing

To estimate your inventory before mailing, you must know how many units will be sold in the first part of your campaign. If you have sold a similar product in the past, you can develop an estimate based on the relationship between the amount of your advertising and results achieved in the past. Let's assume that you have sold an electronic calculator, and now you are selling a newer model of that calculator. If you spent $10,000 in the first advertising campaign and sold 5000 calculators, you know that it cost $10,000 divided by 5000, or $2, to sell each calculator. If the initial stages of your new campaign call for $5000 for advertising, you might estimate that you would sell 5000 divided by $2, or 2500 units, in the initial stage of this campaign.

This method works fine for those items on which you have previous results. However, if you are selling an item for the first time, you will have to use your best judgment to arrive at the number of units you should carry in initial inventory. Study the efforts of your competitors. Usually you can get some idea about demand from the amount of their advertising and whether their advertisements are repeated. If they are, chances are demand is great, and you can estimate toward the high side. On the other hand, if your competitors are not advertising in every medium available and not advertising every single month, chances are demand is not that great, and your initial estimate of sales should be just slightly above breakeven.

Adjusting Your Required Inventory after Initial Response

This is an important step since you now have some reasonably accurate data to go on. Use the forecasting methods outlined in other chapters to estimate what the total response from a particular ad or direct mailing will be. You should continue to monitor your inventory as your campaign proceeds. Be very watchful for decreasing sales. One technique is to plot the trend line of sales from month to month, along with the amount of advertising you are doing every month. In this way, if total sales are increasing, but you are paying more and more to get each customer, you will know that demand is declining, even as your sales are still going up, and you can adjust your inventory requirements accordingly.

Ordering

Ordering has to do with when to buy and how much to buy at a single time. When considering when to place your order, you should consider the amount of time necessary to prepare the order—and the time it takes for whoever is going to fulfill your order to receive the order from you if you are not going to fulfill yourself. If the item is a manufactured item, you must also add the manufacturing time. Finally, don't forget the time it takes between the shipment of the manufactured product and receipt at

Weeks after receipt of first order	1	2	3	4	5	6	7	8	9	10	11	12	13	14	15	16	17	18	19	20
Cumulative % of total number of units sold (similar product)	1.3	7.6	28.0	56.3	69.0	77.7	83.3	86.7	89.7	92.7	94.3	95.3	96.3	97.0	97.7	98.3	98.7	99.0	99.3	99.7
Cumulative number of units to be sold after receipt of first order (new product)																				
Cumulative number of units sold after receipt of first order (actual)																				

Figure 17-1. Forecast of orders based on the results of a prior campaign selling a similar product.

your facilities. It is frequently a good idea to "pad" this ordering period to allow for an error either in your calculations or for delays in manufacturing or shipping.

Let's stop here and go back and look at an example. Let us say you're selling a product through a direct mail campaign. You have sold a similar product before and you know that you received a 3% return from your mailing of 10,000 direct mail packages. If this new mailing is also for 10,-000, you can estimate that you will sell 300 units of the product. That's good information to have, but you would also like to know how these ordered units will be spaced out over the length of the campaign. Since you have sold a similar item in the past and you have fairly accurate records, you can use this information as shown in Figure 17-1. If the product is a new one and you have no prior data which to compare it, use Figure 17-2 to estimate orders. Please keep in mind that these figures are for estimates only, and that actual results may differ considerably from your estimate, depending upon the product, time of year, type of mailing, and various other factors. You will also have to estimate what the total response from your mailing will be. This will be a little trickier if you have no prior data to compare it with, and the best advice I can give you is to caution you to not be overly optimistic in your sales forecast. Try to use the closest product that you've sold or have heard about to come up with a reasonable figure.

Let's assume your total estimate is 300 in total orders to be received from the direct mail campaign in either case. You can use a "how goes it" check as the weeks of your campaign go by simply taking the total number of orders received at that particular time and dividing them by your estimated percentage. For example, using Figure 17-1, if in your seventh week you have received 255 orders, divide 255 by the cumulative percent-

Weeks after receipt of first order	1	2	3	4	5	6	7	8	9	10	11	12	13	14	15	16	17	18	19	20
Cumulative % of total number of units sold	50.	75.	85.	87.	88.	90.	92.	95.	96.	97.0	97.5	98	98.2	98.4	98.6	98.8	99.0	99.3	99.6	100
Cumulative number of units to be sold (forecast)																				
Cumulative number of units sold (actual)																				

Figure 17-2. Estimate of orders in a direct mail campaign for a new product.

age forecast, 83.3%. 255/83.3% gives us 306, which is slightly higher than the total forecast of 300. In a similar fashion, if you got 255 orders in the seventh week of your campaign with a new product, using Figure 17-2, you would divide by your estimated percentage of 92, which would result in a total orders-to-be-received forecast of 277 units, which is 23 units below the 300 you originally estimated. Naturally, as the campaign proceeds and the weeks go by, your forecast can be adjusted and will be more accurate relative to the final number. Once you have calculated the total number of units that will be sold, you subtract those that have been sold to date to arrive at the remaining number you need. In this way, you can check the original order that was placed to see whether you will need to order more units or whether you already have a sufficient number of units on hand.

We now return to the question of when to order. If, for the particular item in question, your order preparation time is one day, the manufacturing time is 19 days, delivery time is seven days, and you add a pad of 10%, you come out with a 30-day lead time, assuming that your supplier can begin manufacturing immediately upon receipt of the order. As the weeks progress and you use the charts in Figures 17-1 and 17-2 to compute the total demand for your product, you can tell whether you are going to be short, and if you are, make some decision about when to order, how much risk you are assuming if you do not have sufficient product to cover your orders, and whether you must write letters to your potential customers to give them the option of getting their money back under the FTC 30-day rule.

To help you decide how many units you should order, you have your forecast, which tells you on an ongoing basis whether your inventory is going to fall short. But that isn't the only consideration when you decide on how many units to order. Other factors you must consider are those that add cost to the merchandise because of the way you order. For example, every time you put an order together it costs money. If you make a telephone call to confirm the order, it costs money. The processing of the order costs money, and receiving, handling, and transportation of the merchandise also cost money. These costs are reduced when you order a larger quantity of the product at one time. Finally, you must consider availability of storage space, insurance on the inventory once you own it, and the fact that until it is sold, you have money invested in the product that is not bringing you a return on your investment.

There is a formula that will permit us to calculate the economic order of quantity as an optimum quantity to purchase:

$$O = \frac{\sqrt{2QC}}{A}$$

In this formula, O = the order size, Q = the annual quantity of the product in units, C = the cost of placing the order, and A = the annual cost of carrying a single unit of stock for one year.

Let's look at an example. Let us say that you sell 5000 units of product every year. The average cost of placing a single order of product from your supplier is $50, and to carry a single unit of product in your warehouse, including insurance and other costs, costs $1 per year. In this case, the order quantity

$$O = \frac{\sqrt{(2 \times 5000 \times \$50)/}}{\$1} = \sqrt{500{,}000}$$

which equal approximately 707 units as your optimum order quantity. If the demand in a certain project is for less than 707 units, you order the entire amount at once. On the other hand, if the demand is some multiple of 707 units, you may wish to place two orders to try to achieve that economical order quantity that we have calculated to be 707.

Receiving

Receiving pertains to the initial processing and handling of the goods you have purchased and will eventually sell to your customers. To minimize mix-ups and ensure that things go smoothly on the receiving end, you should require your vendor—who manufactures and supplies the goods you're going to sell—to mark each case with your purchase order number and the item number according to its catalog and the quantity enclosed in the package. You should also instruct your suppliers not to mix different orders or units in one package. With proper marking in packing, it is easier to log in the material that you receive and much easier to keep track of it as you take it, warehouse it, and put it into inventory. At this point, until your goods are properly warehoused, you should stress security; make sure that the goods are well guarded and that you take an immediate count of all the material received.

Warehousing

Warehousing is putting the goods in storage until you retrieve them to fulfill customer orders. Many beginning mail order operators warehouse in their garages or homes. In fact, I know one mail order businessman who built a $100,000 business, drives an Alfa Romeo sports car, and still keeps his entire inventory in two rooms of his home. It is fairly easy to develop shelf and deck storage from wood or steel shelves or racks, which should be marked clearly with their contents. Here again, you are concerned with security, because this is valuable merchandise. At some point it should be protected with alarm systems and insured for its full value.

Mail Opening, Reading, and Sorting

The majority of your mail will contain orders, along with cash, checks, postal money orders, and letters to you. Your customers will expect to receive their orders as quickly as possible. You will also receive complaints, questions about merchandise that has been ordered and not yet received, and other mail that needs attention. If this mail comes in large quantities, you should make sure that the most important mail is attended to first. In most cases your customers' orders should get first priority, but you also want to make certain that other letters are handled expeditiously. Do not leave your customers dangling when they ask for information about an order. If the order is overdue, be sure to check *immediately* to ensure that the order has been sent out. Even Joe Cossman once slipped and failed at first to send an ant farm to his customer, Caroline Kennedy, who was ordering from the White House. You will also receive a considerable amount of business mail in which other people offer their services to you, and it should be separated from your customer mail.

Responding

Responding has to do with the result of your mail opening, reading, and sorting. It naturally falls into several classes, the major one, of course, being order fulfillment, which is the central act of the entire subject we've been discussing. It means simply that you send the product in return for the money received from your customer.

However, you may have to respond to a complaint or inquiry about a prior order, in which case you have several options, listed in increasing order of expense.

1. Form letters and using the customer's letter itself
2. Computer letters
3. Personal letters
4. Telephone calls

Form Letters and Using the Customer's Letter Itself.   A preprinted form letter is shown in Figure 17-3. All the usual replies are indicated on the single sheet and you simply check the reply applicable to answer the question asked by your customer. The advantages of this form of re-

DEAR CUSTOMER:

Please excuse this form letter, but through its use we are able to expedite your order or answer your question. It also enables us to reduce our costs, and we pass these savings on to you.

The checked comment is applicable to your order or question.

_____ Shipment has been made and your order is on the way. Please allow two weeks for delivery.

_____ Your check was not signed. Please sign the check enclosed and return it to us so that we may ship your order.

_____ Your check was returned for insufficient funds. Please check with your bank and send us a new check so that we may ship your order.

_____ We did not receive your order. Please recheck your records to make sure the information you reported to us is correct.

_____ The item you ordered is temporarily out of stock. It will be shipped as soon as possible, or if you like, we will substitute another item or return your money.

_____ The item you ordered is no longer sold by us. A check for the amount of your order is enclosed.

_____ The amount of money you sent us for your order was insufficient to cover the entire cost. Please send us an additional $_____ so that we can fill your order as soon as possible.

_____ We do not stock the item you inquired about.

_____ The size or color of the items you orderes is no longer in stock. The following are still available: _____

_____

If you like, we will substitute one of these if you will circle the one that you would like. Alternatively, we will return your money. Please let us know your desires.

Sincerely,

Manager,
Customer Relations

Figure 17-3. A preprinted form letter for responding to customer inquiries.

sponse are that it's quick, you do not have to stop to compose a different letter or answer to every different letter coming in from your customers, and it is extremely efficient. It has been estimated that as many as 80 to 90% of all communications from customers can be answered by a form letter with no difficulty. The major disadvantages here are the impersonality and the fact that some questions simply cannot be answered by form letters.

An alternative technique is to write on the customer's letter itself. You can make a photocopy of the customer's letter with your reply so you have something for your file. This can be done in handwriting, is very personalized, and you need not try to make your form letter answer a question or solve a problem for which it was not designed. The major disadvantage here is that if you hire someone to do this chore for you, you have less control over what is said to your customer than if you put a form letter together and simply have the individual check one of the approved answers you have already written.

Computer Letters. The computer letter is somewhat more personal than the form letter, although the data are really prewritten, as with the form letter. The major advantage of the computer letter is, then, that you have a form letter that looks personalized. I would not recommend this operation unless you have ready access to a computer and have more money to spend. It is usually not for the beginner. And that's the biggest disadvantage: the money.

Personal Letters. Occasionally personal letters will be required. Personal letters cost money and if you must dictate them yourself, they cost a lot of money because they take your time as well as the time of someone to type the letter and send it to your customer. Sometimes it's unavoidable. For example, when the customer has a solid complaint because you have made a major error, that must be rectified. Occasionally this can be done simply by having the owner or president of the company send a letter to the individual who has been wronged. In this case, it is worth it because you want to keep your customer. And besides, your customer deserves it. However, don't make this action the norm. It is an expensive way to go.

Telephone Calls. Telephone calls are perhaps the most expensive of all, though they are perhaps the most satisfying to a complaining customer. What can better calm an irate customer than a personal telephone call from the president of the mail order company? But some type of paperwork is usually necessary to follow it up anyway, so telephone calls should be reserved for extreme cases.

Location Controlling

Assuming that the response is order fulfillment, location control is the next step in the fulfillment process. It means that you must locate the merchandise to be sent to the customer. You have several alternatives

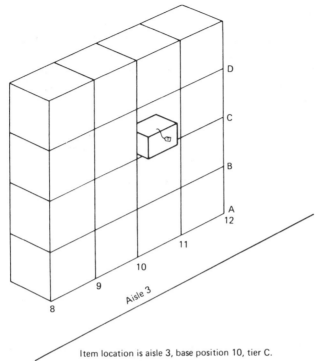

Item location is aisle 3, base position 10, tier C.

Figure 17-4. A three-dimensional location system.

here. If you don't have much of a product line, of course, there is no problem whatsoever. However, once your product line and inventory become extensive, a three-dimensional location system is generally called for. It identifies the location not only by aisle, but also by base position in that aisle and the tier height (see Figure 17-4). The box containing the merchandise itself (or, if it is a large item, the item itself) should be tagged with additional information confirming the contents. A computerized system, which maintains the exact location of your stock along with a running inventory of what is in stock and what is not, is also possible. We'll cover the computerized system shortly.

Inventory Withdrawing

Now that you've located the stock, the next step is withdrawal of the inventory. There are several different options here. One is called *gang-picking*: Similar items of inventory are located together and picked up at the same time. Another option is *individual order pick,* where one person fills a single order by going directly to the location and picking it up. Then there is the *sequel zone pick,* where several different individuals, each working a specific group of product numbers or zones, fill the order by forwarding it from zone to zone in a mobile container. There is also *order disassembly and reassembly,* where a computer disassembles the order into separate suborders and then reassembles the order at a given packing station. Finally, there is a system called *automatic pick,* used for high-volume fulfillment operations. At first you are probably going to use individual order pick, but as you grow, you should sit down and consider each of the options I mentioned against your situation and cost. You will be able to find individuals to help you with this decision in the classified sections of *Direct Marketing* and *ZIP* magazines.

Packing

Having withdrawn your inventory, you assemble the individual items ordered, put them together, box and wrap them, label them, and get the package ready for delivery to the carrier. Naturally this is an important step; if you fail to pack the items well and they are damaged, your customer will be rightfully indignant, even if you replace the order, because of the time delay involved. If your operation becomes fairly large, you can use a conveyor system to transport the order to the packing stations and then complete the packing prior to shipping. However, for most operations, a standard size packing table is perfectly adequate.

Metering and Shipping

The final step in the fulfillment process is metering and shipping, where you apply the postage and ship it out. At this stage you should have a scale to ensure accurate weights, and if a great deal of material is going out, get a postage meter from the U.S. Post Office. The meter is an economical, fast, and easy way to apply postage to your packages, but don't use one until your business is well established and you have sizable mailings every day. More and more mail order companies are shipping by UPS (United Parcel Service), and parcel post is becoming limited to heavier parcels or those too large to be serviced by UPS. You should also consider the different classes of shipping, depending upon the weight and size of the mailing. For example, fourth class mail takes a long time to be delivered but is the cheapest for many types of mail order merchandise. Accurate scales are very important, especially for large volume shipments. If you send out 10,000 packages, each with 2¢ more postage than necessary, you've wasted $200.

SHOULD YOU ACQUIRE A COMPUTER FOR YOUR MAIL ORDER OPERATION?

It is generally not beneficial to acquire a computer when you're first starting unless your operation is one that begins immediately with a huge volume of business. Let's face it: That's highly unlikely. However, once your business has grown to a certain size, a computer can yield certain benefits. You may be able to reduce costs in the clerical handling of orders; in inventory location and withdrawal; in sorting of certain types of mailings to meet with the U.S. Postal Service's discount requirements for various types of mail; in maintaining records; and in many, many other functions, including meeting the FTC's 30-day rule. Frankly, it is extremely difficult to accomplish fulfillment in a large-volume operation without a computer. However, before you jump into buying one, consider first that the computer is going to cost you some money and there are things you have to learn about it. This is another reason you should not get a computer at first—you will have enough on your hands in learning the mail order business without learning a computer system as well. You should also look at your present operations and compare them with what the computer will save you, as offered by whatever company is going to sell or lease you a computer.

Sometimes a computer is not for all of your fulfillment operations, but simply for some of them. Perhaps you want to use a computer only for inventory control and back-order processing. Or you may want to use the computer not only for your fulfillment operations, but also for your list maintenance and other similar activities. In any case, it is important that you look at not just one computer but several, and talk to several competitors. Have them look at your operation, make estimates, and show you where their computer can save you money. Also, ask them for the names of other businesses in your area that have purchased or leased these computers so you can talk with them and see what problems they have had and what benefits the use of the computer has given them. At some point along the line, if you are doing well and your company is successful, you should consider computerizing your fulfillment operations. You should also compare costs of the in-house use of your own computer against those of having a company provide computer services for you. To paraphrase one Los Angeles company, "You may need computing, not a computer."

USING A FULFILLMENT COMPANY

Another option you have in fulfillment that we have not yet discussed is engaging a company that specializes in fulfillment to handle your entire fulfillment operation. These firms can handle as much as you desire—taking your inquiries, turning everything around, sending the orders out to your customers, and sending you the money. Or you can work out a deal where you handle the orders and instruct them where to send the orders. You can find such companies in the classified section of *Direct Marketing* or *ZIP* magazine, or check Appendix D of this book and contact the direct marketing club in your area. They should be able to tell you what local fulfillment companies are doing business.

When you use a fulfillment company, you must give up some of the profit you would otherwise take for yourself. You also lose a certain amount of control of your business. However, again, you should find out what these services will cost and weigh that against what you are doing at the present time by yourself. Sometimes it's actually cheaper to go with a fulfillment company, especially when you consider that your time can be used in some other more creative way, which may be more important in making money for you. If your strengths are in writing copy, developing new ideas, finding new products, or other aspects of marketing, why waste time trying to do something at which you may not be as good?

SUMMARY

In this chapter we've discussed the entire fulfillment process—what it is and why it is very important in obtaining satisfied customers and repeat business. Fulfillment won't be a real problem for you until you start to grow. Also, you can avoid some fulfillment problems by drop-shipping. But at some point, fulfillment is going to be a major factor in whether your business grows or not. In this chapter you learned the 11 essential fulfillment steps—estimating required inventory before mailing, adjusting the required inventory after initial response, ordering, receiving, warehousing, mail opening, reading, and sorting, responding, location controlling, inventory withdrawing, packing, and metering and shipping.

We also talked about the advantages of the use of the computer in your fulfillment operations, and finally, whether you should use the fulfillment services of another company. You will want to reread this chapter before you start to expand.

18

Selling through Your Own Mail Order Catalog

CATALOGS ARE YOUR TICKET TO MAIL ORDER SUCCESS

Catalogs are certainly one way to reach success in mail order selling. They are advantageous in ways unmatched by other methods of mail order selling. Earlier in this book we discussed how repeat business will create big profits for you. The use of catalogs will result in that repeat business and will allow you to amortize the selling expense of all the items offered in one mailing. The importance of this amortization is easily seen in a comparison with a campaign in which you have only one product to offer. Each mailing containing your promotion costs a certain amount. It takes a certain fixed amount of money to stuff and mail the envelopes and do everything else associated with placing the promotional material advertising your product in the hands of your prospective customer. Now compare that with being able to offer 10, 20, 30, 50, 100, or more products to your customer simultaneously. The cost of this mailing may change very little, perhaps only by a few cents, depending upon the cost of the catalog itself. But instead of offering one product to your customer, you offer many. In addition, you have increased your chances of receiving higher dollar amounts from a single order.

There are many, many people who have succeeded in mail order through the use of catalogs, and three of them are worth noting here since two have written books specializing in this aspect of mail order. One is Roger Horchow, who once worked for Neiman-Marcus and wrote the book *Elephants in Your Mailbox,* published by Times Books. The second is Gerardo Joffe, who founded both Haverhills and Henniker's in San

Francisco and wrote *How You Too Can Make at Least $1 Million (but Probably Much More) in the Mail Order Business.* But certainly one of the greatest successes was Len Carlson, who, with a rubber stamp bearing a person's name and address, a product still sold, founded Sunset House, which grew to be perhaps the greatest of the specialty catalog houses.

WHAT CATALOGS DO FOR YOUR CUSTOMER

Clearly there must be some major advantage to catalog ordering or catalogs would not be so successful. Here are just a few.

Easier Than Store Ordering

Ordering through a catalog is much easier than store ordering today. There is no hassle with salesclerks, waiting your turn in line, finding a parking place, and generally getting worn out through a full day's shopping downtown. With the increase in gasoline prices, it is also probably less expensive to order through a catalog than in a retail store.

Shopping at Leisure

Using your catalog, your potential customer can sit back, relax, and browse through the various types of merchandise you are offering. Further, your potential customer does this at ease for as long as he or she wants, being unhampered by store opening or closing hours, traffic, or the need to be somewhere else shortly.

Material All in One Place

Through the use of a catalog, especially a catalog dealing with a specialized type of merchandise, your potential customer sees all the different things he or she may be interested in gathered in one place. In many cases, it would be impossible to gather all the merchandise offered in a catalog under one roof in a normal retail store. But in a catalog, it is possible, and the millions of customers who purchase through catalogs realize this.

Hard-to-Get Material Available

In some cases, your potential customer realizes that the products seen in a catalog cannot be purchased anywhere else. For this reason, your catalog is eagerly awaited and orders frequently come in almost immediately after your customer receives your mailing. This is one of the primary reasons I buy from catalogs. In a catalog I found a rare book I had looked for for years after I had written numerous bookstores and others in an unsuccessful attempt to locate it. L st week I received a specialized catalog covering books on a certain topic. Not only was the book I was looking for advertised, but a new reprint of the book was offered at a much lower price than that of the original edition.

Thorough Product Description

Today, in the hustle and bustle of shopping in stores, few merchants or salespeople have the time—or seem to enjoy—explaining in detail the various products offered for sale. Many would prefer that you buy now and ask questions later. But in a catalog, the space is available to explain your product in some detail, and your potential customer appreciates it. Indeed, it is almost a paradox that though the customer cannot see or touch the product at the time of ordering, he or she frequently understands far more about it and what it can and cannot do than a person who goes to purchase a similar item in a store.

For all of the above reasons, catalog selling in mail order is growing at an astronomical rate. In fact, although there is a growth in retail selling that roughly follows the increase in population, catalog selling is growing at twice the rate of selling through retail stores.

THE INCREDIBLY WIDE SPECTRUM OF CATALOGS

Catalogs represent an extremely wide spectrum of products and items. A catalog can be a single sheet typed at a typewriter and reproduced by a cheap offset process, or it can be extremely expensive, glossy, and multicolored, intended for a customer market segment that drives Rolls Royces and jets around the world. We're going to look at some examples of different catalogs and the products they sell. Note the differences in layout, in how the catalogs are structured, in artwork, and in various other aspects that depend upon the intended market, the prices of the products, the cost of the catalog, and, of course, the types of product that are offered for sale.

Figure 18-1 is from a catalog for cheese lovers from the Wisconsin Cheesemakers Guild, 6048 West Deloit Road, Milwaukee, Wisconsin 53219. This 48-page catalog is a multicolored, mouth-watering display of

GIFT 503—CROWNING GLORY . . . $5.95
An inviting 8" x 8" gift pack of 17 party-time cheeses. Squares of ched-dar and tilsit, wedges of sharpy, ham, smoky, blue, swiss-bit, salamee. Spreads of bluette, caraway, swiss, red pepper and garlic. Treets of spice, smoke, onion and sharp cheddar. 1 lb. in all. The crowning glory at cocktail time, snack time, anytime. Shipping weight 2 lbs.

GIFT 316
BABY GRAND
MUSIC BOX . . . $13.95
Plays the all-time classic, "We've Only Just Begun". Petite baby grand piano has a see-thru top for watch-ing the tinkling musical mechanism go 'round and round. Comes with 12 snackin' good Cheese Guild cheeses. 3-4 lbs. in all. Shipping weight 2 lbs.

GIFT 384—SUPER KISS . . . $4.50
A super gift that young-sters or oldsters will get a kick out of. It's the sweetest kiss a wife, gal friday, granny, or your sweetheart will receive this Christmas. 11 ozs. of 100% pure chocolate. (not just an imitation flavor). Comes in silvery foil, inserted in a rich red gift box. Shipping weight 1 lb.
Not available May thru Sept.

GIFT 527
HOLIDAY PACK . . . $7.50
Give this cheerful cheese assortment. Four 3-1/2 oz. wedges of Wisconsin cheese cheddar, brick, colby, swiss on rye. 2/3 oz. wedges of swiss-bit, salamee, ham, sharpy. One oz. Treets of sharp, spice, blue and smoke. 12 of the Guild's all-time favorites. Shipping weight 2 lbs.

Kiss
for
You

SUPER KISS

Figure 18-1. A page from the Wisconsim Cheesemakers Guild catalog.

hundreds of cheeses, which, I believe, is probably irresistible to those who consider cheese a delicacy. Figure 18-2 shows a shoe catalog from Hanover of Hanover, Pennsylvania 17331. This catalog is also in full color and advertises everything from simple loafers through western boots, shoes crafted of kid, and other specialties. The appeal here is status as well as a good buy. Figure 18-3 is from one of the fabulous catalogs for high-technology electronics products put out by Joe Sugerman's JS&A, One JS&A Plaza, Northbrook, Illinois 60062. This catalog is printed on slick paper and is in black and white, as well as color. Each and every product offered in the catalog has a full page of technical information. To

El Dorado

The lizard look in fashion leather.

Hanover El Dorado Slip-Ons are designed for timeless appeal with the contemporary flair of the lizard vogue. Sleek, trim, continental styling is accented by chain and bit ornamentation on a leather saddle strap. Easy-going comfort from fine leather uppers, leather-lined quarters, soft-cushioned vamp linings, and prime leather outsoles.

Style 2587 Spice Brown Leather Uppers Lizard Print Front **$36.95**	**Sizes and Widths** Combination Last Full Sizes and Half Sizes B—9 to 11 & 12 D—7 to 12 & 13
Style 3587 Black Leather Uppers Lizard Print Front **$36.95**	E—7½ to 11 EEE—7½ to 11

The Cobras

Exotic Genuine Patent Leather.

Four ways to look dashing—four eye-catching styles masterfully crafted by Hanover shoemakers in exotic patent leather. Good looks plus the great comfort of mellow leather quarter and tongue linings, genuine leather outsoles. And, they're so easy to care for. Just wipe with a damp cloth.

Style 5851 Blue Smooth Patent Leather Uppers with Flag Blue Cobra Print Plug **$42.95**	**Style 5852** Brown Smooth Patent Leather Uppers with Brown Cobra Print Plug **$42.95**	**Sizes and Widths** Combination Last Full Sizes and Half Sizes **Styles 5850 & 5852**
Style 5850 Black Smooth Patent Leather Uppers with Black Cobra Print Plug **$42.95**	**Style 5853** Beige Smooth Patent Leather Uppers with Sandpiper Cobra Print Plug **$42.95**	B—9 to 11 & 12 C—8½ to 11 & 12 D—7 to 12 & 13 E—7½ to 11 & 12 EEE—7½ to 11 **Styles 5851 & 5853** D—7½ to 11 & 12 EEE—7½ to 11

Genuine Patent Leather

Keeps that smooth 'n bright look.

Easy does it with these handsome patent leather shoes from Hanover. Just wipe with a damp cloth and they look like new again. The perfect dress shoe for the busy man. Hanover construction assures the comfort of genuine leather quarter linings and outsoles. Fine styling is crafted into every pair.

Style 5566 White Smooth Patent Leather Uppers **$42.95**	**Sizes and Widths** Combination Last Full Sizes and Half Sizes C—8½ to 11 & 12
Style 3566 Black Smooth Patent Leather Uppers **$42.95**	D—7½ to 11, 12 & 13 E—7½ to 11
Style 2566 Dark Brown Smooth Patent Leather Uppers **$42.95**	

Figure 18-2. Hanover Shoe Company catalog offerings.

Sleep
Sheep

*We may have found
a way to improve
your sleep forever.*

New Zealanders discovered that sleeping under sheep's wool induced sleep.

The story we are about to tell you may seem rather incredible. And indeed it is. But if you'll have an open mind, what you will learn may indeed change your life.

There is a new product manufactured in New Zealand that is selling very well. It's called the Woolrest—a bed pad made of thick wool. You simply place it over your mattress and then cover it with your bottom sheet as you normally do when you make your bed.

SLEEP INDUCING

Sheep's wool has always had an outstanding reputation for keeping you warm in winter and cool in summer. That is why wool seat covers are so popular. But wool has another property known by New Zealanders for many years. Namely—wool induces sleep.

In New Zealand, for example, a way to cure insomnia was to cover yourself with a sheepskin rug. For some very unscientific reason, the hypnotic quality of the wool encouraged sleep. Counting sheep was another technique that was often recommended. But it was the development of the Woolrest bed pad that suddenly turned an old wive's tale into fact.

DIFFERENT EXPERIENCE

Sleeping on a Woolrest is a different sleeping experience. Whether you sleep on a hard or soft mattress, the Woolrest apparently radiates a feeling of comfort and relaxation from the wool fibers which mold, massage, and conform to your entire body.

Scientific tests conducted by Dr. Peter Dickson of Ohio State University proved that the Woolrest pad indeed helped induce sleep. Testimonials from people who owned them clearly demonstrated that Woolrest not only induced sleep but also provided great relief for backaches, arthritis, and rheumatism. Its natural fibers tend to alleviate the pain and pressure caused by these illnesses and thus make sleep come easier and deeper.

Frank Thornton, a Seattle Washington dental technician, had trouble sleeping for six years. He purchased a Woolrest pad and has

been able to sleep through the entire night practically every night. According to Thornton, "I felt a sensation of buoyancy from the Woolrest. I have read in literature that a person sleeps more restfully with natural fibers surrounding their body." Thornton has already purchased seven Woolrest pads for his entire family.

There are hundreds of other testimonials we could mention from the thousands who have purchased them, but one thing is clear. Using a Woolrest pad you know that the rest of your life will be spent sleeping comfortably, with a minimum amount of sleeplessness. Certainly, there will be nights when it will be difficult to go to sleep. But with the Woolrest those nights will be fewer, shorter and without the tradeoff of taking sleep-inducing drugs.

WARM IN WINTER

In the winter the Woolrest holds your body heat and thus keeps you warmer. You'd expect that. But in summer it keeps you cooler through a process of moisture absorption by absorbing up to one-third of its weight in moisture to keep your body cool and dry.

Will the Woolrest work for you? We're willing to prove it with no risk on your part. Order one for a 45-day sleep test. When you receive it, closely examine the surface. Feel the thick pure woven pile of natural New Zealand wool. Place it on your bed and then cover the pad with your regular bottom bed sheet—either fitted or plain.

JUST A FEW DAYS

That night go to sleep on it. But don't judge the effectiveness until you've slept on it for at least a full month. You should actually notice the difference in just a few days, but after a month you'll turn from being skeptical like we were, to a real enthusiastic believer. If not, we'll understand. After all it may not work for everybody. Just return it within the 45-day sleep trial and you'll receive a prompt and courteous refund including the $4 delivery charge. The Woolrest washes easily

in your washing machine and has a limited five-year warranty. Complete instructions come with each pad. Sleep on a Woolrest and experience what we mean at no risk or obligation. Order one, today.

To order, credit card holders call toll free and ask for product by number below or send check plus $4 delivery for each pad ordered.

Twin Size (0025C)	**$129**
Full Size (0026C)	**179**
Queen Size (0027C)	**209**
King Size (0028C)	**269**

The New Zealand wool used exclusively in the Woolrest could be a major reason for its effectiveness. Here's why.

Most sheep are raised in countries where temperature extremes cause their wool fibers to become brittle, rigid and often cracked at the ends. In Australia sheep are often raised in the dusty outback where temperature and rainfall can vary greatly.

In New Zealand however, the sheep enjoy a year-round temperate climate and graze in lush green pastures. Their wool fibers are thick and vibrant with good shape retention .

NEW ZEALAND WOOL

The Woolrest uses only the best New Zealand wool. The fibers are actually woven onto a pure wool blanket base and thoroughly washed and tufted.

We have mentioned the importance of New Zealand wool for good reason. Just as there are several grades of sheepskin seat covers, we suspect eventually there will be several grades of wool pads. None will ever compare to the wool used in the Woolrest.

Figure 18-3. One product from the JS&A catalog.

698   US Army M1 Helmet with liner and chin strap, used, good. $10.00

1460   WWII German Army Steel Helmet, M1935. Repainted with Infantry Decals. Complete with good liner and chin strap, used, excellent $50.00

1463   US Navy WWII Gunners Helmet. This is the big blue-gray one which went over the head set. Complete with liner. Unused, very good. $10.00

1530   French Mercenary Infantry Helmet, very good, no liner $10.00
1531   French Colonial Infantry Helmet, very good no liner $10.00
1532   French Chasseurs Light Infantry Helmet, very good, no liner $10.00
1533   French Infantry Helmet, very good, no liner $10.00

2043   Rare US Army Helmet Liner. Must be experimental. Has removable plastic suspension. The headband is soft leather with Velcro adjustments. The headband goes over and around the head. Adjustable for both height and circumference. Unusual. Used, excellent. $7.50

659   US Army Camouflage Helmet Cover, reversable green to brown. Has Brush Loops, used, very good. $3.00 each
660   US Viet Nam Green Helmet Cover with brush loops, excellent, unused. $3.00 each

2166   Helmet Net for the WWII US Helmet. Small mesh. Desert Khaki color. Complete with instruction tag. Used, very good. $2.50
2431   Original US Army WWII Helmet Net. Small mesh. OD Green. With original OD Elastic band and instruction card. Unused, excellent $7.95

668   French WWII Army Helmet, no liner, used, good. $7.00.
1466   Very scarce French WWI Army Helmet. 3 piece shell. A hard to find genuine WWI helmet. Good condition with some rust around the sides. No liner. Scarce, used.   Just $8.00
1512   French WWII Army Helmet. These are the later one piece type. Complete with liner. Used, good. $12.00

ORIGINAL REPAIR PARTS FOR THE US HELMET LINER
1567   Adjustable Neck Band for US WWII and Korean War Helmet Liners, new unused. . 75c each
1568   Leather Head Band for all US Helmet Liners, new unused. $3.00
1811   Adjustable Neck Band for the Helmet Liner, adjustable in two directions for the Viet Nam issue. Used, very good. $1.50
1812   Non-adjustable Neck Band for Korean War and early Viet Nam issue Helmet Liner, new unused. .50¢ each

2287   US Army Russet Leather Head Band for the steel helmet Liner. Early WWII issue with the light kakhi cloth backing. Unused, excellent. $3.50

B. W. TRADING COMPANY   BOX 692   NEWARK, OHIO 43055   Page 23

Figure 18-4.   A page from the B.W. Trading Company catalog for military collectors.

read it is an education in itself. Figure 18-4 is a page from B. W. Trading Company, Box 6092, Newark, Ohio 43055, a catalog for military collectors. It is reproduced by a simple offset process in black and white and is much less expensive than the other catalogs I've discussed. Nevertheless, it brings in big sales for this firm. Figure 18-5 is a page from a catalog that contains literally hundreds of different pieces of cutlery from Arlene's, 3736 Nilswood Drive, P.O. Box 3096, Irving, Texas 75062. You can see from this catalog why someone who is interested in buying a knife would rather go here than to a retail store. Few retail merchants can stock such a wide variety of products profitably. The books shown in Figure 18-6 are just a few of more than 400 titles that my friend Melvin Powers offers through his company, the Wilshire Book Company, 12015 Sherman Road, North Hollywood, California 91605. Melvin started with but a single book on hypnotism and built his business to the point where more than one of his titles has sold more than one million copies, mostly through the mail. Interested in self-improvement through tapes? Figure 18-7 shows a catalog put out by Potentials Unlimited, 4808 Broadmoor S.E., Grand Rapids, Michigan 49508. Tapes on every conceivable subject are listed to help the buyer with personal problems and self-improvement. Each tape sells for about $10, which is a bargain to the customer, but a good-sized markup over cost and profitable to the company as well. Did you think you had to buy stationery from your local printer? Figure 18-8 is one page from a multicolored catalog put out by Stationery House, and, as you might expect, it contains nothing by stationery. Stationery House is at 1000 Florida Avenue, Hagerstown, Maryland 21740. In the market for office supplies? Figure 18-9 shows the Business and Institutional Furniture Company catalog. No matter where you are located, you can buy the supplies you need from the Business and Institutional Furniture Company, 611 Broadway, Milwaukee, Wisconsin 53202. Thousands of office supply items are listed, and orders from business have built this company to a multimillion-dollar enterprise. Is good health your bag? Take a look at Figure 18-10, which is a page from the U.S. Health Club, Inc., catalog of natural foods, vitamins, and health aids. This company is located in Yonkers, New York 10701. You can imagine how this catalog must supplement retail sales. Figure 18-11 is part of a very famous catalog from Edmund Scientific Co., 101 East Gloucester Pike, Barrington, New Jersey 08007. Edmund Scientific started with just a few pages some years ago and today lists more than 4000 scientific products for hobbyists, schools, and industry in this catalog, which contains more than 112 pages. Do you make presentations or give seminars? Figure 18-12 is from the unique catalog put out by Lansford Publishing Company, Inc., 1088 Lincoln Ave-

World's Most Versatile Knives

The official knives of the Swiss Army... Each one is made by Swiss craftsman under quality controlled conditions. The blades, hot drop-forged from the finest stainless steel Sweden has to offer.... are rustproof, tarnishproof, and honed to razor sharpness. On the brilliant red handles is the famous silver crest, the sign that identifies each knife as the real thing. They make a treasured gift any man or boy would be proud to own and show to his friends. They are superb!

NEW! the "President"

... the original Swiss army knife

The Hallmark of the original Swiss Army Knife

It's hard to believe that one knife can do so many different things, but seeing is believing. This super Swiss knife contains 15 different attachments that perform some 24 different operations. Everything from a toothpick to a magnifying glass. Weighs 5 ounces & is 3-1/2 inches long. What a gift for the man or boy who has everything! #346-PRESIDENT (Sold in stores for $45.00) OUR PRICE ... $39.95

the "Champion"

This superbly made beauty features 15 different attachments and they perform a total of 17 different operations. 3-1/2" closed. #146A-CHAMPION   Our Price - $33.00

the "Executive"

Only 2-1/4" long, this magnificient tiny executive knife features blade, file, scissors that really work, toothpick and tweezers! #623-EXECUTIVE as shown above ... $11.25 ea....2 For $21.00 #623A-Without tweezer & toothpick... $9.95 ea.....2 For $19.00

the "Traveler"

Ideal size for travel. Features 6 pieces that perform some 8 different operations. 3-14/". #134K-TRAVELER......$14.95 (2 for $27.95)

FILET FISH THE EASY WAY!

You'll filet fish like an expert with this superb filet knife. Designed by a nationally known fisherman, it features a thin, flexible 6" blade of the finest forged stainless steel. It's hollow ground on one side, and flat on the other for effortless cutting. The top of the blade has about one inch of razor sharp cutting edge at the point for gutting. Tough, durable laminated handle is not affected even by salt water. Used by experts. Leather sheath included. Form grip handle. #C-430 WORLD'S FINEST FILET KNIFE, made in Germany.. $15.95

HAND FORGED RAZOR SHARP STAG HANDLE CLOSE-OUT PRICE

Here's a super Solingen hunting knife at A SPECIAL PRICE! We purchased the entire stock from a famous German knife manufacturer. 4-3/4" razor sharp blade hand forged from the finest high carbon steel. Genuine stag handle. Made for that camper, hunter, fisherman, and hiker.... Just the right size for all purpose use. Genuine leather case that fits on belt. A real beauty, and the price is right. Sold in stores for $14.95. Sold at Arlene's for only $10.95. YOU SAVE $4.00! #420-SOLINGEN HUNTING KNIFE .... ; $13.50

Figure 18-5. A page from Arlene's catalog displaying Swiss army knives.

SECRET OF PERFECT PUTTING

$2

Here's the key to perfect putting and lower scores. You will learn never-before-told secrets to improve your game. You must start putting like a pro or you pay absolutely nothing. For the first time "the secret of perfect putting" has been a n a l y z e d . R e a d t h i s book. It's a must.

SECRET OF SECRETS

$4

Make the impossible dream come true. You have a sleeping giant within you who can do anything. U. S. Andersen tells you how you can awaken this giant— the potential power of your subconscious mind. Step by step, you are taught the mental magic that is the dynamic source of all success.

SEVEN DAYS TO FASTER READING

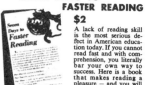

$2

A lack of reading skill is the most serious defect in American education today. If you cannot read fast and with comprehension, you literally bar your own way to success. Here is a book that makes reading a pleasure — and you will never read fast and effortlessly unless you enjoy it.

IMPOTENCE AND FRIGIDITY

$3

Dr. Edwin W. Hirsch presents his theories for the speedy diagnosis and treatment of impotence and frigidity. He rejects the psychoanalytic approach to such problems and contends that sexual activity is basically a reflex response. He uses actual case histories to illustrate his points. This book has helped many achieve a satisfying sexual relationship.

SEX WITHOUT GUILT

$2

Unquestionably, this is the most reassuring book on sex ever written, and it should be required reading for all those who are married or contemplate marriage. Dr. Albert Ellis, the world's foremost sexologist, has dedicated this book to the countless men and women who fight a losing battle against feelings of guilt.

SUCCESS-CYBERNETICS

$4

Cybernetics is a magic word today. It has changed American life more than anything else, and you can use it to change yours. This book will teach you how to program your brain with techniques and ideas that will allow it to operate at its highest capacity— and you will solve problems and attain your ambitions with scientific precision

10 DAYS TO A GREAT NEW LIFE **$3**

Get a pencil and some paper and write down all the goals you would like to achieve. That's all you have to do to begin taking giant steps on the road to success. Utilizing sound and proven psychological principles, William E. Edwards explains how this simple act sets in motion a goal-directed chain of events. You literally write your own ticket to your chosen destination.

THERAPY THRU HYPNOSIS **$3**

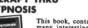

This book, containing many interesting case histories, describes in detail how hypnotism has been used to alleviate a variety of emotional problems such as: impotence, premature ejaculation, frigidity, enuresis, insomnia, nightmares, anxiety, obesity, alcoholism, depression, compulsions, shyness, menstrual pain and nervous headaches.

THINK AND GROW RICH

$3

The legendary Napoleon Hill, advisor to two presidents and a friend of the richest and most famous man of the 20th century, spent 20 years compiling the case histories and money-making methods contained in this book. No man ever utilized more success techniques, and the result was predictable. This book has become one of the best sellers of all time.

THREE MAGIC WORDS

$3

Just three words—and an idea so simple, so startling, so unique, it can change your life and make you happy as you have never been before. This unusual book by U. S. Andersen offers you the key to the inner peace and serenity that is locked within you.

THE SEXUALLY ADEQUATE FEMALE **$2**

A woman can be very passionate and still suffer from frigidity. Frank S. Caprio, M.D., an eminent psychiatrist, explains the physical and emotional causes of frigidity, how it can be cured, and how to achieve a satisfying sexual relationship. This book is a classic in the field of sexology.

THE SEXUALLY ADEQUATE MALE

$3

Impotence has become a disorder associated with modern civilization. The stress of everyday living can negatively permeate one's sexual activity. Frank S. Caprio, M.D., an eminent psychiatrist, explains the physical and emotional causes of impotence, how it can be cured, and how to achieve a satisfying sexual relationship. This book is a classic in the field of sexology.

YOU CAN ANALYZE HANDWRITING

$2

A practical tool for self-knowledge and personal power. A complete course in graphology, based on simplified methods. Includes scores of carefully - analyzed samples, emotion matcher, graphoguides and other aides. Carefully arranged for step-by-step progress.

YOUR SUBCONSCIOUS POWER

$3

The existence of the subconscious mind has been known for some time, but it is just beginning to be accorded the tremendous power it wields. Using its unlimited capacity to achieve anything the mind of man can imagine, there is literally nothing you cannot accomplish if you learn to utilize your subconscious.

YOUR THOUGHTS CAN CHANGE YOUR LIFE

$3

Do you feel cheated?... Yes, literally cheated... because people with less talent than you seem to achieve success, happiness and contentment with apparent ease? Successful people follow positive programs, and this book offers you step-by-step instructions which will lead you to your goals.

Practical stimulating books to help you achieve success, happiness and wealth.

Figure 18-6. Selections from the Wilshire Book Company catalog.

Potentials Unlimited Self-Hypnosis Tapes

The Educational Series

MEMORY

Everybody has a good memory. It is the nature of your subconscious mind to remember everything you've ever heard or learned. Yet, too often, by repeated unconscious self-suggestion, you cripple your memory facilities.

Rid yourself of both negative thoughts and the "I Can't Remember" syndrome. Play this tape; enjoy full use of your facilities of memory, recall and retention *now*.

Recommended Book: "How to Develop an Exceptional Memory," $4.00.

*SELF-HYPNOSIS CAN CHANGE YOUR LIFE

This is a self-hypnosis tape, containing complete instructions on how to give yourself suggestions, along with detailed procedures for entering into a state of self-hypnosis.

Using it, you will be guided into a state of hypnosis with key phrases and statements so you can utilize this level of mind any time you choose. When you've reached a good depth, there's a quiet space where you can enter your *own* suggestions into your mind. Then, after a bit, you're gently guided back to awakening consciousness. Repeated use of this tape will help you develop into a *good* self-hypnosis subject!

Recommended Books: "Self-Hypnosis, A Conditioned Response," $4.00; "Hypnosis and Self-Hypnosis," $3.00; "Hypnotism Made Practical," $3.00.

*GOOD STUDY HABITS

More concerned parents purchase this tape for their children than any other tape we offer. The results are amazing! Attitudes toward school and learning do a dramatic turnabout. Studying *can* be fun; learning *can* be enjoyable. Now is the time to bring out the hidden potential in your child.

Recommended Books: "Student's Guide to Better Grades," $2.00; "Exam Secrets," $2.00.

*FASTER READING

The average high school graduate reads under 300 words a minute. There are dozens of speed reading courses on the market that can increase this speed and comprehension to thousands of words per minute.

This tape contains the same techniques used in courses costing upwards of $300, and produces the same results for substantially less money!

Recommended Book: "Seven Days to Faster Reading," $3.00.

CONCENTRATION

Mind moves from one thought to another. Then another. And no sooner do you start on one thought than your attention is diverted to something else. Is your mind undisciplined and cluttered? Does it move so quickly from one thought to another that you exhaust easily? To discipline your mind, and bring thoughts into logical patterns, you must learn *concentration*.

This tape provides the key to logical, organized mental ability to concentrate on single thoughts, and to keep thinking of them until you're ready to discharge them from your mind. Before you discharge *this* thought, order this tape!

Recommended Book: "Practical Guide to Better Concentration," $2.00.

TAKING EXAMS

Do you feel a sinking feeling in your stomach when the tests are being passed out, and the instructions given? Do you freeze up during exams, even when you know the materials and you're well-prepared? Fear so paralyzes your mind that nothing flows. It doesn't have to happen again, ever. This tape will help you overcome your fear.

Recommended Book: "Exam Secrets," $2.00.

The Fear Series

When fears begin to control and grip our minds, we become a slave to them. Soon, they can grow to the point where they control our entire lives.

Each tape in this special Fear Series first unlocks the chains that bind your mind, places you into a deep state of relaxation, and then proceeds — through sophisticated visualizations and imagination techniques — to systematically remove fear from your life — and remove it forever.

Order individual fear tapes separately.

Overcoming the fear of:

**FLYING
WATER
DRIVING
DEATH
CROWDS
HEIGHTS
CLOSED-IN PLACES
FEAR OF FEARS**

Recommended Book: "How to Analyze and Overcome Your Fears," $3.95.

Potentials Unlimited

M80

Figure 18-7. From the Potentials Unlimited catalog of self-hypnosis tapes.

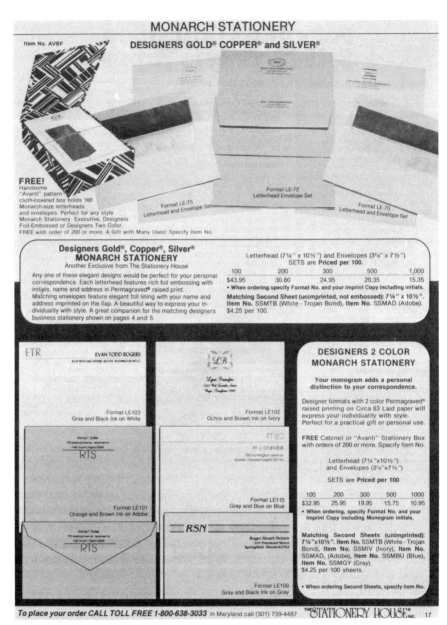

Figure 18-8. Letterheads available from The Stationery House.

408

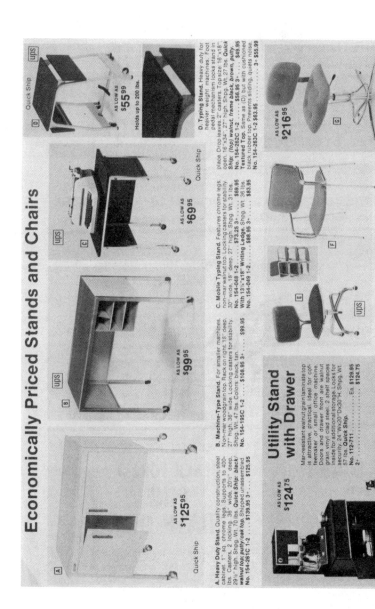

Figure 18-9. Page from the Business and Institutional Furniture Company catalog.

409

DOES DULL DRY SKIN AROUND YOUR EYES MAKE YOU LOOK OLDER?

Now make your eyes younger looking by softening and lubricating the dull dry skin around them!

This beauty cream has been specially formulated for safe, gentle yet effective use around the eyes. It is a combination of rich natural organic oils, including Almond, Avocado and Safflower oil. Rub .n to soften and protect the ultra sensitive areas around the eyes. Can be used before applying tints or shadow . . . and especially useful to keep this delicate skin soft and supple, even if you use no other eye makeup. Don't let dry dull skin around your eyes make you look older. Keep skin lubricated with this Eye Beauty Cream, by Orjene.

EYE BEAUTY CREAM

Catalog #290 **$3.50**

All Natural, Stimulative
QUEEN HELENE

MINT JULEP SHAMPOO

Concentrate
"A Drop or Two — More Lather for You!"

Only a drop or two of this highly concentrated Green Mint Julep Shampoo will lift off and rinse away modern day grit, smog dirt accumulations and loose flaky dandruff. May be diluted to make a full quart of superb all natural shampoo. Guaranteed Results!

4 oz. .....$1.50   16 oz. $4.50

Catalog #250

When husband and wife share the mutual satisfaction of physical fulfillment, love is enriched, new joy and happiness result. Here is a marital aid which has often been recommended by marriage counselors for fuller mutual contentment. Gives greater buoyancy, alignment and elevated support. Inflatable to desired height. Comes complete with washable zippered cover and instruction booklet.

SPECIAL PILLOW Cat. #771   **$7.95**

COMPLETE WITH SATIN COVER   Extra Zippered Covers available at $3 29 each . . . order Catalog #771-C

NEW!
From Queen Helene
FACE THERAPY

This pH-4 acid-balanced astringent face tonic restores the natural pH balance of your skin. Tightens pores, leaves an invisible film to protect your skin against bacteria. Imparts a tangy, stimulating, alive feeling.

Recommended to men as an aftershave lotion, and to women with sensitive skin, as a protective coating that restores the "acid mantle" of the skin, which soaps and detergents may wash away. Also recommended for teenagers. Try it! You'll be glad you found this simple skin treatment.

Catalog #387 8 oz. **$2.19**

QUEEN HELENE

BALSAM
PERU
One Minute Hair Conditioner

THE FAVORITE IN THE BEAUTY SHOP
NOW AVAILABLE FOR HOME USE

For the first time you can use this superb product at home. Guaranteed to restore the natural acid-alkali balance to fine, damaged, over-processed hair. Adds EXTRA STYLE-HOLDING POWER to hair. Makes combing easier. Gives a natural healthy sheen plus extra body and resiliency to hair. Speeds up care for wigs and hair pieces either human hair or synthetic. . . . Guaranteed Results!

CATALOG #270
4 oz. ....$1.50 16 oz. $4.50

44

QUEEN HELENE

BLACK FOREST
PINE BATH OIL

Just add a spoonful of fragrant PINE BATH OIL to your bath water, and settle down into a relaxing, refreshing tub. Let cares be soothed away like magic. A concentrate of pure vegetable oils blended with imported pine needle extract (with chlorophyll) from the Black Forest of Europe. You'll be amazed how soft your skin will look. One bottle good for over 20 luxurious baths. Try a bottle today . . . you'll love it!

CATALOG #271
4 oz. bottle...... **$1.50**

Figure 18-10. Items available from U.S. Health Club, Inc., catalog.

410

Metric Triple Balance is designed for speed and ease of operation. Sensitive, sturdy and parallax free, this balance is magnetically damped (two permanent alnico magnets mounted at the end post to provide friction-free damping) and insensitive to out-of-level conditions. An end-reading. Attachment weights, available as an accessory, fit conveniently in the balance base. Beams: 0-500g; 0-100g; 0-10g. Sensitivity: 0.1g. Capacity: 610g, without attachment weights; 2610g, with attachment weights. Ideal for field work. 6" x 6" x 18". Stainless steel platform.

Triple Beam Balance   K71,695 $89.95

Weigh Either Grams Or Ounces By The Flip Of A Switch. The accurate weight is displayed by the LCD digital display and it can be in either ounces or grams by the flip of the switch. The weighing tray is made of easy to clean plastic and measures 6⅛" x 4½". Has a capacity of 70 oz. or 1999 grams. Uses a 9V battery (not included) and there's an AC adapter plug (adapter not included). A postage/calorie/carbohydrate chart is included.

Digital Postal Scale   K33,066 $89.95
AC/Adapter   K33,135   11.99

Read Angles And True Vertical Levels Instantly. Inclinometer replaces bulky levels. Make precision readings to 90" in any quadrant easily. Simply place on the surface to be checked. Sensitive to ½ of 1°. Chip-proof plastic housing is unaffected by the heat or cold. Angle and grade chart printed on back, 3" edge. Attaches magnetically to square. Maintenance-free.

Inclinometer   K33,417 $13.95

WEIGH AND MEASURE
ACCURATELY WITH THESE IDEAS

English Micrometer Caliper Has Precision Carbide Faces. Measures 0 to 1 inch with accuracy of 0.0001 inch. Parallelism to 0.005 inches. Vernier scale on the barrel is numbered every 0.0001 inch. The thimble scale is in thousands is numbered every 5. Adjustment nut, locking clamp and case.

Micrometer Caliper   K60,524 $44.95

Economy Gram And Ounce Scale. A quality scale at a price you can afford! Comes with a 4 inch tray & stands 6 inches tall. Calibrated 0-16 oz. in 0.5 oz. subdivisions & 0-500 grams in 10 gram divisions.

Economy Gram And Ounce Scale
     K90,053 $17.95

Mix And Measure With These Handy Disposable Plastic Cups. Convenient and sanitary. Cups are available in 1 oz. and 6 oz. sizes. Marked in both English and metric measurements. Smooth beaded, non-spill pouring lip.

1 oz. (100 cups)	K60,365	$5.50
1 oz. (4 pkg. or more)	Each	5.00
6 oz. (100 cups)	K70,625	17.50
6 oz. (4 pkg. or more)	Each	15.50

A High Quality Instrument At An Affordable Price! Balance comes complete with two weight sets: Avoirdupois 1/16, ⅛, ¼, 1 and 2 ounce. Metric: 2, 5, 10, 20 and 50 grams. Has a 0.5 gram sensitivity. Balance measures 10½" x 3" x 4½".

Double Pan   K71,168 $54.95

Ohaus Dial-O-Gram 1600 Single Pan Balance. Three weights are easily attached to the balance. It has a 2610 gram capacity with a 10 gram dial. Balance comes complete with a patented Ohaus tare poise-internally threaded with a flat spring. This precision instrument is accurate even when it's not leveled! Has a 0.1 gram sensitivity. 19" x 7" x 8".

Single Pan Balance   K72,466 $169.95

Economy Vernier Caliper Features Inside And Outside Jaws. Comes complete with depth gauge and roller adjustment. It is graduated 1/16 inch to 5 inches and 1 millimeter to 120 millimeter. An accurate measuring instrument that reads to 1/128 inch and 0.1 millimeter.

Economy Vernier Caliper
     K40,598 $8.95

Inexpensive Student English Micrometer. This finely constructed measuring instrument is the perfect micrometer for the beginner. Reads to .001". Adjustable anvil. Capacity 0-1". Accuracy .001.

Student Micrometer   K60,666 $14.95

Figure 18-11. Some products sold through the Edmund Scientific Co. catalog.

Break-Even Analysis

Designed to present an important tool in pricing, estimating profit and loss potential of products and operations, determining the impact of financial leverage, and other areas. Transparencies include plotting the cost functions, completing the break-even chart, the mathematical model, calculating the break-even point, different ways of plotting the same break-even chart, how the break-even point changes with selling price, break-even charts with realistic cost functions, break-even charts with alternate base lines, and comparing firms with varied cost structures.

9 transparencies, teacher guide.
W235TJK $125.95

Macro-Economics

Popular series designed to provide the instructor with diagrams necessary to explain macro-economics. Titles include: propensity to consume, disposable income and personal consumption, saving and investment, investment and consumption; inflationary and deflationary gaps; effect of an increase in savings; effect of an increase in investment; effect of an increase in government spending; effect of a tax cut.

10 transparencies.
T5000JK $89.95

Macro-Economics Wall Charts

Charts include the same information as Macro-Economics overhead transparencies. Each chart is printed on washable plastic printing paper and measures 35 by 45 inches.

10 lecture charts.
5000JK $135.95

Cost and Revenue

Set includes: schedule of firm's costs; cost curves for the firm; schedule of best profit for firm under competition; best profit for individual firm under competition; types of competition; schedule of marginal revenue; marginal revenue curves; schedule of marginal cost curves; equilibrium under monopoly; equilibrium under perfect competition.

12 transparencies.
T4000JK $89.95

Cost and Revenue Wall Charts

Charts include the same information as Cost and Revenue overhead transparencies. Each chart is printed on washable plastic printing paper and measures 35 by 45 inches.

12 lecture charts.
4000JK $135.95

Supply and Demand

Titles include: demand curve and demand schedule; individual supply curve and aggregate demand; the supply curve and supply schedule; individual supply and aggregate supply; interaction of supply and demand; demand shift, supply shift; elasticity of demand; long-run equilibrium.

10 transparencies.
T3000JK $89.95

Supply and Demand Wall Charts

Charts include the same information as Supply and Demand overhead transparencies. Each chart is printed on washable plastic printing paper and measures 35 by 45 inches.

10 lecture charts.
3000JK $135.95

Money and Banking

Based on the latest data, transparencies present the federal reserve system; federal reserve districts; commercial banks and branches; credit policy; creation of bank deposits; factors of money supply; nation's money supply; income velocity of money; and money supply as a percent of GNP. Includes numerous booklets and charts.

15 transparencies, teacher guide.
T1005JK $195.95

Principles and Applications of Cost-Benefit Analysis

Surveys the nature, principles, approaches, and selected applications of cost-benefit analysis.

27 transparencies, teacher guide, resource materials.
1112JK $295.95

Return on Investment: A Short Course

Deals with the nature and applications of one of the most important business/financial concepts, including discussion of the following topics: ROI versus risk, balance sheet, income statement, analyzing ROI, improving ROI, payback, proceeds per dollar invested, time value of money, net present value, internal rate of return, and practice problems.

24 transparencies, lecture notes, supplementary booklets, article reprints.
1583JK $309.95

Figure 18-12. Transparencies from the Lansford Publishing Company catalog.

nue, P.O. Box 8711, San Jose, California 95155. This catalog contains hundreds of audiovisual products and transparencies on every conceivable subject. Lansford sells to both individual presenters and major corporations and universities around the world. Figure 18-13 shows a catalog put out by the U.S. Government Printing Office, Washington, D.C. 20402, to sell books. Yes, even Uncle Sam is selling by catalogs! Are you a sportsman? Take a look at Figure 18-14 from Cabela's, 812 13th Avenue, Sidney, Nebraska 69160. This catalog features everything for the sportsman and every item is displayed in color. You've heard about Henniker's, founded by Gerardo Joffe, and in Figure 18-15 is a page of this full-color catalog of quality items. Henniker's is now located at 12755 State Highway 55, Minneapolis, Minnesota 55441. Figure 18-16 is perhaps the most fabulous of all: Neiman-Marcus of Dallas, Texas 75221. The page shown is in full color and is, of course, printed on the highest-quality glossy paper available. If you read closely, you will see the items shown start at a low of $3900 and go all the way up to $24,000. And you thought you couldn't sell high-priced items by mail!

In the tradition of Sunset House, Figure 18-17 shows a page from another company selling relatively low-priced items to hundreds of thousands of customers. This is from Hannover House, Hannover, Pennsylvania 17331. Figure 18-18 is from Campmor, 810 Route 17 North, P.O. Box 999, Daramus, New Jersey 07652. Like Cabela's in Figure 18-14, Campmor sells to sportsmen. But unlike Cabela's, its 88-page catalog is printed in two colors with line drawings instead of photographs. Still, this lower-cost catalog doesn't stop Campmor from selling successfully to its customers. You can even buy flowers through catalogs, as the Spring Hill Nurseries catalog, from 100 West Elm Street, Tipp City, Ohio, 45371, demonstrates in Figure 18-19. Or if you're hungry, consider these pages: from the House of Almonds, P.O. Box 11125, Bakersfield, California 93389 (Figure 18-20); from Pfaelzer's 4501 West District Boulevard, Chicago, Illinois 60632 (Figure 18-21); or from Figi's, Inc., Marshfield, Wisconsin 54449 (Figure 18-22). If you need tools of any type, consult the catalog put out by J. Cheaps and Sons, Cheaps Pond Par, Box 7199, Warrensville, Ohio 44128, in Figure 18-23. Interested in expensive jewelry? Richard Thalheimer at Sharper Image now puts out several specialized catalogs in addition to his more general one. The page shown in Figure 18-24 is from one of these catalogs that Sharper Image publishes from 406 Jackson Street, San Francisco, California 94111. Crafts are certainly sold by mail and by catalog, as demonstrated in Figure 18-25, which is from the Craft Basket, Colchester, Connecticut 06415.

Now let's look at how you can become a success in catalog selling.

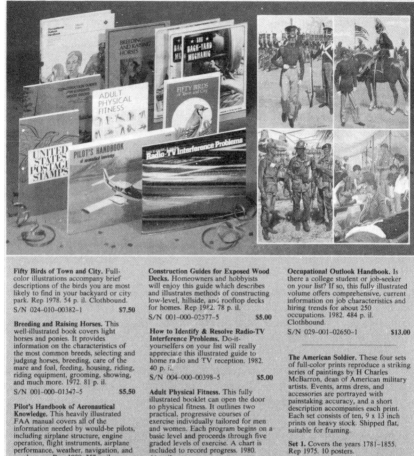

Fifty Birds of Town and City. Full-color illustrations accompany brief descriptions of the birds you are most likely to find in your backyard or city park. Rep 1978. 54 p. il. Clothbound.
S/N 024-010-00382-1   **$7.50**

Breeding and Raising Horses. This well-illustrated book covers light horses and ponies. It provides information on the characteristics of the most common breeds, selecting and judging horses, breeding, care of the mare and foal, feeding, housing, riding, riding equipment, grooming, showing, and much more. Rev 1980. 81 p. il.
S/N 001-000-01347-5   **$5.50**

Pilot's Handbook of Aeronautical Knowledge. This heavily illustrated FAA manual covers all of the information needed by would-be pilots, including airplane structure, engine operation, flight instruments, airplane performance, weather, navigation, and much more. Rev 1980. 257 p. il.
S/N 050-011-00077-1   **$10.00**

The Back-Yard Mechanic Set. These three volumes can help even a novice mechanic with the routine maintenance and repair chores which are part of auto ownership. Everything from changing the oil to basic dent removal is illustrated with step-by-step instructions. All three volumes are included in this money-saving set, or you may order them individually in the **Consumer Aids** section of this catalog.
S/N 008-070-00475-5   **$9.50**

Construction Guides for Exposed Wood Decks. Homeowners and hobbyists will enjoy this guide which describes and illustrates methods of constructing low-level, hillside, and rooftop decks for homes. Rep 1982. 78 p. il.
S/N 001-000-02577-5   **$5.00**

How to Identify & Resolve Radio-TV Interference Problems. Do-it-yourselfers on your list will really appreciate this illustrated guide to home radio and TV reception. 1982. 40 p. il.
S/N 004-000-00398-5   **$5.00**

Adult Physical Fitness. This fully illustrated booklet can open the door to physical fitness. It outlines two practical, progressive courses of exercise individually tailored for men and women. Each program begins on a basic level and proceeds through five graded levels of exercise. A chart is included to record progress. 1980. 64 p. il.
S/N 040-000-00026-7   **$4.50**

United States Postage Stamps Set. This specially priced collection includes the basic postage stamps manual and all supplements issued to date. It illustrates and describes all U.S. postage and special service stamps issued through 1978. Looseleaf and punched for a three-ring binder. Individual components of the set are sold separately in the **Hobbies** section of this catalog.
S/N 039-000-00267-1   **$21.00**

Occupational Outlook Handbook. Is there a college student or job-seeker on your list? If so, this fully illustrated volume offers comprehensive, current information on job characteristics and hiring trends for about 250 occupations. 1982. 484 p. il. Clothbound.
S/N 029-001-02650-1   **$13.00**

The American Soldier. These four sets of full-color prints reproduce a striking series of paintings by H Charles McBarron, dean of American military artists. Events, arms dress, and accessories are portrayed with painstaking accuracy, and a short description accompanies each print. Each set consists of ten, 9 x 13 inch prints on heavy stock. Shipped flat, suitable for framing.

Set 1. Covers the years 1781-1855. Rep 1975. 10 posters.
S/N 008-020-00226-7   **$6.00**

Set 2. Covers 1863-1963. Rep 1975. 10 posters.
S/N 008-020-00227-5   **$6.00**

Set 3. From 1775-1965, filling in the gaps left in the first two sets. Rep 1975. 10 posters.
S/N 008-020-00225-9   **$6.00**

Set 4. Depicts peacetime activities, 1776-1975. 1978. 10 posters.
S/N 008-020-00760-9   **$6.00**

Figure 18-13. Catalog of books from the U.S. Government Printing Office.

Figure 18-14. A page from Cabela's sportswear catalog.

Figure 18-15. Items from Henniker's catalog.

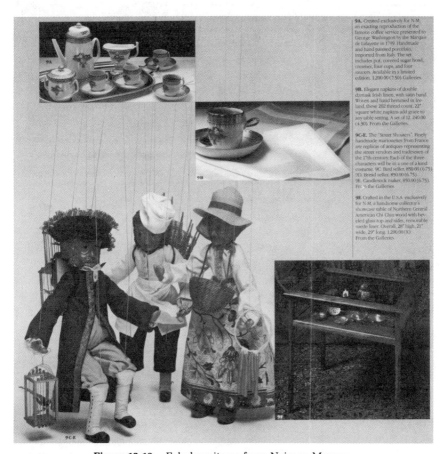

9A. Created exclusively for N-M, an exacting reproduction of the famous coffee service presented to George Washington by the Marquis de Lafayette in 1709. Handmade and hand painted porcelain, imported from Italy. The set includes pot, covered sugar bowl, creamer, four cups, and four saucers. Available in a limited edition. 1,200.00 (7.50) Galleries.

9B. Elegant napkins of double damask Irish linen, with satin band. Woven and hand hemmed in Ireland, these 202 thread count, 22" square white napkins add grace to any table setting. A set of 12, 240.00 (4.50). From the Galleries.

9C-E. The "Street Shouters". Finely handmade marionettes from France are replicas of antiques representing the street vendors and tradesmen of the 17th century. Each of the three characters will be in a one of a kind costume. 9C. Bird seller, 850.00 (6.75). 9D. Bread seller, 850.00 (6.75). 9E. Candlestick maker, 850.00 (6.75). From the Galleries.

9F. Crafted in the U.S.A. exclusively for N-M, a handsome collector's showcase table of Northern Central American Chi Chin wood with beveled glass top and sides, removable suede liner. Overall, 28" high, 21" wide, 29" long. 1,200.00 (X) From the Galleries

Figure 18-16. Fabulous items from Neiman-Marcus.

417

UNICORN IN FRAMED GLASS
Legendary medieval creature (said to bring you good fortune) against a setting sun in a field of flowers. Lead frame. 10½x4½".
Unicorn Plaque;
E539148 . . . . $2.99

ADJUSTABLE CLIP-ON BEDLAMP
For that wonderful pastime, reading in bed! Bracket adjusts to clamp right onto your headboard, bulb swivels a full 360° for maximum comfort. Styrene, incl. on/off, 6' cord, 25W bulb.
E524165—Clip-on Lamp . . . . . ~~$14.99~~
SALE $9.88

LEATHER PATCHWORK HANDBAG
can be dressed up or down. Roomy shoulder bag can shed strap, change to foldover clutch or metal handle pocketbook. Fully lined, has a deep outside pocket 11½x11".
E470385—Leather Bag . . . . . ~~$9.99~~
SALE $8.88

SPECTACULAR VALUE!

Digital quartz watch worth 4 times this amount!

• Stylish slender lines, elegant yet sporty
• Precision crafted for accurate readout of hour, minute, seconds, day, date
• Color-flaired for contemporary fashions

It's about time the digital quartz watch acquired the fashion impact discerning people demand! Ours is sleek, simply sophisticated, priced so low you can order more than one! Tells hour, minute, seconds, day and date. Specify navy, red, black, brown or beige.
Digital Quartz Watch;
E848606B . . . . Each $4.88; 2 for $9.00

Perfect TV View . . . From Any Angle!

HANDSOME SOLID BRASS "KEY" RACK
A key idea when it comes to keeping your daily assortment of keys in a memorable and handy spot. This gleaming brass beauty has four hooks to accommodate all the keys members of your household want to dangle from it. So attractive it looks great anywhere. 4½x1½" h.
E552562—Key Rack $1.99

VIEWING COMFORT "AS THE TABLE TURNS"
Fantastic idea! A TV lazy susan for all-angle viewing, from anywhere in the room. No more straining to shift so-called portables. Ball bearing glides turn the "susan" at a touch while giving a solid base for your TV and protection for your furniture. Solid hardwood with fruitwood finish, decorative scalloped edges. 21x12x¾".
E541326—TV Lazy Susan . . . . . . ~~$19.99;~~ SALE $17.88 **13**

Figure 18-17. A page from the Hannover House catalog.

418

CARIBOU MOUNTAINEERING CRICKET

Cricket day pack features large rectangular main compartment, zipper enclosed outside pocket, full length nylon coil two-way zipper with padded shoulder strap. main compartment measures 14" x 9" x 6". Material is 8 oz., 420 denier super k-kote. Nylon pack cloth. wt 12 oz. Cu. in. 1128. Colors: Burgundy, Royal, Red.

No. 171766 $15.99

LITTLE SPRUCE CHILDS DAY PACK

Jr. Tear Drop Pack made of a durable oxford nylon pack ideal for active children. Comfortable to wear while bicycling, skiing or hiking. nylon coil self repairing zippers. Water resistant coating. Capacity: 400 cu. in. Size: 13" x 8" x 3½". Wt. 3.5 oz.

No. 170147 $6.50

COLLEGIATE DAY PACK

Constructed or durable, heavy duty waterproof Cordura nylon, the Collegiate loads through the front panel, which opens on 3 sides, allowing complete access to the inside. Front panel zippered pocket has an organizer for student needs consisting of 3 pen pockets, comb pocket, calculator pocket, notepad pocket, velcro closed money pocket, and zippered envelope pocket for pencils, keys, change and assorted small items. Leather reinforced padded adjustable shoulder straps. Carry-Hang loop at top. 6" deep x 13" wide x 16" high. Weigth: 15.5 oz. Volume: 1248 cubic inches. Color: Navy and Grey.

No. 170425 $19.99

CHILD'S SCHOOL PACK

Same as collegiate day pack except designed for the 5-12 year old age group. Constructed of durable waterproof pack cloth nylon. Adjustable padded shoulder straps. Carry-hang loop at top. 4" deep x 11" wide x 13½" high. Weight: 6.5 oz. Volume: 594. cubic inches. Color: Royal Blue.

No. 170400 $13.99

THE MOHAWK WITH THE ULTRA PAD SYSTEM

Mohawk converts in seconds from a climbing sack to a weekend backpack. The conversion is accomplished through the use of side pockets and a built in extender stuff sack that is large enough for a winter sleeping bag. In use the stuff sack is held tightly in place by an adjustable floating hood. Top stabilizer straps attach to the hood and pull the stuff sack forward for better balance.

The Mohawk now comes equipped with the Ultra-pad load support system. The Ultra-pad is a cloth covered foam pad with P.V.C. stiffeners that is attached to the backwall of the pack. Held securely in place by Velcro tabs, it supports heavy loads quite comfortably, but it is easily removed to double as a warm seat on a cold belay ledge or in a snowy field. In an emergency the pad can be used to improvise a splint. Comes with 9 lashing points and ice axe loop. Cu. In 2000-4500. Side pockets 10"x6"x4". Color: Navy.

No. 181301 $89.90

WILDERNESS EXPERIENCE

TRAVEL ARETE

Same high quality design as Arete with three important differences. Side mounted hand grip allows pack to be carried like a suitcase. Entire back opens via a double pull YKK coil zipper revealing internal storage area for shoulder strap. Top and bottom "D" rings allow shoulder strap to be connected providing an extremely useful, 3 way system either as an internal frame, suitcase or sling it over the shoulder like a duffle. Size 26"x14"x8". Wt. 4 lbs. 15 oz. Cu. In. 4310.

181299 $119.00

JANSPORT TRAVEL GREAT ESCAPE 1 AND 2

Made of 11-ounce cordura nylon with a tough, tear-resistant Ballistic Cloth bottom, the Great Escape is a backpack and suitcase in one package. The internal parallel stayes provide support, while internal compression straps make it easy to balance the contents. The full-panel-access zipper locks for extra security. The padded waist belt stows away and the shoulder pads can be zipped out of the way so the pack can be carried as a suitcase, using either the sturdy shoulder strap on the side or the leather-reinforced handle at the top. And the outside pockets provide plenty of space for your passport and other small items. With new passport pocket.

Great Escape: Weights: 3 lbs., 14 oz., Total Cu. In.: 3948, Colors: Burgundy, Grey, Navy

No. 184185 Great Escape I $79.00

Great Escape II—For Ladies or Smaller Individuals

No. 184176 - 3,660 Cu.In. $78.00

SUPER VALUE

ONLY $65.00

CAMPMOR TRAVEL PACK

The ultimate value in a travel pack. Large main compartment with interior compression straps measuring 24"x14"x8", two exterior front pockets measuring; top 10½"x10½"x 2.5", bottom 10½"x6½"x2½", two side pockets measures 12"x5½"x3". Travel Pack has two exterior front compression straps with Fastex quick release buckles; four urethane lash tabs; nylon webbinghaul loop zips away with shoulder straps. Back suspension contours snugly to the back of hips. Padded shoulder straps zip out of sight and padded waist belt with Fastex quick release buckle that stuffs away. Carrying handle on side pocket with detachable shoulder strap. Made from 11 oz. coated cordura and ballistics bottom. Color: Navy or Smoke. Cu. in 3,700. Wt. 3 lbs. 2 oz.

No.185274 $65.00

Figure 18-18. The coupon catalog of items for sportmen.

419

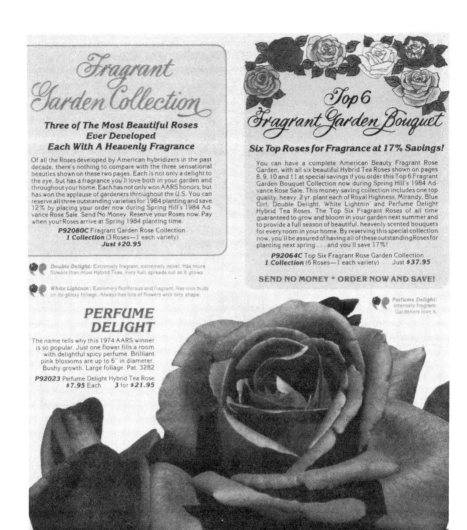

Figure 18-19.   Flowers from the Spring Hill Nurseries catalog.

420

D Six 6.5 oz. tins of selected almonds, **roasted salted, blanched roasted salted, cheese, hickory smoke, barbecue and ranchero** - a treasure of flavor - each tin comes with a resealable lid and is hand packed in a handsome gift box. You will delight anyone who receives this gift.

Order Gift No. F3-46
$18.95 + $1.90 Del. Chg.

Case Price · Save $5.95

Four Flavor Treasures at this special by-the-case price.

Order Gift No. F3-905
$70.95 + $6.50 Del. Chg.

D
Flavor Treasure

— over the years certain sizes and combinations seem to hold their popularity. The tinned gifts listed here are in that category. The resealable lids help maintain freshness.

E **Half Case** (not pictured) Half as many bags as below (one each instead of two of the six flavors.)

Order Gift No. F3-908 $29.95 + $2.30 Del Chg.

Buy 12 pounds and save $3.05.

Twelve pounds of crunchy, tasty flavored almonds. Two one pound bags each of roasted salted, blanched roasted salted, hickory smoke, barbecue, cheese and ranchero flavored almonds. Each bag is topped with a red ribbon to create great "extra gifts" for the holidays.

Order Gift No. F3-907 $54.95 + $6.50 Del Chg.

E **Case Variety**

F **Wicker Bonanza**

F Eight ounces each of four of our all time favorite flavored almonds: cheese, hickory smoke, roasted salted, blanched roasted salted in a handsome four compartmented handwoven wicker tray as an added value!

Order Gift No. F3-906 $16.95 + $1.65 Del Chg.

Figure 18-20. From the House of Almonds.

421

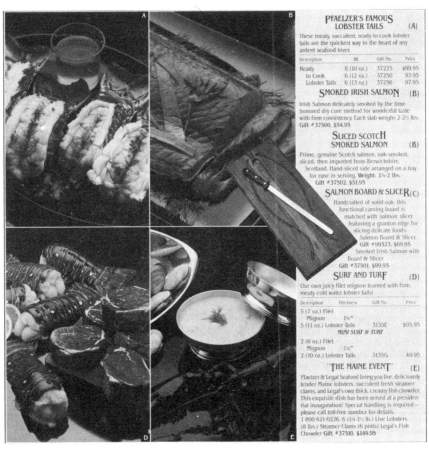

Figure 18-21. Food from Pfaelzer's.

Paradise Cake
GIFT 169 $8.50

A "slice of Hawaiian Paradise"—and you will believe it when you sample this delightful blend of Macadamia Nuts, baked with the juicy chunks of Pineapple. Everyone on your gift list will be thrilled to receive this 1¼ lb. Macadamia Nut Pineapple Loaf. Don't forget to include yourself on the top of the list.

AVAILABLE
YEAR 'ROUND

GIFT BOXED
SHIPPED TO ONE ADDRESS

Gift **471** (Case of Four)
$28.95........Save **$5.05**

Gift **473** (Case of Eight)
$54.95........Save **$13.05**

"I'm writing to express total gratitude and to compliment you on your very prompt service."
Mrs. William Kiger
Fillmore, IN

Rum Crunch Cake
GIFT 332 $11.95

Bakery-fresh, moist and delicious! Rum Crunch Cake is one of our tastiest offers ever. A delicate hint of rum flavors this deliciously-moist sponge cake specialty. For a crowning flavor, it's covered with the sweetest, crunchiest mixture of toasted coconut, chopped nuts, butter and sugar. The irresistible flavor and moistness of this cake makes it a gift that's sure to please. There's a full two and a half pounds to eat and enjoy. Available October thru April.

GIFT BOXED
SHIPPED TO ONE ADDRESS

Gift **377** (Case of Four)
$44.95........Save **$2.85**

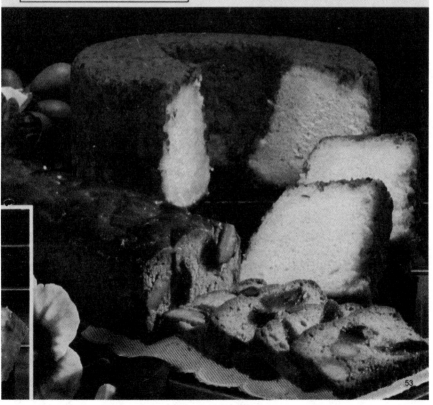

Figure 18-22. Cake from the Figi's Inc., catalog.

Make Your Own Signs With This Router Template Set

We offer two complete sets of letter and numeral templates. One set makes 1½"; the other, 2½" tall figures. The adjustable template clamp is self-aligning and the system is self-spacing for professional results.

These templates need 7/16" and 5/8" diameter guide bushings, available in our bushing kit below. For an interesting variety of results, use ¼" to ½" cove, straight cut or V-groove bits with your router.

55442 - Router Template Set .. **$21.95**
55467 - Template Set + Edge/Bushing
    Kit **(Save $3.90)** **$35.00**

Edging And Bushing Kit For Your Router

Expand the uses of your router. With our kit, you can now trim laminates and edge irregular surfaces. And you'll use the kit's bushings with the letter template set above, as well as with dovetail jigs, mortising templates and other router accessories.

Kit includes a universal base plate to let you fit the roller edge guide and bushings to your router and three bushings: 9/16, 7/16 and 5/8".

55459 - Edging/Bushing Kit .. **$16.95**
55467 - Edging/Bushing Kit +
    Template Set
    (Save $3.90) **$35.00**

6 Outlet Power Bar Convenient And Safe

The six 3-prong outlets will take a 15 amp, 1875 watt load. Circuit breaker stops overload. On-off switch and pilot light to tell you whether power is on, are extra safety features. 6', 3 wire (14 AWG) jacketed cord with molded grounding plug. UL listed.

53181 - 6 Outlet Bar **$24.95**
Buy 2 or more (Save $1 ea.) .... **$23.95 ea.**

Figure 18-23. Tools found in J. Cheaps and Sons catalog.

424

Figure 18-24. Jewelry from the Sharper Image catalog.

Figure 18-25. Crafts by mail from the Craft Basket catalog.

426

MERCHANDISE SELECTION

As I told you earlier in this book, selection of your products for mail order is always very important. However, in the product selection for a catalog, there are other factors you must consider. For one thing, all of your products should have something in common. You should segment the products according to some common factor that appeals to your customers. If you look at the catalog examples mentioned earlier, you will see, in every case, that the catalog has some common theme running through it. Some of these examples are obvious. Arlene's knife catalog carries only knives and similar items. The Edmund Scientific catalog carries items that appeal to the curious lay person, and to the professional. The International Entrepreneurs Association small business catalog appeals to people who are or wish to become entrepreneurs. In every case, the catalogs' common theme is the keynote of product selection for the catalog.

You must still look to your competition to see what's going on in the marketplace and to maximize your chances of success. To do this in the catalog business, you should get the catalog of every possible competitor. Certain items will be found in more than one catalog, an indication that the item is more successful and has a greater chance of success in your catalog as well.

Once you have decided on certain of these products because of their popularity, you must get the manufacturer's name and address. There are several ways you can approach this problem. First, you must ascertain whether the product is manufactured here or abroad, and if it is manufactured abroad, in what country. Usually the simplest and most direct method is simply to buy one of the products yourself and examine it to find out its source. If it's from the United States, start with a directory like the *Thomas Register of Manufacturers*, mentioned earlier. If it's a foreign product, you might consult some of the directories we talked about earlier such as *Hong Kong Enterprises, Made in Europe,* or others. Or, you could take the product directly to a commercial attaché at the consulate or embassy of the country from which the product originated. Once you locate the company that manufactured the product, you should write to ask for information as to the quantity discount. And here we deviate from the standard guideline of a 300 to 400% markup. You probably will not be able to get it. Also, if the product is already popular and carried by several different mail order firms, you will be unlikely to get the exclusive right to sell the product unless you can guarantee sales larger than those of all of your competitors combined. Therefore, look for a discount of about 50% from your selling price, larger for greater quantities. You can also find out about drop-shipping, which may be acceptable for your catalog sales where it cannot be if you have a single product or very limited product line. Clearly you will want to know about quantities on hand, how quickly your order can be filled, and how quickly larger repeat orders can be filled.

You cannot be successful by offering only products obtainable from other mail order houses or through other sources, so many of your products should be unique, and you should try to get exclusives on them. The basic idea here is this: If you have certain products that can be obtained only from your catalogs, the customers buying these products and wanting to buy other products that are available elsewhere will buy these other products from you, since they are already buying from you.

GROWING INTO SUCCESS

Most successful catalog operations *grow* into success—sometimes slowly, sometimes more quickly, but it is always a growing process. It is unwise to try to be a giant catalog house right away. It is better to pattern your success after such successes as Len Carlson's or Joe Sugarman's. On the other hand, people like Roger Horchow have made it into the instant big-dollar catalog business. However, remember that Roger Horchow could afford to—*and did*—lose $2 million in his first year of operation. Gerardo Joffe recommends the rule of thumb that you should have at least 25,000 of your own customers before you attempt to publish a real, honest-to-goodness catalog. My own feeling is that you can get into a catalog much earlier, depending upon your definition of a catalog and remembering that a catalog can also be a simple listing and description printed by off-set of the various items in your product line.

COST CONTROL

You cannot have a profitable catalog if you continue to carry products that are not profitable to you. Therefore, you must keep constant track of which products are selling well and which are not. You eliminate those that are not selling and continue to experiment with new products. Just as with classified, space, or other types of advertising, you can figure out a breakeven for a particular product in your own catalog. Your costs would include the cost of preparing the art, the printing, mailing, paper, and so forth. If the product doesn't do better than break even, either drop the product or try to change the copy, graphics, or positioning to improve the results. There is no trick here. You simply track the results in your catalog and drop or change those that do not do well.

COPY AND GRAPHICS

As with other types of advertising and promotions that you use, copy and graphics are extremely important in catalogs; they count as much as product selection in any equation that yields success. Depending on how fancy a catalog you are going to produce and whether you are going to put the catalog together by yourself or have a company that is experienced in this type of work put it together for you, the price you pay will vary widely. However, there are many factors that enter in here that you must consider. For example, on one hand you may find that the stock, glossy photographs supplied by the manufacturer are totally unsuitable for a catalog operation. Why is this? For one thing, this photograph is taken of the product only; it may not illustrate the particular appeal that you decide to make clear to your customer. Also, you're displaying more than this one single product in your catalog, and all these different products must fit together to support your central theme. With the many different styles of photography, different viewpoints, and so forth that may be illustrated in the different photographs supplied by various manufacturers, you may end up with a hodgepodge of illustrations that will do anything but give your catalog the unified support of a single theme. On the other hand, for some products this differing photography will not disrupt your theme and not only can you use the manufacturer's photographs, but you can integrate them with your own and still be effective in selling. For some types of catalog you can do your own work and not hurt sales. An example is in Figure 18-4, B.W. Trading Company's catalog of military collector's items. These items, such as military helmets, equipment, and surplus, are bought in large quantities both here and in Europe, and generally no photographs are supplied. The photographs in this catalog do not represent the ultimate in art photography, but this has relatively little effect on the sales of these products, since most of the customers either recognize the product they are buying or need only to be reminded through an illustration or a simple photograph what the product looks like. As a guideline, if you have no prior experience, look at what your competition is doing. If the competition isn't using an expensive catalog, you probably don't need one either. Note also that the copy for a catalog is usually much more limited than that for a space advertisement unless the item is relatively expensive and you intend to spend much more selling space on it. An example is JS&A's electronics catalog. The basic principles of copywriting still apply here. In fact, many very famous copywriters such as Maxwell Sackheim got their start in writing copy for catalogs such as Sears and Roebuck.

COLOR VERSUS BLACK AND WHITE

Again, we have the trade-off between color and black and white. Generally color will sell better than black and white, but the big question is whether the additional costs bring in more profits. There is no universal answer to this question. In fact, for some items, color may have no effect on the number of items ordered. My advice here is to go slowly and consider your product carefully. Again, take a look at the competition. If none of your competition is using color, there is probably a good reason. The reverse is also true. So as a starting point, you may use the competition as a guide. Once you are established, you can begin to experiment. Full color is almost required for certain types of product, such as clothing, food, home furnishings, or jewelry. For other types of product, you can test after you start making money, are established, and can afford to experiment.

THE ORDER FORM, ONE OF THE MOST
IMPORTANT PARTS OF THE CATALOG

The order form is one of the most important parts of your catalog. This is not to say that your potential customers cannot order without it, because they can. But it is convenient to order with an order form and it provides much important information. With this information you can track what is happening with your customers, your business, and your products. It is important that you design an order form that has all the information you need. Figure 18-26 is a checklist for order forms. If you follow this checklist, you can't go very far wrong.

Your Name and Address. This is of first importance. Even though your address is contained elsewhere in the catalog (and most definitely should be, for when the order form is gone, that address won't be there any longer), you should always have a place on the order form where your name and address are clearly shown.

A Place for Your Customer's Name and Address. Include a space that clearly shows where your customer is to fill in his or her name and ad-

1. Your name and address
2. A place for customer's name and address
3. A place for quantity
4. A place for your stock number
5. A place for full description of the items ordered
6. A place for unit price
7. A place for the number of units wanted
8. A place for the total price
9. A place for packing and shipping cost (you should help your customer to estimate this by geographic area, weight, or number of units ordered)
10. A place for insurance cost (you must help your customers estimate total cost here also)
11. Sales tax if applicable in your state
12. A place for Visa or Master Card information, including card number, interbank number, and expiration date, if applicable

Optional information depending on your circumstances
1. Your telephone number
2. A place for your customer's telephone number
3. A place where your customer can list the addresses of friends to receive a free copy of your catalog
4. Your catalog number (if you send out more than one catalog yearly)

Figure 18-26. A checklist to follow in preparing your order forms.

dress. There are various alternatives to leaving a blank space. One is to leave a space that allows the customer to attach the label you have used to address the catalog. Special address labels are available for this purpose. Another is to use a computer to address the order form beforehand. In any case, it is a very important part of your form, for without this information, you cannot even fulfill the order.

A Place for Quantity. Very frequently your customer will want to order more than one of a particular product and, if so, you should be sure that the form allows him or her to do so. Also, the existence of such a place will encourage the customer to ask, "Do I want more than one?"

A Place for Your Stock Number. This is the number you have assigned to the goods in your catalog. It will help you to identify what your customer wants faster than if you ask only for a description.

Description. You should allow sufficient space for a full description of the item ordered, including size, color, and other details when appropriate, even though a number is listed. The number can be changed through the dropping of a single digit, but it is much more difficult to make a mistake in the description, so it provides a double-check.

Unit Price.   This is the price of one single item. If your customer is going to order more than one, he or she simply multiplies the number by the unit price.

Packing and Shipping Costs.   You should make some provision for packing and shipping costs unless you intend to pay all the postage. Usually this is a varying amount that depends upon the weight of the package and the shipping distance. However, many mail order firms make it easier for their customers by simply figuring out an average, based on sales price. If the size and weight of your units do not differ greatly, this is a reasonably good solution to the problem.

Insurance Costs.   If the item is lost in transit, either you or your customer must be responsible for the insurance. For big-ticket items, insurance is probably a must, and many companies require their customers to pay an additional amount to cover this cost. Again, you need to tell your customer how much to send, depending upon total value of the products ordered.

Sales Tax If Applicable.   If your state has a sales tax and your customer is living within the state, you will be required to collect this tax. As explained earlier, you will be expected to pay it to your state at periodic intervals.

Charge Card.   A charge card will increase your sales, both because of convenience and because it gives credibility and an easy method to pay for costly items.

Optional Items.   Some items are just a good idea to include, but your decision must take your own circumstances into account. For example, many companies will ask for the page number of the item in addition to the catalog number and description to nail the material down and make certain that the item is, in fact, the item ordered. It also makes it easier for the person checking to find the item. In addition, if you are sending out many different catalogs, it may be a good idea to have your customer indicate which catalog it is. This also lessens the chances of confusion both in ordering and recording information about what your customer has ordered. If you have a toll-free number by which your customer can order, by all means include it on the order blank. It makes ordering much easier and will boost the number of your sales. The order blank is a good place to reiterate the fact that you have a toll-free number. In fact, even if you don't have one, it's a good idea to list your telephone. You'll get some orders this way. It is an excellent idea to advise your customers that their friends can receive the same catalog if they will include their names and addresses, and then allow space for them to do so. This is a way of obtaining potential customers' names at no cost, and you should certainly take advantage of it.

The order form currently used by Edmund Scientific Company is shown in Figure 18-27. Edmund has a number of innovations here—in addition to those required on the checklist just given you—that are worth looking at. First, note that there are two order forms, which extend the life of the catalog since many people will not order once the initial order form has been used. Also note that Edmund has printed the customer's name in the space for the customer's name and address with a computer. In Figure 18-27b, the back of the order form is illustrated. It includes a letter from the president, a guarantee, and information as to where the customer can write to receive additional catalogs. But the order form doesn't end here. Figure 18-27c is on a separate page and gives instructions to the customer on how to order, including the telephone number, the fact that the goods are also sold direct in a retail outlet, and all details necessary to place the order. In addition, on the right-hand side of this sheet, you can see that Edmund gives three ways to stay on its catalog mailing list and again reiterates the direct order telephone line. On the back of this sheet (Figure 18-27d), there is additional information about the company, including the fact it is international, its foreign locations, and the store hours for its retail outlet in this country. Finally, Figures 18-27e and 18-27f show the envelope for sending in the order. In Figure 18-27e, the front side of the envelope, is the standard information with the address of Edmund Scientific preprinted. On the reverse are some final instructions regarding filling out the order blank, adding the packing and guaranteed delivery charge, and signing the check or money order. Below this it reads, "Tell your friends we'll send a free catalog to names listed below." And finally, below that, are some comments and quotes from customers, and to the right yet another product is advertised. Not an inch of space is wasted.

HOW TO STIMULATE ADDITIONAL SALES
WITH YOUR CATALOG

Just because a catalog is a catalog, many mail order operators overlook ways of stimulating additional sales through devices they may ordinarily use when selling a single product. Some of these items to stimulate your sales have already been discussed in earlier chapters. Others will be new

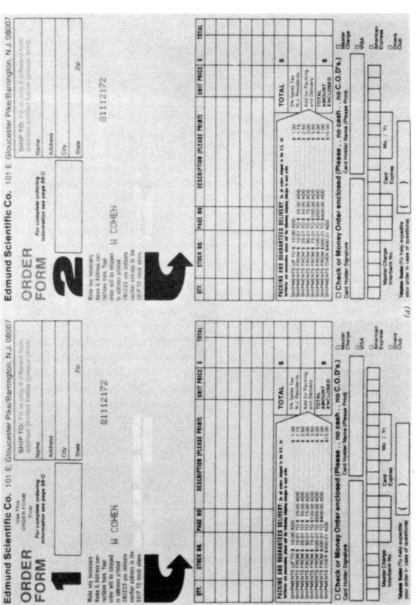

Figure 18-27. The order form for the Edmund Scientific Company: (a) front of the form; (b) back of the form; (c) a separate page telling you how to order; (d) a page of information about the company's international division; (e) the front of the order envelope; (f) the back of the order envelope.

(b)

Figure 18-27. (Continued)

HOW TO ORDER

3 WAYS TO STAY ON OUR CATALOG MAILING LIST!

1 The easiest way to stay on the Edmund Scientific catalog mailing list is to purchase from our catalog. Unless you indicate that you do not wish to be sent further catalogs, you will automatically receive future editions of the catalog, FREE!

2 If more than one individual in your business or household will be ordering from the catalog, unless each individual wishes to receive a separate copy of the catalog, it is best to order under one name where possible. Check to be sure that your address is correct on your order form, too.

3 If you are moving, or if you would like your next catalog sent to another address, either note that information on the order form provided, just beneath the printed address or send us the new address under separate cover. Remember, if you would like a colleague, friend or relative to receive a catalog, please fill out the special 'Send a Catalog to a Friend' portion of the return envelope.

Three Easy Ways To Shop From The Edmund Catalog

SHOP BY MAIL **Be sure to use the Edmund Order Blank, when you have one,** and fill it out completely. Specify quantity, stock no., page no., description and unit price for each item. If package quantity, please indicate PKG and no. of packages in quantity column. Please print your name and street address. To avoid mailing list duplication always use the same name and initials on all orders. Use zip codes—yours and ours (08007) to speed delivery of your order. See page 56-D for international ordering information. NOTE: Do not request Product Information on your order form. This only delays your order.

SHOP BY PHONE **24-HOUR PHONE SERVICE for Master Charge, VISA, Diners Club, & American Express**

DIRECT LINE TO ORDER DEPARTMENT . . . (609) 547-8900
A CONVENIENT WAY TO ORDER
Always Open-24 Hrs. A Day; Seven Days A Week

When you call this number, your order will be recorded. Please have all your ordering information ready before you call (same information as is required for shopping by mail). Be sure to give us your telephone number so if there are any questions, we can get back to you.

Our Telex is open 24-Hours, too. The number is 831-584.

Product Information If you require additional information not stated in the catalog, please call our Main Switchboard, weekdays, 8am to 4:30pm EST/EDT. **(609) 547-3488.**

Adjustments & Delivery Information For Adjustments & Delivery Information, ask for our **CUSTOMER SERVICE DEPARTMENT.** For Product Information & Technical Assistance ask for our **CUSTOMER SERVICE DEPARTMENT.** For questions regarding Open Billing, ask for **ACCOUNTS RECEIVABLE.**

SHOP IN PERSON **Our factory store is located in Barrington, N.J.** (See page 56-D for more information) near Philadelphia, Pa. and Atlantic City, N.J. Come in and visit us. All items in this catalog, plus more, are on display.

CREDIT CARDS **We accept Mastercharge, VISA, American Express and Diners Club.** Charge card purchases are shipped to the cardholder only. On all charge orders please be sure to state your card number, expiration date, and interbank number (Mastercharge only). Your signature is also required.

HOW TO ORDER **Send your personal check, money order or charge card information.** Please do not send cash or postage stamps. For ALASKA, HAWAII, U.S. POSSESSIONS Orders: Personal checks delay orders because of slow clearance in those areas. Send money order or cashiers check only.

PACKING AND GUARANTEED DELIVERY **Please use the Packing & Guaranteed Delivery Chart** to determine the appropriate charge. This charge includes postage costs, insurance, guaranteed delivery and careful individualized packing & handling by Edmund Scientific. To compute this charge, simply find the range within which the dollar amount of your order falls on the chart and add the accompanying charge. For example, if your order totals $14.95, this falls within the $10.01 to $25.00 shipment range. The charge for an order in this range is $1.75. You would then add $1.75 to the box to the right of the chart on the order form.

On all orders shipped to the U.S., its territories & possessions, please add the following charges in each order:

SHIPMENTS UP TO $ 10.00 ADD	$ 1.30
SHIPMENTS FROM $ 10.01 TO $ 25.00 ADD	$ 1.75
SHIPMENTS FROM $ 25.01 TO $ 50.00 ADD	$ 2.50
SHIPMENTS FROM $ 50.01 TO $ 75.00 ADD	$ 3.00
SHIPMENTS FROM $ 75.01 TO $100.00 ADD	$ 3.50
SHIPMENTS FROM $100.01 TO $200.00 ADD	$ 4.00
SHIPMENTS FROM $200.01 TO $400.00 ADD	$ 7.00
SHIPMENTS OVER $400.01 ADD	$15.00

PURCHASE ORDERS **Purchase orders must be signed by an authorized person.** If confirming, please indicate. ALL PURCHASE ORDERS WILL BE SHIPPED F.O.B. Barrington, N.J.—the Packing and Guaranteed Delivery chart does not apply to Open Accounts. If you request special shipping (air mail, parcel post, special delivery, etc.) such costs should be authorized on your purchase order. Terms are net 30 days. We reserve the right to assess a 20% re-stocking charge for merchandise returned after 30 days. To establish credit send one bank and two commercial references, unless your company is well-rated in Dun & Bradstreet. Credit checks normally takes 4 to 6 weeks. If in a hurry, please send us your check, as well as your references with your first order.

PRICES **Prices in this catalog are effective September 1, 1980** and supercede all previous catalog prices. We strive to maintain the lowest possible prices in compliance with Wage & Price Guidelines established by the President, and will try our best to deter future increases. Prices in this catalog are subject to change without notice. Sometimes it is necessary for us to increase prices on selected items due to increase in prices to us. Thank you for your understanding.

HOW TO PURCHASE A GIFT CERTIFICATE **Birthdays, anniversaries, Christmas, graduations** . . . if you can't decide on a gift for someone special, why not let them browse through our catalog. We will send a gift certificate (any amount, $10 or over) along with a gift card with your best wishes and a FREE Edmund catalog. Great for prizes and awards, too! Gift certificate requests should be sent: Attention Gift Dept.

MORE THAN ONE CATALOG? **Do you receive more than one catalog in the mail?** If so, please send us the label(s) from the catalogs you do not want. This will enable us to give you better service and also save money by eliminating duplication. After you've returned the label why not give the extra catalog to a friend?

A CONVENIENT WAY TO ORDER
DIRECT ORDER TELEPHONE LINE
(609) 547-8900
24-Hour Telephone Service For Credit Card Customers
Always Open- 24 Hrs. A Day 7 Days A Week

(c)

Figure 18-27. (Continued)

Figure 18-27. (Continued)

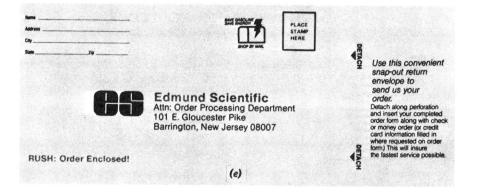

Figure 18-27. (Continued)

here. Use this list as a checklist as you go through your catalog to make sure you have at least thought about doing these things to boost your sales from the catalog that you have put together.

1. *Money-back Guarantee with a Free Trial Period.* Don't forget that, just as in other mail order selling, the strongest guarantee will boost your sales, and a free trial period of one sort or another is also good for products you sell from a catalog.

2. *WATS Telephone Orders.* It's a definite plus if you can offer your customers the capability of ordering through a toll-free line. Here again, profitability is what counts. You will pay extra for the toll-

free line, so you must make this trade-off of additional cost against the additional sales you will make.

3. *You Need Not Carry Every Credit Card in the World.*   However, accepting Visa and MasterCard, the most often used credit cards in the United States, will greatly increase your sales.

4. *Discounts Tied to the Size of the Order.*   A discount tied to the size of the order will frequently get your customer to increase the order. Therefore, consider offering discounts for orders as they increase in magnitude.

5. *Free Gifts Tied to the Size of the Order.*   People like to get something for nothing and if you offer free gifts, even though they may not be very expensive, it will have a positive impact on increasing the size of your customer's order on almost every order that you receive.

6. *Sweepstakes.*   We talked about this in an earlier chapter. It can be particularly important with a catalog because of the seasonal nature of some of them, such as Christmas catalogs. If your customers don't order at once from such catalogs, they won't be ordering at all. Therefore, sweepstakes, or anything else that encourages your customers to send their orders in immediately will have a positive effect and will boost your catalog sales.

HOW FREQUENTLY SHOULD YOU MAIL YOUR CATALOG TO YOUR CUSTOMERS?

There are two right answers to this important question. One is always to test to see what is most profitable for you, considering the fact that every time you send a catalog out you should get money back in sales. At the same time, there is a cost associated not only with the mailing, but with the printing and producing of the catalog itself. However, there's another right answer: Keep mailing a catalog to your customer as long as he or she continues to purchase from you. Many people who are vitally interested in a particular subject will order the same day that your catalog comes in, throw that catalog out, and wait for the next catalog before ordering again. Not everyone will keep the catalog over a period of time. However, a useful concept to understand with catalog sales is that of the half-life of your catalog. The half-life concept refers to that period from the time you send the catalog to your customer until you get half the total orders you can expect from that specific catalog. In general, the half-life of a catalog is three or four months, but that is not a standardized figure and will vary significantly, depending upon type of merchandise, the type of catalog, your firm, your market segment, and environmental variables. So you must test to discover the half-life. Once you have half-life computed, you will know fairly easily about the success of a particular catalog and the products, and that knowledge will help you decide when to mail a new catalog to your customer.

THE INCREDIBLE OVERWRAP
AND WHAT IT WILL DO FOR YOU

The catalog overwrap is a relatively new idea. Basically, it is a four-page sheet stapled to the outside of the catalog. The overwrap is a great place to try new product ideas without making major changes in your catalog, remembering that changing the interior is going to run into money every time. The four-page overwrap can be changed for much less money. It's a good place to feature incentives to order, such as sweepstakes and free gifts. The overwrap is also an outstanding place for a letter to your customer. It has been discovered that a letter inside the catalog is the least read of any material in your catalog. But on the outside, your letter is read. You can be certain that you will reach your target audience. Now, you may not wish to include an overwrap at first, especially if your catalog itself is rather skimpy. But once your catalog begins to fill out substantially, think about using the overwrap. It's a great device.

HOW TO GET SAMPLE CATALOGS IN YOUR FIELD

Sample catalogs are a source of ideas as well as information on what your competition is doing. You can get sample catalogs by writing to various mail order companies. But how do you locate them? One way, of course, is to keep your eyes open while perusing magazines that are of interest to your customers. You will see your competition in these magazines and you can write for catalogs. Directories of catalogs are available too. Here are four such directories that list thousands of mail order companies offering catalogs.

> *The Great Book of Catalogs,* by Steve and Betsy Pinkerton. American Autocrafts, Inc., 135 Oak Terrace, Lake Bluff, Illinois 60044.

> *The Wholesale by Mail Catalog,* by Lowell Miller, executive producer, and Prudence McCullough, editor. St. Martin's Press, 175 Fifth Avenue, New York, New York 10010.

The Worldwide Mail Order Shopper's Guide, by Eugene V. Moller. Wilshire Book Company, 12015 Sherman Road, North Hollywood, California 91605.

The Great Catalogue Guide. Direct Mail/Marketing Association, 6 East 43rd Street, New York, New York 10017.

SUMMARY

In this chapter we've discussed important points about selling through your own mail order catalog. First, we've considered the advantages of selling through catalogs both to you and to your customer. Then we've looked at a variety of different catalog samples in totally different businesses, offering totally different types of products. Finally, we've considered factors that lead to success in mail order catalog selling, including product selection, cost control, use of copy and graphics, making the decision between color and black and white, the great importance of the order form, use of various boosters to increase sales by catalog, and such decisions as how frequently you should mail your catalog and whether to use the catalog overwrap device. Finally, I've listed four sources where you can obtain sample catalogs to get ideas, check to see what your competition is doing, and compare products.

19

A Potpourri of New Mail Order Ideas and Techniques

Mail order is plunging ahead at an incredibly rapid pace. Almost every day new opportunities are born and presented to the prospective mail order entrepreneur. This chapter illustrates some of these new ideas and techniques you can use to build big profits in your mail order business.

GETTING GREAT RESPONSE
WITH A LETTER THAT LOOKS LIKE A TELEGRAM

You could get a high rate of response if you could send a personal telegram to every potential customer. Can you imagine the impact of such a mailing? The problem, of course, is that a mailing consisting of telegrams would be prohibitively costly. However, a new type of mail telegram was developed several years ago and is available for your use. An example of this system, known as a Tell-a-Gram, is shown in Figure 19-1. This type of presentation has some major advantages. Obviously it arouses interest and will almost guarantee that the addressee will read the copy you send. Your message is certainly given added credibility because it is far more believable when the recipient knows you have spent more money to send it. Like a telegram, it conveys importance and a sense of urgency. Although I haven't tried these yet myself, I know that mail telegrams probably generate consistently higher response rates than other types of mailing. They have other advantages. They permit effective personaliza-

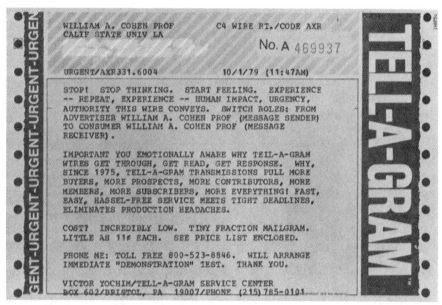

Figure 19-1. An example of a Tell-a-Gram, by the Scan Form Company.

tion by name. The method allows you to tailor certain key copy that you want to go into every telegram and eliminates other copy by computer. With the use of a priority service, which allows the mail telegram to arrive much earlier than would normally be the case, it will help you in avoiding missed deadlines or making up time if you are late. The flexibility of this system is really tremendous, and you can think up different uses for it. You can use it for requesting payments on past-due accounts, for announcing new products or new campaigns, for changing prices, for promoting sales or special offers, for advising and directing members or distributors of your mail order company, for sending press releases. And, of course, you can use it for conducting short surveys for urgent marketing decisions. If you are interested in using such a system, here are three companies that can help you:

Tell-A-Gram. Scan Forms, Inc., 181 Rittenhouse Circle, Bristol, Pennsylvania 19007.

Western Union Electronic Mail, Inc., 1651 Old Meadow Road, McLean, Virginia 22102.

Action Gram, Agawam Associates, Inc., 51 Summer Street, Rowley, Massachusetts 01969.

ALERTING YOUR CUSTOMERS OF
UPCOMING IMPORTANT MAIL WITH A POSTCARD

Another new technique that can greatly increase your response over what you might normally get is to alert your customers of upcoming important mail with a postcard. An example is shown in Figure 19-2, a *Reader's Digest* postcard announcing an upcoming sweepstakes. The advantage of this system is that the card is more likely to be read than the contents of an envelope that must be ripped open. If your customer can be presold with the postcard, he or she will be looking for the envelope containing your material when it comes. The bottom line is that your response will be increased. Of course, the cost is greater. You must discover through testing whether the additional profits are worth the additional expense or not.

SELLING YOUR PRODUCT WITH POSTCARDS

It is also possible that you can sell products by postcard. Now, you don't have much room to sell on a postcard, so you must use the space you have very cleverly. Certain products and services that require long descriptions cannot be sold this way. But some lend themselves to this type of promotion, and, as is shown in Figure 19-3, it can be done very effectively and inexpensively. In the promotion in the figure, the company, S.C. Patents, has indicated that there have been 14 patents issued after mine that the U.S. Patent Office has classified as being identical to my patent. Naturally, most inventors will want to know whether their patents dominate those issued after theirs. Why? Because if so, they could collect a royalty. So the company offers to send a copy of each later patent classified with my patent at a cost of $35, plus $1 for each patent copy. This simple copy on this inexpensive postcard brings a very high rate of response.

YOU MAY HAVE A PRODUCT YOU CAN DROP-SHIP
TO OTHER DEALERS, OR DROP-SHIP FOR THEM

You may have a product you can sell not only directly to your ultimate customer, but also at a discount to other mail order dealers, and allow them to sell—actually, compete—with you. This isn't as farfetched an idea as it may sound and it allows for greatly increased distribution. One

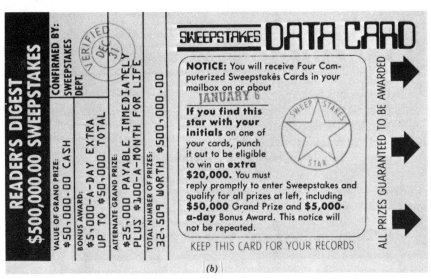

Figure 19-2. The Reader's Digest sweepstakes alert card: (*a*) personalized front; (*b*) back.

DATA BASE EXPANSION NOTICE

An expanded computer search of your Patent No. $\underline{3803639}$ shows that there are ____14____ patent(s), issued after your patent, that the U.S. Patent Office has classified identically with your patent (same class and subclass).

You will undoubtedly want to know:
1. Whether your patent dominates the later issued patent(s); and
2. Any state of the art advances shown by the later patent(s).

We will send you a copy of each later patent identically classified with your patent at a cost of $35.00 plus $1.00 for each patent copy if you will return this card with your remittance of $ ____14.0____ to:

SC Patents, Inc.
P.O. Box 2327
2001 Jeff Davis Hwy. (Suite 1012)
Arlington, VA 22202

We automatically refund $1.00 for each later patent that is your own. Full refund if all later patents are your own

____703-979-7232

SCP-34

Figure 19-3. Patent update service sold by postcard.

company that does this is Wilshire Book Company. Figure 19-4 is a letter Melvin Powers has sent out showing the discount for his books and describing circulars advertising his many book titles through which other mail order dealers can sell his products. As I advised earlier, it is not wise to sell products under these conditions unless you have a catalog or you have other products in your product line that you control. Someone then offers your products as an adjunct to his or her product line. Other than that, the dealers offering your products can't make a profit because of the smaller size of the market and an insufficient markup. However, if the dealer is already selling by mail, it does make sense to sell a product such as Melvin's, and it will make sense also for other dealers to sell many of your products. You do this by promoting your product to them. Many will be delighted to include your product in their product line, and both of you will profit.

YOU CAN NOW SELL YOUR PRODUCT THROUGH SOUND

Here's a new product to assist you in your promotions that wouldn't have been possible several years ago. It's a recording of your advertisement on a sheet of plastic. It works like a regular record and is played by your cus-

Melvin Powers

W *ilshire Book Company*

12015 Sherman Road, No. Hollywood, California 91605

(213) 875-1711
(213) 983-1105

YOU CAN MAKE MONEY SELLING QUALITY PAPERBACK BOOKS BY MAIL
I HAVE FOR 25 YEARS AND I'M WILLING TO SHARE MY SECRETS

Yes, you can do just that by using our book circulars. We'll sell you
these circulars at reasonable prices and ship them postpaid. Examine
the titles--books for every reading taste.

YOU GET A WHOPPING 50% OFF THE PRICES SHOWN IN THE CIRCULARS

Enclose these inserts with your direct mail solicitations, with your
orders and with all your outgoing mail. Then sit back and watch the
orders pour in.

ORDERS DROP-SHIPPED SAME DAY RECEIVED

As the orders come in, send us your addressed labels, your remittance,
and indicate on the back of each label the names of the books to be
shipped. We'll process your order the same day we receive it. Or we're
willing to sell you the books and you do your own shipping. In either
case, our discount is 50%. Send us the postage you receive.

SAVE MONEY WITH UNIMPRINTED CIRCULARS -- INCREDIBLY LOW COST

Set the wheels in motion. Order these circulars, including your
remittance. Circulars will be sent immediately. Simply stamp your
name and address in the blank space.

HOW TO WRITE A HIT SONG MAILER	$10 per 1,000 postpaid
HOW TO WRITE A HIT SONG MAILER	$1 per 100 postpaid
JOIN THE WINNERS' CIRCLE MAILER	$10 per 1,000 postpaid
JOIN THE WINNERS' CIRCLE MAILER	$1 per 100 postpaid
MAGIC MAILER - selling 23 books	$10 per 1,000 postpaid
MAGIC MAILER - selling 23 books	$1 per 100 postpaid
SELF-IMPROVEMENT MAILER - selling 333 books	$30 per 1,000 postpaid
SELF-IMPROVEMENT MAILER - selling 333 books	$3 per 100 postpaid

ACT TODAY FOR TOMORROW'S PROFITS

This could be one of the best investments you'll ever make. I'm pleased
to discuss your individual mail order needs and I welcome the opportunity
to meet you if you are in the Los Angeles area. This is my 25th year
servicing mail order companies. I'm as close as your telephone and I'm
available for consultation. I will answer your letters promptly.

WILSHIRE BOOK COMPANY

Melvin Powers

Melvin Powers, President

Figure 19-4. Wilshire Book Company circular selling to other mail order dealers.

tomer on standard audio equipment, so your customer not only sees your visual material, but actually gets your message through sound. This innovation does a lot of good things for you. The addition of sound to your message gets your audience involved: Your prospective customers will listen, and they'll also remember. There are all sorts of possibilities here, and many large companies are using these techniques right now, including Time-Life, the National Geographic Society, Xerox, American Red Cross, and Sears, as well as small companies and churches.

According to a leading company in this business, Eva-Tone Sound Sheets, the impact of sound often costs no more and sometimes costs less than ordinary printed insertions, and you add excitement and uniqueness to any message for less than the price of a telephone call. Eva-Tone says that you can test this type of custom-made advertising for less than $225. To get a complete packet that shows you some examples of the company's recordings and how they work, as well as giving information on how Eva-Tone will record your campaign promotion for you, write to Eva-Tone Sound Sheets, P.O. Box 7020, Clearwater, Florida 33518-7020, and ask for their idea kit. You will be pleasantly surprised, and it may give you a whole new outlook on the kind of creative promotion that can be done through the mail.

SELL YOUR PRODUCT AT LOW COST BY SHARING THE COST WITH OTHER ADVERTISERS

Another great new idea is cooperative mailing, which means that a direct mail advertisement going to a prospective customer contains not only promotional materials from you, but also those from other mail order dealers. The advantages of this system are several. First, you share the cost of using the mailing list. Second, you share the tremendous cost of postage. Third, you probably reduce your printing costs. Figure 19-5(a), (b), and (c) are examples from a package of postcards in which one side is the advertisement and the other side is a self-addressed, stamped indicia, enabling the potential customer to fill the card out and send it to the dealer. These cards either are bound together or come in booklet form so that one customer may see 50, 100, or more cards all at one time and all from different advertisers. Your potential customers, who have been selected because of certain factors they have in common and a probable interest in your product, go through the entire list and fill out response cards to those advertisements they find interesting. There are many different kinds of mailings of this type, and to recommend specific advertisers, let me again remind you of SRDS. Look in the *Direct Response*

No. 527 Denim

No. 524 Mesh

No. 526 Ramie/Cotton

No. 522 Denim/Mesh

ADJUSTABLE CAPS (with emblems)

USE FOR: Safety awards, incentive for production goals, product promotion, advertisement, conventions, company picnics, trade shows, attendance awards.

Choose the cap that fits your need. Send us a copy of your logo or a rough pencil sketch and we'll do the rest. Your emblem expertly made and sewn on the best caps available. NYLON JACKETS WITH EMBLEMS ALSO AVAILABLE.

PLEASE FURNISH THE FOLLOWING INFORMATION:

- Copy for Emblem _____
- Color _____ • How Many _____ • Style No. _____

COLORS: Royal Blue, Navy Blue, Red, Black, Orange, White, Gold, Kelly Green and Brown.

Price includes one 1-color emblem sewn on front of cap. (Minimum Order — 72)

CARDINAL™
CAP & JACKET CO.

HIGHWAY 460-9   BOX 1430
GRUNDY, VA 24614

ALASKA, HAWAII and VIRGINIA
CALL COLLECT 703/935-4545
TOLL FREE 800/336-0551

72	144	288	432	864	1728
$4.10 each	$3.65 each	$3.50 each	$3.40 each	$3.30 each	$3.20 each

(a)

(b)

Figure 19-5. Examples in a package of postcard: (*a*) adjustable caps; (*b*) a trade show exhibit booth; (*c*) machinery for fast plastic packaging.

Two low-cost portable Autobag® systems for fast plastic packaging.

We'll mail full facts on portable Autobag® packaging systems.

□ One operator cuts bagging/ sealing time in half.

□ Bags air-opened for easy loading.

□ Both use Autobag plastic bags on rolls; plain or printed in up to six colors.

□ Easy. Anyone can operate them.

(c)

H-55A. Semi-automatic bag-ger loads/heat seals up to 8,000 bags per shift.

H-25. Loader-sealer for short runs. Rated 10-18 bags per minute.

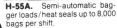

AUTOMATED PACKAGING SYSTEMS, INC.

8400 Darrow Road □ Twinsburg, Ohio 44087 □ (216) 425-4242

Technical Representatives and Demo Centers throughout the U.S. and Canada.

Fill out flip side. Get facts. Fast!

Figure 19-5. (Continued)

section of their business publications volume and check for cooperative mailings. As with magazines or newspapers, one factor of the cost is going to be the circulation. Picking the right cooperative mailing is just as easy. If you have a product that appeals to doctors, look for a cooperative mailing that goes to doctors.

PEOPLE MAY READ YOUR LETTER IF YOU TELL THEM NOT TO

Here's an innovative way to get your customers to read your follow-up letters. Look at Figure 19-6. This is a follow-up letter for a Mellinger promotion. Note that more than half the front page of the letter has been X'ed out, and above it is printed in block letters, "Don't bother to read this letter. Just let me lend you a copy of the *Complete Mellinger Guide to Mail Order Money-Making*." And yes, sure enough, many potential customers will read every single word, and then turn over the second page, which isn't crossed out at all, and read that too. This type of promotion uses a psychological principle of great power. So, make a big X that draws attention to the copy over it, and then tell your customer not to read. He or she will probably disregard your instructions.

Don't bother to read this letter.

Just let me LEND you a copy of

the complete Mellinger Guide

to Mail Order Money Making.

Dear Friend:

Since you're paying no attention to my first suggestion, maybe I can get you to act on the second one.

I'm not going to _give_ my Guide to you. I'm not going to _sell_ it to you. I'm not going to cut the price to induce you to buy it.

You take a full week to read it. But it won't take that long because some people who started reading it were so impressed with the profits they could make that they finished it in one night. It's that good!

You'll be fascinated with the ease in starting a money-making business in spare time at home. You will see how I give you access to new mail-order products--how they can be drop shipped (which means no investment in merchandise)--where to advertise--even how to get FREE ADS in magazines.

Also, the very exclusive feature of your membership in Mail Order Exchange is explained--how it gives you 14 actual samples of products that sell by mail--how its monthly Trade Bulletins provide names and addresses of suppliers with the products that they offer, new postal regulations to keep you abreast of changes and stories about successful M.O.E. Members.

The Guide and my full year's consultation service are based upon my better than 30 years first hand experience in over $20 Million, mail order sales. Could you ask for more competent advice?

The idea for "Guide Borrowing" is the result of reports of many M.O.E. members who loaned their Guides to friends. They too wanted Guides for their own use. And, speaking of friends, after you look over everything that I send you, talk it over with your family or business advisors. Get

(please read other side)

Figure 19-6. A unique way to get your letter read: Tell the customer not to read it!

451

- 2 -

the benefit of their opinions. Then you can make your decision. If you decide to keep the Guide and enter the profitable mail order business, you can depend upon my full support to make you a big success.

If you decide that my plan is not for you, return the Guide within seven days after you receive it--just as you would return anything else that you would borrow and the loan of the Guide won't cost you a cent!

Let me repeat that I don't want you to buy my Guide. I don't want you to send me a $10.00 deposit. I just want you to borrow my Guide for a week on this liberal proposition. Send me a deposit of only $5. I'll trust you for the entire worth of the Guide if you will trust me.

Michael Braverman and I had this mutual trust and here is what this 22 year old man reported after he had my Guide less than six months:

> His product was a desk lighter that sold for $5.88.
> Acting upon our advice, he received much free adver-
> tising. First month's sales $3,117.00 and 400 cash
> customers. For the following 12 months he expected
> his earnings to be $30,000.00.

Please do not think that I promise that you will make $30,000 during the first year. All I promise now is to send you the complete Guide post-paid upon receipt of your deposit. And, if you don't see greater money making possibilities in mail order than what you are doing, fire the Guide back--our check for your deposit will go in the next mail to you.

So, use the enclosed "Guide Borrowing Request". Fill it in and mail it to me with your deposit in the enclosed postage paid envelope. Do it while this offer is open and give yourself a look into the inner plans of a business that is making fortunes for many others.

                                                 Sincerely,

BLM   :C2   President

Figure 19-6.   (Continued)

GET YOUR CUSTOMER INVOLVED
AND HE OR SHE WILL RESPOND

One of the new techniques discovered by mail order operators is that customers who are involved respond much more frequently than customers who are not. Figure 19-7(a) is a letter from the United States Marine Corps, and 19-7(b) is the card that goes with the letter. You will notice that, in the upper right-hand corner of the letter, there are two stamps affixed to the letter, one saying "yes" and one saying "no." In smaller letters on the "yes" stamp appear the words "I'm interested." And in smaller

HEADQUARTERS · UNITED STATES MARINE CORPS · WASHINGTON, D.C. 20380

Dear Sir:

It's the tough choice -- the Marine Corps. We're a small, elite branch of the Service. We aren't for everyone.

Saying yes to the Marines means choosing hard training and challenge. It also means saying yes to some great benefits. These stamps are your way to say yes to the Marines. You just affix the stamp of your choice to the enclosed reply card. Because we're the tough choice, we'll understand if you say no.

But ... before you make the decision, take a good look at the Marine Corps. What makes it the elite Corps? What can you gain on the tough team?

The Marines offer you the same great benefits as the other military services: skill training for a better job -- in or out of the Marines; good salary; promotions; free housing and food; medical and dental care; a chance to go on to higher education. But there's something extra for you as a Marine.

That extra is a pride and spirit unique to the Corps. Our training is rugged. Our recruiting is selective. We want the best; we train you to be the best. We don't make a lot of promises. What we do promise is challenge and hard work ... plus the prestige and recognition that come with the uniform.

We have a poster we'd like to send you. If the Marine spirit grabs your imagination, you won't want to miss getting your copy.

We're getting a lot of requests for it. To make sure you

(over, please)

(a)

Figure 19-7. A "yes/no" letter from the Marine Corps: (*a*) The letter, including stamps to indicate your choice; (*b*) the enclosed card, on which the stamp is to be placed.

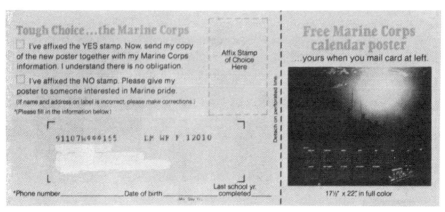

Figure 19-7. (Continued)

letters on the "no" stamp appear the words "I am not interested." About midway down the card in Figure 19-7(b) you will see a space that says "Affix stamp of choice here." Now obviously, if someone's not interested, he or she is simply not going to use the "no" stamp at all. Why in the world would someone respond with a "no" stamp or any other stamp saying "I'm not interested" in something? The fact of the matter is that people are more likely to use that "Yes" stamp because of the involvement in thinking about the decision. Therefore, the "no" stamp serves a useful purpose. Figure 19-8 shows another type of involvement device. In this example, there is a contest for a prize, and on the top it says, "Your free extra SURPRISE is one of the four described below. To discover which of the four is yours, scratch this spot gently with coin edge or fingernail." To the right of this announcement you'll see a spot that says, "Identification Spot," and if I were to scratch this spot there would be a number. Here again, people are more likely to become interested when they become involved with what you show them, instead of just reading a note spelling out the prize without having to do anything. When your customers become involved, there's excitement, curiosity, and mystery, and many other factors that work to help you make a sale.

DO THE UNUSUAL AND THINK CREATIVELY

In mail order, creativity and doing the unusual pay off. I'm going to show you several good examples here of what I'm talking about.

Your FREE EXTRA SURPRIZE is one of the four described below. To discover which of the four is yours . . .

SCRATCH THIS SPOT
GENTLY WITH COIN EDGE OR FINGERNAIL.

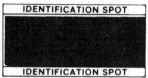

IDENTIFICATION SPOT

IDENTIFICATION SPOT

The number in the Identification Spot (above) will match the number of the FREE EXTRA SURPRIZE you are entitled to (described below).

YOU WILL RECEIVE THIS FREE EXTRA SURPRIZE AUTOMATICALLY IF YOUR $25,000.00 SWEEPSTAKES ENTRY TICKETS AND GEM COLLECTORS APPLICATION FORM ARE MAILED WITHIN THE NEXT 7 DAYS. (You must include this scratch-off sheet so we will know which FREE EXTRA SURPRIZE you are entitled to.) This EXTRA FREE SURPRIZE will be sent to you automatically in addition to, and regardless of, any other prize you may have won.

Free Extra Surprize #79710

Jeweler's Polishing Cloth

Soft specially treated cloth used to protect against dust and smudges, and to polish precious stones and jewelry to fine lustre.

Free Extra Surprize #84569

Black Star of India

Genuine 1-carat Black Star of India, cut and polished. Deep purple-black color punctuated by quadrant star at center. Shipped from our vault accompanied by our Certificate of Authenticity.

Free Extra Surprize #93241

Jeweler's Tweezers

Precision tool of polished steel with etched "safety ribbing" for handling precious stones with optimum security and avoidance of scratches or other damage.

Free Extra Surprize #84773

Investor's Guide Booklet to Precious Stones & Jewelry

Concise pamphlet of practical use to those interested in the various kinds of precious stones, and how they may be valued and acquired for collection and/or investment.

GC-NM/4.80/SURPZ

Figure 19-8. A circular using a scratch-out device.

The first example is in Figure 19-9(a). It appears to be a ripped-off portion of a newspaper, and in the upper left-hand corner are the words, apparently written in ink, "Hi, I thought of you while I read this book. There are some incredible ideas in it a person like you could really capitalize on." And then there's an initial—"J." Well, the only article that you can read in the "ripped newspaper" is a review, entitled, "Ideas and Products That Are Making a Bundle," of a book, *Hottest New Business Ideas,* by Chase Revel. This really isn't a newspaper. In fact, the paper itself is of higher quality than you might have thought. One of the individuals who developed this promotion device with Chase Revel said that one of the problems was to make the ragged edges of the die so that it would appear to be ripped from a newspaper. You can bet that an unusual promotion

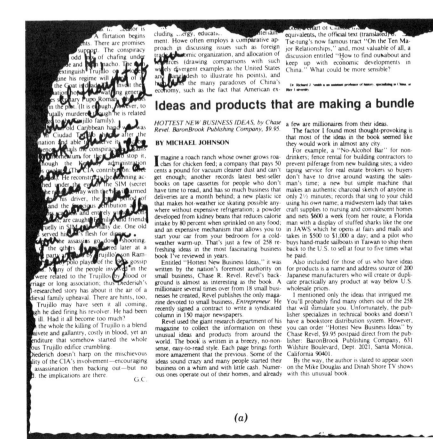

(a)

Figure 19-9. The Chase Revel "newspaper": (a) front view; (b) back of "newspaper."

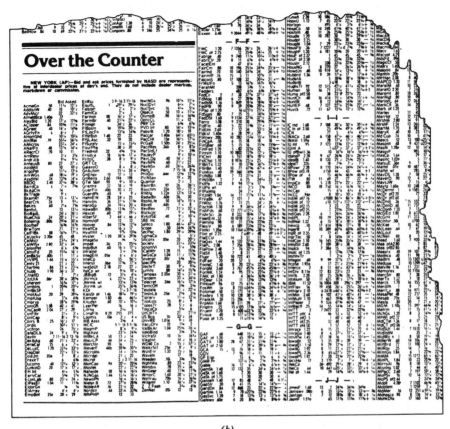

(b)

like this makes money. By the way, if you look at Figure 19-9(b), which is the reverse side, you will see the extent to which the illusion has been carried. Even "daily stock prices" are listed!

Figure 19-10 is from another outstanding promotion, created by Eric Weinstein, president of Revelco, Inc., a list broker and manager. You will see that this promotion appears to be on lined notebook paper, and it's typed in a very strange fashion. You will see hundreds of mistakes in these two short paragraphs. And the bottom line is this—the writer says, "Please pardon all the mistakes, but I've just put up a brand new list and it's so hot I figured you'd rather get the jump on it and hear about it quickly than wait for a printer to get out a fancy promotion. This list is so hot it's burning out the tape drives in our computer. It's a dynamic business buyers' list and here are the particulars. All are paid-up, credit-ap-

July 31, 1979

Mr. John Jones
631 Wilshire Bld.
~~Santa Monica, CA 90401~~

Dear Mr. Jones:

Please pardon alll of the mistakes—but i8ve just put up a ~~NEW~~ BRAND NEW list and it"s ~~so hot it figured you*d rather getthe jump on it & hear about it quickly than wait for a~~ printer to gte out a fancy ~~/~~promotion.

~~This list is so hot its burning out the tape drives in our computer.~~ It8s a dynamite busness buyers list and heres the parti caulars—allare PAID UP CREDIT APPROVED BUYERS ~~OF PERSSONEL, SALES DAN MANAGEMENT PROGRAMS, ETC. AND ALL KINDS~~ OF FORMATES—print, cassette, film an video tape—ALL ARE DISCRETIONARY CHECK SINERS OF MEDIUM AND LARGE ⊗ COMPANIES. A recency of !0 omnths or ~~less'!. Mostly phone derived (70% with the balance direct mail).~~ 80% are MULTIPLE BUYERS. Its called ~~a~~/the APPLIED CONCEPTS Business Buyers List and the average ~~unit of purchase is $350. Thats a lot of money—this list is fresh~~ ~~XoXX~~ red hot, and certain to become a proven money-maker for any quality offer.

try a test soon.

Sincerely,

Eric Weinstein
~~P.s. The quantity/ is 25M & the price is 55 per—how about~~
some business?

Figure 19-10. Eric Weinstein's "mistake"-filled letter. The recipients took notice!

proved buyers of personal sales and management programs, etc., of all kinds of formats, print, cassette, film and videotape. All are discretionary check signers of medium and large companies. A recency of ten months or less! Most are phone derived (70% with the balance direct mail). 80% are multiple buyers. It's called the Applied Concepts Business Buyers' List and the average unit of purchase is $350. That's a lot of money. This list is fresh, red hot, and certain to become a proven money-maker for any quality offer. Try a test soon. Sincerely, Eric Weinstein. P.S. The quantity is 25,000 and the price is $55 per. How about some business?"

Did I say earlier that a good response may be 3%, 4%, 5%, or even less than 1%? Well, Eric Weinstein got an incredible 21.6% response with this letter. Along with the order, many people told Eric, "Why don't you hire a secretary, for crying out loud?" That's creativity.

If you've flown on an airplane, you know what I have shown in Figure 19-11. Yes, this is a sanitary bag, also known as a barf bag, used in case you get motion sickness while flying. But my gosh! What is that on the side of it? "Super film developing offer, only $1.79." Can you imagine that? Here we have an advertisement on the side of a barf bag! Remem-

Figure 19-11.   An advertisement on the back of a sanitary bag.

ber that people must have flown for 50 years in airplanes without ever seeing anything on the side of a barf bag, and here we have a full-page advertisement. This kind of creativity is what pays off. Think of the unusual that hasn't been done before. It will make you money.

DO YOU WANT TO ATTEND EVERY MAJOR MAIL ORDER CONFERENCE IN THE COUNTRY?

It would probably be physically impossible to attend every major mail order conference across the country, even if you could afford it. And believe me, the cost would not be small. In addition to paying the conference fees, which are $200 or $300 or more, you would have to travel back and forth across the entire country and pay the air fares and hotel bills. Fortunately, it's not necessary, for there's a company that makes tapes of every single major mail order conference—Hoke Communications, 224 Seventh Street, Garden City, New York 11535. Hoke Communications publishes a catalog called *Ideas in Sound,* which contains hundreds of different tapes made of every single conference, course of instruction, and almost anyone who has stood before a microphone to say something about direct mail or mail order. This catalog is available to you by writing to Hoke Communications.

CAN YOU USE A PRIVATE MAIL MONITOR SERVICE?

In the course of your business you may find a use for a private mail monitor service, which can do several things for you. First, it can tell you if your mail is being delivered. Second, it can tell you how long it takes for your mail to be delivered so that you can decide when is the optimum time for mailing. And third, it can tell you if your list is being protected against unauthorized use. Remember that if you rent a list, you are renting it for one-time use only, and someone else has the authority to use your list depending on the number of times he or she are paying for it. What does a service like this cost? Well, here's one company that will monitor your mail in 27 cities for $200 a year—U.S. Monitor Service, 43 Maple Avenue, New York, New York 10956. Write and ask for additional information if you're interested.

SAMPLES OF ENVELOPES AND OTHER RESPONSE VEHICLES, AS WELL AS TIPS ON HOW TO PUT THEM TOGETHER AT NO CHARGE

In your business you're going to be using envelopes very, very frequently, but other response vehicles may be your key to higher response rates. *Response vehicles* refer to different types of envelopes, postcards, and so on, which are folded or not folded, two-piece, three-piece, four-piece, or more, self-addressed, stamped, and all combinations thereof. Manufacturers will provide idea kits and other information to assist you. Here are several companies that supply such kits at no charge. Write and ask them for the kit and other information.

Tension Envelope Corporation, 19th and Campbell Streets, Kansas City, Missouri 64108.

Champion Printing Company, Box 148, Gross, Ohio 45061.

Visual Promotions, Inc., 49 West 45th Street, New York, New York 10036.

Webcraft, Route 1 and Adams Station, Box 185, North Brunswick, New Jersey 08902.

SELL BY SMELL

I talked earlier about selling by sound, but how about selling by smell? Is this possible? Well, in today's world of high technology, it is. A company called 3M developed this product—3M's is called Scratch 'n Sniff—and it is quite unique. Almost any fragrance, aroma, or scent can be encapsulated and put right on the printed page by this process, called microfragrance technology. It is printed directly by an overlay process. In the process, tiny globules of material are imprinted over the normal printing. When these globules are scratched, the fragrance held within is released. 3M currently has more than 100 different fragrances, including pineapple, pear, cucumber, orange, strawberry, peach, and banana. If you are interested in this material, write and request information from 3M Company, Microproducts, Building 220-6W, St. Paul, Minnesota 55101. An example of strawberry Scratch 'n Sniff is shown in Figure 19-12. The kind of fuzzy area is where the granules have been implanted. But don't scratch it because we haven't used the process in this book!

HAND-ADDRESSED ENVELOPES

Personalization is certainly the key in mail order and in direct mail, and one way you can obtain it is to have your addressing done by hand. Naturally, it is more expensive, and perhaps you have to hire students to keep your costs down. But in this day in which labels, computer letters, and so forth are the norm, a handwritten envelope stands out and it will probably stand a good chance of being opened.

Because of the large amount of direct mail I get, I don't always open the printed ones, but if I see something handwritten, I will definitely open it and read what is inside. Recently I received such a handwritten envelope. The envelope was marked "Personal." I opened it to find an apparently typewritten sheet, signed "Anonymous." Actually, rather than typewritten, it was offset typewriting. What was it selling? A system for winning at the stock market. I didn't order the system, but I certainly read the letter, and I bet with the right list it would bring a good response.

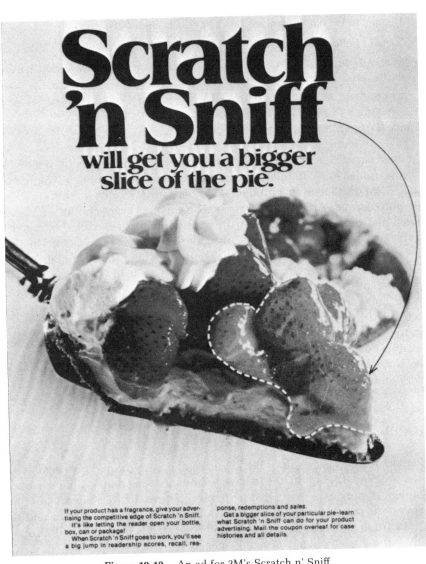

Figure 19-12. An ad for 3M's Scratch n' Sniff.

A SPECIAL P.I. DEAL FOR *PARADE MAGAZINE*

Parade Magazine offers a special per inquiry, or P.I., deal. Now when *Parade Magazine* does this, you should probably sit up and listen, because it goes to 21 million households, and according to their descriptive advertisement, you can get 10,000 to 20,000 requests for your catalog, brochure, or booklet through *Parade's* eight-times-a-year Information Center. The advertisement costs you nothing up front since it's a per inquiry deal. Here's how it works. Write to *Parade Magazine* and ask for complete information. They will send it to you, along with an Information Center credit application. You fill out the application completely, and *Parade Magazine* then makes the decision whether to run your ad. If it does, according to *Parade,* you will receive approximately 10,000 to 20,000 requests for free material you are offering, or 1000 to 3000 orders if the reader is required to send money. About two weeks after the issue date you will begin receiving gummed, pressure-sensitive labels arranged in zip code order, one for each request made as a result of the advertisement contained in the Information Center. What's your cost? Well, it's not free, but it's pretty small. Remember, the Information Center is published eight times a year. To find out the exact dates and further information, write to *Parade Magazine* at Parade Publications, Inc., 750 Third Avenue, New York, New York 10017, and ask about advertising in their Information Center.

CREATIVE HELP BY MAIL

In an earlier chapter I talked about doing your own creative work, including both copy and art, and about different sources of other work. Here's a company that will actually consult with you and do the creative work by mail, no matter where you're located in the United States: T.M. Creative, 223 Old Hook Road, Westwood, New Jersey 07675. The members of T.M. Creative have a total experience of nearly a century in the business and have sold just about everything under the sun in mail order, including "how to" books, books on gardening and flower arranging, sports and hobby books, fix-it books, books on architecture, mystery books, and so forth. They have also sold seminars, courses, audio cassettes, dictionaries, encyclopedias, and so forth; and they've worked for such firms as Prentice-Hall, McGraw-Hill, Columbia Broadcasting System, the American Management Association, and other major companies. So if you're living in an area of the country where you cannot sit down with someone who can write your direct mail letters for you or do your artwork, write to T.M. Creative and ask for complete information about their creative conference by mail program.

MAKE MONEY BY GIVING YOUR CUSTOMERS
A WHOPPING GOOD DEAL

Sometimes you can make money by giving your customers such an incredibly good deal that they cannot get it anywhere else. Such an opportunity is shown in Figure 19-13. This is an offer to the subscriber of *Moneysworth*—to renew the subscription *for life* for $9.95. Now that's incredible when you realize that most lifetime subscriptions today cost several hundred dollars. This is a whopping good deal, and if you read through the letter contained in Figure 19-13, you will see just what a good deal it really is. Now you may ask yourself, how can *Moneysworth* do this? Well, one explanation is given about the interest rate on $9.95, and while I don't want to say this may be untrue, there are other reasons that *Moneysworth* can make money while giving you this bargain. Remember that in offering a lifetime subscription for $9.95, the publication will get its number of subscribers to soar. In fact, even now, *Moneysworth* has grown to where it has millions of subscribers. When a newspaper or any other advertising medium has such a large number of subscribers, the advertising rates go up tremendously because it is reaching many more customers. You know this from being an advertiser and reading earlier portions of the book. In addition, *Moneysworth* has a list of several million subscribers, all seeking money-making opportunities, so it can rent its list. And you can bet there are many people who are interested in renting a list like this. The bottom line is that everyone wins—the subscribers to *Moneysworth,* who get a lifetime subscription so cheaply, the advertiser, who now has a much larger medium for reaching his or her potential customer, and *Moneysworth* itself, which, in spite of giving a huge bargain, will make a lot of money.

INCREASE YOUR SURVEY RESPONSE
BY GIVING MONEY AWAY

It is said that you can't give money away, but that isn't totally true, and *Advertising Age* and a few other companies have proved it in a rather strange fashion. In Figure 19-14 is a survey sent to the subscribers of *Advertising Age.* Attached to it, although not shown, since I presume that every one of my readers knows what a dollar bill looks like, was a brand

251 WEST 57TH STREET   NEW YORK, NY 10019

Dear Moneysworth Subscriber,

Here's an incredible piece of news: If you'll renew your subscription now, but immediately, we'll let you do so at the *unreal rate of $9.95—FOR THE REST OF YOUR LIFE!*

You read right: We'll let you renew your subscription at $9.95 *FOR THE REMAINDER OF YOUR NATURAL LIFETIME!*

How can we afford to do this? Why are we making this ludicrously low-priced offer when other periodicals charge *up to $500* for lifetime subscriptions?

Ironically, it's because of the current economic downturn: Present high interest rates make this offer possible.

The interest, alone, on your $9.95 Lifetime Subscription prepayment now covers the cost of postage, our biggest expense in fulfilling your Moneysworth subscription. Thus, we're able to offer you this Lifetime Subscription so cheaply.

This is one of the few instances we know of where a consumer actually benefits from today's rampant inflation and astronomical interest rates.

You, as a Moneysworth subscriber and savvy consumer, can appreciate the beauty of this offer—and the fact that it's irresistible.

There are other reasons, apart from this unprecedented price break, why you should renew your Moneysworth subscription *now*:

• The national economic outlook is baffling and you need all the expert advice you can get—in managing your personal finances, maximizing your spending power, conserving your assets.

• Even at its standard one-year rate, Moneysworth represents an unparalleled bargain. Its competitors charge much more. Consumer Reports, for example, charges $12.00 a year, Money magazine $14.95, etc., etc. And we're offering you *A LIFETIME SUBSCRIPTION FOR LESS THAN OUR COMPETITORS CHARGE FOR A SINGLE YEAR!*

• Our cadre of hard-nosed, deep-digging researchers and reporters file dispatches from all over the world. They provide you with an up-to-the-minute continuum of the most useful, authoritative, wallet-fattening consumer news anywhere.

• Even the modest $9.95 cost of your Lifetime Subscription is tax-deductible—assuming you use your subscription in connection with your investments.

—OVER—

Figure 19-13. *Moneysworth* lifetime subscription offer.

—2—

• Celebrities abound on the pages of Moneysworth.
Contributors to its "Opinion Bank" feature have included:

Jack Anderson, Howard Baker, Isaac Bashevis Singer, Lawrence Welk,
Julia Child, Gay Talese, Bob Hope, Cleveland Amory, F. Lee Bailey,
Henny Youngman, Helen Gurley Brown, Isaac Asimov, Russell Baker,
Charles Schulz, Andy Warhol, Noam Chomsky, Ed Asner, David Reuben,
Ann Landers, Joyce Brothers, Rodney Dangerfield, Craig Claiborne,
Clive Barnes, Alice Cooper, James Coco, Earl Wilson, Frank Church,
Abigail Van Buren, Paul Harvey, Rex Reed, Flip Wilson, George McGovern,
William Sloan Coffin, Jr., Bill Bradley, Don Rickles, Jimmy Breslin, Elizabeth
Forsling Harris, William Kunstler, Cale Yarborough, Bobby Allison,
A.J. Foyt, Colonel Harland Sanders, Art Linkletter, Jackie Gleason, Liberace,
Alistair Cooke, Dan Greenburg, Keir Dullea, Orson Bean, Bob Cummings,
Arthur Godfrey, Rocky Graziano, Hermione Gingold, Arlene Francis,
Benjamin Spock, MD, Eberhard & Phyllis Kronhausen, Pat Boone, Lucille Ball,
Johnny Mathis, Dennis Weaver, Debbie Reynolds, Bob Newhart, Jack
Palance, Ricardo Montalban, James Coburn, Victor Borge, Bill Cosby,
Mario Andretti, Loretta Lynn, Merv Griffin, Robert Goulet, Carol Lawrence,
Red Skelton, Shari Lewis, George Wallace, Paul Krassner, Morris Udall, Bill Dana,
Tom Smothers, Dick Smothers, Marshall Efron, John Simon, Bob Guccione,
George Plimpton, "Catfish" Hunter, Curt Gowdy, Billie Jean King, Ed Mc-
Mahon, George Jessel, Mimi Sheraton, Toots Shor, Bill Graham, Eileen Ford,
Howard Cosell, Reverend Ike, Elizabeth Ashley, President Carter,
Marie Osmond, Jack Dempsey, Bill Blass, Barry Goldwater, Jr., Della Reese,
Monty Hall, Roberta Peters, Dick Clark, Jane Pauley, Nikki Giovanni, Larry
Rivers, Huntington Hartford, Nathaniel Benchley, Oscar Brand, Phyllis Diller,
Allen Ginsberg, Eli Wallach, Ed Muskie, Andy Griffith, Bess Myerson,
Judith Crist, Erskine Caldwell, Jim Backus, Gahan Wilson, Buckminster Fuller,
William Shatner, Paul Winchell, John Travolta, Cher, and George Burns.

Clearly, Moneysworth has it all: celebrities, money smarts, advice and information on how to enrich your life in every way. *AND NOW IT HAS A PRICE FOR LIFETIME SUBSCRIPTIONS ($9.95!) THAT'S LESS THAN COMPETING MAGAZINES CHARGE FOR A SINGLE YEAR!*

To avail yourself of this unprecedented offer—and renew your Moneysworth subscription *FOR THE BALANCE OF YOUR LIFETIME*—simply fill out and return the enclosed Incredible $9.95 Lifetime Subscription Renewal Form in the postage-free envelope. If you like, we'll bill your credit card.

But hurry! Once today's high interest rates drop appreciably —and some experts think this may be soon—this offer will automatically be withdrawn, and this once-in-a-lifetime opportunity will be gone forever.

No sophisticated consumer will pass this up.

Cordially,

R. Clifford Webster
Vice President

MWL 1 © Moneysworth mcmlxxx

Figure 19-13. (Continued)

Advertising Age

The International Newspaper of Marketing • 740 Rush St., Chicago, Ill. 60611 • (312) 649-5200 Telex: 254248 Cable: CRAINCOM

January 18, 1980

Dear Subscriber:

My Editors and I try hard to give you an interesting
and useful publication; but to do even better in the 1980's,
we need reactions directly from people like you. So, we
decided to conduct this special survey of our readers to
learn more about their information interests.

Since you are a part of a small and scientifically
selected sample, your response is vital to the success of
this project. I promise that your answers will be held in
confidence; they will be tabulated in with those of others
in the sample to develop a representative picture of our
subscriber's interests.

Please complete the attached questionnaire and return
it to us in the postage-paid reply envelope; you'll find that
it takes but a few minutes. The sole purpose of the number
on the back of the return envelope is to avoid sending a
second questionnaire to people who complete and return the
first one. If, however, you prefer not to be identified
even for this limited purpose, just cut off the number.

The Editors and I personally will be very grateful for
your help.

Best wishes,

Louis F. DeMarco
Publisher

P.S. The enclosed $1 bill is a small token of our apprecia-
tion for your cooperation.

A PUBLICATION OF CRAIN COMMUNICATIONS INC.

Figure 19-14. *Advertising Age* letter with survey. A $1 was enclosed.

new, crisp $1 bill. You will see this referred to in the P.S. in the letter, which says, "The enclosed one dollar bill is a small token of our appreciation for your cooperation." Can you imagine the psychological impact of this? No one likes to spend time filling out a survey form. On the other hand, what do you do when you get $1 in the mail? Do you send it back? Do you keep it, do nothing, and feel guilty? Or do you complete the survey? Well, tests have proved that a much greater majority of people complete the survey than ordinarily would and it's well worth that crisp dollar enclosed, whether the reader completes the survey or just puts the money in his or her pocket. So you *can* make money by giving money away.

SEND YOUR MAIL IN A PLASTIC BAG

Here's another product made possible by our advanced high technology. The plastic bag shown in Figure 19-15 is from the International Preview Society and they're promoting a classical record club. Although you may not be able to see it, the plastic bag enables whoever is receiving it to see some of the contents that are inside. That's a significant advantage over an opaque envelope. Here's why. Remember, one of the main problems

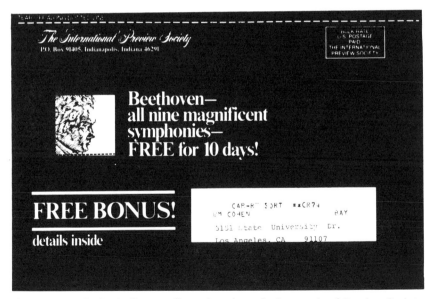

Figure 19-15.   A plastic direct mail envelope from the International Preview Society.

you must overcome in direct mail is getting your potential customer to open the envelope. That's step one. In the case of a plastic envelope, it's like sending a postcard: Your customer doesn't have to open to see. If you are correct in your assumption that you have the material inside to get him or her to read further, you've encouraged him or her to open the envelope in order to do just that. Also, plastic envelopes are new, and so they tend to attract attention. If you are interested in plastic envelopes, one firm that does this type of work is Poly-Flex Corporation, 984 North Broadway, Yonkers, New York 10701. Write and ask for information and samples.

SELL THROUGH OTHER LARGE MAIL ORDER HOUSES

Here's a variation of selling to other dealers. What you do is sell to other large mail order houses that use catalogs, and they sell your product through their catalogs. Where do you get the names and addresses of these firms? Every mail order firm that carries your type of product is a possible candidate to sell your product. How do you approach these companies? Well, you usually won't have to send them the product. What you must send them is a glossy photograph of the product, along with a complete description, price information, and the availability of delivery, as well as drop-shipping information, if applicable. Naturally, you should make your product sound interesting and salable. Remember, catalog space is valuable! By using this methodology, you can really multiply the effectiveness of your campaign and your ability to reach greater numbers in your market. You will have to allow at least a 50% discount to these firms, even higher in large quantity, but the number of units you can sell this way makes it all worth it. This is the one method that Joe Cossman used to sell millions of units of every single product he offered. It's a great way to make a fortune.

THE NEWSPAPER OF DIRECT MARKETING

There is now a bimonthly newspaper called *DM News* giving the latest in news of interest to mail order people. It is published monthly by DM News Corporation, 19 West 21st St. New York, New York 10010. Although the normal subscription rate is $36 per year, it is distributed free of charge to qualified users and producers of direct response advertising. Write for a free copy.

WOULD YOU LIKE TO HAVE A ROBOT TO HELP YOU WITH YOUR TELEMARKETING?

The age of robotics is here, and a computer called Hal has been invented to help you with your mail order campaigns by phone. Hal the computer can be programmed to make or receive telephone calls and to carry on a two-way conversation with the other party. Hal works by communicating a prerecorded message designed to get qualified leads for your product or service. But Hal does more. He can ask questions and record the answers to these questions for you. He will dial telephone numbers that you program him to dial . . . automatically . . . and will then begin to prospect for you for sales leads. Few prospects can resist talking to a real honest-to-gosh robot. But if the other party does hang up, Hal simply goes on to the next number and doesn't feel rejected at all. If you want to try Hal out, there is currently a toll-free number available; 1-800-645-RIKA, or in New York, 1-516-351-1100. Or, for complete information, you can write to RIKA Communications, Inc., 150 Broadhollow Road, Suite 100, Melville, New York 11747.

WANT A MONITOR SERVICE TO CHECK YOUR MAILINGS?

Television, radio, newspapers, and other media have been checking their mailings and services for years. Now there is a private service available that has decoy names available in 26 cities. When mail addressed to the decoy name is received, the date received is noted on the envelope and it is returned to you unopened by first class mail. In this way you can monitor your mailings and know whether your mail was delivered, how long it took to be delivered, whether all inserts were included in the mailing piece, whether there were any printing errors, and whether the use of your list was authorized. For complete details, write U.S. Monitor Service, 86 Maple Avenue, New York, New York, 10956.

ASSISTANCE IN AVOIDING CHECK AND CREDIT CARD FRAUD BY MAIL

Larry Schwartz and Pearl Sax got so badly stung in their own direct marketing operations that they decided to put a stop to it. They researched every technique possible and tested most in their own mail order business. The result was not only savings for them but also the creation of *Credit Card and Check Fraud Stop-Loss Manual* and a special newsletter to keep everyone up to date as to the latest safeguards and the latest scams being employed. If you'd like information about either their manual or their newsletter, write them at the Fraud and Theft Information Bureau, 630 East Ocean Avenue, Boynton Beach, Florida 33435.

TWO DIRECT MARKETING NEWSLETTERS

There are many newsletters on direct marketing. Craig Huey, whom I mentioned earlier as being president of Infomat, Inc., is also a publisher of a very fine newsletter called *Direct Response*. For a sample copy, write *Direct Response*, 25550 Hawthorne Boulevard, Suite 304, Torrance, CA, 90505. From Florida, copywriter and consultant Galen Stilson publishes *Mail Order Connection*, which would be hard for me to criticize since I am a consulting editor. For a sample copy write Stilson and Stilson, P.O. Box 1075, Tarpon Springs, Florida 34286-1075.

ENVELOPES OF ANY SHAPE OR TYPE

Envelopes come in certain standard sizes and types, and if you order from your printer, the styles that are available may be extremely limited. If you want envelopes that are difficult to locate on short notice, or even custom envelopes, try Golden State Envelope, 1741 North Ivar Avenue, Los Angeles, California 90028. This is the firm that developed the listing shown in Figure 19-16. Meanwhile, Transo Envelope Company has developed a free booklet, *90 Testworthy Envelope Ideas for Direct Response*, and has samples and case histories of creative ideas that businesspeople in every industry have used to cut postage, production, and operational costs as well as other inexpensive promotional money-makers. Write Dick Sonheim, Transo Envelope Company, 6501 San Fernando Road, Glendale, California 91201.

LIST ENHANCEMENT

List enhancement is the latest thing in improving the results of your mailings, and it is all made possible by the very latest in computer technology. List enhancement is based on the principle that the more you know about your customers and the likelihood of their making a mail order purchase, the greater your chances of making a sale. Market Data Retrieval, 59 East Van Buren Street, Suite 2506, Chicago, Illinois 60605,

GENERAL INFORMATION

Envelope Styles

A. Commercial Envelopes. Made with and without windows, in a variety of papers; for correspondence, invoices, checks, etc. Windows save time and help to avoid mis-matching correspondence and envelopes that have been separately addressed.

B. Open Side (OS) or Booklet Envelopes. Opening and flap on the longer side.

C. Open End (OE) Envelopes. Opening on the shorter side. Includes coin and catalog envelopes.

D. Expansion Envelopes. For sales literature, forms, and other bulky correspondence.

E. Baronial Envelopes. More formal open side envelope with deep pointed flap. Frequently used for invitations, greeting cards, etc.

F. Invitation Envelopes. Similar to Baronials except that they come in larger sizes and have square flaps.

G. Bankers' Flap and Wallet Flaps. These special flaps are usually available on commercial-style envelopes and are used for bulky correspondence. Larger sized flap makes it possible to seal very full envelopes.

Closure Styles

A. Latex Gum. There are three styles of latex sealing gum:

1. **Redi-Seal** (generally for commercial-style envelopes). Gum in two places: On the regular flap and on a special second flap which turns up and presses to the first flap to seal the envelope.

2. **Self-Seal** (generally used on coin, catalog and booklet envelopes). Gum on the flap and on the back of the envelope. Bring the flap and the back together and the envelope is sealed.

Note: Styles 1 and 2 have a shelf life of 6-8 months, depending on storage (all gummed envelopes should be kept in a cool, dry place).

3. **Peel & Seel.**® Latex gum on flap, covered by waxed paper. Remove the paper and the envelope seals anywhere on the back. Extended shelf life. Easy to print.

B. Clasp. Metal tabs let you open and close the envelope several times before final sealing.

C. String-and-Button. Offers unlimited ability to open and close the envelope. Typically used for inter-office communication, but lends itself to many other applications.

D. Touch n' Tac. Similar to self-seal, but more durable. Lets you open and close the envelope many times.

Envelope Styles

Closure Styles

MAILING ENVELOPES

Commercial (Letter-Size) Envelopes
- Hard-To-Find™ stock items such as 8⅝" 24 lb. White Wove regulars; IBM (3½" x 7⅜") size envelopes; #10s in colors.
- 6" x 11⅛" (the NEW #15). Available in White or Brown Kraft. Largest envelopes that fit the post office profile (anything larger requires a surcharge on mail of one ounce or less).
- Redi-Seal Commercial Envelopes (double flap style, latex gumming). No moisture required. Easy to print. #6¾ and #10 regular and standard window envelopes.

Window Envelopes
- #12 and #14 standard left hand window envelopes; 24 lb. White Wove.
- #10 standard right hand window envelopes (1⅛" x 4½"; ⅞"R, ½"B).
- 6" x 9" open side envelopes with standard left hand window; 24 lb. White Wove.
- 8⅝" Check envelopes (two window positions), 24 lb. White Wove; inside tint.
  "A" Window: 1⅛" x 4¾"; ⅝"L, ¹³⁄₁₆" B.
  "B" Window: 1" x 4"; 1"L, ¾"B.

Note: Windows in Color: Available in commercial, booklet, and open end envelopes on custom basis. Window material colors: Blue, Green, Rose, Smoke, Yellow.

Catalog Envelopes
- Hard-To-Find™ sizes (for example, 8½" x 10½" and 10" x 15").
- Colors: 9" x 12" in 24 lb. Colored Wove; 9" x 12" and 10" x 13" in Carnival Kraft.
- Grey: Most popular sizes in Grey Kraft.

Jumbo Envelopes
- Available from stock in 28 lb. Brown Kraft. Open end style. Sizes up to 22" x 27". Stocked with no gum on flap. Gum, clasp, string-and-button closures and latex gum available. White, Gray, Manila and Tyvek jumbos also available.

Tyvek Envelopes
- The light, super-strong envelope used by such companies as Federal Express. Tyvek envelopes save money on postage and UPS charges. So strong almost nothing can tear them. Available in most sizes, #10 through #14 and 6" x 9" through 12" x 15½". First class borders and air mail borders available on most sizes.
- These envelopes are made in a variety of seal gums: Regular gum, self-seal, and Peel & Seel® . Selected sizes available in Grey and Brown Kraft colors.

Figure 19-16. Listing of envelope styles from Golden State Envelope.

Bubble-Lined Mailers
- Heat sealable, 70 lb. Gold Kraft polyethylene bubble-lined envelopes. Their lighter weight saves postage when compared to boxes and comparable "heavy" bags. Heat seal makes the package water resistant and pilfer-proof. Reduces chance of damage during shipping.

Peel & Seel® Envelopes
- 6" x 9" through 12" x 15½" in 28 lb. White, 28 lb. Brown Kraft, 32 lb. Manila and 32 lb. Grey Kraft.
- The self-sealing envelope with extended shelf life. Easier to use and print than the double latex self-seal envelopes. Just pull the release liner off the latex gum on the flap and the envelope is ready to seal.

Air Mail Border Envelopes
- #10 light weight (13 lb. opaque with inside tint) **regular and window;** Tyvek #10s and most sizes from 6" x 9" through 12" x 15½".

First Class Border Envelopes
- Paper: 9½" x 12½" OE and 10" x 13" OE 28 lb. White and Brown Kraft, regular gum.
- Tyvek: Most sizes from 6" x 9" through 12" x 15½" and the #14 commercial (open side).

Squares, Baronials, Invitations
- Square envelopes, 24 lb. White, from 5" x 5" through 9½" x 9½". Most standard sizes of baronials and invitations.

Chipboard Mailers
- Made of .030 White or .040 Kraft Board, these mailers offer solid protection for photos, catalogs, artwork samples and ad mats without the use of corrugated stiffeners. Locking flaps.

Expansion Envelopes
- For mailing material such as sales literature, catalogs, price lists (where this material exceeds approximately 1" in thickness). Many sizes. Open end and open side.

Interoffice Envelopes
- Standard copy versions of both a #11 Regular Manila envelope with no gum on flap (no string-and-button) and 10" x 13" Brown Kraft with either string-and-button or Peerless Tac (like a self-seal but lasts longer).

Copy Machine Window Statement Envelopes
- 4⅝" x 6" open side, 24 lb. White Wove. The window is 1¼" x 3⅞"; 1" Left x 1⅞" Bottom. No printing. Standard "Thank You" behind window.

W-2 Envelopes
- Two styles and sizes:
  "A" Version: 3⅛" x 8⅝" 24 lb. White Wove; inside tint. Top Window (1" x 3", ½" L x 2⅜" B); Bottom Window (1¼" x 2⅞", ½" L x ½" B).
  "B" Version: 4" x 8" 24 lb. White Wove; inside tint. Top Window (⅞" x 3½", ⅝" L x 2¼" B); Bottom Window (1⅜" x 3⅝", ⅝" L x ⅝" B).

Proxy 2 Compartment Envelopes
- 9" x 12" 28 lb. White envelopes. In addition to a full 9" x 12" compartment to carry an annual report (for example), there is a 3⅛" deep, 8½" wide data card pocket. Window is 1¼" x 3¼", 3¾" L x 6" B. Plain. Easily printed.

Miscellaneous
- Payroll Envelopes (for cash distribution): 3⅛" x 5½" coin envelope with a 5⅝" perforated flap.
- Theater Envelopes: 2" x 4½" 20 lb. White Wove open side envelope.

FILING / STORAGE / SHIPPING

Packing List Envelopes
- Poly packing list envelopes. Most standard sizes and copy.

Bubble-Lined Mailers
- See description under "Mailing Envelopes".

Chipboard Mailers
- See description under "Mailing Envelopes".

File Jackets
- Colored Vertical File Jackets: 9½" x 11¾" OS, 11 pt. colored stock. Back of jacket extends ½" above front and has 1" reinforcement. No expansion; thumbcut on front. Shrinkwrapped 10 per package: One each of Red, Blue, Yellow, Pink, Orange, White, Green, Tan, Purple and Brown. 10 packages per box. Minimum 10 packages.
- Escrow Jackets: Flat file jacket designed for holding a number of loose documents. 100 lb. White stock. Letter size: 9½" x 11⅞". Legal size: 9½" x 14⅞".
- Employee's Personnel File Jacket: 11 pt. Manila double top. Provides a complete personnel record. Headings include Payroll Information, General Information, Employment History and Confidential Personnel Record. May be used in conjunction with standard vertical file folders. 9½" x 11¾".
- Punched Tape Jackets: 11 pt. Manila one piece jacket with 3½" x 7" pocket (left or right side). Diagonally cut front flap. 9½" x 11¾".

Jumbo and Tyvek Jumbo Envelopes
- Up to size 22" x 27" open end. Paper envelopes: 28 lb. Brown Kraft, 28 lb. White Kraft, 32 lb. Manila and 32 lb. Grey Kraft. Tyvek envelopes: 20 lb. Tyvek (super-strong material).
- Used to store and ship artwork, negatives, etc. Usually stocked with no gum on seal flap. Regular gum, self-seal, clasp and string-and-button closures all available at extra charge and on 4 to 6 week basis.

Job Ticket Envelopes
- Two sizes: 8¾" x 11¼" open end, and 9½" x 12" open end. Both with no flap and tab. 100 lb. tag plain.

X-Ray or Negative Preservers
- Stock size: 14½" x 17½" OE, Brown Kraft, plain. Also, many custom sizes and styles, including "kangaroo", some terminal digit styles, and simulated expansion envelopes.

X-Ray Shipping Envelopes
- 15" x 18" OE 28 lb. Brown Kraft, string-and-button. Cardboard insert provided.

Double Pocket Plate Files
- For handling and storing artwork, negatives, duplicator masters and printing plates. Available in 3 sizes:

FLAT	FOLDED
15⅜" x 21½"	15⅜" x 10¾"
16½" x 21½"	16½" x 10¾"
18¾" x 23"	18¾" x 11½"

Tyvek Envelopes
- Super-strong, light weight envelopes. Used by such companies as Federal Express. Tyvek envelopes save postage and keep your documents from being damaged. Virtually impossible to tear. (See "Mailing Envelopes".)

Packaging Envelopes
- Optical parts/small parts envelopes: From 1½" x 2" to 6" x 12" open end; 20 lb. White, no gum on flap. Also available with **cellulose lining** to reduce scratching and retard tarnishing.

Miscellaneous
- Jewelry Repair Envelopes (two sizes):
  1. 3⅛" x 5½" open end, with 5⅜" flap, perforation; plain.
  2. 3½" x 6½" open end, with 5⅞" coupon flap, perforation; plain.
- Metal Tab Envelopes: Leak-resistant construction for minerals or grain samples.
- Florist Card Envelopes: 2½" x 4¼" 24 lb. White plain, no eyelet.
- Meter Record Envelopes: 12" x 12" 32 lb. Brown Kraft, plain. Used for storing and mailing circular graphs and charts.

Figure 19-16. (Continued)

will take your customer list and match it against their business data bases. As a result, you can obtain a profile of all your customers, including 20 different data elements such as SIC code, location, employee size, sales volume, and job title. Now you know who your best customers are according to their data elements and can do your mailings in accordance with these profiles. Further, you can mail to prospects other than your current customers based on the characteristics that your best customers exhibit. For complete information about this service, write to Market Data Retrieval.

SUMMARY

In this chapter I've given you twenty different and innovative techniques, special methods, and money-making ideas that you can incorporate into your mail order operation. Remember that mail order rewards the creative and innovative operator with success. If you can think of a new twist or a new idea from one of the concepts I have shown you, or from one of the idea kits or catalogs you receive from someone else, it can make you a fortune. But don't forget—as with everything else in mail order, you must test to make sure that your idea is profitable before you sink large sums of money in it.

Mail Order Management and Record Keeping

Good management and accurate record keeping are an essential, but unglamorous, part of your mail order business. Why are management and record keeping essential? First, there's maintenance of a positive cash flow, which requires them over the long run. The basis of mail order is testing. But testing can be done accurately only if you keep good records. Throughout your business career you will be making various decisions based on what you must do to earn a profit. These decisions are also influenced by the records that you keep. Finally, you will need to keep good records for tax purposes. Not only must you pay taxes, but to know what deductions you are eligible for and to take every deduction you can legally take, you must keep good records—and that is true even if you use an accountant.

In this chapter we're going to discuss six essential records and how to keep them. In addition, you will be shown sample copies of each of the necessary forms to keep these records. The six types of records we're going to discuss are the daily inquiry/order sheet, advertising response sheet, customer card file, inventory status sheet, weekly expense record, and weekly expenses by category.

DAILY INQUIRY/ORDER SHEET

A daily inquiry/order sheet is shown in Figure 20-1. It is used as a running log to keep a record of people and customers who send inquiries to you if you are using the two-step method of selling, or inquire for other

NAME	ADDRESS	AMOUNT	MEDIUM/KEY	INQUIRY REC/FILLED	ORDER REC/FILLED

Figure 20-1. Daily inquiry/order sheet.

reasons, or have placed an order with you. This form can be used for a variety of purposes. It acts as a check to make sure that you fill every order placed and every inquiry that you receive. It also gives you a running account of how long it takes you to fill each order or answer each inquiry. It provides a check to make sure that, when your customers do order, the correct amount that is supposed to be enclosed is received and accounted for. And it can also be used to trace your orders and find out from what medium the customer order originated.

Now let's look at Figure 20-1. It's really quite simple and almost self-explanatory. In the first and second columns you put the customer's name and address at the time the order or inquiry arrives. The amount of money found in the envelope, if any, goes in the third column. The next column is for the medium key, used if the order or inquiry originates from a magazine, a direct mailing, or even a catalog. In the fifth column you write the date the inquiry was received and also the date that you sent literature in response to this inquiry, if applicable. Now, this is how the form is used for a two-step. For the final column, order received/filled, if it's a two-step, you wait until the order is received and go back and use the same line that you started earlier. The order received/filled column is also used if no inquiry was received, but the order was received direct. It takes just a few minutes to fill out the inquiry/order sheet every day, but these few minutes can be worth a lot of money to you as you do a profitability or media effectiveness analysis later on.

ADVERTISING RESPONSE SHEET

The advertising response sheet is shown in Figure 20-2. It allows you to analyze every single advertisement or promotion you do, including a

WHICH ADVERTISEMENT? _____   COST OF ADVERTISEMENT _____   PROFIT _____
MEDIUM _____   KEY _____
DATE ADVERTISEMENT APPEARED _____   DATE FIRST RESPONSE RECEIVED _____
(DATE OF MAILING FOR D.M.)

DAY	RESPONSE	CUMULATIVE RESPONSE	PROJECTED RESPONSE	PROJECTED RETURN (D.M.)	PROFIT (LOSS)
1					
2					
3					
4					
5					
6					
7					
8					
9					
10					
11					
12					
13					
14					
15					
16					
17					
18					
19					
20					
21					
22					
23					
24					
25					
26					
27					
28					
29					
30					
31					

Figure 20-2. Advertising response sheet.

classified ad, a display advertisement, television, radio, or even a direct mailing. It also acts as a sort of "how goes it" sheet, inasmuch as you can compare and project responses on a continuing basis, as well as profit or loss.

The advertising response sheet starts with a description of the advertisement and the product the sheet is analyzing. It's a good idea to cut out a copy of the advertisement and put it on the opposite side of the sheet. Then there'll be no doubt as to which advertisement you're talking about. The medium is the magazine, radio station, television station, or list used to carry your promotion to your prospective customer. Below that is a statement that says, "Date advertisement appeared," or in parentheses, "Date of mailing for DM." "DM" stands for direct mail. In some cases you may not know the exact date that the magazine hit the street with your advertisement. In this case, you will have to use an approximate date. But you should know the exact date of a direct mailing and the date of radio or television appearances. The next column is headed Cost of Advertisement, and, of course, for a direct mailing you would list the cost of your mailing. Below that is a place for you to write the key that we discussed earlier to be used to identify this particular advertisement. Finally, below this is the date that the first response is received from the advertisement you're analyzing. In the far right is space for profit. This is the last figure that you write in at the end of the project, when you receive your final response. It's used later on so you can check the advertisement and compare it with others and its results.

In the lower portion of Figure 20-2, the first column is headed "Day" and is already filled in—Days 1 through 31. However, in actuality, you would continue to fill this out until the last response was received. The second column is Response. All you do here is go back to your daily inquiry sheet and look at the key. Match up the key for this particular advertisement and count the number of inquiries you received over the past week. Write this figure under Response. For the first day the cumulative response will be the same number as that in the Response column, but for the second day, you would add the responses you received in the second day to the cumulative response column, and so on. The next column is Projected Response. Here you use the projection methods I gave you earlier in the book, depending upon the type or medium of advertisement, to project the total response you'll receive. After you have been in the mail order business for a while, you can develop your own formula for projecting response. For example, for a particular type of medium and a particular type of product, perhaps you've discovered that after day 1 you will receive 50% of your total responses. In that case, your total projected response, which goes in the Projected Response column, would be your response for the first seven days multiplied times two. So, if you receive 50 responses in seven days, your total projected response would be 100. The Projected Return column is next, and it is used only for direct mail. In this column, you list, depending upon what your cumulative response is to date, what the projected return is for the total project. You can use the formula that I gave earlier in the book for projecting response. However, as you become more experienced, you can work out your own formula for this as well, because your formula will differ, depending upon many factors, including your business, your customers, the business environment, and so forth. Let's say your response is 50 during the first seven days. If your formula indicates that first seven days' response for a direct mailing of this type would net 25% of the total, you would multiply the response you received during the first seven days by four, since 25% is one-fourth of the total: $50 \times 4 = 200$. You would then look at your total mailing to see what your projected return would be. If your total mailing in this case was 10,000, then 200 divided by 10,000 equals a 2% projected return. In the last column in Figure 20-2, you put your projected profit or loss, based on your responses so far. Let's take a look at that last example of a 2% projected return on our 10,000 mailing. According to the particular situation we might have and the profitability calculations I showed you earlier in the book, let's say that 1% is breakeven and 2% is therefore profitable. List the amount of profit in dollars. On the other hand, let's say that our projected rate of return was only ½% and 1% was breakeven. Then there is a loss. Calculate this loss and write it in parentheses in the right-hand column.

You can see how valuable the advertising response sheet is in seeing the relative value of your different advertisements, and also in predicting success or failure fairly early on. You can also watch how the response situation changes on a continuing basis and later use this information to help in calculating what future projections would be for similar advertisements.

CUSTOMER CARD FILE

The customer card file is shown in Figure 20-3. It's a file card of convenient size, which you can buy at your local variety store. Each customer's file card contains the name and address of the customer, along with the date of first inquiry and the date of first order. Furthermore, as your customer places each order, you log the date, the items ordered, the prices,

NAME _____   DATE OF FIRST INQUIRY _____

ADDRESS _____   DATE OF FIRST ORDER _____

CITY, STATE, ZIP _____

DATE	ITEMS ORDERED	PRICES	TOTAL ORDER	REMARKS

Figure 20-3.   Customer file card.

the total amount of the order, and in the remarks section on the card, anything else you think worth putting down. If the customer's check bounced, you definitely would want to log that. Or if the customer returned his or her merchandise, you would want to log that also. Why? Well, obviously if the customer's check bounced, you want to try to get paid for the product you shipped. On the other hand, if you don't get paid, you don't want to continue to ship merchandise to this customer against bad checks. If a customer returns merchandise once, okay, perhaps there's a reason. But if a customer returns your merchandise continually, then obviously the customer isn't someone you want to do business with. A review of the customer card file will inform you of either situation immediately as you log in the date and the item ordered. Now you may wonder why you list all the items ordered and the prices. As you continue with your business, certain products will be better to encourage customers to place a first order. Other products will be better to encourage larger orders over a period of time from your customer. Remembering that mail order is a back-order business, perhaps you wish to offer a special on these items to attract long-term customers because of this very reason. Further, by a review of your customer card file from time to time, you will notice that after a certain period some customers no longer order at all. This is important information because you want to know what the life of your customer is, and if you're mailing catalogs, fliers, and so forth, you want to know when to stop so as not to waste money. After awhile you will be able to calculate an average life of your customer by reviewing your customer card files. Again, each customer card file takes but a minute or so to prepare, but can be very valuable to you for the future of your mail order business.

INVENTORY STATUS SHEET

The inventory status sheet is shown in Figure 20-4. With a valuable inventory, you will want to know what its status is at all times. You will also want to know when you need it, how much you need, from whom you ordered it, and so forth. All this information and more is contained on the inventory status sheet.

The first item is the inventory description—what exactly the product or material is that you have listed here. The inventory number is your own number that you've assigned to this particular product. The location is where you store this item, whether it is in your plant or someone else's. The lead time is how long it takes to get the item to the customer. Remember that there is a certain amount of lead time associated with every product you order. The rate of usage in Figure 20-4 is an estimate and, of course, is approximate and may change. Unit measure is how the product is ordered—by boxes, pounds, ounces, or whatever. The unit price is also a changeable quantity and you should keep it updated. It is used to allow you to make estimates for planning. The reorder quantity is used if you have calculated an optimum number for reorder over a period of time, as discussed in the section on fulfillment.

The next item on the inventory status sheet is a list of sources, including the name of the firm, the address, and the contact—the name of the person you deal with and his or her telephone number. This allows you to get in touch with these people in a hurry.

The last part of the inventory status sheet starts out with Date, and refers to the date you placed an order. The next column is In Stock—how many of the items are in stock right now. Add. Needed means additional items needed. The next section is headed On Order, and under On Order

INVENTORY DESCRIPTION _____   RATE OF USAGE _____
INVENTORY NUMBER _____   UNIT MEASURE _____
LOCATION _____   UNIT PRICE _____
LEAD TIME _____   REORDER QUANTITY _____

SOURCES   (NAME OF FIRM)   (ADDRESS)   (CONTACT)   (TEL. #)
          (NAME OF FIRM)   (ADDRESS)   (CONTACT)   (TEL. #)
          (NAME OF FIRM)   (ADDRESS)   (CONTACT)   (TEL. #)
          (NAME OF FIRM)   (ADDRESS)   (CONTACT)   (TEL. #)

DATE	IN STOCK	ADD. NEEDED	P.O. #	QNTY.	ON ORDER DATE REC'D	QNTY. REC'D	PLANNED ALLOCATION (Project, Quantity, and Date Req'd)

Figure 20-4. Inventory status sheet.

are four different columns: P.O. Number, which refers to the purchase order; Quantity, Date Received, and Quantity Received. The purchase order number is the number you have used to order this material or product. The quantity is the quantity ordered. The date received is when you get an order. The quantity received is necessary because you won't always get everything you order at one time. Finally, the last column is headed Planned Allocation, and this means what you plan on doing with the inventory recorded under In Stock and Add. Needed. Probably it is for a project or promotional, so you record the quantity needed and the date by which you need it.

Use of the inventory status sheet will allow you to monitor the inventory you need and ensure that it arrives promptly so that you can fulfill the order, not get in trouble with the FTC, and maintain the good will of your customers.

WEEKLY RECORD OF EXPENSES

The weekly record of expenses is shown in Figure 20-5. It is a running record, and every week you should use a new form to keep track of what you buy. The first item is the date. The next, to whom you paid the amount. The third is the item or service you purchased, and the fourth, the check number. (Under check number, if you pay in cash or by credit card or by some other means, you would note that information here. Otherwise, you note the number of the check you used.) Finally, the last column is the amount of the expense in dollars.

Sometimes, when you open your checking account, your bank will give you a form that will have this information on it. The problem is that it will be difficult to use the bank's form since it also involves the remaining amount you have available in the bank. This means you cannot use the form for this purpose unless you always pay by check and never by cash or through charge. Therefore, for most situations, you should not only keep a record in your checkbook of how much is remaining in your checking account, but make use of this weekly record of expenses.

DATE	TO WHOM PAID	ITEM OR SERVICES PURCHASED	CHECK NUMBER	AMOUNT

Figure 20-5.   Weekly record of expenses.

DEDUCTIBLE EXPENSES	TOTAL THIS WEEK	TOTAL PRIOR	TOTAL TO DATE
Advertising			
Bank charges			
Car and truck expenses			
Commissions			
Dues and publications			
Freight			
Insurance			
Interest of business indebtedness			
Inventory			
Laundry and cleaning			
Legal and professional services			
Office supplies			
Pension and profit-sharing plans			
Postage			
Rent on business property			
Repairs			
Supplies			
Taxes			
Telephone			
Travel and entertainment			
Utilities			
Wages			

NONDEDUCTIBLE EXPENSES			
Federal income tax			
Fixed assets			

Figure 20-6. Weekly expenditures by category.

WEEKLY EXPENDITURES BY CATEGORY

The weekly expenditures by category sheet, shown in Figure 20-6, is used in conjunction with the previous sheet. This sheet is most important for figuring out your income tax at the end of the year. Even if you do not do it yourself, but use an accountant, you will save much money and much grief by maintaining this simple log on a weekly basis. What you do is this. At the end of every week, you look at Figure 20-5 and record the expenditures you have made and put them under the appropriate columns, as listed in Figure 20-6. For example, advertising expenditures done during the week in several different newspapers would be totaled and placed under the first column. If you bought a fixed asset—let's say, a new typewriter—this would be logged on 20-5 along with the date, to whom you paid, the check number, and the amount. At the end of the week you would add this fixed asset with any other fixed assets you bought that week and list the total in the nondeductible expenses section of 20-6. The next column is Total Prior, and this means for all the previous weeks of that year. You add the Total Prior column with the Total This Week to result in the Total To Date. The Total To Date is also used on your income tax forms to get the correct amount for your deductions. Note that other spaces are left so that you can log other deductible or nondeductible expenses not listed on the form.

SUMMARY

In this short chapter we've discussed the essential forms and how to use them to enable you to run a profitable and well-managed mail order business. These forms will also enable you to make accurate calculations and projections that will add greatly to your potential for profitability. This system can be used until you become big enough to have a completely or partially computerized operation, as discussed earlier in the book.

High Technology and Buck Rogers Mail Order

More than five years ago I recieved a special credit card from Comp-U-Card, a discount buying service, Comp-U-Card started out with a relatively modest membership, but today they have 1.5 million subscribers and take hundreds of orders every day for their mechandise. On this special credit card is a toll-free number that is dialed in order to place the order. Comp-U-Card acts as a broker for almost all types of merchandise. If a subscriber wants to buy any product, he or she simply dials the toll free number and Comp-U-Card says whether or not the merchandise is obtainable through its service, and if so, its price. If he or she wishes, the subscriber orders this merchandise immediately, using the personal number on the credit card. The merchandise is sent by mail or delivery service and the amount is billed to the subscriber's account We will see shortly how similar systems work using the new high technology of direct-response marketing.

CABLE TELEVISION

Cable TV has been around for some time, but now it is really taking off as a direct-response medium because it offers major advantages for advertisers seeking to sell their products in a direct-response fashion. These include the following:

1. Freedom from the 30-, 60- or 120-second commercial on regular television. As I explained in an earlier chapter, if we wish to advertise on television, these are the blocks of time that are assigned to us; we create an advertisement that will fit into these structured time segments. But through cable we can create advertising for much longer periods of time and they can cost far less. For example, one cable TV home shopping show today runs for an entire 30 minutes. While an advertisement lasting only two minutes during the Super Bowl on a one-time showing may cost close to $1 million, in many areas of the country you can get an entire package of cable TV spots on a local or origination channel for less than $1000.

2. Local access to a national market through satellite. The number of communications satellites that carry cable TV is continually increasing. As a matter of fact, the number has almost doubled in the last two years. In this way, even though it is only a local cable TV station that carries a particular advertisement, through a satellite the advertiser may reach a national or eventually even an international market.

3. Segmentation. Segmentation is one key to marketing success in general. It is one of the big advantages of direct-response marketing. In cable TV, we have market segmentation par excellence since it is a subscriber system. Therefore we have much better information on the demographics and psychographics of the viewers, along with their names, addresses, and phone numbers. In other words, since they are wired into the system, we know exactly what segment of the market our advertising message is reaching. And because we offer specialized shows on these channels, we can be far more selective and segment our market far more precisely than in any regular television broadcast.

4. Interactive television. Interactive television, which we will discuss shortly, is perhaps the ultimate in direct-response marketing. With such a system an individual has all the advantages of feedback in selling to his or her customer without the continually spiraling costs of face-to-face sales.

Cable television has meant an entirely new ball game. It bears more resemblance to direct mail than to regular television because of the segmentation and direct-response attributes. And because of this, it has already attracted numerous direct-response companies and a number of direct-response advertising shows.

Via-Tel Corporation has introduced video mail order. Video mail order is a television catalog in which 50 established direct mail order catalog publishers are participating, to the tune of five minutes each, showing a few of their best and most outstanding products in a show that will run to five hours. These products are divided into five categories, including gifts, fashion, consumer electronics, sporting and leisure activities, and decorative accessories. The customers will order through a toll-free number. The cost to the advertiser is $10,000, but this will include all production costs of putting their five-minute segment together. And since the average cost of the merchandise sold is planned at $75 per unit, the breakeven response for this direct-response medium, which should be compared to other direct-response media, is only .008%.

The Home Shopping Show is another effort along these lines. The Home Shopping Show is a production of New York's Modern Satellite Network. It reaches four million home viewers, three days a week, from 2:00 to 2:30 p.m. The advertiser pays $9000 for a single nine-minute segment, but this segment is played four times over during a 45-day period.

Yet another cable television direct response effort is the Shopping Channel, which is a joint venture of Times Mirror Satellite Programming and Comp-U-Card of America, which I mentioned previously. The Shopping Channel has no advertising or paid sponsorship, since Comp-U-Card makes its money on its annual memberships and its commission of 3 to 5% on each sale. However, it is certainly direct response, and the potential customers viewing the different products displayed on the Shopping Channel can purchase them through a WATS line toll-free number and have the product billed to their account as described earlier for regular Comp-U-Card customers.

Where Is Cable Television, How and Where Is It Going?

At the present time, more than half of all U.S. householders can subscribe to cable television. About half of these actually do. It is estimated that cable television will be the major force not only in direct-response advertising but perhaps in all advertising when market penetration reaches 75 to 80%. Currently, it is a little better than 30%, and it is forecast to reach this magic 75 to 80% figure by the turn of the century.

One sign of this is that cable television revenue doubled since 1979 to 1982 and will double again by 1985. Also, the number of cable satellites in orbit or authorized has increased dramatically in just a few years. In 1982 there were 13 cable satellites in orbit or authorized and 264 transponders. By 1985 this number will increase to 25, with 480 transponders.

The future of television in cable direct response is awesome. Major markets will be on line by 1990, and when combined with interactive ordering systems, which we will talk about shortly, they will involve more sophistication and more sophisticated techniques in marketing. Naturally, many more satellites will be in oribt, and major companies as well as small entrepreneurs will be fully engaged in this type of direct-response advertising. In the foreseeable future, cable television will be a major factor in all marketing activities.

INTERACTIVE SYSTEMS

With interactive systems, you interact with the medium of advertisement or direct response that you are viewing. In the case of television it means actually communicating with your television set. Let's look at some of these systems.

Viewdata

Viewdata began in England and was invented by Sam Fedida, a British research engineer. It has been offered by the British Post Office since 1976. In England the system is called Prestel. Viewdata has other names in other countries. In the United States it's called Viewdata; in Canada, Telidon; in France, Teletel; in Japan, Captain; in Germany, Bildschirmtext. With this system you need only a telephone and a modified television in order to be in business. The subscriber is given a key pad about the size of a hand-held calculator, or in some cases a keyboard. The subscriber keys requests in, the data appear on the television on frames, and this is the way that advertisements are perceived. Frames that can be requested are rented by the advertiser. In this way the buyer can compare prices, receive product descriptions, and order and pay by credit card or by electronic fund transfer. One current limitation of Viewdata is that photos or moving pictures can't be projected or broadcast, but this limitation is being overcome. A leading Viewdata system in the United States was introduced by Knight-Ridder, a newspaper company.

Qube

Qube is a cable interactive television system introduced by Warner-Amex Cable Communications. It started in Columbus, Ohio, and has since expanded to other cities. In Columbus alone it has had more than 30,000 subscribers. In this case all subscribers have their home televisions hooked to the studio by cable, and more than 30 different channels are offered. For Christmas shopping, separate television channels are offered solely for direct-response advertising. Customers watch these presentations and can order merchandise by pressing one of five different response buttons on a small console furnished with the system as designated by the host of the "show."

Other interactive television systems are in the offing, but even without television and only a computer, direct-response advertising will be possible. A system called the Source, offered by Telecomputing Corporation of America and operated by hooking up the owner's computer by telephone lines, started in 1979. This system is very easy to operate and, of course, the display comes on the video display furnished with the owner's computer. The telephone handset is operated by placing it into a special coupler. Then a local access number is dialed through the telephone and the viewer waits for a light to appear on his or her terminal. He or she then types in his or her account number and a special password, and is ready to go. Currently, the Source offers a home shopping service via the Money Saver, which features a 20-to-30% discount over merchandise ordered through the terminal. At the present time no advertising is offered, but you can immediately grasp the potential. The future will probably see more direct-response advertising over one's personal computer.

Videodisc

In 1981, one of the original traditional mail order companies, Sears Roebuck, produced a videodisc catalog for the Pioneer Videodisc Player. A test was conducted with 1000 customers. The catalog consisted of 5600 frames in 19 video motion sequences, which ranged in time from 30 seconds to four minutes. The results of this test were very promising, and Sears plans to continue to develop electronic communication for catalog marketing and to make use of the videodisc in the interactive capabilities coupled with other systems. Futurists are already predicting mail order catalogs that are totally interactive, in which various prices, views, and uses of the products can all be called up and viewed by a sophisticated disc catalog that will even enable holistic viewing. This degree of complexity is as yet in the future, although if the videodisc test run by Sears is any indication, it may happen sooner than we think.

Cassettads

Cassettads are a brand new response medium. They consist of a 90-minute tape with 24 songs hosted by a disc jockey. They also include 24 advertising commercials. The consumer pays a small amount for this tape. He or she may receive it when requesting a special catalog, or it could be a premium received when purchasing another product. The tape also contains coupons to permit direct response for the advertised products, along with reduction on the products ordered. It is estimated that by 1985, 20 million of these tapes will be in circulation. Further, plans are in motion that after 1985 videodisc ads will be constructed in the same fashion, with the consumer paying a reduction in amount that he or she would pay for a regular videodisc.

Ink-Jet

Personalization is the key to winning in direct response; it always has been and it always will be. Ink-Jet imaging is the new method that allows large volumes of personalized mailings. In fact, in one year, 1982, Ink-Jet Systems produced over two billion feet of personalized mailings for direct marketers.

The advantages of Ink-Jet printing are not only that they permit personalization by name and address, but also that the area of personalization has been greatly increased for effective imaging in the same package, including personalization of advertising copy, order forms, locally addressed reply cards and envelopes, temporary ID cards, pressure-sensitive stickers, personalized coupons, and so forth.

Recent developments have permitted such personalization at a relatively low cost not only for the large, multimillion-piece mailings but also for those who are doing mailings as low as 10,000 pieces. This means Ink-Jet will be available for use not only by large companies but by smaller entrepreneurs as well.

Future developments along this line will permit individual catalogs to be sent out based on an individual's past ordering pattern. Mass-produced catalogs will be possible that are not identical but are personalized for each customer. A true breakthrough in mail order printing and catalogs for the future!

In this chapter we've discussed just a few of the recent and near-future developments in this incredibly dynamic and technology-oriented field. Clearly, for mail order, the future has already begun; and the developments in the last 15 years in this exciting field are probably greater in a technological sense than any that have occurred in the previous history of this method of marketing since it first began in the nineteenth century. These new technologies are likely to accelerate even further the fantastic growth of the direct-response industry, representing significant opportunities for entrepreneurs.

A Personal Postscript
from the Author

As I reviewed the material in this book I have just completed, I thought about the hundreds of different topics and techniques we've discussed. I believe that I have told you every single thing that you need to be a success in mail order. I say this based not only on my own personal experience, but also on the experience of hundreds of others who have taken my courses and attended my seminars; I have heard from my students all over the country who have followed my instructions, and I know that these instructions work and lead to success. However, to be successful in mail order, just reading this book is insufficient. You must act. You must actually start a business to reap any benefit from the information I have given you. Further, even though the information is correct and will lead to success, you will find additional secrets in mail order, secrets you cannot get from anywhere but your own experience. And so, the final chapter of this book is really your own and is not contained between these covers. For it is your own adventure in mail order and the secrets and success you will gain from it. You may not become an overnight mail order millionaire, but if you start your business and lay it out according to the instructions that I have given you, whether you are part- or full-time, you can make a good profit, and you will, with all sorts of rewards. Some will be financial. Others will relate to the personal satisfaction that you are making a significant contribution to the joy and betterment of other people who are your customers. The greater service that you render to others, the greater your own rewards, financial and otherwise, will be. To this end, I wish you the tremendous good fortune and success that can be yours.

Appendix A

A Business Guide to the Federal Trade Commission's Mail Order Rule

Contents

 Introduction

 How to Comply With the Rule

 Questions and Answers About the Rule

 Sample Notices

1 Introduction

What is the Mail Order Rule

The Mail Order Rule was issued by the Federal Trade Commission (FTC) to correct growing problems with late or undelivered mail order merchandise. Under this Rule, you have a duty to ship merchandise on time. You also must follow procedures that the Rule requires if you cannot ship ordered merchandise on time.

When there is a shipping delay, the Rule requires that you notify your customers of the delay and provide them with an option either to agree to the delay or to cancel the order and receive a prompt refund. For each additional delay, your customers must be notified that they must send you a signed consent to a further delay or a refund will be given.

Why Was the Rule Issued

The Rule was issued after federal, state, and local consumer protection authorities received thousands of consumer complaints about mail order problems. The major complaints were: failure to deliver merchandise, late delivery of merchandise, failure to make prompt refunds, and failure to answer customer inquiries about delayed or lost orders. For example:

- One consumer wrote about Christmas decorations she ordered in early October that were finally shipped the day before Christmas. This consumer wrote twice to the company about her order, the second time requesting a refund. Both inquiries were ignored.
- Another consumer complained about a company that failed to send a stereo component he ordered with payment in July. By late October, the only communication he received from the company was his canceled check.

Title 16—Commercial Practices

CHAPTER I—FEDERAL TRADE COMMISSION

PART 435—MAIL ORDER MERCHANDISE

Promulgation of Trade Regulation Rule

THE FEDERAL TRADE COMMISSION, pursuant to the Federal Trade Commission Act, as amended, 15 U.S.C. 41, et seq., and the provisions of Subpart B, Part I of the Commission's Procedures and Rules of Practice, 16 CFR 1.11, et seq., has conducted a proceeding for the promulgation of a Trade Regulation Rule concerning Undelivered Mail Order Merchandise and Services. Notice of this proceeding, including a proposed Rule, was published in the FEDERAL REGISTER on September 28, 1971 (36 FR 19092 (1971)). Interested parties were thereafter afforded opportunity to participate in the proceeding through the submission of written data, views and arguments, and to appear and express their views orally and to suggest amendments, revisions, and additions to the proposed Rule.

The FTC received 3,200 similar consumer complaints prior to beginning its rulemaking process. In addition, the President's Office of Consumer Affairs (OCA) received over 1,000 complaints concerning mail order practices, 60% of which concerned non-delivery. OCA complaint statistics for mail order were second only to complaints about autos and auto services.

The rulemaking record contains more than 10,000 pages of complaints regarding mail order sales. State and local agencies urged the Commission to take action to correct these problems. Industry members provided valuable input as to the feasibility and practicality of a mail order rule.

On October 22, 1975, the FTC promulgated the Mail Order Rule, and it went into effect on February 2, 1976.

Why You Should Comply with the Rule

When you comply with the Rule, you are being responsive to your customers. This is beneficial to you and to your customers because it promotes a positive industry image. Compliance creates consumer trust in buying by mail and fosters repeat mail order business. Of course if you ship on time, the requirements of the Rule pertaining to "option notices" do not apply.

Although most members of the mail order industry adhere to the Rule's requirements, there are some who do not. The FTC's Bureau of Consumer Protection monitors consumer complaints to ensure that businesses comply with the Rule. The FTC also provides compliance information, such as this manual, and assistance to all industry members.

AFTER IT HAD CONSIDERED THE SUGGESTIONS, CRITICISMS, objections, and other pertinent information in the Record, the Commission on March 8, 1974, published a revised proposed rule in a notice in the FEDERAL REGISTER (39 FR 9201 (1974)) extending an opportunity to interested parties to submit data, views or arguments regarding the revised proposed Rule. A period of over 90 days was allowed for the submission of written comments on the revised proposal. Written comments of the Direct Mail Marketing Association (DM/MA) were admitted into the Record at a subsequent date and the public was given 30 days to submit written views and comments related to the DM/MA submission (39 FR 40515 (1974)).

The Commission has now considered all matters of fact, law, policy and discretion, including the data, views and arguments presented on the Record by interested parties in response to the Notices, as prescribed by law, and has determined that the adoption of the Trade Regulation Rule set forth herein and its Statement of Basis and Purpose[1] is in the public interest.

Accordingly, the Commission hereby amends Subchapter D, Trade Regulation Rules, Chapter I of 16 CFR by adding a new Part 435 as follows:

Sec.
435.1   The Rule.
435.2   Definitions.

AUTHORITY: The provisions of this Part 435 issued under 38 Stat. 717, as amended, 15 U.S.C. 41, et seq.

---

[1] Statement of Basis and Purpose filed as part of the original document.

2 How to Comply with the Rule

This section of the manual provides **THE TEXT OF THE RULE, WITH EXPLANATIONS OPPOSITE** of how to comply with the Rule.

§ 435.1   The Rule.

IN CONNECTION WITH MAIL ORDER SALES in commerce, as "commerce" is defined in the Federal Trade Commission Act, it constitutes an unfair method of competition, and an unfair or deceptive act and practice for a seller:

(a)(1) To solicit any order for the sale of merchandise to be ordered by the buyer through the mails unless, at the time of the solicitation, the seller has a reasonable basis to expect that he will be able to ship any ordered merchandise to the buyer: (i) within that time clearly and conspicuously stated in any such solicitation, or (ii) if no time is clearly and conspicuously stated, within thirty (30) days after receipt of a properly completed order from the buyer.

(2) To provide any buyer with any revised shipping date, as provided in paragraph (b), unless, at the time any such revised shipping date is provided, the seller has a reasonable basis for making such representation regarding a definite revised shipping date.

(3) To inform any buyer that he is unable to make any representation regarding the length of any delay unless (i) the seller has a reasonable basis for so informing the buyer and (ii) the seller informs the buyer of the reason or reasons for the delay.

(b)(1) Where a seller is unable to ship merchandise within the applicable time set forth in paragraph (a)(1), above, to fail to offer to the buyer, clearly and conspicuously and without prior demand, an option either to consent to a delay in shipping or to cancel his order and receive a prompt refund. Said offer shall be made within a reasonable time after the seller first becomes aware of his inability to ship within the applicable time set forth in paragraph (a)(1), but in no event later than said applicable time.

What to Know When You Make an Offer

When you offer to sell merchandise by mail, the Rule requires you to have a "reasonable basis" for expecting to ship within the time stated in your solicitation.

For example, if you know before advertising your products that your suppliers are on strike and are likely to remain on strike for several months, you do not have a "reasonable basis" for expecting to ship within a month.

The shipping date, when provided in your offer, must be clearly and conspicuously stated:

ADVERTISEMENT
Cardigan Sweaters
S, M, L — Beige or Blue
$29.95 plus tax
Allow 5 weeks for shipment.

If you do not provide a shipping date, you must ship the merchandise within 30 days of receiving a "properly completed" order. An order is properly completed when you receive payment accompanied by all information you need to fill the order. Payment may be made by cash, money order, check, or credit card, according to your company policy. If a credit card is used for a purchase, the order is properly completed when you charge your customer's account.

When you cannot ship on time, you must provide your customer with an "option" notice. The notice must provide an option to cancel the order and receive a prompt refund, or to agree to a delay in shipping. And, as with the original date, you must have a reasonable basis for setting that shipping date.

You must also have a reasonable basis for telling your customers that you do not know when you can ship merchandise. In that case, you must provide the specific reasons for the shipping problem. For example, you could state that a fire destroyed the warehouse holding the goods and you are unable to provide a revised shipping date because you

497

do not know how long it will take to replace the merchandise.

When You Should Send a First Notice

If a shipment is delayed, the Rule requires that you give your customers an option:

- to consent to a delay; or
- to cancel the order and receive a prompt refund.

People in the trade often refer to the notice as a "delay" notice. More accurately, it should be called an "option" notice. You violate the Rule if you only provide a notice of delay without also providing an option to cancel the order.

Remember, you must send the notice after you first become aware that there will be a shipping delay. The notice must be sent:

- before the promised shipping date; or
- within 30 days after you receive the order (if no date was provided in your solicitation).

What a First Notice Must Say

If you provide a revised shipping date of 30 days or less, you must have a reasonable basis for making the change. The notice must inform your customers that non-response is considered consent to be a delay of 30 days or less.

If you are unable to provide a revised shipping date, your notice must state that you cannot determine when the merchandise will be shipped. It must also state that the order will be automatically canceled unless:

- you ship the merchandise within 30 days of the original shipping date and you have not received your customer's cancellation before shipment; or

(b)(i) ANY OFFER TO THE BUYER of such an option shall fully inform the buyer regarding his right to cancel the order and to obtain a prompt refund and shall provide a definite revised shipping date, but where the seller lacks a reasonable basis for providing a definite revised shipping date the notice shall inform the buyer that the seller is unable to make any representation regarding the length of the delay.

(ii) WHERE THE SELLER HAS PROVIDED a definite revised shipping date which is thirty (30) days or less later than the applicable time set forth in paragraph (a)(1), the offer of said option shall expressly inform the buyer that, unless the seller receives, prior to shipment and prior to the expiration of the definite revised shipping date, a response from the buyer rejecting the delay and canceling the order, the buyer will be deemed to have consented to a delayed shipment on or before the definite revised shipping date.

(iii) Where the seller has provided a definite revised shipping date which is more than thirty (30) days later than the applicable time set forth in paragraph (a)(1) or where the seller is unable to provide a definite revised shipping date and therefore informs the buyer that he is unable to make any representation regarding the length of the delay, the offer of said option shall also expressly inform the buyer that his order will automatically be deemed to have been canceled unless (A) the seller has shipped the merchandise within thirty (30) days of the applicable time set forth in paragraph (a)(1), and has

498

received no cancellation prior to shipment, or (B) the seller has received from the buyer within thirty (30) days of said applicable time, a response specifically consenting to said shipping delay. Where the seller informs the buyer that he is unable to make any representation regarding the length of the delay, the buyer shall be expressly informed that, should he consent to an indefinite delay, he will have a continuing right to cancel his order at any time after the applicable time set forth in paragraph (a)(1) by so notifying the seller prior to actual shipment.

(iv) Nothing in this paragraph shall prohibit a seller who furnishes a definite revised shipping date pursuant to paragraph (b)(1)(i), from requesting, simultaneously with or at any time subsequent to the offer of an option pursuant to paragraph (b)(1), the buyer's express consent to a further unanticipated delay beyond the definite revised shipping date in the form of a response from the buyer specifically consenting to said further delay. *Provided, however,* that where the seller solicits consent to an unanticipated indefinite delay the solicitation shall expressly inform the buyer that, should he so consent to an indefinite delay, he shall have a continuing right to cancel his order at any time after the definite revised shipping date by so notifying the seller prior to actual shipment.

(b)(2) Where a seller is unable to ship merchandise on or before the definite revised shipping date provided under paragraph (b)(1)(i) and consented to by the buyer pursuant to paragraph (b)(1)(ii) or (iii), to fail to offer to the buyer, clearly and conspicuously and without prior demand, a renewed option either to consent to a further delay or to cancel the order and to receive a prompt refund. Said offer shall be made within a reasonable time after the seller first becomes aware of his inability to ship before the said definite revised date, but in no event later than the expiration of the definite revised shipping date. Provided, however, that where the seller previously has obtained the buyer's express consent to an unanticipated delay until a specific date beyond the definite revised shipping date, pursuant to paragraph (b)(1)(iv) or to a further delay until a specific date beyond the definite revised shipping date pursuant to this paragraph (b)(2), that date to which the buyer has expressly consented shall supersede the definite revised shipping date for purposes of this paragraph (b)(2).

(i) ANY OFFER TO THE BUYER of said renewed option shall provide the buyer with a new definite revised shipping date, but where the seller lacks a reasonable basis for providing a new definite revised shipping date, the notice shall inform the buyer that the seller is unable to make any representation regarding the length of the further delay.

(ii) The offer of a renewed option shall expressly inform the buyer that, unless the seller receives, prior to the expiration of the old definite revised shipping date or any date superseding the old definite revised shipping date, notification from the buyer specifically consenting to the further delay, the buyer will be deemed to have rejected any further delay, and to have canceled the order if the seller is in fact unable to ship prior to the expiration of the old definite revised shipping date or any date superseding the old definite revised shipping date.

- you receive within 30 days of the original date your customer's consent to the delay.

Your notice must provide this information if the definite revised shipping date is more than 30 days after the original date.

When you are unable to provide a revised shipping date, you must inform your customers of their continuing right to cancel the order by notifying you prior to actual shipment.

What Later Notices Must Say

If you are unable to ship the merchandise on or before your revised shipping date, you must notify your customers again. This is called a "renewed option" notice. This notice must inform your customers of their right to consent to a further delay, or to cancel the order and receive a prompt refund.

The renewed option notice must inform customers that if they do not agree in writing to this delay, their order will be canceled. Unless you receive your customer's express written consent to the second delay before the first delay period ends, you must cancel the order and provide a full refund.

Keep in mind that you do not have to offer a "renewed option" to customers who consent to an indefinite delay in response to the first option notice. But any customer who agrees to an indefinite delay has the continuing right to cancel the order at any time before the merchandise is shipped.

How You Should Send Notices

You should send any option notice by first class mail, and your notice should provide a written means for your customers to respond. A prepaid business mail reply or prepaid postage card meets this requirement.

The notice is most advantageous for you if at some point you have to prove that you complied with the Rule. If the FTC takes action against a company, the firm must be able to show that any other form of notice it used was equal to or better than the written form described in the Rule. For example, an "800" telephone number for customers' use in canceling orders is an adequate substitute, if you can prove that the system met the Rule's requirements. This would include being able to show that the 800 number could readily and consistently be used to cancel an order because you provided adequate and competent staff to take cancellations. You should keep records of all cancellations.

When You *May* Cancel an Order

In some cases you can have an option to cancel an order or to send out another notice. You may make this decision when you are unable to ship merchandise on time or within the delay period to which your customer agreed. But if you decide to cancel the order,

Provided, however, that where the seller offers the buyer the option to consent to an indefinite delay the offer shall expressly inform the buyer that, should he so consent to an indefinite delay, he shall have a continuing right to cancel his order at any time after the old definite revised shipping date or any date superseding the old definite revised shipping date.

(iii) This paragraph (b)(2) shall not apply to any situation where a seller, pursuant to the provisions of paragraph (b)(1)(iv), has previously obtained consent from the buyer to an indefinite extension beyond the first revised shipping date.

[i]t constitutes an unfair method of competition, and an unfair or deceptive act and practice for a seller:...

(b)(3) WHEREVER A BUYER HAS THE RIGHT to exercise any option under this part or to cancel an order by so notifying the seller prior to shipment, to fail to furnish the buyer with adequate means, at the seller's expense, to exercise such option or to notify the seller regarding cancellation. In any action brought by the Federal Trade Commission alleging a violation of this part, the failure of a respondent-seller:

(i) To provide any offer, notice or option required by this part in writing and by first class mail will create a rebuttable presumption that the respondent-seller failed to offer a clear and conspicuous offer, notice or option;

(ii) To provide the buyer with the means in writing (by business reply mail or with postage prepaid by the seller) to exercise any option or to notify the seller regarding a decision to cancel, will create a rebuttable presumption that the respondent-seller did not provide the buyer with adequate means pursuant to this subparagraph (3).

NOTHING IN PARAGRAPH (B) of this part shall prevent a seller, where he is unable to make shipment within the time set forth in paragraph (a)(1) or within a delay period consented to by the buyer, from deciding to consider the order canceled and providing the buyer with notice of said decision within a reasonable time after he becomes aware of said inability to ship, together with a prompt refund.

you must inform your customer of this decision and provide a prompt refund.

Whether you cancel or send another notice, you must inform your customer about it within a reasonable time after you know you cannot ship the merchandise.

[i]t constitutes an unfair method of competition, and an unfair or deceptive act and practice for a seller:....

(c) To FAIL TO DEEM AN ORDER CANCELED and to make a prompt refund to the buyer whenever:

(1) The seller receives, prior to the time of shipment, notification from the buyer canceling the order pursuant to any option, renewed option or continuing option under this part;

(2) The seller has, pursuant to paragraph (b)(1)(iii), provided the buyer with a definite revised shipping date which is more than thirty (30) days later than the applicable time set forth in paragraph (a)(1) or has notified the buyer that he is unable to make any representation regarding the length of the delay and the seller (i) has not shipped the merchandise within thirty (30) days of the applicable time set forth in paragraph (a)(1), and (ii) has not received the buyer's express consent to said shipping delay within said thirty (30) days;

(3) The seller is unable to ship within the applicable time set forth in paragraph (b)(2), and has not received, within the said applicable time, the buyer's consent to any further delay;

(4) The seller has notified the buyer of his inability to make shipment and has indicated his decision not to ship the merchandise;

(5) The seller fails to offer the option prescribed in paragraph (b)(1) and has not shipped the merchandise within the applicable time set forth in paragraph (a)(1).

When You *Must* Cancel an Order

You must cancel an order and provide a prompt refund:

- when your customer does not agree to a delay and exercises the option to cancel an order before it has been shipped;
- when you notify your customer of your inability to ship the merchandise and of your decision to cancel the order;
- when you are unable to ship merchandise before the revised shipping date and you have not received your customer's consent to a further delay;
- when the delay is indefinite and you have not shipped the merchandise or received your customer's consent to an indefinite delay;
- when the definite revised shipping date in the first option notice is more than 30 days after the original shipping date, and you have not shipped the merchandise, nor received your customer's consent to the delay within 30 days of the original shipping date; or
- when you cannot ship on time and do not notify your customers of their options.

All refunds must be sent to the buyer by first class mail. If the buyer paid by cash, check, or money order, you must refund payment within seven (7) days after the order is canceled. For credit card sales, you must make refunds within one billing cycle after the order is canceled. Under no circumstances are you to substitute credit vouchers or script for a refund.

Why You Should Keep Records

If for some reason your company has problems in shipping on time, your customers may begin to file complaints with you, and with local, state, or federal law enforcement agencies. Because the Federal Trade Commission has enforcement jurisdiction under the Mail Order Rule, many complaints are forwarded to the FTC from other agencies.

When the FTC takes action against a company and alleges that it violated the Rule, the company must have records or other documentary proof that will show the steps it took to comply. Systems and procedures for complying with the Rule are carefully reviewed. Lack of such proof creates a rebuttable presumption that the company failed to comply. This means that the seller must be able to show that it used reasonable systems and procedures to comply with the Rule. Consequently, it is in your best interest to establish an accurate, up-to-date record-keeping system.

(a)(4) IN ANY ACTION BROUGHT BY THE FEDERAL TRADE COMMIS-SION, alleging a violation of this part, the failure of a respondent-seller to have records or other documentary proof establishing his use of systems and procedures which assure the shipment of merchandise in the ordinary course of business within any applicable time set forth in this part will create a rebuttable presumption that the seller lacked a reasonable basis for any expectation of shipment within said applicable time.

(d) In any action brought by the Federal Trade Commission, alleging a violation of this part, the failure of a respondent-seller to have records or other documentary proof establishing his use of systems and procedures which assure compliance, in the ordinary course of business, with any requirement of paragraphs (b) or (c) of this part will create a rebuttable presumption that the seller failed to comply with said requirements.

What the Rule Does Not Cover

The following mail order sales are exempt from the Rule:

- magazine subscriptions (and similar serial deliveries), except for the first shipment;
- sales of seeds and growing plants;
- orders made on a collect-on-delivery basis (C.O.D.);
- transactions covered by the FTC's Negative Option Rule (such as book and record clubs);
- mail order photo-finishing; or
- orders made by telephone and charged to a credit card account.

NOTE 1: This part shall not apply to subscriptions, such as magazine sales, ordered for serial delivery, after the initial shipment is made in compliance with this part.

NOTE 2: This part shall not apply to orders of seeds and growing plants.

NOTE 3: This part shall not apply to orders made on a collect-on-delivery (C.O.D.) basis.

NOTE 4: This part shall not apply to transactions governed by the Federal Trade Commission's Trade Regulation Rule entitled "Use of Negative Option Plans by Sellers in Commerce," 16 CFR 425.

NOTE 5: By taking action in this area, the Federal Trade Commission does not intend to preempt action in the same area, which is not inconsistent with this part, by any State, municipal, or other local government. This part does not annul or diminish any rights or remedies provided to consumers by any State law, municipal ordinance, or other local regulation, insofar as those rights or remedies are equal to or greater than those provided by this part. In addition, this part does not supersede those provisions of any State law, municipal ordinance, or other local regulation which impose obligations or liabilities upon sellers, when sellers subject to this part are not in compliance therewith. This part does supersede those provisions of any State law, municipal ordinance, or other local regulation which are inconsistent with this part to the extent that those provisions do not provide a buyer with rights which are equal to or greater than those rights granted a buyer by this part. This part also supersedes those provisions of any State law, municipal ordinance, or other local regulation requiring that a buyer be notified of a right which is the same as a right provided by this part but requiring that a buyer be given notice of this right in a language, form, or manner which is different in any way from that required by this part.

In those instances where any State law, municipal ordinance, or other local regulation contains provisions, some but not all of which are partially or completely superseded by this part, the provisions or portions of those provisions which have not been superseded retain their full force and effect.

NOTE 6: If any provision of this part or its application to any person, partnership, corporation, act or practice is held invalid, the remainder of this part or the application of the provision to any other person, partnership, corporation, act or practice shall not be affected thereby.

NOTE 7: Section 435.1(a)(1) of this part governs all solicitations where the time of solicitation is more than 100 days after promulgation of this part. The remainder of this part governs all transactions where receipt of a properly completed order occurs more than 100 days after promulgation of this part.

§ 435.2   Definitions.

For purposes of this part:

(a) "Shipment" shall mean the act by which the merchandise is physically placed in the possession of the carrier.

(b) "Receipt of a properly completed order" shall mean:

(1) Where there is a credit sale and the buyer has not previously tendered partial payment, the time at which the seller charges the buyer's account;

(2) Where the buyer tenders full or partial payment in the proper amount in the form of cash, check or money order, the time at which the seller has received both said payment and an order from the buyer containing all the information needed by the seller to process and ship the order.

Where to Go for Help

For more information, contact:

- the Federal Trade Commission, Enforcement Division, B.C.P., Washington, D.C. 20580, (202) 376-3475;
- the Direct Marketing Association, 1730 K Street, N.W., Washington, D.C. 20006;
- your local United States Postal Service; and
- your local consumer protection office.

State and local governments also may have requirements with which you must comply. You should consult each agency for information about laws that affect your operations.

Definitions

Provided, however, that where the seller receives notice that the check or money order tendered by the buyer has been dishonored or that the buyer does not qualify for a credit sale, "receipt of a properly completed order" shall mean the time at which (i) the seller receives notice that a check or money order for the proper amount tendered by the buyer has been honored, (ii) the buyer tenders cash in the proper amount or (iii) the seller receives notice that the buyer qualifies for a credit sale.

(c) "Refund" shall mean:

(1) Where the buyer tendered full payment for the unshipped merchandise in the form of cash, check, or money order, a return of the amount tendered in the form of cash, check, or money order;

(2) Where there is a credit sale:

(i) And the seller is a creditor, a copy of a credit memorandum or the like or an account statement reflecting the removal or absence of any remaining charge incurred as a result of the sale from the buyer's account;

(ii) And a third party is the creditor, a copy of an appropriate credit memorandum or the like to the third party creditor which will remove the charge from the buyer's account or a statement from the seller acknowledging the cancellation of the order and representing that he has not taken any action regarding the order which will result in a charge to the buyer's account with the third party;

(iii) And the buyer tendered partial payment for the unshipped merchandise in the form of cash, check, or money order, a return of the amount tendered in the form of cash, check, or money order.

(d) "Prompt refund" shall mean:

(1) Where a refund is made pursuant to Definition (c) (1) or (2) (iii), a refund sent to the buyer by first class mail within seven (7) working days of the date on which the buyer's right to refund vests under the provisions of this part;

(2) Where a refund is made pursuant to Definition (c) (2) (i) or (ii), a refund sent to the buyer by first class mail within one (1) billing cycle from the date on which the buyer's right to refund vests under the provisions of this part.

(e) The "time of solicitation" of an order shall mean that time when the seller has:

(1) Mailed or otherwise disseminated the solicitation to a prospective purchaser;

(2) Made arrangements for an advertisement containing the solicitation to appear in a newspaper, magazine, or the like, or on radio or television, which cannot be changed or canceled without incurring substantial expense; or

(3) Made arrangements for the printing of a catalog, brochure or the like which cannot be changed without incurring substantial expense, in which the solicitation in question forms an insubstantial part.

Effective: February 2, 1976.

Promulgated October 22, 1975, by the Federal Trade Commission.

CHARLES A. TOBIN,
Secretary.

[FH Doc. 75-28203 Filed 70-21-75; 3:45 am]

3 Questions and Answers About the Rule

The FTC receives questions from mail order sellers who want to know how to comply with the Rule. The following questions are those that are asked most frequently.

What to Do When You Start a Mail Order Business

Q: What advice do you give someone who is planning to start a mail order business?

A: The FTC suggests that you do the following:
- Learn the requirements of the Mail Order Rule.
- Familiarize yourself with state laws in areas where you plan to do business. For example, some states, such as Wisconsin, have additional mail order requirements that should be followed.
- Ask experienced mail order sellers for practical hints to help you avoid the pitfalls in mail order business.

Q: How important is it to set up a customer service procedure?

A: An efficient customer service procedure is beneficial to you and your customers. Customers often complain that they have been treated badly by the companies they have contacted. But the number of complaints should drop significantly if your customer service personnel communicate responsively with your customers when they have problems.

Q: Our company has read the Mail Order Rule, but we still have questions about what we can and cannot do. Who should we contact?

A: It depends on whether you need a formal or an informal response.
- You should feel free to write the FTC Enforcement Division to ask questions about the Rule and how your operations are affected. Staff advice is not binding on the Commission, but this advice can be helpful.
- You may obtain a binding advisory opinion from the Commission if you send a specific, written inquiry about the legality of certain conduct. Advisory opinions apply only to proposed conduct, not to conduct that is in practice. The opinions are usually restricted to questions that are not clearly answered by the terms of the Rule. Ask the FTC staff about the procedure for obtaining an advisory opinion.

When You Must Ship an Order

Q: We advertise a shipment date of six weeks. What happens if there is a workers' strike or some other unanticipated event and shipment is delayed? Have we violated the Rule?

A: If you calculated the shipping date correctly in the first place, you have complied with the Rule. But if you discover that a delay cannot be avoided, you must notify your customers and provide the option notice. If you fail to do this, you have unilaterally changed the sales contract and have violated the Rule.

Q: We advertise several products but do not indicate a shipping date in our ads. When must we ship?

A: If your solicitation does not state when you plan to ship the merchandise, the Rule requires that you ship it within 30 days after you receive a properly completed order (that is, when you have received payment and sufficient information to fill the order).

Q: How can we protect our company accounts from customers who bounce checks or do not qualify for credit?

A: Be prompt in depositing checks and checking your customers' credit-worthiness. Remember, the order is properly completed, triggering the 30-day period, when you receive payment and all information needed to process the order. For example, if the buyer does not send enough cash to cover the cost of an order, the order is not properly completed. You may wait for the check to clear before mailing, as long as you ship within the 30-day period.

Q: What about a credit sale?

A: When you receive a properly completed order with a charge account number, the clock starts when you charge your customer's account.

Q: If a customer orders an item which is not in stock when the order is received, can we substitute an item of similar or better quality without the customer's consent?

A: No. The FTC has established that you must obtain your customer's authorization to substitute merchandise different from that ordered.

506

What Items Are Covered

Q: *Are mail order sales between businesses covered by the Rule?*

A: Yes. Mail order transactions between businesses are covered. This would include specialty items, such as calendars, pens, and ashtrays which bear advertising messages and are not sold to the general public.

Q: *Does the Rule cover orders placed by telephone?*

A: The Rule covers those situations in which you solicit orders by telephone and require your customers to mail the order accompanied by payment. If the mail is used to finalize the sale, the Rule applies. If mail is not used, the Rule does not apply.

Q: *Does the Rule cover orders placed over the telephone involving credit card payment?*

A: No. The Rule does not cover charges to a credit card account when the order is placed over the telephone.

What Rule Applies to Unordered Merchandise

Q: *Is it legal to send unordered merchandise through the U.S. Mail?*

A: No. The unordered merchandise statute provides that only two kinds of merchandise can be sent legally through the U.S. Mail without a consumer's prior consent:

- free samples that are clearly and conspicuously marked as such; and
- merchandise mailed by a charitable organization asking for contributions.

Consumers may consider unordered merchandise sent through the U.S. Mail as a free gift. They are not obligated to return it or to pay for it. Also, it is illegal for a company to send any bill or dunning communication seeking payment or return of unordered merchandise.

Why Record-Keeping is Important

Q: *Does the Rule require us to keep records?*

A: No. The Mail Order Rule does not impose record-keeping requirements on mail order sellers. But if you are ever involved in an action with the FTC, you must have records that prove you complied with the Rule. Therefore, it is advisable to establish a record-keeping method that best suits your situation and demonstrates compliance with the Rule.

Q: *How long do we have to keep customer complaint letters?*

A: The Rule does not specifically indicate whether or how long you must keep complaint letters. Complaint letters, when adequately answered, may be used as proof that you complied with the Rule if you are ever questioned. It is probably advisable to keep such correspondence and other records for a period of three to five years.

When the FTC Takes Action

Q: *What actually happens when the FTC receives a complaint against a company?*

A: The staff checks to see whether the company has been advised of the Rule's requirements. If not, then a copy of the Rule with an explanation letter is usually sent to the firm. The FTC evaluates consumer complaints to see whether a pattern of violations is developing. The FTC then contacts the company to determine whether further action is necessary.

Q: *Under what circumstances will the Commission sue a mail order firm for violating the Rule?*

A: If a company is violating the Rule, it runs the risk of being sued. The Commission evaluates many criteria to determine whether an action is in the public interest.

Q: *What are the penalties for violating the Rule?*

A: The FTC Act provides that a person, partnership, or corporation may be liable for civil penalties of up to $10,000 per

Q: What can industry members expect from the FTC in the future?

violation. In addition, the FTC can sue for consumer redress.

A: Because the industry is steadily growing, an increased enforcement presence can be expected. This may mean actions for civil penalties against firms who fail to comply with the Rule. At the same time, the FTC is part of a government-wide effort to encourage industry members to effectively regulate themselves. The FTC is working to assist businesses as they undertake voluntary compliance with the Rule. This manual is part of that effort.

4 Sample Notices

Sample Option Notice

[Rule Section 435.1(b)(1)(ii)]

When you are unable to ship on time and wish to provide a **revised shipping date which is 30 days or less** after the original date, use a form such as this to notify your customers. This form must be sent out by first class mail within a reasonable time after you become aware that there will be a shipping delay. It must be sent before the promised date, or if no date was promised, within 30 days after you receive a properly completed order.

Dear Customer:

Thank you for your order. We are sorry to inform you that there will be a delay in shipping the merchandise you ordered. We shall make shipment by the revised shipping date of (   ). It is quite possible we could ship earlier.

You have the right to consent to this delay or to cancel your order and receive a prompt refund. Please return this letter in the enclosed postpaid envelope with your instructions indicated by checking the appropriate block below.

Unless we hear from you prior to shipment or prior to *the revised shipping date*, it will be assumed that you have consented to a delayed shipment on or before the definite revised shipping date stated above.

Sincerely yours,

Name & Title of Signer
Company Name
Address

Enclosure: Envelope

☐ Yes, I will accept a further delay in shipment of my order for this item until _____ (Insert date which is 30 days or less.)

☐ I cannot wait. Please cancel my order for this item and promptly refund my money.

Please Sign Here

Sample Renewed Option Notice

[Rule Section 435.1(b)(2)(i)-(ii)]

When you are unable to ship merchandise on or before the promised definite revised shipping date, and wish to provide **a new definite revised shipping date,** use a form such as this to notify your customers.

Dear Customer:

We are sorry to inform you that there will be a further delay in shipping the merchandise you ordered. We shall make shipment by *(new definite revised shipping date)*. It is quite possible we could ship earlier.

You have the right to consent to a further delay or to cancel your order and receive a prompt refund. Please return this letter in the enclosed postpaid envelope with your instructions indicated by checking the appropriate block below.

Unless we hear from you prior to the old shipping date to which you previously agreed, it will be assumed that you have rejected any further shipping delay and your order will be canceled and a prompt refund made.

Sincerely yours,

Name & Title of Signer
Company Name
Address

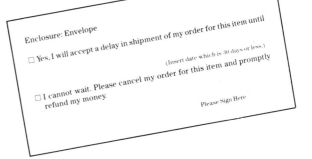

Enclosure: Envelope

☐ Yes, I will accept a delay in shipment of my order for this item until

(Insert date which is 30 days or less.)

☐ I cannot wait. Please cancel my order for this item and promptly refund my money.

Please Sign Here

☆ U.S. GOVERNMENT PRINTING OFFICE: 1983 - 408-216 - 814/1161

Appendix B

The Direct Marketing Association's Guidelines for Ethical Business Practices

*T*he Direct Mail/Marketing Association's Guidelines for Ethical Business Practices are intended to provide individuals and organizations involved in direct mail and direct marketing with principles of conduct that are generally accepted nationally and internationally. These Guidelines reflect DMMA's long-standing policy of high levels of ethics and the responsibility of the Association and direct marketers to the consumer and the community —a relationship that must be based on fair and ethical principles.

*W*hat distinguishes the Guidelines, which are self-regulatory in nature, is that all are urged to support them in spirit and not to treat their provisions as obstacles to be circumvented by legal ingenuity. The Guidelines are intended to be honored in the light of their aims and principles.

*T*hese Guidelines are also part of the DMMA's general philosophy that self-regulatory measures are preferable to governmental mandates whenever possible. Self-regulatory actions are more readily adaptable to changing techniques, economic and social conditions, and they encourage widespread use of sound business practices.

*B*ecause it is believed that dishonest, misleading, immoral, salacious or offensive communications make enemies for all advertising/marketing including direct response marketing, observance of these Guidelines by all concerned is recommended.

Table of Contents

The Terms of the Offer

Honesty
Article #1
All offers should be clear, honest and complete so that the consumer may know the exact nature of what is being offered, the price, the terms of payment (including all extra charges), and the commitment involved in the placing of an order. Before publication of an offer, direct marketers should be prepared to substantiate any claims or offers made. Advertisements or specific claims which are untrue, misleading, deceptive, fraudulent or unjustly disparaging of competitors should not be used.

Clarity
Article #2
A simple statement of all the essential points of the offer should be clearly displayed in the promotional material. When an offer illustrates goods which are not included or cost extra, these facts should be made clear.

Print Size
Article #3
Print which by its small size, placement or other visual characteristics is likely to substantially affect the legibility of the offer, or exceptions to it should not be used.

Actual Conditions
Article #4
All descriptions and promises should be in accordance with actual conditions, situations and circumstances existing at the time of the promotion. Claims regarding any limitations (such as time or quantity) should be legitimate.

Disparagement
Article #5
Disparagement of any person or group on grounds of race, color, religion, national origin, sex, marital status or age is unacceptable.

Standards
Article #6
Solicitations should not contain vulgar, immoral, profane, or offensive matter nor promote the sale of pornographic material or other matter not acceptable for advertising on moral grounds.

Advertising to Children
Article #7
Offers suitable for adults only should not be made to children.

Photographs and Art Work
Article #8
Photographs, illustrations, artwork, and the situations they represent, should be accurate portrayals and current reproductions of the product, service, or other subject in all particulars.

Sponsor and Intent
Article #9
All direct marketing contacts should disclose the name of the sponsor and each purpose of the contact. No one should make offers or solicitations in the guise of research or a survey when the real intent is to sell products or services or to raise funds.

Identity of Seller
Article #10
Every offer and shipment should sufficiently identify the full name and street address of the direct marketer so that the consumer may contact the individual or company by mail or phone.

Solicitation in the Guise of an Invoice
Article #11
Offers that are likely to be mistaken for bills or invoices should not be used.

Postage and Handling Charges
Article #12
Postage or shipping charges and handling charges, if any, should reflect as accurately as practicable actual costs incurred.

515

Special Offers

Use of the Word "Free" and other Similar Representations
Article #13

A product or service which is offered without cost or obligation to the recipient may be unqualifiedly described as "free".

If a product or service is offered as "free", for a nominal cost or at a greatly reduced price and the offer requires the recipient to purchase some other product or service, all terms and conditions should be clearly and conspicuously disclosed and in close conjunction with the use of the term "free" or other similar phrase.

When the term "free" or other similar representations are made (for example, 2-for-1, half price or 1-cent offers), the product or service required to be purchased should not be increased in price or decreased in quality or quantity.

Negative Option Selling
Article #14

All direct marketers should comply with the FTC regulation governing Negative Option Plans. Some of the major requirements of this regulation are listed below:

Offers which require the consumer to return a notice sent by the seller before each periodic shipment to avoid receiving merchandise should contain all important conditions of the plan including:
a. A full description of the obligation to purchase a minimum number of items and all the charges involved and,
b. the procedures by which the consumer receives the announcements of selections and a statement of their frequency; how the consumer rejects unwanted items and how to cancel after completing the obligation.

Negative Option Selling (Continued)

The consumer should be given advance notice of the periodic selection so that the consumer may have a minimum of ten days to exercise a timely choice.

Because of the nature of this kind of offer, special attention should be given to the clarity, completeness and prominent placement of the terms in the initial offering.

Sweepstakes
Article #15

All direct marketers should abide by the DMMA Guidelines for Self-Regulation of Sweepstakes Promotions. Articles #16 through #18 (below) contain the basic precepts of these Guidelines.

Clear and Conspicuous Disclosure of Rules
Article #16

All terms and conditions of the sweepstakes, including entry procedures, the number and types of prizes, the closing dates, eligibility requirements, and the fact that no purchase is required should be disclosed in a clear and conspicuous manner in the promotion.

Devices, check boxes, reply envelopes and the like used for entering the sweepstakes only should be as conspicuous as those utilized for ordering the product or service and entering the sweepstakes.

Prizes
Article #17

All prizes advertised should be awarded. Winners should be selected in a manner that ensures fair application of the laws of chance.

Chances of Winning
Article #18

No sweepstakes promotion, or any of its parts, should state or imply that a recipient has won a prize or overstate the chances of winning.

Price Comparisons
Article #19
Price comparisons may be made in two ways:
  a. between one's price and a former, future or suggested price or
  b. between one's price and the price of a competitor's comparable product.

In all price comparisons, the compared price against which the comparison is made must be fair and accurate.

In each case of comparison to a former, suggested or competitor's comparable product price, substantial sales should have been made at that price in the recent past.

For comparisons with a future price, there should be a reasonable expectation that the future price will be charged in the foreseeable future.

Guarantees
Article #20
If a product or service is offered with a "guarantee" or a "warranty", the terms and conditions should either be set forth in full in the promotion, or the promotion should state how the consumer may obtain a copy. The guarantee should clearly state the name and address of the guarantor and the duration of the guarantee.

Any requests for repair, replacement or refund under the terms of a "guarantee" or "warranty" should be honored promptly. In an unqualified offer of refund, repair or replacement, the customer's preference shall prevail.

Special Claims

Use of Test or Survey Data
Article #21
All test or survey data referred to in advertising should be competent and reliable as to source and methodology, and should support the specific claim for which it is cited. Advertising claims should not distort the test or survey results nor take them out of context.

Testimonials and Endorsements
Article #22
Testimonials and endorsements should be used only if they are:
  a. Authorized by the person quoted,
  b. Genuine and related to the experience of the person giving them and
  c. Not taken out of context so as to distort the endorser's opinion or experience with the product.

The Product

Product Safety
Article #23
Products should be safe in normal use and be free of defects likely to cause injury. To that end, they should meet or exceed current, recognized health and safety norms and be adequately tested, where applicable. Information provided with the product should include proper directions for use and full instructions covering assembly and safety warnings, whenever necessary.

Product Distribution Safety
Article #24
Products should be distributed only in a manner that will provide reasonable safeguards against possibilities of injury.

Product Availability
Article #25
Direct marketers should only offer merchandise when it is on hand or when there is a reasonable expectation of its receipt.

Direct marketers should not engage in dry testing unless the special nature of that offer is disclosed in the promotion.

Fulfillment

Unordered Merchandise
Article #26
Merchandise should not be shipped without having first received a customer's permission. The exceptions are samples or gifts clearly marked as such, and merchandise mailed by a charitable organization soliciting contributions, as long as all items are sent with a clear and conspicuous statement informing the recipient of an unqualified right to treat the product as a gift and to do with it as the recipient sees fit, at no cost or obligation to the recipient.

Shipments
Article #27
Direct marketers are reminded that they should abide by the FTC regulation regarding the prompt shipment of prepaid merchandise, the Mail Order Merchandise (30 Day) Rule.

Beyond this regulation, direct marketers are urged to ship all orders as soon as possible.

Credit and Debt Collection

Equal Credit Opportunity
Article #28
A creditor should not discriminate on the basis of race, color, religion, national origin, sex, marital status or age. If the individual is rejected for credit, the creditor should be prepared to give reasons why.

Debt Collection
Article #29
Unfair, misleading, deceptive or abusive methods should not be used for collecting money. The direct marketer should take reasonable steps to assure that those collecting on the direct marketer's behalf comply with this guideline.

Use of Mailing Lists

List Rental Practices
Article #30
Every list owner who sells, exchanges, or rents lists should see to it that each individual on the list is informed of those practices, and should offer an option to have the individual's name deleted when rentals or purchases are made. The list owner should remove names from the owner's customer or donor lists when requested directly by the individual, and by use of the DMMA Mail Preference Service name removal list.

List brokers and compilers should take reasonable steps to assure that the list owners follow these list practices.

Personal Information
Article #31
All list owners, brokers and compilers should be protective of the consumer's right to privacy and sensitive to the information collected on lists and subsequently considered for transfer.

Information supplied by consumers such as, but not limited to, medical, financial, insurance or court data should not be included on lists that are rented or exchanged when there is a reasonable expectation by the consumer that the information would be kept confidential.

List Usage Agreements
Article #32
List owners, brokers, compilers and users should make every attempt to establish the exact nature of the list's intended usage prior to the sale or rental of the list. Owners, brokers and compilers should not permit the sale or rental of their lists for an offer that is in violation of any of the Ethical Guidelines of DMMA. Promotions should be directed to those segments of the public most likely to be interested in their causes or to have a use for their products or services.

List Abuse
Article #33
No list or list data should be used in violation of the lawful rights of the list owner nor of the agreement between the parties; any such misuse should be brought to the attention of the lawful owner.

Telephone Marketing

(See Articles #9 and #27)
Reasonable Hours
Article #34
All telephone contacts should be made during reasonable hours.

Disclosure and Tactics
Article #35
All telephone solicitations should disclose to the buyer during the conversation the cost of the merchandise, all terms, conditions and the payment plan and whether there will be postage and handling charges. At no time should "high pressure" tactics be utilized.

Use of Automatic Electronic Equipment
Article #36
No telephone marketer should solicit sales using automatic electronic dialing equipment unless the telephone immediately disconnects when the called person hangs up.

Taping of Conversations
Article #37
Taping of telephone conversations should not be conducted without all-party consent or the use of a beeping device.

Telephone Name Removal/ Restricted Contacts
Article #38
Telephone marketers should remove the name of any contact from their telephone lists when requested to do so.

Telephone marketers should not call telephone subscribers who have unlisted or unpublished telephone numbers unless a prior relationship exists.

Fund Raising

(See Article #26)
Commission Prohibition/ Authenticity of Organization
Article #39
Fund raisers should make no percentage or commission arrangements whereby any person or firm assisting or participating in a fund raising activity is paid a fee proportionate to the funds raised, nor should they solicit for non-functioning organizations.

Laws, Codes, and Regulations
Article #40
Direct marketers should operate in accordance with the Better Business Bureau's Code of Advertising and be cognizant of and adhere to laws and regulations of the United States Postal Service, the Federal Trade Commission, the Federal Reserve Board, and other applicable Federal, state and local laws governing advertising, marketing practices, and the transaction of business by mail, telephone, and the print and broadcast media.

Appendix C

A Sample Mail Order Marketing/Business Plan

MARKETING PLAN
California Testing Services

Developed by
Steve Popkin & Mark Varnes

TABLE OF CONTENTS

Used with permission of the authors

Schedule of Business Operations: PERT Analysis Financial Analysis
  A. Projected Years 1, 2, and 3 Income Statement
  B. Projected Year One Income Statement By Month
  C. Breakeven Analysis
  D. Dollar Requirement for Project Test
  E. Business Cycle Graph
Controls and Continuity
Conclusion

Exhibit 1. Topic Outline of Correspondence Program
Exhibit 2. Sample Test Questions
Exhibit 3. Questionnaire Survey
Exhibit 4. Classified Advertisement Draft
Exhibit 5. Classified Section of *American Druggist*
Exhibit 6. Brochure Draft

INTRODUCTION

The purpose of this marketing plan is twofold: (1) to show potential investors and lenders how California Testing Services will operate, why it will be successful, and how the profit structure is determined, and (2) to act as a guiding, measuring, and evaluating vehicle in the implementation of all aspects of California Testing Services.

EXECUTIVE DIGEST

California Testing Services has conducted market research and analysis and has identified a need for an affordable preparatory program for the California State Board of Pharmacy exam. In response to this need, California Testing Services has developed and will market a correspondence program designed specifically for the aforementioned exam. It consists of eight sections and over 5000 sample questions and answers. The price of the program is $295.00 as opposed to $800.00 charged by the one competitor in the market.

The company is owned equally by Steve Popkin and Mark Varnes. Both are pursuing Masters of Business Administration degrees and have much applicable professional experience.

The correspondence program will be marketed via mail order. Advertising in trade journals, pharmacy school newspapers, and foreign newspapers will be done to elicit inquiries from potential buyers.

The financial analysis shows that the project requires a small investment, has a high rate of return on investment, has low overhead, and has low risk.

COMPANY MISSION, SCOPE, AND GOALS

California Testing Services (CTS) is in the test anxiety reduction business. Initially, CTS will strive to be the unit sales leader in preparatory programs for the California State Board of Pharmacy examination by year 3. In addition, CTS seeks a client passing rate of 85%, a client satisfaction rate of 95%, and a product return rate of 10% or less. At the conclusion of year 1, this initial division will be evaluated for the purpose of determining the feasibility of expanding into selected other states. If the evaluation proves positive, expansion into one additional state is anticipated to begin in year 4. If this expansion proves successful, other states will then be studied.

In addition to possibly expanding the pharmacy division, other unsaturated disciplines will be investigated by CTS to determine the feasibility of entering such markets (i.e., psychiatry, nursing, etc.).

The company philosophy is to operate with a minimum amount of risk and overhead.

BUSINESS ANALYSIS

California Testing Services will offer a preparatory correspondence program for the California State Board of Pharmacy exam. The program will include eight separate sections which specifically address the sections on the California State Board of Pharmacy exam (sections are outlined in Exhibit 1). In total, there are over 800 pages and 5000 practice test questions in a multiple choice format. Many questions will appear on the current exam, and most of the remaining ones have been on previous exams (sample questions are shown in Exhibit 2). Includded in the program are test taking techniques and tips.

The program was compiled by Marshall Hankin, doctor of pharmacy and former associate professor of pharmacy at Temple University, School of Pharmacy. Marshall Hankin will assist with the biannual updating of the program. Test questions and information on revised subject matter will be gathered from clients who had just taken the exam. They will be paid a nominal amount. The product is spiral bound with woodgrain vinyl covers. The eight separate sections range from 52 to 137 pages. The price of the program is $295.00 including tax, shipping, and handling.

EXHIBIT 1. Topic Outline of Correspondence Program

Program 100
General pharmacy practice—OTC drug use.

Program 200
Treatment of cardiovascular and respiratory disorders, pharmacology of drugs pertaining thereto.

Program 300
Treatment of gastrointestinal, genitourinary, bone, joint, supportive tissue, dermatologic, neurologic, psychiatric, fluid and electrolytic, and nutritional disordeers. Pharmacology of drugs pertaining thereto.

Program 400
Treatment of infections, oncologic, hormonal, metabolic, pediatric, geriatric, obstetrical and gynecologic, toxicologic disorders. Drug abuse. Literature evaluation. Pharmacology of drugs pertaining thereto.

Program 500
Ethics and the law.

Program 600
Pharmaceutical calculations.

Program 700
Pharmaceutics, biopharmaceutics, pharmacokinetics, compounding.

Program 500 Test (500T)
Substantive highlights law.

Program M
Miscellaneous questions and answers.

EXHIBIT 2. Sample Test Questions

536. The State Board of Pharmacy may *not:* (FALSE STATEMENT)
    A. Sell copies of its lists of licenses to "junk" mailing services.
    B. License "anyone" to sell hypodermic needles and syringes.
    C. Disclose any or all of its records to the public.
    D. Restrict the sale of any OTC drugs to "sale by pharmacist only" after proper hearings.
    E. Pass regulations which control the physician in his use of drugs.

537. A. A member of the Board could, if reappointed, serve a term as long as:
    A. Six years
    B. Eight years
    C. Eight and one-half years
    D. Twelve years
    E. No limit

538. An inspector of the State Board of Pharmacy:
    A. Is not a peace officer.
    B. Cannot make arrests without a warrant.
    C. Cannot seize Rx records without a warrant.
    D. Need not be a registered pharmacist.
    E. Is not liable for "false arrest" if "reasonable cause" existed.

539. Members of the California State Board of Pharmacy:
    A. Must be appointed by the Governor from a list of candidates proposed by the California Pharmaceutical Association.
    B. Must all be registered pharmacists.
    C. Must have their decisions reviewed by the Director of Professional and Vocational Standards.
    D. Must have their appointments confirmed by the State Legislature.
    E. All of the above are incorrect.

540. Prescriptions may *not* be telephoned to a pharmacy by:
    A. A podiatrist
    B. A veterinarian (D.V.M.)
    C. An appropriately designated employee of a physician
    D. An osteopathic physician
    E. An optometrist

SITUATION ANALYSIS

Assumptions

The market for new pharmacists in California is relatively stable. There is an adequate number of pharmacists to fill most positions, but the market is not oversaturated. The overabundance of medical school applicants and the limited amount of medical school space has caused a portion of premed students to turn to pharmacy school as an alternative. This is one factor that contributed to the slight but steady increase in pharmacy school graduates during the past five years. This trend is expected to continue for the next five years.

A significant factor in the market is the foreign pharmacist or pharmacy school graduate who migrates to the United States with hopes of becoming a licensed pharmacist. Each state determines its own eligibility requirements. In 1973, California passed a somewhat permissive law. It requires not only educational equivalency, but also that the applicant have two years of "practical experience" in his or her homeland during the previous five years. Fred Willyerd, State Board executive secretary, observes that the immigrant influx began around 1976, with most emigrating from China, Japan, India, and the Philippines. Two hundred fifty-eight foreigners took the California licensure exam in 1979 as compared to 142 in 1978, 79 in 1977, and 23 in 1976. Because the failure rate among foreign pharmacists is so high—in June 1979, for example, only 32 of 109 passed—many repeat the test. The great influx of foreign pharmacists has caused tension among United States pharmacists. They claim that foreigners have taken away jobs from American pharmacists and lowered the level of competency. In response to this, legislation was passed in 1980 making it more difficult for foreigners to obtain educational equivalency and be eligible to take the licensure exam. Already the percentage of foreigners enrolling in pharmacy school and taking the licensure exam has dropped significantly. Legislators are not being pressured by foreign lobbyists. The fight seems far from over. The outcome will have a definite effect on the buyer profile and market strategy of California Testing Services. Even with these fluctuations, the actual size of the market remains relatively constant. When there are fewer foreign pharmacists, more American pharmacists are attacted to California; and conversely, when there is an abundance of foreign pharmacists, American pharmacists tend not to migrate to California in as great numbers. Statistics show that more American pharmacists migrate to California than to any other state in the country.

According to Bank of America's *Economic Outlook 1982*, California will experience continued moderate economic growth in 1982. The estimated gross state product will be up 12.5% from 1981. This is a 3.5% gain after inflation. Employment, personal income, retail sales, and business revenues will all rise moderately. As has been the case since 1973, the state's economic growth will outpace that of the nation as a whole. In addition, service industries will greatly outpace other industry sectors.

Competition

Morris Cody and Associates currently has a monopoly on the preparatory industry for the California State Board of Pharmacy exam. Morris Cody and Associates is basically a one-man operation with a part-time instructor and secretarial service. The company operates from Van Nuys and San Francisco. Morris Cody, the owner and instructor, purchased the business 11 years ago from Dean Brady of the USC School of Pharmacy.

Morris Cody and Associates offers a classroom course held every night for the last two weeks before each exam and Tuesday and Thursday throughout the year. They also offer a corresponddencce course, or a combination of the two. The materials used in the classroom course are the same as used in the correspondence course. Regardless of which option the individual chooses, the fee is $800.00. Payment may be made by personal check, Visa, or MasterCard.

Morris Cody and Associates does classified advertising in three pharmacy trade journals (see Exhibit 3). Other than a one-page promotional mail piece sent on request, this is theonly advertising done.

The content of the correspondence programs of California Testing Services and Morris Cody and Associates are very similar.

There are two major pharmacy review books that sell for about $25 each, however, they are not specifically gearred to the California State Board of Pharmacy exam.

Company Resources

California Testing Services draws on the marketing expertise of Steve Popkin and Mark Varnes. Both partners possess a bachelor's degree in business administration-marketing. In addition, both are currently pursuing master's of business administration degrees. Steve Popkin and Mark Varnes have had formal academic training in mail order marketing and marketing a new business. Mark Varnes has professional experience in direct sales, graphic design, and budget administration. Steve Popkin has professional experience in copywriting, direct mail campaigns, and general marketing administration.

EXHIBIT 3. Questionnaire Survey

1. Have you taken a *classroom* review course for the California State Board of Pharmacy Exam? yes ( ) no ( )
2. If you answered "no" to question 1, were you aware of a classroom review course for the Californ a State Board of Pharmacy Exam? yes ( ) no ( )
3. Have you taken a correspondencce course for the California State Board of Pharmacy Exam? yes ( ) no ( )
4. If you answered "no" to question 3, were you aware of a correspondence course? yes ( ) no ( )
5. Have you purchased any preparatory books for the California State Board of Pharmacy Exam? yes ( ) no ( )
6. Have you ever taken the California State Board of Pharmacy Exam before? yes ( ) no ( )
7. Are you currently a licensed pharmacist? yes ( ) no ( )
   If yes, in what state are you licensed?_____
8. What pharmacy school did you graduate from?_____
9. Was the California State Board of Pharmacy Exam: (check one)
   ( ) Harder than you had expected.
   ( ) Easier than you had expected.
   ( ) About the same as you had expected.
10. Roughly, what do you feel a fair price is for a correspondence course for the California State Board of Pharmacy? $_____

THANK YOU

California Testing Servicces employs the pharmacological expertise of Marshall Hankin, PhD, on a contract basis. Marshall Hankin is a licensed pharmacist in California and Philadelphia. He is a former associate professor of pharmacy at Temple University, School of Pharmacy. Marshall Hankin has owned and managed a variety of pharmacies in both California and Philadelphia. Through his experience, Marshall Hankin has gained a concrete understanding of the needs and anxieties of the recent graduate as well as the out-of-state pharmacist. When Marshall Hankin moved to California in 1977, he enrolled in Morris Cody and Associates' classroom course before taking the California State Board of Pharmacy exam. This gave him and California Testing Services a working knowledge of the competition's mode of operation, course content, client attitude, and so on. As previously states, Marshall Hankin compiled the original correspondence program and will assist in its updating. In addition, he will be contacted for miscellaneous consulting.

California Testing Services will call on Carl Rosen, western regional manager, Division of MasterCard/Visa, City National Bank. Mr. Rosen, a personal friend of one of the partners, has consented to let California Testing Services offer Visa and MasterCard as a merchant through City National Bank.

Market Potentials, Forecasts, Facts

The potential market size for California Testing Services' preparatory program is the number of applicants for the California State Board of Pharmacy exam. A little background is in order. The California State Board of Pharmacy exam is a two-day test that is administered twice a year: once near the end of October and again near the end of June. The testing location alternates between Hayward, California, and Glendale, California. Using 1977 to 1980 figures, and it rises to approximately 600 in June. Combining the two brings the annual market potential to 1000 units or $295,000 in gross sales. As alluded to earlier, political and environmental factors have an effect on the customer mix but have little effect on the actual size of the market. The past three years' figures show a very slight upward trend in the number of applicants.

California Testing Services' product/service is immune to market saturation and diminishing returns. For the most part, there are a different 1000 people taking the exam annually, thus, the demand begins anew each year.

California Testing Services administered a questionnaire survey to persons taking the October 1981 California State Board of Pharmacy exam. The survey was taken at the test location as persons were leaving the testing room. California Testing Services representatives did not identify themselves as such (questionnaire is shown in Exhibit 3). A quota sampling was used with all exam takers meeting the quota requirements. Forty-two responses were gathered. The results of the survey are shown below.

1. 7% of responddents had taken a classroom review course.
2. 61% of the remainder were not aware of a classroom review course.
3. 16% of respondents had taken a correspondence course.
4. 48% of the remainder were not aware of a correspondence course.
5. 21% of respondents had purchased a preparatory book prior to the exam.
6. 24% of respondents had taken the exam previously.
7. 59% of respondents were currently licensed pharmacists.

8. No geographical concentration was identified.
9. 27% of respondents felt the exam was harder than expected, 54% felt it was about the same as expected, and 19% felt it was easier than expected.
10. The arithmetic mean for a fair price for the California State Board of Pharmacy exam was $197.00. The median was $223.00.

There were not enough respondents to get high confidence level results; however, there were enough to identify trends, opportunities, and concerns in the market. One major opportunity identified was that if California Testing Services could raise the level of awareness of a correspondence preparatory program, it could increase the industry size and its market share significantly.

Due to the monopolistic nature of the industry, Morris Cody and Associates sales are the same as total industry sales. From observation, surveys, and actual claims from Morris Cody and Associates, the current industry size is estimated to be approximately 200 units. Of the 200 units, 50 are estimated to be strictly classroom participants and 150 either correspondence or a combination of correspondence and classroom.

The breakdown of State Board applicants by group, as best determined, is 35% instate recent graduates, 20% out-of-state recent graduates, 30% out-of-state pharmacists, and 15% foreign pharmacists. Thirty percent of the aforementioned groups had previously taken and failed the California State Board of Pharmacy exam.

Market Share

As previously stated, the current size of California State Board of Pharmacy exam preparatory program industry is approximately 200 units. California Testing Services believes that with a sound marketing effort, it can conservatively increase the industry size to 250 units in year 1.

Of the 250 units, California Testing Services forecasts a 40% market share, or 100 units. This equates to a 10% share of the potential market. Of the 100 units, an estimated 50 sales will be new sales, purchases that would not have been made had CTS not been in the market. The remaining 50 sales will be "taken" from Morris Cody and Associates.

California Testing Services conservatively forecasts sales of 135 and 170 units for years 2 and 3, respectively. This represents an estimated 45 and 55% market share after allowing for an annual increase in industry size.

There are three separate and one overlapping market segments for the product/service offered by California Testing Services. These are (1) recent pharmacy school graduates, in and out of state, (2) currently licensed out-of-state pharmacists, (3) foreign pharmacists, and, overlapping, (4) applicants who have failed a recent California State Board of Pharmacy exam.

California Testing Services forecasts that 60% of its first year sales will be from out-of-state pharmacists, 30% from recent graduates, and 10% from foreign pharmacists. Of the aforementioned groups, an estimated 20% will have taken and failed a previous exam.

Morris Cody and Associates' product/service differentiation is the option of a classroom course and the availability of presale communication between Morris Cody and the potential client. This is expected to give Morris Cody and Associates an advantage in the recent in-state-graduate and foreign-pharmacist segments. It is geographically practical for in-state graduates to attend classroom sessions. Foreign pharmacists often have a language communication problem and require extensive personal attention rather than simply written material. In addition, a direct mail piece that is effective for American potential customers may not be as effective for foreign potential customers. They may also require personal persuasiveness before committing to buy. By observation, about half of Morris Cody and Associates' classroom students are foreign. On the other hand, in most cases it is very difficult for out-of-state applicants to relieve themselves of obligations and have the time to attend classroom sessions. California Testing Services believes that its price differential will counteract a portion of Morris Cody and Associates' advantages and

CURRENT MARKETING ORGANIZATION

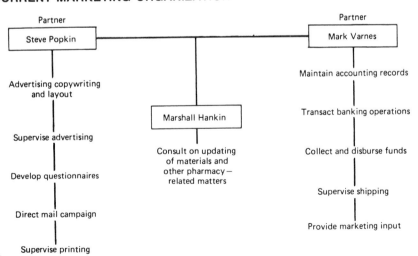

will have an extremely positive effect on the out-of-state market where all things are relatively equal. Within the industry, California Testing Services forecasts (1) 80% market share of out-of-state pharmacists, (2) 20% market share of in-state recent graduates, (3) 50% market share of out-of-state recent graduates, and (4) 30% market share of foreign pharmacists.

MARKETING OBJECTIVES

Quantitative marketing objectives for years 1, 2, and 3 are as follows:

	Year		
	1	2	3
Market share (%)	40	45	55
Inquiries	250	270	325
Unit sales	100	135	170
Closing percentage	40	50	52
Gross sales	$29,000	$39,825	$50,150
Profit before tax	$12,837	$18,409	$23,642

MARKETING STRATEGIES AND PROGRAMS

Advertising

After determining that a mail listing of applicants for the California State Board of Pharmacy exam was not available, California Testing Service chose a two-step advertising approach. The purpose of all its advertising is to motivate potential buyers to send in their names and addresses and receive a direct mail piece giving the details of the offer and an order coupon.

California Testing Services will advertise toward, and elicit sales from, all of the aforementioned four market segments; however, its main thrust and expenditures will be geared toward the out-of-state market.

Out-of-State Pharmacists. To capture this market at the least expense, California Testing Services will do classified advertising in four pharmacy trade journals: *Pharmacy Times, Drug Topics, American Druggist,* and *U.S. Pharmacist.* An estimated 85% of people who read pharmacy trade journals read one of these four journals. The charge for an average

EXHIBIT 4. Classified Advertisement Draft

CALIFORNIA BOARD OF PHARMACY EXAM REVIEW: Pass the California
Board of Pharmacy exam—or pay nothing! Be thoroughly prepared to pass the
exam, then relax. Most complete and least expensive correspondence course
available. You owe it to yourself to find out. For free details, clip this ad and send
it with your name and address to: CALIFORNIA TESTING SERVICES. . . .

classified ad in these journals ranges from approximately $35 to $100 with
the average being $70. Prices are roughly correlated with circulation (see
Exhibit 4 for classified section of *American Druggist* and draft of CTS
classified ad). Morris Cody and Associates advertises in the classified
section of three of the four trade journals mentioned. Each advertisement
will be coded for evaluation purposes. This mode of advertising will also
touch on all other market segments.

Recent Graduates. California Testing Services will place small display
advertisements in pharmacy school newspapers. California has 3 of 72
pharmacy schools: University of Southern California (USC), University
of California–San Francisco (UCSF), and University of Pacifica (UOP).
Ads will initially be placed in three school newspapers for testing purposes. These schools include USC, UOP, and a third out-of-state school
selected on the basis of the size of the school and the California migratory
patterns of the area. This test should indicate anticipated demand from
in-state local, in-state nonlocal, and out-of-state graduates. It was previously stated that California Testing Services forecasts only a 20% market share on in-state recent graduates, however, this represents a greater
actual number than does the 40% share of out-of-state recent graduates.
Initially, advertisements will be laced bimonthly. Depending on the results, thea ds may be expanded in coverage and/or frequency, or eliminated.

Foreign Pharmacists. A small display advertisement will be placed in
the *World Journal,* a daily Chinese-language newspaper. This newspaper
is circulated from San Francisco to SAn Diego and has the largest readership of any newspaper of its kind. From secondary data and observation
of the competition, it was determined that Chinese is by far the predomi-
nant nationality of foreign state board applicants. As with the school
newspapers, this advertisement will initially appear bimonthly. Depending on the results, it will expand in frequency, remain the same, be eliminated and/or inspire advertising on other foreign languages.

Applicants Who Have Failed a Previous State Board Exam. During each examination, a business/advertising card will be placed on the windshield of each car parked at the testing location. The card will give the company name, services provided, and address to write to for more details. An applicant doesn't know for about six weeks whether he or she passed the exam. In that length of time, a brochure or flyer will often get thrown away or lost in a pile. A business card can be put in a wallet or purse for easy retrieval. In addition, a business card is less expensive and is less likely to elicit objections from test or city authorities.

Brochure. As stted, when a potential buyer sends in his or her name and address, he or she will be sent a brochure. In its brochure, California Testing Services attempts to counter the following potential objections.

1. "$295 is a lot of money."
2. "If you charge so much less than your competition, you must be offering an inferior product."
3. "I don't have that much cash on hand."
4. "I wouldn't buy an expensive item through the mail without seeing it first."

In addition to countering objections, California Testing Services attempt to elicit customer response by following the AIDA copywriting approach: grab attention, stimulate interest, create desire, encourage action. (A rough draft of the brochure copy is shown in Exhibit 5.)

A follow-up letter will be sent to a potential customer if an order is not received within two weeks after sending the brochure. Tentatively, the theme of the letter will be anxiety reduction.

EXHIBIT 5. Brochure Draft

MAIN HEADLINE:	PASS THE CALIFORNIA STATE BOARD OF PHARMACY EXAMINATION—OR PAY NOTHING!!!
COMPONENTS: HEADLINE:	DO ANY OF THESE SOUND FAMILIAR?

- I want to move to California, but I can't unless I pass the exam.
- I've been away from the classroom so long, I don't know if I'll remember enough.
- I just graduated, I know the theory, but I don't know what's going to be on the California exam.
- I have a family to support, I can't afford not to pass.

IF THEY DO—WE CAN HELP

A team of pharmacists headed by Marshall Hankin, Ph.D., developed a correspondence program for California Testing Services. We can now offer it to you. The eight separate sections attack the heart of the California State Board of Pharmacy Exam, and will give you confidence entering the testing room.

In total there are over 800 pages and over 5000 questions and answers. Many questions will appear on the actual test. The program is updated after each exam to make sure that you have the most current, accurate material available anywhere. This program was designed specifically to prepare applicants to pass the California State Board of Pharmacy Examination. This is not a book, and cannot be bought in any store.

HEADLINE:　　WOULD YOU PAY $800.00 FOR A PROGRAM LIKE THIS?

Hundreds of pharmacists have—but you don't have to. Morris Cody and Associates have been offering a very similar correspondence program. At last check it was selling for $800.00. Through California Testing Services you pay only $295.00 *including* tax, shipping, and handling. In addition to the cost savings you will, quite frankly, receive a better, more complete program.

HEADLINE:　　HOW CAN WE DO IT3

How can California Testing Services offer a program for $295.00 that sells elsewhere for $800.00?

ANSWER: We don't have:

- A large fancy office building.
- Salespeople and secretaries to answer your calls.
- Needless business equipment.

What we do have is quality personnel to develop, update, and evaluate the program to be sure that it meets your exact needs.

HEADLINE:　　WOULD YOU PAY $295.00 THROUGH THE MAIL—SIGHT UNSEEN?

Would a person of above average intelligence send $295.00 without first seeing the product?

We won't ask you to take our word for the quality of the program, that's why we offer a no risk–double guarantee.

HEADLINE: NO RISK–DOUBLE GUARANTEE

1. If within 30 days, this program does not meet your expectations, send it back for a complete, no questions asked, refund. You can even post date your check for thirty days.
2. If for any reason you do not pass the California State Board of Pharmacy Examination, send the program back for a complete refund. Simply enclose a copy of your Consumer Affairs Board of Pharmacy notice. Take up to 90 days after the exam date.

These kinds of guarantees are unheard of in the industry. Our competition doesn't offer even one money back guarantee. We don't hesitate to offer these guarantees because we believe strongly that this program will be invaluable to you.

HEADLINE: IF YOU HAVEN'T ALREADY SENT IN YOUR ORDER— READ THIS.

```
T
  E
    S
      T
        I
          M
            O
              N
               I
                A
                  L
                    S
```

HEADLINE: DO I HAVE TO SEND A CHECK?

NO. You can send a check or money order, or call toll free 1-800-xxx-xxxx and use your Visa or MasterCard. Either way, we will ship the program to you immediately upon receipt of your order.

HEADLINE: WOULD YOU INVEST $295.00 IN YOUR FUTURE?

$295.00 is still a lot of money, especially these days. But, this $295.00 can allow you to earn well over $30,000.00 as a licensed California Pharmacist. That's quite a return on your investment.

HEADLINE: CALIFORNIA TESTING SERVICES—IT'S WORTH THE
                 PEACE OF MIND FOR THE MOST STUDY TIME—ORDER
                 NOW

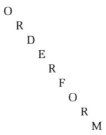

Pricing

As previously stated, Morris Cody and Associates charges $800.00 and
California Testing Services charges $295.00. A low price strategy was
chosen for several reasons.

1. Other than price, there is virtually no product differentiation.
2. Morris Cody and Associates has a reputation, credibility, and per-
    sonal selling; there must be enough of a price difference to out-
    weigh these advantages.
3. California Testing Services hopes to create a submarket of ratio-
    nal, somewhat price-conscious consumers, rather than compete
    head to head for existing customer types; the price differentiation
    will create a new consumer in the market.
4. A strong marketing effort can elicit buyers from untapped areas,
    however, once Morris Cody and Associates copies the marketing
    tactics, California Testing Services is back to square 1.
5. Currently Morris Cody and Associates is practicing "skim" pricing
    in a monopolistic situation. When a competitor enters the market,
    somewhat of an oligopoly will occur and a response will be elicited
    (see Figure 1). If California Testing Services prices closer to $800, it
    may spur a "price war" where each competitor is trying to under-
    sell the other. At $295, California Testing Services is at the oppo-
    site end of the price range. It would not be feasible for Morris Cody
    and Associates to compete on a price basis, thus allowing each
    competitor his own niche in the market place.

6. Protecting the preparatory correspondence program concept and materials is a potential problem. With the emergence of California Testing Services, the high and low price ends of the industry are covered. This will make it more difficult and less attractive for another competitor to enter the market.

7. Surveys have indicated that $800 is well above the initial preceived value for this type of product/service. Two hundred-ninety five dollars is more consistent with perceived value.

8. Oddball pricing (295.00 as opposed to $300.00) is used to promote a "good deal" image.

9. California Testing Services does not believe that the demand for its product is entirely elastic. However, it does feel that, up to a point, a decrease in price will create an increase in sales if accompanied by a sound marketing effort.

A portion of the brochures will be printed with an alternate price, perhaps $395.00. After the completion of the first six-month business cycle, it will begin being tested for profitability against the control price of $295.00. Testing will continue until an optimum price is determined.

Distribution Channel

California Testing Services will sell its product via mail order. This choice was based on several factors.

1. Desire to limit the amount of inventory, overhead, and investment.
2. Desire to limit the amount of administrative and selling time.

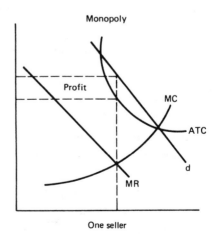

Figure 1

3. The widespread geographical disbursement of potential customers.

4. The pharmacological expertise lies with someone other than the two general partners.

5. The product is an "unsought good."

Further analysis of the appropriateness of this product for mail order is shown below using Dr. Cohen's mail order product evaluation form. It shows that on almost all points the product is rated very good or excellent.

Advertising and Project Evaluation Criteria

The advertising campaign will begin on March 1, 1982. As shown in the financial analysis, forecasted sales for March are 10 units. Forecasted sales for March through June, the first business cycle, are 60 units. Thirty-one units must be sold to break even for year 1. If on April 1, 1982, 5 units are sold, the project will be continued. If sales are less than 5, the project will be discontinued. If on July 1, 1982, sales are above 30 units, the project will be continued; if it's below, it will be discontinued.

If an advertisement fails to pay for itself at the end of any given month, it will be eliminated. If a newspaper advertisement produces four sales in a given month, it will be increased in frequency and/or size for the next month. In this case, advertisements in similar newspapers will be tested.

California Testing Services believes that quantitative criteria are valuable and necessary. However, it will strive to remain flexible enough to respond to fluctuations and unexpected occurrences in the market.

SCHEDULE OF BUSINESS OPERATIONS: PERT ANALYSIS

Phase I
Market survey
R&D product design
Routing (product feasibility)
Complete prototype model
Cost estimates
Preliminary product testing
Pricing and forecast reports
Final report

MAIL ORDER PRODUCT EVALUATION FORM

Instructions: Give each evaluation item
                4 points for an evaluation of excellent
                3 points for an evaluation of very good
                2 points for an evaluation of good
                1 point for an evaluation of fair
                0 point for an evaluation of poor

Multiply the evaluation points times the importance weighting. Only pick new products that have a high point total.

		Importance Weighting		Evaluation Points		Total
I.	**Marketability**					
	1. How large is the potential market?	.03	×	1	=	.03
	2. How important is the need that the product fills?	.08	×	4	=	.32
	3. Can the customer buy the product easily in a store?	.03	×	4	=	.12
II.	**Profitability**					
	1. What is the total and yearly profitability estimate?	.08	×	1	=	.08
	2. Can the item be sold at 3 to 4 times your cost?	.08	×	4	=	.32
	3. Does the product lend itself to repeat business?	.07	×	2	=	.14
	4. What is the ratio of total profit of total investment?	.03	×	3	=	.09
III.	**Investment**					
	1. How much investment will the project require?	.05	×	4	=	.20
	2. How many units must be sold until the investment is recouped?	.04	×	4	=	.16
IV.	**Legal Consideration**					
	1. Is the product strictly legal?	.17	×	3	=	.51
	2. Is the product completely safe?	.09	×	4	=	.36
	3. Can there be any legal repercussion through use or misuse of the product?	.08	×	4	=	.32
V.	**Mailing**					
	1. Can the product be shipped and mailed easily?	.06	×	4	=	.24
	2. Is the product breakable?	.06	×	4	=	.24
	3. Can the product be shipped at low cost?	1.00	×	4	=	.28
					Grand total	3.41

Phase II

Questionnaires
Ads in periodicals and newspapers
Direct mail campaign
Response from ads and direct mail
Direct mail brochures
Orders from customers
Printing and production of review tests
Packaging and mailing of product
Final report

PERT ANALYSIS–PHASE 1

PERT ANALYSIS–PHASE II

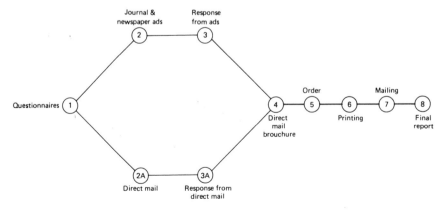

FINANCIAL ANALYSIS

	Year		
	1	2	3
Total net sales	29,500	39,825	50,150
Cost of goods sold	8,667	11,701	14,734
Gross profit	20,833	28,124	35,416
Expenses	*	*	*
	*	*	*
Advertising	4,200	4,200	4,200
Business registration	75	45	45
Post office box	26	26	26
Postage	60	80	100
Envelopes	150	0	0
Brochures	600	0	600
Follow-up letter	35	0	0
M.C./Visa setup	25	0	0
Product updating	200	200	200
Product returns	2,525	5,164	6,503
Misc.	100	100	100
Total expenses	7,996	9,715	11,774
	*	*	*
	*	*	*
Net profit (loss) before taxes	$12,837	$18,409	$23,642

CONTROLS AND CONTINUITY

Formal records of actual results as compared to forecasted results will be compiled monthly for evaluation purposes. This will allow California Testing Services to react to small fluctuations and unexpected occurrences in the market.

Biannually, near the end of June and October, this marketing plan will be reviewed in its entirety. Using primary and secondary data, appropriate changes will be made. By November 30 of each year, a written supplement will be submitted identifying necessary amendments in the original marketing plan.

During off seasons, November to March, California Testing Services will investigate company progress and the feasibility of expansion. Medium and long-range goals and objectives will be determined and evaluated.

Controlling and reviewing the continuity of this plan on a regular basis

Business Cycle Graph

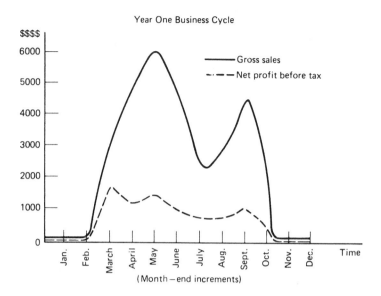

Year One Business Cycle

(Month—end increments)

is extremely important in order to avoid a "marketing myopia" or short-sightedness effect.

CONCLUSION

California Testing Services strongly believes that with an initial investment of $5000 to roughly cover two business cycles, and careful and tenacious administration of its marketing plan, it will become a successful, growing concern.

Projected Year 1 Income Statement by Month

	March	April	May	June	July	Aug.	Sept.	Oct.	Nov.	Dec.	Jan.	Feb.
Total net sales	2950	4425	5900	4425	2360	2950	4425	2065	0	0	0	0
Cost of goods sold	868	1302	1735	1302	694	868	1302	607	0	0	0	0
Gross profit	2082	3123	4165	3123	1666	2082	3123	1458	0	0	0	0
Expenses	*	*	*	*	*	*	*	*	*	*	*	*
Advertising	525	525	525	525	525	525	525	525	0	0	0	0
Business registration	75	0	0	0	0	0	0	0	0	0	0	0
P.O. box	13	0	0	0	0	0	13	0	0	0	0	0
Postage	6	9	12	9	5	6	9	4	0	0	0	0
Envelopes	150	0	0	0	0	0	0	0	0	0	0	0
Brochure	600	0	0	0	0	0	0	0	0	0	0	0
Follow-up letter	0	35	0	0	0	0	0	0	0	0	0	0
M.C./Visa setup	25	0	0	0	0	0	0	0	0	0	0	0
Product updating	0	0	0	0	100	0	0	0	100	0	0	0
Product returns—15%*	382	574	765	574	306	382	574	268	0	0	0	0
Misc.	12	13	12	13	12	13	12	13	0	0	0	0
Total expenses	1788	1156	1302	1121	936	913	1133	810	100	0	0	0
Net profit (loss) before taxes	294	1967	2863	2002	730	1169	1990	648	(100)	0	0	0

* Product returns are applied to the month in which they are sold.

543

Breakeven Analysis

Selling price	$295.00
Variable costs	
Product reproduction	40.00
State sales tax	17.70
Shipping	5.00
Packaging	2.00
800 tel. # $(0.10 \times 295) \times (0.50)$	14.75
MasterCard/Visa $(0.05 \times 295) \times (0.50)$	7.38
Total variable costs	$86.78
Gross profit per unit	$208.22
Fixed costs	
Advertising	4,200.00
Business registration	75.00
Post office box	26.00
Postage	60.00
Envelopes	150.00
Brochures	600.00
Follow-up letter	35.00
Updating product	200.00
Misc.	100.00
Total fixed costs	$5,446.00

Total fixed costs	÷	Gross profit per unit	=	Breakeven quantity
$5446.00		$208.22		26.155

Additional units needed to compensate for 15% product return: 4.62
Adjusted breakeven quantity: 31 units

Dollar Requirement for Project Test

Advertising	$525.00
Post office box	$ 13.00
MasterCard/Visa setup charge	$ 25.00
Business registration	$ 75.00
Artwork/typesetting for envelopes and brochure	$250.00
Misc.	$ 50.00
Total	$938.00

APPENDIX D

Mail Order Associations

Association of Direct Marketing Agencies, 342 Madison Avenue, New York, New York 10173, (212)687-2100.

Business Professional Advertising Association, 205 East 42nd Street, New York, New York 10017, (212)661-0222.

Chicago Association of Direct Marketing, 333 North Michigan Avenue, Chicago, Illinois 60601, (312)977-9600.

Cleveland Advertising Club, Cleveland Plaza, Cleveland, Ohio 44115, (216)241-4807.

Direct Marketing Association, Inc., 6 East 43rd Street, New York, New York 10017, (212)689-4977.

Direct Marketing Association of North Texas, c/o Epsilon Data Management, 13628 Beta Drive, Dallas, Texas 75234, (214)392-2717.

Direct Mail/Marketing Club of Atlanta, c/o Southern Bell, 3400 Peachtree Road, Suite 1333, Atlanta, Georgia 30326, (404)262-3400.

Direct Marketing Association of Detroit, The Dy-Dee Service, 9106 Fullerton, Detroit, Michigan 48238, (313)933-2026.

Direct Marketing Association of Washington, Daly Direct Marketing, 918 16th Street, N.W., Washington, D.C. 20006, (202)659-2927.

Direct Marketing Club of Des Moines, c/o Metromail Advertising Company, P.O. Box 500, Mt. Pleasant, Idaho 52641.

Direct Marketing Club of Indianapolis, 9245 North Meridian, Indianapolis, Indiana 46260, (317)846-1286.

Direct Marketing Club of Kansas City, c/o 3209 West 68th St., Shawnee Mission, Kansas 66208, (913)236-6669.

Direct Marketing Club of St. Louis, c/o Creative Office Systems, 1601 Washington Ave., St. Louis, Missouri 63103, (314)436-2800.

Direct Marketing Club of New York, c/o Mailmen Inc., 342 Madison Avenue, New York, New York 10173, (212)986-4862.

Direct Marketing Club of Southern California, c/o Transo Envelope Co., 6501 San Fernando Road, Glendale, California 90015.

Direct Marketing Association of Tulsa, c/o Kraftville, Box 800, Tulsa, Oklahoma 74101, (800)331-7290.

Direct Marketing Creative Guild, March Direct Marketing, 485 Madison Avenue, New York, New York 10017, (212)286-0460.

Direct Marketing Credit Association, c/o Grolier Enterprises, Sherman Turnpike, Danbury, Connecticut 06816, (203)797-3500, ext. 3642.

Direct Marketing Idea Exchange, 475 Park Avenue South, Room 3500, New York, New York 10016, (212)924-1200.

Envelope Manufacturers Association, 1 Rockefeller Plaza, New York, New York 10020, (212)255-5885.

Florida Direct Marketing Association, c/o The Buren, Inc. 6600 NW 21st Avenue, Ft. Lauderdale, Florida 33309, (305)975-0113.

Fulfillment Management Association, 25 West 43rd Street, New York, New York 10036, (212)262-8800.

Houston Direct Mail/Marketing Club, 1801 Walker Avenue, P.O. Box 2622, Houston, Texas 77001, (713)652-2100.

Hudson Valley Direct Marketing Club, cflo Winston & Sherman, 18 East 42nd Street, New York, New York 10017, (212)532-2700.

Honored Million Club of New York, c/o Accredited Mailing Lists, Inc., 3 Park Avenue, New York, New York 10016, (212)889-1180.

International Mail Advertising Associations, 7315 Wisconsin Ave., 818 E., Washington, D.C. 20014, (301)654-7030.

Long Island Direct Marketing Association, Abelow Response, Inc., 430 West Merrick Road, Valley Stream, New York 11580, (516)825-0013.

Louisville Direct Mail/Marketing Association, 1821 Spring Drive, Louisville, Kentucky 40205, (502)459-0635.

Marketing Communications Executives, 2130 Delancy Place, Philadelphia, Pennsylvania 19103, (215)732-9340.

Mid-American Direct Marketing Association, A-1 Direct Mail Service, Inc., 9101 "F" Street, Omaha, Nebraska 68127, (402)339-5100.

Midwest Direct Marketing Association, c/o the Webb Co., 1999 Shepard Road, St. Paul, Minnesota 55116, (612)690-7200.

National Mail Order Association, 5818 Venice Boulevard, Los Angeles, California 90019, (213)934-7986.

New England Direct Marketing Association, Small Business Service Bureau, P.O. Box 1441, Worcester, Massachusetts 01601, (617)756-3513.

New Jersey Direct Marketing Club, 20 Nassau Street, Princeton, New Jersey 08540, (609)924-9488.

Ohio Direct Mail and Marketing Association, c/o Robert Silverman, Inc., 1375 Euclid Avenue, Cleveland, Ohio 44115, (216)771-6332.

Ohio Valley Direct Marketing Club, c/o Vortec Corp., 10124 Carver Road, Cincinnati, Ohio 45242, (513)891-7474.

Pacific Northwest Direct Marketing Club, c/o Portland Mailing Services, 1438 NW Hoyt, Portland, Oregon 97209, (503)221-0707.

Parcel Shippers Association, 1211 Connecticut Avenue, NW, Washington, D.C. 20036, (202)296-3690.

Philadelphia Direct Mail Club, 754 North Reingold, Philadelphia, Pennsylvania 19130, (215)232-6711.

Phoenix Direct Marketing Club, Paralegal Institute, P.O. Drawer 33903, Phoenix, Arizona 85067, (602)263-7950.

Rocky Mountain Direct Marketing Club, Marketing Communications, 2369 S. Trenton Way Drive, Denver, Colorado 80321, (303)751-0433.

San Francisco Advertising Club, Transo Envelope Co., 1600 64th Street, Emeryville, California 94608, (415)654-7851.

Upper Midwest Direct Marketing Club, c/o Mailhouse, 210 North Second Street, Minneapolis, Minnesota 55401, (612)339-8701.

U.S. Electronic Mail Association, Harvard Square, Box 43, Cambridge, Massachusetts 02138, (617)742-2500.

Women's Direct Response Group, Cambridge Scientific Abstract, 5161 River Road, Bethesda, Maryland 20816, (301)951-1403.

Women's Direct Response Group, P.O. Box 5134, FDR Station, New York, New York 10150, (212)765-6500, ext. 356.

Women's Direct Response Group, c/o Wesley Lists, 3227 N. Frontage Road, Suite 2703, Arlington Heights, Illinois 60004.

Women's Direct Response Goup, c/o Unimail List Corporation, One Lincoln Plaza, New York, New York 10023, (212)580-3000.

APPENDIX E

Some Mail Order Advertising Agencies

Arau and Goldberg, 425 15th Street, Philadelphia, Pennsylvania 19102.

Ben Franklin Advertising, Inc., 1424 Lincoln Boulevard, Santa Monica, California 90401.

Cinamon Associates, Inc., 29 Harvard Street, Brookline, Massachusetts 02146.

Dickinson Direct Response, Inc., 67 Federal Avenue, Quincy, Massachusetts 02169.

Direct Marketing Agency, Inc., 733 Summer Street, Stamford, Connecticut 06901.

The DR Group, Inc., 522 Fifth Avenue, New York, New York 10036.

Franklin and Joseph, Inc., 237 Mamaroneck Avenue, White Plains, New York 10605.

Grizzard Advertising, Inc., 1144 Mailing Avenue SE, Atlanta, Georgia 30315. Iversen-Norman Associates, 175 Fifth Avenue, New York, New York 10010.

Januz Advertising Inc., P.O. Box 1000, Lake Forrest, Illinois 60045.

Ketchum, Macleod, and Grove Direct Marketing, Four Gateway Center, Pittsburgh, Pennsylvania 15222.

Loch Arbour Direct, Inc., 100 Main Street, Allenhurst, New Jersey 07711.

Nelson–Panullo–Jutkins Direct Marketing, 147 Richmond, El Segundo, California 90245.

Paul Muchnick Co., 5818 Venice Building, Los Angeles, California 90019.

Ogilvy and Mather Direct Response, Inc., 675 Third Avenue, New York, New York 10017.

Alan H. Rosenberg Associates, Inc., 310 Madison Avenue, New York, New York 10017.

Robert Silverman, Inc., 1375 Euclid Avenue, Cleveland, Ohio 44115.

Smith-Hemmings-Gosden Direct Response Advertising, 3360 Flair Drive, El Monte, California 91713.

William Steiner Associates, Inc., 19 W. 44 Street, New York, New York 10036.

APPENDIX F

Some Sources of Mailing Lists

Advanced Management Systems, Inc., 9401 Wilshire Boulevard, Suite 660, Beverly Hills, California 90212.

Ed Burnett Consultants, Inc., 2 Park Avenue, New York, New York 10016.

Business Mailers, Inc., 640 North LaSalle Street, Chicago, Illinois 60610.

Dependable Lists, Inc., 257 Park Avenue, South, New York, New York 10010.

Direct Marketing Corporation of America, 3700 Wilshire Boulevard., Los Angeles, California 90010.

Dunhill International List Company, 2430 West Oakland Park Boulevard, Ft. Lauderdale, Florida 33311.

Dun's Marketing Services, 3 Century Drive, Parsippany, New Jersey 07054.

InfoMat, 25550 Hawthrone Boulevard, Suite 304, Torrance, California 90505.

Hank Marshall Marketing Company, P.O. Box 2729, Laguna Hills, California 92653.

List Mart, 2210 Wilshire Boulevard, Suite 700, Santa Monica, California 90403.

Market Compilation and Research Bureau, Inc., 11633 Victory Boulevard, North Hollywood, California 91609.

Market Data Retrieval, Ketchum Place, Westport, Connecticut 06880.

National Business Lists, Inc., 162 North Franklin Street, Chicago, Illinois 60606.

Alvin B. Zeller, Inc., 475 Park Avenue South, New York, New York 10016.

Zeller-Letica, Inc., 15 East 26th Street, New York, New York 10010.

Index